World Civilizations

SEVENTH EDITION

Volume II: Since 1500

For Gracie, an historical event

—Philip Adler

To Joel, Eric, Ethan, Ellie, and Lauren

—Randall L. Pouwels

World Civilizations

SEVENTH EDITION

Volume II: Since 1500

Philip J. Adler

East Carolina University, Emeritus

Randall L. Pouwels

University of Central Arkansas, Emeritus

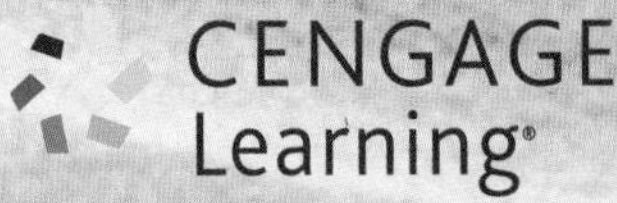

Australia • Brazil • Japan • Korea • Mexico • Singapore • Spain • United Kingdom • United States

***World Civilizations, Volume II: Since 1500*, Seventh Edition**
Philip J. Adler, Randall L. Pouwells

Product Director: Suzanne Jeans

Product Manager: Brooke Barbier

Senior Content Developer: Kate Scheinman

Content Coordinator: Cara D. Swan

Product Assistant: Katie Coaster

Media Developer: Laura Hildebrand

Marketing Manager: Valerie Hartman

Market Development Manager: Kyle Zimmerman

Senior Content Project Manager: Jane Lee

Senior Art Director: Cate Rickard Barr

Manufacturing Planner: Sandee Milewski

Senior Rights Acquisition Specialist: Jennifer Meyer Dare

Production Service: Integra

Cover Designer: Sarah Bishins

Cover Image: Colorful mural showing farmers and agriculture on bandstand in Parque Central. Credit: Tim Bewer/Lonely Planet Images/Getty Images.

Compositor: Integra

Library of Congress Control Number: 2013932746

Student Edition:

ISBN-13: 978-1-285-44282-2

ISBN-10: 1-285-44282-2

Cengage Learning
200 First Stamford Place, 4th Floor
Stamford, CT 06902
USA

Printed in the United States of America
1 2 3 4 5 6 7 17 16 15 14 13

Brief Contents

Contents

Maps

Preface

WORLD CIVILIZATIONS is a brief history of civilized life since its inceptions some five thousand years ago. It is meant to be used in conjunction with a lecture course in world history at the introductory level. The authors, who bring nearly sixty total years of classroom experience to its writing, have constantly kept in mind the needs and interests of freshman and sophomore students in two- and four-year colleges and universities.

World Civilizations deals with the most noteworthy civilizations in world history while attempting to walk a middle line between exhaustive detail and frustrating brevity. Its narrative embraces every major epoch, but the treatment of topics is selective and follows definite patterns and hierarchies. It deliberately tilts toward social and cultural topics, as well as toward the long-term processes that affect the lives of the millions, rather than exclusive attention being given to the acts of "the captains and the kings." The evolution of law and the formative powers of religion on early government, for example, receive considerably more attention than wars and diplomatic arrangements. The rise of working classes in cities is accorded more space than the policies of governments. The authors have emphasized providing students with the basic details needed to grasp and appreciate the distinguishing features of individual civilizations, while also demonstrating how humans fabricated new strands of global connectivity through the six ages covered in the text. Selectivity, of course, is forced on authors of any text, but the firm intent to keep this a concise survey necessitated a particularly close review of the material. Dividing a brief narrative into fifty-three short chapters both gives the instructor considerable leeway for including additional material or expanding the topics and also makes it likelier that students will read the assigned material. This approach has been relatively successful and has found sufficient favor among many teachers to justify the appearance of this seventh edition.

CHANGES IN THIS EDITION

The table of contents in this seventh edition again reflects a significantly increased amount of non-Western coverage, has been reorganized more chronologically, and shows increased coverage of worldwide trade and exchange. More material on Africa, Asia, and the Pacific has been added, and we have given less emphasis and space to European political history. New or partly new chapters have been added to accommodate these additions.

The Images of History feature that was introduced in the sixth edition has been retained to attract student's interest. We have incorporated a new box feature, called The Historian's Craft, to introduce students to some of the methods historians use to inform their understanding of the past. See also the section on Pedagogy for a complete list of important updates to the many pedagogical features found within the text.

The authors and editors have undertaken three major aims in this edition: (1) to provide additional matter that illustrates how the world has become increasingly globalized and interdependent; (2) to include more coverage of the non-Western world and the important initiatives of non-Western peoples, even through the West's recent expansionary age; and (3) to give a greater and sharper focus on the importance of women in history.

Following are the many chapter-specific changes in this edition:

Chapter 1 has an updated Worldview Map. 1.3: Origins of Agriculture and Pastoralism.

Chapter 3 includes the first of the new Historians Craft boxes, Learning about History from Language.

Chapter 4 has new material on the prehistoric civilizations of Central Asia, previewing the origins of the Silk Road.

Renamed The Settlement of the Americas and the Pacific Islands, Chapter 7 has an added section on ancient Austronesians' migrations into Oceania and the Indian Ocean. The chapter has a new Images of History box on the ancient Lapita culture of the ancestral Polynesians.

Chapter 8 has a new box feature on Neolithic Europe. A second addition is a Historians Craft box on oral traditions as sources of historical evidence.

Chapter 9 takes a closer look at women's roles in Hellenistic society and includes a new Patterns of Belief box, Greek Women "Gone Mad": Feminine Power in the Religious Realm.

Chapter 10 includes a new section that examines Rome's expanded presence in the classical world and includes evidence from the *Periplus of the Erythraean Sea*.

In addition to the core material on classical India, Chapter 12 has been expanded to include information about Parthian and Sassanid Persia. As in previous chapters, the aim of this one is to elucidate the growing networks of trade and migration that occurred throughout the Eurasian and African worlds of antiquity.

The so-called "Father" of the Silk Road is the subject of a new box in Chapter 13, bringing more attention to the emergent globalism of the classical era.

This edition has endeavored to focus more attention on domestic life and women's roles. Therefore, Chapter 14 has new information about everyday home life among the Inca.

Although the Society and Economy box on women's rights, as defined by the *Quran*, in Chapter 16 is not a new one, it contains new material.

Chapter 18 has additional material to reinforce Africa's place in the Old World economy during the classical and late classical ages.

Chapter 19 retains the Arts and Culture box but changes its attention from poetry to the diary of Lady Murasaki Shikibu for its information about birth practices and the religious taboos and rites that surrounded them in eleventh-century Japan.

Because Chapter 20 has a box on the medieval European village of Wharram Percy, a Historians Craft box on archaeology has been added to the chapter. The chapter also adds some new material on the "northern" trade routes pioneered by the Vikings and their settlement of what came to be Russia.

Although the subject matter remains the same, the Evidence of the Past box on pre-Hispanic Tenochtitlán has been rewritten and updated in Chapter 22. Portions have been revised to bring the chapter more into line with the major themes.

New material in Chapter 25 focuses attention on African initiative in the era of the slave trade with a Law and Government box about Queen Mpande Nzinga's wars of resistance to the Portuguese enslavement of her people.

Again emphasizing global themes, Chapter 26 has added information about China's expansion during the Ming era. Highlighting this is a new box on Zheng He, the fourteenth-century explorer of the Indian Ocean.

Chapter 30 combines the old Chapters 30 and 31 from previous editions because they both concern eighteenth-century liberalism. It also includes another one of the new Historians Craft boxes. This one briefly discusses the challenges the historian faces in trying to use written primary sources. Again calling attention to the importance of women, a new Images box highlights the actions of women in the French Revolution.

In Chapter 32 on the early Industrial Revolution is a new box on Florence Nightingale, "the Lady with the Lamp," whose work during and after the Crimean War helped pioneer modern health care practices.

On "Advanced Industrial Society" in the nineteenth century, Chapter 33 has a new box on the Great Exhibition of 1851. It emphasizes the great technological breakthroughs of the Industrial Revolution, as exemplified most conspicuously in the Crystal Palace.

Because in certain respects, European imperialism in India predated that in Africa, the old Chapters 36 and 37 have switched places in this edition. A new chapter in the last edition, we have extended Chapter 35 (formerly Chapter 37) to include more information about India through much of the *Raj*. The added material includes details about early Indian Nationalism and the Congress Party.

Again emphasizing local initiative, Chapter 36 includes a new box on African resistance and the role religious beliefs sometimes played in African responses to colonial force.

Many women who helped lead the national and revolutionary movements in Latin America have been forgotten. However, Chapter 38 has a new box recalling the contributions of three women, Dolores Jiménez y Muro, Clorinda Matto, and Narcisa Amália de Campos.

Chapter 39 covers the revolution in the sciences that occurred in the early twentieth century. However, achievement in the sciences often has had a social dimension, and in keeping with that, we have added a new box that demonstrates how scientific prowess sometimes runs in families. The one in this chapter considers the famous Curies—Pierre, Marie, and daughter Irene.

Chapter 41 considers the social, political, and cultural consequences that World War I had on Western civilization. A new Arts and Culture box looks at several examples of modernist art and shows how new notions of reality, changed by the war, appeared in the arts.

Chapter 42 has a new box that looks at Nuremburg race laws as the legal "justification" for racism in Nazi Germany.

Chapter 44 has some additional material on the Meiji era in Japan and a new box on the noted early Japanese reformer, Fukuzawa Yukichi.

Again taking up the theme of social history and changing gender roles, a new box in Chapter 45 is devoted to "Rosie the Riveter" and the U.S. Home Front in World War II.

Chapter 49 contains added material on the jihadist movements in Africa and the improving outlook for the economies of some of its nations.

Chapter 50 includes a new Arts and Culture box on The Solitude of Latin America: Nobel Lecture by Gabriel García Márquez in 1982.

With so much of the world's attention drawn to the so-called Arab Spring over the past two years, Chapter 51 has a new box that summarizes the changes that have occurred up to the time of the printing of this edition.

With the ever-growing importance of the Internet, Chapter 53 contains a new box on its likely future as an instrument of communication in the world. The section on the gender gap has been rewritten and updated. A new box, 2010 United Nation Millennium Development Goals: A Progress Report, also has been added.

ORGANIZATION OF THE SEVENTH EDITION

We have retained the six-part arrangement of previous editions, and all parts have been named to reflect both chronological and global themes. However, one of the main points of reference is the relative degree of contact among civilizations. This ranges from the near-perfect isolation of the preclassical age (100,000–500 B.C.E.) to close and continual interaction (as in the late twentieth-century world). Within each part, attention is drawn to these themes in the introduction to each chapter and the description of each part. The number of chapters has been reduced further to 53.

The second organizing principle is the prioritization of certain topics and processes. We generally emphasize sociocultural and economic affairs and keep the longer term in perspective, while deliberately minimizing some short-term phenomena. In terms of the space allotted, we emphasize the more recent epochs of history, in line with the recognition of growing global interdependence and cultural contact.

From its inception, *World Civilizations* has been meant as a world history and contains proportionately more material on non-Western peoples and cultures than many others currently in print. (In this respect, "Western" means not only European but also North American since the eighteenth century.) After an introductory chapter on prehistory, we look first at Mesopotamia,

Africa and Egypt, India, Central Asia, China, (Native) America, and the Pacific. In these river-valley, mountainous, and maritime environments, humans were first successful in adapting nature to their needs on a large scale. Between about 2500 B.C.E. and about 1000 B.C.E., the earliest civilizations matured and developed a culture in most phases of life—a fashion of thinking and acting that would be a model for as long as that civilization was vital and capable of defending itself. Elsewhere, in Africa, Central Asia, the Pacific Islands, and in the Americas, similar processes were under way. However, in two noteworthy respects, these regions provided exceptions to the pattern by which people learned to produce food for themselves. In Africa's case, people of the Sahara region domesticated livestock, most likely cattle, before they learned to grow and depend on crops. Also unlike the patterns established in the Old World, early Native American farmers of the Western Hemisphere developed forms of agriculture that did not depend on the floodwaters of major rivers. In Central Asia and the Pacific Islands, nomadism, based on herding in the former case and on fishing combined with agriculture in the latter one, became the prevalent forms of subsistence.

By 500 B.C.E., the Near Eastern civilizations centered in Egypt and Mesopotamia were in decline and had been replaced by Mediterranean-based civilizations, as well as new ones in Africa, Asia, and the New World, which drew on the older civilizations to some extent but also added some novel and distinctive features of their own. First the Greeks, then the Romans, succeeded in bringing much of the world known to them under their influence, culminating in the great Roman Empire that reached from Spain to Persia. For Europe, the greatest single addition to life in this era was the combination of Judeo-Christian theology and Greco-Roman philosophy and science.

In the millennium between 500 B.C.E. and 500 C.E., the entire globe underwent important change. Western and Central Asia became a potpourri of ideas where monotheistic religions took root. First Judaism, then Christianity and Zoroastrianism appealed to the growing numbers of urbanites. Further south and east, Buddhism and Jainism challenged India's Hindu religion and philosophy, while China recovered from political dismemberment to become the permanent chief factor in East Asian affairs. In the early centuries C.E. both Buddhist and Hindu civilizations appeared for the first time in both mainland and insular Southeast Asia as India's merchant classes traded with and settled in these regions at that time. Japan emerged slowly from a prehistoric stage under Chinese tutelage, while the southeastern part of the Asian continent attained a high civilization created in part by Indian traders and Buddhist missionaries.

In the Mediterranean, starting about 800, an amalgam of Greco-Roman, Germanic, and Jewish-Christian beliefs called European or Western Christianity had emerged after the collapse of Roman civilization. At the same time, the emergence of Islam created what many scholars believe was the first truly "world" civilization—at least to the extent that the Eurasian and African landmasses encompassed the world that was known to "Old World" peoples at that time. Rivaling the great civilizations of Asia and considerably surpassing that of Europe, the great empire of the Abbasid caliphs in Baghdad (750–1258 C.E.) acted as a commercial and intellectual bridge that transcended regional barriers from China to Africa and Europe. Therefore, among the many lands and peoples bordering the Indian Ocean, the spread of Islam along the highways of commerce contributed to the emergence of sophisticated maritime civilizations in Western Asia, Southeast Asia, India, and East Africa. In West Africa, the great Sudanic civilizations of Mali and later Songhay and Bornu were likewise solidly based on an Islamic foundation. Despite isolation from the Old World, Native Americans of the New World created a series of highly sophisticated civilizations in the high Andes Mountains of South America, in Mesoamerica, and in the southwestern and eastern parts of what now is the United States.

By 1500, Western civilization began to rise to a position of a temporary worldwide domination, marked by the voyages of discovery and ensuing colonization. In the next three centuries, the Europeans and their colonial outposts slowly wove a web of worldwide commercial and technological interests, anchored on military force. Our book's treatment of the entire post-1500 age gives much attention to the impacts of Western culture and ideas on non-Western peoples, and vice versa. In particular, it looks at the African civilizations encountered by early European traders and what became of them, southern Asia under the Raj, and the Native American civilizations of North and Latin America and their fate under Spanish conquest and rule.

From 1700 through World War I, Europe took the lead in practically every field of material human life, including military affairs, science, commerce, and living standards. This was the age of Europe's imperial control of the rest of the world. The Americas, much of Asia, Oceania, and coastal Africa all became formal or informal colonies at one time, and some remained under direct European control until the mid-twentieth century.

In the nineteenth and twentieth centuries, the pendulum of power swung steadily away from Europe and toward first North America, then Russia, Japan, and the non-Western (particularly Asian) peoples. As we enter a new millennium, the world not only has shrunk but has again been anchored on multiple power bases. A degree of equilibrium is rapidly being restored—one that combines Western science and technology with those Asian, African, and Native American social values and intellectual traditions that go back to the preclassical era and whose resilience has enabled them to endure the West's imperial era.

Our periodization scheme, then, is a sixfold one:

- From Human Origins to Agrarian Communities, c. 100,000–500 B.C.E.
- Classical Civilizations of the World, 500 B.C.E.–800 C.E.
- The Post-Classical Era, 800–1500 C.E.
- Expanding Webs of Interaction, c. 1400–1800

- Revolutions, Ideology, the New Imperialism, and the Age of Empire, 1700–1920
- Towards a Globalized World, 1914–Present

PEDAGOGY

From the first edition through this one, an important feature of *World Civilizations* has been its division into a number of short chapters. Each of its fifty-three chapters is meant to constitute a unit suitable in scope for a single lecture, short enough to allow easy digestion and comprising strong logical coherence. Each chapter contains a variety of pedagogical elements intended to help students learn and retain important information.

- Thematic features and photographs are keyed to the five broad text themes: Society and Economy, Law and Government, Patterns of Belief, Science and Technology, and Arts and Culture. All chapters have one or more boxed feature inserts, some of which are based on biography, many others on primary sources. To encourage readers to interact with the material as historians would and to compare themes across chapters, each boxed feature concludes with Analyze and Interpret questions. A global icon has been added throughout the chapters as a way to highlight discussions of global developments and movements.
- Two additional boxed features, Evidence of the Past and the Images of History, spotlight artifacts and material culture. Once writing became common, of course, some materials that you will see in Evidence of the Past are written primary sources, but we point out to you, where appropriate, their roots in oral traditions. We also include some eyewitness accounts for analysis.
- The new Historians Craft boxes briefly describe some of the methods and sources on which professional historians rely to illuminate the past. These include: historical linguistics, archaeology, oral traditions, and written documents.
- A chapter outline and a brief chapter chronology help students focus on the key concepts in the material they are about to encounter.
- Chapter summary encapsulates the significance of the chapter's concepts.
- A Test Your Knowledge section at the end of the chapter provides a brief—and unique—self-test. Reviewers tell us that their students rely on these tests to assess their understanding of each chapter and to prepare for quizzes and exams. New questions have been added to most chapters.
- The For Further Reflection section at the end of each chapter follows the objective Test Your Knowledge questions. The intent of these essay-type questions is to impel students to think beyond the "merely" objective knowledge required for successfully completing the Test Your Knowledge section. The idea, of course, is to exhort them to review, interpret, and apply that knowledge as a technique for arriving at a better understanding of developments as seen from the perspective of their regional and

(possibly) global implications. These questions vary in difficulty. They ask students to use their imaginations, as well as their fact-based understanding of the subject, and they sometimes require that students search for additional information outside of what the text affords (for example, in class lectures).

- Key terms appear in boldface type and are repeated at chapter end in an Identification Terms list.
- Parenthetical pronunciation guides of unfamiliar names appear within the text, facilitating ease of reading.
- Color illustrations, many of them new, and abundant maps appear throughout the text. We include Worldview maps that show global developments. Descriptive map and photo captions encourage readers to think beyond the mere appearance of each visual and to make connections across chapters, regions, and concepts. And critical-thinking questions encourage students to work with and read maps as a historian might.

Additional text-specific pedagogical elements include the following:

- An end-of-book Glossary with a pronunciation guide provides explanations of unfamiliar terms and pronunciation guidance for the more difficult among them.
- Part introductions and Worldview maps highlight the major civilizations discussed in that part of the text. At the end of each part, there is a Worldview chart comparing the same civilizations, color-coded to the same groups in the part-opening map and affording a nutshell review of their accomplishments according to the text's five major themes. A Cross-Cultural Connections section at the end of each Worldview encourages thinking beyond regional borders.
- Finally, like the For Further Reflection questions placed at the end of each chapter, essay questions have been added to each Worldview section to exhort students to think "globally," to draw on their understanding of two or more chapters contained in each part. Appropriately, we have called this review section Putting It All Together.

SUPPLEMENTS

A wide array of supplements accompanies this text to assist students with different learning needs and to help instructors master today's various classroom challenges.

Instructor Resources

MindTap Reader (ISBN: 9781285772981) MindTap Reader is Cengage Learning's re-imagination of the traditional eBook, specifically designed for how students assimilate content and media assets in a fully online—and often mobile—reading environment. MindTap Reader combines thoughtful navigation ergonomics, advanced student annotation support and a high level of instructor driven personalization through the placement of online documents and media assets. These features create an engaging student reading experience further enhanced through tightly integrated web-apps (e.g. social media, note-taking, utilities) that ultimately deliver a holistic learning tool driving immediacy, relevancy and engagement for today's learners. MindTap Reader is available within CourseMate.

Online PowerLecture with Cognero® (ISBN: 9781285455051) This PowerLecture is an all-in-one online multimedia resource for class preparation, presentation, and testing. Accessible through Cengage.com/login with your faculty account, you will find available for download: book-specific Microsoft® PowerPoint® presentations; a Test Bank in both Microsoft® Word® and Cognero® formats; an Instructor Manual; Microsoft® PowerPoint® Image Slides; and a JPEG Image Library.

The *Test Bank,* prepared by Edward Shelor of Georgia Military College and offered in Microsoft® Word® and Cognero® formats, contains multiple-choice and essay questions for each chapter. Cognero® is a flexible, online system that allows you to author, edit, and manage test bank content for World Civilizations, 7e. Create multiple test versions instantly and deliver through your LMS from your classroom, or wherever you may be, with no special installs or downloads required.

The *Instructor's Manual,* prepared by Rico Chapman of Jackson State University, contains for each chapter: chapter outlines and summaries, lecture topics, suggested student activities, and essay/discussion topics. The *Microsoft® PowerPoint® presentations,* prepared by Susan Maneck of Jackson State University, are ready-to-use, visual outlines of each chapter. These presentations are easily customized for your lectures and offered along with chapter-specific Microsoft® PowerPoint® Image Slides and JPEG Image Libraries. Access your Online PowerLecture at www.cengage.com/login.

CourseMate Cengage Learning's History CourseMate brings course concepts to life with interactive learning, study, and exam preparation tools that support the printed textbook. History CourseMate includes an integrated eBook, interactive teaching and learning tools including quizzes, flashcards, videos, and more, and EngagementTracker, a first-of-its-kind tool that monitors student engagement in the course. Learn more at www.cengagebrain.com.

CourseReader CourseReader is an online collection of primary and secondary sources that lets you create a customized electronic reader in minutes. With an easy-to-use interface and assessment tool, you can choose exactly what your students will be assigned—simply search or browse Cengage Learning's extensive document database to preview and select your customized collection of readings. In addition to print sources of all types (letters, diary entries, speeches, newspaper accounts, etc.), their collection includes a growing number of images and video and audio clips.

Each primary source document includes a descriptive headnote that puts the reading into context and is further supported by both critical thinking and multiple-choice questions designed to reinforce key points. For more information visit www.cengage.com/coursereader.

Cengagebrain.com Save your students time and money. Direct them to www.cengagebrain.com for choice in formats and savings and a better chance to succeed in your class. *Cengagebrain.com,* Cengage Learning's online store, is a single destination for more than 10,000 new textbooks, eTextbooks, eChapters, study tools, and audio supplements. Students have the freedom to purchase a-la-carte exactly what they need when they need it. Students can save 50 percent on the electronic textbook and can pay as little as $1.99 for an individual eChapter.

Student Resources

Book Companion Site A website for students that features a wide assortment of resources to help students master the subject matter. The website, prepared by Patricia Ali of Morris College, includes a glossary, flashcards, learning objectives, chapter summaries, and tutorial quizzes.

Doing History: Research and Writing in the Digital Age, 2e (ISBN: 9781133587880) Prepared by Michael J. Galgano, J. Chris Arndt, and Raymond M. Hyser of James Madison University. Whether you're starting down the path as a history major, or simply looking for a straightforward and systematic guide to writing a successful paper, you'll find this text to be an indispensable handbook to historical research. This text's "soup to nuts" approach to researching and writing about history addresses every step of the process, from locating your sources and gathering information, to writing clearly and making proper use of various citation styles to avoid plagiarism. You'll also learn how to make the most of every tool available to you—especially the technology that helps you conduct the process efficiently and effectively. The second edition includes a special appendix linked to CourseReader (see previous page), where you can examine and interpret primary sources online.

The History Handbook, 2e (ISBN: 9780495906766) Prepared by Carol Berkin of Baruch College, City University of New York, and Betty Anderson of Boston University. This book teaches students both basic and history-specific study skills such as how to take notes, get the most out of lectures and readings, read primary sources, research historical topics, and correctly cite sources. Substantially less expensive than comparable skill-building texts, *The History Handbook* also offers tips for Internet research and evaluating online sources. Additionally, students can purchase and download the ***eAudio*** version of The History Handbook or any of its eighteen individual units at www.cengagebrain.com to listen to on the go.

Writing for College History (ISBN: 9780618306039) Prepared by Robert M. Frakes, Clarion University. This brief handbook for survey courses in U.S. history, Western Civilization/European history, and world civilization guides students through the various types of writing assignments they encounter in a history class. Providing examples of student writing and candid assessments of student work, this text focuses on the rules and conventions of writing for the college history course.

The Modern Researcher, 6e (ISBN: 9780495318705) Prepared by Jacques Barzun and Henry F. Graff of Columbia University. This classic introduction to the techniques of research and the art of expression is used widely in history courses and is also appropriate for writing and research methods courses in other departments. Barzun and Graff thoroughly cover every aspect of research, from the selection of a topic through the gathering, analysis, writing, revision, and publication of findings and present the process not as a set of rules but through actual cases that put the subtleties of research in a useful context. Part One covers the principles and methods of research; Part Two covers writing, speaking, and getting one's work published.

Reader Program Cengage Learning publishes a number of readers, some containing exclusively primary sources, others devoted to essays and secondary sources, and still others provide a combination of primary and secondary sources. All of these readers are designed to guide students through the process of historical inquiry. Visit Cengage.com/history for a complete list of readers.

Custom Options

Nobody knows your students like you, so why not give them a text that is tailor-fit to their needs? Cengage Learning offers custom solutions for your course—whether it's making a small modification to *World Civilizations* to match your syllabus or combining multiple sources to create something truly unique. You can pick and choose chapters, include your own material, and add additional map exercises along with the Rand McNally Atlas to create a text that fits the way you teach. Ensure that your students get the most out of their textbook dollar by giving them exactly what they need. Contact your Cengage Learning representative to explore custom solutions for your course.

Rand McNally Historical Atlas of the World (ISBN: 9780618841912) This valuable resource features more than seventy maps that portray the rich panoply of the world's history from preliterate times to the present. They show how cultures and civilization were linked and how they interacted. The maps make it clear that history is not static. Rather, it is about change and movement across time. The maps show change by presenting the dynamics of expansion, cooperation, and conflict. This atlas includes maps that display the world from the beginning of civilization; the political development of all major areas of the world; expanded coverage of Africa, Latin America, and the Middle East; the current Islamic World; and the world population change in 1900 and 2000.

ACKNOWLEDGMENTS

The authors are happy to acknowledge the sustained aid given them by many individuals during the long incubation period of this text.

Phil Adler's colleagues in the history department at East Carolina University, at the annual meetings of the test planners and graders of the Advanced Placement in European History, as well as in several professional organizations—notably the American Association for the Advancement of Slavic Studies—are particularly to be thanked.

In addition, we thank reviewers of the sixth and seventh editions of our book:

Patricia Ali, Morris College
Steven Bachelor, Fairfield University
Stefan Bosworth, Hostos Community College
Robert Caputi, Erie Community College—North Campus

John Fielding, Mount Wachusett Community College
Thomas Hafer, John Jay College
Kenneth Heller, McLennan Community College
Robert Hendershot, Grand Rapids Community College
Cathy Itnyre, Copper Mountain College
Mark Klobas, Scottsdale Community College
David Marley, Vanguard University
Brandon Marsh, Bridgewater College
Kate Martin, Cape Cod Community College
Cherry McCabe, Simpson University
Brendan McManus, Bemidji State University
Barbara Moss, Georgia Highlands College
Andrew Oleary, Bristol Community College
R. Edward Shelor, Georgia Military College
Steven Stofferahn, Indiana State University
David Weiland, Collin County Community College

We would also like to acknowledge Brooke Barbier's contribution as Product Manager, Kate Scheinman's as Senior Content Developer, and Jane Lee's as Senior Content Project Manager.

And special thanks go to Joel B. Pouwels, Ph.D., for her important suggestions for and contributions to the chapters on Latin American civilizations.

About the Authors

PHILIP J. ADLER taught college courses in world history to undergraduates for almost thirty years prior to his recent retirement. Dr. Adler took his Ph.D. at the University of Vienna following military service overseas in the 1950s. His dissertation was on the activity of the South Slav émigrés during World War I, and his academic specialty was the modern history of Eastern Europe and the Austro-Hungarian empire. Fulbright and National Endowment for the Humanities grants have supported his research. Adler has published widely in the historical journals of this country and German-speaking Europe. He is currently Professor Emeritus at East Carolina University, where he spent most of his teaching career.

RANDALL L. POUWELS earned his B.A. in history at the University of Wisconsin and his Ph.D. in history at UCLA. His Ph.D. dissertation was on the history of Islam in East Africa. His book *Horn and Crescent: Cultural Change and Traditional Islam on the East African Coast, 800–1900* (Cambridge, 1987) has become a standard work on African history. The *History of Islam in Africa* (Athens, Oxford, and Cape Town, 2000) was jointly edited with Nehemia Levtzion of Hebrew University, Jerusalem. Widely praised in reviews, it was selected by Choice as an Outstanding Academic Title for 2001 and was made a selection of the History Book Club. In addition, Pouwels has written numerous articles and reviews on East African history, the history of Islam in Africa, and historical methodologies. His other research interests include the history of the Middle East, the Indian Ocean, and the history and archaeology of Native Americans. Over the years, his work has been supported by grants and fellowships from Fulbright-Hays, the National Endowment for the Humanities, the Social Studies Research Council, the National Geographic Society, and the American Philosophical Society. He has taught African history for over twenty years at LaTrobe University in Melbourne, Australia, and at UCLA. He retired at the end of 2009, and is now an Emeritus Professor of African and Middle Eastern History at the University of Central Arkansas.

NOTE ON USAGE AND SPELLING

Throughout the work, the Pinyin orthography has been adopted for Chinese names. The older Wade-Giles system has been included in parentheses at the first mention and retained in a few cases where common usage demands it (Chiang Kai-shek, for example).

Introduction to the Student: Why Is History Worth Studying?

HUMAN ACTIONS TEND TO FALL into broad patterns, whether they occurred yesterday or 5,000 years ago. Physical needs, such as the need for food, water, and breathable air, dictate some actions. Others stem from emotional and intellectual needs, such as religious belief or the search for immortality. Human action also results from desires, such as literary ambition or scientific curiosity, or the quest for political power over others, rather than from absolute needs.

History is the record of how people have tried to meet those needs or fulfill those desires. Many generations of our ancestors have found that familiarity with that record can be useful in guiding their own actions. The study of past human acts also encourages us to see our own present possibilities, both individual and collective. This may be history's greatest value.

Many people are naturally attracted to the study of history, but others find it difficult or (even worse) "irrelevant." Some students—perhaps yourself—dread history courses, saying that they can see no point in learning about the past. My life, they say, is here and now; leave the past to the past. What can be said in response to justify the study of history?

People who are ignorant of their past are also ignorant of much of their present, for the one grows directly out of the other. If we ignore or forget the experience of those who have lived before us, we are like an amnesia victim, constantly puzzled by what should be familiar, surprised by what should be predictable. Not only do we not know what we should know, but we cannot perceive our true possibilities, because we have nothing to measure them against. The nonhistorical mind does not know what it is missing—and, contrary to the old saying, what you don't know can definitely hurt you!

A word of caution here: this is not a question of "history repeats itself." This often-quoted cliché is clearly nonsense if taken literally. History does *not* repeat itself exactly, and the difference in details is always important. But history does exhibit general patterns, dictated by common human needs and desires. The French Revolution will not recur just as it did 215 years ago. But, as we know all too well, people still depose their leaders and rise up in arms to change the way they live. Some knowledge of and respect for those patterns has been a vital part of the mental equipment of all human societies.

But there is another, more personal reason to learn about the past. Adults who are historically unconscious are confined within a figurative wooden packing crate, into which they were put by the accident of birth at a given time and in a given place. The boards forming the box restrict their freedom and block their view in all directions. One board of the box might be the prosperity—or lack of it—into which they were born; another, their physical appearance, race, or ethnic group. Other boards could be their religion, whether they were born in a city slum or a small village, or whether they had a chance at formal education (about three-fourths of the world's children never go beyond the third year of school). These and many other boards form the boxes into which we are all born.

If we are to fully realize our potential as human beings, some of the boards must be removed so that we can see out, gain other vistas and visions, and have a chance to measure and compare our experiences with others outside. And the smaller our "global village" becomes, the more important it becomes to learn more about the world beyond the campus, city, state, and country in which we live. An introductory course in world history is an ideal way to learn about life outside the box.

As a good student, your best resource is your own sense of curiosity. Keep it active as you go through these pages. Remember, this and every other textbook is the beginning, not the end, of your search for useful knowledge. Good luck!

P. J. A.
R. L. P.

Note: Some of you may at first be confused by dates followed by bce, meaning "before the common era," and ce, meaning "common era." These terms are used to reflect a global perspective, and they correspond to the Western equivalents bc (before Christ) and ad (*anno Domini*). Also, a caution about the word century is in order: the phrase *seventeenth century* CE refers to the years 1601 to 1699 in the common era, and the phrase *first century* BCE refers to the years 99 to 0 bce With a little practice, these terms become second nature and will increase your fluency in history.

PART IV

Worldview Map IV Peoples of the World, *c.* 1400

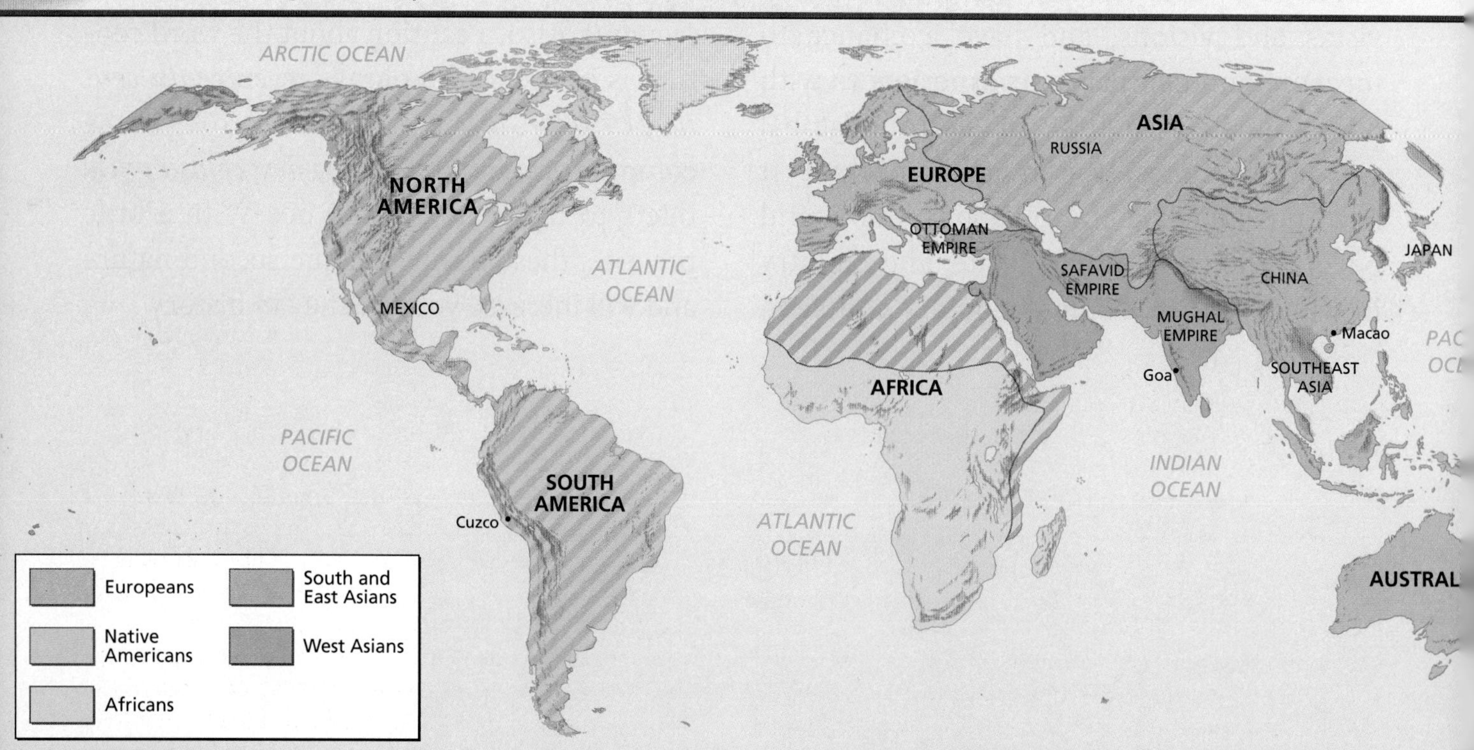

Expanding Webs of Interaction, c. 1400–1800

Within two hundred years of 1400 C.E., a host of events or processes contributed to an atmosphere of rising confidence in the power of governments and their supportive institutions. In the political and military realm, the Mongol yoke in Russia was lifted; the Ottoman Turks, victorious at Constantinople, failed in an attempt to seize Vienna and central Europe; the Hundred Years' War had ended and the French recovery commenced. After suffering horrific mortality rates, the civilizations of Eurasia and Africa finally recovered from the ravages of the Black Death, and maritime trade increased significantly in all of the three oceans girdling the entire world. Indeed, it can be said that for the first time trade and contacts among the world's civilizations had become truly global.

But aside from these general developments, the centuries that came between about 1400 and 1800 usually are heralded as the beginning of the modern era because of two specific complexes of events: the questioning of traditional authority in the West, manifested in the Protestant Reformation, and European and Chinese voyages of discovery that revealed the possibilities of the globe to the imaginations of some Europeans and Asians. Both of these contributed, in different ways, to the expansion of China's and Europe's reach and authority that took place in this four-hundred-year time span, until Europeans began to claim a prerogative to decide the fates of others as almost a God-given right. This tendency was particularly striking in Eastern and Southeast Asia and the American colonies, where the native Amerindians either were obliterated or virtually enslaved by their overlords. But it was also the case—although in a much more limited way—in eastern and southern Asia, the coast of Africa, and the island or Arctic peripheries of a world, which was larger and more varied than anyone had formerly supposed.

The difference between 1400 and 1850 in this regard might well be illustrated by comparing the Aztecs' Tenochtitlán, which amazed the envious Hernán Cortés, with the sleepy, dusty villages to which Mexico's Indians were later confined. Similarly, one might compare the army of the Persian Safavid rulers of the early sixteenth century that reduced the mighty Mughals to supplicants for peace with the raggedy mob that attempted—in vain—to stop a handful of British from installing themselves on the Khyber Pass three centuries later. The West by 1800, whether represented by Spanish freebooters or Oxford-educated British bureaucrats, seemed destined to surpass or be invincible against what one unrepentant imperialist called the "lesser breeds." Part Four examines the massive changes that were slowly evincing themselves during these four centuries of heightening interactions. The European voyages of discovery of the fifteenth and sixteenth centuries, the opening of maritime commerce across the Indian and Atlantic oceans, and the resultant Columbian Exchange and the slave trade are the subjects of Chapter 22. Chapter 23 considers in detail the successful challenges to the authority of European monarchs and the Roman Catholic hierarchy and their permanent effects on Western sensibilities. Challenges to religious authority inevitably led to other confrontations. This chapter also examines the ideas of absolutism and constitutionalism, as well as their expressions in religious warfare and the desire for stability, which became the cornerstones of modern governments. Chapter 24 shifts the focus to Asia, where the rise and fall of the great Muslim empires of central Asia and India are discussed. Chapter 25 focuses on the continuities and changes that Africa experienced in this era of global expansion and the slave trade. China's centuries of glory following the ejection of the Mongols through the early Qing Dynasty are analyzed in Chapter 26. The history of Japan and Southeast Asia before 1700 follows in Chapter 27. Finally, the Iberian colonies of America and their struggle for independent existence are outlined in Chapter 28.

Our Worldview Map IV, Peoples of the World, indicates the most significant development in the period after 1400, the dramatic enlargement of the areas of the globe where Europeans and East Asians colonized and settled among indigenous peoples.

22 A Larger World Opens

I have come to believe that this is a mighty continent which was hitherto unknown. —CHRISTOPHER COLUMBUS

Mid-1400s	Portuguese begin voyages of exploration
1492	Christopher Columbus reaches Americas
1498	Vasco da Gama arrives in India
Early 1500s	Transatlantic slave trade begins
1519–1540	Spanish conquer Aztecs and Incans
1522	First circumnavigation of globe completed
1602	Dutch East India Company founded

CHAPTER OUTLINE

The unparalleled overseas expansion of Europe in the later fifteenth and early sixteenth centuries opened a new era of intercontinental contacts. What were the motives for the rapid series of adventuresome voyages? They ranged from Christian missionary impulses to the common desire to get rich. Backed to varying degrees by their royal governments, Portuguese, Spanish, Dutch, French, and English seafarers opened the world to European commerce, settlement, and eventual dominion. Through the **Columbian Exchange** initiated in 1492, the New World entered European consciousness and was radically and permanently changed by European settlers. In most of the world, however, the presence of a relative handful of foreigners in coastal "factories" (as trading stations were called) or as occasional traders meant little change to traditional activities and attitudes. Not until the later eighteenth century was the European presence a threat to the continuation of accustomed African, Asian, and Polynesian lifestyles.

MARITIME EXPLORATION IN THE 1400s

The Vikings in their graceful longboats had made voyages across the North Atlantic from Scandinavia to Greenland and on to North America as early as 1000 C.E., but the northern voyages were too risky to serve as the channel for permanent European expansion, and Scandinavia's population base was too small. Four hundred years later, major advances in technology had transformed maritime commerce. The import of new sail rigging, the magnetic compass, and the astrolabe (an instrument used to determine the altitude of the sun or other celestial bodies) from Asia; a new hull design; and systematic navigational charts enabled Western seamen, led by the Portuguese, to conquer the world's oceans. Firearms of all sizes backed up their claims to dominion over their newly discovered territories. By the end of the fifteenth century, the map of the Eastern Hemisphere was gradually becoming familiar to Europeans.

Knowledge of the high cultures of Asia was current by the early 1400s. Muslim traders had long before established an active commerce with southern and eastern Asia—by their command of the Indian Ocean routes and the famous Silk Road through central Asia—and had served as intermediaries to Europe (Chapter 16). Marco Polo's great adventure was well known even earlier, after the appearance of his book about his many years of service to Kubilai Khan.

Most of Europe's luxury imports had long come from Africa, China and India, while the Spice Islands (as they were called by Europeans) of Southeast Asia had been the source of the most valuable items in international exchange (see Map 22.1). In the fourteenth century, this trade was disrupted, first by the Ottoman Turkish conquest of the eastern Mediterranean and then by the breakup of the Mongol Empire, which had formed a single unit reaching from China to western Russia.

Security of transit across Asia was threatened, as was the Europeans' long-established and profitable interchange of goods with the Arabs and Persians. In 1453, the great depot of Eastern wares, Constantinople, fell into the hands of the Ottomans. With direct access to this old gateway to the East now lost, Europeans became more interested than

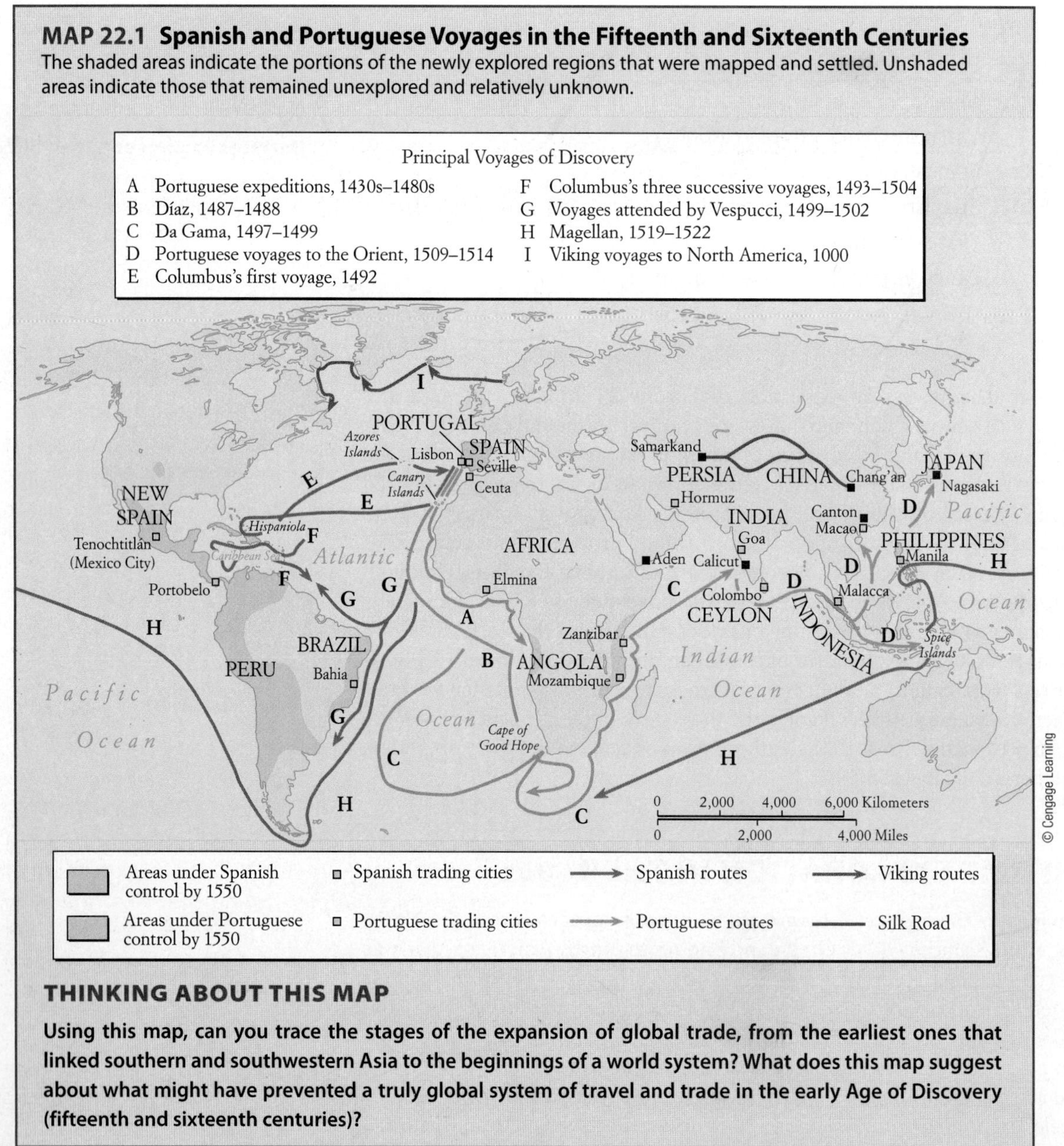

MAP 22.1 Spanish and Portuguese Voyages in the Fifteenth and Sixteenth Centuries
The shaded areas indicate the portions of the newly explored regions that were mapped and settled. Unshaded areas indicate those that remained unexplored and relatively unknown.

THINKING ABOUT THIS MAP

Using this map, can you trace the stages of the expansion of global trade, from the earliest ones that linked southern and southwestern Asia to the beginnings of a world system? What does this map suggest about what might have prevented a truly global system of travel and trade in the early Age of Discovery (fifteenth and sixteenth centuries)?

ever in finding a direct sea route to the East by circumnavigating Africa and so making it possible to bypass the hostile Ottomans.

OVERSEAS EMPIRES AND THEIR EFFECTS

First the Portuguese and the Spanish and then the Dutch, English, and French created overseas empires that had far-reaching effects both at home and abroad.

Portuguese Pioneers

In the middle of the 1400s and under the guidance of the visionary **Prince Henry the Navigator** (1394–1460), tiny and impoverished Portugal sponsored a series of exploratory voyages down the west coast of Africa and out into the ocean as far as the Azores (about one-third the distance to the Caribbean) in a search of African gold and pepper. In 1488, the Portuguese captain Bartolomeo Díaz made a crucial advance by successfully rounding the Cape of Good Hope. Some years later, **Vasco da Gama** (VAHS-coh duh GAH-mah) sailed across the Indian Ocean to the west coast of India. (For a closer look at da Gama's exploits, see the Evidence of the Past box.) Trying to follow a new route around the southern tip of Africa that took him far to the west, Pedro Alvarez Cabral got blown all the way across the Atlantic, making landfall in Brazil, which he promptly claimed for Portugal. By 1510, Portuguese flags were flying over Goa in India and Macão on the coast of China (see Map 22.1). In 1511, the extraordinary admiral Afonso da Albuquerque seized the great port-depot of Malacca at the tip of the Malay Peninsula. With the capital of their Indian Ocean empire in Goa, the Portuguese became the controllers of the most profitable sea trade in the world.

The Portuguese empire was really only a string of fortified stations called "factories," from which the Portuguese

EVIDENCE OF THE PAST

Vasco da Gama's First Contacts in East Africa

One of the most daring of all the explorers sailing in the name of Portugal or Spain was Vasco da Gama, the first to round the tip of Africa and sail on to India. Da Gama made landfall on the Indian coast in 1498 before returning safely to Lisbon the following year. He kept a detailed diary of his epoch-making voyage, from which the following comments on the non-Muslim peoples of the East African littoral are taken.

> These people are black, and the men are of good physique, they go about naked except that they wear small pieces of cotton cloth with which they cover their genitals, and the Senhores [chiefs] of the land wear larger cloths. The young women in this land look good; they have their lips pierced in three places and they wear some pieces of twisted tin. These people were very much at ease with us, and brought out to us in the vessels what they had, in dugout canoes….
>
> After we had been here two or three days there came out two Senhores of this land to see us, they were so haughty that they did not value anything which was given to them. One of them was wearing a cap on his head with piping worked in silk, and the other a furry cap of green satin. There came in their company a youth who, we gathered from gestures, came from another far country, and said that he had already seen great vessels like those that carried us. With these signs we rejoiced greatly, because it seemed to us that we were going to reach where we wanted to go….
>
> This land, it seemed to us, is densely populated. There are in it many villages and towns. The women seemed to be more numerous than men, because when there came 20 men there came 40 women …. The arms of these people are very large bows and arrows, and assagais [short stabbing spears] of iron. In this land there seemed to be much copper, which they wore on their legs and arms and in their kinky hair. Equally used is tin, which they place on the hilts of daggers, the sheaths are of iron. The people greatly prize linen cloth, and they gave us as much of this copper for as many shirts as we cared to give.

ANALYZE AND INTERPRET

What seems to have been the attitude of the East Africans toward these European strangers? To what do you attribute this view? From where do you suppose the previously seen "vessels" had come? To what kinds of material technology does it appear the Africans had access? Where do you think they got it?

Source: Harry Stephan, ed. *The Diary of Vasco da Gama (Travels Through African Waters 1497–1499)* (Sydney: Phillips, 1998), 32–33.

brought back shiploads of the much-sought-after spices, gold, porcelain, and silk obtained from their trading partners in East Africa and the Southeast Asian mainland and islands. They paid for these imports initially with metal wares, cloth, and trinkets, and later with firearms and liquor. The Lisbon government was the initiator and main beneficiary of this trade because Portugal's small upper and middle classes were unable to pay sufficiently to outfit ships for the expeditions.

The era of Portuguese leadership was brief. The country was too poor and its population too small to maintain this lucrative but thinly spread empire. By the late 1500s, the aggressively expanding Dutch merchants had already forced Portugal out of some of its overseas stations. Previously independent Portugal was incorporated into Catholic Spain in 1580, which gave the Dutch and English Protestants an excuse to attack the Portuguese everywhere. Eventually, by the end of the seventeenth century, Portugal was left with only Angola and the Kongo kingdom in West Africa, plus Mozambique, Macão, Goa, Brazil, and a few additional enclaves and scattered trading posts around the Indian Ocean rim.

How did a relative handful of European intruders establish themselves as regionally dominant authorities in these distant corners of the globe? In the Indian Ocean and Southeast Asia, the patterns established by the Portuguese were followed by all of their successors. The European outreach was seaborne, and control of the sea was the crucial element. Local populations that tried to resist quickly learned that it was not profitable to confront the European ships with arms because the Europeans would generally win. Their naval cannon, more advanced methods of rigging, more maneuverable hulls, better battle discipline, and higher levels of training assured them of success in almost all engagements. The intruders avoided land warfare unless and until mastery of the surrounding seas was assured, and in that case, land warfare was rarely necessary.

After an initial display of martial strength, the newcomers were usually content to deal with and through established local leaders in securing the spices, cotton cloth, silk, and other luxuries they sought. In the normal course of events, the Europeans made treaties with paramount regional rulers that assured them a secure place in the export market. A kind of partnership thus evolved between the local chieftains and the new arrivals, in which both had sufficient reasons to maintain the status quo against those who might challenge it.

The Portuguese frequently made the mistake of alienating the local population by their brutality and their attempts to exclude all competition, but the Dutch and, later, the British were more circumspect. Unlike the Portuguese, they made no attempt until the nineteenth century to bring Africans and Asians to Christianity. As a general rule, after the sixteenth-century, Portuguese missionary efforts had subsided, and the Europeans interfered little with existing laws, religion, and customs unless they felt compelled to do so to gain commercial ends. Such interference was rare in both Asia and Africa. There, the European goal was to derive the maximum profit from trade, and they avoided anything that would threaten the smooth execution of that trade. The Spanish and Portuguese empires in the Americas were a different proposition, however.

The Spanish Empire in the Americas

By the dawn of the sixteenth century, a newly unified Spanish kingdom was close behind, and in some areas competing with, Portugal in the race for a world empire. A larger domestic resource base and extraordinary finds of precious metals enabled Spain to achieve more permanent success than its neighbor. The Italian visionary, Christopher Columbus, was able to persuade King Ferdinand and Queen Isabella to support his dream of a shortcut to the "Indies" by heading west over the Atlantic, which he thought was only a few hundred miles wide. The first of Columbus's Spanish-financed voyages resulted in his discovery of the American continents. He made three more voyages before his death and was still convinced that China lay just over the horizon of the Caribbean Sea.

By then, the Spanish crown had engaged a series of other voyagers, including Amerigo Vespucci, who eventually gave his name to the New World that Columbus and others were exploring. In 1519–1521, the formidable Hernán Cortés conquered the Aztec Empire in Mexico. Soon, Spanish explorers had penetrated north into what is now Florida, California, and Arizona. By the 1540s, Spain controlled most of northern South America as well as all of Central America, the larger Caribbean islands, and the South and Southwest of what is now the United States.

Perhaps the greatest of these ventures was the fantastic voyage of **Ferdinand Magellan**. Starting from Spain in 1519, his ships were the first to circumnavigate the world. A few survivors (not including the unlucky Magellan) limped back into Seville in 1522 and reported that the world was indeed round, as most educated people already thought.

Like the Portuguese, the Spaniards' motives for exploration were mixed between a desire to convert non-Christians to the Roman Catholic Church and thus gain a strong advantage against the burgeoning Protestants (see Chapter 23) and the desire for wealth and social respectability. Land, too, was increasingly in short supply in Europe, especially for the younger offspring of the nobility and the landed gentry. Gold, God, glory, and acquiring land were the motives most frequently in play. By whatever motivation, however, the middle of the 1500s saw the Spanish adventurers creating an empire that reached as far as the Philippine Islands. The Spanish crown claimed its share of treasures found by the explorers under royal charters. Indian gold and silver (*bullion*) thus poured into the royal treasury in Madrid. Those metals, in turn, allowed Spain to become the most powerful European state in the sixteenth and seventeenth centuries.

A PORTUGUESE GALLEON. In what kind of vessel did the early explorers set sail? Ships such as these opened the trade routes to the East and to Brazil and the Caribbean for the Lisbon government in the sixteenth and seventeenth centuries. Later on, two or three rows of cannons gave them heavy firepower as well as cargo space.

Whereas the Portuguese were primarily interested in quick profits from the trade in luxury items from the East, the Spanish explorers came in search of wealth and status denied them in Spain. Those who succeeded did so by confiscating land and workers from among the indigenous population. The priests who accompanied them set up missions among the native population to convert them and to force them into servitude. Finding that *El Dorado* and the much-dreamed-of cities of gold and silver were mirages, the Spanish immigrants gradually created agricultural colonies in much of Middle and South America, using first Amerindian and then African slave labor. The Spanish colonies thus saw the growth of a multiracial society—Africans, Amerindians, and Europeans—in which the Europeans held the dominant political and social positions from the outset. The dominance of the whites was to assume increasing importance for the societies and economies of these lands both during their three hundred years as colonies and later as independent states.

The African Slave Trade Opens

The European export of slaves from Africa commenced in the fifteenth century. When the Portuguese ventured down the West African coast, they quickly discovered that selling black house slaves to the European nobility could be a lucrative business, but the slave trade remained small in scale through the 1490s and began to grow only when slaves started to be shipped across the Atlantic. By the mid-1530s, Portugal had shipped moderate numbers of slaves to the Spanish Caribbean and to its own colony of Brazil, and the trans-Atlantic trade remained almost a Portuguese monopoly until into the next century. At that time, Dutch, French, and then English traders moved into the business and dominated it throughout its great expansion in the eighteenth century until its gradual abolition.

Few European women traveled to the Americas in the early years of colonization, so the Spaniards often married Amerindian or African women or kept them as concubines. As a result, *mestizos* (the offspring of Amerindians and whites) and *mulattos* (the children of Africans and whites) soon outnumbered Caucasians in many colonies. The same thing happened in Portuguese Brazil, where over time a huge number of African slaves were imported to till the sugarcane fields that provided that colony with its chief export. Here, the populace was commonly the offspring of Portuguese and African unions, rather than the Spanish-Indian mixture found to the north.

Dutch and English Merchant-Adventurers

Holland. When Portugal's grip on its Indian Ocean trade began to falter, the Dutch Protestant merchants combined a fine eye for profit with religious zeal to fill the vacuum. In the late sixteenth century, the Netherlands gained independence from Spain. Controlling their own affairs after that, the bourgeois ship owners and merchants of the Dutch and Flemish towns quickly moved into the forefront of the race for trade. By the opening of the seventeenth century, Amsterdam and Antwerp were the major destinations of Far Eastern shippers, and Lisbon had fallen into a secondary position.

Dutch interest in the eastern seas was straightforward and hard edged. They wanted to accumulate wealth by creating a monopoly of demand, buying shiploads of Southeast Asian luxury goods at low prices and selling the goods at high prices in Europe. Many of the Asian suppliers were Muslims, and their relationship with the Catholic Portuguese had been strained or hostile. They preferred to deal with the Dutch Protestants, who were simply businessmen with no desire to be missionaries. If the suppliers were for one or another reason reluctant to sell, the Dutch persuaded them by various means, usually involving Dutch superiority in naval gunnery.

The Dutch focused on the East Indies spice and luxury trade, but they also established settler colonies at Cape Town in South Africa, in New Amsterdam across the Atlantic, and on several islands in the Caribbean. These colonies were less attractive to the Dutch than trade and eventually were surrendered to other powers, such as England. New Amsterdam became New York at the close of the first of two naval wars in the seventeenth century that made England the premier colonial power along the East Coast of the future United States.

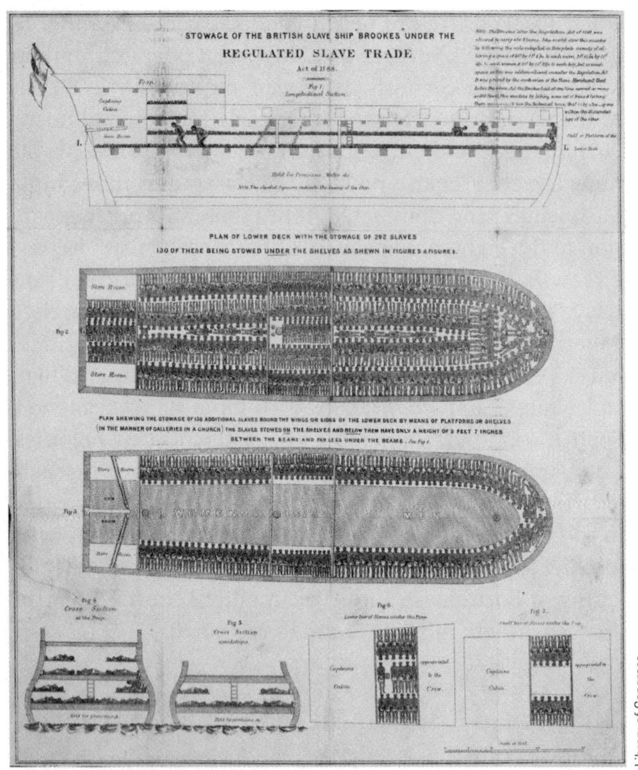

PLAN OF A SLAVE SHIP. This engraving shows how slaves were transported on a "tight packer" slave ship. Africans were crammed below decks with barely enough space to move. Even basic functions were difficult and diseases were a constant threat to all on board.

How did such a small nation (Holland did not possess more than 2.5 million people at this juncture) carry out this vast overseas enterprise while it was struggling to free itself from its Spanish overlords? A chief reason for the Dutch success was the **Dutch East India Company**. A private firm chartered by the government in 1602, the company had a monopoly on Dutch trading in the Pacific. The company eventually took over the Portuguese spice and luxury trade in the East, which proved to be an enormous bonanza for its stockholders. A partnership would be set up for one or more voyages, with both costs and profits split among the shareholders, while minimizing risks for all. The traders hired captains and crews who would be most likely to succeed in filling the ship's hold at minimal cost, whatever the means or consequences. Later in the seventeenth century, the focus of attention shifted from importing spices and luxury goods to the alluring profits to be made in the trans-Atlantic trade in African slaves.

England. The English colonial venture was slow in getting started. When the Portuguese and Spaniards were dividing up the newly discovered continent of America and the Far Eastern trade, England was just emerging from a lengthy struggle for dynastic power called the War of the Roses (see Chapter 21). Starting in the 1530s, the country was then preoccupied for a generation with the split from Rome under Henry VIII and its consequences (see Chapter 23). Then came the disappointing failure of Sir Walter Raleigh's "Lost Colony" on the Carolina coast in the 1580s and a war with Spain.

Only in the early 1600s did the English begin to enter the discovery and colonizing business in any systematic way. Like the Dutch, the English efforts were organized by private parties or groups and were not under the direction of the royal government. The London East India Company (often called the British East India Company), founded in 1600, is a good example. Similar to its Dutch counterpart, it was a private enterprise with wide political as well as commercial powers in dealing with foreigners and with its own military resources.

After two victorious wars against the Dutch in the 1650s and 1660s, the English were the world's leading naval power. The East Asian colonial trade was not important to them, however, and they soon gave up their attempts to penetrate the Dutch monopoly in East Indian luxuries, choosing to concentrate on India. (The only important English station in Southeast Asia was the great fortress port of Singapore, which was not acquired until the nineteenth century.)

English colonies in the seventeenth century were concentrated in North America and the Caribbean, and an odd mixture they were. The northern colonies were filled with Protestant dissidents who could not abide the Anglican Church regime: Puritans, Congregationalists, and Quakers. Maryland was a refuge for persecuted Catholics. Virginia and the Carolinas began as real-estate speculations. They were essentially get-rich-quick schemes devised by nobles or wealthy commoners who thought they could sell off their American holdings to individual settlers at a fat profit. Georgia began as a noble experiment by a group of philanthropists who sought to give convicts a second chance.

Elsewhere, the English were less inclined to settle new lands than to make their fortunes pirating Spanish galleons or competing with the Dutch in the slave trade. What the Dutch had taken from the Portuguese, the English seized in part from the Dutch. This was equally true in the New World, where the English and French superseded the Dutch challenge to Portuguese and Spanish hegemony in the Caribbean in the eighteenth century.

France. The colonial empire of France parallels that of England. Although they were relatively late in entering the race, the French sought overseas possessions or trade factories throughout the world to support their prospering domestic economy. From Canada (as early as 1608) to the west coast of Africa (as early as 1639) and India (in the early eighteenth century), the servants of the Bourbon kings contested both their Catholic coreligionists (Portugal, Spain) and their Protestant rivals (Holland, Britain) for mercantile advantage and the extension of royal powers. Thus, the French, too, reflected the seventeenth-century trend of allowing state policies to be dictated more by secular interests than by religious adherences.

MERCANTILISM

During this epoch, governments attempted to control their economies through a process later termed ***mercantilism***. Under mercantilism, the chief goals of economic policy were: a favorable balance of trade (with the value of a country's exports exceeding the cost of its imports) and increasing the size of a country's gold and silver reserves. To achieve these goals, the royal government constantly intervened in the market and attempted to secure advantage for itself and the population at large by carefully supervising every aspect of commerce and investment. England, France, Holland, and Spain all practiced mercantilism, but it was most successful in northern Europe, where commercial capitalism already was well established. There, trading and joint stock companies excelled at prudent investing in commerce and manufacturing. In contrast, Spain became impoverished of gold and silver when its kings chose to finance wasteful wars of religion.

As for colonial policy, mercantilism held that only goods and services that originated in the home country could be (legally) exported to the colonies and that the colonies' exports must go to the home country for use there or re-export. Thus, the colonies' most essential functions were to serve as captive markets for home-country producers and to provide raw materials at low cost for home-country importers. Reaction against mercantilism's restrictions led to contraband trade routes (to Spanish America), to demands for free trade (in regions where capitalism was most robust), and to political independence (North and South America). Today, the pendulum continues to swing between the extremes of free trade and state intervention.

THE COLUMBIAN EXCHANGE

The coming of the Europeans to the New World resulted in important changes in the resources, habits, and values of both the Amerindians and the whites. Scholars call this the Columbian Exchange. Among the well-known introductions by the Europeans to the Western Hemisphere were horses, pigs, cattle, sheep, and goats; iron; firearms; sailing ships; and, less tangibly, the entire system of economics we call capitalism.

But the Columbian Exchange had another side: a reverse flow of products and influences from the Americas to Europe and through Europe to the other continents. Educated Europeans after about 1520 became aware of how huge and relatively unknown the Earth was and how varied the peoples inhabiting it were. This knowledge came as a surprise to many Europeans, and they were eager to learn more. The literature of discovery and exploration became extraordinarily popular during the sixteenth and seventeenth centuries. (See Evidence of the Past box.)

From this literature, Europeans learned, among other things, that the Christian moral code was but one of several; that the natural sciences were not of overwhelming interest or importance to most of humanity; that an effective education could take myriad forms and have myriad goals; and that viewpoints formed by tradition and habit are not necessarily correct, useful, or the only conceivable ones. Initially just curious about the Earth's other inhabitants, upper-class Europeans gradually began to develop a certain tolerance for other peoples' views and habits. This tolerance slowly deepened in the seventeenth and especially the eighteenth century as Europe emerged from its religious wars. The previously favored view that unknown peoples were probably *anthropophagi* (man eaters) began giving way to the concept of the "noble savage," whose unspoiled morality might put the sophisticated European to shame.

Contacts with the Americas also led to changes in Europe. Some crops such as sugarcane and coffee that were already known in Europe but could not be grown profitably there were found to prosper in the New World. Their cultivation formed the basis for the earliest plantations in the Caribbean basin and the introduction of slavery into the New World. In addition, a series of new crops were introduced to the European, Asian, and African diets. Tobacco, several varieties of beans and peas, potatoes, squashes, rice, maize, bananas, manioc, and other agricultural products stemmed originally from American or Far Eastern lands. First regarded as novelties—much like the occasional Indian or African visitor—these crops came to be used as food and fodder.

The most important for Europe was the white (or Irish) potato, an Andean native, which was initially considered fit only for cattle and pigs but was gradually adopted by northern Europeans in the eighteenth century. By the end of that century, the potato had become the most important part of the peasants' diet in several countries. The potato was the chief reason European farms were able to feed the spectacular increase in population that started in the later 1700s.

So much additional coinage was put into circulation in Europe from the Mexican and Peruvian silver mines that it generated massive inflation. In the seventeenth century, the Spanish court used the silver to pay army suppliers, shipyards, and soldiers; and from their hands, it went on into the general economy. Spain suffered most in the long run from the inflation its bullion imports caused. Moreover, with its tiny middle class and ideological opposition to the new sciences, Spain resisted technological innovation and industrialization. So when the rest of Europe began industrializing, Spanish gold and silver went into the pockets of foreign suppliers, carriers, and artisans rather than into domestic investments or business. This situation would prove fateful in the next century.

In a period of inflation, when money becomes cheap and goods or services become dear, people who can convert their wealth quickly to goods and services are in an

EVIDENCE OF THE PAST

A Tour of the Aztec Capital, Tenochtitlan

Bernal Diaz de Castillo (1492–*c.* 1580), one of Cortes' soldiers in Mexico, wrote the *True History of the Conquest of New Spain* and published it in 1576. Diaz de Castillo describes both his amazement and his foreboding upon seeing the magnificent Venice-like island city of Tenochtitlan.

> Gazing on such wonderful sights, we did not know what to say, or whether what appeared before us was real, for on one side, on the land, there were great cities, and in the lake ever so many more, and the lake itself was crowded with canoes, and in the Causeway were many bridges at intervals, and in front of us stood the great Tenochtitlan, and we did not even number four hundred soldiers!
>
> And we well remembered the words and warnings given us by the [enemies of the Aztecs] . . . that we should beware of entering Tenochtitlan, where they would kill us, as soon as they had us inside . . . .
>
> [Montezuma gave permission for Cortes and his men to visit the market plaza at Tlatelolco and the main pyramid at Tenochtitlan.]
>
> On reaching the market-place, . . . we were astounded at the great number of people and the quantities of merchandise, and at the orderliness and good arrangements that prevailed . . . . [The market contained: gold, silver, precious stones, feathers, cloaks, and embroidered goods; cotton goods, chocolate, sisal (hemp) cloth, ropes and sandals; animal skins, tanned and untanned; beans, vegetables, fruits, and herbs; fish, turkeys, rabbits, deer, ducks, little dogs; cooked food such as cake and tripe; pottery of all sizes; honey and other sweets; timber and wooden furniture; pitch-pine for torches; paper made of tree bark, tobacco, cochineal for dye; bronze axes; gourds and wooden jars. After leaving the market, the Spaniards then climbed the great temple, where Montezuma awaited them.]
>
> Cortes . . . addressed Montezuma through Doña Marina: ' . . . I beg of you to show us your gods . . . .' [The Spaniards were escorted into] a sort of hall, in which there were two altars . . . There were some smoking braziers . . . in which they were burning the hearts of three Indians, . . . sacrificed that day; the walls of that shrine were so splashed and caked with blood that they and the floor too were black. Indeed, the whole place stank abominably . . . .
>
> [Cortes said:] 'Lord Montezuma, I cannot imagine how a prince as great and wise as your Majesty can have failed to realize that these idols . . . are not gods but evil things, . . . devils . . . .' [Cortes further suggested erecting a cross and a shrine to Our Lady in one section of the hall.]
>
> Montezuma, however, replied in some temper . . . : '[I]f I had known that you were going to utter these insults I should not have shown you my gods. We hold them to be very good. They give us health and rain and crops and weather, and all the victories we desire. So we are bound to worship them and sacrifice to them, and I beg you to say nothing more against them.' [Cortes changed the subject.]

ANALYZE AND INTERPRET

Which of the Tlatelolco market items were native to the New World? What intangible cultural elements alluded to in this selection did the Spaniards introduce from Europe? How did Montezuma explain the practice of human sacrifice?

Do you think that the Aztec Triple Alliance had turned this religious practice into an imperial instrument of terror?

Gianni Dagli Orti/The Art Archive at Art Resource, NY

RIVERA'S GREAT TENOCHTITLAN. Muralist Diego Rivera's portrayal of Mexican Pre-Columbian civilizations, painted in the 1920s on the walls of the National Palace, took this from Diaz de Castillo's depiction of the Great Tenochtitlan. The National Palace in which the mural is on display is just one block from the ruins of the main temple described.

Source: J. M. Cohen, trans., Bernal Diaz del Castillo, *The Conquest of New Spain* (New York, Viking Penguin, 1963).

enviable position. Those whose wealth is illiquid and cannot be easily converted are at a disadvantage. As a result, the landholders—many of whom were nobles who thought it beneath them to pay attention to money matters—lost economic strength. The middle classes, who could sell their services and expertise at rising rates, did well. Best off were the merchants, who could buy cheap and sell at higher prices. But even the unskilled or skilled workers in the towns were in a relatively better position than the landlords: Wages rose about as fast as prices in this century.

In many feudal-remnant areas, where serfs paid token rents in return for small parcels of arable land, the landlord was dealt a heavy blow. Prices rose for everything the noble landlords needed and wanted, while their rents, sanctioned by centuries of custom, remained about the same. Many of them had been living beyond their means for generations, borrowing money wherever they could with land as security. Unaware of the reasons for the economic changes and unable to anticipate the results, many landlords faced disaster during the later sixteenth century and could not avoid bankruptcy when their long-established mortgages were called. Much land changed hands at this time, from impoverished nobles to peasants or to the newly rich from the towns. Serfdom in the traditional pattern became impractical or unprofitable. Already weakened by long-term changes in European society, serfdom was abolished in most of Western Europe.

EUROPEAN IMPACTS ON THE WORLD AND VICE VERSA

How strong was the European impact on the Amerindian cultures of the Western Hemisphere and on the peoples of the Far East, sub-Saharan Africa, and the Pacific Rim? Historians agree that it was enormous in some areas but much less so in others. The trading factories of the Portuguese and others on the African and Asian coasts had minimal impacts on the lives of the peoples of the interior. Only in exceptional circumstances was the presence of the Europeans a prominent factor in local people's consciousness. Even in the areas most directly affected by slaving such as Senegambia, the Nigerian delta, and Angola, the consensus of recent scholarly opinion holds that there was considerable variation, largely depending on local traditions, demography, and political circumstances. In many cases, the slave trade undermined social and political structures and destroyed entire civilizations, such as Kongo and Ngola. In other locations such as Dahomey and the tiny states of the Niger Delta, new societies were created that depended on the trade. Almost everywhere, however, the commerce in human beings took away the youngest and most productive members of African societies, raised the frequency and level of violent conflict, and destroyed local craft production.

The fate of the Amerindians in Spain's American settler colonies was quite different in these respects. Although the Spanish crown imposed several regulatory measures to protect the Indians after 1540, little could be done to inhibit the spread of epidemic disease (smallpox, measles, and influenza) in the Amerindian villages. Because they had not been exposed to childhood diseases such as measles and smallpox, they had no immunity to the diseases brought by the newcomers, whereas the Spaniards were much less affected by the Amerindian maladies. During the sixteenth century, successive waves of smallpox epidemics killed an estimated 80 to 90 percent of native populations in Mexico and Peru.

As with the exchanges in agricultural products, the stream of external influences was not simply one way—from Europe to the rest of the world. In the Americas, a noticeable degree of change was wrought in the Spanish and Portuguese culture by prolonged exposure to Amerindian and African habits and attitudes. An example would be the adoption of maize culture by the mestizo and Spanish populations in Mexico. Another would be the incorporation of Amerindian irrigation techniques.

In another part of the early imperial world created by the voyages of discovery, the architecture of the Dutch colonial town of Batavia (Jakarta) was soon converted from the trim and tight homes and warehouses of blustery Amsterdam to the different demands of the Javanese climate.

Perhaps it is most accurate to say that in the settler colonies of the Western Hemisphere and South Africa, the local peoples were extensively and sometimes disastrously affected by the arrival of the whites, but in the rest of the world, including most of sub-Saharan Africa, the Asian mainland, and the South Pacific islands, the Europeans were less disruptive to the existing state of affairs. Sometimes local peoples even succeeded in manipulating the Europeans to their own advantage, as in West Africa and Mughal India. This would remain true until the nineteenth century. Promoted by industrialization at that time, the European impacts multiplied, became more profound, and changed in nature so as to subordinate the indigenous peoples in every sense.

Racism's Beginnings

Africans came into European society for the first time in appreciable numbers during the fifteenth century. At that time, the first faint signs of white racism appeared. The first slaves from Africa were introduced to Europe through Muslim channels. Their rich owners mostly regarded them as novelties, and they were kept as tokens of wealth or artistic taste. Some free black people lived in Mediterranean Europe, where they worked as sailors, musicians, and actors, but they were not numerous enough for the average European to have any firsthand contact.

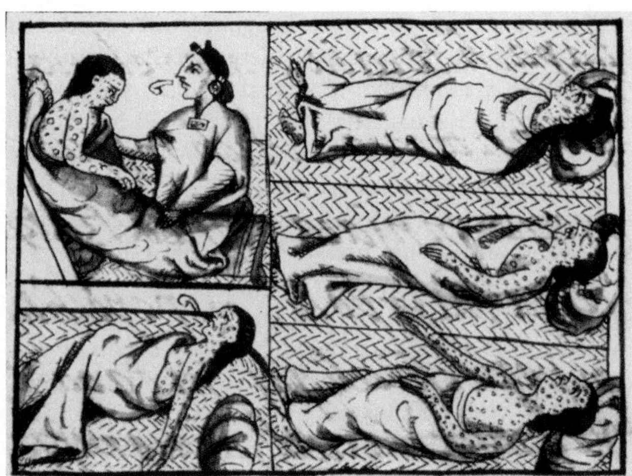

Florentine Codex/Science Source/Photo Researchers

AZTEC SMALLPOX EPIDEMIC. When Europeans arrived in the Western Hemisphere, they introduced diseases to which they were immune but to which Native Americans had no natural defenses. This sixteenth-century illustration depicts Aztecs dying of smallpox following the arrival of Hernán Cortés and his Spanish army in 1519.

Many Europeans thought of black people in terms dictated either by the Bible or by Muslim prejudices imbibed unconsciously over time. The biblical references were generally negative: Black was the color of the sinful, the opposite of light in the world. "Black hearted," "a black scoundrel," and "black intentions" are a few examples of the mental connection that was made between the color black and everything evil and contemptible. The Arab slave traders in both West and East Africa who supplied some of the European as well as the Asiatic markets were another source of prejudice. They were contemptuous of non-Muslim Africans of western Sudan or the East African coast in whose flesh they had dealt for centuries before the European trade began. These merchants' point of view was easily transferred to their Italian and Portuguese partners. However, once the European slave trade became big business in the seventeenth century, white racism became the mental cornerstone of a pervasive and viciously exploitative slave-based economy in many parts of the Western Hemisphere.

SUMMARY

The explosive widening of Europe's horizons in the sixteenth century, in both the geographic sense and the psychological sense, was one side of the Columbian Exchange. First the Portuguese and the Spanish created their colonial empires—then the Dutch, the English, and the French after them. The original objective of the government-funded explorers was to find new, more secure trade routes to the East, but soon their motives changed to a mixture of enrichment, missionary activity, and prestige: gold, God, and glory.

The import of great quantities of precious metals created severe inflation and promoted the rise of the business or commercial classes. The discovery of customs and values that were different from those of Europeans gradually induced Europeans to adopt new attitudes of tolerance. The overseas expansion also added important new foods to the European diet.

For the non-Western hosts, this colonial and commercial outreach had mainly negative consequences, although circumstances varied from place to place. In Spain's American colonies, the indigenous peoples were almost wiped out by disease and overwork. In West Africa, East Africa, and the Asian mainland, the European trading presence had little overall effect on ordinary life at this time. Racism's beginnings, however, can be traced to its roots in the African slave trade commencing in this era.

IDENTIFICATION TERMS

Test your knowledge of this chapter's key concepts by defining the following terms. If you can not recall the meaning of certain terms, refresh your memory by looking up the boldfaced term in the chapter, turning to the Glossary at the end of the book, or accessing the terms on the CourseMate website at **www.cengagebrain.com.**

Columbian Exchange
Dutch East India Company
Ferdinand Magellan
mercantilism
Prince Henry the Navigator
Vasco da Gama

FOR FURTHER REFLECTION

1. Considering the technological advantages that Asian civilizations had over those of Europe, what reasons might explain why it was Europeans and not Asians who embarked on world-girdling voyages of discovery? In fact, is there any evidence that Asians did attempt such voyages? What became of them?

2. Once Europeans "discovered" the Americas, what did they hope to find? Why did they not have expectations of discovering great mineral resources in Asia? What about Africa?
3. On what parts of the world did European expansion have fewer effects than it did on others? Why do you think this was the case?
4. Was there, or had there ever been, a "Columbian-like Exchange" among the civilizations of Eurasia and Africa? In thinking about other or previous movements of people, ideas, and resources, what, if anything, was different about the Columbian Exchange?
5. Why did African contact with Europeans not cause plagues among them as it did among Native Americans?

TEST YOUR KNOWLEDGE

Test your knowledge of this chapter by answering the following questions. Complete answers appear at the end of the book. You may find even more quiz questions on the CourseMate website at **www.cengagebrain.com.**

1. The fifteenth- and sixteenth-century voyages of exploration were stimulated mainly by
   a. European curiosity about other peoples.
   b. the determination to obtain more farming land for a growing population.
   c. the individual explorers' hopes of enrichment.
   d. the discovery that the Earth was in fact a sphere without "ends."
   e. new technology.
2. Which of the following was not proved by Magellan's epic voyage?
   a. The globe was more compact than had been believed.
   b. The globe was indeed spherical.
   c. A sea passage existed south of the tip of South America.
   d. The islands called "Spice Lands" could be reached from the East.
   e. The journey was a long and difficult one.
3. Which of the following nations was most persistently committed to converting the natives of the newly discovered regions to Christianity?
   a. Spain
   b. Holland
   c. England
   d. Portugal
   e. France
4. What is the correct sequence of explorer-traders in the Far East?
   a. Spanish, English, French
   b. Spanish, Portuguese, Dutch
   c. Dutch, English, Spanish
   d. Portuguese, Dutch, English
   e. Spanish, Portuguese, English
5. The first to engage in the slave trade were the
   a. Dutch.
   b. Portuguese.
   c. Danes.
   d. English.
   e. Spanish.
6. Which of the following reasons was least likely to be the motive for a Dutch captain's voyage of discovery?
   a. A desire to deal the Roman Church a blow
   b. A search for personal enrichment
   c. A quest to find another lifestyle for himself in a foreign land
   d. The intention of establishing trade relations with a new partner
   e. The desire to serve as a middleman between East Asia and Europe
7. Mercantilism aimed first of all at
   a. securing financial rewards for the entrepreneurs.
   b. allowing the impoverished a chance of rising in society.
   c. bringing maximum income to the royal throne.
   d. securing a favorable balance of foreign trade.
   e. developing a wide range of products for export.
8. Which proved to be the most important of the various new foods introduced into European diets by the voyages of discovery?
   a. Tomatoes
   b. Rice
   c. Potatoes
   d. Coffee
   e. Wheat
9. The sixteenth-century inflation affected which group most negatively?
   a. Landholding nobles
   b. Urban merchants
   c. Wage laborers
   d. Skilled white-collar workers
   e. Church officials
10. The most devastating effects of pandemics on the native population brought about by European discovery occurred in
    a. India.
    b. Latin America.
    c. West Africa.
    d. Southeast Asia.
    e. North America.

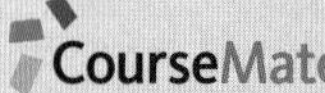

Visit the CourseMate website at **www.cengagebrain.com** for additional study tools and review materials for this chapter.

Religious Division and Political Consolidation in Europe 23

I have often been resolved to live uprightly, and to lead a true godly life, and to set everything aside that would hinder this, but it was far from being put in execution. I am not able to effect that good which I intend. —MARTIN LUTHER

CHAPTER OUTLINE

1517	Posting of the Ninety-five Theses
1534	Act of Supremacy (England)
1540s	Calvinism spreads through much of Europe
1588	English defeat Spanish Armada
1593	Henry IV restores peace in France
1618–1648	Thirty Years' War; Treaty of Westphalia
1649–1651	Civil War in England
1653–1658	England under Oliver Cromwell's Commonwealth
1660	Restoration of Charles II in England
1661–1715	Reign of Louis XIV in France
1688–1689	Glorious Revolution; William and Mary
1533–1584	Ivan IV, the Terrible (Russia)
1640–1688	Frederick William, the Great Elector (Prussia)
1682–1724	Peter I, the Great (Russia)
1713–1740	Frederick William I (Prussia)
1740–1786	Frederick II, the Great (Prussia)
1740–1748	War of the Austrian Succession
1740–1780	Maria Theresa (Austria)
1756–1763	Seven Years' War

The split in Christian belief and church organization that is termed the Protestant **Reformation** brought enormous consequences in its wake. Its beginning coincided with the high point of the Age of Discovery by Europeans. Altogether, religious upheaval, warfare, and capitalism helped shift the balance of power in sixteenth- and seventeenth-century Europe, which in turn caused some longtime powers to decline and energetic new nations to emerge.

While the Roman Catholic Church reasserted the absolute sovereignty of the church and the papacy, in lands that remained Roman Catholic, monarchs claimed an authority (called *royal absolutism*) that made them answerable only to God. Particularly in France and Spain, the church and the state became partners in power. In Protestant domains, on the other hand, the roles of the church in providing spiritual leadership and the monarchy in governing became contested issues.

THE REFORMATION

The upheaval called the Reformation of the early sixteenth century had its roots in political and social developments as much as in religious disputes. The longstanding arguments within the Christian community had already led to rebellions against the Roman Catholic Church on several occasions. In the major instances in thirteenth-century France, fourteenth-century England, and fifteenth-century Bohemia, religious rebels (the official term is *heretics*, or "wrong thinkers") had battled the papal church. Eventually, all of them had been suppressed or driven underground. But now, in sixteenth-century Germany, **Martin Luther** (1483–1546) found an enthusiastic reception for his challenges to Rome among the majority of his fellow Germans.

Luther and the German National Church

Why was the church in the German lands particularly susceptible to the call for reform? The disintegration of the German medieval kingdom had been followed by the birth of dozens of separate little principalities and city-states, such as Hamburg and Frankfurt, that could not well resist the encroachments of the powerful papacy in their internal affairs. Many of the German rulers were angry at seeing the tax funds they needed sometimes used for goals they did not support. These rulers were eagerly searching for some popular basis to challenge Rome. They found it in the teachings of Martin Luther.

In 1517, a major indulgence sales campaign opened in Germany under even more scandalous pretexts than usual. Much of the money raised was destined to be used to pay off a debt incurred by an ambitious noble churchman, rather than for any ecclesiastical purpose. Observing what was happening, on October 31, 1517, the chaplain at Wittenberg University's church, Martin Luther, announced his discontent by posting the famous **Ninety-five Theses** on his church door. In these questions, Luther raised objections to papal indulgences and to the whole doctrine of papal supremacy.

Luther's youth had been a long struggle against the conviction that he was damned to hell. Intensive study of the Bible eventually convinced him that only through the freely given grace of a merciful God might he, or any person, reach immortal salvation.

The Catholic Church, on the other hand, taught that humans must manifest their Christian faith by doing good works and leading good lives. If they did so, they might be considered to have earned a heavenly future. Martin Luther believed that faith alone was the factor through which Christians might reach bliss in the afterlife. It is this doctrine of **justification by faith** that most clearly distinguishes Lutheranism from the papal teachings.

Portrait of Martin Luther (1483–1546) 1529 (oil on panel), Cranach, Lucas, the Elder (1472–1553)/Galleria degli Uffizi, Florence, Italy/The Bridgeman Art Library

MARTIN LUTHER. This contemporary portrait by Lucas V. Cranach is generally considered to be an accurate rendition of the great German church reformer in midlife. Both the strengths and weaknesses of Luther's peasant character are revealed.

As the meaning of Luther's statements penetrated into the clerical hierarchy, he was implored, then commanded, to cease. Instead, his confidence rose, and in a series of brilliantly forceful pamphlets written in the German vernacular, he explained his views to a rapidly increasing audience. By 1520, he was becoming a household word among educated people and even among the peasantry. He was excommunicated in 1521 by the pope for refusing to recant, and in the same year, Emperor Charles V declared him an outlaw.

Threatened by the imperial and papal officials, Luther found the protection of the ruler of Saxony, as well as much of the German princely class. With this protection and encouragement, Luther's teachings spread rapidly, aided by the newly invented printing press and by the power and conviction of his sermons and writings. By the mid-1520s, Lutheran congregations, rejecting the papal authority, had sprung up throughout most of Germany and Scandinavia.

Calvin and International Protestantism

It was not Luther, the German miner's son, but **John Calvin** (1509–1564), the French lawyer, who made the Protestant movement an international theological rebellion against Rome. Luther always saw himself as a specifically German patriot, as well as a pious Christian. Calvin, on the contrary, detached himself from national feeling and saw himself as the emissary and servant of a God who ruled all nations. Luther wanted the German Christian body to be cleansed of papal corruption; Calvin wanted the entire Christian community to be made over into the image of what he thought God intended.

Calvin believed that the papal church was hopelessly distorted. It must be obliterated, and new forms and practices (which were supposedly a return to the practices of early Christianity) must be introduced. In ***The Institutes of the Christian Religion*** (1536), Calvin set out his beliefs and doctrines with the precision and clarity of a lawyer. His most dramatic change from Rome and Luther was his insistence that God predestined souls. That is, a soul was meant either for heaven or hell for all eternity. Calvin believed that humanity had been eternally stained by Adam's sin and that most souls were destined for hellfire. Those who were not were God's **Elect**.

Swiss School, (17thcentury)/Bridgeman Art Library

JOHN CALVIN. This Swiss portrait of the "pope of Geneva" in his younger days depicts Calvin in a fur neckpiece. This bit of bourgeois indulgence probably would not have been worn by an older Calvin.

Despite its doctrinal fierceness, Calvin's message found a response throughout Europe. By the 1540s, Calvinists were appearing in Germany, the Netherlands, Scotland, England, and France, as well as Switzerland. Geneva had become the Protestant Rome, with Calvin serving as its priestly ruler until his death in 1564.

More than Lutherans, the Calvinists thought of the entire community, lay and clerical alike, as equal members of the Christian church on Earth. Calvinists also insisted on the power of the congregation to select and discharge pastors at will, inspired by God's word. They never established a hierarchy of clerics. There were no Calvinist bishops but only presbyters, or elected elders, who spoke for their fellow parishioners in regional or national assemblies. The government of Calvin's church thus included both clerical and lay leaders. The combination gave the church's pronouncements great political as well as moral force.

By around 1570, Calvin's followers had gained control of the Christian community in several places: the Dutch-speaking Netherlands, Scotland, western France, and parts of northern Germany and Poland. In the rest of France, as well as Austria, Hungary, and England, they were still a minority, but a growing one. Whereas Lutheranism was confined to the German-speaking countries and Scandinavia and did not spread much after 1550 or so, Calvinism was an international faith that appealed to all nations and identified with none. Carried on the ships of the Dutch and English explorers and emigrants of the seventeenth and eighteenth centuries, it continued to spread throughout the modern world.

The English Reformation

In England, the reform movement had its origins in the widespread popular resentment against Rome and the higher clergy. As we have seen, a group called the Lollards had already rebelled in the 1300s against the clerical claims to sole authority in interpreting the word of God and papal supremacy. The movement had been put down, but its memory persisted in many parts of England.

But it was the peculiar marital problems of **King Henry VIII** (1490–1547) that finally brought the church in England into conflict with Rome. Henry needed a male successor, but his elderly Spanish wife, Catherine of Aragon, had failed to produce one. Therefore, he wanted to have the marriage annulled by the pope (who alone had that power) so that he could marry some young Englishwoman who might produce the desired heir.

The pope refused the annulment because he did not wish to impair the close alliance of the Catholic Church with the Spanish monarchy. Between 1532 and 1534, Henry intimidated Parliament into declaring him the "only supreme head of the church in England"—the **Act**

THE CALVINIST CHURCH. This painting is by a Dutch sixteenth-century master, Hendrik van Steenwyck, who portrays the "purified" interior of the Antwerp cathedral after it was taken over by Calvinists.

of Supremacy of 1534. Now, as head of the **Anglican** (English Protestant) **Church**, Henry proceeded to marry the tragic Anne Boleyn. Much other legislation followed that asserted that the monarch, and not the pope, was the determiner of what the church could and could not do in England. Henry went on to marry and divorce several more times before his death in 1547, but he did secure a son, the future King Edward VI, from one of these unhappy alliances. Two daughters also survived: the half-sisters Mary and Elizabeth.

Henry's actions changed English religious beliefs very little, although the Calvinist reformation was gaining ground in both England and Scotland. But under the sickly boy-king Edward (ruling 1547–1553), Protestant views became dominant among the English governing group, and the powerful oratory of John Knox led the Scots into Calvinism (the Presbyterian Church).

At Edward's death in 1553, popular support for Mary (ruling 1553–1558), the Catholic daughter of Henry VIII's first, Spanish Catholic wife, was too strong to be overridden by the Protestant party at court. Mary restored Catholicism to its official status during her brief reign. Protestant conspirators were put to death—hence, she is called "Bloody Mary" by English Protestants.

Finally, the confused state of the English official religion was gradually cleared by the political skills of Mary's successor, the political genius **Queen Elizabeth I** (ruling 1558–1603). She ruled for half a century with great success. (See the Law and Government box.) She arrived at a compromise between the Roman and Protestant doctrines, which was accepted by a steadily increasing majority and came to be termed the *Church of England.* It retained the bishops, rituals, and sacraments of the Roman Church, but its head was the English monarch, who appointed the

A PROTESTANT VIEW OF THE POPE. Clothed in hellish splendor and hung about with the horrible symbols of Satan, the Roman pope is revealed for all to see in this sixteenth-century cartoon.

LAW AND GOVERNMENT

Elizabeth I of England (1533–1603)

In the late sixteenth century, England became for the first time a power to be reckoned with in world affairs. What had been an island kingdom with little direct influence on any other country except its immediate neighbors across the Channel gradually reached equality with the other major Western military and naval powers: France and Spain. But England's achievement was not just in military affairs. It also experienced a magnificent flowering of the arts and a solid advance in the economy, which finally lifted the nation out of the long depression that had followed the fourteenth-century plague and the long, losing war with France.

The guiding spirit for this comeback was Elizabeth I, queen of England from 1558 until her death in 1603. The daughter of Henry VIII and his second wife, the ill-fated Anne Boleyn, Elizabeth emerged from a heavily shadowed girlhood to become one of the most beloved of British lawgivers. Elizabeth was an intelligent, well-educated woman with gifts in several domains. One of her most remarkable achievements was that she managed to retain her powers without a husband, son, or father in the still very-male-oriented world in which she moved.

Born in 1533, she was only three years old when her mother was executed. She was declared illegitimate by order of the disappointed Henry, who had wished for a son. But after her father's death, Parliament established her as third in line to the throne, behind her half-brother, Edward, and her Catholic half-sister, Mary. During Mary's reign (1553–1558), Elizabeth was imprisoned for a time, but she was careful to stay clear of the hectic Protestant-Catholic struggles of the day. By so doing, she managed to stay alive until she could become ruler in her own right.

Her rule began amid many internal dangers. The Catholic party in England opposed her as a suspected Protestant. The Calvinists opposed her as being too much like her father Henry, who never accepted Protestant theology. The Scots were becoming rabid Calvinists who despised the English's halfway measures in religious affairs. On top of this, the government was deeply in debt.

Elizabeth showed great insight in selecting her officials and maintained good relations with Parliament. She conducted diplomatic affairs with farsightedness and found she could use her status as an unmarried queen to definite advantage.

Philip of Spain, widower of her half-sister, Mary, made several proposals of marriage and political unity that Elizabeth cleverly held off without ever quite saying no. She kept England out of the religious wars that were raging in various parts of Europe for most of her reign, but in one of these wars, against her ex-suitor Philip, the Virgin Queen led her people most memorably.

In 1588, after long negotiations failed, Philip sent the Spanish Armada to punish England for aiding the rebellious Dutch Calvinists across the Channel. The queen rallied her sailors in a stirring visit before the battle. The resulting defeat of the Armada not only signaled England's rise to naval equality with Spain but also made Elizabeth the most popular monarch England had ever seen.

A golden age of English literature coincided with Elizabeth's rule, thanks in some part to her active support of all the arts. Her well-known vanity induced her to spend large sums to ensure the splendor of her court despite her equally well-known miserliness. The Elizabethan Age produced Shakespeare, Marlowe, Spenser, and Bacon. By the end of the sixteenth century, English literature for the first time could hold a place of honor in any assembly of national arts.

Elizabeth's version of Protestant belief—the Church of England—proved acceptable to most of her subjects and finally settled the stormy waves of sixteenth-century English church affairs. By the end of her long reign, "Good Queen Bess" had become a stock phrase that most people believed in, from barons to peasants.

ELIZABETH I OF ENGLAND. The Armada Portrait, perhaps the most famous, was painted by an anonymous artist in the late sixteenth century. Elizabeth was vain, despite being no beauty, and was always receptive to flattery, without in the least being influenced by it in matters of state.

ANALYZE AND INTERPRET

Given that an unmarried queen was considered a political risk, what reasons of state could have impelled Elizabeth to remain "the Virgin Queen"? What political capital did she make out of creating the hybrid Church of England that otherwise would have been denied her?

bishops and their chief, the archbishop of Canterbury. However, the strict Calvinists, called **Puritans**, were not happy with this arrangement and wished to "purify" the church by removing all remnants of popery.

Other Early Protestant Faiths

The followers of a radical sect called **Anabaptists** ("rebaptizers") believed in adult baptism, a priesthood of all believers, and a primitive communism that included sharing worldly possessions. After their efforts to establish a republic in the Rhineland city of Münster were bloodily suppressed, the Anabaptists were driven underground. Their beliefs continued to evolve, and they emerged much later in the New World as Mennonites, Amish, and similar groups.

Yet another Protestant creed emerged early in Switzerland. Founded by *Ulrich Zwingli* (1484–1531), it was generally similar to Lutheran belief. The inability of Zwingli's adherents and the Lutherans to cooperate left Zwingli's stronghold in Zurich open to attack by the Catholic Swiss. The use of bloody force to settle religious strife was an ominous note. It was to become increasingly common as Protestant beliefs spread and undermined the traditional religious structures.

THE COUNTER-REFORMATION

Belatedly realizing what a momentous challenge was being mounted, the papacy finally came to grips with the problem of Protestantism in a positive fashion during the 1540s. Pope Paul III (serving 1534–1549) moved to counter some of the excesses that had given the Roman authorities a bad name and set up a high-level commission to see what might be done to "clean up" the clergy. Eventually, the Roman Church decided to pursue two major lines of counterattack against the Protestants: a thorough examination of doctrines and practices—such as had not been attempted for more than one thousand years—combined with an entirely novel emphasis on instruction of the young and education of all Christians in the precepts of their religion. These measures together are known as the **Counter-Reformation**.

The *Council of Trent* (1545–1563) was the first general attempt to examine the church's basic doctrines and goals since the days of the Roman Empire. Meeting for three lengthy sessions, the bishops and theologians decided that Protestant attacks could be met by clearly defining what Catholics believed. But the council's work had an unintended negative effect on the desired reunification of Christianity: The doctrinal lines separating Catholic and Protestant were now firmly drawn, and they could not be ignored or blurred by the many individuals in both camps who had been trying to arrange a compromise.

The founding of the **Jesuit Order** was the most striking example of the second aspect of the Counter-Reformation. In 1540, Pope Paul III accorded to the Spanish nobleman **Ignatius of Loyola** (1491–1556) the right to organize an entirely new religious group, which he termed the *Society of Jesus*, or *Jesuits.* Their mission was to win, or win back, the minds and hearts of humanity for the Catholic Church through patient, careful instruction that would bring to everyone the word of God and of his deputy on Earth, the pope. Furthermore, the *Index* of forbidden books was created and the Inquisition was revived to ensure that no Catholic deviated from that doctrine (Chapter 20). These institutions greatly expanded the Roman Catholic Church's powers to censor the writings and supervise the beliefs of its adherents. Both became steadily more important in Catholic countries during the next century.

RELIGIOUS WARS AND THEIR OUTCOMES TO 1600

The Counter-Reformation stiffened the Catholics' will to resist Protestants' attacks, which had almost overwhelmed the unprepared Roman authorities. By 1555, the **Peace of Augsburg** had concluded a ten-year civil war by dividing Germany into Catholic and Lutheran parcels, but it made no allowances for the growing number of Calvinists or other Protestants.

In the rest of Europe, the picture was mixed by the late 1500s (see Map 23.1). England went through several changes of religious leadership, but it eventually emerged with a special sort of Protestant belief as its official religion. Scandinavia became Lutheran in its entirety, almost without violence. Austria, Hungary, and Poland remained mostly Catholic, but with large minorities of Calvinists and Lutherans. Spain and Italy had successfully repelled the Protestant challenge. Russia and southeastern Europe remained almost unaffected, being either hostile to both varieties of Western Christianity (Russia) or under the political control of Muslims. In two countries, however, the issue of religious affiliation was in hot dispute and caused much bloodshed in the later 1500s.

France

France remained officially Catholic but developed a large Calvinist minority among the nobility and the urbanites. For a brief time, the Catholic monarchs and the Calvinists attempted to live with one another, but costly religious wars began in the 1570s that threatened to wreck the country.

After some years, the Calvinists found a politician of genius, Henry of Navarre, who profited from the assassination of his Catholic rival to become King Henry IV of France. In 1593, he agreed to accept Catholicism to win the support of most French. He became the most popular king in French history. His Protestant upbringing inspired the Calvinist minority to trust him, and he did not disappoint them.

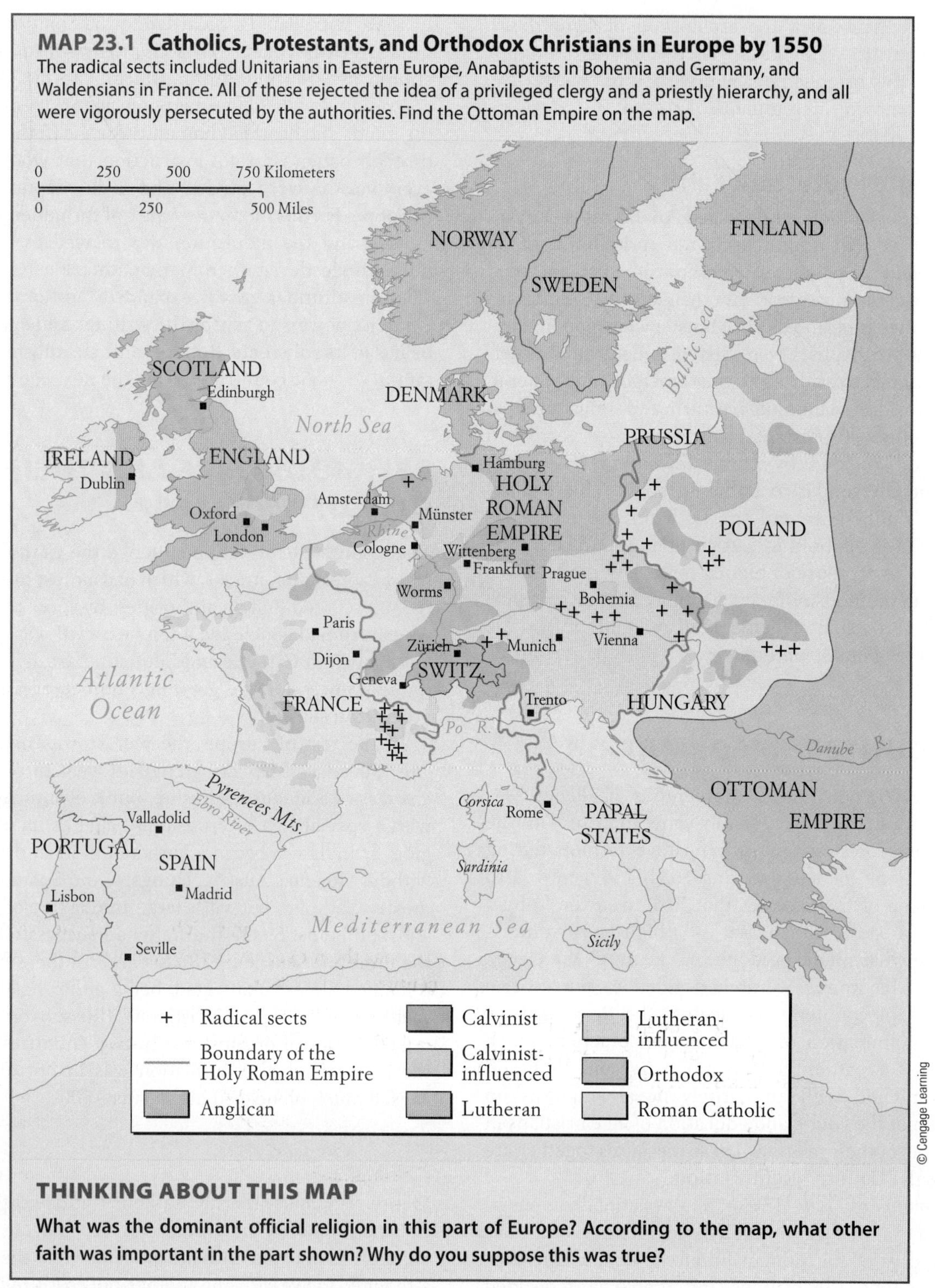

MAP 23.1 Catholics, Protestants, and Orthodox Christians in Europe by 1550
The radical sects included Unitarians in Eastern Europe, Anabaptists in Bohemia and Germany, and Waldensians in France. All of these rejected the idea of a privileged clergy and a priestly hierarchy, and all were vigorously persecuted by the authorities. Find the Ottoman Empire on the map.

THINKING ABOUT THIS MAP

What was the dominant official religion in this part of Europe? According to the map, what other faith was important in the part shown? Why do you suppose this was true?

In 1598, Henry made the first significant European attempt at religious toleration by issuing the **Edict of Nantes**. It gave the million-or-so French Calvinists—the Huguenots—freedom to worship, to hold office, and to fortify their towns. The Edict held for the better part of a century, during which France rose to become the premier power in Europe.

The Spanish Netherlands

The Spanish Netherlands (modern Holland and Belgium) were ruled from Madrid by the powerful King Philip II. He had inherited an empire that included Spain, much of Italy, and the Low Countries in Europe, plus the enormous Spanish overseas empire begun by the voyages of Columbus. Philip was a man with a mission, or rather two missions: the reestablishment of Catholicism among Protestants and the defeat of the Ottomans (see Chapter 24). These missions imposed heavy demands on Spanish resources, which even the flow of gold and silver out of the American colonies could not fully cover. Philip could not handle a revolt in the Netherlands that broke out in the 1560s. The Netherlands were a hotbed of both Lutheran and Calvinist doctrines, and its large middle class was much disturbed at the Spanish aliens' attempt to enforce on them the Counter-Reformation and papal supremacy.

The revolt held Philip's feared professional army at bay. While Philip saw himself as the agent of legitimacy and the Counter-Reformation, the English aided the Dutch rebels militarily and financially. In the mid-1580s, the friction came to a head. Philip became incensed at the execution of the Catholic Mary, Queen of Scots, by order of Elizabeth, who had imprisoned this rival for England's throne. With the reluctant support of the pope, Philip prepared the vast Armada of 1588 to invade England and conquer that country for the "True Church."

The devastating defeat of the Armada gave a great boost to the Protestant cause everywhere: It relieved the pressure on the Huguenots to accept Catholic overlordship in France, it saved the Dutch Calvinists until they could gain full independence some decades later, and it marked the emergence of England as a major power. Spain remained the premier military power long after the Armada disaster, but the country in a sense never recovered from this event. Henceforth, the other powers were able to keep Spain in check until its inherent economic weaknesses reduced it to a second-line nation by the end of the seventeenth century.

THE LEGACY OF THE REFORMATION

The Protestant movement made a deep impression on the general course of history in Europe for centuries. It is one of the chief reasons European history is conventionally divided into "modern" versus "medieval" around 1500. The religious unity of all Western Europe under the Roman pope was irrevocably shattered, and with the end of such unity inevitably came political and cultural conflicts. For a century and a half after Luther's defiance of the papal command to be silent, much of Europe was engaged in internal acrimony that wracked the continent from the Netherlands to Hungary.

Some of the other long-term cultural changes that resulted from the Reformation included the following:

1. *Higher literacy and the beginning of mass education.* In much of Protestant Europe in particular, the exhortation to learn and obey Scripture provided an incentive to read that the common folk had never had before. The rapid spread of printing after 1520 accelerated this change even more.
2. *Emphasis on individual moral responsibility.* Rejecting the Catholic assurance that the clergy knew best what was necessary and proper in the conduct of life, the Protestants underlined the responsibility of individual believers to determine what they must do to attain salvation.
3. *Increase in conflicts and intolerance.* Much of Europe fell into civil wars that were initially set off by religious disputes. These wars were often bloody and produced much needless destruction by both sides in the name of theological truth. Religious affiliation greatly exacerbated dynastic and emergent national conflicts.

THE BIRTH OF THE NATION-STATE

Europe during the seventeenth century saw the birth of the modern state as distinct from the domain of a ruling monarch. The powers attached to a governing office began to be separated from the person of the occupant of the office. This separation allowed the creation over time of a group of professional servants of the state, or bureaucrats—people who exercised authority not because of who they were, but because of the offices they held. Religious conflict between Protestant and Catholic continued but gave way to political-economic issues in state-to-state relations. The maritime countries of northwestern Europe became steadily more important thanks to overseas commerce, while the Central and Eastern European states suffered heavy reverses from wars, the Turkish menace, and commercial and technological stagnation.

The Thirty Years' War

The Thirty Years' War, which wrecked the German states and was the most destructive conflict Europe had seen for centuries, arose from religious intolerance, but it quickly became a struggle for territory and worldly power on the part of the multiple contestants. It began in 1618, when the Habsburg Holy Roman Emperor attempted to check the spread of Protestant sentiments in part of his empire. By 1635, the war had become an international struggle beyond consideration of religion. The Protestant kings of Scandinavia and the Catholic French monarchy supported the Protestants, whereas the Spanish cousins of the Habsburgs assaulted the French.

For thirteen more years, France, Holland, Sweden, and the German Protestant states fought on against the Holy Roman Emperor and Spain. Most of the fighting was in Germany. But finally, a peace, through the **Treaty of Westphalia**, was worked out in 1648 after five years of haggling. The big winners were France and Sweden, while the losers were Spain and, to a lesser degree, the Austrian-based Habsburgs. From 1648 on, Germany ceased to exist as a political concept and broke up into dozens, and then hundreds, of small kingdoms and principalities (see Map 23.2).

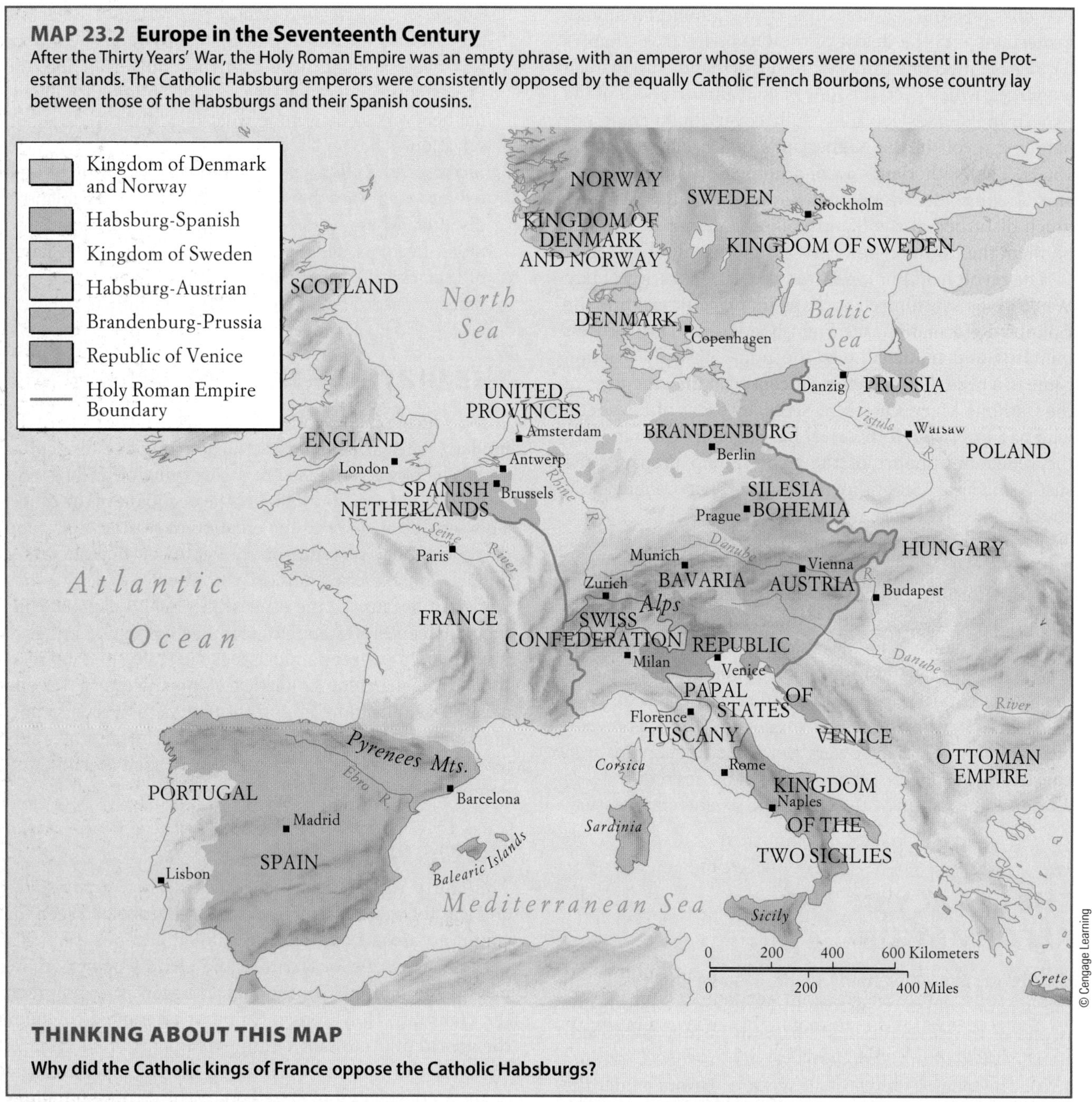

MAP 23.2 Europe in the Seventeenth Century
After the Thirty Years' War, the Holy Roman Empire was an empty phrase, with an emperor whose powers were nonexistent in the Protestant lands. The Catholic Habsburg emperors were consistently opposed by the equally Catholic French Bourbons, whose country lay between those of the Habsburgs and their Spanish cousins.

THINKING ABOUT THIS MAP

Why did the Catholic kings of France oppose the Catholic Habsburgs?

The Treaty of Westphalia was the first modern state treaty. From start to finish, its clauses underlined the decisive importance of the sovereign state, rather than the dynasty that ruled it or the religion its population professed. Theological uniformity was replaced by secular control of territory, and population as the supreme goal of the rival powers. For Spain, the ultimate results were almost as painful, although the war was not fought on Spanish territory. The Dutch Protestants gained full independence from Madrid, and the tremendous military and naval advantages that Spain's government had once possessed had all been used up; it was now condemned to second rank in European and world affairs.

THE THEORY AND PRACTICE OF ROYAL ABSOLUTISM

The theory of royal absolutism existed in the Middle Age, but the upheavals caused by the Hundred Years' War and the Black Death in the fourteenth century (see Chapter 20), followed by the wars of religion, had weakened the powers of the monarchies. Now, in the seventeenth century, they got back to the business of asserting their sacred rights.

The outstanding theorist of absolutism was a French lawyer, Jean Bodin (zhahn boh-DAN), who stated that "sovereignty consists in giving laws to the people without their consent." Sovereignty cannot be divided; it must remain in the hands of a single individual or institution. Bodin insisted that the French monarch had "absolute power" over his people. Bodin found his most potent and effective adherent in **Cardinal Richelieu** (rish-LYOU; 1585–1642), the prime minister for the young King Louis (LOO-ee) XIII in the 1620s and 1630s.

Richelieu was the real founder of absolute monarchy in France and, despite being a prince of the Roman Catholic Church, Richelieu believed wholeheartedly in the primacy of the state over any other earthly institution. *Raison d'état* (ray-ZOHN day-TAH; reason of state) was sufficient to justify almost any action by government, he thought. The state represented order, the rule of law, and security for the citizenry. If it weakened or collapsed, general suffering would result. The cardinal set up a cadre of officials (**intendants**: ahn-tahn-DAHNTS) who kept a sharp eye on what was happening in the provinces and reported to the king's ministers. The cardinal-minister used them to check the independence of the provincial nobles, particularly the Calvinist Huguenots (OO-geh-nohs). He used armed force on several occasions and executed rebels. Before his death in 1641, Richelieu had handpicked as his successor as chief minister Cardinal Mazarin (mah-zah-REHN), who had the same values as his master. The new king, **Louis XIV** (ruling 1643–1715), was just five years old, so the government remained in Mazarin's hands for many years. The young Louis was brought up to believe that kingship was the highest calling on earth and that its powers were limited only by God.

Louis XIV (1638–1715) in Royal Costume, 1701 (oil on canvas), Rigaud, Hyacinthe (1659–1743)/Louvre, Paris, France/Giraudon/The Bridgeman Art Library

LOUIS XIV. This masterful portrait by the court painter Rigaud shows Louis as he would have liked to appear to his subjects. The "well-turned leg" was considered to be an absolute essential for royal figures. Louis's wig and ermine cape were also necessities for a king.

French Government Under Louis XIV

The late seventeenth and eighteenth centuries were the Age of France or, more precisely, the Age of Louis XIV. Not only in government, but also in the arts, the lifestyle of the wealthy and the highborn, military affairs, and language and literature, France set the pace. What Florence had been to the Renaissance, Paris was to the European cultural and political world of the eighteenth century. Louis XIV was the incarnation of absolute monarchy, believing in divine right, which said that the monarchy's powers flowed from God. He allegedly once said, "I am the state," a statement he truly believed. He saw himself as not just a human being with immense powers and prestige but as the very embodiment of France. He took kingship seriously, working twelve hours a day trying to govern a country that was notoriously difficult. In this task he was greatly aided by a series of first-rate ministerial helpers, each of whom made major contributions to the theory and practice of his chosen field.

To govern as he believed he should, Louis had to nullify the independent powers of the aristocrats in the provinces. He did this by forcing them to come to Versailles (vayr-SIGH), his magnificent palace outside Paris, where they vied for his favor and he could keep them under a watchful eye. By his death, the previously potent nobles had been reduced to a decorative, parasitic fringe group, with few real powers.

Although Louis kept the peace for the first thirty-five years of his reign, his overpowering thirst for glory led him to provoke four conflicts with England, Holland, and most of the German states in the last twenty years. The most important was the final one, the War of the Spanish Succession (1700–1713), in which France tried to seize control of much-weakened Spain and its empire, but was checked by a coalition led by England. The war bankrupted France and was extremely unpopular. The signing of the **Treaty of Utrecht** in 1713 ended the hostilities. France succeeded only in placing a member of the Bourbon (boor-BOHN) family (the French dynasty) on the Spanish throne, but under the condition that Spain and France would never be joined together. England emerged as the chief winner, having gained control of part of French Canada and the key to the Mediterranean, Gibraltar. England's biggest prize, however, was Spain's concession of the rights to trade with her possessions in the Caribbean. The war began the worldwide struggle between England and France for mastery of Europe, but the Treaty of Utrecht helped vault England into a position that enabled her to become the world's greatest imperial and industrial power over the next two hundred years.

VERSAILLES. The views from the garden side, with the Grand Fountain in the foreground. The palace lies a few miles outside Paris and is now one of the most visited tourist centers in Europe.

Strengths and Weaknesses of French Absolutism

Louis XIV gave all of Europe a model of what could be accomplished by a strong king and a wealthy country. With the help of his officials, the king kept a constant watch on the country as a whole. Anything that happened in the provinces was soon known at the Palace of Versailles and received a royal response. The palace was awe-inspiring, serving to reinforce Louis's prestige and power in visible fashion. Originally a mere hunting lodge, Louis reconstructed it into the largest and most impressive secular structure in Europe. It was surrounded by hundreds of acres of manicured gardens and was large enough to house the immense court.

But problems also persisted. Finance was always the sore point for aspiring kings, and Louis and his successors spent huge amounts of cash in their quest for military and civil glory. A helter-skelter system of concessions for tax collection in the provinces did not work well. Worse, with the government legally prevented from taxing the Church and the nobility, Louis's common subjects were forced to bear the entire burden of his and his successors' extravagances. The French peasants slowly became aware of the contrasts between the taxes they had to bear and the exemptions enjoyed by the clergy and the nobility. When that discontent was later joined by the resentment of the middle-class townspeople, the potential for revolution would exist.

REVOLT AGAINST ROYAL ABSOLUTISM: SEVENTEENTH-CENTURY ENGLAND

Two British political philosophers formed the basis of public debate on the nature of government during the tumultuous seventeenth century. In his book, *Leviathan*, Thomas Hobbes (1588–1679) thought that the pregovernmental "state of nature" had been a riotous anarchy. Recognizing the need to restrain violence, according to him, early societies gave birth to the idea of the state and to the state's living embodiment, the monarch. Most significant, however, was that Hobbes implied that the state and the monarch derived their sovereignty from the people, rather than from God. Nevertheless, he remained pessimistic about the future of the people.

Hobbes's uncompromising pessimism about human nature was countered at the end of the seventeenth century by the writings of John Locke (1632–1704). In his most famous work, the *Two Treatises of Civil Government*, Locke said that all men (though not women) possess certain natural rights. Some of those rights were voluntarily given up to form a government that would protect and enhance the remaining ones: the rights to life, liberty, and property. No princes could interfere with such rights or claim to have one-sided powers to define the citizenry's welfare. When they did, they surrendered all claims to citizens' support, and they could righteously form a new government.

The Stuart Monarchy

At the death of Queen Elizabeth in 1603, the English crown passed to Elizabeth's nearest male Protestant relative, the Stuart King James VI of Scotland, who became James I of England (ruling 1603–1625). James was a great believer in absolutism and the divine right of kings and quickly alienated the English Parliament with his insistence that the Crown should have sole control over taxes and the budget. This plus his lack of respect for English customs made him highly unpopular by the end of his reign.

The England that James ruled, however, was rapidly developing into a society in which the commercial and professional classes were becoming used to exercising power. The merchants and municipal officials who were represented by Parliament's House of Commons insisted on their rights to have final input on taxation and much else in national policy. They were armed with a four-century-old tradition of parliamentary government.

Another topic of debate between the king and his subjects was the proper course in religious affairs. James had been brought up as a Calvinist but had agreed to adopt Anglicanism as king of England. In truth, many people believed that he sympathized with Rome, which made the Anglicans nervous and appalled the Puritans.

James died in 1625 and was succeeded by his son, Charles I (1625–1649). The son turned out to be as difficult as his father. When the Commons attempted to impose limits on his taxing powers, he refused to honor the ancient custom of calling a Parliament at least every third year. He appointed an archbishop of Canterbury who many people believed was a sympathizer with popery. Finding that Parliament would not cooperate with him, he sent it home in 1629 and ruled without its advice and consent.

Charles's marriage to a French Catholic princess had stirred up much resentment, and his high-handed attitude toward the Calvinist clergy finally offended his Scot subjects so badly that in 1640, they rose in revolt. Charles needed money—lots of it—to raise an army against them. That meant that he had to impose new taxes, which in turn meant that he had to summon Parliament. When the representatives came together, they passed a series of restrictive laws on the royal powers. When the increasingly radical Parliament insisted on direct control of military affairs, Charles raised an army of royalist supporters, and this action led to the beginning of civil war in 1642.

Civil War: Cromwell's Commonwealth

Britain divided about evenly between supporters of the king and supporters of Parliament. After several years of intermittent struggle, the war ended with Charles's defeat. Parliament then tried the king for treason. After a parliamentary trial, he was found guilty and beheaded in 1649.

After the king's execution, Parliament debated at length the question of where sovereignty lay, and it concluded by declaring that England was a commonwealth—that is, a republic with no monarch. Its executive was the chief organizer of the triumphant Puritan army, Oliver Cromwell, who had gained a deserved reputation as a man of iron will and fierce rectitude. For five years, he ruled and imposed his stern Calvinist Protestantism as Lord Protector (1653–1658). When he died, few people wanted to hear more about Puritan government. Cromwell's rule had also become unpopular because of the high taxes he levied to put down rebellions against English rule in Catholic Ireland and Calvinist Scotland. A maritime war with Holland in the 1650s brought England far along the road to control of the seven seas and also conferred the rich prize of the former Dutch colony of New Amsterdam in North America.

When Cromwell's weak son attempted in vain to fill his father's shoes, parliamentary negotiations with the exiled son of Charles I were begun. After eighteen months, the **Restoration** was completed with the return of King Charles II (ruling 1660–1685) to his native land.

Restoration and the Glorious Revolution of 1688

The pendulum of power in British government had swung decisively toward the House of Commons during the revolutionary era, and Charles made his peace with the Commons by establishing the beginnings of the ministerial system. The king appointed several of his trusted friends to carry out policy, but these men had to answer to parliamentary questioning. Gradually, this informal arrangement became a fundamental part of government and was formalized when the party system got under way in the eighteenth century. From it came the modern British cabinet, with its collective responsibility for policy and its reliance on parliamentary votes of confidence to continue its authority as a government.

Charles cared little about religion, but when it became clear that the aging and childless Charles would be succeeded by his Catholic younger brother, James, the English viewed their new king with a great deal of suspicion. James II (ruling 1685–1688) made things worse by flinging insult after insult at the Protestants in and out of Parliament. So long as the king had no Catholic children to succeed him, the English could grit their teeth and wait for the elderly man's death. But in 1688, his young second wife unexpectedly produced a healthy baby son who would be raised a Catholic and would presumably rule Britain for many years.

Practically all of England rebelled against James in the **Glorious Revolution of 1688** that ended the Stuart male line on the English throne. James again went into French exile, while parliamentary committees stepped into the vacuum. After brief negotiations, William of Orange, the husband of James's daughter, Mary, was invited to rule England jointly with his wife as William and Mary (1689–1702).

Significance of the Glorious Revolution.

The revolution against James Stuart had been political and constitutional, not military or economic. Sovereignty shifted from the monarch to his or her subjects, as represented by their elected Parliament. From now on, England was a constitutional state. The king or queen was the partner of Parliament in matters of high policy, both domestic and foreign.

The most concrete result of the Glorious Revolution was the **Bill of Rights**, which was adopted by Parliament in 1689. Its most important provisions spelled out the rights and powers of Parliament versus the Crown:

- Law was to be made only by Parliament and could not be suspended by the king.
- Members of Parliament were immune from prosecution when acting in their official capacities.
- The king could not impose taxes or raise an army without prior approval by Parliament.

In addition, the Bill of Rights ensured the independence of the judiciary from royal pressures, prohibited standing armies in peacetime, extended freedom of worship to non-Anglican Protestants, and stipulated that the throne should always be held by a Protestant.

Mary's younger sister, Anne, succeeded William and Mary on the English throne. Like William and Mary, she died without surviving children. Parliament exercised its new powers by inviting the Duke of Hanover, a distant German relative of King James I and the nearest male Protestant relation to the deceased queen, to become King George I (ruling 1714–1727). George thus introduced the **Hanoverian Dynasty** to Great Britain.

ABSOLUTISM EAST OF THE ELBE

East of Germany's Elbe River, absolute monarchy was able to develop more completely, largely because of the rural, farm-based economies that lingered there longer than in Western Europe. Monoculture estates lasted much longer than in France, England, and Sweden. The social cleavage between lord and peasant was perpetuated by the rising profits the landlords were able to wring from their large estates. The struggle between noble landowners and the royal government was resolved in Eastern Europe when the monarchs surrendered control over the peasants to the landlords in return for the landlords' loyalty and service to the Crown. As time passed, the once-weak monarchs steadily gained power through control of the armed forces.

Moreover, no effective middle-class voice was ever heard in constitutional affairs east of the Elbe. Why? The towns were too few and too impoverished, and the small urban populations never gained self-government and economic freedom as in the West. Accordingly, the royal dynasts were gradually able to subordinate all classes and interests to themselves.

Prussia's Rise

As we have seen, after the Thirty Years' War (1618–1648), much of Germany was in a state of economic decay and political confusion. The three hundred-odd German states and statelets were divided along religious lines: About half were Catholic and half Protestant. Neither accepted the other, and distrust and animosities were always present. Notwithstanding these issues, in the middle of the seventeenth century, Frederick William, the **Great Elector** (ruling 1640–1688), a man of iron will and great talent, succeeded in uniting Prussia, Brandenburg, and some small areas in western Germany into a single government that was known thereafter simply as Prussia. The Great Elector tripled the government's revenues and then spent much of the increase on his prize: a new professional army. In return for the nobles' agreement to allow him control over national affairs and their agreement to serve in the powerful new army that Frederick William was creating, he handed the peasants over to the noble landlords. He never allowed the Prussian middle classes to play the crucial role they had in Western Europe. They could not strike a "deal" with either king or nobles to guarantee their own rights. They had to pay the taxes from which the nobles' lands were exempt, and their social and political status remained much lower than that of the Prussian nobility, the *Junkers.*

After Frederick William's death, his grandson, Frederick William I (ruling 1713–1740), was even more intent than his grandfather on building the finest army in Europe. During his reign, Prussia was aptly called "an army with a country." The series of notable Hohenzollern monarchs culminated in the eighteenth century with Frederick II, the Great (ruling 1740–1786), who is generally seen as one of the most talented kings in modern history. Frederick II cleverly associated the Prussian monarchy with a reviving German sense of national unity. With him began the "German dualism," the century-long contest between Austria and Prussia for leadership of the German-speaking people—the most numerous in Europe.

The Habsburg Domains

Prussia's rival for eventual political supremacy over the fragmented Germans was Habsburg Austria. Based in Vienna, the **Habsburg Dynasty** (HABS-berg) ruled over three quite different areas: Austria proper, Bohemia (the present-day Czech Republic), and Hungary (see Map 23.3). The dynasty had acquired Hungary and Bohemia through lucky marriages in the sixteenth century. However, against its southern and eastern flanks, the Ottoman Turks were still a menacing foe, and they mounted an invasion that reached the outskirts of Vienna in 1683. The Ottomans' attack was beaten off, and the counterattack against the Ottomans went well at first, but the Turks were able to recoup their strength temporarily. The Treaty of Karlowitz in 1699 (see Chapter 24) eliminated the threat of a Turkish invasion of central Europe, and Austria became a leading power.

This new power, however, had a flaw that became apparent with time. Ethnically, the empire of Austria was the least integrated of all European countries. It included no fewer than ten different nationalities. As late as the mid-eighteenth century, the Habsburg lands resembled a "salad" of nations and regions that had little in common except rule by the dynasty in Vienna. Maria Theresa (1740–1780) and her son Joseph II (ruling 1780–1790) did much to modernize the Austrian armed forces and civil bureaucracy. She slowly welded the various provinces and kingdoms into a single entity under a centralized government headquartered in the impressive royal city. Much later, in the mid-nineteenth century, the Austrians turned east and south to realize their version of colonial expansion. By so doing, they encountered the Turks, who had sunk into second-level status. But Europe's diplomats agreed to let the Turks continue to control southeastern Europe (the Balkans), to avoid the inevitable conflicts that would ensue if the Turks were pushed aside and replaced by others. First among those contenders were the newly powerful Russians.

MAP 23.3 The Growth of the Austrian Empire, 1536–1795

By an extraordinary stroke of luck, the Vienna-based Habsburg family painlessly acquired the crowns of both Bohemia and Hungary when the last king of both those monarchies fell, childless, on the field of battle against invading Turks in 1526. The surviving widow and heir was a Habsburg princess.

THINKING ABOUT THIS MAP

What happened that explains the success of Austria's expansion into the Balkans after 1600?

THE BELVEDERE IN VIENNA. This palace was built by and for Prince Eugen of Savoy, greatest of the Habsburg generals in the wars of the late seventeenth and early eighteenth centuries. It is a perfect example of Austrian baroque architecture.

RUSSIA UNDER THE TSARS

Russia's government rose from centuries of retardation and near-disintegration to attain great power status in the eighteenth century (see Map 23.4). Until the 1200s, Russia had been an independent Christian principality based on the impressive city of Kiev (kee-YEV), with extensive trading and cultural contacts with both western and Mediterranean Europe through the Baltic and Black seas. The Russians had been converted to Orthodox Christianity by Greek missionaries in the late 900s and had remained closely attached to Constantinople for the next three centuries.

MAP 23.4 From Muscovy to Russia, 1584–1796

The "gathering of the Russian lands" by the Muscovite rulers was facilitated by their acting as the Mongols' agents for centuries and then defeating them and the aggressive Lithuanians and Poles in the late 1400s. Later acquisitions were based on the alleged rights of Moscow to reclaim what it had once ruled.

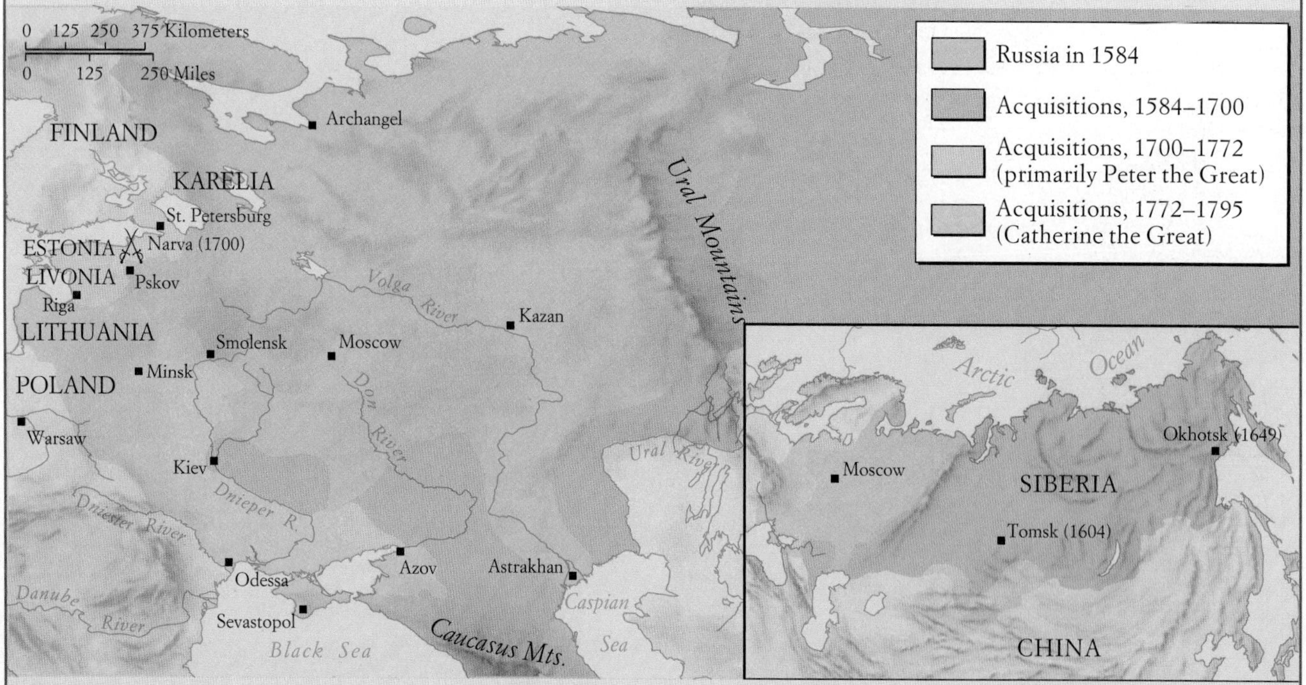

0 125 250 375 Kilometers
0 125 250 Miles

Russia in 1584
Acquisitions, 1584–1700
Acquisitions, 1700–1772 (primarily Peter the Great)
Acquisitions, 1772–1795 (Catherine the Great)

FINLAND
KARELIA
Archangel
St. Petersburg
ESTONIA
Narva (1700)
LIVONIA
Pskov
Riga
LITHUANIA
Smolensk
Moscow
Kazan
Volga River
Ural Mountains
POLAND
Minsk
Warsaw
Kiev
Don River
Ural River
Dnieper R.
Dniester River
Danube River
Odessa
Azov
Astrakhan
Sevastopol
Black Sea
Caucasus Mts.
Caspian Sea
Arctic Ocean
Moscow
Okhotsk (1649)
SIBERIA
Tomsk (1604)
CHINA

THINKING ABOUT THIS MAP

What changes helped enable the Russians to expand into the Black Sea and Caucasus regions under the Muscovites and the Romanovs?

But in 1241, the fierce Mongols conquered the principality of Kiev and settled down to rule the Russians for the next 240 years (see Chapter 18). During that period, Russia's formerly numerous contacts with both Eastern and Western Europe were almost completely severed or neglected, and the Russians retrogressed in many ways. Their governmental institutions also deteriorated. Moscow came through cunning, perseverance, and good luck to overshadow its rivals even during the Mongol era. The *Mongol Yoke*, as the Russians call it, was finally thrown off in a bloodless rebellion led by Moscow in 1480. Trade relations were eventually established with the West, but beyond some raw materials and some exotic items such as ermine skins, there seemed little reason to get involved in trading with this alien society. Militarily and politically, it had nothing to offer the West, and whatever technical and cultural progress was made in Russia during these centuries almost always stemmed from Western sources. The Russians were in any case not inclined to welcome Western ideas and visitors.

The Orthodox Church had been crucially important in keeping alive national identity during the Yoke, and their distrust of Western Christians was strong. Russia experienced almost nothing of the consequences of the Protestant revolt against Rome or the Renaissance. The Renaissance glorification of individuality, examination of the human potential, and the daring to oppose had no impact east of Poland. In religious affairs, the Russians either were ignorant of or rejected the changes Western Christianity had undergone. The Russian clergy had accepted the role of partner of the civil government in maintaining good order on Earth. Unlike the papal or Protestant West, Orthodox clerics saw their role as helper and moral partner of the government in the mutual and interdependent tasks of saving Russian souls and preserving the Russian state.

The expansion of the Muscovite principality into a major state picked up its pace during the sixteenth century. Tsar Ivan IV, or **Ivan the Terrible** (ruling 1533–1584), brushed aside the Mongol remnants in a program of conquest that reached the Pacific shores as early as 1639. Russia was brought into formal contact with China for the first time—and thus began a difficult relationship along the longest land border in the world.

Like the countries of Western Europe, Russia adopted a form of divine-right monarchy in the seventeenth century. Already in the previous century, Ivan the Terrible had established a brutal model by persecuting all who dared question his rights. Those who did not flee and who chose to remain often paid with their lives for nonexistent "treason" or "betrayal." He bullied and terrified the Russian upper classes in a fashion that would have certainly led to revolt in other countries of the age.

The ancient dynasty of Kievan princes died out in the seventeenth century, and various nobles vied with armed force for the vacant throne. Once in power, recovery under the new **Romanov Dynasty** (ROH-mah-noff; 1613–1917) was fairly rapid. Peter I, the Great (ruling 1682–1724), is the outstanding example of Russian royal absolutism. Like Ivan IV, he was in no way inclined to share power, and the impact of the human whirlwind called Peter on stolid, isolated, and conservative Russia is impossible to categorize. He was the first Russian ruler to recognize how primitive Russia was in comparison with Europe. He brought thousands of foreign specialists, craftsmen, artists, and engineers to Russia on contract to practice their specialties while teaching the Russians. These individuals had inordinate influence on the country's progress in the next century.

Defeating the Swedes and the Poles, Peter established a new capital at St. Petersburg to be Russia's long-sought "window on the West," through which all sorts of Western ideas and values might flow. He began the slow, state-guided modernization of what had been a backward economy; he built a navy and made Russia a maritime power for the first time; and he also encouraged such cultural breakthroughs as the first newspaper, the first learned journal, the *Academy of Sciences*, and the first technical schools. But Peter's cruelty bordered on sadism, and his personal life was filled with excess. In any event, he remains the watershed figure of Russia's long history.

PETER THE GREAT. The great reformer–modernizer of backward Russia, painted in the early years of his reign.

Portrait of Peter the Great (1672–1725) (oil on canvas), French School, (18th century)/Chateau de Versailles, France/Giraudon/The Bridgeman Art Library

SUMMARY

As much as the discovery of the New World, the Protestant movement gave birth to the modern era in the West. The protests of Luther, Calvin, and many others against what they saw as the unrighteous and distorted teachings of the Roman papacy had immense long-term reverberations in Western culture. Among Calvinists, the material welfare of the Elect on Earth was linked to their quality of being saved—a link that would gradually produce what later generations called the "Protestant ethic." The Catholic response was the Counter-Reformation, which, spear-headed by the Jesuits, eventually reclaimed much of the Protestant territories for the Roman Church. Exceedingly bloody warfare broke out, and Europe entered the Modern Age in a flurry of fierce antagonisms among Christians. From the early seventeenth century on, doctrines of faith took an ever-decreasing role in forming state policy. The Catholic but anti-Habsburg French replaced Spain as the prime force in military and political affairs. Under the guidance of Richelieu and the long-lived Louis XIV, France became the role model for the rest of the aspiring absolutist monarchies on the Continent.

The English Revolution, sparked by the attempts of the Stuart kings to emulate Louis XIV, ended in clear victory for the anti-absolutist side. Led by the Puritan rebels against Charles I, the wealthier, educated segment of the English people successfully asserted their claims to be equal to the Crown in defining national policies and the rights of citizens. The Glorious Revolution of 1688 cemented these gains. The idea of a society that was contractual rather than authoritarian in its political basis began to emerge. Along with this came the ideal of a state that guaranteed liberty and legal equality for all its subjects.

The Eastern European dynasties were able to grow and foil the occasional efforts to restrict their royal powers because neither of the two potential secular counter-forces—the limited urban classes and the nobility—could find ways to substitute themselves for the throne. The rise of the Prussian Hohenzollern kingdom began in earnest in the mid-1600s when the Great Elector cleverly made his petty state into a factor in the Thirty Years' War, which culminated in the reign of his great-grandson Frederick II. The weaknesses of the Habsburg state were partially addressed by the efforts of Empress Maria Theresa, who brought a degree of centralization and uniformity to the government. But Austria's great problem—its potentially competing nationalities—remained. After an obstacle-filled climb from obscurity under the Mongols, the Muscovite principality "gathered the Russian lands" in the 1500s, and the Russian nobility, once all-powerful, were reduced by the various devices of the tsars to more or-less willing servants of the imperial throne.

IDENTIFICATION TERMS

Test your knowledge of this chapter's key concepts by defining the following terms. If you can not recall the meaning of certain terms, refresh your memory by looking up the boldfaced term in the chapter, turning to the Glossary at the end of the book, or accessing the terms on the CourseMate website at **www.cengagebrain.com.**

Act of Supremacy of 1534
Anabaptists
Anglican Church
Bill of Rights of 1689
John Calvin
Counter-Reformation
Edict of Nantes
Elect
Queen Elizabeth I
Glorious Revolution of 1688
The Great Elector (Frederick William)
Habsburg Dynasty
Hanoverian Dynasty
King Henry VIII
Ignatius of Loyola
The Institutes of the Christian Religion
intendants
Ivan the Terrible
Jesuit Order
justification by faith
Louis XIV
Martin Luther
Ninety-five Theses
Peace of Augsburg
Puritans
Reformation
Restoration (English)
Cardinal Richelieu
Romanov Dynasty
Treaty of Utrecht
Treaty of Westphalia

FOR FURTHER REFLECTION

1. What differences are there between a religious heretic and a religious reformer?
2. Why did the sixteenth-century religious reform movements succeed whereas previous attempts at reform failed?
3. Did religious reform then open way to greater tolerance of other people's values and principles? Be sure to cite specific examples to support your answer.
4. What seems to have been the main differences between royal absolutism as it was practiced in Western Europe and as it was practiced in Eastern Europe?
5. What theological and historical reasons might there have been behind the Russian clergy's opposition to Western ideas? Aside from their opposition, what other possible reasons might explain Russian resistance to Western ideas?

TEST YOUR KNOWLEDGE

Test your knowledge of this chapter by answering the following questions. Complete answers appear at the end of the book. You may find even more quiz questions on the CourseMate website at **www.cengagebrain.com**.

1. Luther's anger over the sale of indulgences led to
   a. his decision to seek the pope's removal.
   b. his decision that he must challenge papal domination.
   c. the posting of the Ninety-five Theses.
   d. his excommunication by the pope.
   e. the Council of Constance.
2. Which of the following practices or beliefs is associated with Calvinism?
   a. The basic goodness of humans
   b. Predestination of souls
   c. Religious freedom for all
   d. Indulgences
   e. The rejection of good works as necessary for eternal salvation
3. Henry VIII's reform of English religious organization occurred
   a. after study in the Holy Land.
   b. for primarily religious-doctrinal reasons.
   c. for primarily political-dynastic reasons.
   d. at the urging of the pope.
   e. after he experienced a vision of the Archangel Gabriel.
4. To combat the challenge of Protestantism the Roman Catholic Church
   a. trained Catholic soldiers to fight religious wars.
   b. increased the power of the Inquisition.
   c. created the Jesuit Order.
   d. created the Dominican Order.
   e. founded new Catholic universities in Protestant lands.
5. The Edict of Nantes
   a. gave Protestants in France a degree of official toleration.
   b. expelled all Protestants from Catholic France.
   c. brought civic and legal equality to Protestants in France.
   d. ended the war between Catholic France and Protestant England.
   e. established religious tolerance between Spain and France.
6. The founder of absolute monarchy in France was
   a. Jean Bodin.
   b. Louis XIV.
   c. Cardinal Mazarin.
   d. Cardinal Richelieu.
   e. Henry IV.
7. *Raison d'état* was used to
   a. buttress the power of the French monarchy.
   b. justify the alliance between the Spanish monarchy and the Roman Catholic church.
   c. reinforce the pope's authority in Europe.
   d. reinforce the pope's authority in France.
   e. deny freedom of religion in Italy.
8. The message conveyed by Hobbes's *Leviathan* was, in brief, that
   a. man would find his way to a better future.
   b. man could make more progress once religion was abolished.
   c. man was irredeemably stained by original sin.
   d. man needed a powerful government to avoid anarchy.
   e. man by nature would do good if taught to do so.
9. East of the Elbe, the feudal landlords of the fifteenth through seventeenth centuries
   a. maintained or increased their local powers and prestige.
   b. regularly overthrew the royal governments.
   c. suffered a general decline economically.
   d. practically became extinct with the rise of urban life.
   e. had little to do with the peasants under their control.
10. A great difference between Ivan IV, the Terrible, and Peter I, the Great, is
    a. the savagery of the first and the subtlety of the second.
    b. the minimal successes of Ivan and the tremendous ones of Peter.
    c. the tender consideration shown to the nobles by Peter.
    d. the degree to which they incorporated Western ideas into their country.
    e. their views about the concept of absolute rule.

CourseMate

Visit the CourseMate website at **www.cengagebrain.com** for additional study tools and review materials for this chapter.

The Gunpowder Empires of Western and Southern Asia 24

He who cannot love another human being is ignorant of life's joy. —SA'ADI

CHAPTER OUTLINE

c. 1250	Osman founds the Ghazi Ottoman state
1300s–1500s	Ottoman Empire expands and flourishes
1453	Mehmed the Conqueror seizes Constantinople/Istanbul
1520–1566	Reign of Suleiman the Magnificent
1500s–1722	Safavid Empire in Persia
1556–1605	Reign of Akbar the Great of India
1587–1629	Reign of Shah Abbas the Great of Persia
1500s–mid-1800s	Mughal Empire in India

At the time when Europe slowly began finding its way out of centuries of feudal disintegration to early statehood and East Asian governments experienced challenges from both external and internal rivals, Islamic empires in Asia and Africa were experiencing seemingly endless upheavals. If it can be said that the Islamic world experienced a middle age of governmental evolution and consolidation, it was from about 1300 to 1600. Muslims in Turkey (the Ottomans), Iran (the Safavids), and India (the Mughals) innovated new forms of government based on Sufi brotherhoods and new methods of waging war involving the use of gunpowder. (Hence, scholars have labeled them the gunpowder empires.) Until the late seventeenth century, more often than not they proved to be more than a match for European challengers.

In Chapters 15 and 16, we looked at how Islam expanded rapidly in the tropical zone between Spain and India. Within remarkably few decades, Arab Bedouin armies carried the message of Muhammad the Prophet from Mecca in all directions on the blades of their conquering swords. The civilization that sprang from this message and conquest was a mixture of Arab, Greek, Persian, Egyptian, Spanish, African, and Southeast Asian—the most cosmopolitan civilization in world history.

In the thirteenth century, the capital city of the Abbasid caliphs remained at Baghdad, but by then the Islamic world had become severely fractured into dozens of competing, quarreling states and sects. More devastating still, in that century, the Mongols swept into the Islamic heartland in central and western Asia, destroying every sign of settled life in their path and establishing brief rule over half the world (see Chapter 18). After their disappearance, the Ottoman

Turks gave Islam a new forward thrust. By the 1500s, the Ottomans had succeeded in capturing Constantinople and reigned over enormous territories reaching from Gibraltar to Iraq. Farther east and somewhat later, the Safavids in Persia and the Mughals in India established Muslim dynasties that endured into the early modern age.

THE OTTOMAN EMPIRE

The Mongols had smashed the Persian center of Islam in the 1250s, conquered Baghdad in 1258, and left the caliph as one of the corpses of those who had dared oppose them. At that time, the all-conquering intruders intended to wipe out the rest of the Islamic states that reached as far as Spain. One of these was the Ottoman principality in what is now Turkey, which took full advantage of the Mongols' defeat at Ain Jalut to maintain its independence. (See Chapter 18.)

The arrival of the Ottoman Dynasty in Asia Minor and its subsequent rise to the status of most powerful state in the Islamic world was the partial consequence of two developments that had preceded it. The first of these was the Turkification of the caliphate that had begun as early as the ninth century C.E. The nomadic Turkish tribes began migrating from their homelands in the steppes of central Asia early in that century, and soon, large numbers of them inhabited the eastern lands of the Abbasid caliphate. Faced with increasing challenges to their authority from Kharijites and Shi'ites, the Abbasid caliphs were forced to rely on the skills of these fearsome fighters to help quell revolts. Soon, Turkish troops under Turkish commanders were largely staffing the armies of the caliphate, but the real power resided in Baghdad under the Seljuk sultans (see Chapter 16). Once in power in Baghdad, the Seljuks resumed the Muslim offensive against the rejuvenated Byzantine Empire in the eleventh century. In 1071, a crucial Seljuk victory over the Byzantines at the Battle of Manzikert gave the Turks direct access to Asia Minor for the first time. They established the Rum sultanate in eastern Asia Minor and continued their *jihad* against the Christian enemies to the west.

The second important development was the growing importance of the **dervish**, or Sufi (SOO-fee), orders in Islam. As explained in Chapter 16, many Muslims embraced mystical forms of Islam after the death of al-Ghazzali (al-gah-ZAH-lee) in 1111 C.E. Many dervishes/Sufis formed religious associations or brotherhoods (*tariqas*: tah-REE-kahs). In most cases, these were organized around a central religious figure, or *shaykh* (shake), whom the dervishes believed possessed extraordinary spiritual authority and who was responsible for the spiritual and intellectual direction of his followers. Typically, too, the dervish order was organized into grades, much like a secret society (like the Masons in Western Europe), and initiates graduated into higher levels of the order as they were allowed access to secret knowledge known only to members of these higher levels.

The Ottoman Empire began around 1250, when a Turkish chieftain named Osman (AHS-man)—after whom the dynasty was named—and his group of followers entered into the service of the Rum sultans of eastern Asia Minor. Osman was given a small fiefdom in western Asia Minor to wage jihad against the Byzantines. Thus, the empire began as a *ghazi* state—that is, one made up of **ghazis** (GAH-zees), or frontier warriors, whose express purpose was waging holy war against the Christians. Osman's tiny state was initially organized around two dervish orders, and besides being a warlord, the authority of Osman and his early successors appears to have come from their positions as shaykhs of one or both of these dervish orders.

Osman succeeded in becoming independent when the Mongols destroyed the Rum sultanate soon after it overran Baghdad. By the time he died, Osman had established a core Ottoman state that included most of western Asia Minor through continual warfare against both his Muslim and non-Muslim neighbors. His son and successor, Orhan (ruling 1326–1359), continued this policy of expansion, and he began the conquest of what remained of the Byzantine Empire on the Balkan Peninsula.

More important, as the Ottoman ghazi state continued to grow, Orhan reorganized it along feudal lines. Landed estates were parceled out among the commanders of the mounted army. Orhan was also noted for creating the system by which the growing numbers of various nationalities and religious groups were absorbed into the burgeoning Ottoman Empire. Each group was organized as a *millet*—that is, as a separate minority under the leadership of an appointed shaykh, who answered directly to the sultan and his officials. Each millet was allowed a degree of self-regulation under its shaykh, and its rights were protected.

By the 1450s, the empire had grown to include all of Asia Minor and most of the Balkans south of modern-day Hungary. Of the Byzantine Empire, only the great capital of Constantinople remained. After several failed attempts to capture the great fortress city of the Christians on the western side of the narrow waterway separating Europe from Asia, Sultan **Mehmed** (MEH-mehd) **the Conqueror** (ruling 1451–1481) succeeded in taking this prize. A long siege weakened the Christians' resistance, and the sultan's new bronze cannon destroyed the walls. In 1453, the city finally surrendered. Under the new name of Istanbul, it became the capital of the Ottoman Empire from that time forward. By the reign of **Suleiman** (SOO-lay-man) **the Magnificent** (ruled 1520–1566), Hungary, Romania, southern Poland, and southern Russia had been added to the sultan's domain, while in North Africa and the Middle East, all of the Islamic states from Morocco to Persia had accepted his overlordship (see Map 24.1). At this stage, Ottoman military power was unmatched in the world.

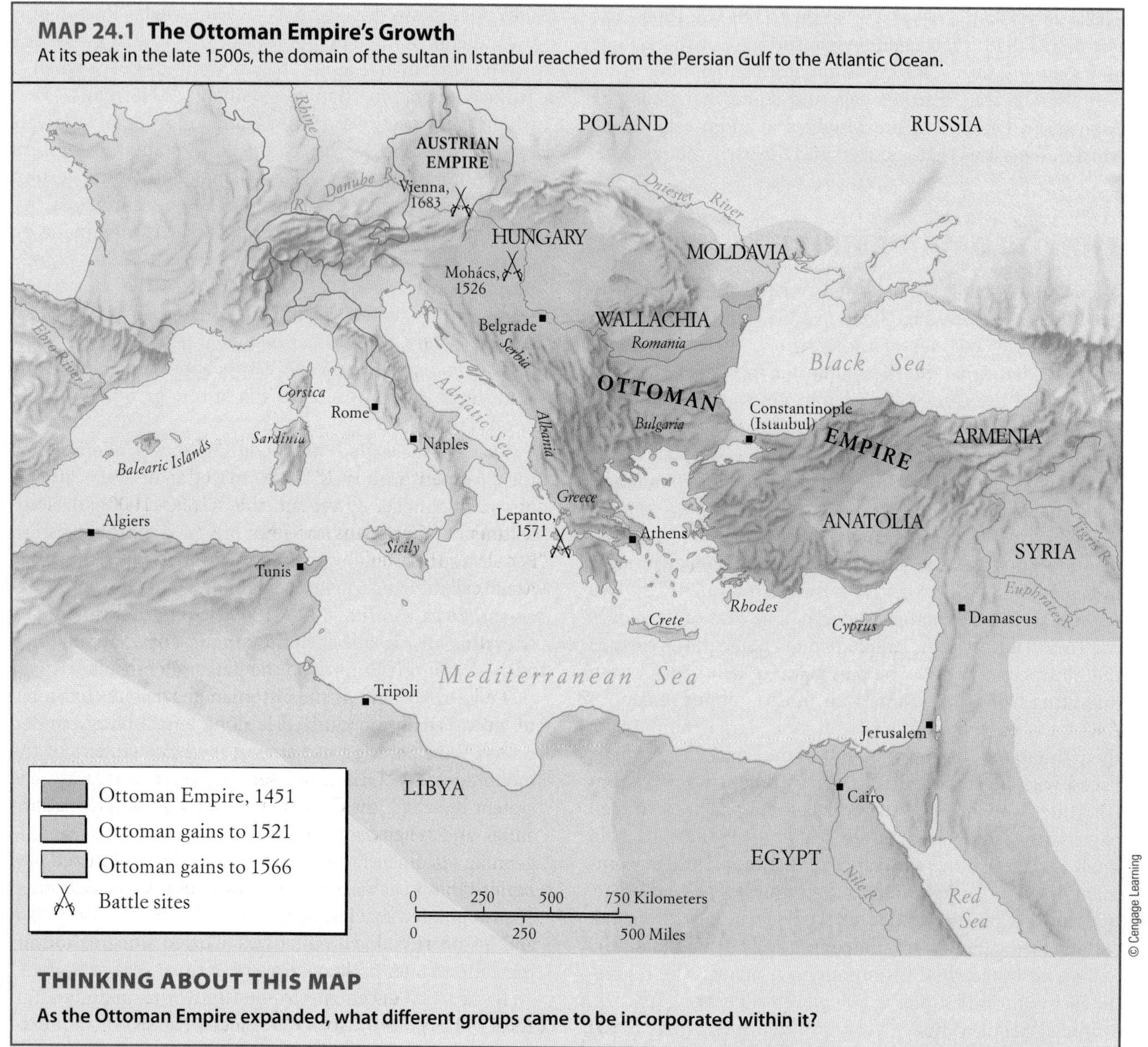

MAP 24.1 The Ottoman Empire's Growth
At its peak in the late 1500s, the domain of the sultan in Istanbul reached from the Persian Gulf to the Atlantic Ocean.

THINKING ABOUT THIS MAP

As the Ottoman Empire expanded, what different groups came to be incorporated within it?

Ottoman Government

Ottoman glory reached its apex during the reign of Suleiman the Magnificent, a sultan whose resources and abilities certainly matched any of his fellow rulers in an age of formidable women and men (Elizabeth I of England, Akbar the Great in India, and Ivan the Terrible in Russia). The government he presided over was divided into a secular bureaucracy, a religious bureaucracy, and a chancery called the **Sublime Porte**—after the gate in the sultan's palace near where it was located. At the head of all three stood the sultan. The officials of the Sublime Porte were what we would call the civil government, and it was composed of many levels of officials from the **Grand Vizier** (vih-ZEER; prime minister) down to the lowliest copyists. Most members of the secular bureaucracy originally were non-Muslims who had converted to the Muslim faith.

The religious bureaucracy was parallel to the secular one. Its members were collectively the *ulama* (oo-la-MAH), or learned scholars of the law, the *Shari'a*, which was derived from the holy book of Islam, the *Qur'an*. The sultan appointed a high official, called the **Shaykh al-Islam**, as the head of this vast bureaucracy. The religious bureaucracy lent its great moral authority to the work of the Sublime Porte; it was, in effect, a junior partner of the government. In the ordinary course of events, conflict between the two was unthinkable.

The army was an arm of the secular bureaucracy. The Ottoman army was far superior to European militaries by virtue of its professionalism and discipline. At its heart were the well-trained and well-armed **Janissaries**, an elite infantry corps. The Ottomans used a system called the **devshirme** (duv-SHEER-muh) to staff the Janissary units of the army and other high positions within the sultan's administration. Essentially this system was based on seizing Balkan Christian boys at a tender age, converting them to Islam, and giving them unlimited chances to advance themselves in both army and government. The system was designed to create new units for the army and the Sultan's palace, staffed by servants whose only loyalty was to the sultan. Some of the most brilliant leaders of the Ottoman state in the sixteenth through eighteenth centuries were these willing slaves of the sultan (as they proudly termed themselves), recruited from the infidels.

Through the devshirme, the Ottoman state for many years successfully avoided the weakening of the central authority that was inevitable with the kind of feudal system Orhan had created in the fourteenth century. Instead, by the time of Mehmed and Suleiman, the bulk of the standing army was a mobile, permanent corps that could be shifted about throughout the huge empire controlled by Istanbul. Therefore, aside from the cavalry corps, most soldiers came to depend on salaries paid directly to them by the central government. The Janissaries and other new infantry corpsmen remained loyal to the central government alone because of their lack of local connections and the fact that they rarely remained in one place very long.

MEHMED THE CONQUEROR. The conqueror of Constantinople is portrayed in this Turkish miniature smelling a rose (symbolizing his cultural interests), as well as gripping a handkerchief (a symbol of his power).

As long as the Janissaries conformed to this ideal, the Ottoman governmental system operated smoothly and effectively. The provincial authorities obeyed the central government or were soon replaced and punished. But after about 1650, when the professional army was able to obtain land and develop the connections to purely local affairs that landholding entailed, a lengthy period of decline commenced.

Non-Muslims Under Ottoman Rule

The treatment of non-Muslims varied over time. In the early centuries of Ottoman rule (1300–1600), official treatment of Christians and Jews was generally fair. These "People of the Book" were distinctly limited in what we would call civil rights, could not hold office, could not proselytize for converts or bear arms, and suffered many other disadvantages, but they were not forced to convert to Islam and could run their own civil and cultural affairs on the local and even provincial level. They were taxed, but not excessively. Until the seventeenth century, the public lives of minorities within the millet system seem to have assured them more security than most Jews or Muslims living under Christian rule could expect. On the other hand, the brutality with which the Ottomans treated defeated opponents and the forceful application of the devshirme proved the limits of Ottoman tolerance for the rights of subject populations.

The majority of the Balkan population was Orthodox Christian. Under Turkish rule, the Balkan peasants were almost always decently treated until the seventeenth century. They were allowed to elect their own headmen in their villages; go to Christian services; and otherwise baptize, marry, and bury their dead according to their traditions. Like other non-Muslims, they were more heavily taxed than Muslims, but they were allowed to own land and businesses and to move about freely.

In the course of the seventeenth century, however, the condition of the Balkan Christians deteriorated badly for several reasons, including the central government's increasing need for tax funds, the increasing hostility toward all infidels at Istanbul, and a moral breakdown in provincial and local government. "The fish stinks from the head," says an old Turkish proverb, and the bad example of the harem government in the capital was having effects in the villages.

During the eighteenth century, the condition of the Balkan Christians had become sufficiently oppressive that they began looking for liberation by their independent neighbors, Austria and Russia. From now on, the

Ottomans had to treat their Christian subjects as potential or actual traitors, which made the tensions between the sultan's government and his Christian subjects still worse. By the nineteenth and twentieth centuries, the treatment of Christian minorities—such as the Greeks, Armenians, and others—at times was about as bad in the Islamic Near East as any people have ever had to endure. Unfortunately for the Balkan states today, these old hatreds that Ottoman rule brought to the region remain the primary source of the ethnic and religious conflicts that continue to plague it.

The Zenith of the Ottoman Empire: Suleiman and After

The Ottoman Empire reached its peak during the reign of Suleiman the Magnificent in the sixteenth century. Many consider Suleiman to have been the empire's greatest ruler. Even in a dynasty that had many long-reigning sultans, the length of Suleiman's rule was remarkably long—from 1520 to 1566. His was an outstandingly stable rule in which it seemed that everything the sultan attempted to accomplish succeeded.

Immediately, when Suleiman came to the throne at twenty-six years of age, he was successful in extending control over all of North Africa. For many years, the Spanish and the Portuguese had attacked and occupied the port cities of Morocco and Algeria. To deal with them, Suleiman formed an alliance with a corsair by the name of Khair ad-Din Barbarossa. The attacks that followed by the combined fleets of Khair ad-Din and the well-armed Ottomans were effective in pushing the Iberians out of Tunis and Algiers. Suleiman also seized the island of Rhodes, which the Christian Knights of St. John hitherto had defended successfully against the Ottomans for centuries. With these victories, Suleiman came close to rivaling ancient Rome in lands conquered by winning complete control over the entire Mediterranean Sea region. In southeastern Europe, the sultan's huge army seized the cities of Belgrade and Budapest. Suleiman's next—and boldest—move was against the capital of the Austrian Empire, Vienna. After a siege that lasted through the summer in 1529, autumn and colder weather finally obliged Suleiman to make an orderly withdrawal. Although the attack failed, it marked the crest of a long wave of Ottoman expansion in Europe.

As they had stacked conquest on top of conquest, the Ottoman sultans increasingly had come to be regarded by Muslims all over the world as the new caliphs of the Muslim *Umma* (see Chapter 15). With the golden age of the Abbasids long past, Muslims needed a powerful ruler who could assume the responsibilities of religious leadership that were essential to Islam. Ottomans such as Mehmed and Suleiman filled that need admirably. Besides his attacks on Christian Europe, for example, Suleiman defeated a powerful Safavid Shi'ite state in Iran (see following discussion) and managed to occupy Iraq. He also took charge of making the crucial arrangements for the annual pilgrimages to Mecca. In addition, he remodeled the Tomb of the Prophet Muhammad in Medina and the famous Dome of the Rock mosque in Jerusalem.

Despite the continued conquests and the unprecedented levels of prestige and influence achieved by the sultanate under this monarch, harbingers of future problems were already surfacing during Suleiman's reign. He introduced new practices that were followed by the sultans who came after him, all of which ultimately proved disadvantageous to the empire. For example, after the demoralizing losses of his favorite Grand Vizier and his son, Mustapha, to harem intrigues (see Evidence of the Past box), Suleiman showed less and less interest in the day-to-day details of governing than had been the case beforehand. He withdrew from daily meetings of his ***divan***, or royal council, allowing his new Grand Viziers to assume power, if not actual responsibility. The annual jihads and conquests continued, but Suleiman and his successors again deferred to their viziers and other military officials (who were given the title of *pasha*) for their execution.

The remainder of the sixteenth century and most of the seventeenth amounted to a stalemate between the Islamic East and the Christian West. This period saw growing difficulties for the Ottomans and the other great Muslim empires—especially in their dealings with the West. Yet there was little or no actual loss of territory. In 1683, the Ottomans even managed to again muster sufficient resources for a second attack on Vienna. This assault failed, but unlike the failure of the first one in 1529, this one was followed by a disastrous defeat at the hands of a Habsburg army led by Eugen (OY-gun) of Savoy. Finally, in 1699, the Ottomans were forced to sign the **Treaty of Karlowitz**, a momentous document that, after centuries of continuous expansion, forced the Ottoman sultan for the first time to cede territory to his European opponents.

THE MUSLIM EMPIRES IN PERSIA AND INDIA

In the sixteenth and seventeenth centuries, the Sufi and Shi'ite divisions, which had existed within the theology of Islam for many centuries, became noticeably stronger. The Sufi mystics sought a different path to God than orthodox Muslims (see Chapter 15). Some of the Sufis of central Asia adopted the historical views of the Shi'ites, who reject all of Muhammad's successors who were not related directly to him by blood or marriage. In the eighth century, as we saw in Chapter 16, this belief resulted in a major split between the Shi'ite minority and the Sunni majority, who believed that the caliph (or successor to the Prophet) could be anyone qualified by nobility of purpose and abilities. From that original dispute over

EVIDENCE OF THE PAST

Harem Intrigue in the Death of Suleiman's Favorite Son

The following is an eyewitness account of a visit with Suleiman by Ogier Ghislain de Busbecq, who had been sent as the Austrian ambassador to the court of the sultan near the end of his reign. As can be seen, Busbecq was impressed by the sultan.

Take particular note of the hint of intrigue in the sultan's harem with the account of the scheme of Roxilana, his favorite wife, to have Suleiman's favorite son, Mustapha, put to death. Throughout history, many women have been excluded from positions of power. However, women such as Roxilana and Kosem Sultan have used informal means to wield power that even princes and office-holding males might envy.

> The Sultan was seated on a rather low sofa, no more than a foot from the ground and spread with many costly coverlets and cushions embroidered with exquisite work. Near him were his bows and arrows. His expression, as I have said, is anything but smiling, and has a sternness which, though sad is full of majesty . . .
>
> . . . He is beginning to feel the weight of years, but his dignity of demeanor and his general physical appearance are worthy of the ruler of so vast an empire. . . . Even in his earlier years he did not indulge in wine or in those unnatural vices to which the Turks are often addicted. Even his bitterest critics can find nothing more serious to allege against him than his undue submission to his wife [Roxilana] and its result in his somewhat [hasty] action in putting Mustapha . . . to death, which is generally [blamed on Roxilana's] employment of love potions and incantations. It is generally agreed that, ever since he promoted her to the rank of his lawful wife, he has possessed no [slave wives], although there is no law to prevent his doing so. He is a strict guardian of his religion and its ceremonies. . . . For his age—he has almost reached his sixtieth year—he enjoys quite good health, though his bad complexion may be due to some hidden malady; and indeed it is generally believed that he has an incurable ulcer or gangrene on his leg. The defect of complexion he remedies by painting his face with a coating of red powder.

Superstock/Glow Images

KOSEM SULTAN AND SERVANTS. The mother of two Ottoman Sultans, Murad IV (ruled 1623–1640) and Ibrahim I (ruled 1640–1648). Kosem Sultan (*c.* 1589–1651) was the consort of Sultan Ahmed I (ruled 1603–1617), and one of the most powerful women in Ottoman history.

ANALYZE AND INTERPRET

What effect did the death of Mustapha seem to have on the great sultan?

Source: From Edward Foster, trans., *The Turkish Letters of Ogier Ghiselin de Busbecq, Imperial Ambassador at Constantinople, 1554–1562* (Oxford: Clarendon Press, 1927), 58–59, 65–66.

succession gradually emerged a series of doctrinal differences. Much of Islamic history can be visualized best within the framework of the rivalry between the Shi'ite and Sunni factions.

The Safavid Realm in Persia

Within the Islamic world, the greatest rival of the Ottoman Empire after the sixteenth century was the **Safavid Empire** of Persia. Therefore, it is ironic that they shared similar origins. The embryonic Safavid state, the first independent Iranian state since the Sassanians, began in the region of Tabriz, west of the Caspian Sea. Like the Ottoman ghazi state, it was organized around a Turkish Sufi association. This brotherhood took its name from its founder, Safi ad-Din (shortened as "Safavid"), who claimed to be a descendant of Muhammad. By the fifteenth century, however, the Safavid state came to differ from the Ottoman orders in one important aspect: It converted to Shi'ite Islam.

The Safavids became a major threat to the Ottomans when they evolved a militant theology that advocated the supremacy of Shi'ism through the force of arms. Spreading their views through propaganda, they converted many Turkish tribes in Iran, Syria, and eastern Asia Minor. These Shi'ites took over much of the Persian Muslim state, and from that base, they waged frequent wars on their Sunni competitors to the west. In the early 1500s, a leader named Ismail, claiming to be a representative of the hidden Shi'a Imam, succeeded in capturing much of Persia and Iraq—including Baghdad—and made himself *shah* (king). With these successes, Ismail proclaimed Shi'ism to be the official cult of the Safavid state. Thus was founded the Safavid Empire, which lasted for two centuries and was a strong competitor to the Ottomans, who were Sunni Muslims (see Map 24.2). This doctrinal opposition to Sunni Islam and political rivalry with the Ottoman Empire became especially sharp by the early seventeenth century, and it reached its height during the reign of Shah Abbas the Great (ruling 1587–1629), the greatest of the Safavid rulers.

The European opponents of the Turks—who were then still established deep in central Europe—aided Shah Abbas in his conflicts with Istanbul. Several foreigners occupied high positions in his government because Abbas strove to avoid favoring any one group within his multiethnic realm. His beautifully planned new capital at Isfahan was a center of exquisite art and crafts production, notably in textiles, rugs, ceramics, and paintings. The Safavid period is considered the cultural high point of the long history

MAP 24.2 Safavid and Mughal Empires

The Safavid Empire, shown at its maximal extent around 1625 under Shah Abbas I, was crushed by Ottoman and Afghani attacks in the 1720s after two centuries of independent Shi'ite rule. The Mughal Empire, shown at its maximal extent around 1700, included most of north and central India until the late eighteenth century, when losses to the Hindu Marathas and the British intensified.

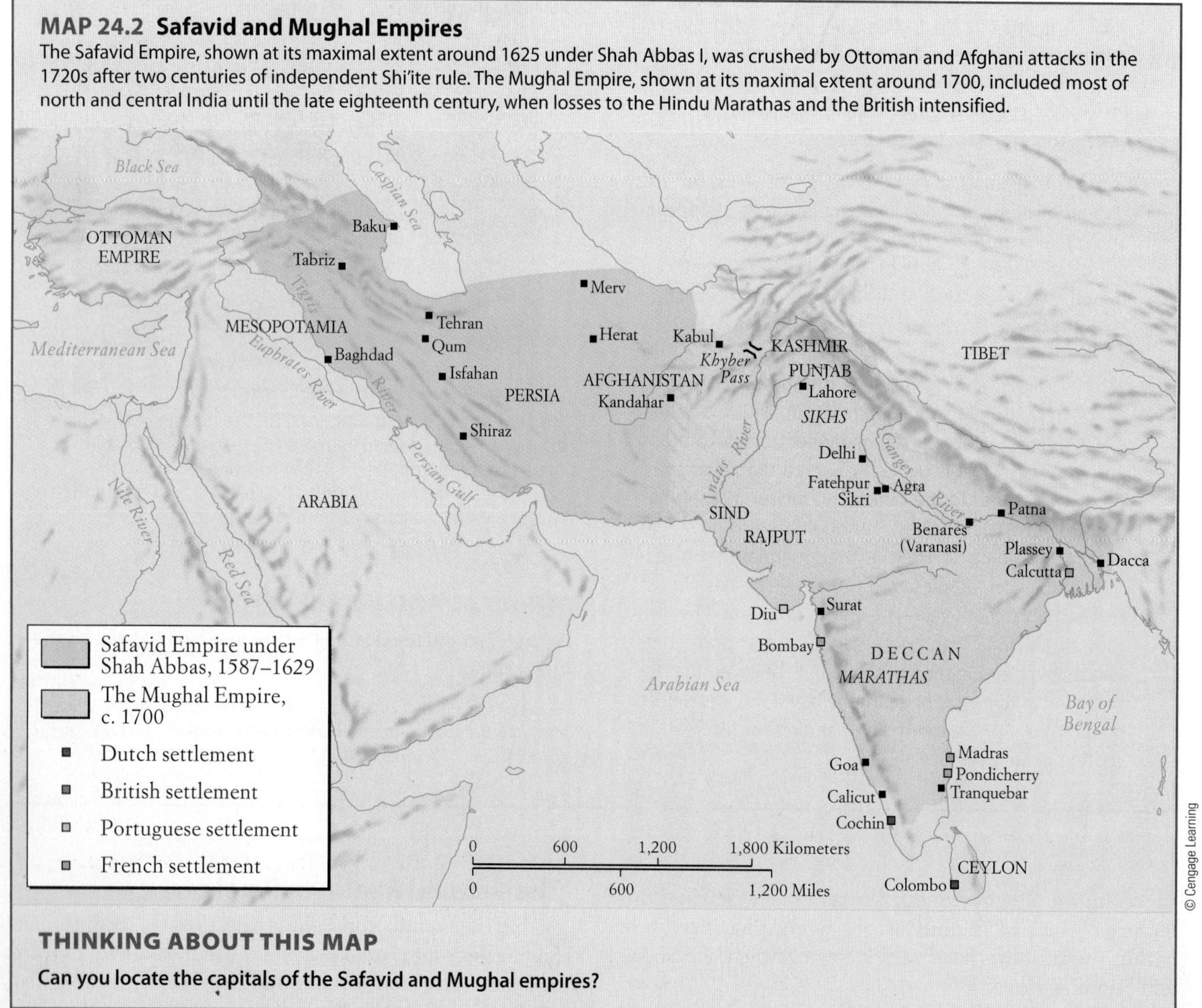

THINKING ABOUT THIS MAP

Can you locate the capitals of the Safavid and Mughal empires?

of Persia and the Iranian people. Also, just as in the case of Suleiman the Magnificent, the reign of Abbas represented the high point of Safavid rule in Persia. Following his reign, a gradual decline resulted from encroachments by highly independent Turco-Iranian tribesman. Making things even more complicated were the gradual and caustic influences of European imperialists. The empire slowly lost vigor and collapsed altogether in the 1720s under Turkish and Afghani attacks. It is worth noting that, like the European Christians, the various subdivisions within Islam fought as much against each other as against the infidels. A common religion is rarely able to counter the claims of territorial, economic, or military advantage in the choice between war and peace.

The Mughal Empire in India

When we last looked at the Indian subcontinent in Chapter 12, we commented on the gradual revival of Hindu culture under the Gupta Dynasty in the fourth and fifth centuries C.E. and the golden age that ensued. Very early in Islam's history, during the late 600s, Arabs and Persians had moved into the Indus Valley and seized the province of Sind at its lower extremity. This was the beginning of a long, ongoing struggle between Hindus and Muslims in the northwest borderlands. Out of this struggle, eight hundred years after the province of Sind was captured, a branch of the Turks known as the **Mughals** (MOO-guls) created in northern India one of the most impressive Muslim empires in world history.

The word *Mughal* is a corruption of the name *Mongol*, to whom the Turks were distantly related. Muslims from central Asia had raided and attempted to invade northern India since the 900s but had been repulsed by the dominant Hindus. As was seen in Chapter 12, in the early 1200s, the Delhi sultanate was established by a Turkish slave army operating from their base at Ghazni in Afghanistan. Within a century, the sultanate controlled much of the Indian subcontinent, reaching down into the Deccan. Divorced from their Hindu subjects by every aspect of culture, language, and religion, the sultans and their courts attempted at first to convert the Hindus and then, failing that, to humiliate and exploit them.

The original dynasty was soon overthrown, but other Central Asian Muslims succeeded it, all of whom fought among themselves for mastery even as they extended their rule southward. Aided by continuing disunity among their Hindu opponents, Mongols, Turks, Persians, and Afghanis fought for control of the entire width of the Indian subcontinent from the Indus to the Ganges. At last, a leader, Babur, who was able to persuade his fellow princes to follow him, arose from the Afghan base. Brilliantly successful battle tactics allowed him to conquer much of the territory once ruled by the Delhi sultans. By the time of his death in 1530, he had established the Mughal Muslim Indian Dynasty. This man's grandson and successor was **Akbar the Great** (ruling 1556–1605). Akbar was the most distinguished Indian ruler since Ashoka in the third century B.C.E. He was perhaps the greatest statesman Asia has ever produced.

Akbar earned his title "the Great" in several different ways. He splendidly fulfilled the usual demands made on a warrior-king to crush his enemies and enlarge his kingdom. Under his guidance and generalship, the Mughal Empire came to control most of the subcontinent—the first time a central government had accomplished this feat since the days of the Mauryan kings. Second, despite being illiterate, he completely reorganized the central government, developed an efficient multinational bureaucracy to run it, and introduced many innovative reforms in society. Third and most strikingly, Akbar practiced a policy of religious and social toleration that was most unusual in the sixteenth century. He was at least formally a Muslim, ruling a Muslim-dominated empire, but he allowed all faiths—including Christianity—to flourish and to compete for converts in his lands.

Because most of his subjects were Hindus, Akbar thought it particularly important to heal the breach between them and the Muslim minority. His initiatives toward creating an ethnically equal society were remarkable. He married a Hindu princess, and Jahangir, one of his sons by a Hindu woman, eventually succeeded him. Hindus were given equal opportunities to obtain all but the highest government posts, and members of the Hindu warrior caste called *Rajputs* became his willing allies in governance. By repealing the odious poll tax (*jizya*) on non-Muslims, Akbar earned the lasting gratitude of most of his subjects. The sorrow that existed among both Muslims and non-Muslims at Akbar's death was the most sincere tribute to his character.

MOSQUE OF SHAH ABBAS I (1611–1638). Persian architecture of the Safavid period differed significantly from that of the Ottoman. The heavier styles favored by the latter betray a significant Byzantine influence. The Safavid style, on the other hand, was characterized by its relative lightness, intricate surface work, extensive use of blue tiles, *iwans*, and the oversized *qibla*, seen in this mosque built by Shah Abbas the Great at Isfahan.

ARTS AND CULTURE

The *Rubaiyat* of Omar Khayyam

Perhaps the most-quoted poem in the English language is a nineteenth-century translation of a twelfth-century Persian philosopher, who may or may not have written the original. The *Rubaiyat* of Omar Khayyam is a collection of four-line verses that became associated with his name long after his death in 1122. Edward Fitzgerald, who had taught himself Persian while passing his days as a Victorian country gentleman, published them in 1859 in a free translation. Instantly finding a public, the *Rubaiyat* was reprinted several times during Fitzgerald's life and many more since then.

The poem speaks in unforgettably lovely words of our common fate. Morality is all too often a negation of joy. Death comes all too soon; in wine is the only solace. The verse story, of which only a fragment is given here, opens with the poet watching the break of dawn after a night of revelry:

1
Awake! for Morning in the Bowl of Night
Has flung the Stone that puts the Stars to Flight
And lo! the Hunter of the East has caught
The Sultan's Turret in a Noose of Light.

2
Dreaming when Dawn's Left Hand was in the Sky
I heard a Voice within the Tavern cry,
"Awake, my Little ones, and fill the Cup
Before Life's Liquor in its Cup be dry."

7
Come, fill the Cup, and in the Fire of Spring
The winter Garment of Repentance fling
The Bird of Time has but a little way
To fly—and Lo! the Bird is on the Wing.

14
The Worldly Hope men set their Hearts upon
Turns Ashes—or it prospers; and anon,
Like Snow upon the Desert's dusty Face
Lighting a little Hour or two—is gone.

15
And those who husbanded the Golden Grain
And those who flung it to the Winds like Rain
Alike to no such aureate Earth are turn'd*
As, buried once, Men want dug up again.

16
I think that never blows† so red
The Rose as where some buried Caesar bled;
That every Hyacinth the Garden wears
Dropt in its Lap from some once lovely Head.

19
Ah, my Beloved, fill the Cup that clears
Today of past Regrets and future Fears—
Tomorrow?—Why, Tomorrow I may be
Myself with Yesterday's Sev'n Thousand Years.

20
Lo! some we loved, the loveliest and best
That Time and Fate of all their Vintage prest
Have drunk their Cup a Round or two before,
And one by one crept silently to Rest.

21
And we, that now make merry in the Room
They left, and Summer dresses in new Bloom,
Ourselves must we beneath the Couch of Earth
Descend, ourselves to make a Couch—for whom?

22
Ah, make the most of what we yet may spend,
Before we too into the Dust descend;
Dust into Dust, and under Dust, to lie,
Sans Wine, sans Song, sans Singer, and—sans End!

23
Alike for those who for TODAY prepare,
And those that after a TOMORROW stare,
A Muezzin from the Tower of Darkness cries
"Fools! your Reward is neither here nor there!"

24
Why, all the Saints and Sages who discuss'd
Of the Two Worlds so learnedly, are thrust
Like foolish Prophets forth; their
Words to Scorn Are scatter'd, and their Mouths are stop'd with Dust.

25
Oh, come with old Khayyam, and leave the
Wise To talk; one thing is certain, that Life flies;
One thing is certain, and the Rest is Lies;
The Flower that once has blown for ever dies.

ANALYZE AND INTERPRET

Do you sympathize with the poetic point of view? Why or why not? Would a Sufi mystic or a Christian monk have agreed with it? Given the religious origins and foundation of Islamic societies, how do you suppose such a point of view would have been accommodated?

Source: *The Rubaiyat of Omar Khayyam*, trans. and ed. Edward Fitzgerald (New York: Dover, 1991).

*"Aureate Earth..." means that once buried, the body is no golden treasure.
† The verb "to blow" here means "to bloom."

Midway in his long reign, around 1580, Akbar decided to build an entirely new capital at Fatehpur Sikri (FAH-tay-poor SIHK-ree), some distance from the traditional royal cities of Delhi and Agra. This palace-city was soon abandoned and is now a ruin, but its beauty and magnificence were famous throughout the Muslim world. The court library reputedly possessed more than twenty-four thousand volumes, making it easily the largest collection of books in the world at this time. Akbar's love of learning encouraged sages of all religions and all parts of the Asian world to come to his court at his expense as teachers and students. His cultivation of the official Persian language brought new dimensions to Indian literature. The ties with Persian culture enabled by the language contributed substantially to the revival of a sense of national unity among Hindus, which they had lacked since the Gupta era.

Society and Culture in Mughal India. India under the Mughals remained a hodgepodge of different peoples, as well as different religions and languages. Besides those under Mughal rule, there were still many tribal groups, especially in the rain forest regions of the eastern coast, whom neither Hindus nor Muslims considered fully human and often enslaved.

The caste system continued to be refined in constant subdivisions among Hindus. Although the Muslims never acknowledged the caste system, it did serve as a useful wall to minimize frictions between subject and ruler. Despite

IMAGES OF HISTORY

Mughal Succession

Beginning with Jahangir, Akbar's son, every Mughal ruler rebelled and seized power from his father, usually imprisoning him in his palace until his death. To ensure that there would be no danger from rivals, the new emperor also had all his brothers murdered. Nevertheless, care had to be taken to legitimize the succession, so the new ruler sometimes had portraits like this one painted, where the line of succession is represented.

Shah Jahangir

Shah Akbar

Shah Jahan

Mughal Emperor Akbar (*center*) symbolocally passing his crown to his son, Jahangir, and to his grandson, Shah Jahan. *c.* 1630 (vellum). Bichtir (fl. 1620).

extensive business and administrative dealings between the two religious communities, social intercourse was unusual at any level. Even among the majority Hindus, culturally based barriers existed that had nothing to do with caste.

A new religion, derived from the doctrines of both Hindu and Muslim, arose in the Far North during the seventeenth century. At first dedicated to finding a middle ground between the two dominant faiths, it eventually became a separate creed, called the religion of the **Sikhs** (seeks). Generally closer to Hindu belief, the Sikhs fought the last Mughal rulers and dominated the northwestern Punjab province. (They currently represent perhaps 5 percent of the total population of India, and still strive for full autonomy on either side of the India-Pakistan border.)

After Emperor Aurangzeb (OR-ahng-zehb; ruled 1668–1707), the governing class was almost entirely Muslim again, and aspiring Hindus sometimes imitated their habits of dress and manner. Many foreigners—especially from the Middle East—came into the country to make their fortunes, often at the luxurious and free-spending courts, not only of the emperor but also of subsidiary officials. Prevented by imperial decrees from accumulating heritable land and office, the Muslim upper class took much pride in funding institutions of learning and supporting artists of all types.

In the fine arts, the Mughal rulers made a conscious and successful effort to introduce the great traditions of Persian culture into India, where they blended with the native forms in literature, drama, and architecture. The quatrains of Omar Khayyam's ***Rubaiyat*** (ROO-buy-yat), which have long been famous throughout the world, held a special appeal for Mughal poets, who attempted to imitate them (see the Patterns of Belief box for an excerpt from the *Rubaiyat*).

The **Taj Mahal** (tahj mah-HAAL), tomb of the much-loved wife of the seventeenth-century emperor Shah Jahan (jah-HAHN), is the most famous example of a Persian-Indian architectural style. But it is only one of many, as exemplified by the ruins of Fatehpur Sikri, the equally imposing Red Fort at Agra, and a whole series of mosques. Much painting of every type and format, from book miniatures to frescos, also survives from this era and shows traces of Arab and Chinese, as well as Persian, influence. By this time, Muslim artists were ignoring the ancient religious prohibition against reproducing the human form. The wonderful variety of portraits, court scenes, gardens, and townscapes is exceeded only by the precision and color sense of the artists.

The Muslims had an extensive system of religious schools (*madrasa*), while the local Brahmins took care of the minimal needs for literacy in the Hindu villages by acting as open-air schoolmasters. Increasingly, the Muslims used the newly created Urdu language (now the official language in Pakistan) rather than the Sanskrit of the Hindus.

Like the Safavid Persians to their west, the Mughals were an exceptionally cosmopolitan dynasty, well aware of cultural affairs in and outside of their own country and anxious to make a good impression in foreign eyes. They welcomed European travelers. Like Marco Polo's reports about Kubilai Khan's China, sixteenth- and seventeenth-century tales of visitors to the Great Mughal were only belatedly and grudgingly believed. Such cultivation and display of luxury were still beyond Europeans' experience.

The Mughal Economy. The existing agrarian system was but slightly disturbed by the substitution of Muslim for Hindu authority. Beginning with the Delhi sultans, courtiers and officials were awarded a parcel of land apposite to their dignity and sufficient taxes to allow them to maintain a specified number of fighting men and their equipment. This system of rewarding individuals who rendered either civil or military service to the state was called the *mansabdari* (mahn-SAHB-dah-ree). Some *mansabdars* maintained small armies of five, or even, ten thousand men. When the sultanate weakened, they established themselves as petty kings, joining the universal fray in northern India for territory and prestige. This system was carried over into the Mughal period. Perhaps half of the mansabdars under Akbar were Hindus, creating a loyalty to the imperial government that continued even under Aurangzeb's determined Islamic regime.

The peasants on the mansabdar's domain were somewhat better off than their contemporary counterparts in Europe or China. Most of them were tenants rather than outright proprietors, but they were not yet haunted by the shortage of agrarian land that would arrive, as it did in China, during the later eighteenth century. Village tradition, the caste system, and government tax collectors restricted their freedoms. The latter were generally no worse than in other places, and their demand for one-third to one-half of the crop was bearable if the harvest was productive.

Taj Mahal, built 1647 (photo), Lahori, Ustad Ahmad (fl. 1630-47)/Agra, Uttar Pradesh, India/The Bridgeman Art Library

THE TAJ MAHAL. This seventeenth-century tomb was designed in Indo-Persian style as the resting place of the beloved wife of Mughal emperor Shah Jahan. Building commenced in 1632 and was completed eleven years later. Four identical facades surround a central dome 240-feet high. Gardens and the river that flows beside it supplement the whole complex.

SUMMARY

The three principal Muslim Empires that occupied most of the Asian continent between 1250 and 1800 were able to hold their own militarily and culturally with their Chinese, Hindu, and Christian competitors. Often warring among themselves, they were still able to maintain their borders and prestige for two to six hundred years. After the terrible destruction rendered by the Mongols, the Muslims of the Middle East absorbed their invaders and rebuilt their cities. Chief and most enduring among their states were those of the Ottoman Turks and the Indian Mughals. The Ottomans profited from the Mongol destruction of Baghdad and the Rum sultanate by erecting their own powerful ghazi state and even eventually took Constantinople (Istanbul) for their capital. Under a series of warrior-sultans, the Ottoman leaders extended their power to the gates of Vienna before internal weakness drove them back in the 1700s. By the nineteenth century, the Ottomans had become so weak that they were sustained only by the rivalry of the major European powers. Thus, the dreaded sixteenth-century empire of Suleiman had been degraded to "the sick man" of Europe—so called by a British statesman.

For two centuries, the Shi'ite dynasty of the Safavids reclaimed grandeur for Persia and Iraq, where they ruled until they were brought down by the superior power of their Sunni rivals in Istanbul. The Mughals descended on Hindu India in the early sixteenth century and set up one of the few regimes in Indian history that successfully managed to rule most of this intensely varied subcontinent. Under the extraordinary Akbar the Great, the regime reached its apex, only to decline slowly during the following century.

IDENTIFICATION TERMS

Test your knowledge of this chapter's key concepts by defining the following terms. If you can not recall the meaning of certain terms, refresh your memory by looking up the boldfaced term in the chapter, turning to the Glossary at the end of the book, or accessing the terms on the CourseMate website at **www.cengagebrain.com.**

Akbar the Great
dervish
devshirme
divan
ghazis
Grand Vizier
Janissaries
Mehmed the Conqueror
Mughals
Rubaiyat
Safavid Empire
Shaykh al-Islam
Sikhs
Sublime Porte
Suleiman the Magnificent
Taj Mahal
Treaty of Karlowitz

FOR FURTHER REFLECTION

1. What circumstances in the Byzantine and Abbasid empires seem to have enabled the Ottoman Turks to rise to power and to expand their control over the region formerly occupied by the Byzantine Empire?
2. Considering the historical rivalry that existed between Sunni and Shi'ite Islam, how did the rise of the Ottoman and Safavid empires help fix the current boundaries between Shi'ite Iran and the predominantly Sunni regions to the west of it?
3. How do you evaluate Akbar the Great's policies of tolerance toward other religions in Mughal India? How did they differ from the policies of previous (and later) Muslim rulers of India? How did Akbar demonstrate tolerance? Did he completely solve the conflicts between Muslims and the followers of other Indian religions? Why not?

TEST YOUR KNOWLEDGE

Test your knowledge of this chapter by answering the following questions. Complete answers appear at the end of the book. You may find even more quiz questions on the CourseMate website at **www.cengagebrain.com.**

1. Taken together at their height, the Ottoman, Mughal, and Safavid empires
   a. could be termed a united political territory.
   b. represented the greatest military and political power in the world.
   c. all were militarily weaker than Renaissance Europe.
   d. represented a reconsolidation and resurgence of Islamic power.
   e. enjoyed the highest standard of living for their citizens in the world.

2. The Ottoman Empire began
   a. as a Shia dervish order.
   b. as a ghazi frontier state.
   c. as a Byzantine state.
   d. subordinate to the Abbasid caliphs.
   e. as a combination of three formerly competing dynasties.
3. Women at the courts of the Ottoman sultans
   a. exercised authority guaranteed to them by Islamic law.
   b. sometimes could hope to move into the sultanate upon the death of a reigning sultan.
   c. were treated as little more than sex slaves.
   d. enjoyed a certain amount of informal power and influence.
   e. rarely had the "ear" of the male ruling elite.
4. The treatment of non-Muslims in the Balkans under Ottoman rule
   a. deteriorated sharply in the seventeenth and eighteenth centuries.
   b. improved as the powers of the sultan diminished.
   c. tended to become better the farther away they were from the capital.
   d. depended entirely on the whims of the ruling sultan.
   e. deteriorated for a short time in the seventeenth century, but by 1900 was much improved.
5. Suleiman the Magnificent accomplished all of these except
   a. driving the Europeans out of North Africa.
   b. conquering Vienna.
   c. remodeling several monumental buildings.
   d. assuming leadership of the Islamic Empire.
   e. taking charge of the arrangements for the pilgrimage to Mecca.
6. Shi'ite Islam
   a. eventually disappeared in the world.
   b. displaced both Hinduism and Sunni Islam in popularity in Mughal India.
   c. rejected the prophetic vocation of Muhammad.
   d. became the dominant sect in Iran.
   e. eventually displaced Sunni Islam in popularity in the Ottoman Empire.
7. The Ottoman and Safavid empires were similar in one respect: They both were
   a. governed by a sultan and a Grand Vizier.
   b. organized in their beginnings around a Sufi order.
   c. organized to fight as holy warriors against Christian infidels.
   d. weakened by the demoralizing effects of harem intrigues.
   e. based on the Sunni sect of Islam.
8. The Muslim rulers of the Safavid Dynasty were
   a. the conquerors of Constantinople.
   b. the allies of the Mughals in India.
   c. a Persian family that converted to Shi'ite Islam.
   d. the first conquerors of Persia for Islam.
   e. militant warriors who cared little for the arts.
9. The attitudes and policies of Akbar the Great regarding Hindus were that of
   a. tolerance.
   b. religious fanaticism.
   c. a desire to secularize them if he could not convert them.
   d. indifference.
   e. disdain.
10. The Taj Mahal
   a. was built by Shah Akbar the Great as his tomb.
   b. was built by Shah Jahan as a mausoleum for a favorite wife.
   c. was reconstructed from an old palace of Ashoka the Great.
   d. is a mosque.
   e. is a Hindu temple.

CourseMate

Visit the CourseMate website at **www.cengagebrain.com** for additional study tools and review materials for this chapter.

25 Africa in the Era of Expansion

We are people because of other people. —SOTHO PROVERB

1340–1591	Songhay Empire
1498–1698	Portuguese domination of East African Swahili states
1650–1870	Height of Atlantic slave trade
1652	Dutch East India Company founds Cape Colony, South Africa
c. 1770–1840	Extensive migrations in South and East Africa
1832	Sayyid Sa'id, Sultan of Oman, founds sultanate of Zanzibar
1830s	French begin to assert control over North Africa
1840s	Christian missionaries and explorers begin to move into interior
1850s–1860s	French begin extending their control up the Senegal River

CHAPTER OUTLINE

The centuries that followed the first appearance of Europeans in Africa were ones of both decline and growth for Africans. These centuries in African history, until about 1880, are often characterized as the era of **Informal Empire**—that is to say, the era when Europeans remained content with limited involvement in Africa. Until then, Europeans were confined to the coastal regions. Conquest and the creation of formal colonies, especially of the continent's vast interior, was something in which European governments were not prepared to invest blood and treasure. Interest remained limited to commerce, and permanent settlement was out of the question for most Europeans. Therefore, Europeans had by far their greatest, and perhaps most destructive, impact on the coastal regions. Africans living there or in the near interior experienced the greatest changes, especially where the effects of the slave trade were felt.

However, describing the history of the entire African continent entirely in terms of the European presence would be a gross misrepresentation of Africans and their history. Many other things were happening in Africa that had little or nothing to do with Europeans. While the European presence in Africa was an important and growing factor in African history during the centuries before 1880, Africans continued to control their own futures and to find continuities with their own rich histories to guide their lives and destinies. One especially noteworthy occurrence was the rise and decline of African states and kingdoms. The era saw the appearance of hundreds of states of all sizes. We cannot review all of them here, but we briefly take note of only a few dozen exceptionally significant ones.

NEW STATES APPEAR

The beginning of the early modern era in world history saw the appearance of the great West African Sudanic empires in Songhay and Bornu, as well as the city-states among the Hausa people of northern Nigeria. The region that includes Lake Victoria and the northern end of Lake Tanganyika also saw new and powerful kingdoms emerge. Around that same time and in the following century, the ancient Swahili city-states of the East coast, as well as Great Zimbabwe, saw significant developments as a result of external threats from the expanding Europeans and the Omani Arabs.

West African States, Old and New

The Niger River city of Gao was already the focus of central Sudanic trade at the time of Ghana's greatness in the western Sudan. It remained in the shadow of its more powerful western Sudanic neighbors through the centuries of Mali's greatness; and in fact, realizing its importance, Mansa Musa subjugated Gao in 1325. Its dominance of the Niger River trade and most of the major trans-Saharan routes to the east of Timbuktu enabled it to exercise great commercial and military power. This power was realized when its first great king, Sonni Ali (1464–1492), employed a strategy that combined coordinated attacks of a robust cavalry of armored warriors with a sturdy navy of river canoes to extend his conquests for creating the core of what became the **Songhay Empire** (song-GEYE). Under Sonni Ali and his successors, Songhay eventually became the mightiest of the great Sudanic states of West Africa.

Askia (ahs-KEE-yah) **Muhammad the Great** (1493–1528) continued his predecessor Ali's expansionist ways. But, as important as his conquests were, Askia Muhammad's most lasting contribution to West African history lay in his support of Islam. Following the example of the great Malian emperors, Mansas Musa and Sulayman, Muhammad was an enthusiastic Muslim who gave Muslim scholars (*ulama*) important positions in his state apparatus; enforced orthodox practices among his subjects; built mosques; and subsidized book production and scholarship in the intellectual centers of Gao, Timbuktu, and Jenne.

Despite the works of Muhammad and his successors, simultaneous attacks by non-Muslim Mossi peoples from the south and Tuareg (TWAH-rehg) Berbers from the north gravely weakened the Songhay state during the 1500s. Its final overthrow came when Moroccan forces invaded it in 1591.

Other Sudanic states, like Mali and Songhay, that were based on trade and Islam were those of Futa Toro (FOO-tah TOH-roh), Futa Jallon, Bornu, and the city-states of the Hausa. The first two of these were located in present-day Senegal and Sierra Leone. These small states were sixteenth- and seventeenth-century creations of *Fulani* (foo-LAH-nee) and *Tukolor* (TOO-kuh-lohr) cattle pastoralists that resulted partly from resistance to the spread of Islam and partly as a response to opportunities to establish trade partnerships with the Europeans on the coast.

The roots of the **Bornu** kingdom were in a previous, more loosely organized state called *Kanem.* Situated to the east of Lake Chad, and like its contemporary and more famous western neighbor Mali, the ancient Kanemi state was a product of the trans-Saharan trade and Islam's march southward from North Africa (Chapter 17). Sometime around the fifteenth century, sultans of the Sefawa (SEH-fuh-wah) Dynasty of the Kanemi state were replaced by a new dynasty of the Mai (rhymes with "eye"). Near the beginning of the fifteenth century, and suffering from repeated attacks from the neighboring Bulala peoples, the king Mai Daud reorganized the kingdom and gave it the new name of Bornu. Throughout its long history, Kanem-Bornu, as it is sometimes called, grew wealthy from the control of the caravan routes of the central Sahara that went northward to Libya, as well as the northeast and eastern routes to Egypt and the Nile River valley. Its Muslim sultans had reputations for exceptional piety and for promoting Islamic literacy and law among their subjects.

Resembling the Swahili of East Africa, the **Hausa** (HOW-sah) people of the northern region of what is now Nigeria did not organize themselves into a unified state until the nineteenth century. Historically, Hausaland was blessed with good soils, so most Hausa were farmers. From ancient times, other Hausa also had a reputation as skilled traders and craftsmen who specialized in growing the valuable kola nut and in producing fine textiles and leather goods, all of which they traded throughout West and North Africa. Their largest political entity was the city-state, of which Kano, Katsina, Zaria, Daura, and Gobir were the largest. A local king called the *Sarki (SAHR-kee)* and his counselors governed each city-state, organized its defense, and oversaw the marketplace, which was the economic mainstay of the state. Each was an integral part of the international trade that extended through the western and central Sudan, and maintained connections with the forest kingdoms, such as Benin and Oyo, to their south.

In the savanna and rain forest of western-central Africa, a series of smaller kingdoms also formed between 1300 and 1600. One of particular note was the Ngola (Ng'-OH-lah) kingdom, located just south of the Kongo in what is now the nation of Angola. Here, chieftaincies formed and kingship later evolved from the control certain clans exercised over rainmaking shrines and their carefully guarded, secret knowledge of iron making. Exercising power that was crucial to farmers, they forced other clans to pay tribute for their services. By 1500, they had molded their people into a single kingdom under one ruler, the *Ngola.*

The kingdom of Kongo was the largest of West-Central kingdoms, and it is from its name that the modern Republic of the Congo is named. The kings (called *Manikongo*) exercised power from their capital of Mbanza

Kongo, which was based on near-monopolistic controls over iron making and regional trade in salt and copper, both of which were abundant in the region. The Kongolese people were highly skilled in cloth making from bark, and traded it widely throughout the region. The natural wealth of the land, derived from abundant rainfall, rich soils, and the ready availability of fish, added to the prosperity of its people and the monarchy.

The Lakes Kingdoms

Soon before or after 1500, pastoralist clans called the Nilotes (neye-LAHTS) from the southernmost regions bordering the Nile River began a steady drift into areas inhabited mostly by Bantu speakers around lakes Kivu, Victoria, and Tanganyika. These Nilotes had a religious tradition that included a kind of spiritual leader called the *roth* or *rwoth*, who in some circumstances could wield considerable political powers. Once they settled around the lakes—and as a result of mixing with the Bantu, a division of labor between farmers and cattle herders, and the greater availability of resources and trade—a number of large, substantial kingdoms came into existence by the seventeenth century that seem to have originated under the "roth-ship." **Bunyoro-Kitara** seems to have been the most powerful of these—one that dominated neighboring kingdoms such as Karagwe, Burundi, and **Buganda**. By the late eighteenth century, however, Buganda started to eclipse Bunyoro, and by the time the first Europeans arrived, its king, the *Kabaka*, ruled a kingdom that included most of the modern nation of Uganda.

The Swahili, the Portuguese, and Oman

East Africa felt the most direct impact of Arab and Swahili traders, who had long preceded the Europeans in slaving and other commerce in African goods. Swahili towns such as Paté (PAH-tay), Mombasa (Mohm-BAH-sah), Zanzibar, and Kilwa were busy entrepôts in the Indian Ocean trade for centuries before 1500 (see Chapter 17). In these coastal regions, the Swahili-speaking people had developed a highly cosmopolitan lifestyle, with trading networks that extended along a broad stretch of the coast from Mogadishu to Mozambique as well as into the interior. The urban Swahili were Muslims, whereas most of the hinterland peoples continued to follow local religious beliefs and practices. These city-states were commercial in nature, trading across the Indian Ocean as partners of their fellow Muslims in southern and eastern Arabia, Iraq, Iran, and India.

In 1498, Vasco da Gama sailed for the first time around Africa's southern Cape of Good Hope on his voyage to India (see Chapter 22). In the following decades, the Portuguese attempted to dominate the gold and ivory trade of East Africa. Ultimately they failed, but they built major fortresses at Mozambique and Mombasa, and for nearly two centuries they controlled these major cities, plus other commercial centers at Paté, Lamu, Malindi, Pemba, Zanzibar, and Kilwa.

Except for cooperation from the sultans of Malindi in the 1500s, there was considerable Swahili resistance to this foreign invasion. Much of it was religiously based: Both the Portuguese and the Swahili saw their conflict as one between Catholic Christians and Muslims. With help coming from the Imamate of Oman (in southeastern Arabia), by the 1660s, the Swahili and their Arab allies were able to challenge Portuguese ascendancy in East Africa and the western Indian Ocean. Except for Mozambique, by 1698, the Omani had replaced the Portuguese as the paramount power in East Africa. In the following two centuries, the Swahili and the Arabs—with the help of inland peoples such as the Kamba (KAHM-bah), the Nyamwezi (Nyahm-WAY-zee), and the Yao (YAH-oh)—opened new trade routes to the East African interior. Most of this was based on ivory and other animal by-products, but in the eighteenth century, slaves became another of East Africa's chief exports (see discussion this chapter).

EUROPEAN IMPRESSIONS

Unfortunately for Africans, in the fifteenth and sixteenth centuries, Europeans arrived on Africa's coasts at about the very time that some of the continent's most powerful kingdoms were in decline or undergoing political changes. As a result, the European explorer-traders perceived the kingdoms of Africa as subservient and backward. This impression was reinforced by the Africans' relative lack of knowledge in military and technological matters, and later by the readiness of some of the African kings and chieftains to allow the sale of competing or neighboring people into slavery—a practice that had been commonplace in Europe for a thousand years but that Christian and Jewish teaching had by that time effectively forbidden.

The Europeans (largely the Portuguese in the first century of contacts) concluded that the Africans were backward in their sensitivity and degree of civilization and that it would not be wrong to take advantage of them. Africans were perceived as not quite human, so what would have been a despicable sin against God and humanity if it had been done back home in Lisbon was quite forgivable in Africa. This callousness was undoubtedly reinforced by the desperate nature of business enterprise in the first centuries of the colonial era, when it is estimated that Europeans who went to the African coast had a 25 percent mortality rate per year. It was not an affair that encouraged second thoughts on the morality of what one was doing.

Other Europeans who as slavers came into contact with Africans shared the Portuguese attitude. Early attempts to convert the Africans to Christianity were quickly subordinated to business interests by the Portuguese and never attempted at all by their English, Dutch, and French successors until the nineteenth century. Europeans rationalized their tendency to see Africans as a source of profit rather than as fellow human beings by using everything from biblical quotations to Arab and Berber Muslim statements reflecting their own prejudices. The basis of European (and later American) racism directed against dark-skinned peoples is to be found in these earliest contacts and the circumstances in which they were made.

THE ERA OF INFORMAL EMPIRE

Long after the first Europeans had arrived on the coasts of West Africa in the second half of the fifteenth century, they had penetrated very little into the enormous depths of the continent or into the interior life of the people. Aside from the Dutch at the Cape of Good Hope and the Portuguese colony of Angola, Europeans in the three centuries after 1480 established no permanent settlements. Instead, trade was often conducted by sailors right on coastal beaches. Fortified trading posts such as the famous Elmina (ehl-MEE-nah) Castle on the Gold Coast (present-day Ghana) were founded at wide intervals. Staffed by a literal handful of European traders and their African employees, these trading stations, or **factories** as they were called, naturally had a strong impact on African life in areas near the coasts. However, the farther one went inland from these European enclaves, the less effect they had. African leaders usually dealt with the white traders on an equal or even advantageous basis, because the whites depended entirely on the African leaders to gather slaves, gold, pepper, and animal by-products that the interior produced for export.

In contrast to the Americas and Asia, most of Africa's interior remained free from outside interventions. The chief reason seems to have been the ability of the early traders to get what they wanted without having to establish permanent settlements or long-term relationships. Of course, what they originally came for was gold and a list of exotic products for which Africa was the only source. In this sense, the early African experience with the Europeans was similar to that of the Southeast Asian peoples: minimal and highly selective contact. Soon, however, slaves took the place of gold as the most profitable and most pursued item of trade. Coastal peoples in mutually profitable fashion delivered both slaves and goods to the Europeans, who saw no persuasive reason to risk the dangers of a long journey into unknown territory to get what African middlemen would deliver—for a price. There was certainly profit enough for all, and the coastal peoples and their rulers possessed sufficient authority and knowledge of trading practices to know how to deal with the newcomers.

The model established in the 1400s by the exploring Portuguese was followed closely by their several successors along the western African coast. The European traders could not and did not simply overwhelm the Africans and seize what they wanted. Europeans did not possess any real military advantage over Africans until the late nineteenth century. Moreover, any such attempt at the use of force would have resulted at the very least in stopping all future trade. And for the entire four centuries of European precolonial contact with West Africa, the Portuguese, Dutch, British, French, and others were engaged in commercial competition, which African leaders could at times manipulate to their own advantage.

Also discouraging permanent settlement were the devastating diseases that were endemic. With its tropical climate, Africa was afflicted more than Europe by fevers such as malaria, cholera, sleeping sickness, typhus, and typhoid fever. The western coast in particular had long had the reputation of being a "white man's graveyard." A recent authority on the question estimates that the mortality rate among white traders and seamen on the West African coast might have surpassed even that of the African slaves shipped across the Atlantic: 25 to 50 percent per year! Adding to such formidable obstacles were the oppressively hot climate and the unknown and difficult terrain. To protect their middleman positions in trading with Europeans—who seemed always to have been willing to think the worst of Africans and their "strange" ways—coastal peoples often gave false accounts of savage peoples inhabiting the interior, who supposedly lay in wait to murder any innocent traveler or explorer who turned up in their midst. Such, then, were the unfortunate origins of the image of Africa as the "Dark Continent"—an image that was difficult to dispel and that persists to some degree even today among the ignorant.

As noted in Chapter 3, Africa's geography and climate made traveling inward from the coast especially difficult. Thanks to the tsetse fly (the primary carrier of "sleeping sickness"), horses and mules were unable to survive throughout most of the central and southern two-thirds of the continent, and the wheel was unknown in equatorial Africa before Europeans introduced it. All goods of whatever nature depended on human muscle for transport. The interior plateaus drop off sharply to the coastal plains, creating rapids and waterfalls that made long-distance river transport impossible in much of the continent. Only the Nile, the Niger (NEYE-jer) in the west, and the Congo in the central region are sporadically navigable far into the interior. All three of these rivers were controlled by substantial states when the Europeans arrived, and the Nile Valley was in Muslim hands.

The Slave Trade and Its Results

Slavery was an old institution that was found at some time or another among virtually all peoples—even Africans—and it long predated transatlantic trade. In ancient and medieval times, unfortunates of all ethnic backgrounds—including Greeks, Turks, Mongols, Africans, and various Slavic peoples—filled the demand for slaves. War and poverty provided the primary reasons for enslaving human beings, whereas ethnic and racial prejudices had contributed to it only indirectly. Ancient and medieval slavery also took many forms. It was formally recognized in the *Qur'an*, for example, yet Muslims were encouraged to treat their slaves with compassion and to free those who converted to Islam. Among Africans, slavery was usually closely akin to indentured labor or even a sort of remote kinship.

In Africa, the slave trade existed long before the arrival of Europeans south of the Sahara. Berber and Arab Muslims transported thousands of slaves from that broad region called the Sudan, moving them across the Saharan Desert and the Red Sea, and to a lesser extent from East Africa and across the Indian Ocean. Despite this prior trade, no topic in African history has been as sensitive and controversial as the extent and results of the transatlantic slave trade (see Map 25.1). The European settlement of the Western Hemisphere and its establishment of plantation systems there created the demand for cheap labor. Their first choice to meet that need was Native Americans, but diseases destroyed up to 90 percent of the Native American population and forced the Europeans to look elsewhere. Given the prior existence of slavery, it cannot be said that racism, per se, motivated their initial choice of Africans to replace Native Americans; more obvious contributing factors in the beginning were the Africans' ability to survive the harsh transatlantic crossing and to resist disease. However, the brutality of the system of trade and transport and the form of slavery in which slaves were reduced to chattels helped engender racism, and racist assumptions about Africans provided the excuses on which the "system" was based.

The Portuguese were the first to engage in the business of slavery. They purchased the first slaves from the region of the Senegal River around 1448, and the slave trade

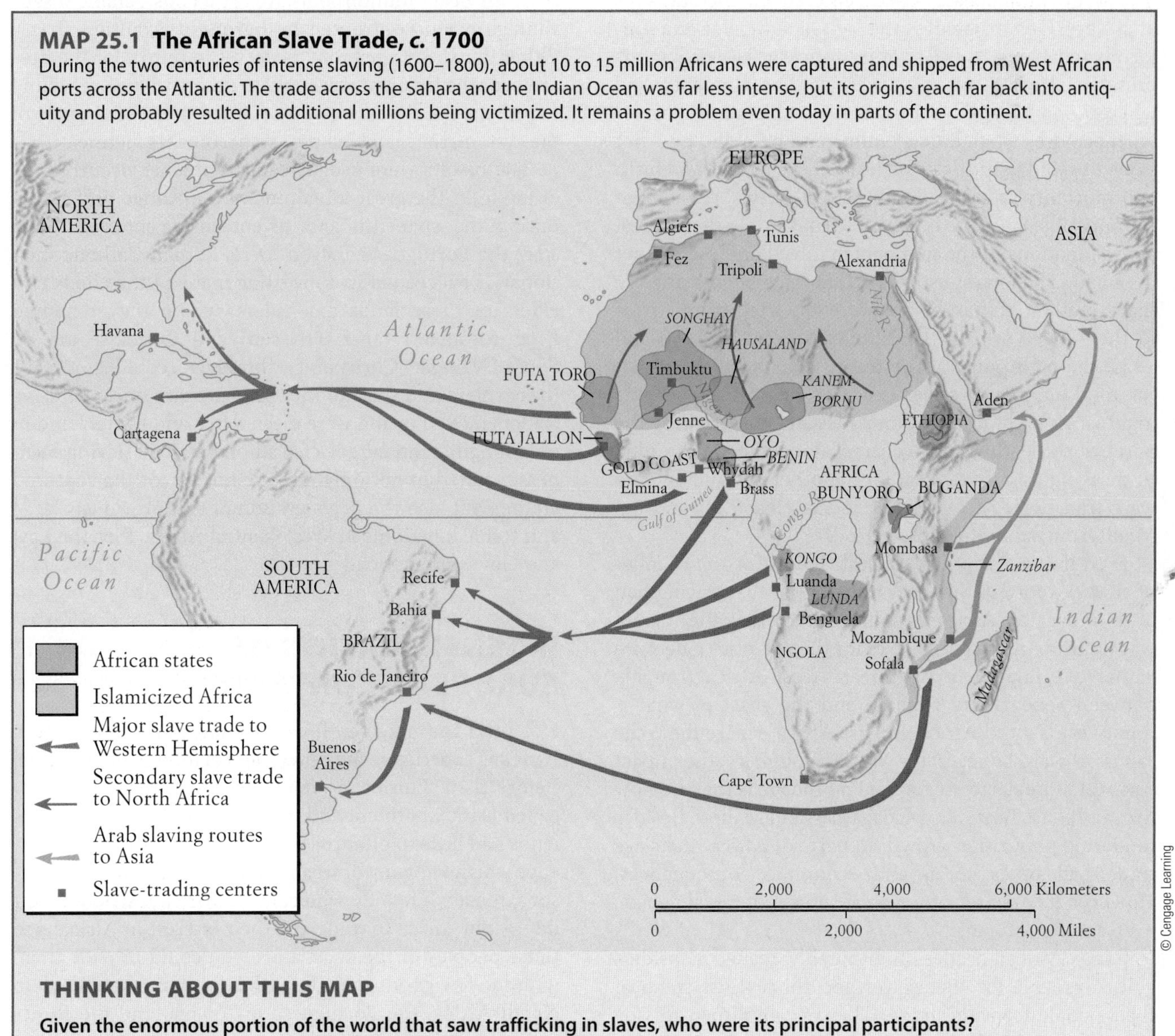

MAP 25.1 The African Slave Trade, *c.* 1700

During the two centuries of intense slaving (1600–1800), about 10 to 15 million Africans were captured and shipped from West African ports across the Atlantic. The trade across the Sahara and the Indian Ocean was far less intense, but its origins reach far back into antiquity and probably resulted in additional millions being victimized. It remains a problem even today in parts of the continent.

THINKING ABOUT THIS MAP

Given the enormous portion of the world that saw trafficking in slaves, who were its principal participants?

continued more or less haphazardly until the early 1500s, probably numbering no more than a few hundred slaves per year. By 1520, however, Portuguese immigrants established sugar plantations on the offshore islands of Príncipe (PRIHN-see-pay) and São Tomé (SAH-oh toh-MAY), to which slaves soon were soon being exported. Until about 1640, relatively few slaves were exported to the New World, but the demand quickly increased thereafter, and the Dutch replaced the Portuguese for a few decades of the seventeenth century as the principal dealers and transporters of slaves. (A Dutch ship sold the first slaves to the colony of Jamestown, Virginia, when tobacco was first being tried there as a cash crop.) By the end of the seventeenth century, the English, French, Danes, and others began challenging the Dutch near-monopoly. The following century saw the trade at its zenith, and after the founding of the Royal African Company in 1672, the English quickly came to dominate it until 1807, when Parliament finally banned it.

The greatest debates have centered on the statistics of slavery. One problem is the lack of sufficient and uniformly reliable data, and another concerns issues of interpretation. How many slaves were sold and bought? And where? And how did these numbers change over time? Furthermore, what crucial information might one not expect to find in the data, such as census figures and birth and mortality rates? Given these difficulties, refinement is impossible, and one is driven to make only the crudest approximations of the numbers involved and the impact they had. The lowest estimates that have been made are that 8 million human beings were exported from Africa to the New World in the 220 years between 1650 and 1870, the high point of the trade. Others calculate that the total number of slaves exported might have been as high as 40 million, if one includes in those figures the number of deaths that occurred along the way. Added to these figures are estimates of another 3.5 million who were transported from Africa to the Near East and the Mediterranean in the same period.

Even if one accepts the lowest figures for the number of slaves exported, this does not suggest that slaving had little impact on African populations or that the impact was uniform in all areas. Slaves for the Atlantic trade were gathered primarily in two areas: West Africa (roughly between Senegal and Nigeria) and the coast of what is now West Central Africa. In East Africa, where the trade ran northward by sea to the Muslim countries, the impact was still more narrowly focused on the areas that are now Mozambique, Tanzania, Madagascar, and Malawi. Besides hindering population growth in parts of Africa, the slave trade had other social and economic consequences. However, its precise nature is the subject of much debate, even among Africans.

Some African leaders indisputably reaped considerable advantage for themselves and for at least some of their people from the trade. They accomplished this by becoming active partners with whites in securing new human supplies and by using the proceeds of the trade in ways that increased their material prestige and power. Leaders especially prized firearms, which they then used to enhance their power to gather more slaves. This trade specifically helped create—or at least enhance—the power of several kingdoms of varying size, particularly those of the so-called Slave Coast, which included the littorals of what now are the African nations of Togo, Benin, and Nigeria. African states that benefited particularly from the slave trade in this region included the kingdoms of Dahomey and Oyo, as well as the Niger Delta city-states of Bonny, Brass, Calabar, Nembé, and Warri.

Slaving and the raids or local wars that it generated were also indisputably a major cause of the chaotic bloodshed observed and condemned by nineteenth-century Europeans. Above all, firearms were responsible for this situation. Guns were needed not only to hunt for slaves but also to defend oneself from would-be slave hunters. Africans often found themselves at a considerable disadvantage when confronted by Europeans wanting slaves: Either they had to provide the slaves in return for the firearms, or the firearms were sold to others who were willing to provide the slaves. If people refused to become a part of the system, they could expect to become its victims.

The results were usually catastrophic, as occurred for example in the great kingdoms of the Kongo and Ngola during the sixteenth and seventeenth centuries. Soon after the Portuguese arrived there, Roman Catholic missionaries succeeded in converting many of the chiefs and elders of these lands and rulers, whom they renamed King Affonso I (ah-FAHN-soh) and Queen Anna de Sousa Nzinga. Christianity, however, could not save these rulers and their unfortunate peoples once the slave traders moved in and were given a free and brutal hand in obtaining human cargoes for shipment. The slaving business resulted in not only massive misery for the captured victims but also the degeneration of two previously large and stable kingdoms in West Central Africa. (See the Law and Government box.)

INTENSIFICATION OF EUROPEAN CONTACTS

Not until the nineteenth century did most sub-Saharan Africans experience the heavy hand of foreign domination. Before then, Europeans remained indifferent to the so-called Dark Continent and believed that its people and its lands had little to offer the world in terms of either knowledge worth knowing or wealth worth having. For these reasons, most white men who came to Africa restricted their interest in Africa to trade and their interest in Africans to those peoples of the coastlands who could provide them with the few goods they desired. Except for the French in North Africa, the Portuguese in Angola, and the **Boers** of Dutch descent in South Africa, the Europeans saw no

LAW AND GOVERNMENT

An African Queen and a Formidable Woman

In the late sixteenth century, Portugal was the sole European nation involved directly in the African gold and slave trade. However, within a few decades, her position increasingly came under threat by England, the Netherlands, and France. Forced to concede her slave operations in West Africa, Portugal directed more of its operations to the Kongo and Ngola kingdoms in West Central Africa.

Although women rulers were not the norm in Africa, one notable exception was Queen Nzinga Mpande of the Ngola kingdom. (See Map 25.1.) Little is known about her early life, but as a favored daughter of the Ngola (King) Kilaunji, she was destined someday to occupy an important place among the Mbundu people of the Ngola state. Most of what we know about her comes from records of Portuguese governors and envoys to her court. She was born around 1583 and died in 1663. Altogether, her life spanned a period when the Portuguese and Dutch threatened her kingdom both through conquest and by highly destructive slave raiding among her people. To negotiate a peace, her brother, the *Ngola* Mpande (um-PAHN-day), sent her as an envoy to negotiate with the Portuguese in 1618. Nzinga's primary objectives for the meeting were (1) to persuade the Governor to agree to withdraw a fortified base he had built on Mpande's land, (2) to put a stop to raiding by his African allies, the Imbangala, and (3) to return some of Mpande's captive subjects. Remarkably, at the meeting the governor, João Correia de Sousa, agreed to Nzinga's demands and the two representatives signed a peace treaty on more or less equal terms. A well-known story that came out of this meeting was that Correia de Sousa did not extend the courtesy of providing Nzinga a chair on which to sit, hoping to gain the psychological advantage. To gain back the advantage, Nzinga, a formidable negotiator, ordered one of her servants to kneel so she could sit on him. (This scene is recreated in the accompanying engraving.) Later, in 1623, she poisoned her brother, the king, and assumed the throne herself.

Despite the treaty, the Portuguese failed in the end to honor the agreement and the slave raids soon recommenced. To fight them, Queen Nzinga Mpande joined forces with another African people, the Jaga, and turned the tables on her enemies by persuading other African peoples to rebel. For the next fifteen years, fighting continued with neither side able to gain the advantage. Finally, the balance began tipping in Nzinga's favor when two other enemies of the Portuguese, the Dutch and the Kongo king Garcia II, joined her cause. With their help, in 1648, Queen Nzinga's armies largely destroyed the Portuguese army and the Dutch seized the Portuguese coastal town of Luanda. In 1656, the hostilities ceased and a peace was worked out, this time with lasting effect. Although she was forced to surrender much of her kingdom, Queen Nzinga fully retained her independence. This formidable queen died in 1663.

ANALYZE AND INTERPRET

Why did the Dutch regard the Portuguese (and Spain) as enemies? (Hint: see Chapter 23.) What reasons might the Kongo king have had to join an alliance with Nzinga and the Dutch? What particular skills did Queen Nzinga show in her struggles with the Portuguese?

NZINGA MPANDE (*c.* 1583–1663) MEETING CORREIA DE SOUSA. Nzinga was the queen of the Ndongo kingdom in Angola. The generic looks of the people and landscape in the image suggest that the artist did not witness this meeting, but instead reconstructed the scene from an account given by an actual eyewitness. Note that she is shown seated on one of her servants.

reason to take any interest in, much less disturb, the patchwork of kingdoms that existed mostly in the interior of the continent. The result was that, in 1800, Europeans knew hardly more about the interior than their ancestors had known in the fifth century. Not even the basic geography of the river systems was understood, and the quest for the sources of the Nile, which lasted until the 1860s, was one of the great adventure stories of the Victorian era.

From 1800 onward, this indifference and ignorance changed gradually. Several reasons account for this change. The first of these was humanitarian. After centuries of being steeped in the inhumanity of the slave trade, Europeans—first and especially those who were most involved in it, the English—simply rediscovered their conscience in the 1790s. A movement to end the slave trade and slavery arose out of late-eighteenth-century Christian evangelism. This was particularly true with the appearance of the Wesleyan (Methodist) movement among the new urban poor of Britain's early Industrial Revolution. Men such as John Wesley and Thomas Fowell Buxton led a vigorous **Anti-Slavery Movement**, which soon acquired many supporters in high places. They persuaded the British Parliament in 1807 to officially end the slave trade, the United States in 1808, and other European nations after the Napoleonic Wars.

To enforce these laws, Britain used its powerful Royal Navy to patrol the coastal areas of West and East Africa, where the trade was most active. Colonies were established at Freetown in Sierra Leone (by Britain) and Libreville in what is now Gabon (by France) for slaves who had been freed through these measures. Right behind these reformers came missionaries who were anxious to convert these freed slaves and other Africans for God and Christ. Missionary societies were begun in Europe and America to train men and women to go into the "field" as evangelists to minister to the souls of Africans and as medical missionaries to minister to their bodies.

Another reason for the changed attitudes was simple curiosity: the desire to explore the world's last great unexplored regions. The most noted of the nineteenth-century journeyers into the African interior were either missionaries such as David Livingstone or explorer-adventurers such as the Frenchman René Caillé (reh-NAY CAH-yay), the German Heinrich Barth, the Englishman Richard Francis Burton, and the Anglo-American Henry Morton Stanley. The sharply competitive search for the source of the Nile River was largely responsible for opening knowledge of the vast interior of East Africa in the 1860s and 1870s to the outside world, while the exploration of the Niger and Congo basins did the same for West and Central Africa. Livingstone was the first European to be acknowledged as having crossed the entire African continent east to west, although there is evidence that he was preceded by half a century by a Portuguese explorer. The journalist Stanley, made famous by his well-publicized search for an allegedly lost Livingstone, went on to become a major African explorer in the 1870s and, as an agent of the king of the Belgians, Leopold II, "opened up" the Congo to colonial status.

Finally, there were two other factors that will be discussed in greater detail in the next chapter: the profit motive and rising nationalism. Commercial interest in Africa was not new in the nineteenth century, but previously most had believed that Africa possessed little more to offer the world than slaves, gold, and animal by-products such as ivory and skins. That perception changed when the gold and slave trade began winding down and the Industrial Revolution in nineteenth-century Europe and America created new needs for industrial raw materials and markets for its finished manufactured goods (Chapters 32 and 34). After having witnessed firsthand the effects of

THE EXPLORER DAVID LIVINGSTONE AND HIS MEETING WITH STANLEY. In 1869, the *New York Herald* sent Henry Morton Stanley (*left*) to search for the famous Scottish missionary-explorer who had not been heard from for several years. In 1871, Stanley found an already ill Livingstone (*inset and right*) at Ujiji on Lake Tanganyika. Together, they explored the northern part of the lake and some of its rivers. After parting, Livingstone continued his exploration of the regions to the east of the lake and finally succumbed to malaria in 1873.

the slave trade in East and Central Africa, Livingstone, perhaps unwittingly, contributed to this new interest in Africa when he observed that if "Christianity and commerce" might be offered, Africans would be weaned away from the slave trade. Trading companies such as Britain's Royal Niger Company and various firms operating out of northern Germany and Marseilles, France, began marking off their respective "spheres of influence" all over Africa, wherein they exercised monopolistic control of trade in highly sought-after local products such as palm oil (the principal lubricant of the First Industrial Revolution).

Gradually, then, as the nineteenth century passed and new forms of interest in Africa developed, the conditions for the sudden late-nineteenth-century competition among the major European powers—called the "Scramble for Africa" (see Chapter 36)—fell into place.

North Africa

Another factor that motivated Europeans to seek colonies in Africa and other parts of the world was nationalism. As a ploy to shore up a weak and unpopular monarchy, the French government hoped to stir up nationalistic feelings by embarking on a new course of conquest unseen since the days of Napoleon. Beginning in 1830, using the threat of piracy as an excuse, France launched invasions of Morocco and Algeria. Morocco remained theoretically independent under its sultan, who was supervised by a "resident-general" appointed by the French government in Paris. Less heavily populated and less stable, Algeria was easily seized from a decaying Turkish administration and made into a formal French colony as early as 1847. Eventually, more than a million French immigrants settled on the region of rich soil between the Atlas Mountains and Algeria's Mediterranean coast. Algeria became the sole African region in which this type of intensive, agriculturally oriented European settlement occurred—until diamonds and gold were discovered in late-nineteenth-century South Africa. Europeans treated the Arabs and indigenous Berbers in Algeria as unwelcome foreigners in their own country, and many were required to work the lands of absentee landlords for meager pay. Nearly the same process occurred later in neighboring Tunisia. Thus, by the later nineteenth century, the whole western half of Africa north of the Sahara was within the French orbit.

The eastern Mediterranean coast of Africa had still been part of the dying Ottoman Empire, but the Turkish regents had been able to exercise little real control over these lands for centuries and could not defend them successfully from European ambitions for long. In 1798, Napoleon invaded Egypt, and once combined Turkish and British arms expelled him, the Ottoman sultan appointed the Albanian Muhammad Ali as the viceroy of Egypt. In the years afterward, Muhammad Ali succeeded in establishing himself and his successors as a quasi-independent regime. In 1821, he extended Egyptian control into the

PORTRAIT OF ABD AL-QADIR. The Algerian Abd al-Qadir led an Islamic resistance to the French invasion of North Africa for many years.

Sudan. In 1869, during the reign of his son and successor, the Khedive Ismail (keh-DEEV iss-MAH-ihl), the French completed the construction of the Suez Canal. In 1882, fearing Egyptian seizure of this strategically vital asset, the British invaded and added Egypt to their worldwide empire. For their part, the Italians took over the (then) wastelands of Libya in 1911.

In all of these lands, Islam was the religion of the great majority. As both the local leadership and the Turks in Istanbul proved themselves unable to act effectively in the face of aggressive Europeans, Islam underwent a revival in many parts of the Islamic world (see Chapter 34), including Africa. Sometimes this revival took the form of *jihads*, holy wars to expel Christian "infidels." In the thousand years since Islam had first been introduced to Africa, it had become fused with local forms of economic and cultural life. Therefore, when Europeans invaded Africa, threatening to impose an alien religion and culture, religion provided a natural foundation for organizing resistance.

Without question, the hardest fought and longest lasting of these struggles was the jihad of Abd al-Qadir (AHB-dal-KAH-deer) in Algeria. Like others who led similarly inspired wars in Africa (see the following West Africa section), Abd al-Qadir was a local leader of a

Sufi brotherhood; more specifically, he was a **marabout** (MAH-rah-boot), a charismatic leader of holy men who inhabited a complex of monastery-like lodges among the desert and mountain Berbers. Abd al-Qadir was able to base his struggle against the French on his personal religious charisma and on effective use of the preexisting network of lodges. The jihad began in 1841, and by 1847, Abd al-Qadir was captured and exiled; however, the jihad continued until 1879 before the French finally prevailed against this "proto-nationalist" struggle, which in many respects presaged the Algerian war of independence in the 1950s (Chapter 49).

West Africa

By the early nineteenth century, the French and the British were the leading European powers operating in West Africa, each having created respective "spheres of influence" in which their merchants carried out business under the protection of their governments. In these areas, the slave trade had been the major occupation of Europeans and their African collaborators for centuries. After slaves were banned by acts of Parliament from British ships in 1807 and from British imperial territory in 1834, the principal slaving centers moved southward into the Portuguese colony of Angola. Here the trade continued to flourish until the U.S. Civil War removed a major destination and the abolition of slavery in Brazil in 1888 eliminated the most important one. (The U.S. Congress prohibited the importation of slaves in 1808, but they continued to be smuggled into the southern United States even during the Civil War.)

As the new "legitimate trade" replaced the slave trade, agricultural exports from Africa and imports of European metal, cloth, and manufactured goods became its foundation all over Africa. In their few locations in West Africa, the French and British, as well as the Portuguese, had staked out monopolistic control of local markets along the coast and the banks of the major rivers of the region. The French were largely concentrated along the Senegal River and the British in the lower Niger River basin (Nigeria), the Gold Coast (Ghana), Sierra Leone, and the Gambia. The vast interior remained unaffected for the most part, although events there ultimately became a major influence on the decision of the French to conquer the West African interior.

Beyond the coastal regions, Islam was the dominant religion in West Africa long before the nineteenth century (Chapter 17). The great medieval commercial empires of Mali and Songhay and others had played important roles in this process in West Africa: Mosques were built, Arabic literacy spread, and Muslim traders carried Islam ever farther into the coastal hinterlands. Despite conversions, however, many African Muslims clung to ancestor veneration, spirit possession, sacrifice, and divination rites that were rooted in their pre- or non-Islamic past. Even rulers of Muslim states allowed practices to persist that were forbidden by Islamic law, such as allowing their own subjects (who were Muslims) to be sold as slaves to Europeans and the collection of illegal taxes.

Werner Forman/ Art Resource, NY

A MINIATURE HAUSA *QU'RAN* OF THE SIXTEENTH-TO-SEVENTEENTH CENTURY AND THE PERIOD BEFORE THE JIHAD OF USMAN DAN FODIO. This design was used for "magical" purposes, such as a form of fortune telling, and indicates the "unorthodox" forms of Islam that developed as Islam penetrated south of the Sahara and against which Usman dan Fodio and al-Hajj Umar fought.

Beginning in the seventeenth century, the first of a series of holy wars began in the region of Senegal and Guinea in response to these shortcomings. Others followed across the western and central Sudan over the next two centuries, but the most important of these were the jihads of Usman dan Fodio (UHS-mahn dan FOH-dee-oh) and al-Hajj Umar Tal (al-HAJ oo-MAHR TAHL) in the nineteenth century.

The jihad of Usman dan Fodio began in the 1790s and arose from a dispute between a Muslim holy man, Usman dan Fodio, and the king of a Hausa city-state called Gobir. The Hausa are a people found in the northern part of modern Nigeria. Like the Swahili of East Africa, they lived in city-states (see Map 25.2). Usman dan Fodio began preaching against the local Habe (HAH-bay) ruler of Gobir (goh-BEER), whom he accused of infidelity. A crisis finally led to the declaration of a holy war, and between 1804 and the time of Usman's death in 1817, a series of jihads vanquished not just Gobir but all of the city-states of Hausaland and even the neighboring countries of Nupe (NOO-pay) and Ilorin (ih-LOH-rihn) in northern Yoruba country to the south. With the capital of his new "caliphate" at Sokoto (soh-KOH-toh), the Islamic empire Usman created consisted of several satellite emirates, each of which centered on the major Hausa states and all of which were governed by Islamic law. Although dan Fodio died soon after the completion of his jihad, his son, Muhammad Bello, succeeded him. His competence and long life put his father's accomplishment on a stable foundation, and the Sokoto caliphate endured through the colonial era.

The success of the jihad of Usman dan Fodio inspired similar Islamic revolutions to the west, particularly among the Tukolor (TOO-kuh-lohr) people in the area between the Niger and Senegal rivers. Whereas the previous holy wars fought by dan Fodio and others were directed against

MAP 25.2 Africa in the Nineteenth Century

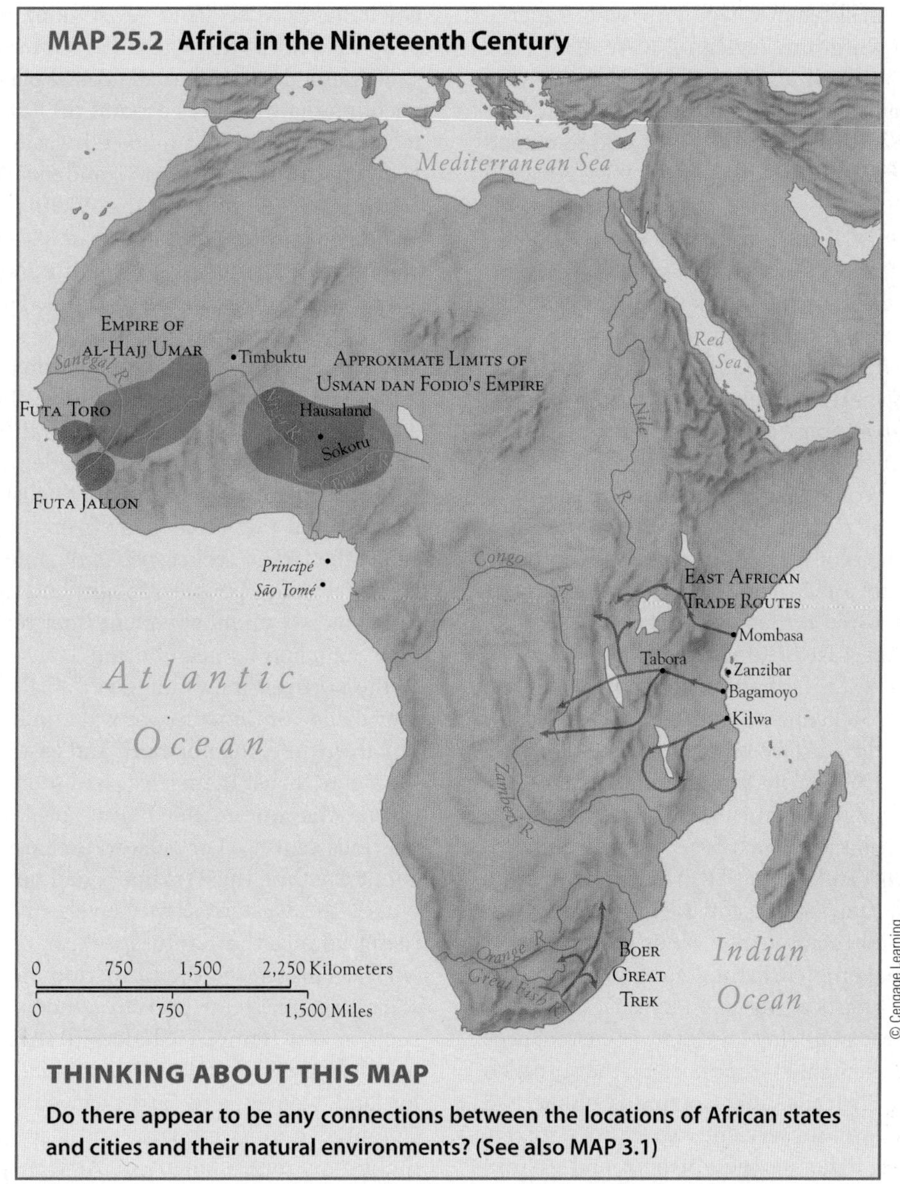

THINKING ABOUT THIS MAP

Do there appear to be any connections between the locations of African states and cities and their natural environments? (See also MAP 3.1)

the non-Islamic practices of local rulers, the jihad of al-Hajj Umar Tal followed a more deliberate plan of conquest and Islamic state building. Umar left his native Futa Toro (FOO-tah TOH-roh) in 1826 to set off on the pilgrimage, and after spending several years at the court of Muhammad Bello, he returned to Futa Jallon (FOO-tah JAHL-lahn) on the headwaters of the Senegal River. There he set up a school and began building a circle of followers, until the 1840s, when he launched his jihad against neighboring Islamic states to the east.

By the 1860s, he had managed to extend his conquests as far as the Upper Niger, where he forced many to convert to Islam and established the Islamic Shari'a as the backbone of his government. These wars got him into difficulties with the French, who had established themselves on the lower reaches of the Senegal River to the west of Umar's growing empire. Louis Faidherbe (fay-DEHRB), the governor of Senegal, feared Umar's designs on French holdings and used Umar's ambitions as a reason to extend control farther up the river. As we shall see in Chapter 36, with imperial ambitions of their own in this region of West Africa, the French were able to exploit divisions among Umar's sons and resentments against his forced conversions to their considerable advantage in the 1880s and 1890s, and to extend their own colonial empire to include most of West Africa.

South Africa

The Cape Colony in extreme southern Africa was the other large area, along with Algeria, where whites settled in some numbers before the late nineteenth century. Cape Town was founded in 1652 when the **Dutch East India Company** decided to establish a colony in South Africa as a place where company ships making the long voyage to and from the East Indies could take on supplies of fresh meat and vegetables and where their sick could receive attention. Although the Dutch colonists sent by the company were originally required to provide these services, soon many demanded—and got—the company's permission to settle new farmlands to the east of the Cape. These so-called Boers (BOHRS; Dutch for farmers) founded new western Cape settlements at Stellenbosch and Graf Reinet (grahf REYE-net) and steadily displaced the indigenous cattle-herding Khoikhoi (KOY-koy) peoples they encountered.

From the beginning, relations with African peoples were almost never conducted on a basis of racial equality. As Boer migrants, or **Trekboers** (TREHK-bohrs), moved ever-farther inland, they swept aside the indigenous peoples and dispossessed them of their lands and livestock. Labor was a perpetual problem in the colony, so slaves were imported from other parts of Africa, Indonesia, India, and Madagascar. Some racial mixing inevitably occurred, producing a new social element in Cape society: the so-called **Coloureds**. Slaves, Africans, and Coloureds either had to accept a permanently subservient role in Boer society or flee, as many did, living on the northern and eastern fringes of Cape Colony and occasionally raiding Boer farmsteads for cattle on the eastern frontier.

Until the recent past, when majority rule was introduced in South Africa, the Boers maintained an old myth that their ancestors had preceded Bantu-speaking Africans in settling South Africa. In fact, archaeological and linguistic evidence indicates that Khoisan (koy-SAHN) peoples had inhabited southern Africa for tens of thousands of years, and Bantu-speaking peoples had been present in South Africa since as early as the fourth century (Chapter 17). Essentially village dwellers, the Bantu-speaking peoples were economically more diversified than the Khoisan and Khoikhoi. They had an iron-based technology and lived as mixed farmers, supplemented by livestock breeding. Gradually, they occupied the eastern Cape and the inland high plateau, where rainfall levels could support their way of life. As for their political organization, available evidence suggests that until the eighteenth century, these Bantu-speaking peoples had lived in loosely organized paramount chieftaincies. The Zulu (ZOO-loo) and closely related peoples, such as the Xhosa (KHOH-sah), steadily pushed southward along the broad coastal plain, until they finally encountered the Boers around the Fish River in the eighteenth century. What followed was a military stalemate. Neither Africans nor Boers could push the other aside.

In 1815, as part of the Vienna settlement of the Napoleonic wars, Britain occupied the Cape, and the colony became subject to English law and slightly more liberal ideas about racial relations. Having enjoyed substantial self-government, the Boers of the eastern frontier resented British efforts to bring order and more humane treatment of Africans. In particular, they resented British efforts to restrict slavery and cut off much of the supply of free labor on which the Boers depended. Beginning in 1836, in an effort to escape the English, the Boers started a northward migration away from the Cape in what was called the **Great Trek**. Once in the interior, they drove out the local Sotho peoples, fought and defeated the mighty Zulu, and set up independent Boer republics (the Orange Free State and its neighboring Transvaal [TRANS-vawl]) to the north of the Orange and Vaal (vawl) rivers, where they could continue the old ways undisturbed.

Meanwhile, the northern and eastern areas into which the Boers thrust themselves had seen considerable transformations among the Bantu-speaking Africans in the previous century. For reasons that are still being debated, about the time the Trekboers had begun their expansion out of the western Cape, levels of conflict had begun rising among the Bantu-speaking peoples of Southeast Africa. This caused the formation of powerful states that were organized for warfare under formidable leaders such as the famous **Shaka** (SHAH-kah) of the Zulu people, as well as others. Continual raiding by Africans for land, women, and cattle, as well as by Boers and even Coloured groups for land and slaves triggered massive flights and resettlement of African populations. Many

SOCIETY AND ECONOMY

Tippu Tib and the Zanzibar Slave Trade

Tippu Tib, whose real name was Hamed bin Mohammed al-Murjibi, was born in Zanzibar sometime in the 1830s, and became one of the most successful clove-plantation owners and caravan traders in East Africa at a time when, although outlawed, the slave trade was at its peak. His mother was an Omani Arab of the ruling class, and his father and grandfather were Swahili who had participated in some of the earliest trading caravans to the distant interior. Consequently, Tippu began his career by working for his father, and by 1865, he went into the caravan business for himself. By that time, many of the elephant herds nearer the coast were hunted out, but he soon found the perfect solution to the collection of ivory and slaves. The answer, of course, was to carry his business farther inland—west of Lake Tanganyika in the western Congo basin—where ivory was still available in sufficient quantities to make the journey of many months worthwhile. Over and above that, he conquered the local Rua peoples and was able to force tribute to be collected in ivory, thus avoiding the necessity of having to purchase it. Through a policy of warfare and conquest, the problem of transport was resolved by forcing captives into slavery. Once back on the coast, they were sold along with the ivory they had borne on their backs for more than one thousand miles.

Bojan Brecelj/Historical/Corbis

TIPPU TIB. Tippu was only the best known of the East African slave traders. The slave trade from Madagascar, the coast, and its hinterland had existed since the tenth century. However, it reached its apogee in the nineteenth century, with many Arabs and Swahili participating in it.

By 1883, Tippu had established himself and about a dozen close clansmen as local rulers throughout the Congo basin. He used the profits from this commercial empire to purchase clove *shambas* (plantations) on Zanzibar. One historian claims that he eventually owned seven plantations and around ten thousand slaves.

During his lifetime, Tippu became a familiar person to many European explorers of that era. Generally, he managed to maintain good relations with them. In 1887, at the height of the European scramble to establish colonies in Africa, and realizing how the balance of power between the Europeans and the sultan of Zanzibar had been shifting, he took on the role of governor of the Stanley Falls area of Belgian King Leopold II's newly created "Congo Free State." (For more about the Scramble for Africa, see Chapter 36.)

Tippu Tib returned to Zanzibar for the last time in 1895, where he retired. He wrote an autobiography in Kiswahili, which was eventually translated and published in Great Britain. In 1905, he died of malaria in Zanzibar Town.

ANALYZE AND INTERPRET

Who was primarily responsible for the African slave trade? Were men like Tippu perpetrators of the nefarious business or merely opportunists?

of these sought the protection of the powerful warlords, whereas other areas became depopulated. To escape the pressures of warfare, some migrated out of South Africa altogether and fled into other regions of southern and East Africa (Map 25.2).

As for Boer–British relations, all went well for a time, because the Boer republics and the British Cape Colony were situated far apart. In 1879, fearing the reputation of the Zulu, the British Army succeeded in eliminating them as a threat to the occupation of Natal by Europeans in

Shackling of Black Miners hands during a break, in a diamond mine in Cape Town (engraving) (b/w photo), French School, (19th century)/Bibliotheque Nationale, Paris, France/Archives Charmet/The Bridgeman Art Library

SHACKLING AFRICAN DIAMOND MINERS. Prospectors in South Africa found the richest diamond-mining district in the world in the 1860s. Massive amounts of hard labor were required to bring the mines into production, leading directly to much harsher working and living conditions for the Africans who supplied this labor.

what is known as the **Zulu War**. Moreover, in the 1860s, the long-standing European perception that Africa had little value changed permanently when diamonds were discovered at Kimberly. Soon after, in the 1880s, rich veins of gold were also found on the Rand in the Transvaal. The diamond and gold fever suddenly cast Africa in a new light: It was a continent rich in natural wealth waiting to be exploited by anyone or any imperial power bold enough to do whatever it took to seize it.

Seyyid Barghash, Sultan of Zanzibar, d. 1888. (From a photograph.)

Seyyid Barghash (c.1834–88), Sultan of Zanzibar, from 'The History of Mankind' by Prof. Friedrich Ratzel, pub. in 1904 (engraving), English School, (20th century)/Private Collection/The Bridgeman Art Library

SULTAN BARGHASH. A proud Arab, Sultan Barghash tried resisting European interference in the slave trade of Zanzibar. In the end, he was forced to submit to ending the slave trade and became dependent on the British for his political survival.

East Africa

Although slaving had formed a small part of this coastal trade for many centuries, it is unlikely that the volume of the East African trade had ever approached that of the West African business, whether Arab or European. The demand for slaves changed suddenly, however, in the eighteenth century. Almost a century after the **Omani Arabs** (oh-MAH-nee; from Oman, in southeastern Arabia) expelled the Portuguese and occupied all points of the coast north of Mozambique, the French settled the Indian Ocean islands of Mauritius (moh-RIH-shus) and Réunion (ray-YOO-nyohn). Plantation economies in the Persian Gulf and on Mauritius and Réunion created an unprecedented demand for slaves, most of which were obtained from the central African interior and exported through Kilwa Kivinje and Zanzibar.

Further encouragement of the East African trade was provided in 1832 when the Sultan of Oman, **Sayyid Sa'id** bin Sultan al-Busaidi (SAHY-yihd sah-EED bin sool-THAN al-boo-sah-EE-dee), moved the headquarters of his sultanate to Zanzibar. After developing what came to be known as the **Zanzibar** (ZAN-zi-bahr) **Sultanate**, Sayyid Sa'id and his successors extended their control over the entire Swahili coast of East Africa. However, theirs was a commercial empire above all else. All coastal trade was directed through Zanzibar, where the sultans collected a standard 3 percent duty. Sayyid Sa'id encouraged the creation of a plantation economy in East Africa, so Arabs and Indian immigrants displaced the local Swahili in Zanzibar and large numbers of slaves were employed in cultivating cloves. Inland from many coastal towns, too, Arabs and local Swahili alike turned to plantation farming, where grains were cultivated for export. Under such a growing demand, trade in slaves and ivory soon reached inland beyond the East African lakes region as far as Uganda and the eastern Congo River basin. In 1873, the trade was finally ended when the British convinced Sa'id's son to agree to permanently abolish the export of slaves. However, the practice of slavery continued in East Africa until finally it, too, was ended during the colonial period.

SUMMARY

In many ways, Africa was in transition from the seventeenth through the late nineteenth centuries. Most parts of the interior of the continent remained relatively unaffected by any European efforts to control or alter the lands and lives of its peoples. For one thing, before the last quarter of the nineteenth century, Europe simply did not possess the power to conquer such a vast continent; for another, it lacked any will to do so. European interest in Africa remained entirely commercial, and as long as there were plenty of Africans who were willing—or whom Europeans could persuade—to supply the slaves and exotic tropical products they demanded, there was no reason for Europeans ever to think of wasting money and manpower on conquest. In the one place where Europeans did settle before the nineteenth century, South Africa, the relatively few hunting and pastoralist peoples the Europeans met in the western Cape were easily defeated.

However, in the late eighteenth century, once these white settlers encountered the much more numerous and advanced Bantu-speaking peoples in the northern and eastern parts, their advance was halted. Therefore, European governments showed no official interest in colonizing Africa during the first great Age of Imperialism, when attention was directed primarily to Asia and America. The only exception was France, which began the conquest of North Africa. There they found that Islam could be a major obstacle to conquest, a fact of which they were to be reminded repeatedly later when they launched the conquest of the Sudan.

All of the reasons Europeans had for official disinterest in Africa changed after about 1880, in what is called the age of the New Imperialism. As will be seen in Chapter 36, all of the major European powers experienced dramatically changed attitudes toward Africa and the potential difficulties and responsibilities that empire building there would entail. All of the major powers, and a couple of minor ones as well, would engage in carving up what one empire builder, King Leopold II of Belgium, called "this magnificent African cake."

IDENTIFICATION TERMS

Test your knowledge of this chapter's key concepts by defining the following terms. If you can not recall the meaning of certain terms, refresh your memory by looking up the boldfaced term in the chapter, turning to the Glossary at the end of the book, or accessing the terms on the CourseMate website at **www.cengagebrain.com.**

Anti-Slavery Movement
Askia Muhammad the Great
Boers
Bornu
Buganda
Bunyoro-Kitara
Coloureds
Dutch East India Company
factories
Great Trek
Hausa
Informal Empire
marabout
Omani Arabs
Sayyid Sa'id
Shaka
Songhay Empire.
Trekboers
Zanzibar Sultanate
Zulu War

FOR FURTHER REFLECTION

1. Why do you think estimating the number of Africans exported into slavery might be controversial? If you were a scholar trying to make such an estimate, what challenges would you expect to encounter?
2. Why were Europeans, for the most part, so disinterested in Africa for so many centuries? How and why did this begin to change in the nineteenth century?
3. What factors contributed to state building in Africa (see also Chapter 17)? How did the introduction of the slave trade alter this? Why did it destroy some kingdoms and help to create others in their place?

TEST YOUR KNOWLEDGE

Test your knowledge of this chapter by answering the following questions. Complete answers appear at the end of the book. You may find even more quiz questions on the CourseMate website at **www.cengagebrain.com.**

1. An early rival to the Buganda kingdom in what is now Uganda was
   a. the Kongo kingdom.
   b. Benin.
   c. Bunyoro-Kitara.
   d. Zanzibar.
   e. the Hausa city-states.
2. Which of these kingdoms developed out of a previous form of religious leadership?
   a. The Hausa
   b. The Swahili
   c. Bunyoro-Kitara
   d. Benin
   e. The Zulu
3. South Africa was colonized in 1652 by settlers sent by
   a. the Dutch East India Company.
   b. the Portuguese government.
   c. missionary societies.
   d. Omani Arabs.
   e. Oman.
4. What can be said about the slave trade?
   a. It had positive effects on some African societies.
   b. It had negative effects on some Africans.
   c. The exact numbers who were sold into slavery are uncertain.
   d. The firearms that were sold to cooperative Africans reduced the amount of violence the slave trade brought.
   e. answers a, b, and c
5. During the colonial era, what non-African religion made the biggest gains in Africa?
   a. Islam
   b. Buddhism
   c. Hinduism
   d. Christianity
   e. Shinto
6. One major cause of the West African jihads was
   a. the practice followed by Muslim rulers of allowing non-Muslims to settle among Muslims.
   b. continued observance of non-Islamic practices among West African Muslims and their rulers.
   c. the practice followed by Muslim rulers of allowing non-Muslims to marry Muslim women.
   d. continued involvement of West Africans in the slave trade despite Islamic injunctions against it.
   e. slave raiding conducted among Muslims by non-Muslim coastal peoples.
7. The jihadist activities in West Africa were partly
   a. a reaction to the increased levels of violence caused by the slave trade.
   b. inspired by an expected return of Muhammad.
   c. inspired by Islamic revivalism in Arabia and the Islamic heartlands.
   d. inspired by the resistance of Abd al-Qadir to the French invasion of Algeria.
   e. a reaction to growing activities by Christian missionaries in Africa.
8. The Dutch who founded the Cape Colony in South Africa in 1652 came there for what purpose?
   a. To spread Christianity among the Africans
   b. To create a station where Dutch East India Company ships could take on supplies
   c. To conquer the local African population and seize their livestock
   d. To seek freedom of religion
   e. To trade and seek other new economic opportunities among the African population
9. What colonial power succeeded the Portuguese in most of East Africa by the late 1600s?
   a. the Spanish.
   b. the English.
   c. the Omani Arabs.
   d. the French.
   e. Indians.
10. The coastal cities of East Africa in the nineteenth century
    a. already had centuries of trading history by the time they were put under Omani rule.
    b. were already part of Christian culture.
    c. had never before experienced foreign contacts.
    d. were enclaves of Arab colonists.
    e. exported no slaves.

CourseMate

Visit the CourseMate website at **www.cengagebrain.com** for additional study tools and review materials for this chapter.

26 China from the Ming Through the Early Qing Dynasty

Great wealth is from heaven; modest wealth is from diligence. —CHINESE FOLK TRADITION

1368–1644	Ming Dynasty
1400s	Maritime Expeditions
1500s	First contacts with Europeans
1644–1911	Qing Dynasty
1700s	Economic growth; population rises; trade increases

CHAPTER OUTLINE

The ages of China do not coincide with those of Europe. China had no Middle Age or Renaissance of the fourteenth century. The outstanding facts in China's development between 1000 C.E. and 1500 C.E. were the humiliating conquest by the Mongols and their overthrow by the rebellion that began the **Ming Dynasty**. For more than two hundred years, the Ming rulers remained vigorous, providing the Chinese with a degree of stability and prosperity that contemporary Europeans would have envied. But the sustained creative advance in the sciences and basic technologies that had allowed China to overshadow all rivals during the thousand years between the beginning of the Song and the end of the Ming dynasties (600–1644) was slowly drawing to a close. The West was overtaking China in these areas, but as late as the eighteenth century, this was hardly evident to anyone. Possessed of an ancient and marvelous high culture, China was still convinced of its own superiority and was as yet far from being forced to admit its weaknesses.

MING CHINA, 1368–1644

The Ming was the last purely Chinese dynasty. It began with the overthrow of the hated Mongols, who had ruled China for one hundred years. Founded by the peasant Zhu Yuanzhang (joo yuwen-chahng), who had displayed masterful military talents in leading a motley band of rebel armies, the Ming would last three hundred years. Zhu, who took the imperial title Hongwu (hung-woo; ruling 1368–1398), was an individual of great talents and great cruelty. In many ways, his fierce ruthlessness was reminiscent of the First Emperor. He built the city of Nanjing (Nanking) as his capital near the coast on the Yangzi River. His son and successor, Yongle (yuhng-leh), was even more talented as a general and an administrator. During Yongle's twenty-two-year reign (1402–1424), China

MAP 26.1 The Empire Under the Ming and Qing Dynasties

By the time of the Ming Dynasty, China had reached its modern territorial extent, with the exception only of Tibet and the far western deserts. Beijing and Nanjing alternated as the capital cities. At the height of the empire under the Qing Dynasty in the middle of the eighteenth century, both Tibet and the huge desert province of Sinkiang came under its control.

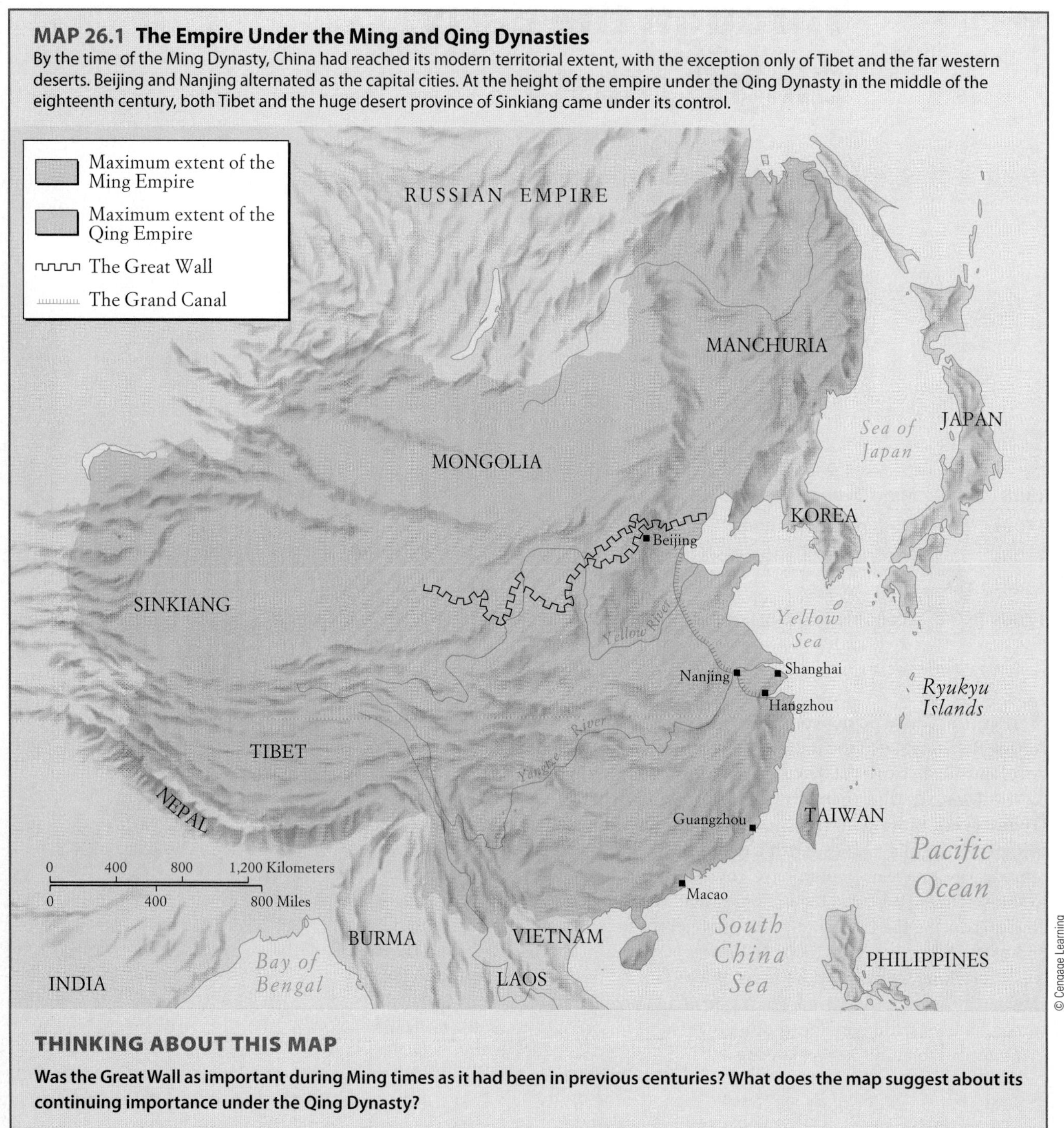

THINKING ABOUT THIS MAP

Was the Great Wall as important during Ming times as it had been in previous centuries? What does the map suggest about its continuing importance under the Qing Dynasty?

gained more or less its present heartlands, reaching from Korea to Vietnam and inward to Mongolia (see Map 26.1). The eastern half of the Great Wall was rebuilt, and the armies of China were everywhere triumphant against their Mongol and Turkish nomad opponents.

In the Ming era, China generally had an effective government. One sign of this was the sharp rise in population throughout the dynastic period. When the Ming took power, bubonic plague (the same epidemic that was simultaneously raging in Europe; see Chapter 20) and Mongol savagery had reduced the population to about 60 million—the same size it had been in the Tang period five hundred years earlier. The population rose to perhaps 150 million by 1600, the most dramatic rise yet experienced by any society.

This new population necessitated an equally dramatic rise in food supply. The old center of Chinese food production, the Yangzi basin in south-central China, was not able to meet the demand. A new area for rice cultivation in the extreme south near Vietnam was developed during the Ming, and some new crops from the Americas such as corn, squash, peanuts, and beans made their way into Chinese fields via the trans-Pacific trade with the Portuguese and the Spanish. Interestingly, the Irish or white potato, which would become the staple food crop of northern European peasants in the eighteenth century, was introduced in China but did not catch on. Because rice has greater nutritional value than the potato, this turned out to be a boon for China.

MING POTTERY MAKERS. The late Tang through the Ming eras saw significant developments in Chinese society. There were notable developments in the size and sophistication of its cities, technological innovation, and cultural efflorescence. A key to its manufacturing and commercial sectors was the organization of craftsmen, like these potters, into imperial workshops and guilds (*cohong*).

ECONOMIC PROGRESS

Commercial activity steadily increased until it was probably more commonplace in China than in any other country of the world by the 1600s. A larger percentage of the labor force was directly engaged in buying, selling, and transporting goods than in any other land. The merchants remained quite low on the social ladder but were acquiring sufficient money to provide them with a comfortable and cultivated lifestyle.

Commercial contact with the Europeans started in the early 1500s with the coming of the Portuguese into the Indian and, soon, Pacific oceans. Originally welcomed, the Portuguese behaved so badly that the Chinese quickly limited them to a single port: Macao (mah-COW). (See Dealing with Foreigners discussion this chapter.) In return for silver the Spanish introduced from the Americas in 1571, European traders could obtain luxurious and exotic goods that brought exorbitant prices from European nobles, who coveted them for the prestige they conveyed. A merchant who could take a few crates of first-class Chinese porcelain tableware back to Europe could make enough profit to start his own firm.

Urbanization and Technology

The Ming period also saw an enormous increase in the number of urban dwellers. Some Chinese cities, serving as marketplaces for the rural majority and as administrative and cultural centers, grew to have several hundred thousand inhabitants; one or two possibly had more than a million at a time when no European town had a population of even 100,000. In these Chinese metropolises, almost anything was available for money, and the kind of abject poverty that would arise later was probably still unknown. In general, the villagers and city dwellers of Ming China seem to have been decently housed and fed.

Historians have often asked why China, with its large, financially sophisticated commercial class and a leadership role in so many ideas and techniques, did not make the breakthrough into a mechanical mode of industry. Why, in other words, did the Chinese fail to make the leap from the "commercial revolution" of the later Ming period to an "industrial revolution" of the kind that began in the West a century later? Various answers have been proposed, but no single one is satisfactory. The Chinese esteem for artists and scholars and the tendency of such people to place little emphasis on accumulation of material goods must be part of the explanation. Engineers and inventors were never prominent in China's culture, even though Chinese science and technology led the world until at least the 1200s. Also, the Confucian ethos did not admire the capitalist entrepreneur or his activities. It was the retention of the old, not the invention of the new, that inspired properly educated Chinese. In the end, we can only attest that China did not experience an industrial-technical breakthrough. If it had, China and not Western Europe would have been the dominant power of the world in the past three centuries.

THE MING POLITICAL SYSTEM

As always since Han times, the Chinese government culminated in the person of an all-powerful, but not divine, emperor, who ruled by the mandate of Heaven through a highly trained bureaucracy derived substantially from talented men of all classes and backgrounds. Hongwu, the peasant rebel commander, brought militaristic and authoritarian ways to the government he headed. This first Ming ruler divided China into fifteen provinces, subdivided into numerous counties, an arrangement that has survived almost intact into the present day. He made occupations hereditary and classified the population into three chief groups: peasants, soldiers, and workers. Supposedly, the class into which people were born would determine the course of their lives, but this was much truer on paper than in reality. China was far too vast and the bureaucracy far too small to allow this restrictive and nontraditional theory to be successfully put into practice.

But the emperor's powers during the early Ming were probably greater than ever before. Hongwu created a corps of palace eunuchs, men without families who had been raised since boyhood to be totally dedicated servants of the ruler. They served as his eyes and ears, and during periods of weak leadership, the eunuchs often exercised almost dictatorial powers over the regular officials, because they alone had direct access to the emperor. This practice, of course, led to much abuse, and the eunuchs were hated and feared by most Chinese. Curiously, the eunuchs never seem to have attempted to overthrow a legitimate ruler, although some Ming emperors practically turned the government over to them. The imperial corps of eunuchs lasted into the twentieth century, though their powers were much diminished by then.

After a brief sojourn in Nanjing during the rule of the first Ming emperor, the government was returned to the northern city of Beijing (bay-jing), which was originally built by the Mongols. In its center was the **Forbidden City**, a quarter-mile-square area of great palaces, offices, and living quarters for the higher officials. No ordinary person was ever permitted within its massive walls. The Forbidden City was expanded several times during the Ming, until it came to house more than twenty thousand men and women, who served the emperor or his enormous official family. Its upkeep and the lavish entertainments and feasts that were regularly put on for thousands were a heavy burden on the whole country.

The Bureaucracy

The basis for entry and success in the bureaucracy remained the same as it had been for the last 1,500 years: mastery of the Confucian philosophy and ethics. Confucianism grew stronger than ever. Many schools were founded solely to prepare boys for the government service exams. The first Ming emperor immediately reinstated these exams, which had been suspended by the Mongols. Their essentials would not change until the twentieth century. The exams were administered every other year at the lowest (county) level and every third year at the provincial capitals. Each candidate was assigned a tiny cubicle in which he slept and ate under constant surveillance when not writing his essays during the three to five days of the examination.

EXAMINATIONS FOR GOVERNMENT POSTS. This seventeenth-century painting shows the examinations for government posts in progress. Despite years of preparation, few candidates were successful at the higher levels.

Only a tiny minority was successful in obtaining an official post even at the province level. The most distinguished of these would then compete for the central government posts every third year, and the successful ones were considered the most prestigious of all of the "men of Han." Unchanged for centuries, the exams influenced all Chinese education and kept what we now call the *curriculum* to a very narrow subject range. After basic reading, writing, and arithmetic, most Chinese schooling was aimed only at preparing students for the civil service examinations. It consisted of a good deal of rote memorization and required extensive knowledge of the various interpretations of Confucian thought. Imagination, creativity, and individuality were definitely not desired.

Over the long term, this limited education put China's officials at a distinct disadvantage when confronted with situations that required flexibility and vision. On the other hand, the uniform preparation of all Chinese officials gave the country an especially cohesive governing class—the mandarins (see Chapters 6 and 13)—and conflicts generated by differing philosophies of government were rare or nonexistent. Until recently, civil upheaval and antagonism never occurred within the governing class—only between it and some outer group (usually foreigners, eunuchs, or provincial usurpers). This unity of view and the loyalty it engendered were valuable in preserving China from threatened disintegration on repeated occasions.

In the early Ming period, both the government and most of the educated population agreed on the vital principles of a good civic life and how to construct it. All officials, from the emperor down to the minor collector of customs in some obscure port, were accepted by the masses as their proper authorities. The ever-recurring question of how to meet the modest demands of the peasantry for survival without alienating the often rapacious landlord-officials was handled effectively. Unfortunately, this harmony declined in later years, as weak emperors ignored the examples set by the dynasty's founders.

DEALING WITH FOREIGNERS

The Mongols and other nomadic peoples on the northern and northwestern frontiers were still a constant menace after they had been expelled from China proper. Much of the large military budget of Ming China was spent on maintaining the two thousand miles of the Great Wall, large sections of which had to be rebuilt to defend against potential invaders. To do this job, a huge army—well more than a million strong—was kept in constant readiness. The main reason for moving the capital back to Beijing from Nanjing was to better direct the defense effort.

The rulers at Beijing followed the ancient stratagem of "use the barbarian against the barbarian" whenever they could, but twice they miscalculated, and the tribes were able to put aside their squabbles and unite in campaigns against the Chinese. The first time, the Mongols actually defeated and captured the emperor, liberating him only after payment of a tremendous ransom. The second time, they smashed a major Chinese army and overran Beijing itself in 1550. Eventually, both incursions were forced back, and the dynasty was reestablished.

With the Japanese, relations proceeded on two planes: that of hostility toward pirates and smugglers and that of legitimate and beneficial exchange. From the fourteenth century, pirate-traders (there was little distinction) from Japan had appeared in Korean and north Chinese waters. Gradually, they became bolder and often joined Chinese pirates to raid coastal ports well into the south. Because the Japanese could always flee out of reach in their islands, the Chinese could only try to improve their defenses, rather than exterminate the enemy fleets. During the sixteenth century, the Beijing government actually abandoned many coastal areas to the pirates, hoping that this tactic would enable them to protect the rest.

Otherwise, the Ming period was a high point in cultural and commercial interchange between China and Japan. Direct Chinese–Japanese relations concentrated on trading between a few Japanese *daimyo* and Chinese merchants, a private business supervised by the respective governments. Several of the shoguns of Japan (see Chapter 27) were great admirers of Chinese culture and saw to it that Japan's doors were thrown widely open to Chinese ideas as well as artifacts.

The trading activity with the Japanese was exceptional, however. Generally speaking, China's rulers believed that the Empire of the Middle needed little from the outside world. A brief but significant excursion onto the Indian Ocean trade routes seemed to underline this conviction. The **Maritime Expeditions** of the early 1400s are a notable departure from the general course of Chinese expansionist policy, in that they were naval rather than land ventures. Between 1405 and 1433, huge fleets traveled south to the East Indies and as far west as the coast of Africa. The expeditions were sponsored by the government, and at the emperor's order, they stopped as suddenly as they had begun. The fleets made no attempt to plant colonies or to set up a network of trading posts. Nor did the expeditions leave a long-term mark on Chinese consciousness or awareness of the achievements and interests of the world outside. (See the Society and Economy box.)

The Maritime Expeditions were a striking demonstration of how advanced Chinese seamanship, ship design, and equipment were and how confident the Chinese were in their dealings with foreigners of all types. Although China certainly possessed the necessary technology (shipbuilding, compass, rudder, sails) to make a success of overseas exploration and commerce, the government decided not to use it. The government's refusal was the end of the matter. The large mercantile class had no alternative but to accept it because the merchants had neither the influence at court nor the high status in society that could have enabled the voyages to continue. In this sense, the failure to pursue the avenues opened by the expeditions reflects the differences between the Chinese and European governments and the relative importance of merchants and entrepreneurial vision in the two cultures.

Contacts with Westerners during the Ming era were limited to a few trading enterprises (mainly Portuguese, Spanish, or Dutch) and occasional missionaries (mainly Jesuits from Spain or Rome). The Portuguese soon made themselves offensive to Chinese standards of behavior. The missionaries got off to a considerably more favorable start. They made enormous efforts to empathize with the Confucian mentalities of the upper-class Chinese officials and to adapt Christian doctrines to Chinese psyches. Several of the missionaries were well-trained natural scientists and were able to interest their hosts in their religious message via demonstrations of Western mechanical and technical innovations.

Outstanding in this regard was *Matteo Ricci* (mah-TAY-yoh REE-chee; 1551–1610), a Jesuit who obtained access to the emperor thanks to his scientific expertise, adoption of Chinese ways of thought, and mastery of the difficult language. Ricci and his successors established a Christian bridgehead in China that for a century or more looked as though it might be able to broaden its appeal and convert the masses. But this was not to be. (See the Science and Technology box for some of Ricci's remarks on Chinese technology and his insights into Chinese culture.)

SOCIETY AND ECONOMY

Zheng He and Ming-Era Internationalism

Starting in 1405, and on six subsequent occasions, gigantic fleets of Chinese junks numbering up to 317, some more than 400 feet long and 150 feet across, set sail from Nanjing China under the command of **Zheng He** (chung-huh). Estimates are that these armada's crews totaled upward of twenty-seven thousand sailors and soldiers. The largest ships had up to nine masts and could hold up to one thousand soldiers, deckhands, interpreters, navigators, merchants, physicians, priests, scribes, and cooks.

At the time it was an unprecedented display of naval power. Its purpose was to "show the flag" of the Yongle Emperor in the ports and kingdoms of Southeast Asia and the rest of the most prosperous trading region in the world at that time, the Indian Ocean. By the time the Emperor put a sudden end to these voyages in 1433, China had become a naval power without equal and the Emperors in Nanjing had the fear and respect of rulers in South and Southeast Asia, the Middle East, and East Africa—all of which Zheng had visited at one time or another on behalf of his master.

Zheng He was born in 1371 to a Muslim family in western China at a time when Ming influence was just starting to reach the region. When Ming armies reached Yunan, Zheng's home district, they captured him and brought him to the capital at Nanjing where he was castrated and made a eunuch to a Ming prince, Zhu Di, who later became the Yongle Emperor. The prince befriended Zheng He, and in time made him his head eunuch. After the disaster of the Mongol invasions, the young emperor wanted to return to the glories of China's Tang and Song dynasties. China's first ocean-going junks had been built during the Song era, but the Yuan emperors had taken the initiative of sending the first fleets to Southeast Asia and India to install Chinese trade emporia in those regions. It was the Yongle Emperor's wish to reestablish the Chinese presence and to develop a more extensive trade network in these locations. When he encountered resistance from his Confucian court officials, he entrusted his friend and chief eunuch to build and lead the fleet.

Zheng He's voyages were a great success, but on his last voyage he died in India. The fleet was disbanded upon its return to Nanjing, and the explorations ceased. The question then is, why? The answer is that court politics were behind it; by 1433, the Confucians had persuaded the emperor that the growing power and influence of the merchants needed to be curtailed. China also had a history of **xenophobia**—a suspicion of foreigners and foreign ways—stemming from long-held Chinese notions of cultural superiority and the advantages of agrarian values over commercialism. So upon the death of the Yongle Emperor, the great treasure ships were sunk and new laws were passed that made the possession of any ship with more than two masts a crime. In time, even the records of Zheng He's fleets and travels were burned.

Sean Yong/Reuters

ANALYZE AND INTERPRET

What might have been the long-term effects of these voyages had they not been stopped? How might history have been changed?

ZHENG HE'S SHIP. This is a full-size replica at the site of the shipyard where original ship was built in Nanjing, China.

SCIENCE AND TECHNOLOGY

Chinese Inventions

In the sixteenth century, an Italian priest named Matteo Ricci was invited by the emperor to reside at the court in Beijing in the capacity of court astronomer. Ricci had learned Chinese and drew on his learned background in the sciences to both instruct and entertain his hosts. His journals were published shortly after his death in 1610 and gave Europeans their first eyewitness glimpse of the Ming Dynasty civilization and the first knowledgeable insight into Chinese affairs since Marco Polo's report three centuries earlier.

> All of the known metals, without exception, are to be found in China.... From molten iron they fashion many more things than we do, for example, cauldrons, pots, bells, gongs, mortars ... martial weapons, instruments of torture, and a great number of other things equal in workmanship to our own metalcraft....
>
> The ordinary tableware of the Chinese is clay pottery. There is nothing like it in European pottery either from the standpoint of the material itself or its thin and fragile construction. The finest specimens of porcelain are made from clay found in the province of Kiam and these are shipped not only to every part of China but even to the remotest corners of Europe where they are highly prized.
>
> Finally we should say something about the saltpeter, which is used in lavish quantities in making fireworks for display at public games and on festival days. The Chinese make them the chief attraction of all their festivities. Their skill in the manufacture of fireworks is really extraordinary and there is scarcely anything which they cannot cleverly imitate with them. They are especially adept at reproducing battles and in making rotating spheres of fire, fiery trees, fruit, and the like, and they seem to have no regard for expense where fireworks are concerned....

The art of printing was practiced in China at a date somewhat earlier than that assigned to the beginning of printing in Europe.... It is quite certain that the Chinese knew the art of printing at least five centuries ago, and some of them assert that printing was known to their people before the beginning of the Christian era....

> Their method of making printed books is quite ingenious. The text is written in ink, with a brush made of very fine hair, on a sheet of paper which is inverted and pasted on a wooden tablet. When the paper has become thoroughly dry, its surface is scraped off quickly and with great skill, until nothing but a fine tissue bearing the characters remains on the wooden tablet. Then with a steel graver, the workman cuts away the surface following the outlines of the characters, until these alone stand out in low relief. From such a block a skilled printer can make copies with incredible speed, turning out as many as fifteen hundred copies in a single day. Chinese printers are so skilled at turning out these blocks that no more time is consumed in making one of them than would be required by one of our printers in setting up a form of [moveable metallic] type and making the necessary corrections....
>
> The simplicity of Chinese printing is what accounts for the exceedingly large number of books in circulation here and the ridiculously low prices at which they are sold. Such facts as these would scarcely be believed by one who had not witnessed them.

ANALYZE AND INTERPRET

Why do you think the Chinese did not use gunpowder technology in war as in entertainments? In light of what Ricci reports, was the contemporary European preference for metallic type justified?

Source: The Diary of Matthew Ricci, in Matthew Ricci, China in the Sixteenth Century, trans Louis Gallagher, (New York: Random House, 1942, 1970).

MANZHOU INVADERS: THE QING DYNASTY

The end of the Ming Dynasty came after a slow, painful decline in the mid-seventeenth century. A series of ineffective emperors had allowed government power to slip into the hands of corrupt and hated eunuchs, who made decisions on the basis of bribes, without responsibility for their consequences. Court cliques contended for supreme power. The costs of the multitude of imperial court officials and hangers-on were enormous and could be met only by squeezing taxes out of an already hard-pressed peasantry.

Peasant rebellions began to multiply as the government's ability to restrain rapacious landlords declined. The administrative apparatus, which the eunuch cliques at court had undermined, ceased to function. Adding to the troubles was the popularity among the mandarins of an extreme version of scholarly Confucianism that rejected innovation.

The Manzhou (man-choo) tribesmen living north of the Great Wall in **Manchuria** had paid tribute to the Beijing emperor but had never accepted his overlordship. When the rebellions led to anarchy in several northern provinces, the Manzhou saw their chance. The Manzhou governing group admired Chinese culture and made it clear that if and when they were victorious, conservative Chinese would have nothing to fear from them. Presenting themselves as the alternative to banditry and even revolution, the Manzhou invaders gradually won the support of much of the mandarin class. One province after another went over to them rather than face continuous rebellion. The last Ming ruler, faced with certain defeat, committed suicide. Thus was founded the last dynasty of imperial China, the Manzhou or Qing (ching) Dynasty (1664–1911). In its opening generations, it was to be one of the most successful as well.

Qing Government

When the **Qing Dynasty** was at the apex of its power and wealth, China had by far the largest population under one government and the largest territory of any country in the world (see Map 26.1). China reached its largest territorial extent at this time. The Qing had been close to Chinese civilization for many years and had become partially Sinicized (adopted Chinese culture), so the transition from Ming to Qing rule was nothing like the upheaval that had followed the Mongol conquest in the 1200s. Many Ming officials and generals joined with the conquerors voluntarily from the start. Many others joined under pressure or as it became apparent that the Qing were not savages and were adopting Chinese traditions in government. Two individuals, in fact, occupied high positions in the central and even the provincial governments: one Manzhou, the other one was Chinese. Manzhou officials oversaw Chinese provincial governors, and the army was sharply divided between the two ethnic groups, with the Qing having superior status as the so-called Bannermen, who occupied key garrisons.

Like most new dynasties, the Qing were strong reformers in their early years, bringing order and respect for authority, snapping the whip over insubordinate officials in the provinces, and attempting to ensure justice in the villages. The two greatest Qing leaders were the emperors Kangxi (kang-shee; ruling 1662–1722) and his grandson Qienlong (chyen-loong; ruling 1736–1795). Their unusually long reigns allowed them to put their stamps on the bureaucracy and develop long-range policies. Both were strong personalities, intelligent, and well-educated men who approached their duties with the greatest seriousness. Both attempted to keep the Manzhou tribesmen and the ethnic Chinese separate to some degree, although the Manzhou were always a tiny minority (perhaps 2 percent) of the population and were steadily Sinicized after the early 1700s by intermarriage and free choice. Kangxi was the almost exact contemporary of Louis XIV of France and, like him, was the longest-lived ruler of his country's history. From all accounts, Kangxi was a remarkable man with a quick intellect and a fine gift for administration. He retained the traditional Chinese system of six ministries advising and implementing the decrees of the Son of Heaven in Beijing. He did much to improve the waterways, which were always of great importance for transportation in China. Rivers were dredged, and canals and dams built. He was particularly active in economic policy making, both domestically and toward the Western merchants whose vessels were now starting to appear regularly in Chinese ports. After decades of negotiations, Kangxi opened four ports to European traders and allowed them to set up small, permanent enclaves there. This decision was to have fateful consequences in the mid-nineteenth century, when the Beijing government was in much weaker hands.

Kangxi's grandson, Qienlong, was a great warrior and perceptive administrator. He eradicated the persistent Mongol raiders on the western borders and brought Tibet under Chinese control for the first time (see Map 26.1). The peculiar fashion of dealing with neighboring independent kingdoms such as Korea as though they were voluntary satellites of China (tributaries) was extended to much of Southeast Asia at this time. Qienlong ruled through the last two-thirds of the eighteenth century, and we know a good deal about both him and his grandfather because Jesuit missionaries still resided in Beijing during this era. Their perceptive reports to Rome contributed to the interest in everything Chinese that was so manifest in late eighteenth-century Europe.

The early Qing emperors were unusually vigorous leaders, and the Chinese economy and society responded positively to their lengthy rule until the mid-nineteenth century, when the dynasty's power and prestige suffered under a combination of Western military intrusions and a growing population crisis. (This period is covered in Chapter 37.)

QING CULTURE AND ECONOMY

Although the Qing were originally looked upon as foreign barbarians and they exerted themselves to remain separate from the Chinese masses, no break in fundamental cultural styles occurred between the Ming and Qing dynasties. As in earlier China, the most respected cultural activities were philosophy, history, calligraphy, poetry, and painting. In literature, a new form matured in the 1500s: the novel. Perhaps inspired by the Japanese example, a series of written stories about both gentry life and ordinary people appeared during the late Ming and Qing eras. Best known are the *Book of the Golden Lotus* and ***The Dream of the Red Chamber***, the latter a product of the eighteenth century. Most of the authors are unknown, and the books that have survived are probably only a small portion of those that were actually produced. Some of the stories are pornographic, a variety of literature that the Chinese evidently enjoyed despite official disapproval.

Porcelain reached such artistry in the eighteenth century that it became a major form of Chinese aesthetic creation. Throughout the Western world, the wealthy sought fine "china" as tableware and objets d'art and were willing to pay nearly any price for the beautiful blue-and-white Ming wares brought back by the Dutch and English ships from the South China ports. Chinese painting on scrolls and screens was also imported in large amounts, as were silks and other luxury items for the households of the nobility and wealthy urbanites. The popular decorative style termed *chinoiserie* (shin-WAH-seh-ree) reflected late-eighteenth-century Europe's admiration for Chinese artifacts and good taste. The clipper ships of New England made the long voyage around Cape Horn and across the Pacific in the first half of the nineteenth century to reap enormous profits carrying luxury goods in both directions: sea otter furs from Alaska and the Pacific Northwest and porcelain, tea, and jade from China.

During the Ming and Qing periods, far more people were participating in the creation and enjoyment of formal culture than ever before. By the 1700s, China had a large number of educated people who were able to purchase the tangible goods produced by a host of skilled artists. Schools and academies of higher learning educated the children of anyone who could afford the fees—generally members of the scholar-official class who had been governing China since the Han Dynasty.

In this era (from the 1500s on), however, China definitely lost to the West its lead in science and technology, which it had maintained for the previous thousand years. Developing a sensitivity to beauty, such as the art of calligraphy, was considered as essential to proper education in China as mastering literacy and basic math. Painting, poetry, and meditation were considered far more important than physics or accounting or chemistry. This ongoing downgrading of the quantitative sciences and the technical advances they spawned in the West was to be a massively negative turning point in international power relations for China. Aesthetic sensitivities and artistic excellence proved to be little aid when confronted by cannons and steam engines.

Progress and Problems

Among the outstanding achievements of the early Qing emperors were improvements in agriculture and engineering that benefited uncounted numbers of ordinary Chinese. Kangxi, for example, did much to ensure that the South China "rice bowl" was made even more productive and that the Grand Canal linking the Yellow River with the central coast ports and the Yangzi basin was kept in good order. New hybrid rice allowed rice culture to be extended and increased yields, which in turn supported an expansion in population.

Internal trade in the large cities and many market towns continued the upsurge that had begun during the Ming Dynasty and became ever more important in this era. Although most Chinese—perhaps 80 percent—remained villagers working the land, there were now large numbers of shopkeepers, market porters, carters, artisans, moneylenders, and all the other occupations of commercial life. Money circulated freely as both coin and paper, the coins being minted of Spanish silver brought from the South American colonies to Manila and Guangzhou to trade for silk and porcelain.

All in all, the Chinese in the early Qing period were probably living as well as any other people in the world, and better than most Europeans. But this high standard of living worsened in later days, when for the first time the population's growth exceeded the ability of the agrarian economy to allow suitable productive work for it. By the nineteenth century, almost all of the land that had adequate precipitation or was easily irrigable for crops had already been brought under the plow. The major improvements possible in rice farming had already been made, and yields did not continue to rise as they had previously. Machine industry had not yet arrived in China (and would not for many years), and trade with the outside world was narrowly focused and on a relatively small scale that government policy refused to expand. (China wanted few material things from the non-Chinese, in any case.) In the nineteenth century, rural China began to experience massive famines and endemic poverty that were the result of too-rapid growth in population in a technically backward society without the desire or means to shift to new production modes.

MING VASE. This superb example of Chinese porcelain was made in the seventeenth century, possibly for the developing export trade with Europe.

Ming vase with three colour decoration (porcelain), Chinese School/Musee Guimet, Paris, France/The Bridgeman Art Library

SUMMARY

The overthrow of the Mongols introduced another of the great Chinese dynasties: the Ming. Blessed by exceptionally able emperors in the early decades, the Ming imitated their Tang Dynasty model and made notable improvements in agriculture and commerce. Urban life expanded, and the urban bourgeoisie of merchants became economically (but not politically) important. The borders were extended well to the west and north, and the barbarian nomads thrust once again behind the Great Wall for a couple of centuries.

In the classic pattern, however, the Ming's grip on government and people weakened, and the costs of a huge court and army pressed heavily on the overtaxed population. When rebellions began in the northern provinces, the people were encouraged by the promises of change offered by the invading Manzhou in the northeast. Triumphant, the Manzhou leader began the final dynastic period in China's three-thousand-year history—that of the Qing.

The two first Qing emperors were extraordinarily able men, who in the eighteenth century led China to one of the summits of its national existence. The economy prospered, and overpopulation was not yet a problem. In the arts, there was extraordinary refinement and development of new literary forms. But in science and technology, China now lagged far behind the West, and the coming century would be filled with political and cultural humiliations. China entered the modern age unprepared to handle the types of problems that it faced on the eve of the European intrusion: growing impoverishment, military backwardness, and technical retardation. First the Europeans and then the Japanese would find ways to take advantage of these handicaps.

IDENTIFICATION TERMS

Test your knowledge of this chapter's key concepts by defining the following terms. If you can not recall the meaning of certain terms, refresh your memory by looking up the boldfaced term in the chapter, turning to the Glossary at the end of the book, or accessing the terms on the CourseMate website at **www.cengagebrain.com.**

Forbidden City
Manchuria
Maritime Expeditions
Ming Dynasty
Qing Dynasty
The Dream of the Red Chamber
xenophobia
Zheng He

FOR FURTHER REFLECTION

1. Despite the fact that this was an era of expansion for Europeans, China remained unaffected by these developments. Is this statement true or false? Be sure to explain your answer.
2. Was this an era of growth and continued innovation for China, or was it a period of decline?
3. What were the reasons for China's brief period of exploration in the fifteenth century? Why do you think it came to such an abrupt end?

TEST YOUR KNOWLEDGE

Test your knowledge of this chapter by answering the following questions. Complete answers appear at the end of the book. You may find even more quiz questions on the CourseMate website at **www.cengagebrain.com.**

1. The most serious menace to China's stability during the 1300s and 1400s was
   a. the Japanese coastal pirates.
   b. the Mongol conquerors from the north.
   c. the conspiracies of the palace eunuchs.
   d. the invasions of the Vietnamese in the south.
   e. the isolation that caused the Chinese to fall behind the rest of the world.
2. China's Ming dynasty of emperors succeeded what dynasty?
   a. Zhou.
   b. Song.
   c. Tang.
   d. Yuan (Mongol).
   e. Qin.
3. Which Native American food crop did *not* become popular in China?
   a. peanuts.
   b. beans.
   c. squash.
   d. corn.
   e. potatoes

4. The emperor Hongwu initiated a period during which only the _______ had direct access to the emperor.
   a. royal family
   b. leading merchants
   c. government officials
   d. palace eunuchs
   e. military leaders
5. During the Ming/Qing era, China was ruled by a bureaucracy that was
   a. selected on the basis of aristocratic birth.
   b. controlled by a professional military establishment.
   c. dominated by the Buddhist priesthood.
   d. selected on the basis of written examinations.
   e. unconcerned about the Chinese peasantry.
6. During the Ming period, Chinese-Japanese contacts were
   a. thriving on a number of fronts, both commercial and cultural.
   b. restricted to occasional commerce and raids by Japanese pirates.
   c. hostile and infrequent.
   d. marked by the Japanese willingness to accept China's dominance.
   e. exceptional, in that the Chinese adopted Japanese technology.
7. The great Chinese admiral Zheng He was a
   a. Ming emperor.
   b. Mongol.
   c. Muslim eunuch.
   d. Qing emperor.
   e. Mandarin scholar.
8. The replacement of the Ming by the Qing Dynasty was
   a. caused by a Japanese invasion of China and a collapse of the Ming.
   b. a gradual armed takeover from a demoralized government.
   c. carried out by Westerners, who were anxious to install a "tame" government in Beijing.
   d. caused by Western Christian missionaries hostile to the Ming.
   e. the natural result of cultural interaction between the two groups.
9. The outstanding Qing emperors of the eighteenth century
   a. learned much of political value to them from the West.
   b. were cruel tyrants in their treatment of the common Chinese.
   c. split governmental responsibility between Qing and Chinese.
   d. tried hard to expand commerce between China and Europe.
   e. rejected the traditional Chinese bureaucracy in favor of absolute rule.
10. Which of the following did not figure prominently in Qing cultural achievement?
   a. Poetry
   b. Landscape painting
   c. Theology
   d. Fictional narratives
   e. Calligraphy

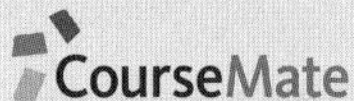

Visit the CourseMate website at **www.cengagebrain.com** for additional study tools and review materials for this chapter.

Japan and Southeast Asia in the Era of European Expansion

27

The white chrysanthemum
Even when lifted to the eye
Remains immaculate. —BASHO

CHAPTER OUTLINE

c. 1200–1600	Malaysians and Indonesians convert to Islam
1521	Portuguese seize control of Malacca
1543	First European contacts with Japan
c. 1600	Tokugawa Shogunate established in Japan
c. 1630s	Christianity suppressed in Japan; foreigners expelled; sakoku begins
1600s–1700s	Money economy and commercial society develop in Japan

Before the 1500s, the Japanese islands' contacts with the outer world were only with Korea and China. The arrival of Portuguese trader–explorers brought change to a substantial segment of society, which adopted Christian belief. But this trend was later reversed by government action, and in a remarkable turnabout, the Japanese entered a long period of self-imposed seclusion.

Southeast Asia also experienced the European outreach, but in a highly localized and restricted manner, linked to the exclusive interest of the newcomers in the spice trade. Only much later, in the nineteenth century, did Europeans begin to develop Southeast Asian colonies.

JAPAN

Although akin to China in some ways, Japan was different in many others. The political power of the emperor in Kyoto was weak throughout early modern times, and Japan became a collection of feudal provinces controlled by clans. In the century between the 1460s and the 1570s, the warrior-nobles (**daimyo**: DEYE-mee-oh) had engaged in a frenzy of the "strong eating the weak." Finally, a series of military strongmen managed to restore order, culminating in the establishment of a type of centralized feudalism: the *Shogunate*.

The first European contacts occurred in the mid-1500s, when traders and missionaries were allowed to establish themselves on Japanese soil. One of the most important trade items brought by the Portuguese was firearms. Another was the Christian Bible. Contacts with Europe were complicated by Japanese distrust of the Christian faith and its hints of submission to an alien culture. The shogun eventually decided that this danger was intolerable. Within a generation's time, Japan withdrew behind a wall of enforced isolation from the world, from which it would not emerge until the nineteenth century.

FIRST EUROPEAN CONTACTS: CHRISTIANITY

The Portuguese arrived in Japanese ports for the first time in 1543, looking for additional opportunities to make money from their active trading with all the Eastern countries. They took Chinese silk to Japan and Japanese silver to China and used the profits from both to buy spices in the South Pacific islands to bring back to Portugal.

One of the first influences from the West to reach the thus-far isolated Japanese was Christianity, which arrived via the numerous Catholic missionaries sponsored by the Society of Jesus (Jesuits). The Jesuit order had been founded to fight Protestantism only a few years previously, and its missionaries were well educated and highly motivated. For opportunities to trade and to acquire new military technologies, a fair number of the daimyo were sympathetic to the Jesuit efforts and converted to Christianity during the 1550s and 1560s. By the year 1600, it is estimated that 300,000 Japanese had converted. That number would have constituted a far higher percentage of the population than do Japanese Christians in modern times.

ARRIVAL OF THE PORTUGUESE. Note the black slave unloading the goods, showing that the Portuguese were already using black labor in their trans-Indian Ocean trade in the first half of the seventeenth century. The Japanese observer is possibly the merchant for whom the goods were consigned, and the monkey is the ship's mascot.

At this time, most Japanese were adherents of either Shinto or one of the many varieties of Buddhism. Why did the ruling group allow the missionaries free access to the people? And why did the Japanese initially prove more receptive to Christianity than had, for example, the Chinese or the Indians? It is impossible to say with certainty. One reason was the personal example of the Jesuits, led by St. Francis Xavier, who greatly impressed their hosts with their piety and learning.

Other changes were under way. In the later 1500s, a movement for Japanese national unity led by Oda Nobunaga (OH-dah noh-buh-NAH-gah; 1523–1582), a feudal lord who had fought his way to regional power, was beginning. In the 1570s, the brutal Nobunaga succeeded in capturing Kyoto and most of the central island of Honshu, but he was killed by one of his cohorts. Following Nobunaga's death, his lieutenant Toyotomi Hideyoshi (toh-yoh-TOH-mee hee-deh-YOH-shee) took over. Aided by the first large-scale use of firearms in Japan, Hideyoshi had visions of Asian, if not worldwide, supremacy. He invaded Korea as a first step toward the conquest of Ming China. Repulsed in 1592, he was in the midst of a second attempt when he died in 1598. After a few years of struggle the formidable warrior and statesman **Tokugawa Ieyasu** (toh-koo-GAH-wah ee-eh-YAH-soo; ruling 1603–1616) seized the baton (see the Law and Government box).

Tokugawa ceased the abortive invasion of the mainland and by 1600 had beaten down his several internal rivals. Thus began the 250 years of the Tokugawa Shogunate, a military regency exercised in the name of an emperor who had become largely a figurehead. Tokugawa "ate the pie that Nobunaga made and Hideyoshi baked" goes the schoolchildren's axiom in modern Japan. He was the decisive figure in premodern Japanese history, using a selective violence against the daimyo to permit a special form of centralized governance.

THE TOKUGAWA SHOGUNATE

Once in power, Tokugawa continued and expanded the changes that Hideyoshi had begun. By disarming the peasants, Tokugawa removed much of the source of the rebellions that had haunted Japan during the preceding century. From this time on, only the professional warrior class, the samurai, and their daimyo employers had the right to own weapons. The daimyo, who were roughly equivalent to the barons of Europe some centuries previously, were expected to spend half their time at the court of the shogun, where they would be under the watchful eyes of the shogun and his network of informers.

In the early 1600s, the Tokugawa shoguns began to withdraw Japan into seclusion from outside influences. Hideyoshi had previously had misgivings about the activities of the Jesuits within his domains, and in

LAW AND GOVERNMENT

Tokugawa Ieyasu (1542–1616)

On March 8, 1616, Shogun Ieyasu died. According to his wish, he was buried in Nikko, a beautiful wood ninety miles north of Tokyo. His tomb stands at the end of a long avenue of great gardens. Posthumously, Tokugawa was given the title, "Noble of the First Rank, Great Light of the East, Great Incarnation of the Buddha." He was already acknowledged as the individual who brought law to a lawless society.

Tokugawa Ieyasu (that is, Ieyasu of the Tokugawa clan) was born in 1642. During the last decades of the sixteenth century, he became an ally of Toyotomi Hideyoshi, the most powerful of all the feudal aristocrats who divided the country among themselves.

When Hideyoshi died unexpectedly in 1598, Ieyasu and another man were the prime candidates to succeed him. Tokugawa assembled a force of 80,000 feudal warriors, and his opponent led a coalition of 130,000. In the decisive battle of Sekigahara in 1600, the outnumbered Tokugawa forces claimed the field. In the next few years, Ieyasu destroyed the coalition's resistance and secured the shogun's office for himself and his second son. Ieyasu's victory was a turning point of great importance. For the next 250 years, the Japanese were forced to live in peace with one another. This "Era of Great Peace" was marked by the Tokugawa clan's uninterrupted control of the Shogunate in Edo (Tokyo), while the semidivine emperor resided in Kyoto and remained the symbolic center of Japanese patriotism.

Ieyasu was an extraordinarily gifted man. Coming out of the samurai tradition of military training, he was nevertheless able to appreciate the blessings of a permanent peace. He carefully redivided the feudal lords' domains throughout the islands to ensure his control over all of them. He established the daimyo as the officials of his kingdom. They were given considerable freedom to do as they pleased in their own backyards, so long as their loyalty to the shogun was not in doubt. Ieyasu and his successors in the 1600s did much to improve and nationalize Japan's economy, particularly among the peasant majority. The *heimin* (high-MIHN), or plain folk, were divided into three basic groups: farmers, artisans, and traders, in that rank order. Farmers were generally regarded as honorable people, whereas traders were originally looked down upon, as in China. At the bottom of the social scale, were the despised common people, who were the equivalent to the Indian untouchables. Unlike the untouchables, however, the commoners were able to rise in status.

In many ways, Tokugawa Ieyasu was the father of traditional Japan. The political institutions of the country did not change in any significant way after him until the late nineteenth century. He lives on in the pantheon of Japan's heroes as a model of military virtue who reluctantly employed harsh and even brutal measures to bring about the rule of law in a lawless society.

ANALYZE AND INTERPRET

Would there have been many alternatives to Tokugawa's method of imposing order in sixteenth-century Japan? What problems may arise from having absolute powers supposedly in one man's (the emperor's) hands, while another actually exercises them? How might this arrangement be compared to similar situations throughout history (for example, the later Abbasid caliphate, as in Chapter 15)?

Portrait of Tokugawa Ieyasu (1543-1616), Japanese, 17th century, Japanese School, (17th century)/Private Collection/The Bridgeman Art Library

TOKUGAWA IEYASU. This portrait was done after the powerful warrior had ensured his position as shogun in 1603.

1587, he had issued an order (which was later revoked) that they should leave. After newly arrived members of the Franciscan Order attempted to meddle in the Shogunate's internal affairs, Tokugawa acted. He evicted the Christian missionaries who had been in the country for half a century and put heavy pressure on the Christian Japanese to reconvert to Buddhism. After Christian peasants supported a revolt in 1637, pressure turned into outright persecution. Death became the standard penalty for Christian affiliation. In a few places, the Christians maintained their faith through "underground" churches and priests, but the majority gradually gave up their religion in the face of heavy state penalties and their neighbors' antagonism.

At the same time, Japan's extensive mercantile contacts with the Europeans and the Chinese were almost entirely severed. Only a handful of Dutch and Portuguese traders/residents were allowed to remain in two ports (notably, Nagasaki, where two Dutch ships coming from the East Indies were allowed to land each year). (See Map 27.1.) The building of oceangoing ships by the Japanese was forbidden. No foreigners could come to Japan, and no Japanese were allowed to reside abroad (with a few exceptions). Japanese who were living abroad were forbidden to return. The previously lively trade with China was sharply curtailed.

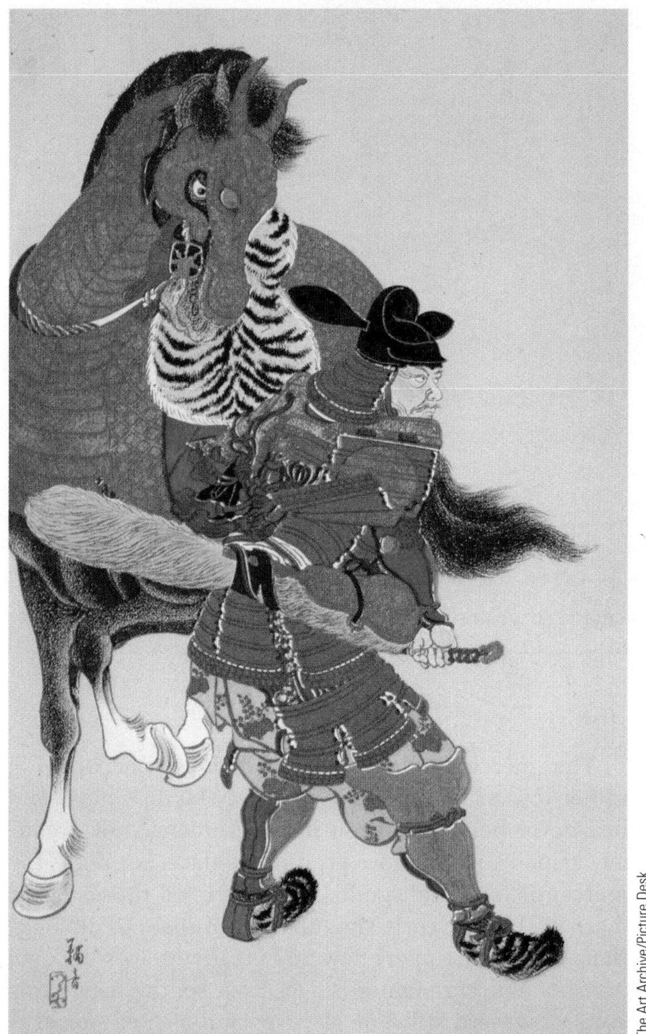

HIDEYOSHI AS SAMURAI. This later illustration of General Hideyoshi allows close inspection of the traditional samurai costume and weapons.

This isolation (called **sakoku** in Japanese history; pronounced sah-KOH-koo) lasted until the mid-nineteenth century. It was a remarkable experiment with highly successful results so far as the ruling group was concerned. Japan went its own way and was ignored by the rest of the world.

Shogun, Emperor, and Daimyo

The Tokugawa shoguns continued the dual nature of Japanese government, whereby the Shogunate was established at **Edo** (EH-doh; later renamed Tokyo), while the emperor resided in the imperial palace at Kyoto and occupied himself with ritual and ceremony as the current holder of the lineage of the Sun Goddess who had created Japan eons previously (see Chapter 19). True power in both a military and a political sense remained with the shogun, who now headed a council of state composed of daimyo aristocrats. An individual who was always a member of the Tokugawa clan acted in the name of the emperor, closely overseeing some twenty large and perhaps two hundred small land-holding daimyo. The daimyo acted both as his agents and as autonomous regents in their own domains. The shogun controlled about one-fourth of Japan as his own fiefdom. This system continued without important change until 1867.

The daimyo were the key players in governance and posed a constant potential threat to Tokugawa's arrangements. As the source of military power on the local level, they could tear down any shogun if they united against him. Therefore, to secure the center, the shogun had to play the daimyo against each other in the countryside. He did this by constant intervention and manipulation, setting one clan against another in the competition for imperial favor. The shogun controlled the domains near Edo or put them in the hands of dependable allies. Domains on the outlying islands went to rival daimyo clans, which would counterbalance one another. Meanwhile, the wives and children of the more important daimyo families were required to live permanently at Edo, where they served as hostages for loyal behavior. The whole system of supervision and surveillance much resembled Louis XIV's arrangements at Versailles in seventeenth-century France.

Economic Advances

Japan's society and economy changed markedly during these centuries of isolation. One of the most remarkable results of sakoku was the great growth of population and

MAP 27.1 Tokugawa Japan
The Japanese islands during the period of *sakoku*, which lasted until the mid-nineteenth century. Key cities, including the Shoganate's capital, Edo, are shown.

THINKING ABOUT THIS MAP

What features of Japan's physical geography might have made social and political unity difficult?

domestic trade. The population doubled in the seventeenth century and continued to increase gradually throughout the remainder of the Tokugawa period. Closing off trade with foreigners apparently stimulated internal production rather than discouraged it, and domestic trade rose accordingly. The internal peace imposed by the powerful and respected government of the Shoganate certainly helped. The daimyo aristocracy had an ever-increasing appetite for fine wares such as silk and ceramics. Their fortress-palaces in Edo and on their domains reflected both their more refined taste and their increasing ability to satisfy it.

The merchants, who had previously occupied a rather low niche in Japanese society (as in China) and had never been important in government, now gradually gained a much more prominent place. Formerly, the mercantile and craft guilds had restricted the access to markets, but the early shoguns forced them to dissolve, thereby allowing many new and creative actors to come onto the entrepreneurial stage. Even so, the merchants as a class were still not as respected as were government officials, scholars, and especially the daimyo and their samurai. Nevertheless, the merchants' growing wealth, which they often lent—at high interest—to

SUNRISE. This wood cut by the famed engraver Hiroshige (1797–1858) shows a typical procession of laborers going to work in a seaside town while the fishermen raise sail and the rice sellers ready their booths for the morning trade along the quay. The long net is presumably for capturing birds that will be put into the cages and sold.

impoverished samurai, began to enhance their prestige. A money economy gradually replaced the universal reliance on barter in the villages.

Commercialization and distribution networks for artisans invaded the previously self-sufficient lifestyle of the country folk. Banks and the use of credit became more common during the later Tokugawa period. Some historians see the growth of a specifically Japanese form of capitalism long before Japan's entry into the world economic system in the later nineteenth century.

Peasants and Urbanites

The condition of the peasants, who still made up the vast majority of the population, improved somewhat under the early Tokugawa regime. Since the beginnings of the Shoganate under the Fujiwara (foo-jee-WAH-rah) clan, the peasantry had been sacrificed to keep the daimyo and their samurai retainers satisfied. In most of the Japanese lands, the peasant was no better than a serf and lived in misery. In the early Tokugawa era, the peasants received some protection from exploitation, and the shogun's government claimed that agriculture was the most honorable of ordinary occupations. But the government's taxes were heavy, taking up to 60 percent of the rice crop, which was by far the most important harvest. In later years, the increasing misery of some peasants led to many provincial rebellions, not against the shogun but against the local daimyo who were the peasants' landlords. These revolts, although numerous, were on a much smaller scale than those that would trouble Manchu (Qing) China in the same nineteenth-century epoch.

Cities grew rapidly during the first half of the Tokugawa period but more slowly later. Both Osaka (oh-SAH-kah) and Kyoto were estimated to have more than 400,000 inhabitants in the eighteenth century, and Edo perhaps as many as 1 million. All three cities were bigger than any town in Europe at that date. The urban population ranged from wealthy daimyo and merchants at the top; through tens of thousands of less fortunate traders, shopkeepers, and officials of all types in the middle; and to many hundreds of thousands of skilled and unskilled workers, casual laborers, beggars, prostitutes, artists, and the unlucky samurai at the bottom. Most Japanese, however, still lived as before in small towns and villages. They depended on local farming, timbering, or fishing for their livelihood and had only occasional and superficial contact with the urban culture. Until the twentieth century, the rhythms of country life and the rice culture were the dominant influence on the self-image and the lifestyle of the Japanese people.

TAMING THE SAMURAI

In the seventeenth and eighteenth centuries, the samurai caste, which had been the military servants of the wealthy daimyo and their "enforcers" with the peasants, lost most of its prestige in Japanese society. Estimated to make up as much as 7 percent of the population at the time of the establishment of the Tokugawa regime, the samurai had now become superfluous.

With the creation of the lasting domestic peace, there was literally nothing for them to do in their traditional profession. They were not allowed to become merchants or to adopt another lifestyle, nor could they easily bring themselves to do so after centuries of proud segregation from the common herd. The Edo government encouraged the samurai to do what they naturally wished to do: enjoy themselves beyond their means. Borrowing a page from the merchants, the samurai tried to outdo one another in every sort of showy display. After a generation or two, the result was mass bankruptcies and social disgrace.

The fallen samurai were replaced in social status by newcomers, who were finding that they could advance through commerce or through the civil bureaucracy. As in the West, this bureaucracy was slowly assuming the place of the feudal barons and becoming the day-to-day authority in governance. The samurai lost out to a new class of people: men who did not know how to wield a sword but were good with a pen. Trained only to make war and raised in the *bushido* (boo-SHEE-doh) code of the warrior, most of the samurai were ill equipped to transition from warrior to a desk-sitting official of the shogun or a daimyo lord. Most samurai seem to have gradually sunk into poverty and loss of status as they reverted to the peasant life of their long-ago ancestors.

TOKUGAWA ARTS AND LEARNING

The almost-250 years of peace of the Tokugawa period produced a rich tapestry of new cultural ideas and practices in Japan. Some of the older ideas, originally imported from China, were now adapted to become almost entirely Japanese in form and content. The upper classes continued to prefer Buddhism in one form or another, with a strong admixture of Confucian secular ethics. Among the people, Shinto and the less intellectual forms of Buddhism formed the matrix of belief about this world and the next. Japanese religious style tended to accept human nature as it is without the overtones of penitence and reform so prominent in Western thought. As before, a strong current of eclecticism blended Buddhism with other systems of belief and practice.

Literature and Its Audiences

Literacy rates were quite high in Japan and continued to increase in the later years of the Tokugawa period, when perhaps as many as 50 percent of the males could read the cheap product of wood-block printing presses and write. This percentage was at least equal to the literacy rate in central Europe in those days and was facilitated by the relative ease of learning the phonetic written language (in distinct contrast to Chinese, the original source of Japanese writing).

Literature aimed at popular entertainment began to appear in new forms that were a far cry from the elegant and restrained traditions of the past. Poetry, novels, social satires, and Kabuki plays were the foremost types of literature. By this era, all of these forms had been liberated from imitation of classical Chinese models, and several were entirely original to the Japanese.

Haiku (HEYE-koo) poems, especially in the hands of the revered seventeenth-century poet Basho, were extraordinarily compact revelations of profound thought. In three lines and seventeen syllables (always), the poet reflected the Zen Buddhist conviction that the greatest of mysteries can only be stated—never analyzed. Saikaku's contributions in fiction matched those of Basho in poetry, also during the late seventeenth century. His novels and stories about ordinary people are noteworthy for their passion and the underlying sense of comedy with which the characters are observed. Saikaku's stories, like Basho's verse, are read today in Japan with the same admiration afforded to them for centuries.

Kabuki (kah-BOO-kee) is a peculiarly Japanese form of drama. It is highly realistic, often humorous and satirical, and sometimes violent in both action and emotions. For its settings, it often used the "floating world," the unstable but attractive world of brothels, shady teahouses, and gambling dens. Kabuki was wildly popular among the upper classes in seventeenth- and eighteenth-century Japan. It was not unusual for a particularly successful actor (males played all parts) to become a pampered "star." Actors were often also male prostitutes, just as actresses in the West were often female prostitutes at this time. Homosexuality was strongly frowned on by the Shoganate authorities, but it had already had a long tradition among the samurai and in some branches of Buddhism.

Adaptation and Originality

In the fine arts, Japan may have drawn its initial inspiration from Chinese models, but it always turned those models into something different, something specifically Japanese. This pattern can be found in landscape painting, poetry, adventure and romance stories, gardens, and ceramics—in any art medium that both peoples have pursued.

The Japanese versions were often filled with a playful humor that was missing in the Chinese original and were almost always consciously close to nature, the soil, and the peasantry. The refined intellectualism common to Chinese arts appeared less frequently in Japan. As a random example, the rough-and-tumble of Kabuki and the pornographic jokes that the actors constantly employed were specifically Japanese and had no close equivalent in China.

The merchants who had prospered during the Tokugawa era were especially important as patrons of the arts. Again, a parallel can be drawn to the European experience, but with differences. The European bourgeoisie became important commissioners of art two centuries earlier than the Japanese merchants and did so in self-confident rivalry with the nobles and the church. Japan had no established church, and the bourgeoisie never dared challenge the daimyo nobility for taste-setting primacy. Nevertheless, high-quality paintings and woodblock prints displaying a tremendous variety of subjects and techniques came to adorn the homes and collections of the rich merchants. In fact, much of what the modern world knows of seventeenth- and eighteenth-century Japanese society is attributable to the knowing eye and talented hands of the artists rather than to historians. Unlike the Chinese, the Japanese never revered compilers of records. There are no Japanese equivalents of the great Chinese histories.

RESPONSE TO THE WESTERN CHALLENGE

In the later Tokugawa, the main emphasis of Japanese thought shifted from Buddhist to Confucian ideals, which is another way of saying that it changed from an otherworldly emphasis to an empirical concern with this world. The Japanese version of Confucianism was, as always, different from the Chinese. The secular, politically pragmatic nature of Confucius's doctrines comes through more emphatically in Japan. The Chinese mandarins of the nineteenth century had little tolerance for deviation from the prescribed version of the Master. But in Japan, several schools of thought contended and were unimpeded by an official prescription of right and wrong. Another difference was that whereas China had no room for a shogun, Japan had no room for the mandate of Heaven. Chinese tradition held that only China could be the Confucian "Empire of the Middle." The Japanese, on the other hand, although confident that they were in that desirable position of centrality and balance, believed that they need not ignore the achievements of other less fortunate but not entirely misguided folk.

What was the significance of this pragmatic secularism for Japan? It helped prepare the ruling daimyo group for the invasion of Western ideas that came in the mid-nineteenth century. The Japanese elite were able to abandon their seclusion and investigate whatever Western technology could offer them with an open mind. In sharp contrast to China, when the Western avalanche could no longer be evaded, the Japanese governing class accepted it with little inherent resistance or cultural confusion.

At the outset of the Tokugawa Shoganate, the Japanese educated classes were perhaps as familiar with science and technology as were the Westerners. Sakoku necessarily inhibited further progress. The Scientific Revolution and its accompanying technological advances were unknown in Japan, and the Enlightenment of the eighteenth century was equally foreign to the cultural landscape of even the most refined citizens (see Chapter 29). From the early 1800s, a few Japanese scholars and officials were aware that the West (including nearby Russia) was well ahead of them in certain areas—especially the natural sciences and medicine—and that much could be learned from the Westerners. These Japanese were in contact with the handful of Dutch merchants who had been allowed to stay in Japan, and they occasionally read Western science texts. "Dutch medicine," as Western anatomy, pharmacy, and surgery were called, was fairly well known in upper-class Japan in the early nineteenth century, although it did not yet have much prestige.

When the U.S. naval commander Matthew Perry arrived with his "black ships" to forcibly open the country to foreign traders in 1853 and 1854, the Japanese were not as ill prepared as one might assume after two centuries of isolation. Aided by the practical and secular Confucian philosophy they had imbibed, the sparse but important Western scientific books they had studied, and the carefully balanced government they had evolved by trial and error, the Edo government, the daimyo, and their sub-officials were able to absorb Western ideas and techniques by choice rather than by force. Instead of looking down their cultured noses at what the "hairy barbarians" might be bringing, the Japanese were able to say, "If it works to our benefit (or can be made to), use it." Unlike China, the West decidedly did not overwhelm the Japanese. On the contrary, they were true to their nation's tradition by showing themselves to be confident and pragmatic adapters of what they thought could be useful to them and rejecting the rest.

SOUTHEAST ASIA

The territories in Southeast Asia that had succeeded in achieving political organization before the appearance of European traders and missionaries had little reason to take much notice of them until a much later era. (See Chapter 19.) Contacts were limited to coastal towns and were mainly commercial. In the 1600s, the Dutch had driven the Portuguese entirely out of the islands' spice trade, and they had established a loose partnership with the local Muslim sultans in Java and Sumatra to assure the continuance of that trade with Europe. After a brief contest with the Dutch, the British, in the form of the East India Company, had withdrawn from the Spice Islands to concentrate on Indian cotton goods. Only in the Spanish Philippines was a European presence pervasive and politically dominant over a sizable area.

Michael S. Yamashita/Encyclopedia/Corbis

HIMEJI CASTLE. This relatively late construction, known as the White Egret to the Japanese, stands today as a major tourist attraction. The massive stone walls successfully resisted all attackers.

Most of the insular Asians were by now converted to Islam, a process that began in the 1200s through contact with Arab and Indian Muslim traders. By the time the Portuguese arrived in 1511, Malacca had become a commercial crossroads of the Indian Ocean and East Asian networks, as well as the most important point of dissemination for Islam throughout the region. From Malacca, the Portuguese extended their control over the Spice Islands. Except for on the island of Bali, the original syncretistic blend of Hindu with animist beliefs that had been India's legacy had faded away. Only in the Philippines was there a Christian element.

If the islands were relatively untouched by the early European traders, the mainland populations were even less so. In the 1700s, the three states of Thailand, Burma, and Vietnam dominated the area. The first two were by then part of the *Hinayana* Buddhist world, whereas Vietnam under Chinese influence had remained with the *Mahayana* version of the faith. The once-potent Khmer state of Cambodia had been divided between the Thais and the Viets by stages during the fifteenth to seventeenth centuries. Nowhere else was there a visible European influence so late as the end of the eighteenth century, but this was to change radically in the next century.

SUMMARY

After a century of unchecked feudal warfare in Japan, three strongmen arose in the late sixteenth century to recreate effective centralized government. Last and most important was Tokugawa Ieyasu, who crushed or neutralized all opposition, including that of the Christian converts who were the product of the first European contacts with Japan in the mid-1500s.

By the 1630s, Japan was rapidly isolating itself from the world under the Tokugawa Shoganate. The chief goal of the Tokugawa shoguns was a class-based political stability, which they successfully pursued for centuries. The shogun controlled all contacts with foreigners and gradually ended all interaction to isolate the island empire for more than two hundred years. The daimyo nobility were carefully controlled by the shogun in Edo, who ruled from behind the imperial throne. Massive social changes took place at the same time as the feudal political structure remained immobile. While urban merchants rose in the socioeconomic balance and peasants became wage laborers, the samurai slowly declined into obsolescence.

The population surged, and the general economy prospered. The arts, particularly literature and painting, flourished. When Japan's solitude was finally broken, the governing elite were ready to deal with the challenge of Western science and technology constructively.

In Southeast Asia, the colonial period commenced with Dutch and Spanish presence in the Indonesian and Philippine Islands, respectively. But as late as the end of the eighteenth century, the Western traders and missionaries had had relatively little impact on the mass of the native inhabitants of the islands and even less on the mainland.

IDENTIFICATION TERMS

Test your knowledge of this chapter's key concepts by defining the following terms. If you can not recall the meaning of certain terms, refresh your memory by looking up the boldfaced term in the chapter, turning to the Glossary at the end of the book, or accessing the terms on the CourseMate website at **www.cengagebrain.com.**

daimyo
Edo
haiku
Kabuki
sakoku
Tokugawa Ieyasu

FOR FURTHER REFLECTION

1. To what do you attribute Japan's repeated efforts at limiting foreign influences? How was this accomplished?
2. How did Japanese attitudes to foreigners compare with China's? Were the reasons the same?
3. In what ways, if any, did Japan's tendency to isolate itself affect its development?

TEST YOUR KNOWLEDGE

Test your knowledge of this chapter by answering the following questions. Complete answers appear at the end of the book. You may find even more quiz questions on the CourseMate website at **www.cengagebrain.com.**

1. The early Christian missionaries to Japan
   a. found a hostile reception.
   b. were mainly Protestants.
   c. made the mistake of trying to conquer the Buddhist natives.
   d. were welcomed and given a hearing.
   e. were evicted from the country within five years of their arrival.
2. The Shinto faith is best described as
   a. the native Japanese religion.
   b. the Japanese Holy Scripture.
   c. a mixture of Christianity and Japanese pagan belief.
   d. a variety of Buddhism imported from Korea.
   e. a reaction to the proselytizing of the Jesuits.
3. The only widely practiced religion in Japan that was *foreign* in origin was
   a. Christianity.
   b. Hinduism.
   c. Buddhism.
   d. Shinto.
   e. Islam.
4. The government system created by the shoguns in the 1600s
   a. allowed the local chieftains called daimyo to rule unchecked.
   b. was an imitation of the Chinese system of mandarin officials.
   c. made the daimyo dependent on the shogun's favor.
   d. used the emperor as military chief while the shoguns ruled all else.
   e. provided imperial protection for the families of the daimyo.
5. Which of the following did not occur during the Tokugawa period?
   a. Japanese elite thought shifted from Buddhist to Confucian patterns.
   b. Japanese formal culture stagnated in its continued isolation from the world.
   c. Trade and economic activity generally increased.
   d. Internal peace and order were effectively maintained.
   e. The elite samurai faded into obsolescence.
6. The reduction of the samurai's influence in public affairs was
   a. carried out through government-ordered purges.
   b. attempted but not achieved during the Shoganate period.
   c. achieved by eliminating internal warfare through a strong government.
   d. achieved by encouraging them to become merchants and landlords.
   e. opposed by the shoguns but supported by the emperor.
7. Kabuki was (and is) a form of Japanese
   a. comedy.
   b. poetry.
   c. drama.
   d. combat.
   e. swordsmanship.
8. Which of the following art forms was an original Japanese invention?
   a. Wood-block printing
   b. Haiku
   c. Nature poetry
   d. Weaving of silk tapestry
   e. The epic poem

9. In general, it can be said of Japanese merchants that they
   a. emigrated in large numbers and established wider trade networks under Tokugawa rule.
   b. always enjoyed high status in Japanese society.
   c. saw little change in their trade throughout the entire period of the Tokugawa Shoganate.
   d. gained in status after the imposition of sakoku.
   e. saw an increase in trade with foreigners as a result of sakoku.
10. Prior to the 1600s, Islam spread among the majority of people in/on
   a. Cambodia only.
   b. Cambodia and the Southeast Asian islands.
   c. the Indian sub-continent.
   d. the mainland areas of Southeast Asia.
   e. the islands of Southeast Asia.

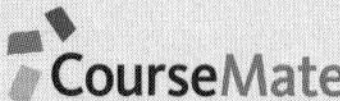

Visit the CourseMate website at **www.cengagebrain.com** for additional study tools and review materials for this chapter.

28 From Conquest to Colonies in Hispanic America

[The conquest] was neither a victory nor a defeat. **It was the dolorous birth of the mestizo people.** —*ANONYMOUS INSCRIPTION AT THE SITE OF FINAL AZTEC DEFEAT*

1520s–1820s	Latin America under Spanish and Portuguese rule
1650s–1750	Stagnation under a weakened Spain
1760–1790	Revival of economy under Charles III
1793–1804	Haitian slave rebellion and independence

CHAPTER OUTLINE

The arrival of the Europeans in the New World started an enormous exchange of crops, commodities, modalities, and techniques. The beginning and most important phase of this exchange was conducted under the auspices of the Spanish conquistadors, who rapidly conquered the Indian populations in the sixteenth century. For the next three years, most of the newly discovered lands were administered by a colonial system that superimposed Iberian Christian economic institutions, habits, and values on existing indigenous ones. The form of colonial lifestyle that gradually evolved in Latin America was the product of the native Indians and the imported black slaves as much as of the whites.

THE FALL OF THE AZTEC AND INCA EMPIRES

We have seen (in Chapter 22) that the initial phase of Spanish exploration in the Caribbean was dominated by the search for treasure. The "Indies" of Columbus were reputed to be lands of gold and spices, waiting to be exploited by the first individual who might happen upon them. Within a few years, however, this image was obliterated by the realities of the Caribbean islands, where gold was nonexistent. The search then shifted to the mainland, and the immediate result was the conquest of the Aztecs in Mexico and the Incas in Peru.

The Aztec capital fell in 1521 to conquistador Hernán Cortés, who began construction of Mexico City with stones from the leveled pyramids. Within a decade, Francisco Pizarro used the tactics of Cortés to conquer the Inca Empire in South America. Pizarro, based in Panama, followed rumors of gold to the south, and by 1532, he had taken the Inca capital, Cuzco. Just as in Aztec Mexico, when the Spanish arrived in Peru, they found many allies to help them overthrow the government in Cuzco, which was engaged in civil war. The viral pandemics of smallpox, measles, and influenza carried by the Spaniards to Mexico and Peru decimated the Indians' ranks while hardly affecting the Spaniards. The generous social assistance programs of the Incas

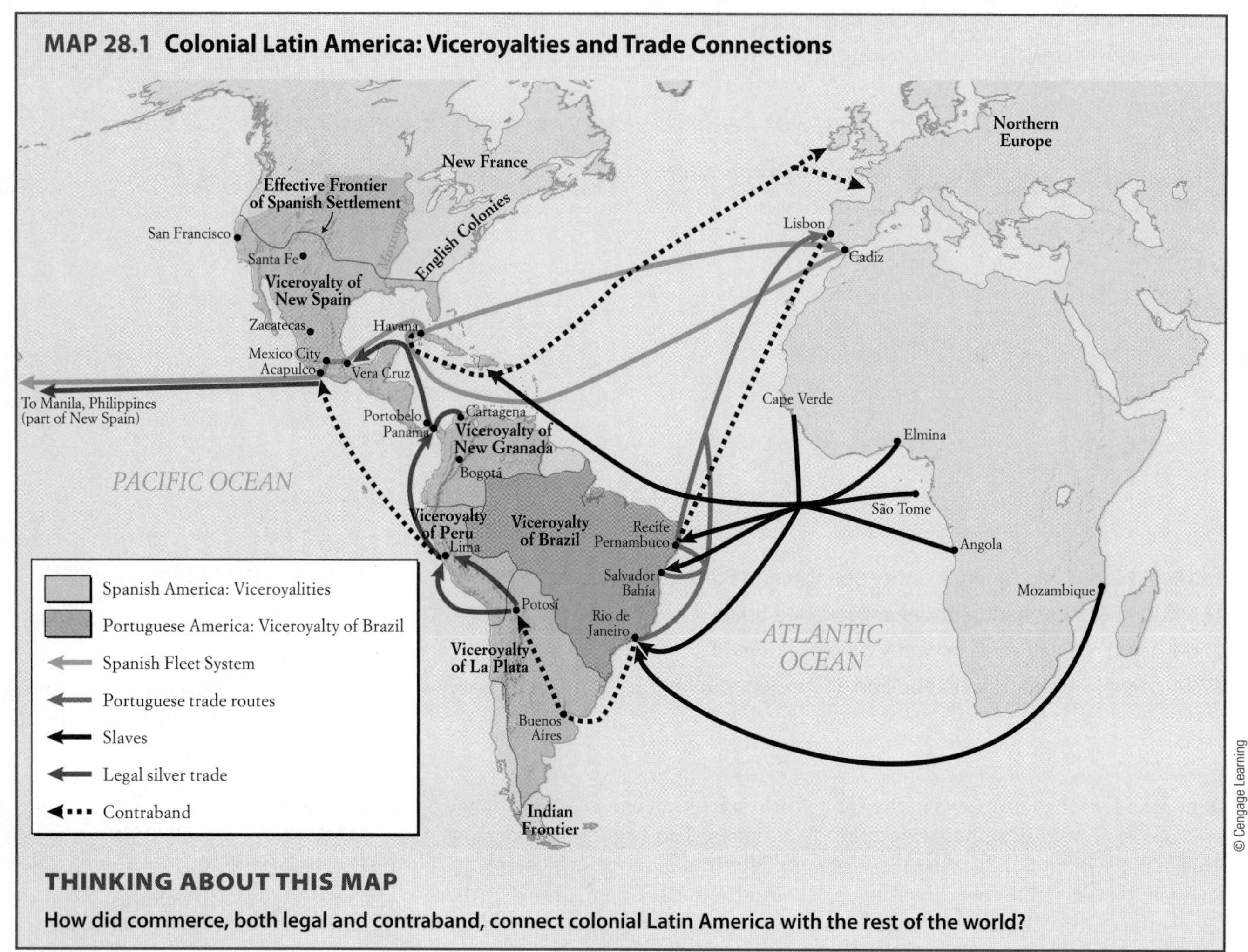

MAP 28.1 Colonial Latin America: Viceroyalties and Trade Connections

THINKING ABOUT THIS MAP

How did commerce, both legal and contraband, connect colonial Latin America with the rest of the world?

(see Chapter 14) were no longer enough to win the active loyalty of the Inca's subjects. Pizarro and his band, which was even smaller than that of Cortés in Mexico, were able to take the Inca king hostage and demolish the regime in a short time in the Peruvian lowlands and valleys. Some of the imperial family and their officials escaped to the high mountains and attempted to rule from there for another thirty years before being crushed.

Spain showed much less interest in colonizing the sparsely populated areas of northern Mexico and southern South America, where no gold or silver had been found. In these areas, recalcitrant Amerindian groups such as the Puebloans of New Mexico and the Mapuche (mah-POO-chay) of Patagonia violently resisted Hispanization. The northernmost reaches of Spanish lands encompassed today's U.S. Southwest but were beyond the practical reach of the viceregal capital, Mexico City. Effectively, the fortified Franciscan mission towns of San Francisco and Santa Fe anchored the northern borders of Spanish colonization (see Map 28.1).

The early Portuguese colonization of Brazil was similar to the Spanish colonization of the areas of Chile and Argentina. Lacking the allure of precious metals and a ready-made Indian workforce, these regions were gradually colonized by merchants and farmers, rather than swiftly conquered by gold seekers or would-be aristocrats. Brazil was named after the first natural resource exploited by the Portuguese: the valuable red dye, called *brazil*, extracted from the Brazilwood tree. The (male) settlers in precarious areas, such as coastal Brazil, arrived without their wives and families. Iberian men freely mixed with indigenous women; their offspring in Brazil were called *mamelucos* (ma-meh-LOO-koez). The offspring of Spaniards and Amerindians were called ***mestizos*** (meh-STEE-soze). The hinterland societies were less class conscious because everyone had to work together to survive.

THE COLONIAL EXPERIENCE

Spain's colonization of the New World focused on the conquered areas of the Aztec and Maya dominions (the colonial Viceroyalty of New Spain) and the Inca Empire (the Viceroyalty of Peru). These areas had treasure in gratifying abundance, both in gold and, in even greater amounts, silver. Here Indian resistance was broken, and the small groups of Spaniards made themselves into feudal lords, each with his Spanish entourage and Indian servants. One-fifth of what was discovered or stolen belonged to the royal government; the remainder could be divided up as the conquistadors saw fit. Agricultural production was greatly enriched by the introduction of draft animals and new crops (wheat, rice, sugarcane, citrus fruits). The survivors of the pre-Columbian empires furnished a ready-made free labor pool, which was accustomed to organized labor for tribute to a central authority.

In this earliest period, until about 1560, the Spanish crown, which in theory was the ultimate proprietor of all the new lands, allowed the conquerors of the Indians (as a reward for the risks and hardships of exploration) the ***encomienda*** (en-koh-MYEN-dah). In theory, the encomienda was the right to demand uncompensated labor from the natives in return for providing them with material necessities and religious instruction. However, this soon led to such abuses that friars charged with converting the Indians to Christianity—most notably the determined Dominican Bartolomé de las Casas—protested vigorously to Madrid. Prompted by these protests, King Charles V and his advisors were the first Europeans to debate the legal and ethical status of conquered peoples (including the first definition of "just war," still a relevant issue today). As a result of the king's debates, the Spanish home government passed idealistic reform laws, including a prohibition against Indian enslavement. Most of these laws were impossible to enforce because of the great distance, and because the encomienda owners opposed and ignored the laws. (See the Society and Economy box). Owing to overwork, malnutrition, and pandemic diseases brought by the whites and unfamiliar to the Indians, Native American populations crashed horrifically (see Chapter 22). By the mid-seventeenth century, the Indian populations had begun to recover but never did so fully. Latin American populations only reached their pre-Columbian levels in the nineteenth century, when the influx of Africans, Asians, and Europeans had created a wholly different ethnic mix.

Friar de las Casas advocated the importation of Africans to alleviate the Native Americans' miserable condition. African slaves were relegated to the lowest echelon of colonial society, with no protections from abusive "owners" (see the Evidence of the Past box). However, slavery in the Iberian colonies included the possibility of buying or otherwise earning one's freedom, creating a growing class of free African Americans. Runaway slaves established communities in the hinterlands. The African cultural and religious influence was particularly strong in the plantation zone (the territory from the Caribbean area to southern Brazil), which was the destination of most slaves.

Colonial Administration

The Spanish administration in most of the Americas and the Portuguese system in Brazil were essentially similar. Under the auspices of the home government, an explorer or conqueror was originally allowed nearly unlimited proprietary powers in the new land. Soon, however, he was displaced by a royal council set up with exclusive powers over commerce, crafts, mining, and every type of foreign trade. Stringent controls were imposed through a viceroy or governor, appointed by the Spanish government in Madrid and responsible solely to it. Judicial and military matters were also handled through the councils or the colonial *audiencia* (high court) in each province. The only hints of elective government were in the bottom ranks of the bureaucracy: the early Spanish town councils (*cabildos*) and the traditional communes of the Indian villages.

Iberian-born nobles (*peninsulars*) dominated the colonial administration. It was highly bureaucratized and mirrored the home government in its composition and aims. A great deal of paper dealing with legal cases, regulations, appointment procedures, tax rolls, and censuses flowed back and forth across the Atlantic. From the mid-sixteenth century, the government's basic aim was to maximize fiscal and commercial revenues for the home country.

Secondarily, the government wished to provide an avenue of upward mobility for ambitious young men in the administration of the colonies. The viceroyalties of New Spain and of Peru were established in the mid-sixteenth century, and the holders of these posts were always peninsulars. A few of them were able administrators; most were court favorites being rewarded with a sinecure with opportunities for wealth. Despite all attempts to ensure Madrid's control over colonial policies, the sheer distance involved and the insecurity of ocean travel meant that the local officials—normally ***criollos*** (cree-OH-yohz; native-born people of Iberian race in Latin America)—had considerable autonomy. Their care of their Indian and mestizo charges varied from blatant exploitation to admirable solicitude.

The Colonies and the Roman Catholic Church

Another Iberian institution was a partner to the civil government in the colonies: the Catholic Church. Filled with the combative spirit and sense of high mission that were a legacy of the long *reconquista* struggle against the Moors, the missionaries were anxious to add the Central and South American Indians to the church's ranks. In this endeavor, the government authorities supported them. A church stood at the center of every town in the new lands; all other buildings were oriented around it. The bishops, nominated by the Crown, were as important in the administration of a given area as the civil governors; cultural and educational matters pertaining

SOCIETY AND ECONOMY

Forced Labor and Debt Peonage in the Spanish Colonies

The luxurious lifestyle of the colonial elites was supported by the labors of their inferiors in the social pyramid: Native Americans, Africans, and mestizos. They toiled in the textile mills and on the haciendas, where conditions—although wretched—were still preferable to working in the mines.

In the 1620s, a Spanish monk traveled through the Spanish colonies in the Americas, making careful observation of what he witnessed, including the workings of Mexican textile mills and how they got their labor.

> "... To keep their [woolen] mills supplied with labor, they maintain individuals who are engaged and hired to snare poor innocents; seeing some Indian who is a stranger to the town, with some trickery or pretense, such as hiring him to carry something ... and paying him cash, they get him into the mill; once inside, they drop the deception, and the poor fellow never again gets outside that prison until he dies and they carry him out for burial.
>
> In this way they have gathered in and duped many married Indians with families, who have passed into oblivion here for 20 years, or longer, or their whole lives, without their wives and children knowing anything about them; for even if they want to get out, they cannot, thanks to the great watchfulness with which the doormen guard the exits. These Indians are occupied in carding, spinning, weaving, and the other operations of making cloth; and thus the owners make their profits by these unjust and unlawful means.
>
> And although the Royal Council of the Indies, with the holy zeal which animates it in the service of God our Lord, of his Majesty, and of the Indians' welfare, has tried to remedy this evil ... and the Viceroy of New Spain appoints mill inspectors to visit them and remedy such matters, nevertheless, since most of those who set out on such commissions aim rather at their own enrichment, ... than at the relief of the Indians, and since the mill owners pay them well, they leave the wretched Indians in the same slavery; and even if some of them are fired with holy zeal to remedy such abuses when they visit the mills, the mill owners keep places provided in the mills in which they hide the wretched Indians against their will, so that they do not see or find them, and the poor fellows cannot complain against their wrongs."

Source: A. Vásquez de Espinosa, *Compendium and Description of the West Indies*, trans. C. Clark (Washington, DC: Smithsonian, 1942).

Spanish royal officials described the plight of the Indians in Peru, who not only paid the tribute tax, but were also condemned to the serfdom of debt peonage; that is, perpetually working off debts forced on them by their masters.

> On farming haciendas, an Indian subject ... earns from fourteen to eighteen pesos a year.... In addition, the hacendado assigns him a piece of land, about twenty to thirty yards square in size, to grow his food. In return the Indian must work three hundred days in the year, leaving him sixty-five days of rest for Sundays, other church holidays, illness, or some accident that may prevent him from working. The mayordomo [foreman] of the hacienda keeps careful record of the days worked by the Indian in order to settle accounts with him at the end of the year.
>
> From his wage the master deducts the eight pesos of royal tribute that the Indian must pay; assuming that the Indian earns eighteen pesos, the most he can earn, he is left with ten pesos. From this amount the master deducts 2.25 pesos to pay for three yards of coarse cloth ... [for] a cloak to cover his nakedness. He now has 7.75 pesos with which to feed and dress his wife and children, if he has a family, and to pay the church fees demanded by the parish priest. But ... since he cannot raise on his little plot all the food he needs for his family, he must get from the hacendado [hacienda owner] each month two bushels of maize, [at] more than double the price if he could buy elsewhere, [an annual total of] nine pesos, which is 1.75 pesos more than the Indian has left. Thus the unhappy Indian, after working three hundred days of the year for his master and cultivating his little plot in his free time, and receiving only a coarse cloak and twelve bushels of maize, is in debt 1.75 pesos, and must continue to work for his master the following year.... [T]he poor Indian ... remains a slave all his life and, contrary to [all] law ... after his death his sons must continue to work to pay the debt of their father.

ANALYZE AND INTERPRET

When enslavement of Amerindians became illegal and obsolete, debt peonage replaced the encomienda system. Was debt peonage an improvement on the encomienda? Explain your answer.

Source: Jorge Juan and Antonio de Ulloa, *Noticias Secretas de América* (Madrid, 1918), 2 vols., I, 290–292, as quoted in Benjamin Keen, ed., *Latin American Civilization*, 4th ed. (Boulder, Colorado and London: Westview Press, 1986), 75–76.

EVIDENCE OF THE PAST

Recovering Life Stories of the Voiceless: Testimonial Narratives by African Slaves

The oral histories of a handful of ex-slaves provide the only first-person accounts of life on the colonial plantations. Sympathetic editors have collected, edited, and published these accounts. The slaves in Cuba and Brazil worked mainly on cash-crop plantations in a variety of capacities. The following selection is from one of the few first-person slave narratives from Brazil. In about 1850, Mahommah G. Baquaqua told his story to one of the abolitionists who had freed him.

> [After being captured as a boy in Africa] I was then placed in that most horrible of places, the slave ship ... [where] we became desperate through suffering and fatigue [as well as hunger and thirst].... We arrived at Pernambuco [Recife, Brazil], South America, early in the morning.... We landed a few miles from the city, at a farmer's house, which was used as a kind of slave market.... I had not been there very long before I saw [the farmer] use the lash pretty freely on a boy, which made a deep impression on my mind....
>
> When a slaver comes in, the news spreads like wildfire, and down come all those that are interested in the arrival of the vessel with its cargo of living merchandise.... I was soon placed at hard labor [by my new master], such as none but slaves and horses are put to. [My master] was building a house, and had to fetch building stone from across the river, a considerable distance, and I was compelled to carry them that were so heavy it took three men to raise them upon my head, ... for a quarter of a mile at least, down to where the boat lay. Sometimes the stone would press so hard upon my head that I was obliged to throw it down upon the ground, and then my master would be very angry indeed, and would say the [dog] had thrown the stone, when I thought in my heart that he was the worst dog; but ... I dared not give utterance in words.

Source: Samuel Moore, ed., *Biography of Mahommah G. Baquaqua, A Native of Zoogao* [sic] *in the Interior of Africa* (Detroit: George E. Pomeroy and Co., 1854), 34–50.

The Cuban ex-slave Esteban Montejo was 103 years old when he told his life story to an anthropologist in 1963. The following passage begins with his birth on a sugar plantation.

> Like all children of slavery, the criollitos, as they were called, I was born in the infirmary where they took the pregnant black women to give birth.... Blacks were sold like piglets, and they sold me right off—that's why I don't remember anything about that place.... At all the plantations there was an infirmary near the [slave quarters]. It was a large wooden house where they took the pregnant women. Children were born there and stayed until they were six or seven years old when they went to live in the slave quarters and to work like everyone else.... If a little black boy was pretty and lively, they sent him inside, to the master's house.... [T]he little black boy had to spend his time shooing flies [with a large palm fan] because the masters ate a lot. And they put [him] at the head of the table.... And they told him: "Shoo, so those flies don't fall in the food!" If a fly fell on a plate, they scolded him severely and even whipped him. I never did this work because I never liked to be near the masters. I was a *cimarrón* [wild, runaway] from birth.

bpk, Berlin/(name of museum)/(name of photographer)/Art Resource, NY

A BRAZILIAN PLANTATION IN 1830. A Portuguese colonist in Brazil planted the first sugarcane there in 1521. Sugar soon became Brazil's economic mainstay, and African slaves were imported to work on plantations like this one overlooking a harbor near Rio de Janeiro.

ANALYZE AND INTERPRET

When Baquaqua and Montejo told their stories, they had lived many years as free men. Do you think that the intervening years might have affected their childhood memories of slavery in any way? What influence might the editors of their published stories have had on the narratives?

Source: Miguel Barnet, ed., *Biography of a Runaway Slave*, trans. W. Nick Hill (New York: Pantheon Books, 1994), 19–20, 22, 38.

to both Europeans and Indians were in their hands. In its lavish baroque buildings and artworks, the church left a long-lasting physical imprint throughout the Spanish and Portuguese colonies. The spiritual imprint was even more profound, continuing to the present day.

THE EARLY ECONOMIC STRUCTURE

International commerce between the Iberian colonies and Europe and Asia connected the colonies to the nascent global economy (see Map 28.1). The major element in the economy of the early Spanish colonies was the mining of precious metals. Everything else served that end. (Brazil, the Portuguese colony, was originally a sugarcane plantation, but later it also emphasized mining.) The agricultural estates, which were first encomiendas and then ***haciendas*** (hah-SYEN-dahs)—rural plantation-villages with wage laborers who were at least technically free—existed primarily to supply food for the mining communities. Handicraft industries made gloves and textiles, prepared foods, and provided blacksmithing services for the same market. There were few exports beyond the produce of the mines and a handful of cash crops such as sugar, tobacco, and indigo.

Rights to export goods for the Spanish colonies were limited to Spaniards; the goods could be carried only in Spanish ships, which left from one port, Seville (later also Cádiz), twice a year. From Latin America, another flotilla laden with the bullion mined the previous year left annually from the Mexican port of Vera Cruz. The restrictions on these flotillas were intended to protect the treasure coming from the Americas from pirates and to restrict what was sent to and taken from the colonies.

The great bonanza of the early years was the "mountain of silver" at Potosí (poh-tuh-SEE) in what is now Bolivia. Next to it came the Mexican mines north of Mexico City. The silver that flowed from the New World to Seville (and from Acapulco to Manila) from the 1540s to the 1640s far overshadowed the gold taken from Moctezuma and the Inca during the conquest period. When the volume declined drastically in the 1640s, the Madrid government experienced a crisis. Production stayed relatively low for a century, but thanks to new technology and increased incentives, it reached great heights in the later eighteenth century before declining again—this time for good.

A HACENDADO AND HIS FAMILY. This nineteenth-century scene shows a Mexican *hacendado*, owner of a large plantation, with his wife and one of his overseers. The elaborate costumes were impractical but necessary for maintaining social distance from the peons.

The input of bullion did not produce lasting constructive results in Spain. Some of it flowed on through royal or private hands to enrich the western European shippers, financiers, merchants, and manufacturers who supplied Iberia with every type of good and service in the sixteenth and seventeenth centuries. Perhaps a third wound up in Chinese hands to pay for the Spanish version of the triangular trade across the Pacific. Spanish galleons left Acapulco, Mexico, loaded with silver and bound for Manila, where they met Chinese ships loaded with silk and porcelain, which, after trans-shipment across Mexico or Panama, wound up in Seville and might be reshipped back to the Caribbean. Less than half of the Spanish silver remained in Spanish hands, but this was enough to start an inflationary spiral in Spain that seized all of Europe by the end of the sixteenth century and brought ruin to many landholding nobles (see Chapter 22).

STAGNATION AND REVIVAL IN THE EIGHTEENTH CENTURY

The later seventeenth century and the first decades of the eighteenth were a period of stagnation and decline in New Spain. The last Spanish Habsburg kings were so weak that local strongmen in Hispanic America were able to overshadow the high courts and municipal authorities of the viceregal governments. The once-annual treasure fleets were sailing only sporadically, and the total supply of American bullion was down sharply from its high point. Several of the larger Caribbean islands were captured by the British, French, or Dutch or were taken over by buccaneers. The import-export controls imposed by the Madrid government were falling apart, because non-Spaniards were able to ignore the prohibitions against trading with the colonies, were granted exemptions, or collaborated with the criollos in smuggling in a systematic fashion. By now, the colonies could produce the bulk of their necessities and no longer had to import them.

At this juncture, the Spanish government experienced a revival when a new dynasty, an offshoot of the French Bourbons, took over in Madrid in 1701 as a result of the War of Spanish Succession (see Chapter 23). Especially under King Charles III (ruling 1759–1788), who figured among the most enlightened monarchs of the eighteenth century, thoroughgoing reform was applied to the Indies.

A form of free trade was introduced, the navy and military were strengthened, and a new system of administrators responsible to the center on the French Bourbon model was able to make Spanish colonial government much more effective. Taxes were collected as they had not been for years, and smuggling and corruption were reduced. The two Spanish American viceroyalties were subdivided into four: New Spain, Peru, New Granada (northern South America), and Rio de la Plata (Argentina and central South America). The officials for these new divisions continued to be drawn almost exclusively from Spain, an affront that the people in the colonies did not easily swallow. Another point of contention was that many criollo clergymen were among the Jesuit missionaries banished by the anticlerical Bourbons from the Iberian empire. Colonists throughout the Western Hemisphere rose up in protest against the expulsion of the Jesuits, who had won the hearts and minds of all, and who from their exile encouraged the emerging sense of Hispano-American identity among criollos and mestizos alike.

The reforms did not benefit the mass of Indian and mestizo inhabitants at all. The Indian population increased—perhaps doubling—in the eighteenth century, creating an irresistible temptation to hacienda owners to press this defenseless and unskilled group into forced labor in the expanding plantation agriculture. The market for the products was not only the seemingly insatiable demand for sugar in Europe and North America but also the rapidly growing population in the colonies. The foreseeable result was an expansion of brutal serfdom, generating a series of Indian uprisings. **Túpac Amaru II**, a descendant of the Inca, led the most notable of these in the 1780s. The viceregal government of Peru was nearly toppled before the revolt was put down. A few years later in the Caribbean island of Haiti (then Saint Domingue), a black ex-slave named **Toussaint L'Ouverture** led an uprising of slaves that ended French dominion on that island. The Toussaint rebellion eventually succeeded in attaining complete independence for Haiti, and it made an indelible impression on both the friends and enemies of the daring idea of a general abolition of slavery.

The oppressed Indians and enslaved blacks were by no means the only Latin Americans who were discontented in the last years of the eighteenth century. Economic policy reforms, however needed, were also sometimes painful to the native-born criollos. With free trade, imports from Europe became considerably cheaper, hurting domestic producers. And the remarkable increase in silver production as a result of new mining techniques (using mercury) and new discoveries did not flow to the benefit of the locals but rather to what was more often now viewed as an alien government in Madrid. The loosening of the former restrictions on trade and manufactures had a distinctly stimulating effect on the intellectual atmosphere of the criollo urbanites. After decades of somnolence, there arose within a small but crucially important minority a spirit of criticism and inquiry, which reflected the stirring of European liberalism we shall examine in Chapter 30.

In the 1770s, the criollo elite witnessed the successful (North) American revolt against Britain, and a few years later, the radical French Revolution doctrines seized their attention. In both of these foreign upheavals, they believed they saw many similarities with their own grievances against their government—similarities that were to be ultimately persuasive for their own rebellion.

COLONIAL SOCIETY AND CULTURE

The Spanish colonists established a social hierarchy imported from Spain and based on racial and religious criteria. In legal terms, the "Spanish" colonials included peninsulars, criollos, and even wealthy European immigrants. These white elites controlled the government, church, military, and the economy. They had a separate justice system from the lower classes. Their lavish lifestyle depended on the labor of a growing mixed-blood population. The upper classes felt both fascinated and threatened by the emerging multiracial reality. They used a pseudo-scientific race-based classification system to support their claims of superiority, to decide whom to allow into the upper classes, and to relegate everyone else to a lower status. (See this chapter's Images of History box for an example of the elite perspective on race and class.) Especially for the mestizo, an individual's place in society was determined by family lineage, social connections, economic standing, and lifestyle, rather than by skin color alone. The celebrated Sister Juana Inés de la Cruz was a mestiza who enjoyed the privileges of an upper-class criolla. There was limited social mobility in both directions. Later waves of immigrants from Europe, having no ties to the original colonizers, were more likely to become merchants or laborers than to be welcomed into the upper classes.

Upper-class peninsulars and criollos re-created Iberian high-society life, distancing themselves from the masses, whom they deemed to be "uncivilized." Social life was centered in the cities and towns because the Spaniards preferred urban life. The elite lifestyle moved at a leisurely pace, consisting of carriage rides and other outings to display their finery, religious ceremonies and festivals, and diversions such as gambling, bullfights, and the popular baroque poetry contests. The elite criollos were secondary in political and social status to the peninsulars, although the American-born descendents of the conquistadors owned ranches and mines and could be wealthier than the peninsulars. These upper-class criollos cultivated intellectual and literary pursuits that enriched the cultural environment. Although the Inquisition prohibited reading novels and other "heretical" material, and the printing presses in Mexico and Lima produced mostly religious material, secular books were nonetheless widely

Sister Juana Ines de la Cruz (1648-95) (oil on canvas), Islas, Andres de (fl.1772) / Museo de America, Madrid, Spain/Giraudon/The Bridgeman Art Library

SISTER JUANA INÉS DE LA CRUZ. Sister Juana is revered as the finest poet of her time in New Spain (Mexico), an extraordinary achievement given the constraints on colonial women. Sister Juana's unique intellectual outlook made her the object of both admiration for her originality and severe criticism for her worldliness.

During the early colonial years, the term *mestizo* was derogatory because it referred to the illegitimate child of a Spanish man and an Indian woman. The Spanish monarchs encouraged marriage between interracial couples, and mestizos rose in status accordingly. At times, they served as intermediaries and interpreters among the elites, the Indians, and other categories of mixed-blood peoples. By law, individuals classified as mestizos were excluded from the universities and from positions in the church and the government. They could be soldiers but not officers, artisans' apprentices but not master craftsmen. Mestizos might also be tenant farmers or hacienda managers. The mestizo ***gaucho*** horsemen of the Argentine pampas (great-plains area) found their niche as providers of contraband cowhides and tallow. The mixed-blood mamelucos of Brazil were intrepid explorers of the western frontiers, who sometimes raided the Jesuit missions to capture Indian slaves. However, it was possible available through contraband, and the criollo intellectuals kept abreast of Enlightenment thought and the latest European literary currents. The monastery or convent was also an option for the criollos. In the more lenient religious orders, the "cells" were more like suites of rooms.

In this strongly patriarchal society, women lacked independent legal status and were expected to obey their fathers, brothers, or husbands unconditionally. Spanish women were carefully protected because their family's honor depended on their irreproachable behavior. The daughters of criollos were married, if possible, to newly arrived aristocratic peninsulars to ensure the family's prestige. Young men were sent to Spain or France for higher education. Young women were given a rudimentary education by tutors at home, and a few learned domestic and social arts at mission schools, but they were denied any higher education. Notions about propriety limited women to religious reading matter. In the final analysis, elite women had three alternatives: marriage, spinsterhood, or the convent. Widows of comfortable financial status were the most independent women in colonial times; they were free to make their own decisions, and they often ran family businesses with great success.

Methods of Throwing the Lasso and the Bolas, from 'Travels in Chile and La Plata' by John Miers, 1826 (litho) (b/w photo), Miers, John (d.1822) (after)/Private Collection/The Bridgeman Art Library

GAUCHOS ON THE ARGENTINE PAMPAS. The gaucho, usually a mixed-blood mestizo, created a lifestyle that blended the cultures of Spanish and Native American horsemen. Gaucho contraband traders, frontiersmen, and soldiers helped shape the history of the River Plate region (today's Argentina and Uruguay).

IMAGES OF HISTORY

Pseudo-Scientific Racial and Class Typologies of Colonial Hispanic America

The Iberian elites linked each socioeconomic rank with skin color, costume, environment, occupation, and degree of acculturation to Spanish norms. Paintings such as these were commissioned by wealthy patrons in the 1700s in an effort to codify and control the new multiracial society—which by that time had far outstripped the old Spanish ideas of race and class. The images shown are four scenes from a series of sixteen paintings by an accomplished portrait painter for the elites. The top two scenes, loaded with markers of high status, depict affluent families headed by Spanish males. The bottom two scenes show lower-class families plying their trades as street vendors. The trappings of the elite are realistically portrayed, in contrast to the stereotypical and erroneous renderings of the multiracial figures' facial features and clothing. The difference in caliber between the two mestiza women (top left and bottom right) illustrates the fluidity in the system.

for mestizos (both men and women) to change categories through marriage, political connections, and accumulated wealth. It was even possible for a mestizo in the right circumstances to purchase a document that certified him as "white," enabling him to live the lifestyle of an affluent criollo. On the other hand, an impoverished mestizo could change his category by adopting Indian dress and living in Indian communities.

Other categories of mixed-blood peoples were more severely restricted than the mestizos because the Spanish (wrongly) assumed them to be violent and unpredictable. They were barred from bearing firearms, and their testimony in court was thought to be less reliable. However, freed slaves could serve in militias established for them. Escaped slaves settled in secluded communities far from the Spanish authorities. African American slaves were at the bottom of the social pyramid. Along with some surviving Amerindians, they toiled from dawn to dusk in the mines, on haciendas and plantations, in sweatshops, and in mills, for little or no pay (see the Society and Economy box). Their only opportunities for rest were the Sunday mass and markets and the occasional festival. Non-Spanish women were less restricted because the Amerindian and African cultures were less patriarchal in origin than that of the Spanish. However, these women suffered sexual exploitation and abuse by their Iberian masters.

The subdued Amerindians lived in a variety of other settings besides haciendas and plantations. The Spanish crown decreed special treatment for the Indians because they were innocents in need of spiritual guidance. Ignoring the unenforceable royal edicts, the colonists often abused their charges. Communally run Indian towns, vestiges of the pre-Columbian empires, were remote from the Hispanic towns and were left intact. The only outsiders they saw were priests and the infamously corrupt tribute collectors. In areas where the Indians had dispersed and a demand arose for their labor in the mines, the Spanish rounded them up and settled them in newly established Spanish-run towns, where clergy saw to their instruction in the Catholic faith and where they were readily accessible for tribute labor. Finally, the religious orders collected Indians in missions, where they received the rudiments of religious indoctrination and were taught useful crafts. Treatment of the Indians in the missions ranged from exploitative to benevolent, but even in the best of cases, they were legally classified as minors and treated as children. Indians were exempt from some taxes, and because they were viewed as children in the eyes of the church, they were beyond the reach of the Inquisition. The Jesuit missions in Paraguay and Brazil protected their Indian charges from capture by ruthless mameluco slave hunters from Brazil.

Superficial similarities between Catholicism and pre-Columbian beliefs helped the Indians throughout the colonies to adopt Christianity. The quite graphic Spanish crucifixes evoked the self-immolation of the ancient creator gods, a source of pre-Columbian rites of human sacrifice. To varying degrees, the Catholic saints were blended with pre-Columbian deities. A group of Indians devoutly praying at a saint's altar in a baroque cathedral might well be paying homage to the Inca or Aztec deity hidden under the statue's skirts. In the Caribbean areas, the Africans equated Catholic saints to Orisha spirits, resulting in syncretic belief sytsems such as Santería, which is still practiced by many Cubans.

SUMMARY

The Iberian conquest of Latin America set the stage for the creation of a new society that blended contributions from Native Americans, Iberians, and later, Africans. As the conquerors and explorers became colonists, they replaced the Aztec and Inca masters at the top of the socioeconomic ladder. The conquerors' thirst for gold and elite status could be quenched only with the labor of the Indians. Some progressive missionaries tried in vain to protect their Indian charges to convert them humanely to Christianity. Unlike the Portuguese and other imperial powers, the Spanish monarchs grappled with the legal issues involved in the enslavement of their Indian subjects. However, few questioned the morality of importing African slaves to the great plantation zones of Brazil and the Caribbean islands.

The colonial experience in Latin America was quite different from that of Asia, North America, or Africa. Many Europeans eventually settled there but remained far outnumbered by the native Indians and the imported blacks, as well as the mestizos and other mixed-blood peoples. The church and government worked together to create a society that imitated that of the mother countries, while remaining different in many essentials. The unique melding of Iberian with Indian and African cultures proceeded at differing tempos in different places. After the flow of American bullion to the Old World tapered off in the mid-seventeenth century, a long period of stagnation and neglect ensued. A century later, the Spanish Bourbons supervised an economic and political revival in Latin America with mixed results. While the economies of the colonies were stimulated, so was resentment against continued foreign rule. By the early 1800s, armed rebellion against the mother country was imminent, inspired in part by the North American and French models.

IDENTIFICATION TERMS

Test your knowledge of this chapter's key concepts by defining the following terms. If you can not recall the meaning of certain terms, refresh your memory by looking up the boldfaced term in the chapter, turning to the Glossary at the end of the book, or accessing the terms on the CourseMate website at **www.cengagebrain.com**.

criollos
encomienda
gaucho
haciendas
mestizos
Toussaint L'Ouverture
Túpac Amaru II

FOR FURTHER REFLECTION

1. Compare and contrast the administrative structures of the British and Spanish colonies. Then explain why the North Americans were more prepared than the South Americans for independent self-government.
2. Enumerate some of the Iberian, Amerindian, and African cultural contributions to the new Latin American reality that emerged during the colonial period.
3. How did the gold and silver from colonial Mexico and Bolivia affect the economies of Spain, northern Europe, and China?
4. What role do you think racism played in the colonial societies of Spain and Portugal?
5. A mestizo baby born to married parents might be registered at baptism as Spanish or Indian, according to the family's circumstances. What factors might determine his or her category?

TEST YOUR KNOWLEDGE

Test your knowledge of this chapter by answering the following questions. Complete answers appear at the end of the book. You may find even more quiz questions on the CourseMate website at **www.cengagebrain.com**.

1. Which of following Spanish terms does not apply to Hispanic American social or ethnic divisions?
   a. Criollo
   b. Menudo
   c. Mestizo
   d. Mameluco
   e. Mulatto
2. Which of the following factors helped bring about the rapid fall of both the Aztec and Inca empires?
   a. The Indians thought Cortés and Pizarro were devils.
   b. The conquistadors lost their Indian allies against the emperors.
   c. The conquistadors bribed Moctezuma and the Incan king to betray their people.
   d. The Indians had steel weapons capable of killing an armored horseman.
   e. Mass numbers of Indians died or were weakened by foreign diseases.
3. Cattle, sugarcane, and wheat were
   a. native to the Andes mountains of South America.
   b. native to Mexico and Central America.
   c. introduced to the New World by Europeans.
   d. native to North America.
   e. introduced to the New World by Africans.
4. Which of these were main features of the colonial system?
   a. Viceroyalties and cabildos
   b. Democratic elections
   c. Free trade among the viceroyalties
   d. The predominance of small farms owned by mulattos
   e. Separation of church and civil government
5. The conversion of Native Americans to Christianity
   a. was not important to Hispanic conquistadores and settlers.
   b. was accomplished quickly and easily.
   c. largely occurred as a result of efforts by Protestant missionaries.
   d. usually was the result of peaceful efforts by Iberian missionaries.
   e. often was preceded or accompanied by violence or disease.

6. One result of the Bourbon reforms was
   a. decentralization of power and more autonomy for the colonies.
   b. vast improvements in the Indians' quality of life.
   c. mercantilism and trade monopolies.
   d. more efficient government and less corruption.
   e. mine closures and the breakup of huge haciendas.
7. The only successful rebellion by slaves in the Western Hemisphere occurred in
   a. Haiti.
   b. Cuba.
   c. Colombia.
   d. Brazil.
   e. Mexico.
8. Which factor led to the discontent of the criollos with colonial rule?
   a. The consolidation of two viceroyalties into one
   b. The peninsulars' exclusion of criollos from the upper echelons of government and society
   c. The expulsion of the Muslim Moors
   d. The Monroe Doctrine
   e. The Black Legend
9. Most of the work in mines and religious missions was done by
   a. African slaves.
   b. Native Americans.
   c. European mine owners and missionaries.
   d. European settlers eager for employment in payment for their passage to the New World.
   e. Slaves and indentured servants imported from East Asia.
10. The colonial mestizos
   a. were exempt from taxation and the Inquisition.
   b. were never nomadic horsemen.
   c. served as links between the Indian and Spanish populations.
   d. were encouraged to attend university.
   e. could be military officers.

Putting It All Together

1. In Parts Two and Three, we saw how civilizations grew together by forming networks of religious and ideological discourse, trade, migration, and even direct interaction. By 1400, would it be accurate to say that, hitherto, the most successful networks had been forged in Asia and parts of Africa? Would it be accurate to say that Western Europe had created such a network by 1400? If so, what were the principal components of the network?
2. What happened to this internal European network between 1400 and 1700?
3. During the Era of Expansion, 1400–1700, what new networks (or communities of discourse) did Europeans create in exploring and settling other regions of the world? Were these networks successful in including Asians, Africans, and Native Americans, with whom Europeans traded and among whom they settled?
4. Many scholars have interpreted this era of expansion as a time in world history when Asian, African, and American civilizations declined or were even subjugated by "superior" Europeans. Did Europeans defeat and subjugate all peoples with whom they came into contact? In what ways did Asian and African civilizations adapt to and even control the effects of the European presence? In fact, is there any evidence that they continued to develop their civilizations and maintain their own networks?

CROSS-CULTURAL CONNECTIONS

Trade and Exchange Networks

Regional trade systems of the Old and New Worlds tied into global network for the first time during the era of European discovery and exploration. However, Europeans' creation of overseas empires and imposition of mercantilist trading rights adumbrate full potential of a worldwide, free-market based system.

Migrations

Europeans: European migration and widespread colonization of Western hemisphere; fewer Europeans settle permanently in Asia and Africa.
Asians: Southwest Asians migrate and settle Asian and African lands on Indian Ocean; Chinese merchants migrate to Southeast Asia; Indians settle East African coast.
Africans: Africans taken as slaves to Brazil, Caribbean Islands, New Spain, British colonies, Europe, India, and Middle East. Dutch settle Cape Colony.
Americans: Pandemics destroy up to 90 percent of Native American population; many cultures disappear. Ancestral Puebloans continue migrations to upper Rio Grande and Hopi Mesa.

Spread of Ideas and Technologies

Europeans: New World crops introduced to Europe; tobacco, potatoes, squashes, and maize have greatest impact. Bananas, yams, sugar, and coconuts introduced from Africa and Asia.
Asians: Some slaves exported to South Africa. Chinese migrations to regions of Southeast Asia. Some Southeast and South Asians convert to Christianity.
Africans: New World crops introduced, especially manioc and maize. Decline in population in regions of West Africa most heavily affected by the slave trade. Some states destroyed and others thrive because of slave trade. Christianity introduced in some regions but survives in few areas beyond sixteenth century. Islam continues advances in West Africa.
Americans: New food crops brought from Old World: citrus fruits, beef, mutton, and spices as well as sheep wool textile weaving. European settlers and African slaves populate areas previously settled by Native Americans. New diseases imported from Europe and Africa. Christianity introduced and many Native Americans and Africans forced to convert.

Worldview IV

Expanding Webs of Interaction, 1400–1700 C.E.

	 LAW AND GOVERNMENT	 SOCIETY AND ECONOMY
EUROPEANS	• Law and government based on class, but effect of religious wars makes them increasingly secular. Absolutist monarchy is the rule. Nobles and landlords rule free peasants in West, serfs in East. State and church still intertwined; religious tolerance considered dangerous to public order by most governments.	• Economy continues to diversify, with strong capitalist character, especially in Protestant nations. Urban middle class prominent in business and commerce. Class divisions and number of impoverished increase, with serfdom common east of Elbe River. Machine industry begins in later eighteenth century.
ASIANS	• ***East Asians:*** Western presence not yet decisive but becoming more apparent. Japan originally welcomes Westerners but then shuts itself off in *sakoku*. China continues as imperial dynasty ruling through mandarin bureaucracy after Manzhou/Qing dynasty replaces Ming in 1600s. • ***South and Southeast Asians:*** India's north and center unified under Mughals in Delhi, with Europeans beginning to occupy coasts after 1700. Western presence not yet decisive but becoming more apparent. Many South Pacific and Southeast Asian territories under Western administration since 1500s. • ***West and Central Asians:*** Government continues along traditional Qur'anic lines, and law follows Shari'a. Ottomans bring Muslim empire to apex in sixteenth century, but cannot sustain momentum after 1700. Safavid Dynasty in Persia has two hundred years of glory but exhausts itself between Ottoman and Mughal rivals.	• ***East Asians:*** Japan prospers and advances while maintaining sakoku isolation. China has last great age under Qing before suffering humiliation from Europeans. • ***South and Southeast Asians:*** Trade brings north and south together. Mughul India still well-organized country, with much commerce with Southeast Asia and islands. Merchants and craftsmen multiply, but everywhere agrarian village is mainstay of economy. • ***West and Central Asians:*** Complex trade further evolves among Muslim countries as well as between them and non-Muslims. Slavery common, mainly from African sources. Wealth from gold mines in West Africa, spices from East Asia, and carrying trade between India/China and West.
AFRICANS	• Mali declines and is replaced by the Songhay Empire. Dynastic change in Kanem; new state of Kanem-Bornu founded west of Lake Chad. Rise of several new states in West African forest zone based on slave trade; others decline when victimized by slave raids. Kingdoms of Kongo and Ngola in West-Central Africa rise and suffer from destructive slave raiding. New states in Natal region of south Africa; Zulu raids and Boer violence force massive migrations. Omani sultanate in Zanzibar; extensive slave raiding in East African interior. In regions in which Islamic orthodoxy is enforced, women increasingly subordinated to males and clan-based property rights curtailed in conformity to Qur'anic principles.	• Arrival of Europeans along coastal regions. Dutch found colony at Cape Town, 1653; expansion eastward forces Khoisan and Khoikhoi out of their native homelands; Boer society divided into whites, blacks, and coloreds. Slave trade and imports of alcohol and firearms highly destructive of many existing African societies. Slave based plantation economy established in parts of West Africa and offshore islands, along Zambezi and Limpopo Rivers, and along East African coast.
AMERICANS	• By the mid-1500s, Spain and Portugal establish Iberian law and viceroyalties from Mexico to Argentina. Native Americans subordinated to minority of whites. Centralized colonial governments committed to mercantilist system and discouragement of autonomy; reversal of policies occurs in later 1700s.	• Most in both North and South America live in agrarian subsistence economy. Mercantilism enforced until later 1700s, with colonial artisans and manufacturers obstructed by Madrid and London. Mining and plantation agriculture dominant large-scale economic activities in the Latin colonies.

 PATTERNS OF BELIEF	 ARTS AND CULTURE	 SCIENCE AND TECHNOLOGY
• Protestant Reform breaks Christian unity; papal church challenged, but regains some lost ground in seventeenth century. Churches become nationalistic, and theology more narrowly defined. Skepticism and secularism increase after 1700, leading to tolerance by end of eighteenth century. Enlightenment dominates intellectual affairs after *c.* 1750.	• Renaissance continues in plastic arts; age of baroque architecture, sculpture, and painting in Catholic Europe. Neoclassicism of eighteenth century led by France. Vernacular literature flourishes in all countries. Western orchestral music begins. Authors become professionals, and arts begin to be democratized.	• Physical, math-based sciences flourish in "scientific revolution" of seventeenth century. Science replaces scripture and tradition as source of truth for educated. Improved agriculture enables population explosion of eighteenth century. Beginnings of the Industrial Revolution in England.
• ***East Asians:*** Christianity briefly flourishes in Japan until suppressed by Tokugawa shoguns in 1600s. Religious beliefs undergo no changes from Buddhism and Shinto. • ***South and Southeast Asians:*** Religious beliefs undergo no changes from Buddhism; Hinduism (most of India, parts of Southeast Asia); Islam. • ***West and Central Asians:*** *Ulama* and Islamic tradition resist evidence of Western economic and technical advances and refute it on doctrinal grounds. Orthodoxy is severely challenged in parts of empire (e.g., Sufi, Shi'a) and becomes defensive.	• ***East Asians:*** Superb paintings and drawings on porcelain, bamboo, and silk created in China and Japan. Calligraphy major art form. *Kabuki* and No plays invented in Japan, and novels in China. Poetry of nature admired. • ***South and Southeast Asians:*** Expansion makes its last surge into Mughal India. High point of Islamic art forms under Ottoman, Safavid, and Mughal aegis. Architecture, ceramics, miniature painting, and calligraphy particular strengths. In India, Taj Mahal, frescoes, enamel work, and architecture are high points. • ***West and Central Asians:*** Turkish and Persian miniature painting appears. Tribal carpet and textile making highly developed.	• Sciences throughout Asia behind Europe by end of period; exceptions in medicine and pharmacy. • ***East Asians:*** China adopts defensive seclusion from new ideas under mandarins. Technology lags, as overpopulation begins to be problem at end of period, further reducing need for laborsaving devices. • ***South and Southeast Asians:*** Some scientific techniques introduced into Southeast Asia by Europeans. Science and new technology lag in India. • ***West and Central Asians:*** Sciences neglected; mental capital derived from Greek and Persian sources exhausted. Technology also lags, with all ideas coming from West rejected. By the end of period, Westerners moving into preferred posts in commerce of Ottoman and Mughal empires.
• Portuguese convert some Africans in coastal upriver areas, but most resist conversion. African Muslims incorporate many local, traditional beliefs into their Islam. *Jihads* enforce Islamic literacy and "orthodox," Sunni Islam across Saharan and sub-Saharan regions of west Africa; Islam makes some inroads into forest states.	• Most Africans continue traditions of fine art and craftwork, both Islamic and non-Islamic, from natural materials. Distinctive, local styles of Islamic architecture and cuisine appear in West and East Africa.	• Aside from new weapons (firearms), very little new technology developed or introduced among Africans.
• Catholicism makes impression on Latin American Indians, but religion remains mixed cult of pre-Christian and Christian beliefs, supervised by *criollo* priesthood and Spanish hierarchs.	• Church in Latin America remains the sponsor of arts, but folk arts derived from pre-Columbian imagery remain universal. Little domestic literature written, but secular Enlightenment makes inroads into educated class by mid-eighteenth century.	• Science and technology in Latin colonies dependent on stagnant mother country and have no importance to masses. Enlightened monarchs of later 1700s make improvements, but these are temporary and partial. In North America, Enlightenment finds acceptance.

PART V

Worldview Map V The World in the Early Modern Era

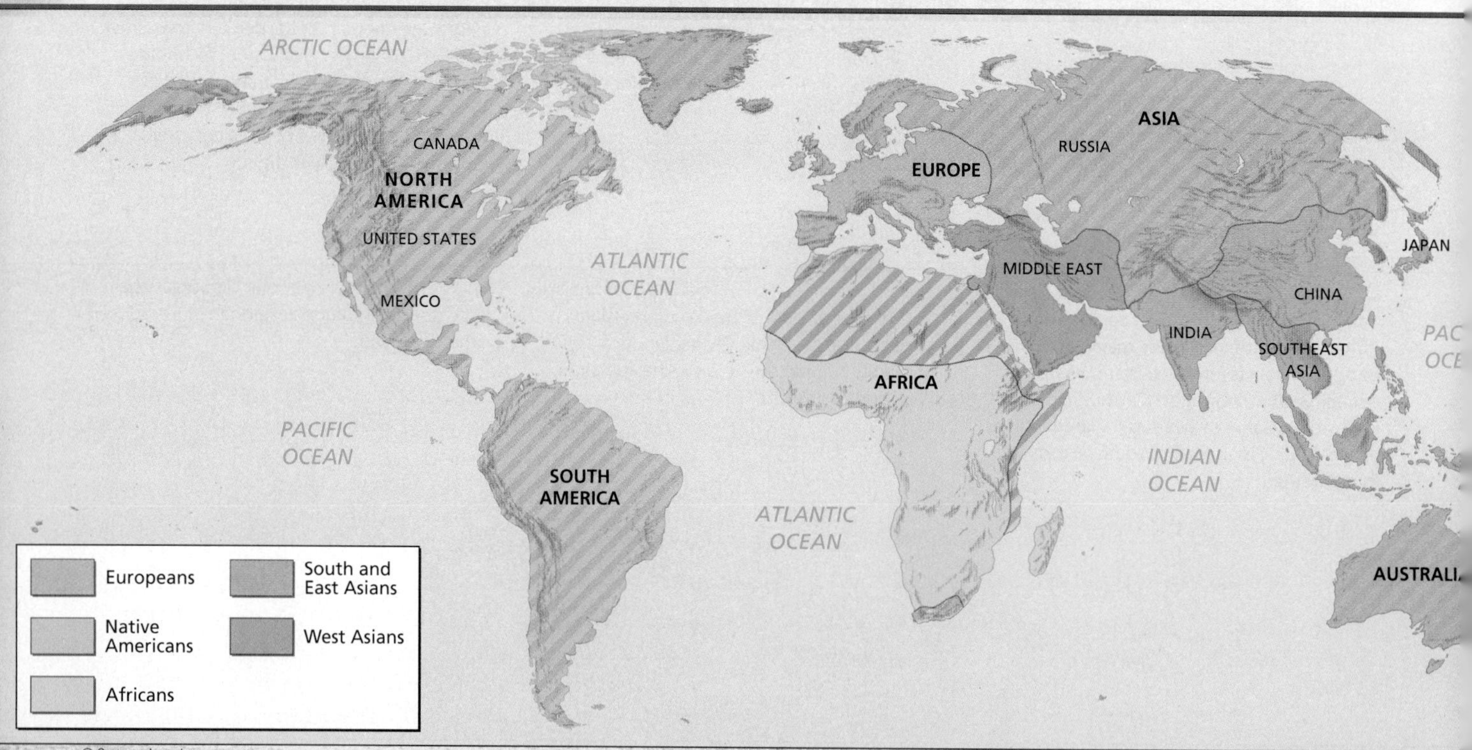

Revolutions, Ideology, the New Imperialism, and the Age of Empire, 1700–1920

After rising secularism had gradually dampened the Europe-wide crisis generated by the Protestant challenge to the papal church, the seventeenth century witnessed the first wave of "scientific revolutions" that would mark modern times. For the first time since the Greeks, the West took the forefront in advances in knowledge about this world and its natural phenomena (Chapter 29).

The same curiosity and willingness to challenge ancient authority that impelled the breakthroughs in natural science were a bit later applied to the "Science of Man," as the eighteenth-century European Enlightenment called it. The Enlightenment was the project of an urban upper class determined to have reason take its rightful place in the halls of government as well as in the school and the home. Filled with a sense of sacred mission, the *philosophes* fought the intolerance and ignorance of the past—most especially the darkness surrounding the established church and the absolutist throne. To some extent, such notions had contributed to the English civil wars of the seventeenth century (Chapter 23), and in the 1770s, they stirred dissidents in England's American colonies to rise up against what they believed were an unrepresentative government and a tyrannical monarchy (Chapter 30).

What they desired in political and constitutional affairs seemingly came to pass in the first flush of the popular revolution in France, but the original reforms were soon overshadowed by a radical democracy and a dictatorship employing terror against all who opposed it. The Napoleonic empire's aggressions confirmed the negative impression gained by most observers outside France and also strengthened the eventual victors' resolve to limit and control both political and social change (Chapter 30).

Following the pattern established in late-eighteenth-century Britain, the rest of Western Europe entered the industrial epoch in the ensuing century by stages. The initial Industrial Revolution was powered by steam and concentrated on a few basic commodity-production processes. Its immediate social repercussions were bitter for the masses of poor laborers in the new towns but were gradually ameliorated (Chapter 31). Advancing industrial development, now powered by the new energy sources of petroleum and electricity, helped bring about further democratization as well as a rising wave of Marxian socialism as the nineteenth century entered its final quarter (Chapter 33). However, the postrevolutionary peace was disturbed by clashes between conservative monarchies and the rising forces of political liberalism, which culminated in the rebellions of 1848 in much of Europe. The short-term failure of most of the 1848 rebellions was caused largely by the new ethnically based nationalism that had arisen in many lands as an indirect result of the French Revolution (Chapter 32).

Meanwhile, with the shift in the military balance of power between the West and the East, Europe became increasingly aggressive overseas. Islamic powers, such as the Ottomans, the Safavids, and the Mughals, were at a disadvantage for the first time in dealing with European powers. Chapter 34 examines the responses of the Islamic peoples of the Near and Middle East to this changed situation. Chapters 35 and 36 consider how the dramatic rise in European aggression in late nineteenth century spilled over into Africa, India, and Southeast Asia and how Africans and Asians responded as Europeans now became their masters in a colonial era that lasted into the mid-twentieth century. Throughout this period of growing European aggression, China, a more unified and powerful state under the Qing Dynasty, managed to resist the outright occupation that Africa and other parts of Asia experienced. Therefore, its story, covered in Chapter 37, presents an interesting case that contrasts significantly when compared with what happened in the states in India, Africa, and Southeast Asia during these centuries. Our examination of this era of discovery and European imperialism concludes with the Iberian colonies of America and their struggle for independent existence, which is outlined in Chapter 38.

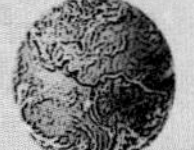

The physical sciences and some of the social sciences also took imposing strides in the second half of the nineteenth century and had various effects on the twentieth and early twenty-first centuries. Therefore, Part Five concludes with a short chapter (Chapter 39) that considers how these advances occurred and the impact they have had on the modern popular consciousness.

Our Worldview Map V, The World in the Early Modern Era, illustrates the ethnic and language groups of the world and the regions in which they were prevalent. Note that there were considerable overlaps. Why do you suppose this was so?

29 The Scientific Revolution and Its Enlightened Aftermath

If I have seen farther than others, it is because I have stood on the shoulders of giants. —ISAAC NEWTON

1543	Nicholas Copernicus, Revolution of the Heavenly Bodies
c. 1575–c. 1650	Francis Bacon, Galileo Galilei, René Descartes
1687	Isaac Newton, *Principia Mathematica*, law of gravitation
1690	John Locke, *Essay Concerning Human Understanding*
1730s–1789	Enlightenment flourishes
1776	Adam Smith, *Wealth of Nations*
1776	Thomas Jefferson, *Declaration of Independence*

CHAPTER OUTLINE

Perhaps the most far-reaching of all the "revolutions" since the introduction of agriculture in the Neolithic Age was the early modern era's change in educated people's thinking about natural phenomena, their laws, and their relation to a presumed creator. This *Scientific Revolution* became fully evident in the work of the eighteenth-century *philosophes*, but its major outlines were drawn earlier, when the focus of European intellectual work gradually shifted away from theology to the mathematical and empirical sciences. By the end of the eighteenth century, it had proceeded so far among the educated classes that a new worldview was taken for granted—one that seriously challenged the medieval conviction that an omniscient God ordained and guided the natural processes, including the life and eternal fate of mankind. While the consolidation of royal absolutism seemed to be rigorously proceeding in most of Europe during the seventeenth and eighteenth centuries, the sciences successfully undermined traditional theology's claims and by so doing countered the royal throne's aspirations for acceptance as God's chosen representative on earth.

THE SCIENTIFIC REVOLUTION OF THE SEVENTEENTH CENTURY

So great were the achievements during this epoch that one of the outstanding modern philosophers said that "the two centuries [that followed] have been living upon the accumulated capital of ideas provided for them by the genius of the seventeenth century." The natural sciences—that is, those based primarily on observed phenomena of nature—experienced a huge upswing in importance and accuracy. A new style of examining phenomena, the **scientific method**, came into common usage. It was composed of two elements: careful observation and systematic experimentation based on that observation. Interpretation of the results of the experiments, largely relying on mathematical measurement, was then employed to achieve new and verified knowledge.

The most significant advances in the sciences came from posing new types of questions rather than from collecting new facts. Different questions led directly to novel avenues of investigation, and those led to new data being observed and experimented with. For example, **René Descartes** (reh-NAY day-CART; 1596–1650), one of the founders of the mathematical style of investigation, wished to take humanity to a higher plane of perfection than ever yet achieved. To do so, he separated the material from the nonmaterial universe completely, insisting that the material world could be comprehended by mathematical formulas that existed entirely apart from the human mind. If that was so, knowledge of these broad laws of number and quantity could provide explanations—hitherto lacking—of observed phenomena. The proper way to understand the material world, then, was to formulate broad generalizations of a quantitative nature and employ them to explain specific events or processes. This approach, in which one went from a general law to a particular example of that law observed by the human mind, was called **deductive reasoning**.

Another method of accumulating knowledge about the natural world was exemplified in the writings of Englishman Francis Bacon (1561–1626). Bacon insisted that contrary to traditional belief, most ideas and principles that explain nature had not yet been discovered or developed but lay buried, like so many gems under the earth, awaiting discovery. Like Descartes, he looked forward to a better, more completely understood world, but this world was to be created through persistent and careful observation of phenomena without any preconceived laws or general explanations of them—a process that became known as **inductive reasoning**.

Bacon was not methodical in his science or his reasoning. His close association with the concept of inductive reasoning is perhaps not really deserved, but his writings did encourage later scientists to practice the **empirical method** of gathering data and then forming generalizations. *Empirical* means the evidence obtained by observation through the five senses, which is then worked up into varying hypotheses (assumptions) that may be subjected to experiment. This style of assembling facts and verifying knowledge blossomed in the seventeenth century and later became a foundation of the sciences.

Background of the Scientific Revolution

Why did the spectacular advances in natural science occur in the seventeenth century rather than earlier or later? There is no single answer to this question. As with most important changes in the status quo of human knowledge, several factors came together at that time to encourage more rapid progress than before, but this is not to say that no progress had been under way previously. It is now accepted that the old view of medieval science as a laughable collection of superstitions and crackpot experiments is quite wrong. The medieval universities harbored many people who seriously undertook to widen the horizons of knowledge and had some success in doing so.

The real problem of medieval and Renaissance science seems to have been not its superstitions but its exaggerated reliance on authority rather than evidence. The great Greek philosophers of science—Aristotle, Ptolemy, Galen, Eratosthenes, and Archimedes—were held in excessive reverence as the givers of final truth. The weakening of this reverence was a precursor of the breakthroughs of the sixteenth and seventeenth centuries.

Stimulated and aided by the reports of the explorers and voyagers in the New World, scholars accumulated a mass of evidence about nature and geography that both amplified and contradicted some of what the traditional authorities had taught. Such evidence could be ignored only at the risk of retarding the power and wealth of the whole exploring society. Still more important, perhaps, was the rapid advance in the mathematical capabilities of Europeans. At the beginning of the sixteenth century, European math was still at the same level as in the seventh century. Only with the recovery of the Greek and Hellenistic mathematical works could it advance into new areas: logarithms, calculus, and decimals. By the mid-seventeenth century, math had become as much a device for theoretical exploration as for counting.

Another mass of data that partly contradicted what the Greeks had believed was the product of new instruments. The new math made possible analyses of the physical world that had never before been attempted. Instruments of all sorts (sensitive scales, pressure gauges, microscopes, telescopes, thermometers, chronometers) came along one after the other to assist in this analysis. It was now possible to measure, weigh, divide, and synthesize the world in ways that explained the previously inexplicable.

THE PROGRESS OF SCIENTIFIC KNOWLEDGE: COPERNICUS TO NEWTON

The rediscovery of the Greco-Roman scientific treatises by the Renaissance scholars from Arabic translations of Greek and Latin originals stimulated curiosity while providing a series of new insights into the makeup of the natural world—insights that contradicted the conventional wisdom of the day. This progress was sharply interrupted by the wars of religion in the sixteenth century, when the focus shifted away from science to clashing theologies.

Only with the exhaustion of those religious antipathies after the Thirty Years' War did scientific endeavors once again take a primordial position in educated men's affairs.

Our emphasis on seventeenth-century events does not mean that modern science commenced then. The acknowledged breakthrough in empirical knowledge of the natural world came a century earlier with the *Revolution of the Heavenly Bodies*, the pioneering treatise on astronomy by Polish scholar **Nicholas Copernicus** (1473–1543). Copernicus cast severe doubt on the traditional and generally accepted theory of an Earth-centered (**geocentric**) universe, which he criticized as unnaturally complex and difficult to understand. Copernicus's observations led him to conclude that the Earth revolved around a fixed sun, a belief first advanced by Hellenistic Greek astronomers. A cautious and devout Catholic, Copernicus published his conclusions only in the year of his death. The church ignored his theory at first, although both Luther and Calvin ridiculed it, but when **heliocentrism** began to win adherents in large numbers, both Rome and the Protestants officially condemned it as contrary to both scripture and common sense.

Two astronomer-mathematicians who emerged a generation after Copernicus also deserve our attention. The first was an eccentric Dane, Tycho Brahe (1546–1601), who spent much of his life taking endless, precise measurements of the cosmic rotation of the visible planets. Using these data, the German **Johannes Kepler** (1571–1630) went on to formulate the *three laws of celestial mechanics*, which showed that the heavenly bodies moved in great ellipses (ovals) around the sun, rather than in the perfect circles that had been believed necessary as the handiwork of a perfect creator. This insight explained what had previously been inexplicable and made Copernicus's proposals still more persuasive.

In the early 1600s, an Italian professor at Pisa named **Galileo Galilei** (1564–1642) used his improvement of the telescope to rewrite the rules of cosmology as handed down from the ancients. His discoveries strongly supported Copernicus's suppositions that the universe was sun centered and that the Earth was a relatively small, insignificant planet in a huge solar system. Not only did Galileo's astronomy force clerical authorities to reconsider the condemned theory of Copernicus, but his physics contributed to the final overthrow of Aristotle's long reign as master physicist. Through his work with falling bodies and the laws of motion, Galileo came close to discovering the fundamental law of all nature: the law of gravity.

When Galileo died in 1642, the whole traditional view of the physical universe as an impenetrable mystery—created by God for his own reasons and not responsive to human inquiries—was beginning to come apart. The limiting horizons to human knowledge and understanding that had been in place for many centuries were steadily receding as the seventeenth century progressed. What was still needed was some overarching explanation of the physical world order. The genius of **Isaac Newton** (1642–1727) put the capstone of the new science in place. While still a student at Cambridge University, he theorized that there must be a "master key" to the edifice of the universe. In the century and a quarter since Copernicus, a great deal had been discovered or strongly indicated about the laws of nature. Still lacking, however, was a universally applicable explanation of the most basic property of matter: motion.

In the 1660s, Newton occupied himself with the study of physics. At that time, he evolved his deceptively simple-looking theorem—the most famous in the history of the world—$E = M^2/D^2$. This was the formula of the law of gravitation, although it as yet lacked mathematical proof. After many more years of research, Newton published his conclusions and their proofs in the ***Principia Mathematica*** in 1687. The *Principia* was the most influential book on science in the seventeenth century and was soon known from one end of educated Europe to the other. (See the Science and Technology box for more on Newton.)

Newton proposed a new universe. The physical cosmos was a sort of gigantic clockwork in which every part played a particular role and every movement and change was explained by the operation of impersonal physical laws. It was humans' proud duty and privilege to identify those laws and in so doing to penetrate to the heart of the universe.

RELIGION AND SCIENCE IN THE SEVENTEENTH CENTURY

How did the official churches react to this challenge to tradition? Both Catholic and Protestant preachers felt that relegating Earth to a secondary, dependent position in the universe was at least an implied rejection of Holy Scripture (the Old Testament story about the sun standing still at the Battle of Jericho, for example). It also downgraded the jewel of God's creation, human beings, who lived on this inferior Earth and were presumably limited to it. The Catholic Galileo was threatened with imprisonment if he did not retract parts of what he had published in one of his books on science. He spent his final years under house arrest by order of the pope.

Were these condemnations justified? Most of the seventeenth-century scientists considered themselves good Christians and made no attempt to rule a divine being out of the universe. A devout Anglican, Newton spent most of his later life embarked on religious speculations and obscure theological inquiries. Descartes, like Copernicus before him, was a Catholic who saw no conflict between what he taught about the nature of the material world and what he believed about the spiritual one. Quite to the contrary, Descartes believed that his speculations only pointed more clearly to the existence of a divine intelligence in the universe.

SCIENCE AND TECHNOLOGY

Isaac Newton (1642–1727)

The man many consider to be the most distinguished scientist of all history, Sir Isaac Newton, was born on Christmas Day, 1642, in Lancashire, England. Best recognized as the discoverer of the law of gravity, Newton was equally famed for his work in optics, higher mathematics, and physics in his own day. He was a distinct exception to the rule that pioneers are not appreciated; his career as both a Cambridge professor and a government official under William and Mary was brilliant and adequately rewarded.

Although his father was a farmer with little property, Newton received an exceptional education. He completed studies at the local grammar school near his home village, with the aid and encouragement of the Anglican vicar, who was a graduate of Cambridge. With this gentleman's recommendation, Isaac won a scholarship to the university in 1661, graduating in 1665 with what would now be called a major in natural science. He wished to go on for a master's degree at once, but an outbreak of plague forced the university to close in both 1666 and 1667, and Newton returned home.

ISAAC NEWTON.

During these years, his great, groundbreaking work on gravity was basically outlined. The notion that all physical being was, so to speak, tied together by a single principle—that of gravity—took shape in the twenty-five-year-old's long studies at his family home in Woolsthorpe. Newton gradually refined and expanded his theory when he returned to Cambridge, first as a master's candidate and then as a professor in 1669. He held this post until his honor-filled retirement in 1701.

Although Newton apparently regarded gravitation as a fact as early as the 1660s, he hesitated in publishing his work until 1687. In that year, his *Principia Mathematica*, or *Mathematical Principles of Natural Philosophy*, was finally published in London and soon afterward in most of the capitals of Europe. Rarely has a scientific book been hailed so universally as a work of genius. At the same time, Newton was bringing out fundamentally important work on the spectrum, proving that light was composed of colored light bands. Newton is also generally credited with being the codiscoverer of calculus, along with his rival Gottfried Leibniz. The two men were working independently, and their quarrel over who was first became one of the Scientific Revolution's less appetizing anecdotes.

In his later years, Newton's dedication to Old Testament studies and theology surpassed his scientific interests. Newton was a master of Greek and Hebrew and spent much energy on his researches into the Old Testament prophecies.

Highly placed friends secured his appointment as warden of the Royal Mint in 1696, a lucrative post that Newton was grateful to have. In 1703, he was elected president of the Royal Society, the premier scientific post in England, and was reelected every year thereafter until his death. The queen knighted Sir Isaac in 1705 for services to his country as well as to the realm of science. Newton died at eighty-five years of age, heaped with honors and substantial wealth. On his deathbed, he is supposed to have said, "If I have seen farther than others, it is because I have stood on the shoulders of giants." After a state funeral, he was buried in Westminster Abbey.

The famous story of the falling apple just may be true; no one will ever know.

ANALYZE AND INTERPRET

Contrast the fashion in which Newton gave his formula on gravitation to the world and the way such an announcement might be made today by modern scientists. Why do you think he chose to use Latin as his vehicle, so late in the 1680s?

But the church's truth, resting as it did on revelation rather than empirical data, was being challenged—at first only tangentially, but later more confrontationally—by the facts being revealed by science. Furthermore, science's truth had no axes to grind for one party or another. It was not linked to politics or to a social group's advantage or disadvantage. It was self-evident and could sometimes be used to benefit the ordinary person—for example, through its conversion to new technology (although the connections between science and technology were as yet almost entirely undeveloped).

Increasingly, educated people were beginning to wonder whether it was more useful to know if the Holy Eucharist should be given in two forms or to know how digestion takes place in the stomach or some similar aspect of the new physical science. Science came to be seen as an alternative to theology in finding useful knowledge and applying it to society's multiple problems.

In this regard, two of the most important thinkers of the seventeenth century were the agnostic Dutch Jew Baruch Spinoza and the pious Catholic Frenchman Blaise Pascal. Spinoza was a great questioner, who after leaving Judaism finally found some measure of peace by perceiving his God in all creation. His rejection of a personal deity earned him a great deal of trouble, but his thoughts influenced generations. Pascal wrote his *Pensées* (PAHN-says: *Thoughts*) to calm a troubled mind and produced a work that has been considered one of the greatest of Christian consolations ever since. The fact that Pascal was highly suspect to the French clerical establishment only added to his later fame.

THE SCIENCE OF MAN

Until modern times, the natural sciences were regarded as a branch of philosophy rather than a separate intellectual discipline, but as a branch of philosophy, they had obtained some respectability. Already in the Renaissance, math and physics began to establish a place in the university curriculum. Their prestige was still relatively low and they could not rival medicine, law, or theology in attracting students, but their own rules of evidence and analysis were being formed.

As the mathematics-based sciences came to be accepted as sources of much theretofore unknown truth, the previous relation between natural science and philosophy underwent a gradual but decisive reversal. Philosophy, which had been the more inclusive discipline, *encompassing* science, now became for many people a *branch* of science. Insomuch as an object of thought could not be measured and weighed, it ceased to be worthy of close attention. Individuals thinking along these lines held that only what could be determined in its existence by the tools of science was reachable by the power of reason and useful to humans. They did not deny that other phenomena that were not measurable and not reachable by reason existed, but they insisted that these phenomena should have only a secondary place in the hierarchy of human values.

Among those phenomena, of course, were religious belief, artistic creativity, wonder, imagination, ethics, and political theory, to mention only a few. None of these could be measured, and none could be brought under uniform and predictable laws. Or could they? A body of thought gradually arose that said that these phenomena, too, might be subject to law, analyzable through mathematical computations, and comprehensible in the same way as physics. The *Science of Man*—not man as an anatomical construct or an example of biological systems but as a thinker, political actor, and artist—began to form. By the early eighteenth century, this science, which we now call social science, was competing with physical science for the attention of the educated classes.

THE ENLIGHTENMENT

Eighteenth-century intellectual leaders saw no reason why what had been done in the natural sciences could not be attempted in the social sciences. They wanted to put history, politics, jurisprudence, and economics under the same logical lenses that had been applied to math and physics. Spurred on by such hopes, the **Enlightenment** was born.

Above all, the eighteenth century in Western Europe was distinguished from what had come before by the attitudes that educated persons exhibited in the affairs of everyday life: the atmosphere of their mental life. Two key characteristics of the Enlightenment asserted themselves again and again: optimism and rationality. Here, *optimism* refers to the belief that change is possible and controllable in society at large, whereas *rationality* refers to the idea that the universe and all creatures within it, especially humans, are comprehensible, predictable, and lawful. The commitment to a rational view of the universe usually embraced a similar commitment to *secularism*—that is, a downgrading or outright rejection of the importance of supernatural religion. The Enlightenment preferred to see humanity as capable of creating its own moral code for its own benefit and in accord with the precepts of a rational mind.

How did this translate to concrete activity? The ways of viewing the physical world that math and physics had introduced were now applied—or an attempt was made to apply them—to the world's social, political, and moral aspects. If physicists could measure the weight of Earth's atmosphere (and they now could), then why could historians not isolate the exact causes of cultural retardation and determine how to avoid them in the future? Why could criminologists not build a model prison and establish a regime there that would turn out completely rehabilitated prisoners? Why could political scientists not calibrate various methods of selecting public officials to ensure that only the best were elected?

Formative Figures and Basic Ideas

Although the movement was a truly international one, the two outstanding progenitors of the Enlightenment's ideals were the Englishmen Newton and John Locke. As we have already seen, Newton was the greatest scientific mind of his age; Locke was the leading mapper of the political path that England embarked on with the Glorious Revolution of 1688 (see Chapter 23).

Newton's greatest contribution to science—related to but even more important than the law of gravity—was his insistence on rational, lawful principles in all operations of physical nature. He rejected supernatural causes as an explanation of the natural world, holding that because nature is rational, human society as part of nature should be rational in its organization and function.

Locke was as much a psychologist as a political scientist; he set forth his view of the mind in the immensely influential ***Essay Concerning Human Understanding*** (1690). Here, he said that the mind is a blank page until experience and environment write on it and mold it. Thus, human nature is dynamic and unfixed; it has been in the past and will be in the future formed by external experience, and this experience is capable of being controlled. So humans are not condemned to repeat endlessly the sin of Adam and the mistakes of the past. They can and must take charge of their destiny; they can perfect themselves.

More than anything else, this faith in *perfectibility* is the distinguishing innovation of the Enlightenment. For the previous seventeen centuries, the Christian idea of guilt from the sin of Adam as an insuperable barrier to human perfection had been the foundation stone of Western moral philosophy. Now, the eighteenth century proposed to move the house off this foundation and erect it anew. Progress, both moral and physical, was reachable and real. The study of history showed how far humans had come and how far they still had to go. The past was filled with error and blindness, but it could be—*must* be—learned from so that it could light the way to a better future.

The reformers believed that those who profited from ignorance and prejudice controlled religious belief, and used it as a tool everywhere to obscure the truth. They took an especially harsh view of the Roman Catholic clergy. Where the church had obtained a monopolistic position in the state and was the official church, the reformers believed that inevitable corruption had made it a parasite that should be cast off as soon as possible and replaced with freedom of conscience and worship.

In the reformers' view, education was the salvation of humankind. It should be promoted at every opportunity everywhere. Insofar as people were educated, they were good. The fully educated would be unerring seekers of the best that life held, defenders of the helpless, teachers of the misguided, and the liberators of the oppressed.

The Philosophes and Their Ideals

The Enlightenment was a view of life, a philosophy, and that meant that it must have its philosophers. Generically known by the French term ***philosophes*** (FIL-oh-sohfs), they included men and women of both thought and action, scientists and philosophers, who were committed to the cause of reform. Despite intense personal differences, they were united in their desire for progress, by which they meant controlled changes.

Several of the outstanding philosophes were French. Paris, and secondarily London, was the center of the Enlightenment's activities (it was a decidedly urban phenomenon), but the philosophes kept in frequent touch with one another through a network of clubs and correspondents that covered the map of Europe (see Map 29.1). They included the Frenchmen Voltaire (Vohl-TAYR; François-Marie Arouet), Baron Montesquieu (MAHN-tehs-kyoo), Denis Diderot (DEE-deh-roh), and Jean-Jacques Rousseau (Roo-SOH); the English and Scots David Hume, Adam Smith, Samuel Johnson, William Godwin, and **Mary Wollstonecraft**; the Germans Josef von Sonnenfels, Gotthold Lessing, and August Ludwig von Schlozer; and the Italians Lodovico Muratori and Cesare Beccaria; but the list could be made as long as one wants. The Americans Thomas Jefferson, Benjamin Franklin, and John Adams belong on this list as well. The Enlightenment had no territorial boundaries, although it was much narrower and shallower in Eastern Europe than in the West and had much less impact on the public conduct of government there. Chronologically, the earliest evidence of enlightened activity in organized fashion dates from the 1730s. The period of most active endeavor ended with the French Revolution's political crises. The high point was in the 1770s and 1780s, when various governments from North America to Russia experimented with, gave lip service to, or fully adopted one after another of the favored ideas of the philosophes.

Beyond the commitment to reform, it is difficult to find a common denominator in these ideas because the philosophes themselves are difficult to categorize. Some of them were the first public atheists, but most were at least outward Christians, and some were pious clergymen. Muratori, for example, was a priest. Most believed constitutional monarchy was the best form of government, whereas others were uncompromising believers in representative government.

In the physical sciences, some believed unreservedly in Bacon's procedure of going to the sense-perceptible data (empirical science), others doubted all knowledge that was not reducible to mathematics, and still others classified quantifiable knowledge as inherently inferior. Some were hopeful of a gradual improvement in human affairs (*ameliorationism)*; others were convinced that nothing important could be accomplished without radical, even revolutionary changes in society.

MAP 29.1 Centers of the Enlightenment, *c.* 1750

The absence of Enlightenment centers in Turkish-controlled southeast Europe and their paucity east of the Elbe and south of the Pyrenees were decisive influences on the future of these regions in the ensuing century. Focused on cities and academies, the Enlightened society was the spearhead of later social and political innovation.

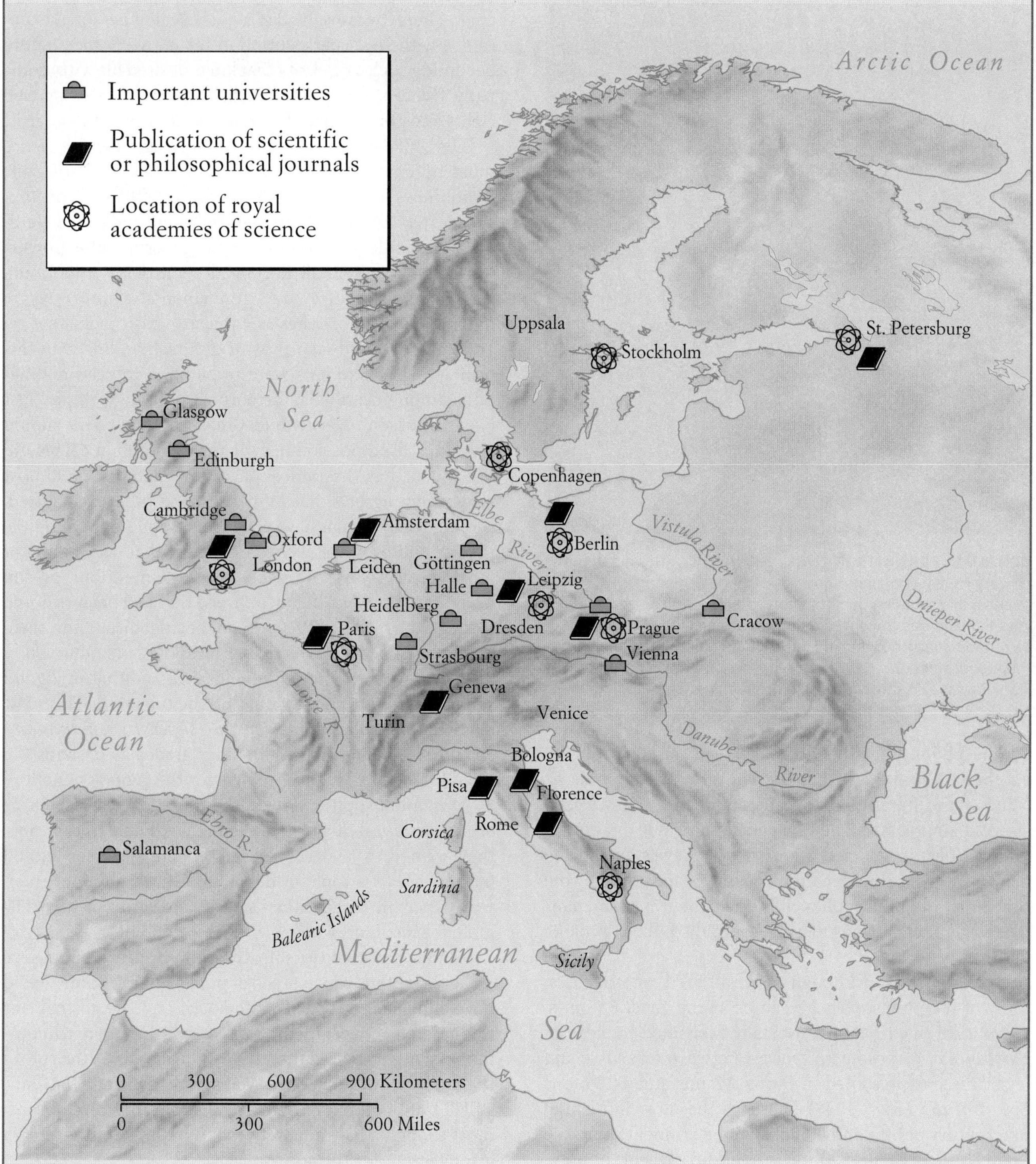

THINKING ABOUT THIS MAP

Why were cities the places most likely to be receptive to new ideas?

BENJAMIN FRANKLIN IN THE LABORATORY. This nineteenth-century French engraving shows the American diplomat-scientist investigating the attraction and repulsion of electrical ions. Franklin was convinced that someday electricity could be rendered useful to humankind. Along with other framers of the American *Declaration of Independence* and the *Constitution*, Franklin was a scientist and a significant Enlightenment figure.

The philosophes did not hesitate to argue with one another as well as with their conservative opponents. Much of the literature of the later eighteenth century consists of pamphlets and newspapers arguing one or another favorite idea. In a society where literacy levels made wide distribution of printed matter a paying proposition for the first time, the philosophes fully used the available channels to get their various messages into the public domain.

Common Goals. Although they differed on specifics, most of the philosophes agreed on many general points. In political theory, they universally acclaimed the idea of a *balance of governmental powers* between executive and legislature, as presented in Baron Montesquieu's famous ***Spirit of the Laws*** (1748)—perhaps the most influential of a century of influential books on government. In it, the French aristocrat argued for the careful division of powers to prevent any one branch from becoming too strong and dictatorial. He thought that of current governments, the British example came closest to perfection in that line (he did not really understand the British system, however), and his ideas strongly influenced the authors of both the U.S. and the French revolutions and their ensuing constitutions.

The *constitutional limitation of monarchic power* was considered an absolute essential of decent government. The brilliant Voltaire (1694–1778), in particular, led the charge here, because he had a good deal of personal experience with royal persecution in his native France before becoming such a celebrity that kings desired his witty company. He, too, admired the British system of ensuring civil rights and condemned the French lack of such safeguards.

The philosophes also agreed that *freedom of conscience* must be ensured at least for all varieties of Christians, if not Jews and atheists as well. "Established" or tax-supported churches should be abolished, and no one faith or sect should be equipped with governmental powers (as was the case in all European countries at this time). All persons should enjoy a fundamental *equality before the law.* The philosophes saw this as a basic right that no government could take away or diminish. In line with this principle, punishments were to be blind to class distinctions among criminals; the baron would be whipped just like the peasant. Meanwhile, those who had talent should have increased possibilities for upward mobility. This did not mean that the philosophes were democrats; almost all of them agreed that humans, being differently gifted, should definitely *not* have equal social and political rights.

The philosophes were convinced that the cause of most misery was ignorance, not evil intentions or sin. They were thus picking up a thread that had been running through the fabric of Western intellectual discussion since the Renaissance: that the main causes of man's inhumanity to man were to be found in ignorance and that in a good society, such ignorance would not be tolerated. This view led the philosophes to call for *state-supervised, mandatory education* through the elementary grades as perhaps the most important practical reform for the general benefit.

Most philosophes viewed the *abolition of most forms of censorship* as a positive step toward the free society they wished to see realized. Just where the lines should be drawn was a topic of debate, however; some of them would permit direct attacks on Christianity or any religion, for instance, whereas others would not.

In addition to censorship, the philosophes did not agree on several other broad areas of public affairs. Some would have abolished the barriers to social equality so that, for example, all government posts would be open to commoners; others feared that this would guarantee the rule of the mob. A few, such as the Marquis de Lafayette (lah-fah-YEHT) and the North Americans, became republicans; most thought that monarchy was a natural and necessary arrangement for the good of all.

Economic Thought: Adam Smith

The outstanding figure in eighteenth-century economic thought was undoubtedly the Scotsman **Adam Smith**

(1723–1790). In his ***Wealth of Nations***, which was published in 1776 and soon became a European best seller in several languages, Smith put forth the gospel of free trade and free markets. Smith is often described as opposing government intervention in the national economy, and that a totally free market could solve all economic problems to the benefit of all. *Laissez-faire* ("let them do what they will") was supposedly his trademark, but this is oversimplification of Smith's ideas. In another work, *The Theory of Moral Sentiments*, Smith emphasized sympathy for others. Looked at as a whole, in his two major works he recognized that human nature has many aspects, some of which come to the fore depending upon the situation. He acknowledged that government intervention in one form or another was necessary for society's well-being.

Smith is, however, rightly credited with being the father of *free enterprise* as that term is used in the modern West. In *The Wealth of Nations*, he laid out in persuasive detail his conviction that an "unseen hand" operated through a free market in goods and services to bring the ultimate consumers what they needed and wanted at prices they were willing to pay. Smith criticized mercantilism, the ruling economic wisdom of his time, for operating to the disadvantage of most consumers. As in so many other instances, his doctrines followed the Enlightenment's underlying conviction that the sum of abundant individual liberties must be collective well-being. Whether this is true, seen from the perspective of the twenty-first century, is debatable; to the eighteenth-century reformers, it was a matter of faith.

In *The Theory of Moral Sentiments*, Smith develops a theory of psychology in which individuals seek the approval of the "impartial spectator" as a result of a natural desire to have outside observers sympathize with them. Rather than viewing *The Wealth of Nations* and *The Theory of Moral Sentiments* as presenting incompatible views of human nature, taken together they represent a more rounded and complete exposition of Smith's thought.

Educational Theory and the Popularization of Knowledge

One of the least orthodox of the philosophes, **Jean-Jacques Rousseau** (1712–1778), was the most influential of all in the vitally important field of pedagogy and educational philosophy. Rousseau was a maverick in believing that children can and must follow their inherent interests in a proper education and that the teacher should use those interests to steer the child in the wished-for directions. Rousseau had little following in his own lifetime, but his ideas strongly influenced some of the revolutionary leaders a few years later and gained more adherents in the nineteenth century. He is now regarded as the founder of modern pedagogical theory.

In the mid-eighteenth century, Europeans were able to profit for the first time from the popularization of science and intellectual discourse that had come about through the Scientific Revolution. The upper classes developed a passion for collecting, ordering, and indexing knowledge about the natural world and humans' relations with it and with each other. The century also saw the initial attempts to make science comprehensible and accessible to the masses.

The most noted of these was the immensely successful French ***Encyclopédie*** (AHN-suh-cloh-pay-dee), which contained thirty-five volumes and thousands of individual articles on literally everything under the sun. Its general editor was Denis Diderot (DEE-dah-roh: 1713–1784), assisted by Jean d'Alembert (dah-lam-BAYR), who saw the work through in fifteen years (1751–1765) against enormous odds. Contributors to the *Encyclopédie* (the first of its kind) included the outstanding intellectuals of Europe. The philosophical articles were often controversial, and their "slant" was always in the direction favored by the more liberal philosophes. (Not the least valuable part of the enterprise was the numerous volumes of illustrations, which are the greatest single source of information on early technology.) The expensive *Encyclopédie* sold more than fifteen thousand copies—a huge number for the day—and was found on personal library shelves from one end of Europe to the other, as well as in the Americas and Russia.

Ideals of the Enlightenment: Reason, Liberty, and Happiness

Reason was the key word in every philosophical treatise and every political tract of the Enlightenment. What was reasonable was good; what was good was reasonable. The philosophes took for granted that the reasoning faculty was humans' highest gift and that its exercise would, sooner or later, guarantee a decent and just society on earth. Liberty was the birthright of all, but it was often stolen away by kings and their agents. Liberty meant the personal freedom to do and say anything that did not harm the rights of another person or institution or threaten the welfare of society.

Happiness was another birthright of all humans. They should not have to defer happiness until a problematic eternity; it should be accessible here and now. In a reasonable, natural world, ordinary men and women would be able to engage in what one of the outstanding philosophes called "the pursuit of happiness" (Thomas Jefferson in the *Declaration of Independence*, see Chapter 30).

All of the ideals of the philosophes flowed together in the concept of progress. For the first time in European history, the belief that humans were engaged in an ultimately successful search for a new state of being here on earth crystallized among a large group. The confidence and energy that were once directed to the attainment of heaven were now transferred to the improvement of earthly life. Progress was inevitable, and it was the individual's proud task to assist in its coming.

Portrait of the Young Voltaire (1694–1778) (oil on canvas), French School, (18th century)/Musee Antoine Lecuyer, Saint-Quentin, France/Giraudon/The Bridgeman Art Library

Jean-Jacques Rousseau, 1766 (oil on canvas), Ramsay, Allan (1713–84)/National Gallery of Scotland, Edinburgh, Scotland/The Bridgeman Art Library

DUAL PORTRAITS: VOLTAIRE AND ROUSSEAU. Two faces of the Enlightenment are shown here, when they were young men. Voltaire's confident smile suited the man who wrote the savagely satirical *Candide*, whereas Rousseau's moral seriousness comes across in this portrait of the author as a young man.

The Audience of the Philosophes

How thoroughly did the Enlightenment penetrate European society? It was not by any means a mass movement. Its advocates, both male and female, were most at home amid the high culture of the urban elite. (See the Society and Economy box on Mary Wollstonecraft.) There were probably more fans of the acid satire of Voltaire in Paris than in all the rest of France and more readers of Hume in London than in all the remainder of the British Isles. It was an age of brilliant conversationalists, and the hostesses who could bring the celebrated minds of the day together were indispensable to the whole movement. In the "salons" of Madame X or Madame Y were heard the exchanges of ideas and opinions that were the heartbeat of the Enlightenment.

The movement hardly ever attempted direct communication with the masses. In any case, most were still illiterate and could not absorb this highly language-dependent message. Others, especially among the peasants, rejected it as atheist or antitraditional. Only the upper strata—the educated professional and

Mary Evans Picture Library/Alamy Limited

WILLIAM (1738–1822) AND CAROLINE (1750–1848) HERSCHEL. William Herschel is credited with many discoveries in astronomy, including Uranus, as illustrated here. However, throughout most of his scientific life, he and his sister Caroline worked closely as a team. Caroline made several discoveries of comets, and in 1828 the Royal Astronomical Society presented her with their Gold Medal for her work.

SOCIETY AND ECONOMY

The Enlightened Woman: Mary Wollstonecraft (1759–1797)

The Enlightenment supported the notion of the equality of the sexes only in general ways, and there was wide disagreement as to the extent and the ways in which women were the equals of men. Most characteristic of that era was the notion that women had a nature specific to themselves, so this produced endless speculation among the philosophes as to what made a woman a woman; what it was that distinguished her from a man; and, once such comparisons were made, what rights could be given to women in a rational, ordered society.

Into this situation stepped one of the few women willing to take a public stance on behalf of her sex: the English intellectual and writer, Mary Wollstonecraft. The courage it took to speak her mind and to live a life independent of social approval required a lifetime of learning to fend for herself. Born the second of six children to an abusive father who squandered his inheritance, at the age of nineteen, Mary was forced to seek her own livelihood. Just four years later, she interceded to help her sister escape a bad marriage by hiding her until a separation could be arranged. To support themselves, Mary and her sister established a school, an experience from which Mary formed her ideas concerning women's education. In 1788, she became a regular contributor of articles and reviews to the radical journal, *Analytical Reviews*. In 1792, she published her *Vindication on the Rights of Woman*, the work for which she became at once both notorious and famous. In this, she dared to advocate the equality of the sexes and expressed opinions that eventually became the foundation of the women's movement. She accused society of breeding and educating women to be helpless "gentle domestic brutes." To the extent that contemporary society considered women to be foolish and devoid of serious thought, Wollstonecraft argued that such was the result of their being "Educated in slavish dependence and enervated by luxury and sloth." Thus, she felt that the key to women's liberation was to be given an education equal to men's. This would permit them to achieve a new sense of self-worth and the chance to put their innate abilities to better uses. In *Maria*, or the *Wrongs of Women*, she went further in asserting that women had strong sexual needs, and that denying them the chance for sexual fulfillment helped to dehumanize them.

bpk, Berlin/(name of museum)/(name of photographer)/Art Resource, NY

MARY WOLLSTONECRAFT.

After setting out in 1792 for Paris, Wollstonecraft met American Gilbert Imlay. The couple, though unmarried, settled down together in Le Havre, where she bore her first child, a daughter. Less than a year later, Imlay abandoned her and their child. Wollstonecraft returned to England for what became the only happy years of what had been a sad and difficult life until then. She began a close friendship with William Godwin, perhaps one of Britain's most "free-thinking" men of the Enlightenment—in short, a perfect soul mate for Wollstonecraft. Although both she and Godwin considered marriage to be a form of social despotism and actually lived apart, Wollstonecraft's second pregnancy drove them to the altar to save their child from the stigma of illegitimacy. In October 1797, she gave birth to a second daughter, whom she named Mary, but the new mother died nearly two weeks later of puerperal fever, an infection caused when portions of the placenta fail to be ejected from the mother's womb.

(As a footnote, Wollstonecraft's daughter, Mary Wollstonecraft Godwin, married Romantic poet Percy Bysshe Shelley and became famous in her own right as the author of the classic horror novel *Frankenstein*.)

ANALYZE AND INTERPRET

Were Mary Wollstonecraft's ideas truly radical? By what standards should we judge them?

merchant; the occasional aristocrat; and liberal-minded clergyman—made up the audience of the philosophes, bought the *Encyclopédie*; and were converted to the ideals of progress, tolerance, and liberty. Most of these adherents would undoubtedly have been appalled by the prospect of revolution, and they had no sympathy for the occasional voice that considered violence against an evil government acceptable.

The Enlightenment was, then, an intellectual training ground for the coming explosion at the end of the eighteenth century. In its insistence on human perfectibility, the necessity of intellectual and religious freedoms, and the need to demolish the barriers to talent that everywhere kept the privileged apart from the non-privileged, the Enlightenment spirit served as an unintentional forerunner for something far more radical than itself: the revolution.

SUMMARY

In the sixteenth century, the Renaissance scholars' rediscovery of classical learning and its methods produced an acceptance of empirical observation as a method of deducing truth about the physical world. This new attitude was responsible for the Scientific Revolution, which was at first confined to the physical sciences but inevitably spread to other things. Inductive reasoning based on observation and tested by experiment became commonplace in the educated classes. Mathematics was especially crucial to this process.

A century later, the confidence that the method of science was adequate to unlock previously incomprehensible mysteries had spread to the social sciences: the Science of Man. The same overreaching law that governed the rotation of the planets operated—or should operate—in politics and government. When that law was finally understood, all would fall into place, and the earth would cease to be out of joint.

The conviction that progress was inevitable and that humans were good and wanted good for others was the product of a relatively small but very influential group of philosophes in Britain, France, and other countries. They were the leaders of a significant transformation of Western thought that was gradually embraced by most members of the educated classes during the course of the eighteenth century. This transformation is termed the Enlightenment. The philosophes were obsessed by reason and the reasonable and saw nature as the ultimate referent in these respects. A phenomenon of the urban, educated classes, the Enlightenment made little impact on the masses but prepared the way for middle-class leadership of the coming revolutions.

IDENTIFICATION TERMS

Test your knowledge of this chapter's key concepts by defining the following terms. If you can not recall the meaning of certain terms, refresh your memory by looking up the boldfaced term in the chapter, turning to the Glossary at the end of the book, or accessing the terms on the CourseMate website at **www.cengagebrain.com**.

Nicholas Copernicus
deductive reasoning
René Descartes
empirical method
Encyclopédie
Enlightenment
Essay Concerning Human Understanding
Galileo Galilei
geocentric
heliocentrism
inductive reasoning
Johannes Kepler
Isaac Newton
philosophes
Principia Mathematica
Jean-Jacques Rousseau
scientific method
Adam Smith
Spirit of the Laws
The Wealth of Nations
Mary Wollstonecraft

FOR FURTHER REFLECTION

1. What historical connections do you see between the Renaissance and the Scientific Revolution? Could the Scientific Revolution have occurred had the Renaissance not preceded it?
2. Why were religious authorities opposed to the new ideas about the nature of the physical universe? Did those new ideas, in fact, contradict the Bible? What intellectual and political weapons could they employ to suppress those new ideas?
3. Consider other civilizations that existed at the time of the Renaissance and the Scientific Revolution. Which ones were more advanced in technology and science than Europe was at the time? What did Europe borrow from those civilizations? Was there much that was new about the European Scientific Revolution that might have distinguished it from scientific and technological thought in those civilizations?

TEST YOUR KNOWLEDGE

Test your knowledge of this chapter by answering the following questions. Complete answers appear at the end of the book. You may find even more quiz questions on the CourseMate website at **www.cengagebrain.com**.

1. The Greek philosopher Aristotle was
   a. a teacher of the Roman Emperor Caesar Augustus.
   b. the source of the major elements of medieval European thought in the physical sciences
   c. the source of the major elements of St. Augustine's thought.
   d. a teacher of Copernicus.
   e. the source of the major elements of the scientific method.
2. Developments in which two sciences were at the heart of the advances of the sixteenth and seventeenth centuries?
   a. Physics and astronomy
   b. Math and chemistry
   c. Math and medicine
   d. Biology and chemistry
   e. Biology and astronomy
3. Kepler's great contribution to science was
   a. his theory of the creation of the universe.
   b. the three laws of celestial mechanics.
   c. the discovery of the planet Jupiter.
   d. his theory of the geocentric nature of the universe.
   e. his development of the empirical method of reasoning.
4. Which of the following did not make his fame as a natural scientist?
   a. Galileo
   b. Spinoza
   c. Copernicus
   d. Brahe
   e. Kepler
5. Newton's conception of the universe is often described as
   a. an apparent order that cannot be comprehended by humans.
   b. an incoherent agglomeration of unrelated phenomena.
   c. a mirage of order that exists only in the human mind.
   d. a machine of perfect order and laws.
   e. complete chaos.
6. By the end of the seventeenth century, educated Europeans were generally
   a. ready to abandon the search for a more intelligible natural science.
   b. considering applying the scientific method to the study of humans.
   c. impelled toward atheism by the conflicts between religion and science.
   d. abandoning Bacon's empiricism for Descartes' inductive reasoning.
   e. returning to religion as the center of their existence.
7. The key concepts of the Enlightenment were
   a. science and religion.
   b. faith and prayer.
   c. optimism and rationality.
   d. democracy and freedom.
   e. community and religion.
8. Which of the following was not a common goal held by the philosophes?
   a. Fundamental equality before the law
   b. A more rigid class system
   c. State-supervised education
   d. Constitutional limitations on rulers
   e. The separation of church and state
9. Which of the following was particularly interested in reforming education?
   a. Rousseau
   b. Diderot
   c. Hume
   d. Voltaire
   e. Montesquieu
10. The Enlightenment is best described as a phenomenon that
    a. was generally limited to an urban, educated group.
    b. was found more or less equally throughout Christendom.
    c. reached quickly into the consciousness of most people.
    d. was generally favorable to the idea of an official religion.
    e. was restricted to the country of France.

CourseMate

Visit the CourseMate website at **www.cengagebrain.com** for additional study tools and review materials for this chapter.

Liberalism and the Challenge to Absolute Monarchy 30

The American Revolution broke out, and the doctrine of the sovereignty of the people came out of the townships and took possession of the State.

—ALEXIS DE TOCQUEVILLE

CHAPTER OUTLINE

1765	British Stamp Act
1773	Boston Tea Party
1774–1792	Reign of Louis XVI
1775	American Revolutionary War begins at Lexington and Concord
1776	*Common Sense*; Declaration of Independence
1789	U.S. Constitution adopted
1789–1791	First Phase of the French Revolution
1792–1794	Second Phase of the French Revolution, The Reign of Terror
1795–1799	Third Phase of the French Revolution
1800–1814	Napoleonic Empire ends the Revolution

Among the most imortant long-term consequences of the Scientific Revolution and the subsequent Enlightenment was the set of beliefs called *liberalism.* It took especially strong root in the Anglo-Saxon countries, where it was also fostered by the events of 1688 and the writings of John Locke (see Chapter 23).

The political revolutions in America and France were different in course and outcome, but they were linked by a common origin in the belief in the inherent freedom and moral equality of men. This belief was at the heart of liberal politics and economics and could not be reconciled with the existing state of affairs in either the American colonies or France in the late eighteenth century. In this chapter, we will look at the linkage of liberal thought with the particular problems of the American colonies and France.

In America, the more radical colonists' discontent with their status grew to the point of rebellion in the 1770s. The term *rebellion* is usually associated with starving workers or exploited peasants. In this case, however, a prosperous middle class led the American Revolution. More than what had happened in the American colonies a few years earlier, the unrest in France challenged every tradition and shook every pillar of the establishment. What started as a French aristocratic rebellion against royal taxes became the milepost from which all modern political and social developments in the Western world are measured.

THE LIBERAL CREED

Where did the liberal creed begin, and what were its essentials? Liberalism was born in the form identified by the modern world in the late eighteenth century. But its roots go back much further, to the Protestant Reformation and the seventeenth-century political philosophers in England. The basic principles of liberalism are a commitment to (1) the liberty of the individual in religion and person and (2) the equality of individuals in the eyes of God and the laws.

Eighteenth-century liberals were children of the Enlightenment and thus especially noticeable in France and England (much less so in central, southern, and Eastern Europe, where that movement had taken only superficial root). They believed in the necessity of equality before the law and freedom of movement, conscience, assembly, and the press. They considered censorship both ineffective and repressive, and they despised the inborn privileges accorded to the aristocracy. They thought that a state religion was almost inevitably corrupt and that individuals should have the power to choose in which fashion they would serve and obey their God.

Liberals originally did not believe in equality for all in political or social matters, but only in restricted legal and economic senses. They subscribed to what we would now call "the level playing field" theory—that is, that all people should have the opportunity to prove themselves in the competition for wealth and the prestige that comes with it. Those who were weaker or less talented should be allowed to fail because this was nature's way of allowing the best to show what they had to offer and keeping them on top. The liberals of the eighteenth century reflected the general optimism of the Enlightenment about human nature.

Like most of the *philosophes*, the liberals believed that the good would inevitably triumph and that humans would recognize evil in whatever disguises it might assume for the short term. They believed that rational progress was possible and, in the long run, certain. They believed that education was the best cure for most of society's problems. The enthusiasm for education carried over to a fascination with new technology that could demonstrate the innate mastery of men over nature.

In matters of government, they sympathized with John Locke and Baron Montesquieu. These men thought that the powers of government must be both spread among various organs and restricted by a checks-and-balances system in which the legislative, judicial, and executive powers were held by separate hands. Liberals believed that representative government operating through a property-based franchise was the most workable and most just system. They rejected aristocracy (even though there were many liberal nobles) as being outmoded, a government by the few for the few. But they mistrusted total democracy, which they thought would lead to rule by the "mob"—those who were uneducated, bereft of any property, and easily misled. They were willing to have a monarchy, so long as the monarch's powers were checked by a constitution of laws, by a free parliament, and by free and secure judges.

In the liberal view, the legislature should be the most powerful branch of government. It should be elected by and from the "solid citizens"—that is, from among the liberal sympathizers: educated and well-off landowners, professionals, merchants, and the lower ranks of the nobles. They all believed that in structure, if not in practice, the government of eighteenth-century England should be the model for the world. They admired its segregation of parliamentary and royal powers, with Parliament holding the whip hand in matters of domestic policies. They thought England after the Glorious Revolution had achieved a happy blend of individual freedoms within proper limits, allowing the responsible and forward-looking elements to retain political and social dominance.

THE AMERICAN REVOLUTIONARY WAR

In this context, it was natural that the British American colonies were strongholds of liberal thought and sympathy. Men such as George Washington, Thomas Jefferson, James Madison, Benjamin Franklin, and many others were ardent supporters of the liberal view. They had pored over Locke and Montesquieu and digested their ideas. They had much less fear of popular democracy than they did of the home country, because the masses of desperate poor who might threaten the continued leadership of the middle- and upper-class liberals in Europe were not present in America.

The American Revolutionary War began with a routine dispute between the British government and its subjects over taxation. Fighting the war of the Austrian Succession (Queen Anne's War) and the **Seven Years' War** (or the French and Indian War), which lasted from 1754 to 1763 in North America, had cost the British government a considerable sum. The added necessity of maintaining a large standing army to garrison Canada and the new American frontiers meant that London would be faced with a budgetary drain for the foreseeable future. Therefore, Parliament imposed a series of new taxes on the colonists, most notably the *Stamp Act of 1765*, which created such a furor that it was quickly repealed. The **Navigation Acts**, demanding the use of British ships in commerce between the colonies and other areas, which had been loosely enforced until now, were tightened and applied more rigidly.

These British demands fell on colonists who, as English men and women, believed they had won the right to be represented in Parliament on matters of taxation during the civil wars of the 1640s and 1688. (See Chapter 23.) Moreover, in the Hanoverian Dynasty era they had become

The Historian's Craft

Written Documents in the Historian's Craft

Previous Craft boxes discuss that unwritten sources—particularly oral sources—are heavily subject to interpretation. This stems partly from the forms such sources take and their purposes, and the interpretation process applies equally to written documents. For example, a written proverb, tale, or poem likely has less historical content, serves different readerships, and has other purposes than a written description of an event.

Moreover, it should be remembered that all people are subject to personal biases, many of which they may be unaware when they write or read a document. It is commonly acknowledged that people see what they want to see and believe what they want to believe. Accordingly, scholars who rely on documents to understand the past must be aware of those biases and take them into consideration. There are usually at least two types of biases: those of the writer and those of the reader. A simple and familiar example of the former would be William Herndon's *Abraham Lincoln: The True Story of a Great Life.* Herndon's account was one of the earliest biographies of the great president, written just twenty-five years after Lincoln's death. Herndon had been Lincoln's law partner in Springfield, Illinois, before Lincoln went to Washington in 1861. Herndon based his portrayal on his own personal recollections and those of others who knew Lincoln well. Other early depictions of Lincoln originated in his campaign for the presidency, in which he was represented as the humble "log splitter," the "honest Abe" image that has remained familiar to most people to the present. Anyone using these sources to understand Lincoln would have to become familiar with their writers. The fact that Herndon was a close friend and associate of Lincoln, on the face of it, would make him a valuable source of information, but the fact that he was a close, personal friend of the president throws suspicion on his accounts. A wise historian would do well to consult other sources to check the truth of Herndon's stories.

Scholars studying documents to understand the past also should be aware of an additional layer of partiality: their own. Taking this into account is, ironically, harder to do than the "fact checking" scholars do about the author of the document because it requires a great deal of introspection. Many factors influence how we see the world and its past, especially our own personal history (such as our values, education, religion, the region where we live, and our gender). The quality of any study that results from the use of primary sources such as written documents (and all others) is as much a product of the scholar's own skill at self-examination and confronting personal biases as of the sources themselves.

ANALYZE AND INTERPRET

What do we mean when we talk about history? Is "history" the *past itself*, or is it the *study* of the past? From what you have learned about historical sources in the Historian's Craft boxes, can we ever really know enough about the past and with a sufficiently high level of certainty to render the further study of the past (i.e, history) unnecessary? Do we really have to be less critical of written documents than other possible sources of history? Please explain your answers.

THE REPEAL, OR THE FUNERAL PROCESSION OF MISS AMERICAN STAMP. This engraving was published in 1766 and gives the colonists' viewpoint on the Stamp Act.

thoroughly accustomed to running their own households. Many now felt that the ministers of King George III were unduly pushing them about, and they resolved to let their feelings be known. The focal point of discontent was in the Massachusetts Bay colony, where maritime commerce was most developed.

The Boston Tea Party of 1773 was a dramatic rejection of the right of the Crown to change the terms of colonial trade in favor of British merchants. When the London government replied to the defiant and illegal acts of the

JULY 4, 1776. This well-known painting by American John Trumbull shows Thomas Jefferson as he presented his final draft of the Declaration of Independence to the Continental Congress in Philadelphia.

Bostonians by sending troops and closing the crucially important Boston harbor, the clash came much closer. One act led to another as the stakes were raised on both sides. The additional popularity of Thomas Paine's radical pamphlet ***Common Sense*** showed how inflamed some tempers had become. So, in April 1775, the "shots heard 'round the world" were fired by the Minutemen in Lexington, and the War for Independence—the first full-blown revolt by a European colony against its home country—was on.

The military outcome was eventually dictated by three factors favoring the rebels: (1) the British logistic effort needed to transport and supply a large army overseas; (2) the ***Alliance of 1778***, which provided aid to the rebels by the French fleet and French money; and (3) the only-halfhearted support given to the Crown's efforts by the sharply split Parliament in London. Therefore, the defeat of General Lord Cornwallis at Yorktown in 1781 spelled the end of armed hostilities, and the Peace of Paris officially ended the war in 1783.

RESULTS OF THE AMERICAN REVOLUTION IN EUROPEAN OPINION

What exactly was the American Revolution? We are accustomed to thinking of a revolution as necessarily involving an abrupt change in the economic and social structures, but this was not the case in the new United States. The existing political, economic, and social circumstances of the citizenry, whether white or black, were scarcely changed by independence. The War for Independence had been won, but this was not at all the same as a revolution.

The real American Revolution was slower to manifest itself and did so only by degrees after 1783. The Paris treaty recognized the thirteen former colonies as a sovereign nation, equal to any other. All of the territory west of the Appalachians to the Mississippi was open to the new nation (see Map 30.1). For the first time, a major state (Switzerland preceded the United States but did not qualify as a major state) would have a republican form of government—that is, one that had no monarch and in which sovereignty rested ultimately in the people at large.

MAP 30.1 North America's Possessors, 1700–1783

The changing balance of power in Europe's affairs was closely reflected in North America in the eighteenth century.

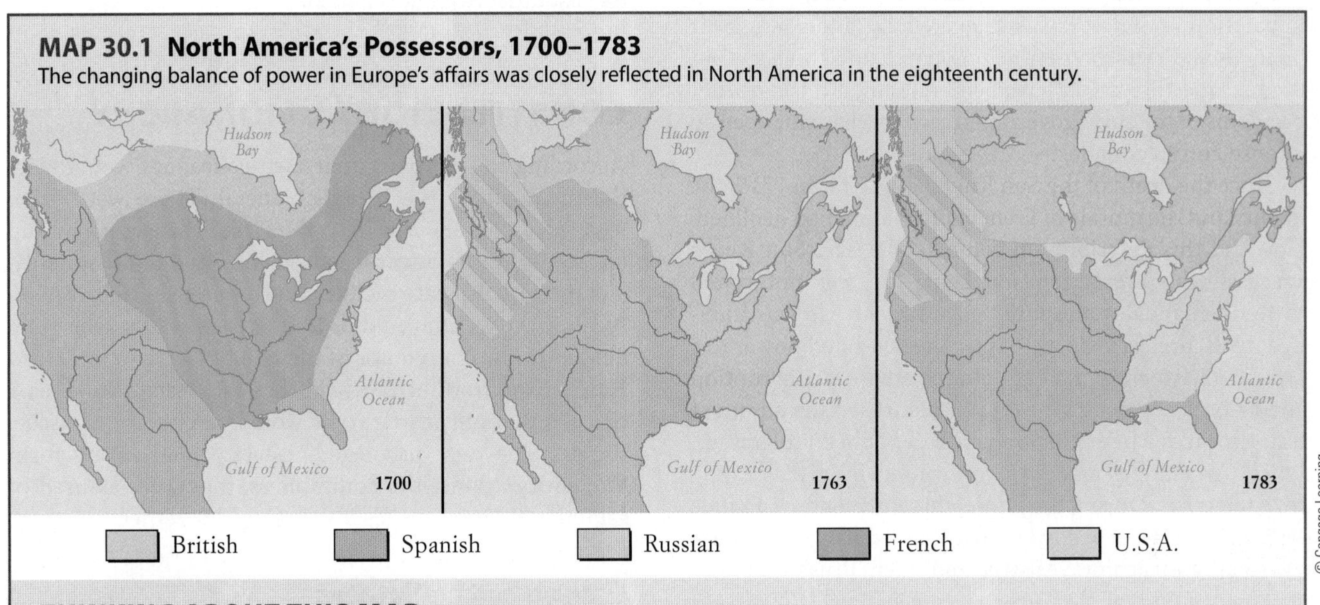

THINKING ABOUT THIS MAP

Can you think of any political developments that might have altered the claims made by the European powers to North American territory?

A few years after independence, the ex-colonists acknowledged the severe shortcomings of the 1781 Articles of Confederation, which had been their first try at bonding the states together. They set about creating a workable, permanent system of government. The outcome of the effort, the U.S. Constitution of 1789, is now one of the oldest constitutions in the world. Men raised in the liberal traditions of the eighteenth century drafted this document. More than the successful war, the American Constitution strongly influenced educated European opinion. Against many expectations, it demonstrated that a large number of men could create a moderate system of self-government with elected representatives and without an aristocracy or a monarch at its head. Many European liberals had informed themselves in detail about the United States. On the continent, the American innovations received the most attention in France. The rebellion had many friends in enlightened society, including some in the royal government who welcomed this weakening of the British winner of the Seven Years' War. Many French officers had been in America and had contact with the leading American figures. The drawing rooms of the Parisian elite were filled with talk about America. Some of it was negative, but much of the talk was enthusiastically favorable. More and more people of high social standing were convinced that the present French monarchic system was in terrible need of reform, and they looked to some aspects of the American experiment for models of what they wished to introduce at home.

THE CRISIS IN FRANCE

Just as the American Revolution had been, the 1789 Revolution in France was triggered by a dispute over finances and taxation between monarch and subjects. But the tax question could have been remedied if the deeper problems of the royal government in Paris had not been so intense and so complex.

Since the death of the Sun King, Louis XIV, in 1715, the quality and the morale of French officialdom had declined. How did this deterioration come about? The Sun King's successor, his great-grandson Louis XV, was not suited to the demands of absolutist government. He was intelligent but, preferring play to work, he delegated power to a group of aristocrats and high-church advisors. Corruption and bribery began to appear in the courts and in administrative offices where it previously had not been tolerated.

The monarchy also was confronted by a ballooning revenue crisis. During the mid-eighteenth century, France engaged in a series of costly and losing wars against Britain overseas and against Austria and then Prussia on the continent (War of the Austrian Succession, 1740–1747; Seven Years' War, 1756–1763). To pay for these, taxes had to be increased, but from whose pockets? The urban middle classes and the peasantry were already paying a disproportionate amount, whereas the state church (the greatest single property owner in France) and the nobles were paying next to nothing, claiming ancient exemptions granted by medieval kings. By the time of Louis XV's death in 1774, the government already was on the verge of bankruptcy.

Louis XV was succeeded by his weak-minded and indecisive grandson Louis XVI (ruling 1774–1792). Louis was in no way qualified to lead an unstable country that was rapidly approaching a financial crisis. Specifically, he could not be expected to limit the vast expenditures that were wasted on the maintenance and frivolities of the royal court at Versailles (such as the amusements of Louis's queen, Marie Antoinette). Nor would he take an effective stand against the rising political pretensions of the nobility. This latter group, acting through their regional assemblies, the *parlements* (pahrl-MOHNT), claimed to be the true defenders of French liberties. In practice, this claim translated into a determined resistance to paying their share of taxes.

When France decided to support the American Revolutionary War in 1778, much of the budget had to be funded by borrowed money at rates of interest that rose higher and higher because of the suspicion that the government would declare bankruptcy and refuse to honor its outstanding debts. Half of the country's revenues had to be paid out just to meet the interest due on current accounts. Faced with the refusal of the nobles and the clergy to pay even a token sum, the king reluctantly agreed to the election of an assemblage that had been forgotten for 175 years: the **Estates General**, or a parliament representing all segments of the society of France. No Estates had been convoked since 1614, because after that time, first Cardinal Richelieu and then Louis XIV had embarked on absolutist royal government.

CONSTITUTIONAL MONARCHY

According to tradition, their own colleagues would elect the members of the Estates General. There were three "estates," or orders of society: the **First Estate** was made up of the clergy, the **Second Estate** consisted of the nobility, and the **Third Estate** included everyone else. Rich or poor, rural or urban, educated or illiterate, all people who were neither in the church nor of the nobility were in the Third Estate. Tradition further held that each estate voted as a bloc, so that only three votes would be cast on any issue. Because the two "privileged" estates could always form a majority against the commoners, they were assured of retaining their privileges if they stayed together.

Calling of the Estates

The first two estates made up only about 3 percent of the total population of France, but the nobles and clergy dominated every aspect of public life except commerce and manufacturing. They were the king's powerful servants and concession holders and had every social privilege imaginable. They lived a life apart from the great majority, with their own customs and their own entertainments, often looking on the commoners with contempt and sometimes fear. Altogether, they held about 40 percent of the real estate in France and an even higher share of income-producing enterprises and offices of all sorts.

Yet, some representatives of the First and Second Estates were liberal-minded individuals who sympathized with the demands for reform. Their leadership and assistance were crucially important to the success of the Revolution's first phase.

Mainly lawyers and minor officials represented the Third Estate, the commoners. A few delegates were peasants, but there were virtually no representatives from the masses of artisans, employees, and illiterate laborers. The Third Estate's major complaints were the legal and social inequalities and their lack of representation in the kingdom. The Estate's guiding principles and its political philosophy were taken straight from the liberal Enlightenment. In the spring of 1789, the elected Estates General convened at Versailles, the site of the royal palace and government. Immediately, a dispute arose over voting. The Third Estate demanded "one man, one vote," which would have given it the majority when joined with known sympathizers from the other estates. The other two orders refused, and the king was called on to decide. After attempting a vain show of force, Louis XVI caved in to the demands of the commoners. Some dissenters from among the privileged then joined with the Third Estate to declare themselves the National Constituent Assembly. On June 20, 1789, they resolved not to disperse until they had given the country a constitution. In effect, this was the French Revolution, because if this self-appointed assembly were allowed to stand, the old order of absolutist monarchy would end.

The National Assembly and Its Constitution

What the Assembly wanted was a moderate constitutional monarchy like England's, but the king's hope to reestablish control and the refusal of most of the nobility and clergy to go along with the Assembly's project made a confrontation unavoidable. The confrontation came in the summer of 1789, beginning with the storming of the Bastille (the royal prison in Paris). For the next several months, the Parisian mob, whipped up by radicals from all over the country, played a major role in the course of political events, which was the first time in modern history that the urban underclass asserted such direct influence. The moderates and conservatives who dominated the Assembly were forced to listen to and heed the demands of the poor, who staged a series of bread riots and wild demonstrations around the Assembly's meeting place.

On August 4, 1789, the nobles who had joined the Assembly made a voluntary renunciation of their feudal rights, effectively ending serfdom and the nobility's legal privileges in France forever. A little later, the Assembly adopted the **Declaration of the Rights of Man and Citizen**, which went much farther than the almost simultaneous first ten amendments—the Bill of Rights—of the American Constitution. The *Civil Constitution of the Clergy*, meaning the Catholic clergy in France, followed this democratic manifesto. It allowed the state to confiscate the church's property and made the priests into (unwilling) agents of the emerging new government—paid by it and therefore controlled by it. This radical act was a misreading of the country's temper because most French were still obedient Catholics and rallied to the support of the church's continued independence. The pope in Rome condemned the Civil Constitution, and resistance against it began the counterrevolution.

By the end of 1791, the Assembly had finished the new constitution. It provided for powers to be shared between king and parliament along the English lines, but with even stronger powers for the parliament. A national election for this new Legislative Assembly was ordained and carried through. Noteworthy, however, was the restriction of the vote to property owners.

JACOBIN TERROR

The conservative monarchic governments of Europe, led by Austria and Prussia, were closely watching what was happening in France, and they were determined to restore Louis XVI to his rightful powers with armed force. A counterrevolutionary war began in the summer of 1792, with armed rebellion in parts of the French countryside and invasion by the armies of Britain, Austria, and Prussia. Combined with the misguided attempt of Queen Marie Antoinette and King Louis XVI to flee the country, the war changed the internal atmosphere of the country all at once. Until 1792, the moderates, who wished to retain the monarchy and to avoid any challenge to the rule of property, had been in control. Now the radical element called the **Jacobins** (JACK-oh-bins: their original headquarters was in the Parisian convent of the Jacobin order of nuns) took over the Legislative Assembly.

The Jacobins were determined to extend the revolution and to put the common man in the driver's seat. They dissolved the Legislative Assembly and called a National Convention, elected by universal male suffrage, into being. In Paris, a self-appointed Jacobin Commune established itself as the legal authority. By early 1793, the war emergency encouraged the Jacobins to institute a *Reign of Terror* against all enemies both within and outside the country. They enacted the former with a mass purge of people based on their social origins or royalist beliefs. Over the next year or so, between twenty-five and forty thousand victims were guillotined, including many women patriots, such as **Olympe de Gouges**, and tens of thousands more were imprisoned or exiled. (See Images of History.)

IMAGES OF HISTORY

Women and the Revolutionary Image

Visual images were particularly important during the French Revolution. Everyone, regardless of class or education, understood the era's vocabulary of visual imagery. Images of women activists advertised public participation by the "gentle sex." When women's political activities were banned as "unnatural," images of women embodied abstractions: liberty, democracy, and France itself.

Gianni Dagli Orti/The Art Archive/Alamy Limited

"TO VERSAILLES, TO VERSAILLES!" This is an image of women's activities at the beginning of the French Revolution in October 1787. A common food protest turned into an angry mob of women who forced others to march with them to the palace at Versailles. Once there, they forced King Louis XVI and his family to return to Paris and face the people. The women's successful mission galvanized Paris, and women became a vivid symbol of rebellion.

The Art Gallery Collection/Alamy Limited

OLYMPE DE GOUGES (1748–1793) was a self-taught journalist and playwright. Her "Declaration of the Rights of Woman and the Female Citizen" (1791) demanded the same rights for women as those granted to men by the National Assembly in 1789. She also criticized the Jacobin National Convention for not being true representatives of the populace. The Revolutionary Tribunal convicted Gouges of provoking dissolution of the convention; she was beheaded in 1793.

Ivy Close Images/Landov

LIBERTY LEADING THE PEOPLE, by Eugene Delacroix (1830). In this celebrated painting, Liberty's dress evokes ancient Greece, the birthplace of democracy. She wears the Roman red cap of the French Revolution's masses. In her right hand, she holds the French flag; in her left she holds a rifle (instead of the traditional pike to represent power). Delacroix used the pictorial vocabulary of the French Revolution of 1789 to portray the Revolution of 1830.

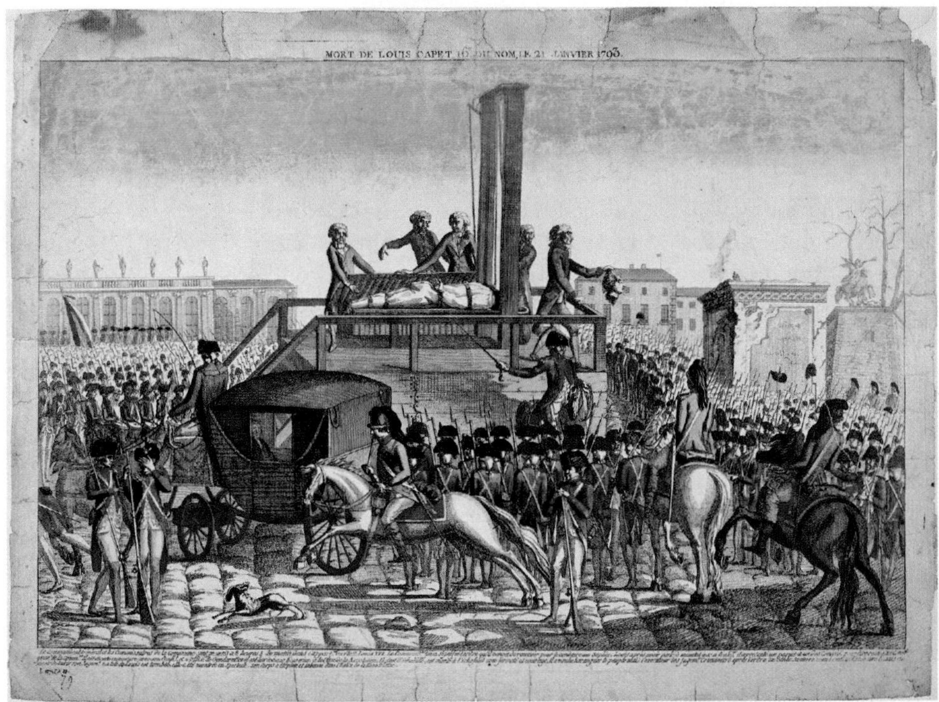

Erich Lessing/Art Resource, NY

THE EXECUTION OF KING LOUIS XVI. It was not the original intention of the Revolutionary Assembly to do away with the Bourbon monarchy. However, the rise to power of the radical Jacobins and the attempted escape by the royal family doomed both the king and Queen Marie Antoinette.

Among the early victims of the Reign of Terror was the king. Held as a prisoner since his foiled attempt to escape France, he was given a mock trial for treason and beheaded in January 1793. Marie Antoinette followed him to the guillotine in October. The killing of the king and queen was an enormous shock to the many Europeans who believed in liberal ideals. From 1793 on, the educated classes of Europe were sharply divided between friends and enemies of the French Revolution, with more and more tending toward the latter camp as the atrocities of the terror were recognized. What had started in 1789 as a high-principled campaign for justice, liberty, and progress had degenerated into a bloodbath.

After September 1792, France was no longer a monarchy but a republic. The National Convention's Committee of Public Safety exercised executive power with dictatorial authority. **Maximilien Robespierre** was its leading member and the theoretician of the Revolution.

The years 1793–1794 were the height of the terror. The Jacobins developed many new ideas and techniques of power that would be imitated in revolutions to come over the next two centuries. Most notable of these were following three points:

- That all men were legally, socially, and politically equal—*Egalité* (eh-GAH-lih-tay)
- That they were free in mind and body—*Liberté* (LEE-bayr-tay)
- That they were, or should be, brothers—*Fraternité* (frah-TAYR-nih-tay)

They elevated reason and patriotism to entirely new heights, making these faculties into virtues that were supposed to supplant the old ones of religion and subservience. They recognized no neutrality, nor would they tolerate neutrals. Those who did not support the people's revolution were necessarily its enemies and would be treated accordingly.

Believing the royal professional military to be a dubious ally, the Jacobins also started the ***levée en masse*** (leh-VAY ahn MAHS; conscript army) to defend the revolution against its enemies. With the aid of many recruits from the former royal forces (such as Napoleon Bonaparte), they developed and used that army so effectively that the French were on the offensive from 1794 onward against the European conservative coalition. And the Jacobins completed the wholesale confiscation and distribution of royal, noble, and clerical land to the peasants, thereby eliminating one of the major causes of complaints in pre-1789 France. The nobility and the church had lost their economic bases. They would never regain them.

REACTION AND CONSOLIDATION

The machinery of terror was quickly dismantled after the execution of Robespierre, as the pervasive fear had become too great for most French, even radicals, to live with. The period of 1794–1795 is termed the *Thermidorean Reaction* against the excesses of the Reign of Terror. The name comes from Thermidor, the new name for August, the month after which Robespierre fell. In place of the Jacobin-led poor who had greatly influenced government policy until now, the middle classes and the wealthy came again to the fore. They chose several of their own to form a new executive, called the **Directory**.

The five directors were soon maneuvering for power and squabbling among themselves, the economic condition of the urban poor grew desperate, and the ongoing war created a severe inflation and a new class of wealthy profiteers. All these fostered discontent among citizens of all classes. These various discontents could be contained only so long as the revolution was winning on the battlefield.

The Bonapartist Era Opens

From 1794 to 1798, French armies seemed irresistible. A young and well-connected general named Napoleon Bonaparte distinguished himself in the campaigns that forced the Austrians and Prussians to make a losing peace with France. In 1798, however, Russia joined the anti-French coalition, and Britain remained an enemy that would not give in. Napoleon persuaded the Directors to send him with a large army to Egypt to cut off the British commercial route to the East and thus induce this "nation of shopkeepers" to make peace. The ill-thought-out Egyptian campaign of 1798–1799 turned into a disaster, but Napoleon saved his reputation by returning home in time and letting his subordinates take the eventual blame. His ambitious wife, Josephine, and his friends had told him that the time was ripe to brush aside the unpopular Directors and take command in France.

Finding little resistance, Bonaparte and his army pulled off the coup d'état of 18 Brumaire, 1799. It made Napoleon First Consul of France, handing supreme civil and military power into his ambitious hands. Confident of his talent and his vast energy, Napoleon pretended to obey a new constitution that was concocted by his agents in the tame legislature. He suppressed all political opposition and solidified his already high standing with the public by carrying out a series of acts, collectively called the **Napoleonic Settlement**. It embraced the following:

- Establishing a *concordat* (CON-cohr-dah: agreement) with the papacy in 1801. This pacified the French clergy and the peasants by declaring that Catholicism was the semiofficial religion, but it also made the Catholic Church and its clergy a part of the state apparatus and put them under strict controls.
- Creating administrative and judicial systems that have survived in France until the present day. Napoleon created a highly centralized network that went far to integrate and standardize the formerly diverse provincial governments and connect the regions more tightly with the capital.
- Granting legal title to the peasants for the lands they had seized previously in the revolution.
- Giving the country new uniform civil and criminal codes of law (the **Civil Code of 1804**).
- Putting the new single national currency and the government's finances in good order.
- Establishing social peace by allowing exiles to return if they agreed to support the new France.
- Crushing Royalist plots to return the Bourbons, and also crushing the radical Jacobin remnants.

FRENCH DOMINION OVER EUROPE

In 1804, Napoleon felt the time was ripe to do what everyone had long expected: He crowned himself monarch of France. His intention was to found a Bonaparte dynasty that would replace the Bourbons. He took the formal title of Emperor, because by then France controlled several non-French peoples. As long as his wars went well, people were tolerant of his excesses, and he could raise vast conscript armies and levy heavy taxes to support their expense.

Napoleon was perhaps the greatest military strategist of the modern era. He devised and led one victorious campaign after another, often against superior numbers, between 1796 and 1809. His implacable enemy was Britain, which actively supported the various coalitions against Napoleon by contributions of troops, ships, and money. War waged between France and Britain almost without interruption for twenty-two years, from 1793–1814. French armies conquered Spain, Portugal, the Italian Peninsula, Austria, Prussia, and Holland—all of which were incorporated into France directly, made into satellites, or neutralized. He also defeated a Russian army sent against France and was on the verge of invading England when his defeat in the decisive naval **Battle of Trafalgar** off the Spanish coast in 1805 put that plan to rest forever.

Napoleon's relations with Russia were always edgy, even after its decisive defeat at French hands in 1807. By 1810, Napoleon was convinced that the tsar, Alexander I, was preparing hostilities again and would form an alliance with the English. He decided on a preemptive strike. In the summer of 1812, the invasion began from a Polish base with a huge army of 600,000. After initial successes against the retreating Russian army, the French belatedly realized that they had fallen into a lethal trap. Exposure and starvation claimed most of those who survived the guerrilla warfare of the long winter retreat from Moscow. Perhaps one-third of the original French force found its way to friendly Polish soil.

PORTRAIT OF NAPOLEON. Though incomplete, this portrait of a still-youthful Napoleon by the artist Jacques David is possibly the most accurate likeness of him that has survived. Most later portraits were done after he had become emperor and tend to romanticize his appearance.

La Grande Armée, Napoleon's magnificent weapon with which he had ruled Europe for the preceding decade, was irretrievably broken despite his frantic efforts to rebuild it. The culminating **Battle of the Nations** at Leipzig in 1813 ended in French defeat at the hands of combined Russian, Prussian, and Austrian forces. Occupied Europe was then gradually freed of French troops and governors. In March of 1814, Paris was surrendered and occupied, and Bonaparte was forced to abdicate and was sent into exile.

NAPOLEON: PRO AND CON

There can be little doubt that Napoleon was an able administrator and selector of talent. In those crucial capacities, he came closer to the ideal "enlightened despot" than any other ruler of his day or earlier. Men of ability could move upward regardless of their social background. Although by no means a revolutionary himself, Napoleon kept the promises that the French Revolution had made to the peasants and to the middle classes. He confirmed—though he may not have originated—many of the liberals' favorite measures, such as the disestablishment of the Catholic Church, equality before the law, and the abolition of privilege by birth. His codes provided a modern, uniform basis for all French law, both civil and criminal (though the subordination of women was kept very much intact). His administrative reforms replaced the huge mishmash that had been the French regional and provincial bureaucracy with a thoroughly rational centralized system. Now power was concentrated in the government in Paris, which appointed and oversaw the provincial and local officials.

The imperial regime developed more than a few blemishes as well. After about 1808, the French government was a dictatorship in which individual liberties depended on Napoleon's wishes. No political parties were allowed, and the press was so heavily controlled that it became meaningless. Political life was forced underground and degenerated into a series of conspiracies. An internal spy system had informants everywhere.

In the occupied or satellite territories that made up the Napoleonic empire (see Map 30.2), governmental policies were often harsh even when enlightened, and patriots who opposed French orders were executed without mercy. The non-French populations were expected to pay new and onerous taxes, to furnish conscripts for the French armies, and to trade on terms that were advantageous to the French. Napoleon also strongly promoted the nationalist spirit that had been so important to the early years of the revolution, but only as long as the subject peoples accepted the leadership of Paris. When they did not, they were regarded as traitors and dealt with accordingly. The Prussian liberals, especially, learned this to their dismay when, in true national spirit, they attempted to reject French overlords after royal Prussia's defeat in 1806.

THE VIENNA SETTLEMENT

With Napoleon exiled to the island of Elba in the Mediterranean, the allies who had united against him went to Vienna to try to work out a general settlement of the extremely complex issues that two decades of war had created. Originally, France was not invited, but the brilliant and slippery Charles de Talleyrand, foreign minister to the now-restored Bourbon monarch Louis XVIII (brother to the last king), used his talents to ensure that France soon received an equal seat at the bargaining table.

In the midst of the discussions in Vienna came the news in February 1815 that Napoleon had fled Elba, landed in southern France, and had issued a call to all of his followers to renew the war. They responded with enthusiasm in the tens of thousands. The Hundred Days' Campaign nearly succeeded but ended in total defeat for the Bonapartists at **Waterloo** in Belgium. This time, Napoleon was shipped off as a prisoner of war to a rock

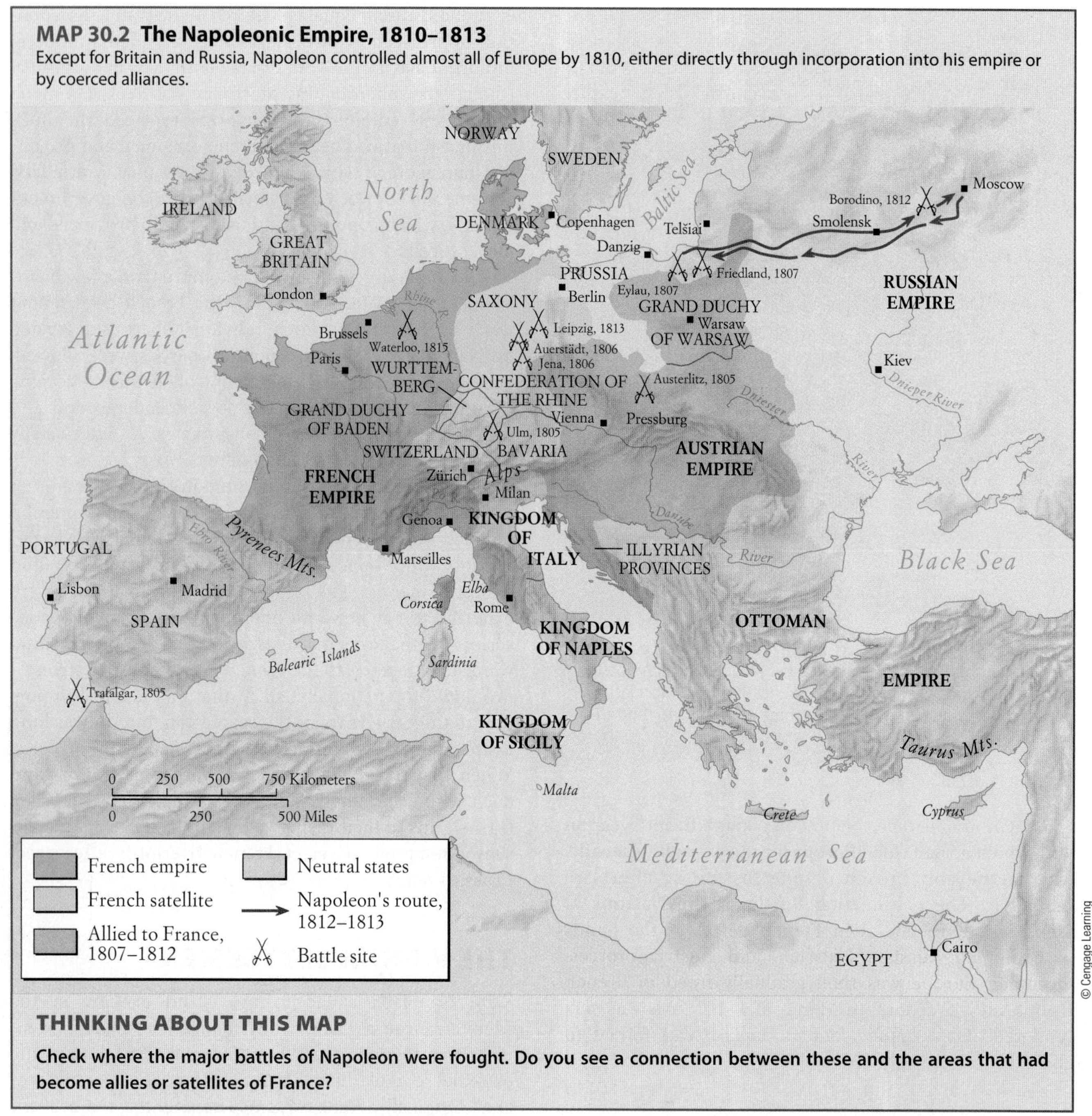

MAP 30.2 The Napoleonic Empire, 1810–1813
Except for Britain and Russia, Napoleon controlled almost all of Europe by 1810, either directly through incorporation into his empire or by coerced alliances.

THINKING ABOUT THIS MAP

Check where the major battles of Napoleon were fought. Do you see a connection between these and the areas that had become allies or satellites of France?

in the South Atlantic, St. Helena, where he lived out the remaining six years of his life, writing his memoirs.

In Vienna, the "Big Four" victors—Austria, Prussia, Russia, and England—were busy working out the political and territorial outlines of a new Europe. Actually, the conservative powers, led by Austria's Prince Clemens von Metternich, hoped to reconstruct the old Europe but found that this was impossible. Too much had happened since 1789; too many hopes had been awakened, borders changed, kings removed, and constitutions issued. In the years since, Europe had experienced a great watershed in political and social history. The "Old System" of European government and society (***l'ancien régime***: LAHN-cee-ahn ray-ZHEEM) could not be reconstructed.

Eventually, the four victors hammered out a series of agreements that collectively gave Europe its political borders for the next hundred years. They were guided in their work by several underlying principles:

1. *Legitimacy in government.* Kings were restored to their thrones, and radical constitutions written by pro-French revolutionaries were thrown out or rewritten to reflect more conservative themes.

2. *International cooperation to maintain peace.* The victors (and soon also France) formed an alliance with regular meetings of foreign ministers. The *Quadruple Alliance* lasted for only a decade, but its principles of international responsibility for peace guided diplomatic meetings throughout the century from 1815 to 1914.
3. *Discouragement of nationalism and liberalism in politics.* The conservative forces saw both nationalism and liberalism as evils brought by the French radicals to Europe. Neither was recognized as a legitimate demand of the citizenry.
4. *Balance of power.* No single state would be allowed to dominate the continent as had France under Napoleon.

Within the framework created by these general principles, what now were the agendas of the four chief victors? Russia had been an important force in the final military defeat of the French, and now under Tsar Alexander (ruling 1801–1825) and his successor, Nicholas I (ruling 1825–1855), it was transformed into a bastion of reactionary and antiliberal forces.

Austria under Prince Metternich also took a leading role in the reconstruction. Metternich fought liberal ideals with all of his considerable skill and energy. However, under his ultraconservative leadership, Austria descended into total paralysis, stagnating intellectually and scientifically.

Prussia originally tended toward liberalism and carried out internal reforms under a group of statesmen who admired the constitutional phase of the French Revolution. But, after the defeat of the French, King Frederick William III succeeded in turning back the political clock for a generation. As a nation, Prussia came out of the wars against France strengthened and expanded, with improved technology and an aggressive entrepreneurial class.

Great Britain was clearly one of the strongest military powers in Europe by 1815, but the British governing class primarily wanted to concentrate on its business interests to take advantage of the big lead it had established since 1780 in the race to industrialize (see the next chapter). By 1825, they had abandoned the Quadruple Alliance system. Having helped establish the balance of power on the continent, they retreated into "splendid isolation" for the next seventy years.

Overall Estimate of the Vienna Settlement

During the later nineteenth century, the treaty made at Vienna was criticized on many grounds. The aristocratic negotiators meeting in their secluded drawing rooms ignored the growing forces of popular democracy, national feeling, liberalism, and social reform. Yet if success is measured by the practical test of enduring peace, it would be hard to find another great international settlement as successful as the Treaty of Vienna of 1815. With the single exception of the Franco-Prussian conflict of 1870, Europe did not experience an important, costly war until the outbreak of World War I in 1914.

SUMMARY

Liberal politics was the product of beliefs dating to the Protestant Reformation and the seventeenth-century English Revolution against absolutism. Its fundamental principles asserted the equality and liberty of individuals in both the moral and the legal sense. Liberals believed that all were entitled to the opportunity to prove their merits in economic competition, but they generally rejected social and political equality as impractical for the foreseeable future.

The British colonies in America were strongholds of liberalism, and those convictions led directly to the rebellion against British rule in 1775. Thanks in part to French military and financial aid and the lukewarm support of the war effort by Parliament, the rebellion was successful: The American republic was born—the first large-scale experiment in liberal politics. Although the War for Independence was won, the true American Revolution took longer to develop. Its paramount expression came in the Constitution of 1789, which made a deep impression on educated Europeans, particularly the French adherents of reform.

Inspired by the Enlightenment and the example of the U.S. Revolutionary War, many French were convinced that the weak and directionless regime of King Louis XVI must change. In 1789, they were able to overcome the stubborn resistance of both king and nobility to bring about a moderate constitutional monarchy. Within two years, however, this situation was turned into a radical social upheaval by the Jacobins and their supporters among the nation's poor.

Invasion and war combined to create the Reign of Terror, led by the Jacobin Committee of Public Safety. This egalitarian dictatorship was overthrown after two years, and a consolidation began under the Directory in 1795. Corruption and incompetence weakened the Directory to a point that allowed a military coup by the young general, Napoleon Bonaparte in 1799.

Napoleon's authoritarian settlement of the revolution's conflicts within France was successful, and his wars in the name of defense of the revolution went well for several years. For a long and important decade, most of Western and Central Europe was under French sway. The 1812 Russia campaign was disastrous, however, and the retreat soon led to defeat in 1814 and its Waterloo sequel. At the Vienna congress of victors, a framework of compromise between reaction against and grudging acceptance of the revolution's principles was worked out; despite its attempt to ignore popular nationalism, it allowed Europe a century of peace and progress.

IDENTIFICATION TERMS

Test your knowledge of this chapter's key concepts by defining the following terms. If you can not recall the meaning of certain terms, refresh your memory by looking up the boldfaced term in the chapter, turning to the Glossary at the end of the book, or accessing the terms on the CourseMate website at **www.cengagebrain.com**.

Alliance of 1778
Battle of the Nations
Battle of Trafalgar
Civil Code of 1804
Common Sense
Declaration of the Rights of Man and Citizen
Directory
Estates General
First Estate
Olympe de Gouges
Jacobins
l'ancien régime
levée en masse
Maximilien Robespierre
Napoleonic Settlement
Navigation Acts
Second Estate
Seven Years' War
Third Estate
Waterloo

FOR FURTHER REFLECTION

1. How does the eighteenth century meaning of the term *liberal* differ from its twenty-first century meaning? Do modern liberals hold the same views as their eighteenth-century forebears? What about modern conservatives?
2. To what extent, and in what specific ways, did documents like the American Declaration of Independence, the French Declaration of the Rights of Man and Citizen, and the American Constitution represent eighteenth-century liberal thought?
3. Was the French Revolution inevitable? Why did it follow the course it did? Could it have remained a relatively bloodless, bourgeois revolution without the radical bloodletting that followed the previous, less violent phase? State the reasons for your answer.
4. To what extent do you think Napoleon's Civil Code conformed to liberal Enlightenment views on government? Again, please state your reasons.
5. Although the Napoleonic occupations evoked resistance, why do you think the principles of the French (and American) Revolution took root in many countries following Napoleon's defeats?

TEST YOUR KNOWLEDGE

Test your knowledge of this chapter by answering the following questions. Complete answers appear at the end of the book. You may find even more quiz questions on the CourseMate website at **www.cengagebrain.com**.

1. Eighteenth-century liberals thought that
   a. all individuals should have equal opportunities to amass wealth.
   b. all individuals should have basic necessities guaranteed to them.
   c. men and women were essentially equal in talents and abilities.
   d. social and cultural position should be about the same for all.
   e. a total democracy was the only government that could succeed in the long run.
2. In matters of religion, eighteenth-century liberals normally believed that
   a. there should be an officially designated and supported faith.
   b. all individuals should have freedom to believe as they saw fit.
   c. the government must have authority over religion because of its connection with politics.
   d. all humans were naturally inclined to evil and sinfulness.
   e. the best religion was one that recognized the worth of humanity.
3. The main reason that the American colonists resented the Navigation Acts and other such laws was that they
   a. believed the taxes were too high.

b. resented Britain's renewed restrictions after years of ruling their own affairs.
c. preferred to trade with countries other than Britain.
d. did not recognize the sovereignty of George III.
e. found that new restrictions placed a tremendous strain on the colonies' meager resources.

4. Which of the following was not a reason for American victory in the Revolutionary War?
 a. The division in Parliament about the conduct of the war
 b. The military mediocrity of the British commanding officers
 c. The better equipment of the American forces
 d. French aid to the rebels
 e. The petty jealousies among the British officers
5. The impact in Europe of the American Revolution can best be summarized as
 a. sufficient to anger conservative Europeans who still believed in the divine right of kings.
 b. important in Great Britain but not acknowledged widely elsewhere.
 c. minimal except among a handful of liberals.
 d. important in a military but not a political sense.
 e. important and influential among the educated classes everywhere.
6. The trigger for the outbreak of revolution in France was
 a. the assassination of the king.
 b. peasant unrest caused by landlord abuses.
 c. an armed rebellion by outraged middle-class taxpayers.
 d. the refusal of the nobles and the clergy to pay their share of taxes.
 e. the frivolous excesses of Queen Marie Antoinette.
7. The opening phase of the French Revolution saw the demand for
 a. a republic.
 b. a military dictatorship.
 c. a representative democracy.
 d. a constitutional monarchy.
 e. an end to civil government that was tied to the Catholic Church.
8. Napoleon came to power in 1799 because of the
 a. public reaction against the Terror of the Jacobins.
 b. complete anarchy in France after Robespierre's fall.
 c. unpopularity of the Directory.
 d. threat of the counterrevolutionaries.
 e. success he had attained in the war against Britain in Egypt.
9. Which of the following did Napoleon not preside over in France?
 a. The signing of a concordat with the Vatican
 b. The creation of a new administrative system
 c. The enactment of uniform legal codes for the whole country
 d. The establishment of a uniform currency
 e. The elimination of the Catholic clergy's influence on French opinion
10. Which of the following was least considered in the negotiations at Vienna?
 a. The right of forcibly deposed monarchs to regain their thrones
 b. The right of working people to determine their form of government
 c. The right of states to retain adequate territory and resources for defense
 d. The responsibility of nations to work together to promote peace
 e. The need to suppress rebellions in the future

CourseMate

Visit the CourseMate website at **www.cengagebrain.com** for additional study tools and review materials for this chapter.

The Early Industrial Revolution 31

Steam is an Englishman. —ANONYMOUS

CHAPTER OUTLINE

1700s	Increase in trade, population, and agricultural production
1750–1850	Change in premarital relationships and family structure
1760s–1820s	First Industrial Revolution in Britain; steam power
c. 1815–1860s	Industrialization of Northwestern Europe
1830	First railroad completed in Britain
Late 1800s	Second Industrial Revolution; petroleum and electricity

The rapid industrial development that gripped Europe in the nineteenth century was a direct outgrowth of the Scientific Revolution and, like that previous event, was not really so much a revolution as a steady accretion of new knowledge and techniques. It was made possible by another "revolution": the transformation of agriculture that took place at the same time. England led in both of these transformations, and the rest of Europe only slowly and unevenly fell into line.

And to what extent were the lifestyles of ordinary people altered during the transition from a preindustrial to an industrial society? We shall see that the change was substantial, but it was gradual in most cases and only really remarkable over a generation or more. Taken all in all, however, the lives of many Europeans changed more in the century between 1750 and 1850 than they had in all the preceding centuries together.

PREREQUISITES FOR THE INDUSTRIAL REVOLUTION

Historians have identified several factors that are necessary for an economy to engage in large-scale industrial production. All of these were present in England by the late eighteenth century:

1. *Upsurge in world trade.* The expanding market for European goods and services created by the new colonies was matched by the large volume of exports from those colonies destined for European consumption. In the eighteenth century, French overseas trading grew more than tenfold, and the English were not far behind. Intra-European trade also grew spectacularly, as the colonial goods were often re-exported to third parties. (See Chapters 35–37.)

2. *Rising population.* The increased demand for imports was largely a result of the rapidly rising population of most of the continent and England. Although the precise reasons for this rise are still in dispute, it is clear that the death rate steadily fell and the birth rate steadily rose in Europe after 1750. The English population, for instance, quadrupled in a century—a phenomenon never before recorded in history from natural increase alone.
3. *Increased flow of money.* Commercial expansion required additional capital. Money was needed to finance the purchase of goods until they could be resold. Many individuals tried to profit from the rising consumption by building new factories, port facilities, and warehouses—all of which required money or credit. Capital was raised by the expanding stock markets, partnerships and speculations, and the issue of paper money backed by the bullion coming from America.
4. *Experienced managers and entrepreneurs.* By the later eighteenth century, several pockets of entrepreneurial expertise could be found, primarily in London, Antwerp, Amsterdam, and other cities of Northwestern Europe. All of these places had already had two centuries of experience in colonial trade. Now they were the home of numerous individuals who had had experience in organizing and managing fairly large enterprises. These people knew how to calculate risks, how to spread them, and how to use the corporate form of organization and insurance to minimize them. They knew how to raise capital, secure credit, and share profit. They were relatively open to new ideas and new technology that promised good returns on investment.

AGRARIAN IMPROVEMENTS

If an industrial society was to be possible, Europe's farmers would have to produce sufficient food to feed the growing urban labor force. To ensure this production, the crop yields had to be increased. Everywhere in seventeenth-century Europe, croplands were tended in much the same way and with much the same results as in the Middle Age. The ratio of grain harvested-to-seed sown, for an important example, was still only about 3 or 4:1, which was far too low. However, with the world becoming ever more interconnected, high-yield New World crops, such as the potato, helped revolutionize agricultural output.

The most important single step toward modernizing farming was the change from open fields to enclosures, which enabled progressive proprietors to cultivate their lands as they saw fit. These newly enclosed fields were capable of producing two crops yearly, whereas only one-third (rather than the traditional one-half) lay fallow. The enclosed-field system originated in Holland, which had the densest population in all of Europe and consequently the most precious agrarian land. The Dutch also pioneered many other new techniques that improved crop yields, including the intensive use of manure fertilizer, rotation between root crops, such as potatoes, and seed crops, such as wheat, the use of hybrid seeds, and land drainage.

From Holland the new agrarian practices spread quickly to Britain, and as it became apparent that landowners using the new methods and crops could make profits equal to those of the industrial manufacturer but at much less risk, many larger landlords took up the new idea of market farming (that is, producing for an urban market rather than for village subsistence). This was the advent of agrarian capitalism, in which reducing unit costs and raising the volume of product were just as important as in industrial production.

Without these improvements in agriculture, the huge numbers of ex–farm laborers required by industry and commerce in the nineteenth century might not have become available. They certainly could not have been adequately fed. Not only were they fed, but many of them were fed considerably better than ever before.

THE METHOD OF MACHINE INDUSTRY

Industrial production is aimed above all at *lessening the unit cost of production through improved technology.* The changes that occurred in late eighteenth- and early nineteenth-century consumption took place not so much because new products were produced but because industrialized technology allowed the production of familiar products in greater quantity and at lesser cost.

For example, one of the chief early products of industry was underclothing for men and women. There was nothing new about its design, raw material, or general method of production. What was new and revolutionary was the much lower price for a shirt or underpants when those items were woven on a machine—a power loom—from textiles that had been spun by machine from flax or cotton that had been cleaned and deseeded by machine. The factory owner could sell to wholesale outlets at much lower unit prices because perhaps five machine-made shirts could be produced for the cost of one previously hand-woven shirt. The wholesaler could then place those five shirts with a single retailer because the price was so low that the retailer could be sure of disposing of all five quickly. Men and women who had previously not worn underclothing because of its high cost were now able and willing to buy several sets.

Most early industrial products were simply variations of previously hand-worked items that had been adapted to a mode of production that used machines for all or part of the process. These products included clothing and shoes, lumber, rough furniture, bricks, coal, and pig iron. Sophisticated or new products came only gradually, when inventors and entrepreneurs had developed a clearer vision of what could be accomplished with the new machinery and had developed a trained labor force.

The Factory

Before the eighteenth century, it was unusual for a single employer to have more than a handful of workers directly on the payroll. Very often, people took in some type of raw material—such as rough bolts of cloth—and worked it up into a finished consumer product in their own homes, working on their own schedules and being paid when they had completed the task assigned. This was commonly called the **putting out system** because the same entrepreneur secured the raw material, found the parties who would work it, and collected the finished product for sale elsewhere. He bore the risks and made all of the profits, while the workers received a piecework wage. Most clothing, draperies, shoes, kitchenware, harnesses, and table utensils, as examples, were made this way in early modern days. The wages earned were an important part of the income of many rural and urban families.

The shift to factory production was as important in changing lifestyles in the Western world as were the industrial products themselves. In the new **factory system**, an entrepreneur or a company gathered together perhaps hundreds of individual workers under one roof and one managerial eye. They were paid on a prefixed pay scale and worked under tight discipline on a single, repetitive part of the production process. See the Society and Economy box for more about labor practices during this era.

No longer did the individual workers function as partners of the employer and have a good deal to say about the conditions and the pay they received. No longer would workers have much to say about how their skills would be employed, the nature of what they were making, or where it would be sold or to whom. All of those decisions and many others were now made exclusively by the employer, the capitalist entrepreneur who controlled the factory (or mine, or foundry, or railroad).

SOCIETY AND ECONOMY

Textile Mills' Labor

Following the victory over Napoleon, a wave of industrial unrest broke over England as the working conditions of early industrial society became intolerable both to the workers themselves and to the awakening conscience of part of the liberal middle classes. In the 1830s and 1840s, a series of parliamentary commissions were charged with investigating the working and living conditions of the factory and mine laborers. Their reports shocked the British public and were followed by some of the earliest attempts to control the "free market" endorsed by the more extreme followers of Adam Smith.

The following is an excerpt from a commission report on child labor, featuring an interview with a witness named Abraham Whitehead. His and other similar testimony led directly to the first child labor law in British history, passed in 1833:

> What is your business?—A clothier
>
> Where do you reside?—At Scholes, near Holmfirth.
>
> Is that not in the centre of very considerable woollen mills?—Yes, I live nearly in the centre of thirty to forty woollen mills....
>
> Are the children and young persons of both sexes employed in these mills?—Yes.
>
> At how early an age are children employed?—The youngest age at which children are employed is never under five, but some are employed between five and six....
>
> How early have you observed these young children going to their work?—In the summertime I have frequently seen them going to work between five and six in the morning, and I know the general practice is for them to go as early to all the mills....
>
> How late in the evening have you seen them at work, or remarked them returning to their homes?—I have seen them at work in the summer season between nine and ten in the evening: they continue to work as long as they can see, and they can see to work in these mills as long as you could see to read....
>
> Your business as a clothier has often led you into these mills?—Frequently.
>
> What has been the treatment that these children received in the mills, to keep them attentive for so many hours at such early ages?—They are generally cruelly treated, so cruelly treated that they dare not hardly for their lives be late to work in the morning.... I have seen them so fatigued, they appear in such a state of apathy and insensibility as really not to know whether they are doing their work or not....

ANALYZE AND INTERPRET

The committee's report was unpopular with many parents of working children because it recommended limiting the hours and types of work they might do. What would you think of this attitude? Is it still true of some parents? Can it be justified?

Source: "The Report of the Committee on the Bill to Regulate the Labour of Children," *British Seasonal Papers* 15 (London: n.p., 1832), 195.

ENGLAND: THE INITIAL LEADER IN INDUSTRIALISM

Why did England take the early lead in the industrial production of goods and services? There were several reasons:

1. *Entrepreneurial experience.* Already in the early eighteenth century, the English were the Western world's most experienced traders and entrepreneurs. The English colonies were spread around the world, and the North American colonies were the biggest markets for goods outside Europe. The national Bank of England had existed as a credit and finance institution since 1603, rates of interest were lower than anywhere else, and the English stock markets were the world's largest and most flexible for raising capital.
2. *Population increase.* As mentioned previously, the English population rose about 15 percent per decade throughout the eighteenth century, generating a huge increase in demand and an equally huge increase in the potential or actual labor supply.
3. *Energy or "Steam is an Englishman."* The key to industrialization as a mechanical process was a new source of energy: steam. The English pioneered the inventions that made steam engines the standard form of mechanical energy during the nineteenth century. All over the world, English steam engines opened the path to industrialized production of goods.
4. *Agricultural improvements.* The improvements in English agricultural production made it possible for the farmers to not only feed the rapidly growing urban sector but also to do so with fewer workers in the fields. The excess rural population then migrated from the countryside, contributing to the growth of the urban sector's demand for foodstuffs.
5. *Key raw materials.* England controlled much of the two basic raw materials of early industry: coal and cotton. The English coalfields were large and easy to access. They provided the fuel for the new steam engines and used those engines extensively to produce coal more cheaply than anywhere in Europe. Cotton came from India, which was by now an English colony, and from the North American colonies. It was carried across the ocean almost entirely in English ships and woven in English factories, and the finished cloth was exported to the rest of Europe without effective competition for a century.
6. *Transportation.* England had the most favorable internal transport system. The geography and topography of England made the country ideal for moving goods to market. Not only were there few natural obstacles to travel and transport, but the river system, connected by canals in the eighteenth century, made transportation cheaper and safer than elsewhere.

As a result of these advantages, it was natural for England to take the lead in industry (see Map 31.1). In the generation between 1740 and 1780, England produced a variety of mechanical inventions, including John Kay's spinning machine, called the *spinning jenny*, and Samuel Crompton's *spinning mule*, which made yarn or thread. By 1800, these machines had been joined by

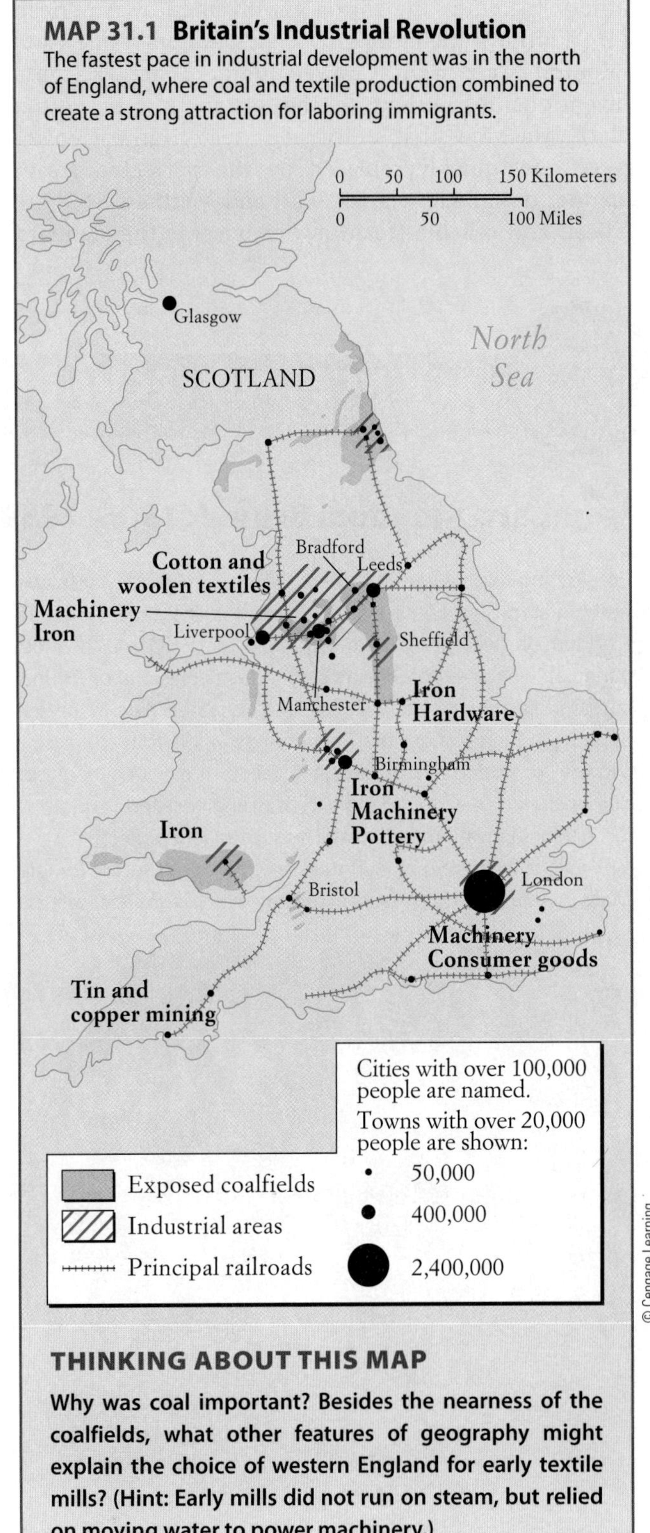

MAP 31.1 Britain's Industrial Revolution
The fastest pace in industrial development was in the north of England, where coal and textile production combined to create a strong attraction for laboring immigrants.

THINKING ABOUT THIS MAP

Why was coal important? Besides the nearness of the coalfields, what other features of geography might explain the choice of western England for early textile mills? (Hint: Early mills did not run on steam, but relied on moving water to power machinery.)

others, including the cotton gin invented by American Eli Whitney, Richard Arkwright's water frame, and Edmund Cartwright's power loom. Together, these inventions revolutionized the production of cotton cloth. Machines that still used water or animal power were now quickly replaced by the perfected steam engines designed by James Watt and Matthew Boulton. Cheap and reliable steam power became the standard energy source of the Western world's machines for the next one hundred years.

Engineers of all sorts, bridge builders, railroad and tramway developers, and mining superintendents—in short, all types of the nineteenth century's burgeoning technical aristocracy—were first and foremost England's contribution to the industrial world. (See the box on Science and Technology as an example.)

SCIENCE AND TECHNOLOGY

Isambard Kingdom Brunel (1806–1859)

Considering that he was the son of French immigrants, there was nothing surprising about his name; yet it is likely that Isambard Kingdom Brunel (IH-sam-bard Kingdom Broo-NEHL) was the most remarkable engineer of Britain's Early Industrial Revolution. Brunel cut his professional teeth while assisting his father, Marc, in the first attempt to tunnel under the Thames River in an effort to create a subway for Londoners. Although it failed, the young engineer demonstrated a well-rounded ability as an engineer and an uncanny instinct for innovation in almost all his subsequent projects.

While still a young man, Brunel saw the bright future for railroads in Britain, so he invested in several lines. His greatest success was the Great Western Railway, a system that he designed to run on an unusual wide-gauge track (7.25 feet). In the end, the wider track proved superior to existing lines because it enabled Brunel to build larger, wider cars to transport heavier freight loads and to give passengers a more comfortable ride. Moreover, it was Brunel himself who designed the track bed and the track itself, the cars, bridges, and tunnels for the line—and, according to one source, even the lampposts for London's Paddington Station, the point of embarkation for the Great Western. However, because of its unorthodox design, later system managers refitted the system with standard-gauge 4-foot tracks. (It should be added that Brunel designed many bridges for his railway projects and that most still exist. One in particular, the Clifton Suspension Bridge, is striking both for its sturdy design and substantial beauty.)

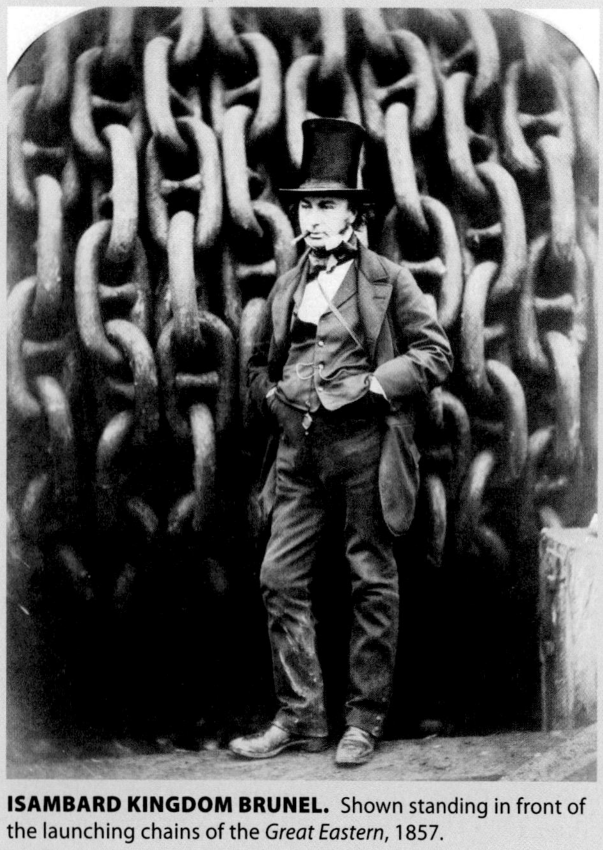

From a purely engineering point of view, Brunel's most original work was in ship design. Even before the Great Western Railway had opened, the engineer proposed to extend it by ship to connect Bristol with New York City. For that, he organized the Great Western Steamship Company. Many people had their doubts because of the mistaken belief that steam-powered ships could not carry enough coal to make so long a voyage and still have space for cargo. Brunel believed that a larger vessel would use proportionally less fuel than a smaller ship. To prove it, he built the first iron ship, the *Great Britain*, and the first steamship, the *Great Western*, that not only reached New York but also did it in record time. Brunel incorporated another design innovation that gave his ships exceptional speed: the screw propeller.

For his contributions to the Industrial Revolution, several dozen statues of Isambard Kingdom Brunel are found around Britain, and he is considered to have been one of his country's greatest engineers.

ISAMBARD KINGDOM BRUNEL. Shown standing in front of the launching chains of the *Great Eastern*, 1857.

ANALYZE AND INTERPRET

What factors in his life might have contributed to Brunel's success? In your opinion, is it likely that just one individual can make such big contributions in several areas today? Do you know of anyone who has?

SPREAD OF THE INDUSTRIAL REVOLUTION

From England, the new processes spread slowly during the eighteenth and early nineteenth centuries. No other country had England's peculiar combination of advantages, but there were other reasons for this tardiness. A major factor was England's attempt to treat industrial techniques as state secrets. These restrictions could not be effectively enforced, and the theoretical knowledge of machine design and technology spread into Northern Europe and the United States after about 1820.

Another factor retarding industrialization was the long Napoleonic wars, which disrupted the normal communications and commerce between the continent and England for the quarter century between 1793 and 1815. It would take another generation before even the more advanced areas of Western Europe could rival Britain in industrial techniques.

By about 1830, the areas on the continent closest to England had begun to industrialize part of their productive capacity. Belgium and northern France began to use steam power first in coal and textile production, the same industries that had initiated the use of steam in England. By the 1860s, industrial techniques had spread to the Rhine Valley—especially the Ruhr coal and iron fields—as well as to parts of northern Italy and the northern United States (see Map 31.2).

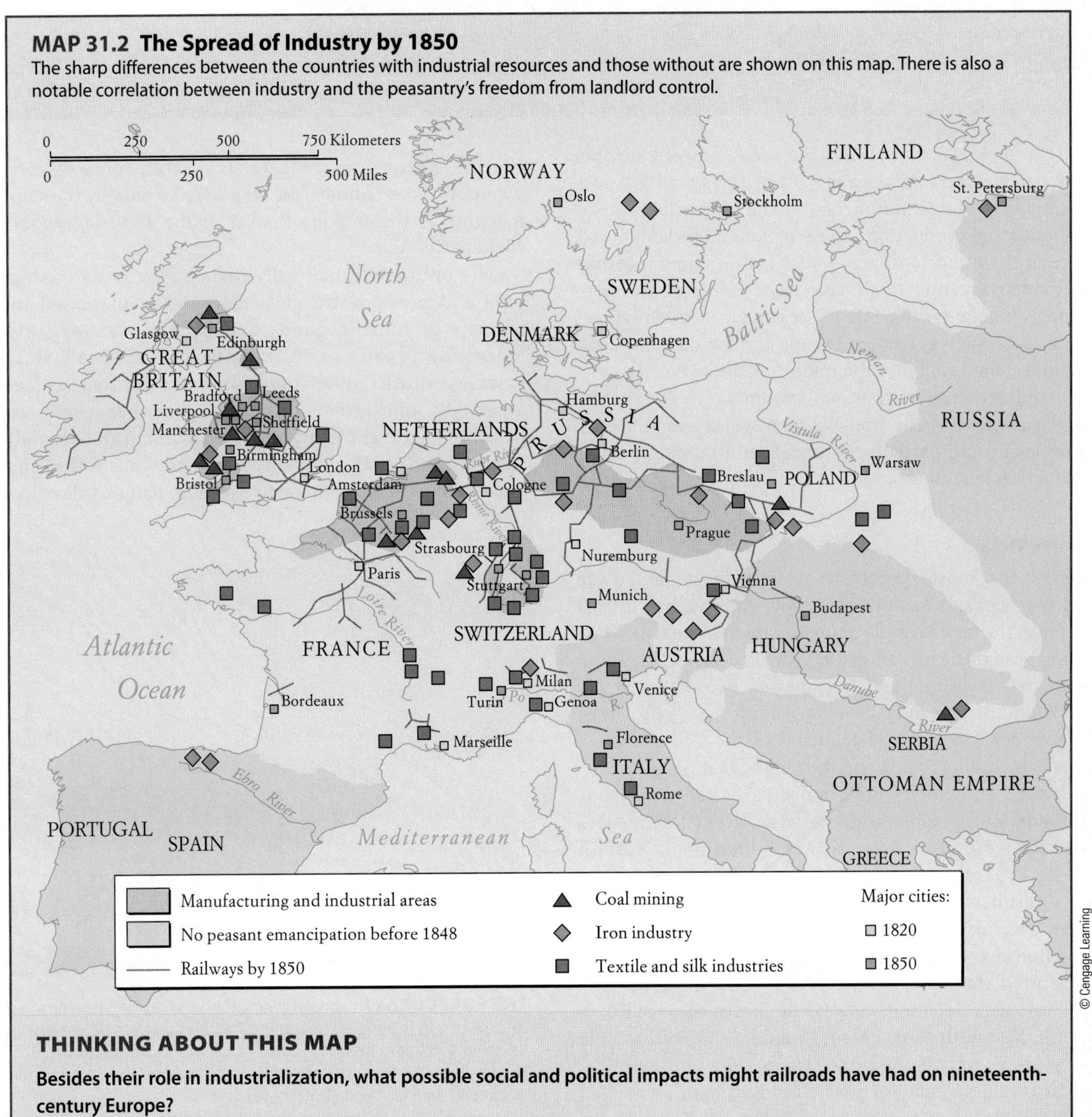

MAP 31.2 The Spread of Industry by 1850

The sharp differences between the countries with industrial resources and those without are shown on this map. There is also a notable correlation between industry and the peasantry's freedom from landlord control.

THINKING ABOUT THIS MAP

Besides their role in industrialization, what possible social and political impacts might railroads have had on nineteenth-century Europe?

Opening Ceremony of the Royal Albert Bridge, Saltash, with a Paddle Steamer Passing Underneath, 1859 (oil on canvas), Robins, Thomas Valentine (fl.1859)/Ironbridge Gorge Museum, Telford, Shropshire, UK/The Bridgeman Art Library

OPENING OF ROYAL ALBERT BRIDGE. Named in honor of Queen Victoria's husband, this span was a design by Isambard Kingdom Brunel and is one of the triumphs of the transport revolution spawned by industrialization.

Nevertheless, even as late as the 1860s, Eastern Europe, Russia, and Iberia (Spain and Portugal), as well as most of Italy, were almost untouched by the industrial lifestyle and industrial production. These regions all lacked one or more of the important factors that had to come together for industrialization to proceed. They became the permanent, involuntary clients of the industrialized regions. Some areas, such as Eastern Europe and the Balkans, were still untouched well into the middle of the twentieth century. Industrialization was not automatic or inevitable, and large parts of the non-Western world are still only superficially and partially industrialized in their essential production techniques.

Railroads

One of the most spectacular results of steam power was the railroad. Again, Britain led the way, but in this instance, the new invention spread rapidly. The first commercial use of steam railroading was in 1830, when a line connected Liverpool and Manchester, two of the newly important British industrial towns. By the 1840s, lines were under way in most countries of the Old and New worlds, including Russia and the United States.

Private companies built most early rail lines, but railroads were costly, and the large debts the owners incurred were often more than the lines could sustain during the frequent downturns in the economic cycle. As a result, many railroads went bankrupt and were taken over by the government. By the 1860s, most railroad lines were in government hands everywhere but in the United States.

The steam locomotive was the heart of a railroad. Yet the locomotive's mechanics were so simple that only a few years after the first one was mounted on its track, it had reached a state of perfection that hardly changed over the next century. Bigger and slightly more efficient locomotives were built, but they were essentially the same machine as the famous Rocket of the 1830 Liverpool–Manchester line.

The railroad dramatically reduced the costs of shipping and personal travel. It also greatly increased the security of moving goods and people over long distances. By as early as 1850, trains were steaming along in excess of fifty miles per hour—a speed that seemed almost diabolical to many onlookers. By that year, it was possible to travel from London to Edinburgh overnight in safety and comfort. Twenty years previously, the same journey had taken four or five jolting, banging days in a

Locomotive Engine, the 'Rocket' in 1830, built by George Stephenson (1781-1848) (aquatint), English School, (19th century)/Bibliotheque des Arts Decoratifs, Paris, France/Archives Charmet/The Bridgeman Art Library

THE ROCKET, 1829. This engraving shows George Stephenson's locomotive as it traveled across the English countryside in 1829. Essentially a steam boiler laid on its side with pistons and wheels, the Rocket quickly outdistanced its stagecoach competitors between Liverpool and Manchester.

stagecoach, and the train cost less as well. The railroad had an impact on the first half of the nineteenth century similar to that of the automobile on the first half of the twentieth—another "revolution"!

PHASES OF THE INDUSTRIAL REVOLUTION

Industrial work and lifestyles did not develop rapidly as a onetime occurrence at the end of the eighteenth century. The changes that began then have continued to the present day, but they can be divided into certain discernible stages.

The **First Industrial Revolution**, which lasted in Europe from about 1760 to 1820, was marked by the predominance of Britain, the central importance of a new supply of energy from steam, and the production of textiles and iron in the factory setting.

The **Second Industrial Revolution** began in the later part of the nineteenth century in various parts of Western Europe and produced modern applied science or technology. The chemical and petroleum industries especially came to the fore in this phase, and a new source of energy was developed: electricity. National leadership shifted gradually from Great Britain to Germany (after its formation in 1871) and the post–Civil War United States.

In our own time, industrial production has spread rapidly into many countries that were previously untouched, or almost so, by these revolutions. At the same time, the older industrial countries in the West have moved on to a postindustrial society, in which the production of goods in factories and their transport by railroad has given way in importance to the provision of services and information relying on electronic transmissions. We are, in fact, living through a Third Industrial Revolution symbolized and powered by the computer.

TRADITIONAL SOCIAL STRUCTURES AND IMPACTS OF EARLY INDUSTRY

During the later eighteenth century in Britain and France (where the records are best preserved), a massive, widespread change in social habits and relationships became apparent. The causes of this change are not well understood, but they seem to be linked with the arrival of Enlightenment science as a primary source of ethical guidance competing with religion. The beginnings of the Industrial Age accelerated changes that had already begun. One striking example is the structure of the family and the household.

The Structure of the Family and Household

For most people, the family they are born into is the most important social institution in their lives. We tend to think of the family as unchanging: a man, a woman, and their children. But is this so? Historians once assumed that, for many centuries before industrialization, the European family had a standard structure that varied little. An extended kin group living under one roof, high rates of illegitimate children, and early universal marriage, so it was thought, characterized this family. Now, however, researchers have established that this stereotype of the preindustrial family is false. The characteristics that were assumed to be commonplace were in fact uncommon during the preindustrial centuries.

Instead, it is now clear that major changes in the family structure took place beginning in the middle of the eighteenth century *before* industry became common.

Three changes were particularly noticeable:

1. A lowering of the average age of marriage from the previous 27 for both men and women to about 22 for women and 23.5 for men by 1850.

The Railway Station, 1862 (oil on canvas), Frith, William Powell (1819–1909)/Royal Holloway and Bedford New College, Surrey, UK/The Bridgeman Art Library

RAIL STATION. This magnificent 1862 illustration by British painter W. Powell Frith captures the bustling activity of a Victorian-era station and the crowds glad to board the "iron horse."

2. A sharp increase in the number of children born outside of wedlock, beginning in the towns but soon becoming common also in the rural areas, where the majority of the population lived.
3. A steady increase in the previously low number of aged persons (older than 60) who had to be cared for by younger generations.

The Place of Children

Until the eighteenth century, only the wealthy or the nobility could afford to give much loving attention to infants or very young children. The reason was simple: The mortality rate for infants and children was so high that it discouraged people from putting much financial or emotional investment into them. In many places, three of five children of ordinary people would normally die before age ten, and another would die before age twenty.

Diseases of every type hit children (and the aged) harder than others. In times of famine, young children were often the first victims. Household and farm accidents of a lethal nature were an everyday affair among children (we frequently hear of children of that era drowning in the farm pond or the well, being kicked by a horse, getting cut by sharp tools, or being burned to death). In those days, when medical care for rural people was nonexistent and hospitals were feared, even minor burns or slight infections would become aggravated and often result in death, weeks or months later.

Therefore, the usual attitude toward the infant was a mix of indifference and a good deal of realistic caution about his or her prospects. Most peasants and workers viewed children younger than age seven or so as debit factors: They demanded time-consuming care and feeding without being able to contribute anything to the family resources. Only after they had become strong and rational enough to do adult work were they looked on as assets.

The urban classes and the wealthy could afford to take a more relaxed attitude toward children's work, but their emotional relations with the young child were about as distant as the peasant's. Urban children died as readily and as unpredictably as rural children. It only made "biological sense" to restrict maternal love and paternal pride to those children who were old enough to have a good chance of a long life. And for most people, the point of having children was to provide a primitive form of social security. Children were expected to see to it that their parents did not suffer the ultimate indignity of a beggarly old age or have to throw themselves on the charity of others when ill or disabled.

At some point between 1750 and 1850, a change became evident because parents began to show what we now consider normal parental love and tenderness toward newborn and young children. This change occurred first in the better-off segment of society and then seeped downward into the lives of the majority. Why did it happen?

Several factors can be identified: the declining child mortality rate, which gradually increased the chances that a child would survive; the rising numbers of middle-class people who did not need the labor but valued children for their own sake; and the influence of educational reformers such as Jean-Jacques Rousseau, Johann Heinrich Pestalozzi, and Friedrich Herbert. These reformers insisted that children should be given more humane education and treated as unformed, responsive individuals rather than contrary creatures whose naturally mischievous ways must be corrected by constant, strict discipline.

Another influence on the attitudes of adults toward young children was the introduction of general public instruction in state-supervised and funded schools, which began in Prussia and Austria, among other places, in the mid-1700s. Clearly, children worthy of being educated at parental tax expense were valuable for more than just serving as attendants in their parents' old age (for which the children needed no education).

Relations Between Men and Women

Marriage among the rural folk and most urbanites was still a contract between two families rather than the result of individual erotic attraction. But this, too, changed during the eighteenth century in Europe. Not only did people marry at an earlier age as the century progressed, but social relations among the young also became considerably freer. In the later eighteenth century, premarital sex without marriage plans seems to have occurred with increasing frequency. Both sexes, in countryside and town, were able to "get away" with behavior that the full weight of social opinion would previously have prevented. Why this happened is a subject of some debate among historians. Some say that a psychological sea-change occurred after 1750 that allowed new freedoms in the sexual sphere. Others—the majority—say that the young people simply seized the increasing opportunities that a more mobile society gave them to get together outside the watchful oversight of pastors, parents, and elders.

For most women, marriage was still the main career option, but demographic changes made it impossible for some women to marry. Although the number of males and females is about equal at birth, unmarried females begin to outnumber males after about age twenty-five. This discrepancy was larger in the past than now because males were affected disproportionately by accidents and violence. Consequently, there were fewer eligible males than females in the age cohort most likely to marry. Many women were never able to marry. These "spinsters" were common in all social strata except the very highest. Their married relatives often took shameless advantage of them, forcing them to work as child watchers, laborers, maids, and seamstresses in return for minimal room and board.

OCCUPATIONS AND MOBILITY

Although most people continued to work directly with and on the land (farming, tending orchards, fishing, timbering, shepherding), the number engaged in urban occupations and nonmanual work was gradually increasing by the 1750s. As methods of agriculture improved, large estates could reduce the number of farm laborers they employed. These displaced persons could normally escape poverty only by moving away to a new life as wage earners in the towns.

Some small minority of these ex-farmers had the intelligence, drive, and luck to take up a skilled trade or nonmanual work, perhaps as bookkeepers, sales clerks, or schoolteachers (for which the only real qualification was semi-literacy). Any who could make their way into these occupations would move upward in the social scale and find the opportunity to better themselves by imitating the manners and ideas of the socially superior classes.

The rapidly increasing overseas commerce of the eighteenth and early nineteenth centuries extended the horizons of ambitious youths, a good many of whom had left their ancestral villages because they saw only too clearly what a miserable future awaited them there. Some of them ended up in one or another of the colonies, but the majority stayed at home, unable to bring themselves to take the leap into the dark that emigration entailed.

Because there were absolutely no government provisions to aid the needy, the threat of unemployment and of literal starvation was often very real. Many young men spent years teetering on the edge of the abyss before they had sufficiently mastered a trade, established themselves in business, or inherited some land to farm so that they could set themselves up as the head of a family household.

Female Occupations

Prior to the nineteenth century, women worked in a wide variety of occupations, but usually as trades apprentices in their own homes. However, the arrival of the Industrial Revolution narrowed their choices. There were essentially only two options: They could stay at home, hoping for a successful marriage to a local youth of their own class, or they could go into service—that is, join the millions of teenaged daughters of peasants and laborers who left home to become live-in servants. Practically every household, even relatively poor ones, had one or more servants. It was not at all unusual for a poor farmer's house to harbor one or two servant girls as well as a male laborer or two. No middle- or upper-class house in the nineteenth century was without its servant staff, mainly females from rural families who came to town to seek work. Sometimes the servants were related by blood or marriage to the household, sometimes not.

Many of these young women left their employers after shorter or longer periods of service, having found a suitable marriage partner with whom to "set up," but many others stayed for life. They remained unmarried, contributing part of their meager wage to support the old folks in the village. Some of these women practically became members of the family and were cared for in their old age, but many were turned out like so many used-up horses when they became too old to work.

By the early nineteenth century, when factory work had become fairly common in Britain, young women also had the option of taking a job tending a machine. Entire families often staffed the earliest factories, but increasingly, young women and children replaced the male adults and family units in the unskilled jobs such as cotton spinning and mechanical weaving. The owners of the textile and shoe mills found that young women would work for lower wages than young men commanded and were more reliable. Many country girls preferred factory jobs—where they could be with their peers and have some freedom in their off hours—to going into domestic service with its many restrictions.

THE MIGRATION TO THE CITIES: URBANIZED SOCIETY

Throughout the Western world, a massive flight to the cities began in the eighteenth century and continued almost unchecked through the twentieth century. Most of the migrants from the countryside were young people in the prime of life. The precise reasons for this **urban migration** varied considerably from place to place and era to era, but three motives underlay it everywhere:

1. *Human curiosity and the desire for change.* The young in every culture are more open to change and more eager to embrace it than their elders. When it became relatively easy to move about and experience new things, new places, and new people, young people took advantage of the changed conditions.
2. *The desire to improve economic and social status.* The variety of occupations that the towns offered, the opportunity to gain at least a minimal education, and the belief that talent and ambition had a freer field in the town than in the ancestral village inspired many persons to move.
3. *The desire to find better marital partners.* Young women in particular—whose prospects of finding desirable husbands in their villages were tightly restricted by their families' demands and social standing and who could not easily rebel—took the opportunity to search elsewhere.

Beyond these subjective motivations, we should note the objective economic fact that, by the nineteenth century, the shift of an entire society from a rural to an urban majority was, for the first time in history, viable and sustainable. The gradual spread of commerce and long-distance communications and financial credit arrangements allowed towns to grow regardless of the local food-producing capacity. Bristol in England, Lyon in France, Brussels in Belgium, and Oslo in Norway, to cite some examples at random, no longer depended on the ability of the agricultural region close by to supply their daily bread and meat. They could—and did—get their supplies from Canada, Denmark, or wherever it was most convenient.

Urban Growth

In the eighteenth century, this urbanization of society was advancing rapidly: Among the metropolises, London's population rose from 700,000 in 1700 to about one million in 1800. Berlin tripled in size to about 175,000. Paris rose from about 300,000 to 500,000 in the same period. In every Western country, the number of towns with populations between 10,000 and 25,000 grew considerably. These towns served as important administrative, cultural, and economic centers for the provinces.

The bulk of the new industry and manufacturing was concentrated in these smaller towns as the Industrial Revolution gradually got under way. Land was cheaper there than in the great metropolises, and the smaller towns were usually closer to the sources of raw materials. Manchester, the English textile center, for example, had a population of about seven thousand in the 1740s. By 1790, the population had risen to about twenty-five thousand, and it gained at least 50 percent every decade for the next half century.

The census of 1851 showed that, for the first time, a majority of the people in England lived in an urban setting (that is, in places with more than five thousand inhabitants). About 25 percent of the population of France and Germany lived in urban areas. But the percentage was lower in Southern and Eastern Europe, where industry was not yet established.

Urban Classes and Lifestyles

In the eighteenth-century towns, especially in Europe, social classes were quite distinct. At the top, dominating politics and setting the cultural tone, was the nobility. In Western Europe and Scandinavia, aristocrats increasingly intermarried with wealthy commoners—bankers, merchants, officials of the self-governing cities—and together they formed the governing group.

Beneath them was the urban upper-middle class, or classes, who included less-wealthy merchants, landlords, tradesmen, and professionals. These well-educated, upwardly mobile men and women constituted what the French called the *bourgeoisie.* Many of them opposed the pretensions of the nobles and their wealthy allies and were on a collision course with the aristocratic governors—a collision that finally exploded in the French Revolution at the end of the century.

TEXTILE MILL WORKERS. This early engraving shows the noisy and dangerous conditions of work in a mid-nineteenth-century mill. The many exposed machinery parts were constantly jamming, often at the expense of a worker's daily wages.

Below the bourgeoisie were the lower-middle classes, also primarily urban, composed of clerks, artisans, skilled workers, and independent shopkeepers. They were desperately afraid of falling back into the class from which they had emerged: the workers who labored in semiskilled or unskilled jobs for an employer. The lower-middle classes mimicked their social betters among the bourgeoisie, a class to which they might ascend with luck, time, and good marriages.

This lower-middle class, more than the still relatively small and fragmented working classes, generated most of the social discontents that marked the late eighteenth and early nineteenth centuries. Only in the later nineteenth century, when the industrial working classes had become much larger and more important in the social structure, did they successfully assert themselves.

PUBLIC HEALTH

Although the lives of ordinary people were improving in several respects, in many areas conditions were hardly better at all. For example, although diet was generally improving, medical and surgical conditions showed little change over the century. Being admitted to a hospital was still almost a death warrant, and the poor would absolutely refuse to go, preferring to die at home. Doctoring was a hit-or-miss proposition, with primitive diagnosis backed up by even more primitive treatment. Surgery was a horror, with no pain deadener but whiskey until well into the nineteenth century. Amputations were the last resort in many cases, and the resultant wounds frequently became infected and killed the patient if shock had not already done so.

Doctors and pharmacists still did not receive formal training in schools of medicine. The trainees completed a haphazard apprenticeship with a doctor, who may or may not have known more than his apprentice. All sorts of quacks were active, bilking the public with their "Electrical Magnetic Beds" and "Elixirs of Paradise." Both the educated and the uneducated had a low opinion of doctors.

Medical facts now taken for granted were unknown then. The functions of many of the internal organs, germ theory, the dangers of infection, and fever treatment were still guesswork or not known at all. The mentally ill were just beginning to be given some treatment besides the traditional approach, under which violent patients were locked up under awful conditions and others were kept at the family home. All in all, the treatment of the human mind and body when they fell ill was hardly improved over what the Romans had done two thousand years previously. Some would say it was worse.

Housing and Sanitation

The most urgent problem facing the industrial towns in the early part of the nineteenth century was sanitation. In the dreary rows of cheap rental housing (hastily built largely by the mill and factory owners as an additional source of income), overcrowding to an incredible degree was commonplace. Even the most basic sanitary facilities were largely missing. Ventilation of interior rooms was nonexistent, and all types of infectious disease ran rampant. Tuberculosis (TB, or consumption) rapidly became the number-one cause of death in nineteenth-century Britain. It bred in the damp, unventilated back rooms and spread easily through the workers' slums, where several people—often unrelated—crowded into every miserable abode. Privacy was impossible for the working class to obtain. Illegitimacy and incest were constant menaces to family cohesion and security. In report after report to the British Parliament in the 1830s and 1840s, shocked middle-class investigators noted that sleeping five and six to a bed was common, that boys and girls in their teens were frequently forced to sleep together for lack of space, and that greedy landlords regularly extracted the maximal rent by having several poverty-stricken families share tiny apartments.

SEVEN DIALS. This 1872 engraving by Gustave Doré captures the irrepressible vitality of the worst slum in London. Seven Dials was known far and wide as a thieves' haven and a pickpocket's bazaar. Some of the stolen wares were brazenly put on display for sale immediately, perhaps to the former owners.

Similar conditions were soon found on the continent as industry spread. For many years, civic authorities were either unable or unwilling to tackle the huge tasks of ensuring decent living conditions for the poorer classes. (Recall that the poor did not yet have the vote anywhere.) Despite the relative youth of the new urban populations, towns and cities normally had a higher death rate than birthrate. Only the huge influx of new blood from the villages kept the towns expanding.

LIVING STANDARDS

As the Industrial Age began, the gap between the living conditions of the European rich and poor became wider than ever before in history. The aristocracy and the handful of wealthy commoners lived a luxurious and self-indulgent life. The higher nobility and court officials were expected to have squadrons of servants, meals with fourteen courses and ten wines, palaces in the towns and manors in the countryside, and personal jewelry whose value was equal to the yearly cash incomes of a whole province of peasants. Great wealth, although almost always hereditary, was thought to be a reward for merit that should be displayed as an intrinsic duty as well as honor.

The lifestyle of the urban middle classes was much more modest, although some of the richest, such as bankers, might have six times the income of the poorer aristocrats. Secure in their solid townhouses, surrounded by domestic servants, the members of the middle classes entertained modestly if at all and concentrated on their counting houses, investments, shops, businesses, and legal firms. They devoted much attention to their extensive families. The wife was expected to be a thrifty, far-sighted manager of the household, and the husband was the source of authority for the children and the bearer of the most precious possession of all, the family honor.

For most people in urban areas, material life was gradually improving, but the lower fringes of the working classes and the many beggars, casual laborers, and wandering peddlers and craftspeople were hard put to keep bread on the table and their children in clothes. Poverty was perhaps never so grim in European cities as in the early nineteenth century, when it became more visible because of the much-increased numbers of abjectly poor, and it had not yet called forth the social welfare measures that would become common by the twentieth century. As industrial work began to become common in the towns, the uprooted ex-peasants who supplied most of the labor often experienced a decline in living standards for a while, until they or their families found ways to cope with the demands of the factory and the town lifestyle. This decline could last for an entire first generation of migrants, and only their children benefited from the often-painful transition.

REFORMS AND IMPROVEMENTS

To the credit of the British aristocrats who still controlled Parliament, as early as the 1820s, after the war emergency had passed, several reform proposals to aid the working classes were introduced. By the 1830s, some of the worst abuses in the workplace were attacked. The **Factory Acts** of 1819 and 1833 limited the employment of young children and provided that they should be given at least a little education at their place of work. (Still, it remained entirely legal for a nine-year-old to do heavy labor for eight-hour workdays and for a thirteen-year-old to work twelve hours a day, six days a week!)

Women and boys under the age of ten were not permitted to work in the mines after 1842. Until then, women and young children did much of the deep underground work, which was highly dangerous and exhausting to anyone. In most textile manufacturing, physical strength was not as important as quickness and endurance. Women and children were paid much less than men demanded, and their smaller size allowed them to move about in the crowded machine halls with more agility than men. Boys as young as seven years of age were employed regularly in twelve- or thirteen-hour shifts until the passage of the 1833 act. The families of young working children often opposed and circumvented the reforms, which threatened to diminish the potential family income. No more substantial reform legislation was passed until the early twentieth century.

Little was done to improve basic sanitation in worker housing until the 1860s. In 1842, a pioneering report by Edwin Chadwick on the horrible conditions in the slums and how they might be corrected through modern sewage and water purification systems began to draw attention. But not until the great cholera scare of 1858, when London was threatened by a major outbreak of this lethal waterborne disease, was action taken. Then the upper and middle classes realized that although epidemic diseases such as cholera might originate in the slums, they could and would soon spread to other residential areas. At about the same time, the restructuring of its primitive sewer system allowed Paris for the first time to manage its waste disposal problem. Led by the English and French capitals, provincial city authorities soon began to plan and install equivalent systems. By the end of the nineteenth century, European city life was again reasonably healthy for all but the poorest slum dwellers.

SUMMARY

Industrial methods of producing goods via machinery entered European life gradually in the mid-eighteenth century, with England as the leader. The English had several natural advantages and social characteristics that enabled them to expand their lead over the rest of the world until well into the nineteenth century. This First Industrial Revolution was largely dependent on two related changes: the increase in agrarian production and the rapid rise in population and attendant demand for consumer goods. Without these, the factory system of concentrated labor under single management and discipline would not have been feasible.

The industrial system spread slowly at first because of the wars and the difficulty of replicating the English advantages. By the mid-nineteenth century, however, industrialization had spread into much of northern and Western Europe and the United States. Coal mining and textiles were two of the initial industries to be affected, and the steam engine became the major energy source for all types of industry. The railroad, introduced in the 1830s, soon effected massive change in the transport of goods and people and contributed to the success of the industrial system in substantial ways. A Second Industrial Revolution commenced in the late nineteenth century, fueled by petroleum and electricity, and a third is currently under way in the provision of services rather than goods.

The social change introduced by mechanized industry took many forms, affecting family relations, occupational mobility, urbanization, and diet. The family was changed by a decreasing age of marriage and a sharp rise in illegitimacy. Children came to be valued as creatures worthy of love in their own right. Several new occupations were opened to both men and women in factories and mills as industry spread, and the traditional servant jobs multiplied in the expanding cities and towns.

Living standards varied from an unprecedented opulence among the rich to an actual decline in the conditions for recent urban migrants. Slums appeared in the new industrial quarters, which were horribly lacking in basic sanitation and privacy. Nevertheless, to the working classes, the attractions of the towns were manifold and irresistible, particularly for those who sought a better life than the traditional social and economic restrictions that the villages offered. A richer and more varied diet even for the poor gradually made itself felt in better health. By the end of the nineteenth century, sanitation and workers' living and labor conditions had visibly improved.

IDENTIFICATION TERMS

Test your knowledge of this chapter's key concepts by defining the following terms. If you can not recall the meaning of certain terms, refresh your memory by looking up the boldfaced term in the chapter, turning to the Glossary at the end of the book, or accessing the terms on the CourseMate website at **www.cengagebrain.com**.

Factory Acts
factory system
First Industrial Revolution
putting out system
Second Industrial Revolution
urban migration

FOR FURTHER REFLECTION

1. Why do we refer to the changes that came with industrialization as amounting to a "revolution"?
2. In what ways did the demand for finished goods like textiles and household wares result in *lower* prices for them? How did this (seemingly) contradict the law of supply and demand?
3. What is capital? What part did capital play in making the Industrial Revolution? Scholars have suggested that there was a relationship between European slavery and its Industrial Revolution. Is this true?
4. What relationship was there between Britain's empire and its Industrial Revolution?

TEST YOUR KNOWLEDGE

Test your knowledge of this chapter by answering the following questions. Complete answers appear at the end of the book. You may find even more quiz questions on the CourseMate website at **www.cengagebrain.com**.

1. The basic aim of industrial production techniques is to
   a. provide more employment opportunities for the labor force.
   b. allow a greater variety of jobs.
   c. lower the unit cost of production.
   d. discipline and organize the labor force more efficiently.
   e. move farm workers into cities to work in factories.
2. Isambard Kingdom Brunel
   a. developed an entirely new form of mechanical energy.
   b. was most noted for his tunnel under London's Thames River.
   c. was a coinventor with James Watt of an improved design for the steam engine.
   d. engineered several improvements to Britain's transportation industry in the nineteenth century
   e. invented a device for raising water from flooded mines.
3. The chief driving force for the Industrial Revolution in eighteenth-century England was
   a. the threat of being overshadowed by France in the world economy.
   b. the invention of an improved source of energy.
   c. the creation of the British overseas colonial empire.
   d. the encouragement of the British government.
   e. the development of the business corporation.
4. The first major industry to feel the effect of industrial production was
   a. lumbering.
   b. railroads.
   c. grain farming.
   d. paper making.
   e. textiles.
5. One effect of the Napoleonic wars was that they
   a. delayed the development of industry on the European continent.
   b. interfered with the colonialist expansion of European nations.
   c. encouraged the upper classes' contempt for profit making.
   d. forced the Europeans to depend on the nations of the Western Hemisphere for industrial goods.
   e. greatly increased the need for raw materials.
6. Around the mid-eighteenth century, the European population
   a. began to rise as a result of declining mortality and rising birthrates.
   b. started to stabilize after a century of steady increase.
   c. tapered off from the sharp decline that had marked the sixteenth and seventeenth centuries.
   d. began to rise as a result of medical breakthroughs against epidemics.
   e. suffered a severe drop because of emigration.

7. Marriage in preindustrial European society could best be described as
   a. a relationship based on love between two people.
   b. a contractual relation formed mostly by economic and social aspirations.
   c. a contractual relation that conformed closely to biological drives.
   d. an economic relationship between two individuals.
   e. a strategy to "cover" the sexual activities engaged in by the young anyway.
8. An important function of children in preindustrial society was
   a. to serve in the landlord's military forces.
   b. to elevate themselves socially and thus honor their parents.
   c. to bring grandsons into the world and so carry on the family name.
   d. to pray for the departed souls of their deceased parents.
   e. to serve as security for their parents in their old age.
9. The putting out system was a/an
   a. early industrial method of manufacturing.
   b. preindustrial form of manufacturing.
   c. centralized method of manufacturing.
   d. improved system of agriculture.
   e. new method of recruiting industrial labor.
10. One effect the improvements in agriculture had in Britain was that it
    a. increased the number of ex–farm laborers available for work in new industries.
    b. decreased the number of farms in Britain.
    c. made farm labor more expensive.
    d. created a greater demand for farm labor.
    e. led to a rise in the duties charged on foreign food imports.

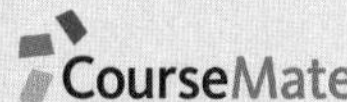

Visit the CourseMate website at **www.cengagebrain.com** for additional study tools and review materials for this chapter.

32 Europe: New Ideas and New Nations

The folk learn more from a defeat than the kings do from a victory. —ALESSANDRO MANZONI

1815–1850	Economic liberalism, conservatism, nationalism, and socialism emerge
1830	July Revolution (France): Louis Philippe (1830–1848)
1832	Reform Act in Great Britain
1848	Popular revolts in France, Austria, Prussia, and Italy
1849–1850	Failure of revolts; conservatives regain control
1851–1871	Louis Napoleon (Napoleon III): Second Empire (France)
1853–1856	Crimean War
1859–1870	Unification of Italy
1861	Freeing of serfs in Russia; Civil War in the United States
1862–1871	Unification of Germany
1870	Franco-Prussian War

The Ancient Regime of pre-1789 Europe could not be brought back. In countries other than France, many of the political, legal, and social reforms that the French Revolution had brought or attempted to bring were delayed or even temporarily reversed. In France, however, the changes since 1789 were too popular to be ignored, and the forces unleashed by the Industrial Revolution in England were going to remake the society of Western Europe by the mid-nineteenth century. New, throne-shaking revolts in 1848 were the direct result of the changes set in motion by industrialization and by the ideas of 1789.

After the defeats of the 1848 uprisings, European liberals and nationalists were in retreat during the next decade, and conservative statesmen were everywhere in control. But only twenty to thirty years later, many of the goals of the liberals had been reached, and nationalism was already one of the givens of policy making. The universal male franchise was introduced in several countries. Governments in many places legalized labor unions, and Russia freed its serfs. The Western world was entering the Second Industrial Revolution and the massive social changes that accompanied it. (See the next chapter.)

CHAPTER OUTLINE

LIBERALISM IN POLITICS AND ECONOMICS

Much of the history of the past two centuries, especially in Europe, has been a reflection of sustained, revolutionary changes in politics and economics. The political revolution was highlighted by events in the United States and in France, which we looked at in previous chapters. The economic revolution was slower and less spectacular, but it was at least as important over the long run. It was generated by changes in industrial production that took place beginning in the second half of the eighteenth century, particularly in Britain; by the conquest of distance through the railroads; and by the immense growth of population in Europe and the United States.

As is often the case, changes in one sphere reinforced changes in the other in all kinds of ways. Two examples will suffice:

1. In the 1790s, during the period of the Directory in France, a tiny group of conspirators tried to eliminate property-based distinctions, and their efforts at sharing equally the products of human labor got nowhere. A generation later, another group of theorists was determined to replace the abuses and exploitation of early capitalism with the humane ideals of equality and mutual care. This was the origin of an organized multinational effort to introduce governmental responsibility for the welfare of the citizenry.
2. The middle classes guided the eighteenth-century political revolution on their own behalf. Later, the more perceptive among them recognized that without the active assistance of much of the laboring classes, they could not gain and hold power against the aristocracy. The industrial laboring classes were growing rapidly but lacked leadership from within their own ranks. Instead, during the later nineteenth century, a partnership grew up in Western Europe between the middle-class reformers and newly enfranchised working-class voters, which brought about substantial improvement in the condition of ordinary people.

The liberal sons and daughters of the Enlightenment everywhere formed a "party of reform," dedicated to changing the traditional class-based system of political representation. By 1815, much had been achieved in those respects in America and France, but the conservative reaction nullified some of those gains everywhere in Europe. Only in France and England was much of the liberal political agenda retained. Parliaments in both countries, similar to Congress in the United States, were responsible to the voters rather than to the king, and freedom of conscience was guaranteed.

The Gospel of Free Enterprise

Another side of the liberal philosophy focused on freedoms in the marketplace and the rebellion against the traditional restrictions imposed by mercantilism. Economic liberalism grew directly from the path-breaking work of Adam Smith, whose ideas were mentioned briefly in Chapter 29. What did Smith's adherents want?

- *Laissez-faire.* If government would only let them alone to do what they saw best fit (laissez-faire), the merchants and manufacturers of every nation would produce goods and services to meet the demands of the market most efficiently and economically.
- *Free trade.* The existing mercantile system of quotas, licenses, and subsidies should be eliminated, and producers should be allowed to trade with any place and anyone at prices that the free market would set.
- *The less government, the better.* As the first two conditions suggest, the economic liberals despised governmental controls of any sort in the economy (even though Smith made certain important exceptions to laissez-faire). They believed that the free market alone would provide proper guidance for policy decisions.

In early-nineteenth-century England, extreme *laissez-fairism* provided the employers of industrial labor with an excuse for the systematic exploitation of the weak. Using theorists such as Thomas Malthus (*An Essay on Population*, published in 1798) and David Ricardo (*The*

THE WANDERER IN THE SEA OF CLOUDS. Caspar Friedrich was the best known and possibly the most technically accomplished of the early generation of Romantic painters. He painted this brooding introspective in 1818.

Iron Law of Wages, published in 1817), liberals believed that the poor would always be poor because of their excessive birthrate and other supposed moral faults, and that it was the well-off people's duty to protect their material advantages by any means they could. Because sympathizers with this line of thought took control of the British House of Commons after the electoral Reform Act of 1832, the British government grew unsympathetic toward the idea of social protection of the lower classes. Only in the 1870s and later did a sufficient number of reformers emerge who rejected this heartless attitude and busied themselves with the improvement of the lot of the poor majority.

CONSERVATISM

The liberals, though gaining strength, were by no means the sole players in the European political field after 1815. Supported by the wave of anti-Napoleonic nationalism, the forces of **conservatism** in Britain and France were powerful for at least a generation, and elsewhere even longer. Conservatism in the first half of the nineteenth century meant one of two things: One was *moderate conservatism*; the other was *reaction.*

Moderate Conservatism

Conservatives of all stripes believed that an official religion was a necessity for instilling proper respect for law and tradition. They could not imagine a state in which church and government were separated by law. They supported a constitution but rejected political democracy as being the rule of the mob. They believed that only those who had a stake in society, evidenced by property, could take on the burdens of self-government.

Moderate conservatism was supported by a large percentage of ordinary Europeans—probably a majority—who had been appalled by Jacobin radicalism and Napoleon's arrogance. The clergy, both Catholic and Protestant, as well as many aristocrats were the leaders of moderate conservatism in much of the European continent. They wished to avoid revolutions in the future by making some necessary concessions now. In economics, they favored the continuation of government controls in trade (especially foreign trade) and industry. They thought that Smith was well meaning but wrong and that without such supervision by the authorities, selfish and greedy entrepreneurs would only harm the national welfare.

Reaction

Reactive conservatism was the rule in Prussia, Austria, and Russia, where few if any political concessions were made to the new social structures being created by the changing modes of production. This led to explosive pressures, which eventually burst forth in the revolts of 1848 and the upheaval of World War I and its revolutionary aftermath.

In Prussia and Austria, the reactionary conservatives ruled for a generation after 1815. They denied a constitution; retained the established church, whether Catholic or Protestant; and maintained strict class distinctions in justice, taxation, and voting rights. Both countries also maintained a form of serfdom until 1848.

In Russia (which meant not only the Russian ethnic groups but also much of what is now independent Eastern Europe), the reactionaries were also in command. Tsar Alexander's successor, Nicholas I (ruling 1825–1855), was a sincere believer in God's designation of autocracy for Russia and a dyed-in-the-wool reactionary. During his reign, Russia was called the *Gendarme* (policeman) of Europe, eager and ready to send troops to put down liberal agitation wherever it might rear its ugly head. All of Europe was split during the entire post-Napoleonic generation between these reactionary forces and their liberal opponents.

NATIONALISM

Besides the struggle between liberal and conservative, another source of conflict appeared in post-1815 Europe: popular nationalist feeling. Modern political **nationalism** has its origins in France between 1792 and 1795, when the Jacobins insisted on the duties imposed on all citizens by patriotism. Later, when the French occupied half of Europe, their subjects' patriotic reaction against the occupier contributed mightily to the growth of nationalism elsewhere.

Early nationalism was generally positive in its goals and tolerant in its outlook. Sometime in the 1840s and later, however, nationalism in much of Europe lost its constructive, tolerant character. This later phase was marked by the rise of negative qualities with which we in modern times are thoroughly familiar: "we" versus "they" and "right" against "wrong"; nationalism as a zero-sum game where one nation's gain is another's loss and vice versa. This nationalism was characterized by a conviction of cultural superiority over other nations. It degenerated to its worst in the Balkans and Eastern Europe, where many distinct peoples lived in mixed communities and regions without clear territorial lines. Here, nationalism soon became an excuse for one war after another in the later nineteenth and early twentieth centuries.

SOCIALISM IN THE PRE-MARX ERA

The earliest socialists were a handful of conspirators in France in the 1790s. All of these preceded Marx. What did these early advocates of **socialism** wish to achieve? Three chief economic goals were involved:

1. *A planned economy.* The unregulated free market was an entirely wasteful, haphazard way of supplying the needs and wants of most people.

2. *Greater equality.* There was too much for the rich, too little for the rest, and too few ways in which that situation could be changed peaceably and fairly.
3. *Ownership of income-producing property by the state rather than private parties.* Only the state was powerful enough to resist the wealthy and ensure that the means of producing wealth were not controlled by a few.

The most influential of the early socialists worked in France. *Henri de Saint-Simon* (1760–1825: ahn-REE duh SANT-see-MOHN) was perhaps the most important of all. He believed further that the state (that is, the government) had the positive duty to look out for those who were unable to look out for themselves—the misfits, the incompetent, and the disabled. Because industrialized production would be so much more lavish than anything previously seen, the economy of scarcity would soon be abolished, and it would be no hardship for the productive majority to care for these "welfare cases." Charles Fourier was an obsessive theorist of technology and organization. His vision of special self-contained units of precisely 1,620 persons living and working together was one of the oddities of early social thought. Fourier was particularly important as a forerunner of feminist equality in work and politics and as the upholder of the demands of the emotional, passionate side of human nature in industrialized society.

Pierre Proudhon (proo-DOHN) was the first modern anarchist (see the glossary about *anarchism*). He believed that the power of the state must be destroyed if men and women were ever to be truly free and capable of living humane lives. He was convinced that government was at best a barely tolerable evil because it was always controlled by the wealthy and was almost always the oppressor of the poor. In 1840, he posed his famous question, "What Is Property?" to which he gave a resounding answer: "Property is nothing but organized theft! It has been stolen from the sole creator of value, the worker, by the owning class. And it should be taken back—by force, if necessary."

In England, utopian socialism's leading figure was *Robert Owen.* Owen was a remarkable man whose hard work and ambition made him a wealthy mill owner at the age of twenty-seven. Inspired by a rugged Christianity, he was convinced that industrial production and a decent life for workers were compatible. At his famous cooperative textile mill in New Lanark, Scotland, Owen put his theories into practice and created a profitable enterprise that also provided well for every need of its workers and their families.

In the 1840s, socialism was still very much an idea or theory of outsiders, condemned as being against the laws of God and man. It was not taken seriously by most middle-class liberals and most economic liberals thundered against it as unnatural. For their part, conservatives thought socialism terribly misunderstood human nature and was foredoomed to fail.

POLITICAL EVENTS TO 1848

In the period just after the Vienna Settlement of 1815 (see Chapter 30), European international affairs were relatively calm (see Map 32.1). The Quadruple Alliance of the victors formed at Vienna was easily strong enough to suppress any attempts to overthrow the peace, as long as its members agreed. Revolts by liberals in Spain (1820) and Italy (1822) were quickly squelched, but a nationalist guerrilla war by the Greeks against their Turkish overlords (1827–1830) was allowed to commence and eventually succeed because it was a special circumstance of Christian versus Muslim. (The Greek rebellion had a special connection to nineteenth-century English literature; see the Arts and Culture box on Lord Byron.)

During this decade, the Spanish-American colonies were also allowed to break away from backward Spain, which was too weak to suppress their revolts by itself. First Mexico and then most of South America rebelled against Madrid and became independent states by 1825. Brazil, Portugal's one colony in the New World, also broke away during this same period (see Chapter 38).

The Liberal States: France and Britain

In an almost bloodless revolution in July 1830, the French threw out their unpopular Bourbon ruler. In his place came Louis Philippe (ruling 1830–1848). Louis gladly accepted from Parliament a moderately liberal constitution, which stated that sovereignty lay in the people, not in the throne.

The **July Monarchy**, the eighteen years of Louis Philippe's reign were a major step forward for liberalism. Citizen rights were granted and usually observed by the government, but those rights were much more extensive for the well-off than for the majority. Social tensions were steadily building. Victor Hugo's great novel *Les Misérables* is the best mirror of this epoch.

Over the protests of the Conservative Party (**Tories**), in 1832, the Liberals in the British Parliament (**Whigs**) passed the most important reform of voting rights since the Glorious Revolution. The **British Reform Act of 1832** stripped away many of the traditional political advantages of the landholding aristocrats and strengthened the previously weak urban middle classes. Overnight, the House of Commons seats were redistributed to increase the representation of urban and industrial districts. Because the Whigs controlled these districts, the composition of the Commons changed drastically. Voting rights also were extended to more members of Britain's middle classes.

By making Parliament into a more representative national body, the British government diminished the danger of revolution. The British middle classes were assured of a Parliament in which their voice would be heard and through which they could attain peaceable, orderly change. Additional Reform Acts in 1867, 1872,

MAP 32.1 Prussia and Austria after the Peace of Vienna, 1815
The center of the continent was the scene of an increasing diplomatic maneuvering for leadership of the German-speaking peoples. Austria and Prussia both emerged victors in 1815, and both were bulwarks of the reaction against French revolutionary ideas.

THINKING ABOUT THIS MAP

What issue served as the source of rivalry between these two German states?

1918, and 1928 gradually extended the vote to men and women of all classes. Revolution and radical socialism never gained much following among the common folk in Britain for that reason.

The Reactionary States: Austria, Russia, and Prussia

In the reactionary countries, the story was different. In Austria, Russia, and the Germanies, the rulers spent the generation after Napoleon attempting to hold back all thought of political liberalism. Through censorship, police and military force, diplomacy, and eventually war, they threw a dam across the tide of reform, which held until 1848. The Austrian emperor, the Russian tsar, and the Prussian king rejected the kind of concessions the French and British governments had made to their citizens. As a result, revolt seemed to many thinking people the only hope of bringing these countries into modern political and economic life.

The Revolts of 1848

Revolts broke out in the streets of working-class Paris in late February 1848 and swept through Europe during the next year. These revolts of the lower classes, combined with an explosion of nationalist conflicts and assertions of popular sovereignty, set all of Europe aflame. Of the major countries, only Britain and Russia were spared.

The revolts did not have a single cause, nor did they have the same outcome. Nevertheless, at least three underlying similarities can be established: (1) The revolts were initially led by middle-class liberals; (2) the workers soon created their own more-violent revolutions against

ARTS AND CULTURE

George Gordon, Lord Byron (1788–1824)

The triumph of the Industrial Age also saw a vigorous reaction against it in the **Romantic movement**, which seized much of Europe during the mid-nineteenth century. Beginning in Britain, this movement first attacked the excessive faith in rationalism that characterized the later-eighteenth-century Enlightenment. By the 1820s, it had become a rejection of the narrow money grubbing that many believed had come into British urban life with the Industrial Revolution. Recognition of the power of the emotions came to be seen as an essential element of all the arts, but particularly the art most given to expression of feeling—poetry. Among the British Romantic poets, George Gordon (Lord Byron) took the first place through not only the magnificence of his verse but also the enormous publicity his unconventional life generated. Several of the finest Romantic poems are from his pen, but Lord Byron's place in history has also benefited from what would now be called successful media exposure.

Born to a dissipated and irresponsible father and a loving but unbalanced mother, Byron's early years were unstable. He was lamed by a clubfoot that grew worse under the attentions of a quack doctor who tried to heal the boy with painful braces. His erratic schooling was successful at least in arousing a love of literature and encouraging his inclination to write. At age sixteen, he fell in love with Mary Chatworth, a girl slightly older than he, whose tantalizing cold-blooded attitude toward her teenage admirer, Byron later said, was the turning point of his emotional life. From this time on, this handsome and passionate man became involved in a steady procession of short- and long-term affairs with women of all descriptions. There is much evidence of sexual ambivalence as well in his relations with men both in Britain and abroad.

Byron's poetic efforts began to see the light of day in 1807, when he was a student at Cambridge. His gifts were equally apparent in his lyrics and in his satires of his detractors, which could be savage. In 1809, he entered the House of Lords (his father had been a minor noble) and soon took off for a two-year visit to the continent. Most of his time was spent in Greece, a place and its people for whom he developed a lasting affection.

The major literary product of his trip was the magnificent *Childe Harold's Pilgrimage*, which became the rage of all London and made Byron's reputation overnight. The long poem beautifully caught the moods of the growing reaction against conventional manners and values, personified in the autobiographical *Childe Harold*. The magnetic Byron now took advantage of his notoriety to enter into one sexual affair after another—an "abyss of sensuality," as he put it, enhanced by both wine and drugs.

Seeking perhaps some stable influence, in early 1815, he suddenly married a rich young woman, but the marriage went awry almost as soon as it commenced. Only a scant year later, his wife was hurrying back to her parents and requesting legal separation despite her just-born daughter. After some squeezing of his in-laws for money, Byron agreed to sign the separation papers; in those days, this was tantamount to an admission of guilt. His social reputation was now destroyed, not only by the scandalous separation but also by dark hints, never denied and much later confirmed, that he had committed incest with his half-sister, Augusta Leigh. In 1816, he left to visit his friend, the poet Percy Bysshe Shelley, in Switzerland. He never set foot in Britain again.

For the final seven years of his life, Byron was mainly in Italy, where he wrote much of his finest work, including the *Don Juan* epic as well as several of his poetic dramas. The Italian years were made happy by his permanent attachment to the young Teresa Guiccioli, the love of his life, who finally released him from the aimless philandering he had engaged in for fifteen years.

In 1823, the Greeks' rebellion against their Turkish overlords attracted Byron's attention, and he hastened to Greece to put his money and energies into the cause. He contracted a lethal fever and died in his adoptive country in 1824. Throughout the rest of the century, his reputation grew, not only as a poet but as the literary symbol of the brave-but-doomed individual who challenges the destiny of ordinary souls and must eventually pay for his temerity by defeat and death. Denied the honor of burial in Westminster Abbey because of his shocking escapades, Byron finally received a memorial stone in the abbey floor in 1969. His beloved Greeks had acted much sooner to memorialize him in their country.

BYRON AS THE GIAOUR. This portrait was painted in 1813, shortly after Lord Byron returned from his tour of the Near East, which produced several of his best poems and established his fame.

ANALYZE AND INTERPRET

Should the character or private life of a great artist influence one's judgment of him or her as an artist? Lord Byron eventually was banned from England for his political and social ideas. Do you think his banning was a legitimate expression of society's condemnation of his private life?

both aristocrats and the middle classes; and (3) national divisions contributed to the failure of the revolts throughout central and Eastern Europe.

Consequences

In instance after instance, during 1848 and 1849, the barely concealed split between the middle class and the lower class enabled the conservative forces to defeat the goals of both in the short term. The liberals got only a conditioned increase in political representation; the workers got nothing.

1. *France.* The Second Republic established by the revolt lasted but three years before Louis Napoleon (Napoleon III), nephew of the great Bonaparte, used the power of the presidency to which he had been elected in 1848 to declare himself emperor. So began the Second Empire in France, which saw the realization of most of the liberals' economic and political goals, but little for the workers.
2. *Prussia.* After a year of wrangling about the exact form and provisions of a liberal constitution for a united Germany, the bulk of the German states reverted to the conservative regimes that had been briefly pushed aside by the revolts. German liberals had suffered a permanent defeat.
3. *Austria.* The new Austrian emperor, Franz Joseph (ruling 1848–1916), relied on his aristocratic advisers to gradually regain control of the revolutionary situation. The Vienna government crushed the separatist independence movements among the Czechs, Hungarians, and Italians within the empire and then intimidated the German liberals in Austria proper. By the summer of 1849, Austria was embarked on a decade of old-fashioned royal absolutism.
4. *Italy.* It is important to remember that Italy was no more than a collection of small kingdoms and the Papal States. Austria controlled the industrial north, the kingdom of **Sardinia-Piedmont** and the papacy divided the middle, and the reactionary kingdom of Naples controlled the south and Sicily. Liberal Italians had long wanted to unite Italy under a constitutional monarchy. They favored the Sardinian kingdom as the basis of this monarchy because it was the only state that had a native Italian secular ruler. Many middle-class Italians, especially those in the northern cities, were anticlerical and antipapal. They viewed the popes as political reactionaries and upholders of class privilege.

In 1848, anti-Austrian and antipapal riots broke out in various parts of Italy. Sardinia declared war on Austria. This proved to be a mistake. The Austrians were decisive victors. Pope Pius IX (in power 1846–1875) was so frightened by the Roman mobs that he opposed any type of liberalism from then on. In 1849, it appeared that a united Italy was as far away as it had ever been.

Thus, the revolts and attempted revolutions had accomplished very little by 1850. Both middle-class liberals and working-class radicals had been defeated by military force or its threat. Yet, within a generation's time, almost all that the middle classes had fought for and even some of the demands of the radicals had come into being in many

Barricades in Marzstrasse, Vienna, 1848 (oil on canvas), Ritter, Edouard (1808–53)/Wien Museum Karlsplatz, Vienna, Austria/ The Bridgeman Art Library

BARRICADES IN VIENNA. Edouard Ritter painted this canvas shortly after the events it depicts in revolutionary Vienna. Bourgeois revolutionaries atop the hill make common cause for a brief interval with the laborers gathered below.

European capitals. The necessity of introducing a more industrialized economy overrode the objections of the old guard. Many of the thousands who were imprisoned for treason or violating public order from 1849 to 1850 would live to see the day when their governments freely gave the rights for which they had long fought.

RUSSIA

The first severe failure of the international alliances set up by the Vienna treaties was the **Crimean War** (cry-MEE-an War; 1853–1856) between Russia on one side and England, France, and Turkey on the other. Expansionary ambitions led Tsar Nicholas I to demand Turkish concessions in southeastern Europe. Once assured of British and French help, the Turks unexpectedly resisted. The conflict was mostly fought on the Crimean Peninsula in the Black Sea (see Map 32.2).

Militarily, the war was a general debacle for all concerned. The Russian commanders and logistics were even less competent than those of the allies; so in time, Russia had to sue for peace. The Peace of Paris of 1856 was a drastic diplomatic defeat for St. Petersburg, and for the next twenty years, Russia was essentially bottled up in the south, unable to gain naval access to the Mediterranean.

MAP 32.2 Europe After 1871

The unification of the Germanies and of the Italian Peninsula had been completed by 1871, but southeastern Europe was still in political flux. A disintegrating Turkey meant that Bosnia would soon fall under Austrian occupation, and a lost war against Russia would force the Ottomans to recognize the independence of Serbia, Montenegro, Romania, and Bulgaria in 1878. In 1912, a new war allowed the kingdom of Albania to emerge from the Ottoman Empire, while Greece and Serbia were enlarged.

THINKING ABOUT THIS MAP

Compare the large map of Europe in 1871 with the small inset map of the Balkans in 1914. Which European power lost some of its territories? Why did this happen?

SOCIETY AND ECONOMY

Florence Nightingale (1820–1910), Public Health Pioneer

Florence Nightingale's accomplishments were remarkable, particularly for a Victorian woman of her class. She pioneered in preventative health care, public health and sanitation, practical nursing education, hospital reform, and the use of statistics to support her reform campaigns.

Known as the "Lady of the Lamp" to British soldiers during the Crimean War, Nightingale came from a wealthy British family with connections in government and high society. The well-educated Nightingale decided in her twenties to study nursing, which she alone saw as a potentially respectable pursuit for young ladies of her status. At that time, secular nursing was a lowly job that required no talent and less training than a chambermaid's. The socially acceptable path for a young lady like Nightingale was marriage, which she rejected, because she preferred to "seize the chance of forming for myself a true and rich life."

Convinced moreover that she could best serve God and humanity as a nurse, Nightingale persevered despite her parents' disapproval of her chosen career. She toured hospitals in Britain and Europe, gathering information about the practice of nursing. Eventually, she prevailed against the era's strict social conventions, completing a practical-nursing course in Germany, and serving brilliantly as superintendant of a London charity hospital.

The outbreak of the tragic Crimean War in 1854 presented her with a greater challenge. New technology—the telegraph and the camera—provided the world's first immediate and graphic frontline war coverage. The British public was particularly outraged to learn of the abominable conditions in British military hospitals, where most deaths were from cholera and typhus, not battle wounds. Pressured by the public to decrease the mortality rates, the Secretary of State for War dared to appoint Nightingale as Superintendent of Nurses in the British Army. She was the first woman named to an official army position and would prove able to tactfully overcome resistance from any resentful administrators.

Nightingale and her first team of nurses spent six months cleaning up the filthy military hospital at Scutari (near present-day Istanbul) and establishing a large kitchen and laundry. Nightingale used her political connections to secure equipment and supplies. The *London Times* supported her work and promoted her reputation. Within a year, the hospital's sewers and drains were sanitized, fresh water was made available, and the death rate fell dramatically. Nightingale believed that moral dissolution among soldiers was the result of a degraded environment. She said, "Give them a book, a game and a Magic Lantern, and they will leave off drinking." Throughout her time in the Crimea, Nightingale was a model of professional comportment. She trained her nurses to high standards of competence, responsibility, and respectability.

It was in the Crimea that Nightingale began developing her unique system of secular nursing. She wrote that nursing is "the proper use of fresh air, light, warmth, cleanliness, quiet, and the proper … diet" while protecting the patient from disturbances. Decades before Louis Pasteur's germ theory of disease was accepted, Nightingale justifiably believed that most suffering arose, not from illness, but from inadequate attention to the patients' well-being (in a holistic sense). Her devotion to the individual soldier brought universal admiration.

Nightingale received a hero's welcome when she returned to England in 1857; she used her fame and influence to press for continued hospital reforms in Britain. She founded the Nightingale School in 1859, which offered the first professional education for nurses. There she continued to develop the Nightingale System of Nursing and wrote the classic textbook *Notes on Nursing.* Many Nightingale School graduates emigrated, spreading her nursing system worldwide. Nightingale wrote hundreds of books and pamphlets to advocate changes in medical care. She died in 1910 at the age of ninety, one of the most eminent figures of the nineteenth century.

ANALYZE AND INTERPRET

Enumerate the ways in which Florence Nightingale's work improved medical care.

Compare Nightingale's definition of nursing with today's image of the profession.

Library of Congress Prints and Photographs Division [LC-DIG-pga-00466]

FLORENCE NIGHTINGALE HOLDING A LAMP. Nightingale's reputation as "The Lady with the Lamp" originated in her habit of personally making night rounds through all the wards in the Scutari hospital for the wounded.

Russia's Great Reforms

The military embarrassment in the Crimea hardened the determination of the new ruler, **Tsar Alexander II** (ruling 1855–1881), to tackle Russia's primary social and economic problem: the question of the serfs. Russia's serfs still lived in almost total illiteracy, ignorance, and superstition. Not only were they growing increasingly resentful of their noble landlords and masters, but they were also an immense drag on the Russian economy. Most had little money to consume anything, nor could they contribute to the nation's capital for desperately needed financial and industrial investments.

In 1859, a determined Alexander commanded a quick resolution of the problem, and in 1861, the tsar issued an order that abolished serfdom in Russia. Altogether, around fifty-five million individuals—serfs and their dependents—were directly affected.

What, then, were the results of the long-sought emancipation? It unfortunately had only a very limited success. Many were disappointed with their allotted portions of land, which were either small or of poor quality. Instead of outright possession of the land, they received only a tentative title, subject to restrictions imposed by the government. The serfs could not mortgage or sell the land without permission from the village council, which was difficult to obtain. So, instead of creating a class of prosperous, politically and socially engaged farmers, the emancipation of the serfs actually made a good many worse off than before.

Besides emancipation, Alexander II presided over several other major reforms in Russian public life. **Russia's Great Reforms** included changes in the army and judicial systems. Most significantly, the central government reorganized local and provincial authority, changing its previously purely appointive nature. It allowed the election of a county commission, called the *zemstvo* board. Originally, the zemstvo boards had few real powers, but they acted as a catalyst of civic spirit and helped the local peasants become aware of what they could do to better their lives.

Seen in the longer perspective, however, Alexander did not think the time ripe for Russia to have a constitution, an elected national legislature, or strong local government bodies. Russia's central authority remained what it had always been—an autocracy (government by a single person having unlimited power). Consequently, every variety of revolutionary doctrine was to be found in the Russian underground by the 1890s, ranging from orthodox Marxism to peasant communes to nihilistic terrorism. As late as 1905, however, the government of the tsar still seemed to be in undisputed control of the illiterate peasants and a small and doctrinally divided group of socialist workers in the towns.

FRANCE

The nephew of the great Napoleon won the presidential election in France that was held in the wake of the 1848 revolt. Riding on his uncle's name and claiming to be a sincere republican, Louis Napoleon was the first modern ruler who understood how to manipulate the democratic franchise to create a near-dictatorship. Within a few months of his election, he imitated his uncle and made himself emperor of the French, as Napoleon III. This *Second Empire* lasted twenty years, which divided into two distinct segments. Until the 1860s, it was an authoritarian regime led by one man's vision. After that, Napoleon gradually liberalized his rule and allowed political opposition. The main reason for the change was his increasingly unpopular and misconceived foreign policy: a frivolous colonial adventure in Mexico in 1863–1864 and failure to stop an aggressively expanding Prussia. To ameliorate these problems, he then had to encourage a previously tame legislature to share leadership responsibilities.

Napoleon was more successful in changing the primarily agrarian France of 1851 into a mixed economy with the firm beginnings of industrial development in place by 1870. By then, capitalist industry was also taking root in many smaller cities, such as Lyon, Marseilles, Nancy, Brest, and Rouen.

Napoleon and his Second Empire came to a disgraceful finish in the **Franco-Prussian War** of 1870, which was the emperor's last foreign policy miscalculation. Foolishly taking the field, he was captured by the enemy, forced to abdicate, and died in quiet exile in England. At the end of the war, the first attempt at socialist revolution had taken place in Paris—the capital city whose residents strongly resented the terms of the peace settlement—but the army crushed the group with great bloodshed. This **Paris Commune of 1871** was extremely unwelcome to the majority of the French. From this time onward, the split between the conservative villagers of the French provinces and the radical workers and intellectuals of "red" Paris that had originated in the French Revolution of 1789 was wide open.

Following the lost war, the monarchists failed to agree on a single candidate. This enabled those who favored a republic to gradually establish themselves in power. By 1875, the **Third Republic of France** was more or less in place; it was a liberal state with a strong National Assembly and a weak presidential executive. A confused mass of political parties ranged across the whole spectrum from extreme reactionaries to Marxists and anarchists. About the only political topic that most French agreed on during the later nineteenth century was the necessity of someday gaining revenge on Bismarck's Germany and reclaiming the "lost provinces" of Alsace and Lorraine (shown on Map 32.4). France's *revanchism* (ray-VAHNSH-ism)—the desire, rooted in wounded national pride, to make up for the loss of national territory by seeking colonial territories abroad—incited France to take part in the "new imperialism" of the leading European powers in the years that lay ahead.

THE UNIFICATION OF ITALY

One of the major changes in the political map of nineteenth-century Europe was the completion of the unification of Italy (see Map 32.3). This had been the goal of two generations of Italian statesmen and revolutionaries, going back to the Napoleonic wars. In the 1860s, unification was thrust through over the opposition of both Austria—which controlled much of northern Italy—and Pope Pius IX.

The father of Italian unification was the liberal-minded aristocrat Count **Camillo Cavour** (1810–1861), who became the prime minister of the kingdom of Sardinia in 1852. Sardinia had long been the best hope of those who wanted a united Italy. However, the center of political gravity in the kingdom had long since moved from backward Sardinia to Piedmont and the modern industrial city of Turin. A believer in **Realpolitik**, or politics based on practical considerations only (and not ideology), Cavour built Piedmont into the leading economic force in Italy, as well as the major political power, during the 1850s.

After forcing Austria to cede control of Vienna to him in 1959, much of the rest of Italy threw in its lot with Piedmont. The newly christened kingdom of Italy, based in Turin, now embraced about half of the Peninsula. The rest was divided among the pope, the reactionary Bourbon king of Naples and Sicily, and the remaining Austrian possessions.

The romantic and popular revolutionary, Giuseppe Garibaldi, now entered the scene, leading a volunteer army through southern Italy, routing the royal government of Naples, and joining Sicily and southern Italy to the Italian kingdom in 1861. A few months later, Cavour died, with the job of unification by conquest almost complete.

MAP 32.3 The Unification of Italy
The triumphs of the 1860s produced an Italian kingdom that was composed of two distinct regions: North and South.

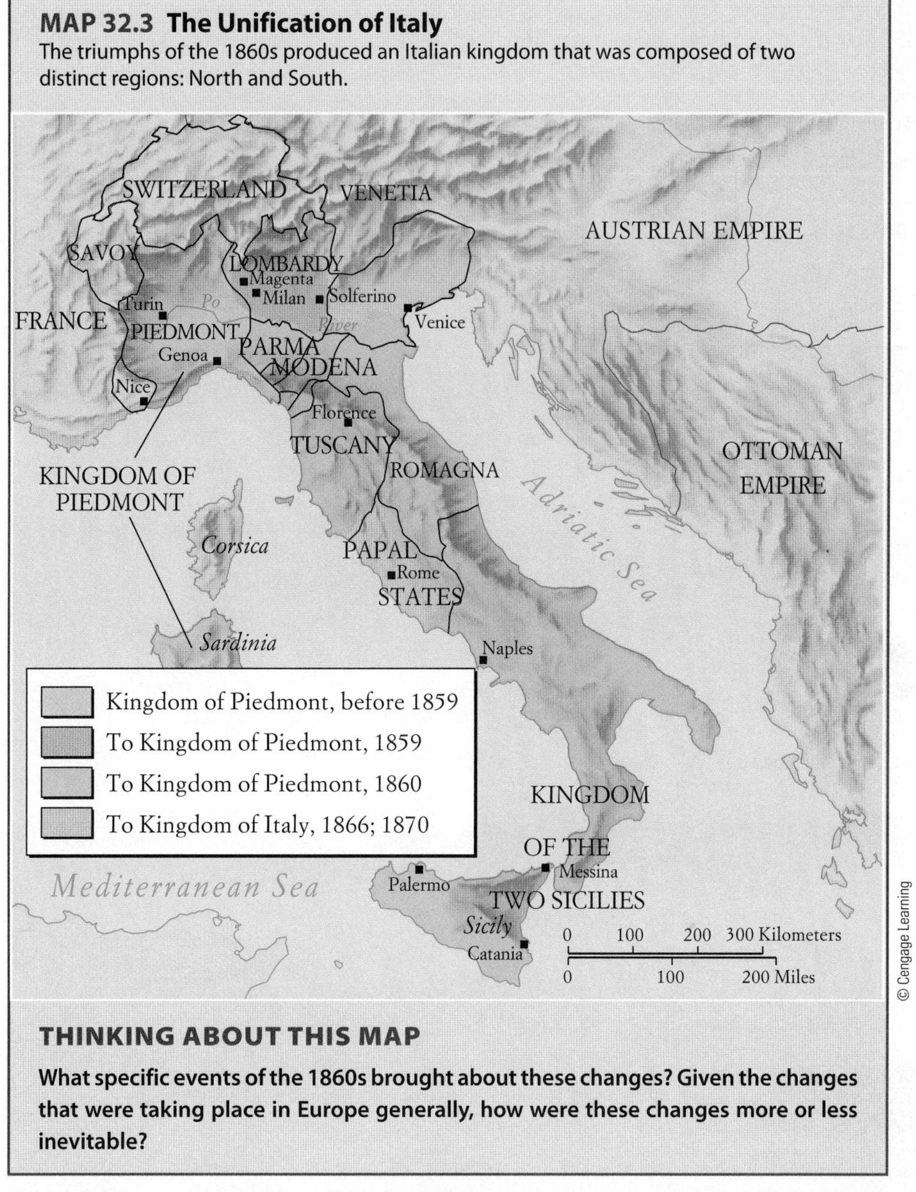

THINKING ABOUT THIS MAP

What specific events of the 1860s brought about these changes? Given the changes that were taking place in Europe generally, how were these changes more or less inevitable?

Two pieces of the picture still remained to be fitted in: the Austrian province of Venetia and the Papal States centered in Rome. Venetia was gained in 1866, as a prize for joining with Prussia in another brief victorious war against Austria. When the Franco-Prussian War broke out in 1870, the Piedmontese quickly annexed the Papal States and made Rome the capital of the new Italian kingdom.

In the two generations that followed, the new Italy was a mixed success story. Lacking all important industrial resources except manpower, Italy was the weakest of the European great powers. This country was in most ways really two distinct countries: the industrializing, urban, liberal North and the agrarian, rural, feudal South.

The south (from Rome southward) and Sicily were controlled by reactionary aristocrats—mainly absentee landowners whose impoverished peasants still lived in serfdom in everything but name. The Catholic Church was all-powerful and an ally of the aristocracy. The south had no modern industry or transport, and no prospects of any. On the other hand, educated, wealthy landowners and a large commercial middle class that lived and worked in good-sized cities such as Turin, Milan, and Venice controlled the north (from Florence northward). These towns, which had ties to transalpine Europe, were rapidly industrializing, producing a proletariat that would soon be one of Europe's most fertile fields for socialist ideas.

THE UNIFICATION OF THE GERMANIES

During the same years that the Italians were attempting to construct one state, the unification of Germany came into being (see Map 32.4). The way Germany was united would have a dominant influence on the later history of the country. It followed the conservative Realpolitik style

MAP 32.4 Unification of the German Empire

After the battle of Königgrätz in 1866, the Austrians were put out of the running for primacy among German speakers. The surrender of French emperor Napoleon III at the head of his army at Sedan completed the task Bismarck had set for himself and the Prussian military.

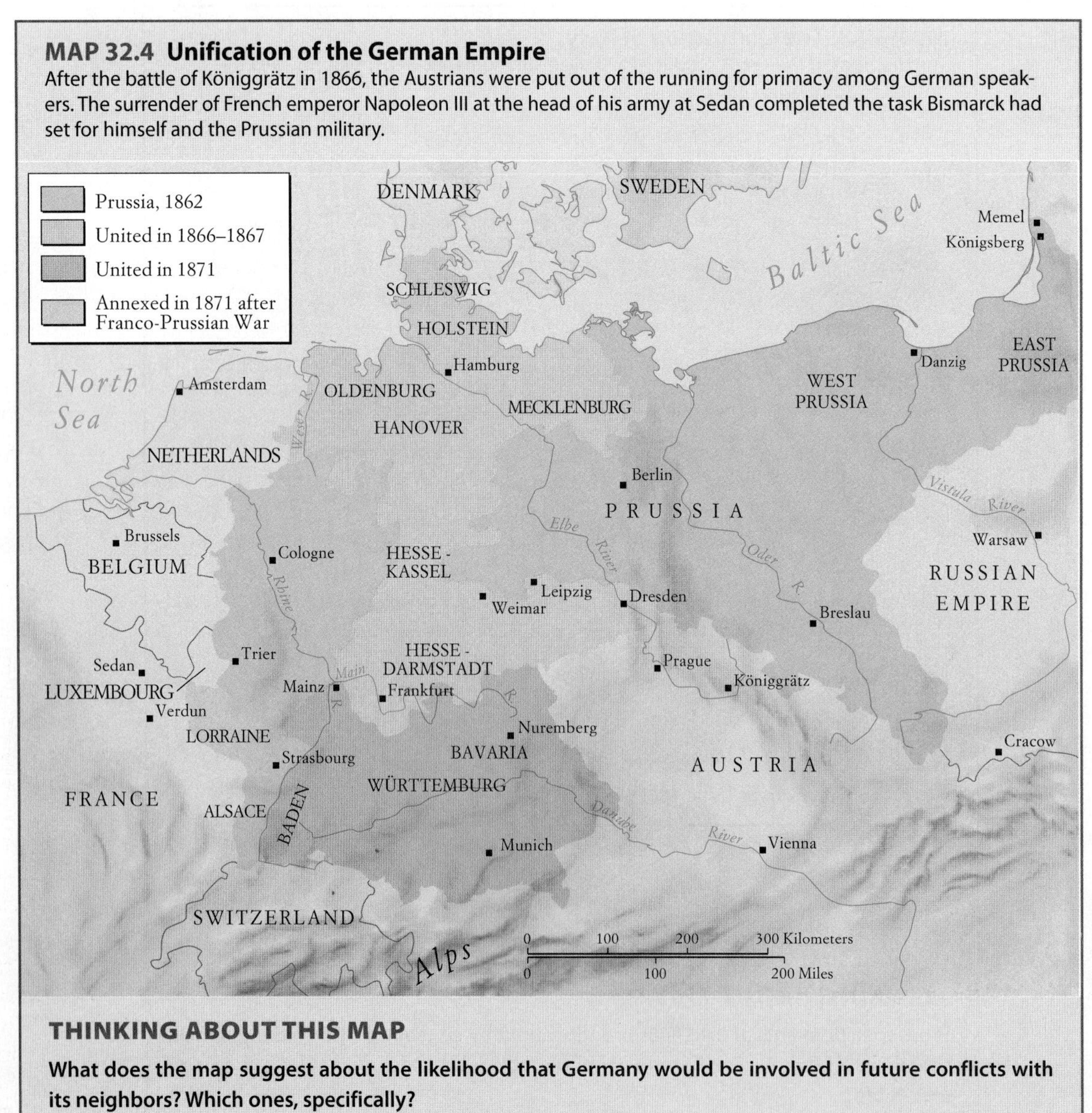

THINKING ABOUT THIS MAP

What does the map suggest about the likelihood that Germany would be involved in future conflicts with its neighbors? Which ones, specifically?

of two men: the Prussian king William I (or Wilhelm I; ruling 1861–1888) and his chancellor and trusted friend, **Otto von Bismarck** (1815–1898). For good or evil, modern Germany was largely the product of Germans' rising sense of nationalism and Bismarck's cunning ability to use it to bring about the creation of a single, powerful national state—Germany.

Like almost all nineteenth-century patriots, Bismarck wished to see the German people united rather than remain fragmented among the sixteen kingdoms and city-states left by the 1815 Treaty of Vienna. Above all, he wanted to complete what many years of Prussian policies had attempted to do with only modest success: to unify all Germans under the political leadership of Berlin. The chief reasons for the failure thus far included lingering distrust between northern (Protestant) and southern (Catholic) Germans left over from previous centuries of sectarian warfare and the determined opposition of Austria.

Bismarck's policy aimed at removing the Austrians from German affairs as soon as possible. To this end, Bismarck provoked Austria into declaring war on Prussia, so that Austria appeared to be the aggressor in the eyes of the other Germans, who tried to remain neutral. The Prussians won the **Austro-Prussian War** of 1866, unexpectedly, in one bloody battle. Instead of seeking territory or money damages, however, Bismarck insisted only that Austria withdraw from German political affairs, leaving the field to Prussia to create a new **Confederation of Northern German States**.

The capstone of Bismarck's policy for unity was to provoke a third war, this one against the traditional enemy west of the Rhine: France. The Franco-Prussian War of 1870–1871 was the result of clever deception by the Prussian chancellor to maneuver the French into becoming the formal aggressor. As Bismarck had reckoned, the southern German states could no longer remain neutral in this situation. Fevered nationalist opinion overrode religious considerations and forced the governments to join the Prussians, as fellow Germans, against the ancient enemy.

Soon, Napoleon III abdicated and France sued for peace. Bismarck now put forward the Prussian king as emperor of Germany, as a wave of national triumph swept the country. The Germans, after all, were the most numerous nation in Europe and had been artificially divided for many centuries. The new Germany, which counted 70 million inhabitants, extended from Alsace (annexed from France) almost to Warsaw and from the North Sea to the Alps, and was intensely nationalistic.

THE MULTINATIONAL EMPIRE OF AUSTRIA-HUNGARY

In the center of the European map stood the Austrian empire. The fourth-largest state in population and third largest in territory, Austria—under the guidance of its longtime foreign minister, Klemens von Metternich—had played a major role in international affairs for a full generation after 1815. After the national-liberal revolts of 1848 had been crushed, a decade of absolutist rule had ensued under the young Kaiser (Emperor) Franz Joseph.

After the defeats in Italy in 1859 and by Prussia in 1866, the emperor had to come to terms with them. He did so in the *Ausgleich* (OWS-glike) of 1867, a compromise that divided Austria into roughly equal halves—Austria and Hungary. Each was independent of the other in everything except foreign policy, defense, and some financial matters. Those living in Hungary were now under the uncompromising domination of the highly nationalistic Hungarians, which they strongly resented. Those in Austria were subordinate to the Austro-Germans, and for a time, the internal affairs of this half of the dual monarchy were more harmonious. But by the 1890s, the "national" question was heating up here as well. The obstructionist minorities in parliament paralyzed the liberal, constitutional government. To get anything done, the emperor had to violate his own constitution and rule by decree. Austria-Hungary became the prime European example of the negative aspects of nationalism.

THE UNITED STATES IN THE INDUSTRIAL AGE

At its independence from Britain, the United States was still an agrarian society, with its four million inhabitants concentrated along the eastern coast. Skilled tradesmen and master craftsmen were in short supply, and 85 percent of the labor force were farmers and agricultural workers. Even in the urbanized areas of New England and the mid-Atlantic region, as late as 1800 there was practically no large-scale commercial production.

By the Civil War, this situation had changed markedly. Thanks to steady waves of immigrants from Europe and slaves from Africa, the United States had more inhabitants than Great Britain—about thirty million. Half a dozen cities had populations of more than 100,000, and farm labor now made up less than half of the total employment. The dependence on British engineering and machinery that had characterized the first generation after independence was now entirely gone. American manufacturers and industrial techniques were rapidly proving that they could compete throughout the world.

New England was the original center of American industry. Factories producing consumer goods, such as textiles and shoes, harnesses and wagons, and metal tools and kitchenware, located there. They took advantage of both the abundant waterpower provided by the many rivers and the large pool of labor from the overcrowded and poverty-stricken rural areas. Mill towns such as Lowell, Massachusetts, and Bridgeport, Connecticut, became common. They were similar in many ways to those in England but less dreary and unsanitary because

PROTEST AND REPRESSION. This engraving illustrates what many middle-class people feared would be the inevitable result of labor organization. In 1891, a labor protest in France resulted in violent suppression at the hands of the police.

of cheaper land and a different building style. Compared to the early industrial towns in Europe where workers for the most part faced exploitation and limited horizons, American towns offered a degree of democracy and social mobility. Although the stories of Horatio Alger ascents from rags to riches were mostly myths, Americans generally did have far more opportunities to improve their condition than were available to the working class in Europe. The belief that a relatively high degree of economic equality and opportunity was and must remain open to Americans permanently shaped American political and social ideals.

THE MODERN NATION-STATE

We have seen that in the quarter century between 1850 and 1875, great political changes occurred in several major European states: Russia, France, Italy, Germany, and Austria-Hungary (review Map 32.2). These changes were accompanied by sweeping changes in the economy and the structure of society. Toward the period's end, the Second Industrial Revolution was in full swing, bringing technological advances that had a direct impact on the everyday lives of everyday people. (See the next chapter.)

What emerged in Europe and the United States during these years was in fact the modern nation-state, in which an ethnic group (the nation) exercises control over a territory (the state) through domination and mass participation in government. Its political-governmental outlines had been initiated in the French Revolution but were not perfected until the industrial-technical breakthroughs of the late nineteenth century. A host of familiar concepts first came into daily life during this period, including the following:

- Mass political parties electing legislatures and executives who were more or less responsible to their voters.
- Mass school systems turning out disciplined, trained minds to take over the technical tasks of a much more complex society and economy.
- Labor unions representing the rapidly increasing numbers of workers negotiating with the representatives of impersonal corporations.

All of these developments were characterized by a large group, a mass or class, coming into a predominant position, whereas the individual and his or her idiosyncrasies, desires, inclinations, and so forth receded into the background.

SUMMARY

The dual revolutions in politics and economics started in the later eighteenth century but matured in the nineteenth. In the era after the Napoleonic wars, Europe divided politically into liberal, conservative, and reactionary segments, all of which were attempting to meet the new challenges thrown up by the Americans' successful revolt against their colonial overlord and the French Revolution.

The liberal spirit that was forcing its way into prominence in France and Britain took a less benign form in economics than in politics. The ideas of Adam Smith and others were selectively adopted by many liberals and used to justify harsh exploitation of the workers. They triggered experiments with socialism that attracted little attention because of their utopian nature and, in most cases, quick failure. The Europe-wide revolts of 1848 mostly failed in the short run, but the forces in society that had touched them off proved too strong to resist, and they triumphed to at least a limited extent in the following generations. Therefore, the 1860s and 1870s produced major changes in almost all of the political and territorial maps of continental Europe.

The modern nation-state with its mass-participatory institutions was coming into existence, although its pace varied from place to place. In Russia, attempts at basic reform fell short because of the Crown's and the nobility's fearfulness and reluctance to allow the people—particularly the newly liberated serfs—a full share in governing themselves. Instead, the aborted political reforms resulted in the growth of a revolutionary movement that would blossom in the early twentieth century. In France, the empire of Napoleon III brought progress internally but failed in foreign policy and was destroyed by the lost war with Prussia. Italy was finally unified in the 1860s, in part voluntarily and in part through conquest by the kingdom of Sardinia-Piedmont. What emerged, however, was two Italies, south and north, that had little in common and would remain isolated from each other for generations.

German chancellor Bismarck was the most successful of the statesmen who attempted to realize national destiny. Unified by war and nationalist fervor, Germans entered into a Prussia-dominated empire after 1871 and immediately became the most potent military force on the continent. One of the countries the new empire surpassed was Austria-Hungary, a former rival that was now defeated militarily and split by conflicting nationalisms. In the United States, steady industrial growth on a regional level in New England was greatly expanded on a national scale after the Civil War. By the end of the century, the American economy rivaled Germany's for leadership of the industrial world. In the last half of the century, the West engaged in a new imperialism that was driven by disparate motives and particularly focused on Asia and Africa. Chapters 35, 36, and 37 deal with this subject.

IDENTIFICATION TERMS

Test your knowledge of this chapter's key concepts by defining the following terms. If you can not recall the meaning of certain terms, refresh your memory by looking up the boldfaced term in the chapter, turning to the Glossary at the end of the book, or accessing the terms on the CourseMate website at **www.cengagebrain.com**.

Austro-Prussian War
Otto von Bismarck
British Reform Act of 1832
Camillo Cavour
Confederation of Northern German States
conservatism
Crimean War
Franco-Prussian War
July Monarchy
nationalism
Paris Commune of 1871
Realpolitik
Romantic movement
Russia's Great Reforms
Sardinia-Piedmont
socialism
Third Republic of France
Tories
Whigs

FOR FURTHER REFLECTION

1. Today, when people use terms like *liberal* and *conservative*, what do they mean? How do these modern terms compare in usage and meaning with their nineteenth-century connotations?
2. Would modern liberals or modern conservatives accept the views of nineteenth-century liberals?
3. Would the positions of British Liberals be considered as liberal or conservative today?
4. What did nineteenth-century socialists seem to have been trying to achieve? Whose interests did they appear to have been representing? Could Smith or Ricardo have been sympathetic to their social and economic agendas?
5. Compare and contrast Cavour's role in unifying Italy with that of Bismarck in creating Germany.

TEST YOUR KNOWLEDGE

Test your knowledge of this chapter by answering the following questions. Complete answers appear at the end of the book. You may find even more quiz questions on the CourseMate website at **www.cengagebrain.com**.

1. Which of the following had its modern birth in the 1789–1814 era?
   a. Constitutional monarchy
   b. Nationalism
   c. Autocracy
   d. Meritocracy
   e. Liberalism
2. The *Gendarme* of Europe was
   a. France.
   b. Great Britain.
   c. Russia.
   d. Germany.
   e. Turkey.
3. Which of the following statements about Florence Nightingale was true? She
   a. was a brilliant administrator.
   b. believed in the germ theory.
   c. was poorly educated.
   d. spent most of adult life in Istanbul.
   e. married a doctor and had children.
4. The most important parliamentary act in nineteenth-century British history was the
   a. passage of the United Kingdom Act.
   b. passage of the Reform Act of 1832.

c. decision to exile Napoleon to St. Helena.
d. passage of the Factory Act of 1819.
e. ousting of the Tories from Parliament.

5. Which country was least affected by the revolts of 1848?
   a. France
   b. Great Britain
   c. Italy
   d. Austria
   e. Prussia
6. The biggest single governmental problem in mid-nineteenth-century Russia was how to
   a. defend the enormous borders against simultaneous attacks.
   b. make the tzar's government more efficient.
   c. bring the military into the modern technical age.
   d. bring the serfs into the national economy.
   e. industrialize the country enough for it to compete with other countries.
7. The Paris Commune was
   a. an attempt to impose a socialist regime under Karl Marx on France.
   b. an imaginative attempt to introduce democracy through popular vote.
   c. an uprising against the imperial government that had lost a war.
   d. a kind of new religion prompted by anti-Christian radicals.
   e. a group of Parisian artists who gathered to support each other in perfecting their craft.
8. Cavour's role in unifying Italy was that of
   a. the diplomat-statesman.
   b. the rabble-rousing tribune of the people.
   c. the military commander.
   d. the right-hand man of the pope.
   e. the author of the Italian constitution.
9. The crucial question for Bismarck as Prussia's chancellor in the 1860s was how to
   a. strengthen the army.
   b. crush the socialists' opposition.
   c. unite the German people politically.
   d. strengthen the constitutional rights of the citizens.
   e. use his military to best effect.
10. One significant aspect of the modern nation-state is
   a. the development of independent thought and action among individuals.
   b. the need for close ties between church and state.
   c. the subordination of the individual to the community.
   d. an increase in social welfare spending.
   e. a greater tolerance for members of opposing groups.

CourseMate

Visit the CourseMate website at **www.cengagebrain.com** for additional study tools and review materials for this chapter.

33 Advanced Industrial Society

Hence all society would appear to arrange itself into four different classes: (1) those that will work, (2) those that cannot work, (3) those that will not work, and (4) those that need not work. —HENRY MAYHEW

1848	Communist Manifesto
c. 1850–c. 1910	Massive emigration from Europe
c. 1870s	Second Industrial Revolution begins
1870s–1914	Urbanization increases; labor unions and mass democratic politics emerge; Marxist socialism strengthens

CHAPTER OUTLINE

Throughout the nineteenth century, the West (that is, Western Europe and the United States) was clearly the dominant factor in world political and military developments. And this colonial subordination of much of the rest of the globe to Europe was a reflection above all of the West's large and increasing lead in technology and economic organization. In the half century between 1860 and World War I, Europe and the United States themselves went through a peaceful change of massive dimensions. As in the eighteenth century, a dual revolution was propelled by a shift in the sources of energy, which was then reflected in social organization and national politics. As the First Industrial Revolution was driven by steam, the Second Industrial Revolution was driven by petroleum and electricity. These two energy sources transformed urban life and made the city clearly the dominant social organism. Urban areas produced new businesses, new organizations of workers, new professions, and new lifestyles.

In these decades, socialism became a major force in several countries for the first time. As enunciated by Karl Marx, it posed a severe threat from below to the combined aristocratic/bourgeois rule that had become the norm in European politics and economies. Also, while the non-Western world was being incorporated into the new financial and commercial system, Europeans were emigrating in massive numbers to selected areas of the globe, primarily for economic reasons. The Americas, and particularly the United States, were the favored destinations.

THE SECOND INDUSTRIAL REVOLUTION

As in the late eighteenth century, population growth and rising demand for consumer goods necessitated new energy sources. Europe's overall population, exclusive of Russia, rose from 265 million to 401 million in the second half of the nineteenth century (see Map 33.1). Despite the stabilization of the average

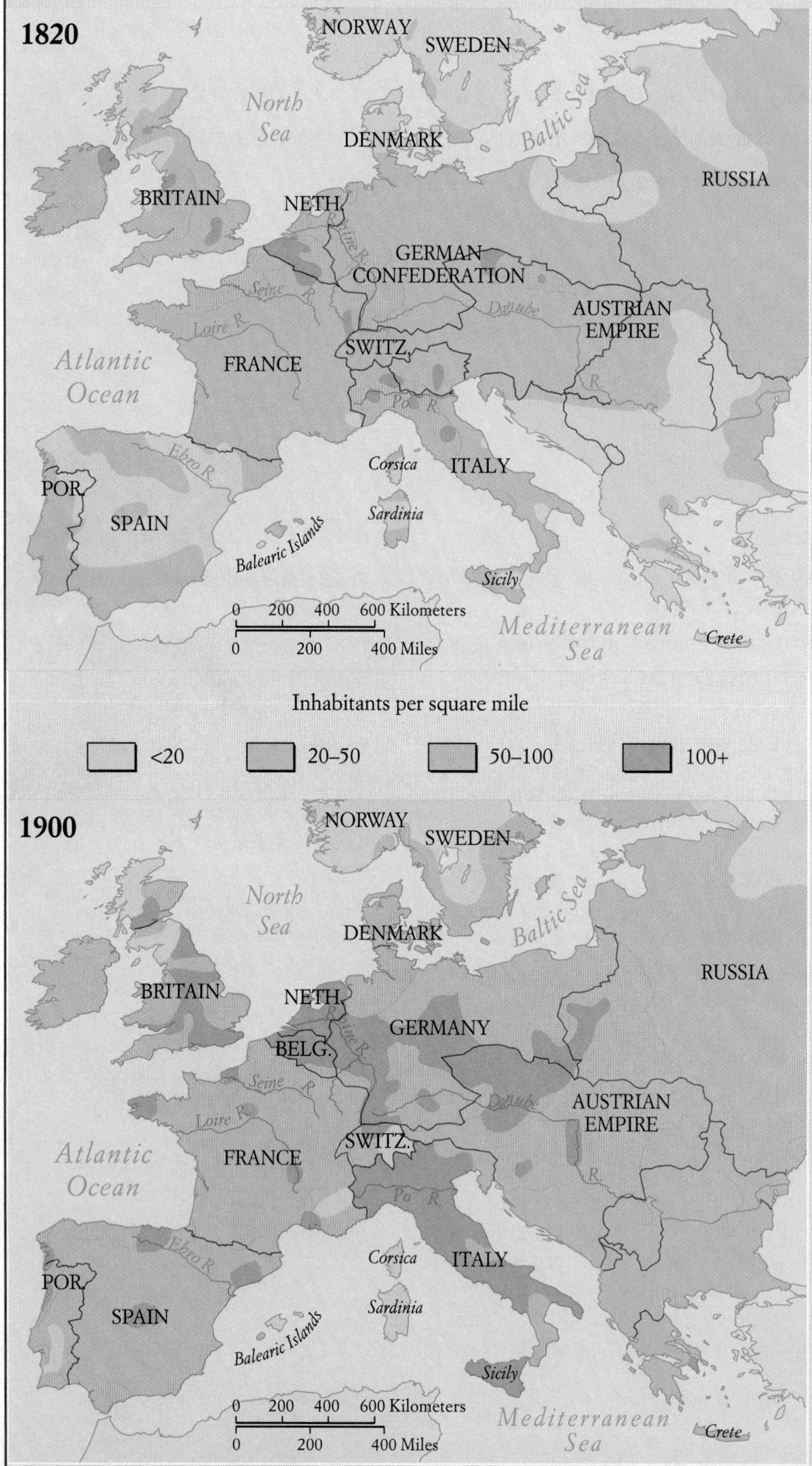

Inhabitants per square mile

<20 | 20–50 | 50–100 | 100+

MAP 33.1 European Population Growth in the Nineteenth Century

The Italian Peninsula and parts of Central and Eastern Europe saw the most dramatic increases in population density during the eighty-year period from 1820 to 1900. In some rural areas in these lands, the lack of industry and the poor soil productivity had created an overpopulation crisis that was only ameliorated by emigration. Government was caught up in conflict with itself; emigration was discouraged and made difficult by national policy (particularly in Russia), while local authorities promoted it. In the latter third of the century, most of the younger male residents of whole villages and counties emigrated to the New World. Some intended to return—and did so—but the majority stayed in their new homelands.

THINKING ABOUT THIS MAP

How do you account for the dramatic growth in Europe's population in this eighty-year span of time?

Western European family at 2.5 children at the end of the century—the Eastern Europeans were substantially more fertile—the previous huge population increase, combined with a sharp rise in real income, created a large market for consumer goods and services of all types.

A definite rise in material standards of living was visible throughout Europe west of Russia. With fewer children's hands now necessary for labor, those who were born at this time profited from better public health and nutrition to live longer, healthier lives. They could and did consume more. Goods that were almost unknown in European workers' houses in the early 1800s now became common: machine-produced footwear and clothes, nursing bottles for babies, gas or electric lighting, and books and newspapers.

Adding to this internal market was the rapidly expanding overseas market, both in the European colonies and in some of the independent nations of America and Asia. The surge of imperial ventures that began in the 1850s brought major increases in the availability of raw materials as well as the number of potential consumers in the Asian and African marketplaces. The volume of world trade shot upward in the later nineteenth century, and the West controlled that trade entirely. Britain, Germany, and the United States were the main beneficiaries.

New Energy Sources

The big lead in industrial production that Great Britain had established in the early nineteenth century gradually narrowed after 1850. Belgium and northern France were the centers of the continent's initial industries, followed by parts of Germany and Italy. After the unification of those two countries, their industrial growth accelerated sharply. As an important example, Germany's steel and iron production exceeded Britain's by 1893 and was almost double British production by 1914.

Whole new industries sprang up, seemingly overnight. Chemicals, oil refining, steamship building, turbines, and electrical machinery, and, toward the end of the 1890s, the automobile industry, are outstanding examples. But perhaps the most important of all the new developments was the taming and application of electricity to both industrial and domestic uses.

Electricity had been recognized as a potentially useful natural phenomenon since the eighteenth century, but no practical use could be made of it then. In the 1870s, this situation changed dramatically as a result of the work of German, American, and French researchers. The development of generators and transformers allowed direct current to be sent wherever desired, cheaply and efficiently, and then transformed into easily used, safe, alternating current. The first big urban power plant was constructed in 1881, and electric power was soon being used to light streets, power trams, and bring artificial light into hundreds of thousands of city homes and factories. Soon after, electrical machinery was being used in thousands of industrial applications. Electric railways and subway systems were introduced in every major European city by the 1890s. Probably no other series of inventions has ever contributed so much to easing the physical labor and improving the material life of ordinary people.

Petroleum was the second new energy source. The internal combustion engine, which drew its power from the controlled explosion of gasoline injected into cylinders, was invented in 1876. Although it was clearly an impressive means of producing energy, its full potential was not apparent until the German engineers Gottlieb Daimler and Karl Benz put the engine on a carriage and connected the cylinder pistons to the wheels. Benz's work in the late 1880s is generally credited with the emergence of the gasoline-powered automobile as a practical, reliable mode of transport, although literally dozens of other German, French, American, and British experimenters also contributed in major fashion to its development.

Petroleum and its by-product, natural gas, were to have many other uses, including lighting, heating, and driving stationary engines and pumps. From petroleum also came a whole range of important new chemicals. Then as now, Europe west of Russia had very little oil and depended on imports from other places. American capital and American exploration and drilling techniques soon led the world in the race for oil production.

The Second Industrial Revolution depended largely on scientific research. The Germans with their well-equipped university and industrial laboratories quickly took over the lead in this area and held it without serious competition for many years. Their carefully organized and well-funded research enabled the Germans to dominate new European industry after 1870. The British, the former leaders, were slow to realize that the rules of industrial competition had changed. They put little money into research, from either government or private hands. By 1890, Britain's technological expertise and innovation were falling steadily behind Germany's, and this growing gap had much to do with the rising competition between the two countries in political and diplomatic affairs.

New Forms of Business Organization

New forms of business organization accompanied the new energy applications. In the first century of the Industrial Age (1760–1860), the standard form of industry had been the private partnership or proprietorship. It was limited deliberately to a small handful of owner-managers, some of whom might work alongside their employees in the office or even on the shop floor. When more capital was needed for expansion, it was borrowed on a short-term basis for specific needs. The public was not invited in, and the banks and investment companies were not partners but only facilitators in arranging funds.

SCIENCE AND TECHNOLOGY

London's Great Exhibition of 1851

The great city of London, the world's industrial and commercial center, buzzed with excitement through the winter and spring months of 1851. Queen Victoria's consort, Prince Albert—a liberal and a progressive by any measure—had formed a committee to plan a **Great Exhibition**, in effect what was to be the world's first international trade fair, to promote the liberal gospel of peace through work and free trade. The project had more than its share of critics. By nature ultranationalist and disdainful of the poor, Tories in Parliament fretted over a feared invasion of Britain's capital city by foreigners and working class "ruffians" from Britain's own rural shires. Others fumed over the proposed site of the exhibition, Hyde Park, a part of the city that the wealthiest Londoners had always monopolized for their own recreation.

Then too there were the interminable arguments over the building to house the exhibits. Altogether, Prince Albert's committee received 245 designs, none of which failed to evoke vociferous condemnation. Finally, however, a radical design was submitted by Joseph Paxton with support from structural engineer Charles Fox, for a massive edifice to be constructed entirely of glass panels over an iron framework. Called the *Crystal Palace*, the design was received with enthusiasm. A construction committee, on which Isambard Kingdom Brunel served (see Chapter 31), oversaw the toil of approximately 2,600 workmen who finished the project in just six months. Glass factories and iron foundries prefabricated it in sections, which then were transported to the building site where it was assembled. When finished, the main building was about 2,000-feet long, intersected by two transepts, and enclosed more than a million square feet. It was built high enough to cover and enclose several of the Park's trees.

Queen Victoria herself opened the Exhibition in June 1851, as pictured here. Politics aside, the Exhibition proved to be a smashing success. Victorians were accustomed to dark interiors in their buildings, so the Crystal Palace, glittering in the sunlight and with its vast and airy interiors—complete with fountains, trees, and even birds—stirred feelings in visitors sometimes approaching the sublime. There were 14,000 exhibits, half of them British and the other half foreign. Among the latter, the empire was heavily represented, as was the United States. The exhibits were a hodgepodge of wonders and contraptions of all sorts: models, industrial machinery, scientific experiments (most notably in electricity), new agricultural machinery, photographic gear, furniture and other domestic items. Oddities were well represented, too—an alarm clock that tossed the sleeper out of bed, for example.

The planning committee took particular care to make the Great Exhibition accessible to everyone. Special trains and ships were laid on from all of Britain's provinces, and there were low admissions days to enable even the poor a chance to see it all. The queen herself was completely captivated and returned frequently to see it. Altogether, there were about six million visits of citizens of all classes and from all over Britain and Ireland, as well as many foreigners. When the committee closed the show in the fall of 1851, £186,437 were taken in as profits. A huge sum at the time, the proceeds were used to construct permanent exhibits in South Kensington, including the Victoria and Albert [Art] Museum, a Science Museum, and the Natural History Museum. The Crystal Palace was sold to a private company, who dismantled it and reassembled it in a part of south London called Sydenham. It continued to be used for special exhibits there until a fire burned it down in 1936.

ANALYZE AND INTERPRET

In what ways did this exhibition exemplify the spirit of 19th century economic liberalism? What else do you know about Prince Albert?

QUEEN VICTORIA OPENS THE GREAT EXHIBITION, 1851. This partial interior view of the Crystal Palace depicts the official opening of the Great Exhibition by Queen Victoria. Note its immense size.

In the **Second Industrial Revolution** (*c.* 1860–1920), the **corporation** rather than the partnership became the standard, and banks, which thus became part owners of the company, often permanently financed the corporation. *Joint stock companies*, whose shares were traded on public stock exchanges in every European capital, were formed to raise huge amounts of capital from the investing public. The shareholders were technically the owners of the company, but, in fact, they had little or nothing to say about management policy, which was the purview of a board of directors with whom the investor normally had no contacts. This separation of ownership and management was one of the most striking changes in business and commerce of all sorts in the later nineteenth century, and it continues to the present.

SOCIAL RESULTS OF THE SECOND INDUSTRIAL REVOLUTION

The Second Industrial Revolution accelerated several trends that had begun during the first. Four were particularly important:

1. *Urbanization.* The outstanding feature in Western demography throughout the nineteenth century was the rapid growth of urban areas. Britain was the first European country to urbanize. In 1851, the census revealed that more than half of the English people lived in towns and cities. (At this time, by comparison, only 22 percent of Americans were urban dwellers.) By 1900, Britain alone had more cities with populations of more than 100,000 than there had been on all of the continent in 1800. Industrial jobs were a major reason for migration to the cities, but they were by no means the only reason. Better education, leisure activities, and marital prospects were also strong incentives.
2. *Organization of labor.* After the failure of revolutions, the workers on the continent rarely attempted to gain better conditions by street riots or mass demonstrations. Instead, they took to organizing labor unions, which would fight for improvements in a legal way and attempt to gain government support against abusive employers. In so doing, the continental workers were following the lead of the British, who had attempted to win reforms in their conditions of life and labor through the **Chartist movement** of the 1840s. Although conservative resistance and police repression frustrated their short-term goals, the Chartists initiated long-term change both in and outside Parliament toward greater democracy and fairer distribution of the country's wealth.

   In the 1870s, Great Britain became the first major country to fully legalize labor unions, giving them the right to strike, picket, and boycott. In the 1880s, France took the same course, and in 1890, Germany did also. By the turn of the twentieth century, all Western European nations except Spain and Portugal had conceded the rights of labor to use all nonviolent means available in the struggle for a better life.
3. *Social reforms.* The unions did give the laboring classes a new and fairly effective way to express their grievances and sometimes win redress for them. By 1914, few workers had to endure the sort of systematically inhumane working conditions that were common during the First Industrial Age. Child labor laws and industrial safety regulations were now common and enforced by both national and local authorities. A few countries had some provisions for worker employment security and pensions. (Bismarck's Germany led in these respects.) The government, if not the employer, frequently even provided worker health and accident insurance.

   The early unions were sometimes socialist in orientation, sometimes not. By the 1890s, however, the Marxist revolutionary socialists were close to taking over the labor movement in several key countries. (The United States was a notable exception; Marxism was never popular there.) This action frightened many employers and their partners in government, and they attempted to suppress or intimidate the socialist leaders. The last decade before World War I saw many bitter disputes between management and labor all over Europe and in the United States. Labor violence was common.
4. *Mass democratic politics.* An important effect of industrial life was the coming of mass politics and parties. In the last third of the century, almost all European governments as well as the United States allowed all of their male citizens to vote, regardless of property qualifications: Germany in 1871, France in 1875, Britain in 1884, and Spain in 1890. Only Russia, Hungary, and Italy stood firm against universal male suffrage as late as 1905. By the outbreak of World War I in 1914, all of Europe had

Suffragette parade, outside the Adelphi Theatre, New York, 1910 (b/w photo), American Photographer, (20th century)/Schlesinger Library, Radcliffe Institute, Harvard University/The Bridgeman Art Library

SUFFRAGETTES. One of the many early twentieth-century demonstrations for women's voting rights, this one in the United States. In most cases, Western countries did not grant female suffrage until after World War I.

male universal suffrage. This advance strongly stimulated the formation of large, tightly organized political parties. Before that time, the people who had the vote were property holders, relatively well educated, and generally aware of the issues of national politics. They did not need an organization to get out the vote, because they knew very well what was at stake in elections and made voting a major part of their public lives.

Now, the much-enlarged number of voters had to be informed about the issues and organized into groups that would identify their interests—and act on them. The vehicle for doing this was a mass political party, equipped with newspapers, local organizations and offices, speakers, and propaganda material. Most of the new voters were men of the working classes, and the new parties concentrated their efforts on them.

SOCIALISM AFTER 1848: MARXISM

The failure of the 1848 revolts inspired much analysis. National antagonisms and the passivity of the country folk were important, but the chief reason, all contemporary observers agreed, was the split between the liberal leaders—professionals and intellectuals—and the urban working classes. This split allowed the conservatives to gain a breathing space after their initial panic and then mount a political and military counterattack that was successful almost everywhere (see Chapter 32).

Why did the split between the middle-class liberals and the workers occur? The liberals generally did not want social reforms. They only wanted to substitute themselves for the conservatives in the seats of political power. The workers, on the other hand, were economically desperate and wished to gain for themselves the type of thoroughgoing change in the alignments of power that the French peasants had won in the wake of the 1789 revolution. When it became clear to the liberals that the workers wanted to go much further down the revolutionary road, they withdrew to the sidelines or actually joined with the conservatives, as happened in Vienna, Paris, and Berlin. In the end, the protection of property meant more than political or social ideals.

Marxist Theory

One close observer of this development was **Karl Marx** (1818–1883). A German Jew whose family had been assimilated into Prussian Protestantism, Marx grew up in the Rhineland town of Trier. Soon after his graduation from the University of Berlin in 1842, he became deeply involved in radical politics. Pursued by the Prussian police, he had to leave his native city and flee to France as a political refugee. There, he came to know his lifelong colleague, Friedrich Engels, the wealthy, radical son of a German industrialist. The two men formed a close working relationship that was ideal for Marx, who devoted his entire adult life to research and writing and organizing revolutionary socialist parties (see Patterns of Belief).

In 1848, Marx and Engels published perhaps the most famous pamphlet in all of European history: the ***Communist Manifesto***. Marx predicted the coming of a new social order, which he called *communism*, as an inevitable reaction against the abuses of bourgeois capitalism. When this order would come, he did not predict, but he clearly expected to see communist society arise within his lifetime. It was equally clear that Marx and Engels expected that communism would be born in a violent revolution by the industrial workers, the proletariat who had been reduced to abject misery and had little or no hope of escaping it as long as capital ruled. The proletarian revolution was inevitable, according to Marx, and the only questions were the precise timing and how those who wished to be on the side of progress and justice might help it along. Marx issued an invitation to all righteous persons to join with the ignorant and miserable proletariat in hastening the day of triumph. Once the revolution of the downtrodden was successful in gaining political power, a "dictatorship of the proletariat" (not further defined) was to be created, which would preside over the gradual transformation to a just society.

What was the ultimate goal of Marxist revolution? According to Marx, it was a communist society, in which private control/ownership of the means of production would be abolished and men and women would essentially be equal and free to develop their full human potential. For the first time in history, said Marx, the old boast of the Greeks that "Man is the measure of all things" would be fulfilled. A society would be created in which "the free development of each is the condition for the free development of all." At the time, no government took notice of the *Communist Manifesto.* During the 1850s and 1860s, Marx and Engels gradually emerged as two of the leading socialist thinkers and speakers. From his London base (England had the most liberal political association and censorship laws in Europe), Marx worked on his great analysis of mid-nineteenth-century industrial society, *Capital* (1867–1873). This work was the basis of Marx's boast that his socialism was scientific, unlike the utopian (that is, impractical) socialism of earlier days.

Marx was a child of his times. The 1840s were the "dismal decade," with widespread depression and years of the crudest exploitation of the workers by greedy or frightened employers. They were frightened because many were being driven to the wall by the relentless competition of the free market. As these small business owners desperately looked for ways to lower production costs, they usually resorted to reducing wages. Because what Marx called a "reserve army" of starving unemployed workers was always ready to work at almost any wage and without job security. Marx was not alone in believing that this condition would persist until it was changed by militant force from below.

PATTERNS OF BELIEF

Karl Marx (1818–1883)

"The critical thing is not to understand the world, but to change it!"

With this maxim as his polestar, philosopher Karl Marx became the most notorious, most quoted, and most influential social reformer of the nineteenth and twentieth centuries. The recent demise of that distortion of his ideas called Soviet communism has put his name and reputation under a heavy cloud from which they may never recover. But for 150 years, Marx and Marxism provided much of the world's dissatisfied citizenry with what they perceived to be their best hope of better times.

Marx was born into a well-to-do Jewish family in Trier, Germany, which at that time was part of the kingdom of Prussia. He studied at the universities of Bonn and Berlin, where his major interest was philosophy, but his interests soon expanded to include economics and sociology, two sciences that were still in their infancies. By the mid-1840s, he was slowly shaping his radical critique of contemporary European society by drawing on all three disciplines: German philosophy, English economics, and French social thought.

Prevented by his Jewish background from realizing his original plan of teaching in a university, Marx returned to Trier after graduating from the University of Berlin. In 1842, he opened a small newspaper, the *Rhenish Gazette*, which was dedicated to promoting social and political reform. He soon got into trouble with the conservative authorities and had to flee to escape arrest. He lived briefly in Paris, where he came to know his lifelong supporter, Friedrich Engels, son of a wealthy German manufacturer. Engels and Marx collaborated on the *Communist Manifesto*, which was published just weeks before the 1848 revolutions.

Soon, Marx aroused the suspicions of the French authorities and had to move on. An attempt to enter German politics as a revolutionary leader failed, and again Marx had to flee his native country, this time to London, where Engels was ready to help. Marx spent the rest of his life in English exile, living in genteel poverty with his German wife and several children.

The world around Marx was in the throes of the first wave of industrialism, and it was not an attractive place for most working people. Air and water pollution were common in the factory towns and in the working-class sections of the cities. Public health was neglected, medical help was restricted to the well-to-do, and welfare facilities of any type were almost nonexistent.

Women and children worked at exhausting jobs for very low pay, and workers were frequently fired without warning to make room for someone else who agreed to work for less. Neither law nor custom protected the workers' rights against their employers, and among the employers, cut-throat competition was the rule. Government intervention to ensure a "level playing field" in the marketplace was unknown. When governmental power was occasionally used, it was always in favor of the status quo, which meant against the workers.

Marx observed this scene closely and was convinced that the situation must soon erupt in proletarian revolution. The explosion would come first in the most advanced industrial countries, which meant at this time Britain, parts of Germany and France, and possibly the United States. While Engels provided financial assistance, Marx dedicated many years to working out a theory of history and social development that would make sense of the chaos and allow a rational hope of a better world in the future. Eventually, he produced *Das Kapital* (or *Capital*), the bible of scientific socialism, which was published in the original German in 1867 and translated into most European languages by the latter nineteenth century. Almost all of the work was done in the Reading Room of the British Museum, which Marx visited with clocklike regularity for decades.

In 1864, Marx organized the International Workingmen's Association. This so-called First International organization lasted only a few years before it collapsed in internal arguments about how the revolution of the proletariat should best be accomplished. Marx was always a headstrong character and was most unwilling to allow others to have their say. Like many prophets, he came to think that any who disagreed with him were ignorant or malicious. Engels was one of the few intimates who remained faithful to the master to the end.

In 1883, Marx died in the same poverty in which he had lived in the London suburb of Hampstead for most of his life. At his death, the proletarian revolution seemed further away than ever, but the movement was slowly growing. It would make giant strides in several countries in the 1890s; and in far-off Russia, a country that Marx held in contempt for its backwardness, a certain Vladimir Ilich Ulyanov, better known as Lenin, was studying *Capital* with an eye toward the Russian future.

ANALYZE AND INTERPRET

What theory or philosophy do you think has taken the place of Marxist socialism as a hope for the world's exploited and oppressed workers? Or do you think that Marxism has not been defeated, but only temporarily rejected as a social philosophy?

Topfoto/The Image Works

MARX AND ENGELS. This rare picture shows Karl Marx with his daughters and lifelong collaborator, Friedrich Engels.

Marxist Organizations

When the Paris Commune arose in the wake of the lost war with Prussia in 1871, Marx mistakenly thought that the dawn of social revolution had come and enthusiastically greeted the radical oratory of the *Communards.* The Commune was speedily crushed, but socialist parties came into being everywhere after 1871 and grew steadily over the next decades. By the end of the century, the industrial working class in most countries had embraced various forms of socialism. Their common denominator was a demand for radical rearrangement of the existing socioeconomic order. Some of these parties were anti-Marxist in doctrine, either preferring some form of anarchism (see the next section) or wishing to operate mainly through labor unions, but most were Marxist and subscribed to the principles laid out in *Capital* by the master.

The most important socialist parties were in Germany, Austria, Belgium, and France. In Southern Europe, they were outnumbered by anarchists and syndicalists (see the next section). In Britain and the United States, no socialist party had a wide following, and in Russia, the Marxists were still a tiny exile group at the end of the century.

RIVALS TO MARXISM

In Mediterranean Europe and Russia, the theory of politics called **anarchism** captured many minds. Anarchism is the rejection of the state and the powers that the modern state exercises over its citizenry. Its followers believe that all government is necessarily prone to corruption. Only such authority as is necessary to avoid conflict over the property or civil rights of the citizens should be surrendered by the citizens to their government. Even then, the least possible authority should be granted, and only on a small-scale, localized basis. Anarchists simply do not trust any government. They believe that sooner or later every government will succumb to the temptation to restrict its citizens' freedoms without just cause.

As a theory, anarchism goes back to the ancient Greeks, but the modern founders of anarchism are Frenchman Pierre Proudhon, whom we encountered in Chapter 32, and Russian Michael Bakunin (1827–1876). Bakunin developed the *propaganda of the deed*, the idea that a dramatic, violent act was the most effective way to gather converts for anarchism. The deeds his followers performed were acts of political terror: They carried out bombings and assassinations in the hopes of shaking the structures of government from the top down. In the two decades between 1885 and 1905—the high point of anarchism—about three hundred notable lives were sacrificed to this belief, including several reigning kings and queens, prime ministers, presidents (including U.S. president William McKinley in 1901), and assorted generals. In the end, it faded and after World War I little was heard of it again until the 1960s.

Syndicalism is a form of political action by the working classes. It is founded on the belief that only the laboring classes and peasants should govern because only they contribute a substantial asset to society through their work. Instead of the political parties, the laborers must create a large-scale association of persons employed in the same type of work. This association, called a *syndicate,* would represent the economic and social interests of the members and confer with other syndicates to find common political means for progress in economics and justice in society. Like anarchism, and unlike communism, syndicalism did not wish to abolish private property but to limit its political power and distribute it more evenly.

Syndicalism was stronger than socialism in Spain and Portugal and was a strong rival to it among the peasantry in Italy and France. Syndicalist government offered the poorly paid and insecure working classes and small peasants a theoretical way upward without going to the socialist extreme of class warfare and the abolition of private property. It never succeeded in establishing control of a national government.

Reform and Revisionism

In Great Britain, the labor force was never much attracted to either socialism or its rivals as solutions to the dual problems of concentrated wealth and concentrated poverty. Instead, British workers in the later nineteenth century focused on gaining higher pay and better working conditions through a moderate reformism that centered on the right to strike and organize unions. In 1906, the reformist, non-Marxist **Labour Party** was formed on a platform of more equitable distribution of wealth. The new party gradually attracted the vote of most union members and much of the lower middle class. It was able to replace the Liberal Party as the main opponent of the Conservatives after World War I.

In the 1880s, Chancellor Otto von Bismarck attempted to crush the appeal of socialism in Germany by an attack on two fronts. First, he outlawed the Marxist socialist party, which had been organized in 1875, claiming that it was a revolutionary group that intended to ultimately destroy the state. Then he tried to show that socialism was unnecessary because the powerful and progressive German state would look out adequately for the workers' welfare. During the 1880s, a series of new laws instituting unemployment insurance, accident and health protection, and worker pensions made Bismarck's Germany the most progressive state in the world in terms of social policy.

The blunt attack on the Marxists did not succeed. After a few years, there were more German socialists than ever, and in 1890, the antisocialist law was repealed as a failure. The German Social Democratic (SD) Party steadily gained votes, attracting not only workers but also the lower middle classes and civil servants. With several newspapers, a tight network of local offices, and an extensive member/financial base in the German labor unions, the German party set the pace for socialists throughout Europe.

In 1899, a leading SD theorist, Eduard Bernstein, published a book in which he claimed that the SDs would soon become strong enough to take over the state in peaceful, constitutional fashion. Socialism would then be introduced through the workings of a parliament and government controlled by the Marxists. Thus, the idea of violent revolution in the streets was outmoded. According to Bernstein, Marx (who had died sixteen years previously) could not foresee that capitalism would be so altered by democracy that the workers would be able to counter it through the ballot rather than on the barricades. The triumph of social justice could and should be obtained without bloodshed.

This idea was heatedly denounced by many in the **Second International**, the Europe-wide association of socialists founded in 1889, but the theory attracted the party leadership in the more industrially advanced countries, especially in Germany and France. By the coming of World War I, **revisionism** (the adaptation of Marxist socialism that aimed to introduce basic reform through parliamentary acts rather than through revolution) was a strong rival to orthodox Marxism as the true path to the workers' paradise.

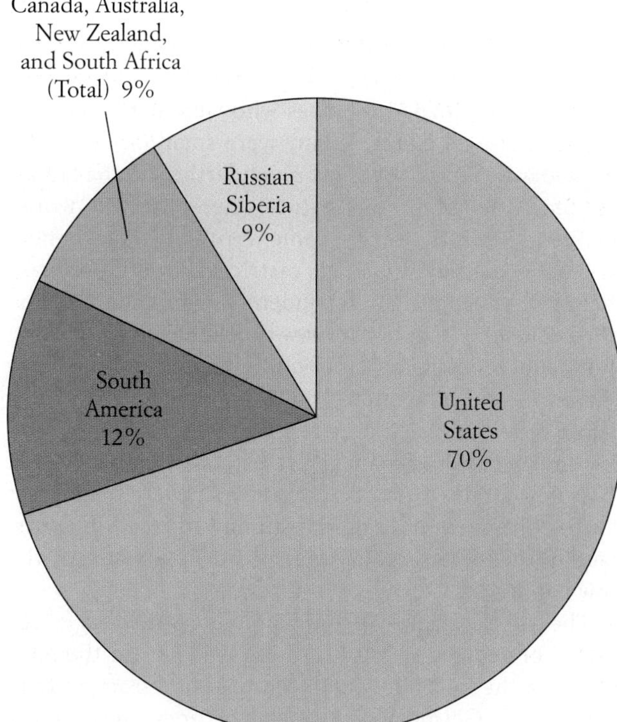

FIGURE 33.1 European Emigrants' Destinations, 1800–1960. The United States was easily the most preferred destination, with South America (mainly Argentina and Brazil) a distant second. What countries did the emigrants leave? Great Britain and Ireland supplied about 33 percent of the total; Italy, about 30 percent; and the rest of Europe, the remainder. The ethnic balance shifted steadily from northern and western Europe to southern and eastern as the nineteenth century matured. At the peak of European emigration in the decade just before World War I, an average of about 1.2 million emigrated annually.

EMIGRATION OVERSEAS

The largest human migration in world history took place from Europe to overseas destinations during the second half of the nineteenth century. What caused this world-reshaping move? In general, the triggers were economic, but the emigrations began with the political upheavals of 1848, when tens of thousands of Germans and Austrians looked to America for the freedoms they feared they would never have in their homelands.

From about 2.5 million in the 1850s, total net emigration from Europe rose each decade until it peaked in the years just before World War I. By then, about 12 million people had left Europe in a ten-year period, a number about equal to the entire population of Scandinavia at that time. The war shut this stream down almost completely, and it never again reached those dimensions. In all, some 60 million Europeans emigrated during the nineteenth century and did not return. (Return to the homeland was common: About one of three emigrants to the United States eventually returned to the home country for reasons ranging from homesickness to deportation.)

Destinations

Where were all of these people headed? The river of emigrants flowed mainly to the New World, but Australia, New Zealand, and Siberia (for Russians exclusively) were also important destinations. The French colony of Algeria and the British colony of South Africa also attracted large groups of emigrants. (See Figure 33.1.)

In terms of proportionate impact on a given nation, Argentina was the most dramatic example of immigration in the world. About 3 percent of the total Argentine population arrived from Europe (mostly Spain and Italy) every year in the early twentieth century—three times the rate that the United States gained from the same source. But in absolute terms, the United States was easily the most popular single destination. It received about 45 percent of the grand total of immigrants worldwide during the nineteenth century.

Why did these emigrants leave? First and foremost, they were seeking better economic conditions. The rise and fall of emigration rates corresponded closely to European business cycles. In hard times, more left for the "land of golden opportunities," but a large proportion left because they were dissatisfied with domestic political and social conditions and had little faith that the future held any more promise than the present.

Types of Emigrants

Who were the emigrants? Most were not the very poor or ignorant. Instead, they were people who had been able to save a little or had relatives who were better off and helped them get a start. Many were small farmers who had too little land to ever get much farther up the ladder and feared for their sons' future when that little would be divided by inheritance. Some were skilled craftsmen, who believed that guild-type restrictions would prevent them from becoming independent entrepreneurs. Some were educated people who saw no chance of fully using their education in a class-bound society. In the later phases of the movement, the poor and ignorant also began to leave, assisted by relatives who had emigrated previously and had managed to establish themselves in their new lands. Unmarried young men were the largest single contingent of emigrants, followed by young girls, usually the sisters or fiancées of males already in the new country.

The ethnic origins of the emigrants varied by chronology of departure. Most of those who left for the New World in the mid-nineteenth century were from Britain, Ireland, and Germany. In the later decades, they tended to be from eastern and southern European countries. By World War I, the Austro-Hungarians, Russians, Poles, and, above all, the Italians supplied the great bulk of the emigrants. A disproportionate number were Jews from the Russian empire (including Poland) who were fleeing ethnic persecution.

LOWER EAST SIDE OF NEW YORK. This "slice of life" shows Mulberry Street, one of the chief street markets in slum New York, in about 1869. Much of the population of such neighborhoods spent little of the day inside their cramped apartments if they could help it.

By the later nineteenth century, in the industrial economies of northern and western Europe, the working classes could find reasonably secure factory and white-collar jobs. Hence, they were less likely to emigrate than the unemployed and underemployed peasants and laborers of eastern and southern Europe. As a rule, the more literate and better prepared went to North America, Australia, or South Africa. South America received mainly those with lesser prospects.

SUMMARY

A Second Industrial Revolution was fueled by the electrical and petroleum industries and the myriad uses to which these new sources of energy were applied in the last third of the nineteenth century. The newly developed corporation replaced the partnership, and banks and joint stock companies became the usual means of raising capital in this same period.

In this second phase of industrialization, mass political parties became commonplace throughout Western Europe. They sometimes represented newly organized labor and were almost always based in the rapidly expanding urban centers. By 1900, most industrial countries had introduced the universal male franchise. These developments contributed to the steady gains of socialism, particularly the Marxist variety after about 1880. Karl Marx's theories posited inevitable class warfare and a revolution of the proletariat against its capitalist oppressors. At the end of the century, this view was increasingly challenged by revisionism or other rivals in the search for a more just distribution of national wealth.

The later nineteenth century also saw the most extensive emigration in recorded history, as up to 60 million Europeans opted to leave their homelands permanently and travel to the New World or other areas for better economic or political prospects.

IDENTIFICATION TERMS

Test your knowledge of this chapter's key concepts by defining the following terms. If you can not recall the meaning of certain terms, refresh your memory by looking up the boldfaced term in the chapter, turning to the Glossary at the end of the book, or accessing the terms on the CourseMate website at **www.cengagebrain.com**.

anarchism
Chartist movement
Communist Manifesto
corporation
Great Exhibition
Labour Party
Karl Marx
revisionism
Second Industrial Revolution
Second International
syndicalism

FOR FURTHER REFLECTION

1. Why do you suppose that Britain, the first nation to industrialize, never experienced the violent revolutions that mainland Europe suffered in the mid-nineteenth century?
2. How did the efforts at social and political reform reflect the changing social and economic climate in early industrial Europe?

TEST YOUR KNOWLEDGE

Test your knowledge of this chapter by answering the following questions. Complete answers appear at the end of the book. You may find even more quiz questions on the CourseMate website at **www.cengagebrain.com**.

1. The Second Industrial Revolution generated
   a. worker revolts in 1848.
   b. capitalist exploitation of workers to the maximum extent.
   c. industrial research and new forms of energy.
   d. mining and iron making.
   e. scientific experimentation.
2. The countries that were in the forefront of the Second Industrial Revolution were
   a. Britain and the United States.
   b. the United States and Germany.
   c. Japan and the United States.
   d. Germany and Britain.
   e. Japan and Britain.
3. Publicly owned corporations and electrical power
   a. were the inventions of individual entrepreneurs.
   b. led to monopolies and nuclear energy.
   c. developed directly from privately owned companies and steam power.
   d. appeared during the Second Industrial Revolution.
   e. appeared during the early Industrial Revolution.
4. Labor unions first gained the legal right to organize and to strike in
   a. Germany.
   b. the United States.
   c. Britain.
   d. Holland.
   e. France.
5. Germany was
   a. the first European nation to allow women to vote.
   b. the first European nation to industrialize.
   c. the first nation to have publically traded corporations.
   d. the second European nation to industrialize.
   e. the first European country to pass laws providing for universal male suffrage
6. Which of the following pairs is logically incorrect?
   a. Karl Marx and scientific socialism
   b. Eduard Bernstein and revisionist socialism
   c. Michael Bakunin and anarchism
   d. Pierre Proudhon and anarchism
   e. All of these are paired correctly.
7. Which of these systems of government would operate only under the auspices of the laboring classes and the peasants?
   a. Communism
   b. Socialism
   c. Anarchism
   d. Legalism
   e. Syndicalism
8. The bulk of the European emigrants of the nineteenth century were
   a. landless laborers seeking a new start in North and South America.
   b. dissatisfied small farmers, businessmen, artisans, and skilled laborers.
   c. Jews and others fleeing political persecution.
   d. relatively successful shop owners, artisans, and white-collar workers.
   e. wealthy families who wanted the benefits of living in the world's most modern nation.
9. Which Western country or countries resisted universal, male suffrage the longest?
   a. Italy and Hungary
   b. Italy
   c. Russia, Poland, and Czechoslovakia
   d. Russia, Hungary, and Italy
   e. France

10. Which of the following was *not* a new phenomenon in the late nineteenth century?
    a. The corporation as the dominant form of business organization
    b. The spread of anarchist philosophy
    c. A dramatic rise in emigration to the United States from Europe
    d. Revision of the Marxist plan of violent revolution
    e. The growth of political parties

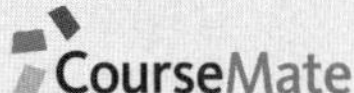

Visit the CourseMate website at **www.cengagebrain.com** for additional study tools and review materials for this chapter.

34 The Islamic World, 1600–1917

The Islamic religion is a religion of unity throughout. It is not a religion of conflicting principles but is built squarely on reason, while Divine revelation is its surest pillar. —SHAYKH MUHAMMAD ABDUH

1500s–1722	Safavid Empire in Persia
1526–1857	Mughal Empire in India
early 1600s	Ottoman decline begins
c. 1700–1830	External attacks on Ottoman Empire
late 1700s	Wahhabist movement begins
1880–1898	Mahdi rebellion in Sudan
1890s	Beginnings of Salafiand Arab nationalist movement

CHAPTER OUTLINE

For the great Islamic empires, the seventeenth and eighteenth centuries were a time of steady social and political decline and loss of power against the West. The European counteroffensive against Islam had begun already in the Middle Ages, as Iberian Crusaders fought for the reconquest of Spain and Portugal, and French, German, and English armies tried to retake Palestine, albeit unsuccessfully. Until the sixteenth century, the civilization and armies of Islam enjoyed the advantage, and there remained a standoff between Europe and the great Muslim empires. But by the mid-eighteenth century, the European Renaissance and the Scientific Revolution, which was perhaps its most important by-product, altered the balance of power in Europe's favor. European fleets invaded the Indian Ocean, defeating the navies of the Ottoman sultans and their Indian allies, and occupied the most important commercial centers from Mozambique to Macao. Slowly, too, the battle for control of the Mediterranean shifted in favor of Venice and the Habsburgs and their Spanish allies after a key naval victory that was fought off the coast of Italy, at Lepanto, in 1571. On land, a "Holy League," organized by the pope in the late 1600s and led by the Ottomans' old rivals, the Habsburgs of Austria, gained the military advantage in the Balkans. By the time of Catherine the Great, Russian armies began driving the Ottomans and Safavids out of their possessions around the Caspian and Black seas.

Since the eighteenth century, Islamic peoples and states have remained on the defensive as Western imperialism and ideas have created steady inroads into their midst. The eighteenth- and nineteenth-century responses of Islam to these incursions are the same paradigms that are still with the world today. The initial responses took the form of state-directed reforms that tried to control and limit the impact of Western ideas, particularly those concerning religion and culture, but the more enduring responses were those broader ones that arose out of Islamic leadership and societies as a whole.

THE DECLINE OF THE MUSLIM EMPIRES

The Strengths and Weaknesses of Ottoman Civilization

The strengths of the Ottomans were most evident during the earlier centuries of their rule, as one would expect, and the weaknesses later. But some of each are clear throughout the long reign of the Ottoman Dynasty, which lasted from about 1300 to 1922. Aside from their military merits, the Ottomans' strengths included extraordinary artistic sensitivity in literature, architecture, and symbolic imagery; a commitment to justice for all, no matter how weak; a tolerance for nonbelievers that was unusual for its time; and a literary language (Turkish with an Arabic-Persian overlay) that was truly an international bond as well as the channel for a rich literature. In economic and administrative affairs, the Ottomans had a far more efficient tax system and better control of their provincial authorities than any European government of the fourteenth through sixteenth centuries. Unfortunately, these institutions were to weaken later on.

Although a vast bureaucracy assisted the sultans, among the Ottomans' weaknesses were a government that depended for the most part on the qualities and energy of one or two individuals—the sultan and the grand vizier. It was no accident that the name of the empire was that of its founding figure, Osman (AHZ-mun; in Turkish, it was called the Osmanli Empire), and of its ruling dynasty. The sultans were not just the principal administrators; the sultanate provided the institutional machinery and energy that kept the empire moving ahead. It was the central fact of the empire. Other weaknesses included a theory of government that was essentially military in nature and needed constant new conquests to justify and maintain itself; an almost complete inability to convert the *Qur'an*-based Shari'a code of law to changing necessities in legal administration; a collective blind eye to the importance of secular education and to all types of technology; and an excessive reverence for tradition, which produced the kind of stagnation that follows from excessive conservatism.

From the middle of the 1700s on, the weaknesses of the Ottoman state in Europe rendered it prey to an increasingly aggressive West. First the Habsburg Dynasty in Vienna and then the Russian Romanovs went on the counterattack against Turkey in Europe, driving back its frontiers step by step (see Map 34.1). In the early 1800s, rising nationalist consciousness among the peoples of the Balkans made them rebel against an Ottoman control that had become increasingly intolerant and oppressive as it declined. The European powers provided them with encouragement and assistance until the Turks' domain was reduced to Bulgaria, Albania, and northern Greece. At that point, about 1830, the external attacks ceased when the aggressors became wary of one another. The "sick man of Europe" was allowed to linger on his deathbed until 1918 only because his heirs could not agree on the division of the estate.

The Decline of the Ottoman Empire

Suleiman's reign (1520–1566) was the high point of the sultan's authority and also of the efficiency and prestige of the central government. Beginning with Suleiman's son and successor, Selim (seh-LEEM) the Sot, many of the sultans became captives of their own viziers and of the intrigues constantly spun within the harem. After 1603, rather than exposing young princes to the rigors of military service, as had been past practice, the sultans began to restrict their sons to being reared entirely within the harem. There, as the sultanate began to decline, the power of the harem and the court bureaucracy grew. More and more, young princes were subject to manipulation by court eunuchs and the sultans' many wives and concubines, who vied for power or to see their sons succeed to the throne. Whichever prince succeeded to the throne, this practice gravely weakened his fitness to rule.

Nevertheless, the empire did not run straight downhill after 1600. Once every few decades, a dedicated grand vizier or a strong-willed sultan attempted to reverse the decay. He would enforce reforms, sweep out the corrupt or rebellious officials in one province or another, and make sure the army was obedient, but then the rot would set in again. By the end of the 1700s, effective reversal was becoming impossible.

Besides the reduced qualities of the sultans, several other factors contributed to the long decline:

1. *Economic.* Starting around 1550, the shift of European trade routes from the Muslim-controlled Near and Middle East to the Atlantic Ocean (and later the Pacific Ocean) dealt a heavy, long-term blow to Ottoman prosperity.
2. *Military.* After the 1570s, the Janissaries and other elite units were allowed to marry and settle down in a given garrison, which gradually eroded their loyalties to the central government and allowed them to become local strongmen with local sympathies, often allying with local craft guilds, in conflict with government interests. Moreover, by the seventeenth century, the Ottomans reached the limits of expansion possible with the types of weapons and organization on which their armies were based. Although the Ottoman armies had been the most innovative in previous centuries (for example, in the use of artillery and firearms), a conservative resistance to further change and the practice of nepotism set in, particularly among the Janissary corps. The repeated failures

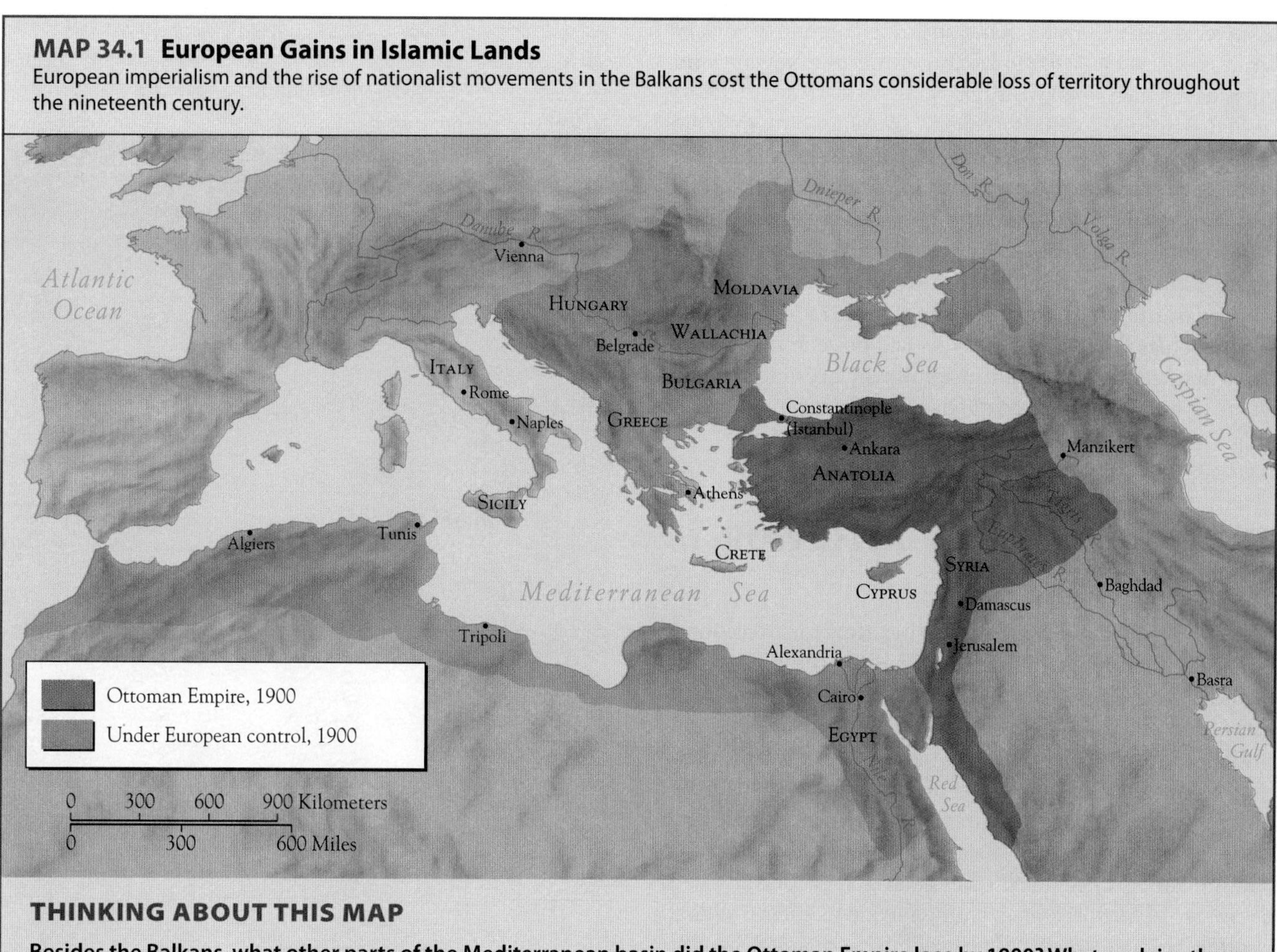

MAP 34.1 European Gains in Islamic Lands
European imperialism and the rise of nationalist movements in the Balkans cost the Ottomans considerable loss of territory throughout the nineteenth century.

THINKING ABOUT THIS MAP

Besides the Balkans, what other parts of the Mediterranean basin did the Ottoman Empire lose by 1900? What explains these losses? On the other hand, what might explain their ability to hold on to the areas they did keep?

of Ottoman armies to win decisively when far from their winter quarters in Istanbul meant that the military initiative passed to the Europeans by the late 1600s.

3. *Technological.* From the seventeenth century on, the Ottomans failed to comprehend how Western technology and science were changing. Increasingly, they found themselves unready when confronted in tests of power. They almost always responded by attempting to ignore the unpleasant realities. They failed to acknowledge or give up old ways when the situation demanded change. This characteristic was spectacularly apparent in military sciences, where the once-pioneering Turks fell far behind the West in all spheres, including training, organization, weapons, and tactics.

SAFAVID AND MUGHAL DECLINE

None of the Safavid rulers who came after Akbar the Great matched his statesmanship. Consequently, by the 1700s, the Safavids had disappeared as a dynasty. In contrast to the Ottomans and Mughals, they had been unable to advance from an empire relying on its original tribal alliance to a centralized bureaucratic empire. Though they had tried, with the help of Georgian Janissary-type infantries, in the end they fell victim to invading Afghan tribesmen and a renewal of tribal competition in Iran through most of the 1700s. At the end of the century, a new dynasty, the Qajars (KAH-jars), established themselves, and under them Iran continued to remain under tribal rule. The Qajars, however, tried with mixed results to bureaucratize Iran in the course of the nineteenth century.

In India, Aurangzeb (aw-rang-ZEB; ruling 1656–1707), though a triumphant warrior, was responsible for reversing the climate of toleration that Akbar had introduced and that had been generally maintained for the ensuing half-century. Aurangzeb was a confirmed Muslim, and he reintroduced a distinctly Islamic character to public life. This change heightened the latent frictions between the ruling class and their Hindu, Zoroastrian, Jain, and (few) Christian subjects. Although his large, efficient, and tax-eating army was too big to challenge directly, Aurangzeb's rule set the stage for eventual rebellion by the Hindu majority, led by the Marathas (muh-RA-thahs) against his weaker successors. The entire eighteenth century witnessed a slow decline of the emperor's powers and prestige and a gradual whittling off of the territory he controlled. The latter condition was the result of both internal (Maratha) and external (European) challengers.

In the expanding empires of the Safavids in Persia and the Mughals in India, the appearance of European explorers and traders during the 1500s did not create much of a stir. At that time, the European presence in India was limited to a relative handful of traders in a few ports such as Goa and Calicut. As will be seen in Chapter 35, what seemed to be an insignificant presence to the rulers of India portended a different future for Indians and neighboring peoples of Southeast Asia.

OTTOMAN SULTAN SELIM III. Selim was the first to institute the permanent and thoroughgoing reforms of the Ottoman military and administration known as the *Tanzimat.*

THE MUSLIM LANDS UNTIL WORLD WAR I

The three Muslim empires of earlier times in Asia were either overthrown or much weakened by the nineteenth century. The Mughals in India, the Safavid Persians, and the Ottoman Turks had been overwhelmed by Western military and financial powers where they came into conflict with them. By the mid-1800s, the British had made most of India an outright colony, and Persia was effectively divided into Russian and British spheres. The Ottomans had repeatedly been defeated by Russia in Europe and had been forced to watch as even the facade of their political overlordship in North Africa faded away and was lost to invading French armies after 1830 (see Chapter 36). Napoleon invaded Egypt in 1798, and while he and his army were expelled by an Anglo-Ottoman alliance in 1804, for all practical purposes, Egypt became independent under its new military governor, Muhammad Ali Pasha (see below). Finally, in 1882, Britain invaded and occupied Egypt, adding that country to its worldwide empire. Only in the Middle East did some substance of Turkish control remain.

Still, these political and military weaknesses were not the only indicators of decline. The Islamic world would have to overcome a series of psychological and technical barriers if it were to regain its equality with the West. The fundamental tradition of Islam, wherever it attained power, was to understand itself as a community of righteous believers who were actively spreading the sole, authentic word of God and establishing his rule on earth. For a thousand years, since the time of the Prophet Muhammad, this viewpoint had been the driving force behind the expansion of the religion around the globe.

From about the mid-eighteenth century, however, this view could no longer be sustained, as the unbelievers took over former Muslim territories from the Balkans to the islands of Southeast Asia. The learned and powerful men of Islam reacted in several ways. Some assumed that e reverses were temporary and that the lands would soon be regained. Others looked—for the first time—to the West for inspiration in technology and, above all, military science, to help them counter and overcome Western superiority.

Unfortunately for Muslim ambitions, the first trend prevailed over the second. The *ulama* and the imams of the Ottoman domains could not accept the secularism of post–French Revolution Europe, but a few grudgingly recognized that Muslim practice would have to incorporate some Western elements if it was not to be utterly overwhelmed. Yet they still believed in the inherent superiority of the community of God (*Dar al-Islam*) over the unbelievers (*Dar al-Harb*). As a result, they only sporadically and inconsistently attempted to adopt some European science and technology without changing the conservative cast of Islamic education and government, which frowned on innovation.

A vast body of traditions and prejudices opposed those few who attempted to bring large-scale Western ideas into Islam. A few Ottoman sultans had come to realize that resisting the West without the assistance of Western science and education would be hopeless. They tried to implement limited reforms, yet they were unable to carry them through against the twin obstacles of tradition and apathy. Consequently, as a cultural and political force in the world, Islam had entered a state of severe decline by the late eighteenth century. Unwilling to adapt to the modern world beyond a superficial level, the Muslim lands seemed destined to a future in which they were the permanent pawns of the European powers.

REFORMS OF THE MUSLIM RULING ELITES

By the 1890s, this inability to resist external pressure had produced four different responses in the Muslim world. The first of these was simply ignoring or rejecting the changes that were occurring. This was the easiest response, and many of the ulama and the general population continued to take for granted the superiority of all things Islamic over other ways and ideas. The second amounted to attempts at accommodation, which began when the ruling elites in the Ottoman Empire, Egypt, and Iran tried to impose limited, largely military, reforms. The third was the beginning of what is now called *Islamic fundamentalism.* The fourth was *pan-Arabism* or *Arab nationalism*, which are related but not identical attempts to create a sense of unity among the Arab peoples of the Middle East and North Africa.

The Tanzimat

The Ottoman Empire was the first Islamic state to try modernizing along European lines, and in many respects, it was the one that experimented the longest and whose attempts ultimately went the deepest in changing its society as a whole. Egypt and Iran also tried to implement similar reforms in the 1800s. However, in each of these cases, the reforms were state-directed—that is, they did not begin as a popular response to the Western challenge—and the ruling elite intended to limit them only to the military sphere.

With the further defeats and losses of territory that came after the Treaty of Karlowitz in 1699, the Ottoman sultans and grand viziers of the eighteenth century finally realized that they had lost the military advantage to the Europeans. To save the sultanate and what remained of the empire, they had to modernize the Ottoman military machinery. As early as 1719, the grand vizier tried introducing reforms that were essentially conservative: The objective was not a wholesale reform of Ottoman society or Islamic institutions, but rather was limited to improving military instruction. Alas, in 1730, a popular uprising against these "Frankish (European) manners" ended his experiment, and the grand vizier paid for his perceived mistakes by being executed. Other similarly brief and unsuccessful experiments were tried in the following decades. Sultan Selim (seh-LEEM) III was the first to initiate far-reaching and successful reforms, later called the **Tanzimat** (TAN-zih-maht; "New Order") **reforms**. Beginning in 1793, he tightened government control over the crumbling and corrupt provinces, and created new schools for the training of officers who were to become the backbone of a new, European-style Ottoman army and navy. European instructors were brought in, books were imported—many from France and reflecting the new thought of the European Enlightenment—and a new library was made available to the students. Again though, in 1807, another uprising of the ulama and the Janissaries deposed Selim and temporarily set back the reforms.

The next sultan, Mahmud II (mah-MOOD; reigning 1808–1839), permanently reignited the reorganization in 1826 when he ended the opposition of the Janissaries and the ulama once and for all after luring them into an ambush. Immediately afterward, he dismantled the Janissary corps, banned the religious (Sufi) brotherhoods, and seized all sources of funding previously controlled by the ulama (*waqfs*, for example: see Glossary). New reforms promptly followed, as the sultan and his viziers created schools for training students in European languages and sciences, and set new controls

Janissary, from 'Costumes of the Various Nations', Volume VII, 'The Military Costume of Turkey', by Thomas MacLean, published c.1800–18 (hand coloured aquatint), English School, (19th century)/Private Collection/The Stapleton Collection/The Bridgeman Art Library

A JANISSARY. This portrait shows a member of the Sultan's Janissary corps as the fighters appeared about the time of Sultan Selim III. At one time the elite of the Ottoman army, the Janissaries had become largely reactionary by the eighteenth century. It was a revolt of the Janissaries that ended Selim's reforms in 1806–1807.

over education, administration, and communications. When Abdul Mejid (AHB-dool meh-JEED) succeeded to the sultanate in 1839, he added even more far-reaching reforms. His **Rose Chamber Rescript of 1839** revolutionized Islamic society by declaring the legal equality of all Ottoman subjects, regardless of religion or ethnicity. In the succeeding decades (1839–1861), Abdul Mejid reinforced the terms of the Rose Chamber Rescript by replacing the moribund feudal estate system with individual land ownership and by creating a new law code modeled on European paradigms along with new courts to administer it equally to all his subjects.

Up to this point, the reforms remained state-directed, but in 1861, the Tanzimat entered a new phase. A new sultan, Abdul Aziz (AHB-dool ah-ZEEZ), proved to be a reactionary who was opposed to further liberalizations of Islamic law and society. By then, the direction and extent of reform had begun to slip from state control. Decades of training Ottoman subjects in European sciences and ideas (including those of Enlightenment liberalism) had created a broader base and momentum for change. A group of young intellectuals and journalists, called the **Young Ottomans**, had started to exert pressure for the political liberalization of Ottoman society. Using European nations as their model, they clamored to replace the sultanate with a constitutional monarchy and parliamentary system. In 1876 when the Sultan Abdul Aziz died, they and other reformers within the government supported Abdul Hamid II (AHB-dool hah-MEED) for the succession, on the promise that he would liberalize the government. The reformers got their constitution, and an election was held for the first time in Ottoman history for the creation of a parliament. Once in power, however, Abdul Hamid proved to be just another autocrat: He ended the Tanzimat by dismissing the parliament and suspending the constitution. Throughout his long reign (1876–1909), he used a vast system of spies to put down all resistance and impose strict control over all Ottoman subjects. He also gradually began to ally the empire with Germany. A nationalist reform party of army officers deposed him in 1909 and set up a military junta in place of the sultanate. Called the Committee for Union and Progress (CUP), it continued to govern using the policies and methods Abdul Hamid had established. More important, perhaps, the CUP led the Ottoman Empire into World War I as an ally of Germany.

Egypt and Sudan Under Muhammad Ali and Khedive Ismail

Appointed as the Ottoman viceroy to Egypt in 1805, **Muhammad Ali Pasha** filled the political vacuum that had been left in Egypt after the forced withdrawal of French forces in 1805. His reign in Egypt was highly unusual for two reasons: (1) its longevity, lasting until 1848, and (2) his success in modernizing the armed forces. He accomplished the first of these goals through bribery and intimidation. Regular gifts of large sums of cash were sent to the sultan and influential members of the Ottoman Court to ensure that he would not be removed from his position. By such methods, he succeeded not only in ensuring that he would remain as Egypt's governor, but also that the position would remain in his family. (The last of his line, King Farouk, was deposed in 1952.)

Far more important for Egypt, though, were Muhammad Ali's reforms. An Albanian by birth, he had served in the Ottoman forces against the French. In those years, he had become utterly convinced of the military superiority of European armies, so to strengthen his position, he implemented a far-reaching program of military reforms similar to what was occurring in Istanbul at that time. Above all, he turned to the French for his models. Missions were dispatched to France to pursue studies in military science, engineering, and medicine. He brought scores of French technicians and officers to Egypt to advise him. He forcefully conscripted thousands of Egyptian peasants, whom he outfitted with the latest weapons, and placed them under the command of Turkish and European officers. To help support these measures, he established munitions industries and created a modern system of schools and public health. He encouraged private landownership, and sugar and cotton were added as important new cash crops.

State monopolies of vital industries, such as sugar refining plus textile, iron, and weapons manufacturing, were established. Emboldened by his successes, the viceroy also expanded his holdings outside Egypt. Much like the ancient pharaohs, he sent his armies up the Nile to occupy the Sudan. The Egyptians founded the city of Khartoum (khar-TOOM) as their primary command center. In 1838, he sent his son to invade Syria, challenging Ottoman authority there. Unfortunately, this aggressiveness against the Ottoman sultanate invited Anglo-French intervention, and the viceroy's navy was destroyed in a battle fought off the coast of Greece in 1839. This disappointment set back the Egyptian reform movement for several decades.

Under Muhammad Ali, foreign investment played a key part in Egypt's modernization. This continued under his successors, particularly in the building of Egypt's railroads and the construction of the Suez Canal, which British and French investors largely capitalized. This created a difficult problem for Egypt's rulers, who were forced to wrestle with the enormous debts they incurred to foreign banks and other investors. The third of Muhammad Ali's sons to rule, Ismail (ISS-mah-il), greatly added to the problem because he loved everything European. It was his fondest desire to make Egypt into a European nation, and he hoped to be accepted by European leaders as one of them. Therefore, when the Suez Canal was opened for the first time in 1869, he spent lavishly on a huge fête, to which he invited all of the European heads of state and royal families. To impress them, he commissioned

MUHAMMAD ALI PASHA, VICEROY OF EGYPT. Many consider Muhammad Ali to have been the founder of modern Egypt. His reforms of the army reached into many other aspects of Egyptian life, including its economy.

the Italian composer, Verdi, to compose an opera, *Aida* (ah-EE-dah), and he rebuilt large parts of Cairo and Alexandria to resemble Paris. Ultimately, he bankrupted his country and was forced to sell Egypt's shares in the Suez Canal Company to Britain. Worse, he was forced by the European powers to turn over the management of Egypt's treasury to a committee made up largely of his principal investors. An uprising of army officers who opposed this European intervention finally forced Britain to occupy Egypt in 1882 to protect its interests in the canal. Britain installed Ismail's son as the new *khedive* (kheh-DEEV: Viceroy), and they remained as a colonial occupier in Egypt until 1922.

The Egyptian occupation of the Sudan led to some unexpected resistance, which also entangled the British. Between 1881 and 1885, Muhammad Ahmad, called **the Mahdi** (MAH-dee; "the Expected One"), led a successful revolt against Egyptian (and British) presence there. Khedive Ismail (kheh-DEEV ISS-mah-il) sent a British officer, General Charles Gordon, as his governor of the Sudan, but Gordon was killed in an assault by the Mahdi's followers at Khartoum. The Mahdiyya (Mahdist rebellion) combined elements of national resistance to foreign rule and Islamic fundamentalist reaction against innovations. Following his victory, Muhammad Ahmad formed a government in which he imposed traditional laws and established courts of Islamic judges to enforce Islamic law. Believing that he was sent as a savior of Islam, he believed he communicated directly with God, so he also modified Islam's Five Pillars to support the principle that loyalty to him was part of true belief. Muhammad Ahmad died of typhus six months after the capture of Khartoum, but the Mahdiyya lasted until British forces finally defeated the rebels in 1898 and set up a protectorate over the Sudan.

Reforms Under the Iranian Shahs

Under the Safavid shahs and the Qajar Dynasty that replaced them in the eighteenth century, Iran did not experience the full impact of growing European cultural superiority and military might that the Ottoman Empire did in the 1700s. Consequently, it did not start down the path of reform until well into the nineteenth century. Shah Nasir ad-Din (NAH-seer ahd-DEEN) was the first Qajar ruler to introduce significant restructuring. Like Selim III and Muhammad Ali Pasha, he tried to reform the shah's army to counter steady Russian encroachment in the Caspian Sea region and British expansion in India. The result was an intensification of military and commercial ties with the West, and gradually Iran was drawn into the world market. As Iranians developed a taste for imports, more turned to growing cash crops, such as tobacco, cotton, and opium, to pay for them.

Under pressure from Britain to lower tariffs, Iran imported a flood of cheap European-manufactured goods, putting indigenous producers out of business. Moreover, for help in building modern transport and communications systems, Nasir ad-Din made overly generous concessions to European firms. In 1890, the granting of a tobacco monopoly to a British firm created a serious crisis when, led by a Muslim cleric by the name of Jamal ad-Din al-Afghani (jah-MAHL ahd-DEEN al-af-GAH-nee), national resistance to foreign interference in Iran broke out. Afghani, fearing Big-Power political intervention in Muslim countries such as Iran, convinced local merchants that the concessions would bring harm to local people and compromise Iran's religious and political autonomy. The shah expelled Afghani from the country in 1891, but he was forced in the end to withdraw the monopoly when another cleric declared a national prohibition on the smoking of tobacco. However, Western control over Iran's mineral and oil rights was established by another concession to the Anglo-Iranian Oil Company, and between 1908 and 1912, Iran began its first exports of oil to the industrial West.

Meanwhile, as happened in Turkey under Young Ottoman leadership in the 1870s, demands for a constitutional and representative government to make it more democratic began circulating among Iran's young, increasingly Western-educated intelligentsia. The catalyst for this movement was Shah Muzaffar ad-Din's (MOO-zah-fahr ahd-DEEN) attempts at punishing Tehran's merchants for price-fixing. The ulama and young intellectuals united in defending the merchants and demanding reforms to curb the shah's actions. Popular support grew so fast that the shah was obliged to capitulate to the protesters' demands for a constitution and a National Assembly (*Majlis*: MAHJ-lees). In 1907, the Majlis convened for the first time, but the shah's willingness to use military force against it effectively weakened it for many years. Although the movement for popular reform ended in a partial failure, nationalist feelings had been born in Iran, and the constitution and the popular movement that supported it remained vivid memories among Iranian reformers that had their echoes in the 1950s and in 1979 (Chapter 51).

TAKING HER COFFEE. This image is of a young Turkish woman having coffee on a sofa, *c.* eighteenth century. Islam forbids the consumption of alcohol; therefore, Muslims often enjoy a concentrated, sugary coffee (so-called Turkish coffee) along with sweets.

SOCIAL AND INTELLECTUAL RESPONSES

Wahhabi Fundamentalism and Jihad

Throughout its long history, Islam has witnessed periodic episodes of revivalism. Sometimes, especially during times when Islam was in crisis, these developments took a decidedly fundamentalist and violent form. At other times, as was the case in the late 1800s, they assumed the character of movements of reform and accommodation. A modern example of the former violent reaction was **Wahhabism** (wah-HAHB-ism), a militant reform begun in the late 1700s when a desert shaykh, Muhammad ibn Ábd al-Wahhab (AHBD-al-wah-HAHB; 1703–1792), joined forces with a tribal leader, Muhammad ibn Saud (sah-OOD; from whom the Saudi royal family is descended). Together, they fought a jihad to purge Islam of Sufis, Shi'ites, and all others whom they accused of introducing innovations, which they believed were responsible for the decline of Islam. Largely inspired by the ultraconservative writing of a late-thirteenth-century theologian, Ibn Taymiyya (teye-MEE-yah; see Patterns of Belief box), the Wahhabis believed that Islam would survive attacks against it by its enemies only by returning to the fundamental sources of the faith, namely the *Qur'an* and collections of oral traditions (called *hadith*) concerning the Prophet Muhammad. Only the example of the primitive Islamic community as it was assumed to have existed at Medina in the time of Muhammad served as an acceptable model for Muslim life to the Wahhabis. Therefore, all Muslims had to be forced to follow that example. Ibn Abd al-Wahhab labeled all who disagreed with this view as heretics deserving of death.

These zealots declared holy war on all neighboring tribes to force them to accept their more purified version of Islam. "Enforcers of obedience" maintained moral order, and they still do so in modern Saudi Arabia. "Objectionable innovations" targeted for destruction even included mosque minarets and grave markers; therefore, they even planned attacks on the tomb of the Prophet Muhammad in Medina. In 1802, they destroyed the tomb of the Shi'ite Imam Husayn at Karbala, Iraq. In 1803, they succeeded in capturing Mecca, the holiest city of Islam, and Medina, where they destroyed the markers of Muhammad's grave. The Ottoman sultan (Mahmud II) sent Muhammad Ali Pasha in 1811 to drive them out. As the original fundamentalist sect of Islam, Wahhabism has inspired many similar violent reactions to change, especially to any innovations originating in the West. In the nineteenth century, to a varying extent, it helped inspire resistance to European ideas and imperialism in Africa and the Middle East.

Today, Wahhabist-inspired fundamentalism is notorious for fueling Islamist terrorism against the United States and other Western nations. Fundamentalism was and is marked by a thoroughgoing rejection of Western influences and Western ideas, including such notions as political democracy, religious toleration, the equality of citizens, and various other offshoots of the Age of Enlightenment and the American and French revolutions. To a fundamentalist (the word is a recent appellation), the task of government is to bring about the reign of Allah and his faithful on earth—nothing less and nothing more. Any obstacles that stand in the way of this process should be swept aside, by persuasion if possible, but by force (jihad) if

THE HAREM OF A CAIRO SHAYKH, c. 1870. The harem was actually the private quarters of a Muslim home, the place where women and children were protected from strangers.

necessary. There can be no compromise with the enemies of God or with their varied tools and facilitators, such as secular schools, mixed-religion marriages, and nonconfessional parliaments. In the rise of Wahhabism in Arabia and the bitter resistance by Abd al-Qadir's followers to the French in Algeria (see Chapter 36), modern Islamic fundamentalism found its first heroes. Many others would come forth in the twentieth century.

The Salafi Movement

Not all who advocated a return to the early community of Islam did so by demanding the wholesale rejection of all things Western. As we saw previously, Muslims who lived under autocratic regimes (such as the Ottomans and the Qajars) agitated for Western-style liberal democracies and constitutional governments to replace the systems they had endured for centuries, but others wanted even more—namely the reform of Islam to permit modern ideas and ways of life to penetrate Islamic societies. Chafing under European occupation of parts of Africa and the Middle East, some Muslim leaders in Egypt and India in the 1890s were distressed that Islamic civilization had fallen hopelessly behind the West, especially in technology and the sciences. One of these concerned leaders was Jamal ad-Din al-Afghani, who urged Muslims to reform themselves to find the strength to meet the challenges of the West. Afghani believed that the key to the future of Islam was to reject blind obedience to religious tradition, and he called for Islam to modernize itself.

It was left to the Egyptian ***shaykh*** **Muhammad Abduh** (AHB-doo) to develop a program of reform. Between 1889 and 1905, Abduh served as the grand *mufti* (supreme legal authority) and as the rector of Egypt's most prestigious mosque university, the Azhar (AHZ-hahr), in Cairo. In these positions, he was able to influence many students and intellectuals to accept limited modifications of Islamic law and thus admit the teaching of new subjects, such as science and geography. Above all, he realized that this change required discarding adherence to tradition that had been the rule since the tenth century. Calling for modernization based on Islamic principles, Abduh and his followers began what came to be known as the **Salafi movement** (SAH-lah-fee). Rather than simply accepting the ways of the past, even the ways of the early community, as Ibn Taymiyya and the Wahhabists had advocated, Abduh called for returning to the days of the "pious ancestors" (*Salaf*, from which Salafi comes) before the tenth century, to the time when Islamic civilization led the world in intellectual experimentation. Firmly adhering to the belief that God favored Muslims, Abduh believed that Allah could not desire to see Muslims in their present state of inferiority and subjection to "Christian" Westerners. Rather, he reasoned, God wished the Muslims to return

PATTERNS OF BELIEF

The Founding Figure of Islamic Fundamentalism and Reform

Many Muslims today consider Taqi al-Din Ibn Taymiyya (1263–1328) to have been the leading intellectual of the ultraconservative Hanbali school of Islamic thought in the Middle Ages. His writings inspired the eighteenth-century Wahhabi movement, an Islamic fundamentalist movement founded by Muhammad ibn Àbd al-Wahhab, and also influenced the reform thought (*Salafi*) of Shaykh Muhammad Abduh and others.

The son of a Hanbali scholar, Ibn Taymiyya received his education in Damascus, where afterward he lived for about fifteen years as a schoolmaster. Living at a time when the Muslim world was divided internally by sectarian differences and under repeated assaults by Christian Crusaders and the Mongol armies, he sought to overcome the problems of Islam. He held that this was to be done by reviving a strictly literal interpretation of the *Qur'an* and Islamic law of the Prophet Muhammad and by opposing customs and innovations he considered to be illegal innovations, such as Sufism and the worshiping of saints. Because of the zeal with which he expressed his opinions, he offended many secular and religious officials. He spent much of his life in various prisons in Cairo, Alexandria, and Damascus, and finally died in prison.

Ibn Taymiyya was convinced of the utter perfection of Islam. Furthermore, as did most ulama, he thought Muhammad had been both the messenger of God and the perfect Muslim. Reasoning thus, to him, later additions to Islam—such as theological speculation, Sufism, and saint worship—detracted from the perfection of Islam as it was in Muhammad's days. To solve current problems, he struggled to revive an understanding of Islam as Muhammad and his close companions (Salafi; hence the adjective *Salafi* sometimes is applied to his revivalism) had originally defined the faith. Although the ulama of all four schools of Islamic law (Shari'a) accepted this last point, where Ibn Taymiyya and most Hanbali scholars differed was in their rejection of every other form of Islam, or sources of Islam other than the *Qur'an* and the traditions of the Prophet. He stated that the goal of a true Muslim was not to think or speculate about God, nor to "know" him, nor love him, nor to seek him in any way. Rather, he thought the only legitimate goals for a Muslim were to carry out God's will through worshiping him and obeying him. Any other form of religious belief and practice for Muslims was mere "innovation" (*bida*)—hence unbelief (*kufr*). Therefore, in his words, it was the duty of every Muslim to wage jihad against anyone who failed to subscribe to these beliefs:

> The command to participate in jihad and the mention of its merits occur innumerable times in the Koran and the Sunna. Therefore it is the best voluntary [religious] act that man can perform ... Jihad implies all kinds of worship, both in its inner and outer forms. More than any other act it implies love and devotion for God, Who is exalted, trust in Him, the surrender of one's life and property to Him, patience, asceticism, remembrance of God and all kinds of other acts [of worship] ... Since lawful warfare is essentially jihad and since its aim is that the religion is God's entirely and God's word is uppermost, therefore according to all Muslims, those who stand in the way of this aim must be fought.

ANALYZE AND INTERPRET

In your experience, how do the views of Ibn Taymiyya compare to the views of religious fundamentalists or revivalists of other religions, such as Christian, Jewish, and Hindu?

Source: Rudolph Peters, *Jihad in Classical and Modern Islam* (Princeton, NJ: Markus Wiener Publishers, 1996), 47–49.

to the days of free intellectual inquiry when they studied all of the sciences. That focus, he believed, would enable them to catch up with the West.

Many of Abduh's ideas spread rapidly in some intellectual circles throughout the Islamic world. Some Muslim scholars advocated similar reforms for the modernization of India, Africa, and Southeast Asia, for example. Unfortunately, though, most ulama continued to ignore all innovations.

Arab Nationalism

Pan-Arabism is an outgrowth of Arab national consciousness that began to be articulated in the late nineteenth century, especially among Lebanese and Egyptian Christians. (Note that the word *Arab* or *Arabic* refers to an ethnic group, not a religious one. There are many Arab Christians in Egypt, Lebanon, and Syria, and they were among the leaders of Arab nationalism.) Ottoman recognition of the equality of all Ottoman subjects in the nineteenth century, regardless of religion, meant that they could no longer refuse admission to missionaries to work among the Christian communities of the empire. The establishment of mission schools in Lebanon and Egypt gradually introduced Christian Arabs to the Enlightenment ideas of political liberalism and nationalism for the first time. In Beirut, editors of a few small Christian newspapers called for increased political self-identity among all Arabs, regardless of religion. These ideas spread rapidly into Syria, Egypt, and Iraq, where they appealed especially to anti-Turkish dissidents who wished to see an end to Ottoman rule. By the 1890s, various vocal Arabic societies had appeared, which advocated political independence from the Ottoman Empire for the Arab provinces.

The reaction of the autocratic Sultan Abdul Hamid to these ideas was predictable: He was able to use his secret police to suppress such talk and hound the leaders of the pan-Arab movement into hiding. Agents were sent disguised as ulama to exacerbate tensions and traditional rivalries between tribes, clans, and families, as well as between Christians and Muslims. These actions were temporarily alleviated when the officers of the CUP deposed the Sultan in 1909, but soon, conservatives within the junta clamped down on Arab aspirations by ordering that all ethnically based organizations be disbanded. None of this action seriously discouraged the Arab nationalist movement, though. In 1905, many were openly promoting the creation of an independent, Arabic-speaking nation, stretching from Iraq to the Suez Canal. By 1913, as the Ottoman Empire was on the brink of entering a world war as an ally of Germany, an Arab Congress met in Paris to hammer out a consensus scheme for an autonomous Arab state. Although the Congress failed to gain the support of the major Western powers that it had hoped for, events during the war soon changed the whole history of the pan-Arab movement, as well as that of the entire Middle East (see Chapter 51).

SUMMARY

Their worldwide expansion in the Age of Discovery brought Europeans into more frequent and, inevitably, more violent contact with other world civilizations. For many centuries beforehand, Muslims and European Christians had fought across religious frontiers in periodic "holy wars." And in these encounters, both intellectually and militarily, the Muslims had generally enjoyed the upper hand. In the centuries following the Renaissance, the balance of power between Europe and the lands of Islam began shifting slowly in favor of the West, and bewildered Muslims responded in several ways that set the pattern for interactions between Western nations and Muslim peoples that has continued to this day. Although these responses differed considerably, they all shared two features: (1) their continued religious base, and because they were religious, (2) the continued assumption of the superiority of all things Islamic, even to a Western civilization that clearly had become wealthier and more powerful.

Because of this assumption, for example, the first responses of the eighteenth and nineteenth centuries to the shift of power were state-directed and limited to relatively insignificant borrowings from Western technology—particularly military technology. Muslim leaders were willing to learn from the West, provided that what they learned did not affect what they believed were rules for living and truths that Allah had mandated. Inevitably, though, such attempts at maintaining a barrier between science and religion had to fail, especially because what the Muslims coveted—science, hence the scientific method—derived from a Western revolution in thought that was highly secular. In the modern era, Westerners learned not to discard their beliefs, but to suspend them in trying to understand and master their world while leaving what happened after death to their faiths. So, in the end, Muslim religious extremists found that their greatest "enemy" was not Western Christianity but Western secularism. Islamic civilization, like the medieval civilization that modern Westerners finally discarded, has struggled to separate religion from everyday life.

IDENTIFICATION TERMS

Test your knowledge of this chapter's key concepts by defining the following terms. If you can not recall the meaning of certain terms, refresh your memory by looking up the boldfaced term in the chapter, turning to the Glossary at the end of the book, or accessing the terms on the CourseMate website at **www.cengagebrain.com**.

Shaykh Muhammad Abduh
the Mahdi
Muhammad Ali Pasha
Rose Chamber Rescript of 1839
Salafi movement
Tanzimat reforms
Wahhabism
Young Ottomans

FOR FURTHER REFLECTION

1. After having been one of the most advanced of the world civilizations for many centuries, why did Islamic civilization in general lose ground to European civilization in the modern era?
2. In your opinion (and, as always, state your reasons), from what you already know about African and other Asian civilizations, is it likely that they would have shared some of the weaknesses of the leading Islamic civilizations of the fifteenth-to-eighteenth centuries? Discuss some of these common weaknesses.
3. Despite their decline vis-à-vis Western civilization, do you think that Islamic civilizations might have continued to grow in other ways?
4. What were some major departures in the ways in which some eighteenth- and nineteenth-century Muslims responded to the threats of Western civilization from past Muslim responses to external threats?

TEST YOUR KNOWLEDGE

Test your knowledge of this chapter by answering the following questions. Complete answers appear at the end of the book. You may find even more quiz questions on the CourseMate website at **www.cengagebrain.com**.

1. A major source of internal trouble for the Ottoman rulers of the eighteenth and nineteenth centuries was/were
   a. the spreading atheism of most of the Turkish upper class.
   b. the professional military units called Janissaries.
   c. the missionaries from Europe in the Ottoman cities.
   d. the attacks from the Mughal Empire of India.
   e. their inability to control their police forces.
2. In eighteenth-century Arabia, the Saudi family
   a. claimed direct descent from Muhammad.
   b. drove out religious extremists.
   c. claimed to be members of the Hashimite clan.
   d. allied themselves with the new United States of America.
   e. rose to power by allying themselves with the Wahhabi fundamentalists.
3. The balance of power between the West and the Islamic lands began shifting during the period of the
   a. Industrial Revolution.
   b. Liberal Revolution.
   c. Reformation.
   d. Renaissance.
   e. Scientific Revolution.
4. Which of the following is/are true about the Tanzimat reforms?
   a. They were initiated and directed by the sultans' government.
   b. They were popularly supported from their inception.
   c. They failed in their objectives.
   d. They were forced on the Ottomans by the European powers.
   e. Both a and d are true.
5. The Rose Chamber Rescript was significant because it
   a. ended the Ottoman monarchy.
   b. advocated the creation of a new, modern army.
   c. established the legal equality of all Ottoman subjects.
   d. banned Islamic law.
   e. ended the feudal system of military estates.
6. An Islamic leader who influenced movements for reform in both Iran and Egypt and who advocated Islamic modernization was
   a. Nasir ad-Din.
   b. Muhammad Abduh.
   c. Mahmud II.
   d. Abdul Hamid II.
   e. Al-Afghani.
7. In Iran, national resistance to a reform-minded government finally gelled around the issue(s) of
   a. government attempts to stop merchants from fixing prices.

b. efforts by the shahs to modernize their armies.
c. attempts by the government to regulate education.
d. government concessions of monopolies to foreigners.
e. both a and b

8. In Iran, a Majlis was a(n)
   a. advisory council to the Shah.
   b. council of religious scholars.
   c. elected Assembly.
   d. building that housed the government bureaucracy.
   e. the shah's personal residence.

9. In many respects, the founder of modern Egypt was
   a. Nasir ad-Din.
   b. Mahmud II.
   c. Selim III.
   d. Muhammad Ali.
   e. Khedive Ismail.

10. The Mahdist uprising in the Sudan was a result of
    a. efforts by the Egyptian Khedive to modernize Sudanese society.
    b. the Egyptian occupation.
    c. the British occupation.
    d. Sultan Abdul Hamid's efforts to suppress Arab nationalism.
    e. the expansion of the slave trade under Egyptian rule.

CourseMate

Visit the CourseMate website at **www.cengagebrain.com** for additional study tools and review materials for this chapter.

India and Southeast Asia Under Colonial Rule 35

We divide, you rule. —MAULANA MOHAMMED ALI TO BRITISH

CHAPTER OUTLINE

1510	Goa becomes seat of Portuguese Indian Ocean empire
1521	Portuguese seize control of Malacca
1603	British East India Company (BEIC) founded
1757	Battle of Plassey; Bengal and Orissa become BEIC possessions
1824–1886	British conquer Burma
1839–1842, 1878–1880	Afghanistan Wars
1856–1857	Great Indian Mutiny
1858	Queen Victoria assumes control of India; BEIC is dissolved
1876	Victoria crowned as Empress of India
1885	Indian National Congress founded in Delhi
1887	French establish Indo-Chinese Union

Beginning with the Portuguese in the fifteenth century, Europeans commenced a spate of global explorations that persisted throughout the next four centuries (see Chapter 22). With much to be won, by the end of the 1500s, direct trade had reached an advanced state with Asia, Africa, and the American hemisphere, and nearly every European nation had found ways of participating in the division of the spoils. Throughout this process, and even after the discovery and settlement of the Americas, Asia continued to offer the richest prizes for those desiring the profits that could be garnered through commerce. The Portuguese were again at the vanguard of a systematic occupation of the principal Indian Ocean and Eastern Asian entrepôts. It was not long, however, before more muscular rivals eclipsed them. The Dutch expropriated the Spice Islands, while the English and the French were forced, for the most part, to focus their efforts on India and other portions of Southeast Asia.

INDIA

In the sixteenth and seventeenth centuries, the period when European military and commercial enterprises in India began, the Mughal Empire was still a viable state. The great Akbar and the next three shahs who followed him—Jahangir, Jahan, and Aurangzeb—could afford to tolerate the presence of foreigners from faraway Europe carrying on trade in their ports, with little heed being given to any hazards they might present. These powerful rulers had built a unified state out of the numerous smaller entities that had preceded them, and the history of India itself was one of a land—not a nation by any standard—that had seen invasions and settlements of one set of exotic interlopers after another. Therefore, what could a few hundred more foreigners matter?

Yet they did matter. The death of the shah in 1707 marked the beginning of the end of effective Mughal administration, and the next 150 years saw a gradual reversal of the conquests of Babur and Akbar, as the centrifugal forces of India's religious and regional differences reasserted themselves and the subcontinent gradually broke up into several dozen minority states, each ruled by its own ***nawab*** (nah-WAHB: Mughal ruling official). It was this breakup that provided an opening for a new set of foreign rulers, the British Empire in India, often called **the *Raj*** (rahj).

The Appearance of the Europeans

The Portuguese were the first Europeans to arrive in India, followed by the Dutch, English, and French. By the end of the 1600s, the Portuguese "factories" except for Goa had been absorbed first by the Dutch and then by the English. After some tentative skirmishing on the seas, the Mughals had settled into a mutually comfortable relationship with the British, centered on trade in goods in both directions, with luxury goods flowing to the West and firearms going in the opposite direction. The privately owned **British East India Company** (BEIC), founded in 1603, was given monopolistic concessions to trade Indian goods—notably tea and cotton cloth—to the West and bring in a few European items in return.

For a long time, the arrangement worked out harmoniously. The Mughal shahs permitted BEIC to trade through two factories at Bombay and Madras. A third, Fort William, was constructed in 1690 on the Hooghly River in Bengal (see Map 35.1), which eventually became the nucleus of the

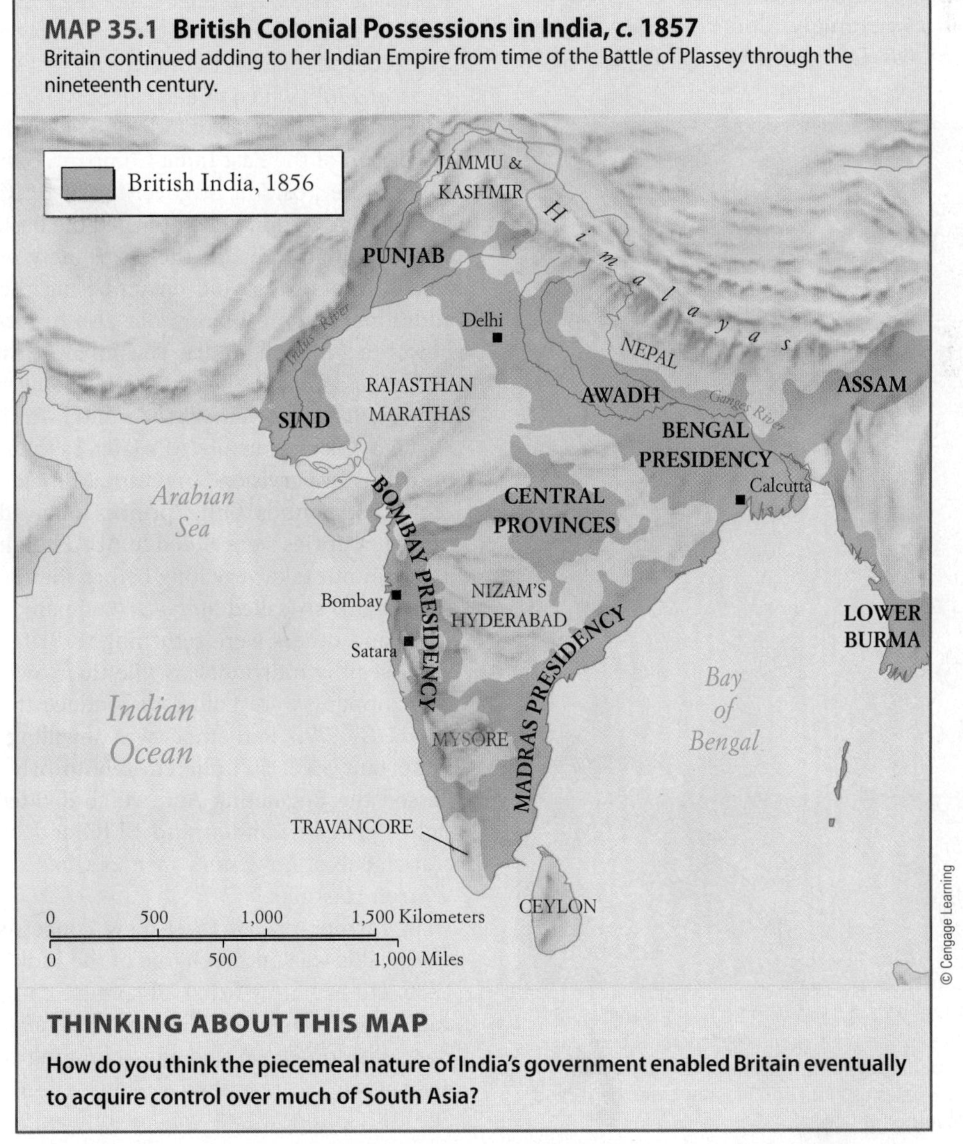

MAP 35.1 British Colonial Possessions in India, *c.* 1857
Britain continued adding to her Indian Empire from time of the Battle of Plassey through the nineteenth century.

THINKING ABOUT THIS MAP

How do you think the piecemeal nature of India's government enabled Britain eventually to acquire control over much of South Asia?

city of Calcutta. By the early eighteenth century, between fifteen and twenty-five merchant ships were making the long annual voyage between England and India. India and the rest of Asia were by then becoming vital additions to the British Empire because they supplied spices, silk, tea, and cotton goods to the growing list of high-value merchandise on which London and Bristol mercantile firms were enriching both themselves and Great Britain. At times, BEIC made large profits. Ironically, however, major obstacles to its profitability were its own employees, who frequently traded on their own accounts at the company's expense.

A second dilemma was that, despite precautions taken to protect this valuable commerce, company factories found the success of their business all too frequently to be at the mercy of local princes. The arrival of the French East Indies Company in the 1670s further complicated the BEIC's predicament and provoked new strains on English–Mughal relations, as Paris was already in competition with London for a colonial empire (an issue that was fought over repeatedly in the Anglo-French wars of the 1700s, including the Seven Years' War). Under the brilliant **Joseph François Dupleix** (doo-PLAYS), governor-general of French possessions in India (1742–1754), the French made an effort to enlist some of the Indian princes as partners in trade and to serve as native go-betweens to assist them in administering their territories. The British then responded similarly. Both the French East Indies and the British East India companies appointed local *rajas* to serve as official "native rulers" through whom they connived to dominate key territories in India. For both sides, Bengal was one of the most crucial prizes to be had. Dupleix recruited Siraj ad-Dawla (sih-RAHJ ad-DOW-lah), the last nawab of Bengal, to despoil the BEIC of its possessions in Bengal. The deciding battle occurred on June 23, 1757, between the forces of Siraj and an army of one thousand British soldiers and two thousand ***sepoys*** (SEE-poys: European-trained Indian troops) commanded by **Robert Clive**. Clive's victory at the **Battle of Plassey** marked a signal defeat of the French East Indies Company and secured BEIC rule in Bengal.

ROBERT CLIVE (1725–1774). Shown here in a general's uniform, *c.* 1764, Clive began his career as a clerk for the British East India Company but made his reputation as a soldier from his leadership at the Battles of Arcot and Plassey. Later, he served twice as the BEIC governor of Bengal.

Life Under Company Rule, 1757–1857

It was Clive's exploits that made the BEIC the most powerful presence in India following Plassey and the ultimate defeat of the French at Pondicherry in 1761. The Treaty of Paris in 1763, which ended the Seven Years' War, surrendered control of much of India to Britain through the intermediation of the East India Company. Subsequently, Clive rose to the position of governor of BEIC possessions in India. As governor, he established the basic framework for British rule in India for the next ninety-odd years. Above all, he wanted to avoid encumbering the company with additional responsibilities, but also to retain the ultimate power in governing India. The policy he established was to make the company the "protecting" power over India, but not the *titular* power. What resulted was indirect rule. He began by placing an ally, Mir Jafar, as the nawab of Bengal, under his "supervision." In return, Mir Jafar gave Clive a gift of 240,000 pounds. Other princes followed this practice as more territories were added to BEIC holdings in India.

It did not take very long before shareholders observed that many so-called *nabobs* (company employees) like Clive and others were returning to Britain from India as very wealthy individuals, while their own investments in the company were failing to produce the expected dividends. By 1773, Parliament was unwilling to trust such an important asset as India entirely to private hands. They passed the Regulating Act, which divided political oversight between London and BEIC and curbed the autocratic style of governors such as Clive and his successor, Warren Hastings.

In furtherance of these new concerns, Lord Charles Cornwallis was put in charge of the Indian possessions in 1786. He began by firing all corrupt company employees and proposed instead that BEIC raise officials' salaries substantially to end the skimming of profits and to discourage the acceptance of bribes from native rulers. English Common Law was introduced into Indian forms

© The Art Gallery Collection/Alamy

"GOING NATIVE." A portrait of a European gentleman in Indian dress seated before an open window, smoking a hookah. British East India Company employees spent years in India, where there were few European women as potential marriage partners. Many, it was said, "went native," forming liaisons with Indian women and adopting Indian lifestyles. Lucknow Company School, early nineteenth century, from an album page.

of land tenure. Most significantly, Cornwallis pronounced that Indian customs and religions were not to be interfered with and were to be respected; consequently, he continued the customary BEIC practice of discouraging Christian proselytizing.

Unfortunately, this policy of tolerance was not to last long. As Britain and other Western nations entered the Industrial Age, bourgeois attitudes toward other civilizations became ever more paternalistic, especially where darker-skinned peoples were concerned. The nineteenth century brought about the end of the slave trade, but it also was the century when the notion of Europe's "civilizing mission" flourished (see Chapter 36). This attitude seemed to receive support when Darwin realized that, in nature, only the fittest survive, an idea which some then applied to ethics and society as a whole (see Chapter 39). When applied to human beings, the result was a pseudo-scientific schematic in which some "races" were deemed superior to others. One especially tragic result of this way of thinking was the growing exploitation of so-called native (i.e., inferior) peoples and a callous neglect of their welfare. Under the British, the much-favored Hindu and Muslim elite (who were allies of BEIC) fared well, but a policy of requiring peasant farmers to grow exportable crops, such as tea and opium, enriched the company but pauperized small farmers and caused occasional severe famines.

Another result of racist thinking was a more aggressive policy of territorial acquisitions in India and neighboring regions. In the years after Plassey, the remaining petty states that remained outside company rule were added to it one after another. After a series of wars, Burma was added to Britain's Indian empire. However, the defeat of

FAMINE VICTIMS. Victims of the 1876 famine sit in Madras. Crops failed disastrously during successive *el niño* events from 1876 to 1979. The British provided no food relief to the victims.

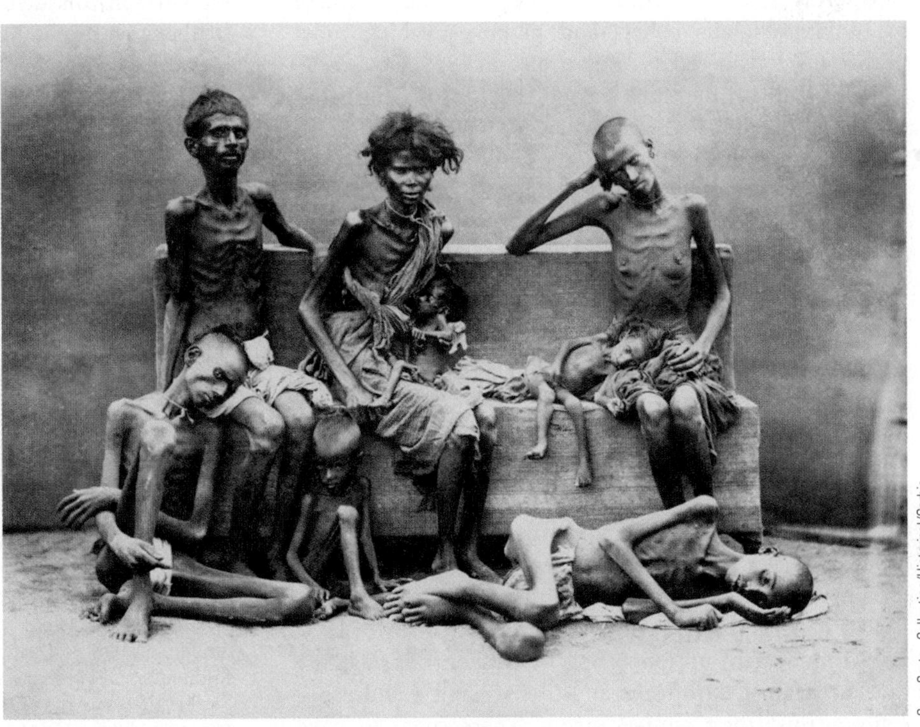
Sean Sexton Collection/Historical/Corbis

the French did not end challenges from other rivals. Often called **The Great Game**, in 1824, BEIC invaded Sind (the Indus region), seizing its ports to discourage Russian designs on southern Asia and its outlets to the western Indian Ocean. This was done because the company had reasons to fear Russian designs on northwestern India, Afghanistan, and Persia. Further military adventures in Afghanistan proved to be much more difficult than Sind and the Punjab (in Northwest India) had proved to be. The first of the **Afghanistan Wars** came to a tragic end when an invading army was forced into a catastrophic retreat from Kabul in the winter of 1842. Out of an army of seventeen thousand Indian sepoys and British officers, only one soldier survived the extreme cold and continual guerrilla attacks by Afghani tribesmen. Two further bids to seize Afghanistan also failed, although the harrowing results of the first war were not repeated. In each instance, the British underestimated their enemy.

A marked increase in the cultural insensitivity of the British occupiers of southern Asia began the generation after Cornwallis's, and it resulted in several mutinies, all of which were mercilessly repressed. Paradoxically, what became paternalism began with good intentions. By the early 1800s, the philosophy of *utilitarianism*, which taught that the greatest good is whatever is best for the greatest number of people, was in vogue among colonial and company administrators. In this spirit, Governor-General George Barlow passed the Charter Act in 1813. Its purpose was to eliminate the rigid separation between Europeans and Indians, so in principle it eliminated discrimination against Indians in the service of BEIC. Unfortunately, this principle was never followed in practice. Also, it eliminated the prohibitions against missionary activity. This form of *cultural imperialism* proved to be highly averse to Indian religious beliefs and practices, which most Europeans considered as "barbarous." In 1829, Governor-General William Bentinck passed the **Act of Abolition**, which eliminated *sati* and allowed Hindu widows to remarry. These measures rankled many Hindus—women included—despite their altruistic intent.

The Great Mutiny of 1857

Although by no means universal, by the 1850s, resentment of the British expansion and their so-called civilizing mission in southern Asia was widespread, particularly among Indian Muslims, high-caste Hindus, and the rank and file of the Indian army. Sepoys in one army unit had already mutinied (1824) when ordered to board ships to transport them to Burma. Mindful of Hindu restrictions against traveling by water, high-caste members had refused their officers' orders. Far worse was yet to come, despite the bloody riposte that followed this minor incident.

The general cause of the **Great Indian Mutiny** of 1857 was years of pent-up rancor felt by native troops against the Raj, against Europeans and their families, and especially against their white officers. There seem to have been two immediate reasons for the revolt. In 1856, the BEIC forcibly annexed the province of Awadh and exiled its nawab to Calcutta. Out of the invading force, about forty thousand soldiers had been from the state and were deeply offended by these actions of the company and its governor, James Dalhousie, giving them reasons to rebel. Further, by the 1850s, British officers spent less time with their soldiers than in the early years of the Raj and were tardy in their responses to rumors concerning their supplies. In 1857, the BEIC had just reequipped the sepoys with new Lee-Enfield rifles. The new weapons required the use of cartridges that had to be bitten before use. Many Indian soldiers believed that the cartridges were smeared with pork fat (forbidden to Muslims) or beef grease (taboo for Hindus). Other rumors had it that pulverized animal bones and cows' blood were mixed into their food, that the caste system was to be abolished, or that they were to be converted to Christianity.

The Great Mutiny began in Awadh when soldiers were humiliated on parade, stripped of their uniforms, and put in leg irons after they refused orders to use the new cartridges. Their comrades massacred their British officers, along with their wives and children, and then seized Delhi and restored the octogenarian Mughal emperor. The mutiny was confined to the Ganges River Valley, and more atrocities were committed. Nevertheless, most regions south of the Ganges Valley and the three main centers of BEIC authority—Calcutta, Madras, and Bombay—remained unaffected. Moreover, most units of the Indian army remained loyal to the British. In the end, the company put down the mutiny with great ferocity.

Realizing that Britons could not continue to rule India without the support of Indians, the Prime Minister, Lord Palmerston, dissolved the BEIC and substituted direct British government over the company's Asian possessions in 1858. To prevent future mutinies, new, more careful

BLOWING MUTINOUS SEPOYS FROM THE GUNS. "Blowing away" was a practice that had been used by the Mughals for rebellious soldiers. Despite this precedent, its use by British soldiers following the Great Mutiny made a mockery of the often-professed "white man's burden." From *The History of the Indian Mutiny*, published in 1858.

IMAGES OF HISTORY

Ceremony for Indian Royalty

The Last Great *Durbar* in June 1911. A *durbar* was a formal imperial assembly held to mark state occasions in India. When Queen Victoria was crowned (in Britain) as the Empress of India, all monarchs that followed her retained the title. However, neither she nor her son and successor, King Edward VII, ever visited India or received their crown (as monarch of India) while actually in India. However, upon Edward's death, King George V arranged to be crowned in India, for which the Great Durbar was called. All the princes of India were required to attend and to render their obeisance to the new emperor. In many respects, the Great Durbar of 1911 marked the apex of the Raj.

Parade of Indian nawabs pay tribute to the new "Emperor."

Reviewing stand on which King George V and Queen Mary sit.

British officers of the Indian army stand at attention.

Elephants trained for use in warfare were marks of authority among the Indian nawabs.

The last Great Durbar in June 1911, Coton, Graham (1926–2003)/Private Collection/Look and Learn/The Bridgeman Art Library

methods of recruitment into the Indian army were put in place. Furthermore, forced Westernization was abandoned. As a last measure of asserting Whitehall's supervision (that of the government in London), in 1876, Prime Minister Benjamin Disraeli arranged to have Queen Victoria crowned as the Empress of India. This set a precedent that was followed by all British sovereigns until Indian independence in 1947 (see the Images of History box).

The Raj to 1915

Had British rule in India been a failure? Much shaken by the mutiny, they dissolved BEIC and transferred power to the government in London. Furthermore, from 1857 on, they were far more loath to modernize their South Asian possessions, particularly if it interfered with local customs. The attempts to substitute the British ways of life for Indian traditions, nevertheless, did produce some beneficial, long-term results. Some believed, for example, that the key to India's future lay in producing a new elite who had been given a Western education and taught the English language. Schools were provided, beginning in 1816 in Calcutta, where young Brahmins received a classical education much like children were given in English private colleges (secondary schools). In time, those who matriculated into these schools produced the so-called **Bengal Renaissance** (see the Society and Culture box).

Known as the period of the Raj, direct rule helped usher in the Industrial Age to India and bound its economy more closely to Britain. The new Industrial era advances in communications and transport technology found their way to India because British policies favored the development of India as a source of industrial raw materials. Roads, railways, bridges, and telegraph lines connected the hinterlands to port cities, where cotton and other primary materials were exported to Britain and where, in turn, finished products could be transported back. India also saw her first factories when cotton mills were opened in the 1850s.

One partial result of these changes was the emergence of a new indigenous, middle class by the 1880s that became increasingly self-aware and willing to assert their interests, if necessary, against Imperial authority. In 1885, this development translated into political action when seventy-two Indian professionals and intellectuals founded the **Indian National Congress** (INC). Although politically moderate during its first twenty years, the INC was critical of Britain's economic exploitation of India through unfair trade practices, high taxations, and restraints placed on native industries. Much like later African complaints (Chapters 36 and 49), INC members above all agitated for a greater share in government for its educated members. By the end of the nineteenth century, the demands of the INC, however, had become more radical, with some openly demanding

SOCIETY AND ECONOMY

Raja Ram Mohun Roy and the Bengal Renaissance

Ram Mohun Roy (1775–1833) was a prominent Hindu scholar and theologian, born to Bengal's most powerful Brahman clan. However, the unorthodox Roy came to condemn Brahman excesses as well as Hindu polytheistic practices. He believed in the unity of God as revealed in the sacred texts not only of Hinduism, but those of Islam, Buddhism, and Christianity as well. From this philosophical premise, Roy became a pioneer in the region's nineteenth-century reformist movement now known as the Bengal Renaissance.

The Bengal Renaissance began after the British East India Company took over Bengal and established schools in Calcutta that provided young Bengalis with a European-style education. Gradually, the schools produced a new elite of Bengali men like Ram Mohun Roy, who interacted easily with members of the British ruling class in business, politics, and religion. Roy worked for the company in his native region of Bengal, where he sometimes conversed with British missionaries and scholars of Asian history and religions, called *Orientalists*. Roy and his reformist cohorts believed in cooperating with the governing regime, ostensibly to defend Hinduism and Indian rights on the Europeans' own terms. Furthermore, the reformers aspired to modernize India by blending the best elements of Indian and British culture. Beginning with Roy's movement and continuing into the twentieth century, Bengal's theologians, scholars, scientists, orators, writers, and social reformers led intense debates about the relative merits of Eastern and Western religious, political, and social systems.

For their part, Christian missionaries condemned Hindu beliefs and rites as idolatrous and evil. To maintain credibility in the religious debates, Roy and the Hindu reformers rejected some social practices that they also considered as irrational, including caste prejudices, the low status accorded women, and dietary restrictions. Roy is best remembered for his campaigns against polygamy, child marriage, and sati. He also advocated property rights for women. Roy founded an early reform society that exerted a lasting influence on India's intellectual revitalization during and after the period of the British Raj. Members of Roy's society established the first English-speaking school in Asia, Hindu College in 1817. As a result, a growing class of English-educated leaders arose to continue the revitalization of India begun by Roy's pioneering generation, and many of its graduates became influential in the Indian nationalist movement.

ANALYZE AND INTERPRET

Some historians liken the Bengali Renaissance of the nineteenth century to the Italian Renaissance of the sixteenth century. What similarities and differences do you see in the two movements? In what ways did Ram Mohan Roy contribute to the Bengali Renaissance?

Indian representation on the viceroy's governing council and even independence. Moreover, it had transformed itself into a modern, mass political party, the first in the country, organizing and agitating for millions of Indians of all classes and religious sects who opposed continued British rule. Significantly, too, for the first time, religion played a part in India's politics. One leader especially, Bal Gangadhar Tilak (TEE-lahk), appealed explicitly to Hindu identity as a force of opposition to continued British rule. About this same time, in 1906, a proposal for the partition of Bengal stirred Hindu opposition and drove Muslims, who favored the division, to organize the All India Muslim League. Muslim apprehensions about Hindu intentions were inflamed further when Tilak began appealing to images of the goddess Kali to excite Hindu support for him in the INC. As will be seen (Chapter 48), religion was to become an even more potent force in the drive for Indian independence in the hands of Mahatma Gandhi, as well as a reason for partition when India finally achieved independence in 1947.

SOUTHEAST ASIA

The territories in Southeast Asia that had succeeded in achieving political organization before the appearance of European traders and missionaries had little reason to take much notice of these visitors until a much later era. Contacts were limited to coastal towns and were mainly commercial. In the 1600s, the Dutch had driven the Portuguese entirely out of the islands' spice trade, and they had established a loose partnership with the local Muslim sultans in Java and Sumatra to assure the continuance of that trade with Europe. After a brief contest with the Dutch, the British—in the form of the BEIC—had withdrawn from the Spice Islands to concentrate on Indian cotton goods. Only in the Spanish Philippines was a European presence pervasive and politically dominant over a sizable area.

Most of the insular Asians were by now converted to Islam, a process that began in the 1200s through contact with Arab and Indian Muslim traders. By the time the

Portuguese arrived in 1511, Malacca had become a commercial crossroads of the Indian Ocean and East Asian networks, as well as the most important point of dissemination for Islam throughout the region. From Malacca, the Portuguese had extended their control over the Spice Islands. Except for on the island of Bali, the original syncretistic blend of Hindu with animist beliefs that had been India's legacy had faded away. Only in the Philippines was there a Christian element.

If the islands were relatively untouched by the early European traders, the mainland populations were even less so. In the 1700s, the three states of Thailand, Burma, and Vietnam dominated the area. The first two were by then part of the Hinayana Buddhist world, whereas Vietnam (under Chinese influence) had remained with the Mahayana version of the faith. The once-potent Khmer state of Cambodia had been divided between the Thais and the Viets by stages during the fifteenth through seventeenth centuries. As late as the end of the eighteenth century, nowhere was there a visible European influence, but this was to change radically in the next century.

In the early nineteenth century, a generation of European administrator-scholars entered colonial careers following the Napoleonic wars (see Chapter 30). These men were products of the Enlightenment and were often sincerely dedicated to humane treatment of their Southeast Asian charges while still being convinced adherents of Western cultural superiority. Foremost among them was **Sir Thomas Raffles**, the founder of Singapore and the first European to take serious interest in the history and archaeology of the precolonial societies. Although Raffles was entrusted with oversight of affairs for only a few brief years in Java, his reforming policies aimed at promoting peasant prosperity and local government autonomy persisted as a model, which was unfortunately not often followed in the century to come.

Indonesia was returned to Dutch rule in 1824 by a treaty that finally settled the ancient Anglo-Dutch rivalry. In the century that followed, Dutch administrators gradually expanded their control, both political and economic, over the hundreds of inhabited islands that make up the "East Indies." The bloody five-year Java War (1825–1830) was the decisive step, establishing Dutch sovereignty once and for all over this most important of the Indonesian lands. Other battles had to be fought in Sumatra and in the Celebes at the end of the nineteenth century. Only then was a true Dutch colony, rather than a trade partnership, created.

In the economic sphere, the Dutch directed a change from a limited spice-export trade with the homeland to an expansive commodity-oriented trade during the mid-nineteenth century. This change was accomplished via the so-called **culture system**, a refined form of peonage through which the peasants were obliged to deliver a major part of their crops to Dutch buyers at minimal prices. This system brought poverty to the Indonesians and great profits for the Dutch and Chinese middlemen, especially from the export of coffee, which replaced spices as the most important crop in the colony. The blatant abuses of the peasant laborers finally led to humanitarian reforms in the latter part of the century, but by this time, Java and Bali had been thrust into a cycle of declining availability of land and a rising population of rural tenants working absentee landlord estates. The resentments thus bred would inspire a tide of nationalist sentiment in the early twentieth century.

Sir Thomas Stamford Raffles (1781–1826), Lonsdale, James (1777–1839)/Private Collection/The Bridgeman Art Library

SIR THOMAS RAFFLES (1781–1826).

The Castle of Batavia, as Seen from Kali Besar West, c.1656 (oil on canvas), Beeckman, Andries (fl.1651)/Rijksmuseum, Amsterdam, The Netherlands/The Bridgeman Art Library

THE CASTLE OF BATAVIA, AS SEEN FROM KALI BESAR WEST, *c.* 1656. Headquarters of Dutch East India Company.

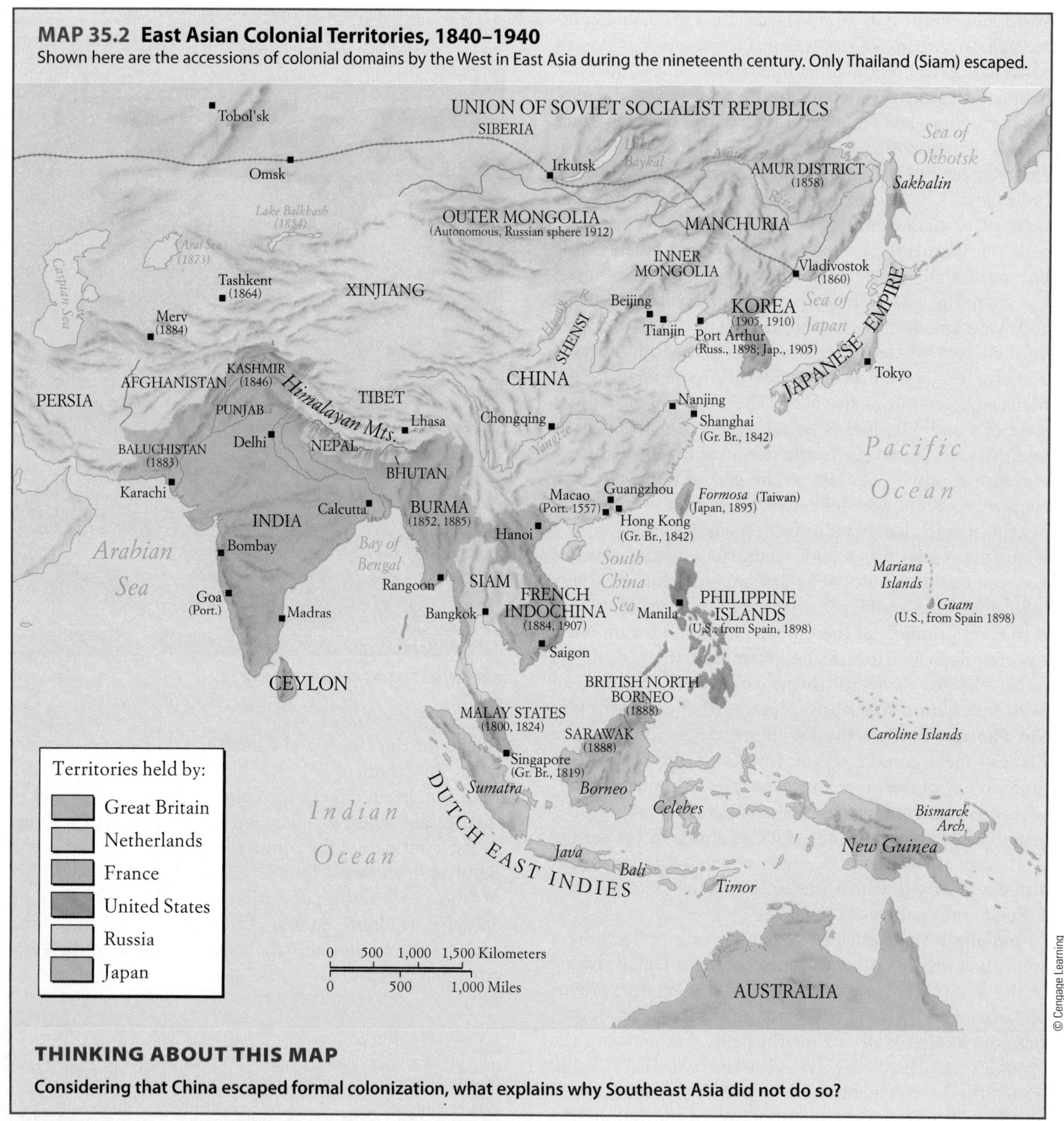

MAP 35.2 East Asian Colonial Territories, 1840–1940

Shown here are the accessions of colonial domains by the West in East Asia during the nineteenth century. Only Thailand (Siam) escaped.

THINKING ABOUT THIS MAP

Considering that China escaped formal colonization, what explains why Southeast Asia did not do so?

In mainland Asia, the assertion of Western colonial power extended first to the Burmese kingdom. As BEIC gradually transformed from a private commercial venture into a colonial government in India, its agents came into conflict with the claims of the Burmese rulers to certain frontier districts. A brief war ensued, with the customary results in favor of the Europeans. The process was renewed twice more in the mid-nineteenth century, and the Burmese eventually submitted to imperial oversight as a province of British India.

The sultans of Malaya (in the lower reach of the long Malay Peninsula) followed a somewhat different route into the imperial camp. Here, the British at Singapore were joined by an influx of Chinese who quickly came to dominate the increasing trade going through the Straits of Malacca. By the 1870s (following the opening of the Suez Canal), this was the world's busiest waterway. Steamships and sailing vessels of many nations carried trade between Asian countries and took part in the long-distance transport between Asia and Europe. The remarkable growth of world markets for tin and rubber, both of which were found in abundance in the Peninsula, also spurred alien business interests there. One after the other, the undeveloped sultanates were peaceably melded into the British *Straits Settlements* with a large population of immigrant Chinese in the mines and plantations. By the opening of the twentieth century, this jerry-built aggregation had become the colony of Malaya.

Vietnam fell under French dominion in this same epoch, largely because of the imperial ambitions of a handful of French leaders, who felt that Paris was falling behind London in the race for colonial riches. A secondary reason was the determination of the Catholic leadership in France to use Vietnam as the portal for the conversion of China to the Roman faith. French missionaries had been engaged among the Viets since the seventeenth century and had made considerable progress by the early years of the nineteenth century. At that time, a successful contestant in the recurrent civil wars that marked Vietnamese history in the nineteenth century subjected them and their converts to an intense anti-Catholic campaign. This was the justification for French military intervention that began in the 1850s and continued at intervals until all of the Union of Indochina—the official name for the colony, which included the present-day states of Vietnam, Laos, and Cambodia—fell under Parisian oversight by the end of the century.

As in Malaya, economic development picked up rapidly after the coming of the Europeans. Capital and steam power brought the great rice-growing area of the lower Mekong River valley into production for the first time, and Vietnam became the premier exporter of rice to world markets. Rubber plantations followed. Unfortunately, the rice fields and plantations were owned either by aliens or by a small clique of aristocrats who were friendly to the French. The economic lot of the Vietnamese villagers deteriorated as a result of the new developments. Just as in Dutch-ruled Indonesia, the visible and growing cleft between the mass of the inhabitants and the European/bourgeois governmental class inspired the rise of strong nationalism among some of the newly educated.

Among the Southeast Asian nations, only Thailand (then still known as Siam) escaped the colonial net and remained independent. How did this happen? It was partly a result of the 1893 agreement between the British in India and the French in Indochina that it would be convenient to maintain a buffer between their respective colonies, and that could only be Thailand. Thai independence was also partly the result of the remarkable vision and diplomatic skills of two nineteenth-century Thai kings: Mongkut (MUHNG-koot; ruling 1851–1868) and his son and successor, Chulalongkorn (CHOO-lah-LUHNG-korn; ruling 1868–1910). The two kings together brought their country into the modern age, introducing a wide variety of Western-style governmental and technical ideas into the traditional Thai culture. These reforms ranged from overhauls of the judicial system to setting up a telegraph line, from abolition of the traditional prostration in the royal presence to the first printing press.

Although the premier foreign influence remained Britain, the Thai kings made it a point to invite advisers from many nations to assist them in their campaign of modernization. Not only were foreigners made to feel secure and well rewarded for their efforts, but the numerous members of the ruling clan were also encouraged to undergo Western education in several different countries before returning to take up their governmental duties. As a result of these policies of openness and technical progress, Thailand entered the twentieth century not only independent but also poised to meet Western cultural imperialism with an awakening sense of Thai national pride and a conviction of equality with the aliens.

SUMMARY

For India and Southeast Asia, most of the eighteenth and nineteenth centuries was a period of transition to colonial occupation or other new forms of Western imperial control. As in Africa, for most of this period, official European interest in Asia remained balanced between merely defending the commercial interests of their nationals and outright colonial occupation. For many years, official British and Dutch interests were buffered by the presence of the British East India Company (BEIC) in India and the Dutch East Indies Company in Indonesia. It was the British company's involvement in the opium trade out of India that eventually entangled Britain in Asia—especially China.

Until 1757 and the victory at Plassey, the BEIC restricted its trade to Bombay, Madras, and Calcutta but faced competition from the French and Dutch. Governors Robert Clive and Warren Hastings were relatively freewheeling in their dealings with Indian princes, preferring to govern *through* them rather than *instead of* them. In those early decades of BEIC rule, officials maintained good relations with the Mughal princes and with Hindus of the higher castes; consequently, many enriched themselves by skimming the trade of their employers and accepting gifts from the nawabs and rajas whom they supported. Most importantly, they maintained a policy of tolerance toward Asians' ancient beliefs and customs.

The Charter Act (1813) and the Act of Abolition (1829) changed the relationships between the British and their Indian subjects. Indians already had plenty of reason to resent British rule, but the cultural arrogance that came with these two regulations greatly worsened those resentments. Territorial acquisitions through conquest and the forceful removal of native rulers, "racial" segregation, missionary proselytizing, and the notion of England's "civilizing mission" to Asians culminated in the Great Indian Mutiny. Consequently, Queen Victoria (the British government) assumed direct rule over southern Asia in 1858 and dissolved BEIC. More tolerant policies were introduced, and Indians formed political associations such as the Indian National Congress, which eventually began calling for the return of self-rule. Although Britain employed more direct methods of governing during the Raj, she also gradually allowed more Indians access to the levers of government. For some, this meant service on the advisory councils of the viceroy and regional governors, and for others as low level government bureaucrats.

As was the case throughout the rest of her empire, Britain tied India's economy ever more to that of the mother country by reducing it to the position of being a supplier of labor and raw materials. Many Indians, for example, were exported to serve as cheap, "coolie" labor in other parts of the Empire. At home, India's native industries were suppressed, and Indian farmers were encouraged to grow "cash crops," such as spices, cotton, and tea for export. The Raj ushered in modern communication and transport, in addition to modern science, technology, and education to India and South Asia. Many urban Indians found new opportunities as students and as employees of the new order.

The Dutch company's loss of Java in 1798 encouraged French involvement in Southeast Asia. When BEIC was dissolved in 1858, Britain became more directly involved. When this occurred, British actions, as well as those of the other European powers, were increasingly driven by the broader imperial concerns outlined in the following chapter: finding new markets for Europe's and colonial India's exports, strategic rivalry (the Straits of Malacca), nationalism, and the urge to export European civilization and Christianity (the white man's burden).

After a series of colonial wars at the end of the century, France, Britain, and the Netherlands added almost all of Southeast Asia to their growing list of overseas possessions. The addition of Germany, the United States, Russia, and imperial Japan to the competition resulted in the seizure of Korea, the Philippine Islands, the islands of the western Pacific, and portions of China. Technically speaking, China did not become an out-and-out colony because it remained self-governing, but large parts of it were occupied.

In Southeast Asia, the colonial period commenced with Dutch and Spanish presence in the Indonesian and Philippine Islands, respectively. But as late as the end of the eighteenth century, the Western traders and missionaries had had relatively little impact on the mass of the native inhabitants of the islands and even less on the mainland.

This situation changed gradually but with increasing rapidity. The nineteenth century saw a transformation of the former subsistence economy of the peasantry and the introduction of direct European control of government both in the islands and on the mainland. By 1900, the entire region, except for Thailand, had become a European colony.

IDENTIFICATION TERMS

Test your knowledge of this chapter's key concepts by defining the following terms. If you can not recall the meaning of certain terms, refresh your memory by looking up the boldfaced term in the chapter, turning to the Glossary at the end of the book, or accessing the terms on the CourseMate website at **www.cengagebrain.com**.

Act of Abolition (1829)
Afghanistan Wars
Battle of Plassey (1757)
Bengal Renaissance
British East India Company
Robert Clive
culture system
Joseph François Dupleix
The Great Game
Great Indian Mutiny
Indian National Congress
nawab
Sir Thomas Raffles
the *Raj*
Ram Mohun Roy
sepoys

FOR FURTHER REFLECTION

1. Why do you suppose that the Mughals initially welcomed European trade? How did these interlopers and the welcome they received fit the pattern of India's long previous experience with outsiders (for example, the Mughals themselves)? In seizing Indian petty, post-Mughal states from their native nawabs, were the Europeans simply being opportunistic? Why might the Europeans (for example, the French and English) have thought it inevitably necessary to dominate these states? Were they right to think this?
2. In what ways did the experience of the British East India Company in India prove to be something of a laboratory that shaped British attitudes and methods for governing non-European subjects throughout their empire? Where else did they apply some of the methods they originated in India?
3. What might have motivated the French to engage in imperialist expansion in Southeast Asia?

TEST YOUR KNOWLEDGE

Test your knowledge of this chapter by answering the following questions. Complete answers appear at the end of the book. You may find even more quiz questions on the CourseMate website at **www.cengagebrain.com**.

1. According to our text, much of the early profits of the British East India Company were
   a. obtained as booty through conquest.
   b. skimmed by company employees.
   c. taken by company directors.
   d. divided among shareholders.
   e. remitted to the Crown.
2. "Going native" meant
   a. joining the armies of Indian princes.
   b. allying with Indian nawabs.
   c. trading with Indian firms.
   d. adopting Indian ways of life.
   e. supporting Indian nawabs and rajas as rulers.
3. A major misstep was taken in 1829 with the passing of the Act of Abolition, which abolished
   a. sati.
   b. the British East India Company
   c. all "native" rule.
   d. missionary activity.
   e. widow remarriage.
4. Among Indians, who seem to have suffered the most from the years of the Raj?
   a. the Mughal princes
   b. the educated elite
   c. small landowners and peasant farmers
   d. merchants and shopkeepers
   e. the Brahmins
5. From what was said in the text, which of the following statements seems to have been true of the *Raj*?
   a. Most Indians benefitted from Britain's "civilizing mission."
   b. Only the Brahmins benefitted, all others suffered.
   c. The government officials of the old Mughal state benefitted as paid bureaucrats, whereas Hindus faced ever more restrictions.
   d. Britain's record in India was a failure from all standpoints.
   e. The rural population probably suffered under the Raj, whereas many urban dwellers found opportunity.
6. The term *civilizing mission* refers to which of the following?
   a. The Indian elites' idea that British civilization was superior to their own.
   b. Some Indians' idea that eventually a new civilization would develop from a mixture of British and Indian civilizations.
   c. Europeans' idea that the Brahmins represented the best of Hindu civilization and that they should promote Brahmanism among Indians of all castes.
   d. Europeans' idea that European civilization should replace the civilizations of Asia, Africa, and America.
   e. Europeans' idea that they were bringing civilization to non-Europeans.
7. The British government seized control over India in 1858 as a result of the
   a. financial failure of the East India Company.
   b. defeat of the French at Plassey.
   c. Act of Abolition.
   d. Great Indian Mutiny.
   e. crowning of Queen Victoria as Empress of India.
8. Which of the following was true of the islands of Southeast Asia by the 1600s?
   a. The Portuguese established control over their trade.
   b. The Dutch established control over their trade.
   c. Most of their trade was lost to China.
   d. Most of their inhabitants had converted to Islam.
   e. both b and d
9. The "culture system" was introduced in
   a. French Vietnam to ensure a supply of rice to the peasantry.
   b. Dutch Indonesia to ensure export profits.
   c. British Malaya to get the rubber plantations started.
   d. the Spanish Philippines to support the Catholic Church clergy.
   e. Japan to facilitate the opening of port cities to Western trade.
10. Thailand's continuing independence is largely attributable to
    a. the conflict between Vietnam and Burma.
    b. the determination of the Thai people.
    c. the protection afforded by the Manchu emperors in China.
    d. the desire for a buffer between India and Indochina.
    e. the desire of the Thai people to modernize their country.

CourseMate

Visit the CourseMate website at **www.cengagebrain.com** for additional study tools and review materials for this chapter.

European Imperialism and Africa During the Age of Industry 36

Take up the White Man's burden—Send forth the best ye breed—Go bind your sons to exile, to serve your captives' need; To wait in heavy harness, On fluttered folk and wild—Your new-caught, sullen peoples, Half-devil and half-child. —RUDYARD KIPLING

CHAPTER OUTLINE

1880s–1914	Scramble for Africa
1884–1885	Berlin Conference
1899–1902	South African War in South Africa
1918–1939	Interwar period, rapid changes in many African societies

The last quarter of the nineteenth century witnessed an extraordinary surge in Western activity in the non-Western world. This reached a climax in the 1870s with a sudden enthusiasm by the major European powers and the United States for seeking new colonies abroad and consolidating old ones; it is often called the **New Imperialism**. The most dramatic manifestation of this New Imperialism was the so-called **Scramble for Africa**, which began around 1882 and lasted until World War I. During these years, about half a dozen European nations engaged in a sudden and furious footrace to lay claims to what the King of the Belgians, Leopold I, called "this magnificent African cake"—a continent in which hardly anyone had shown any interest during the Age of Informal Empire—and that at times threatened to bring them to blows. The Scramble for Africa perhaps remains the most spectacular and irrational example of the New Imperialism, yet much of Asia and the Pacific islands were also the objects of a huge land grab by the United States and Japan as well as the European powers. This chapter explores the background of the New Imperialism and the European colonial period in Africa, and Chapter 37 examines the case of China.

THE BACKGROUND OF THE NEW IMPERIALISM, 1790–1880

Prior to 1880, only Algeria and Cape Colony (South Africa) were under direct European control. By 1914, only Ethiopia and Liberia remained outside formal European control. What factors caused this sudden turn of events?

Rivalry for New Markets

By the last quarter of the nineteenth century, the economic and military situation among the European powers was shifting rapidly. In this era of the Second Industrial Revolution, Britain faced serious competition from other nations for industrial supremacy—especially from Germany and the United States—and its balance of trade went into deficit. Furthermore, Europe as a whole suffered from a depression that lasted from 1873 to 1896. This long depression contributed greatly to the New Imperialism because the Western powers sought new markets for their manufactured goods and sources of raw materials needed to keep their industrial plants operating. In addition, many financiers in Europe and the Untied States sought investment opportunities in new markets that offered endless supplies of cheap labor and little or no competition. In the past, protected "spheres of influence" or colonies—particularly white settler colonies—around the globe had provided outlets of this sort for free capital. Where new markets could be found and opened up to free trade and investment, the opportunities for profits were greater than in the home countries (or so-called *metropoles*).

Strategic Issues

The British government came under intense pressure from industrialists and financiers to secure lucrative markets in India and East Asia from their European rivals. For Britain, obtaining a controlling interest in the Suez Canal, and ultimately control of Egypt itself, was critical to assure easy passage from east to west. For its part, Germany did not even exist before 1871. But once unified, it quickly became a rising industrial power close on the heels of Britain. Otto von Bismarck had little interest in overseas empire: European politics were of greater concern, but he too came under pressure from German industrialists. In addition, international rivalry in Africa provided him another opportunity to keep France isolated and out of any alliances that could threaten German security. Tiny Portugal remained concerned only with protecting its old colonies in Angola and Mozambique against the designs of powerful rivals such as Germany and France. To fend them off, it forged an alliance with Britain.

Nationalism and the Clash of Rival Imperialisms

Competing nationalisms proved to be a compelling force for empire building among the major players. Initially, Bismarck was motivated by the search for German overseas markets, but by the 1880s, the powerful new currents of German nationalism became a greater driving force. Many patriotic Germans felt that no nation could be taken seriously as a great nation if it did not have an overseas empire. Their models, of course, were Britain and France. To have what one official called its "place in the sun," Germany needed to stake its claims overseas along with the other European powers. Pan-Germanism thus made Germany the third-largest colonial power in Africa, after acquiring colonies in what are now Togo, Cameroon, Namibia, and Tanzania.

France, too, acquired its colonies in Africa and Asia out of strong feelings of wounded national honor and the need to assert the glory of France. Most damaging to its national image was the loss of Alsace-Lorraine in the Franco-Prussian War and the British occupation of Egypt; therefore, France felt compelled to compensate with conquests in Africa and Southeast Asia (see Chapter 35). The result was that most of what France added as *French West Africa* and *French Equatorial Africa* was worthless desert and scrubland (see Map 36.1).

Italy, another newly formed nation, sought its share of empire out of a desire to assert national glory. Like France, however, it ended up with little of any real commercial value: desert land in Libya and marginal scrubland (Sahel) in Somaliland and Eritrea. Italy was also the only colonial power to be defeated by an African army in its attempts at conquest in Africa. A war to conquer Abyssinia (Ethiopia) in 1896 resulted in Italian defeat at the Battle of Adowa.

The White Man's Burden

Finally, and by no means least, many well-intentioned folk at all levels of American and European society felt, as Rudyard Kipling expressed in the verse opening the chapter, that it was the so-called **white man's burden** to "civilize" the Asians and Africans. Some, like the missionary David Livingstone, advocated what he termed "legitimate trade" as a substitute for the slave trade. Consequently, Western businessmen and women now came to see Africans and their lands in a wholly new light: they could save Africans from themselves, while bringing them the mixed blessings of the Bible and Western civilization. In other words, what was happening to the non-Western world was not a power play by rapacious foreign exploiters but an act of duty toward fellow humans who—perhaps without acknowledging it—needed the West's magnanimous aid.

THE SCRAMBLE FOR AFRICA, 1880–1914

By the 1880s, sufficient geographic information was available about the interior of the continent to allow the European nations to begin to stake their claims. Belgium and Germany vied with the British in Central and East Africa. The Portuguese took Angola and Mozambique under firm control at this time. The French cemented their hold on West Africa and West-Central Africa. Italy took the area around the Horn of Africa, and King Leopold II of Belgium got the resource-rich Congo basin as his prize. Spain ended up with part of Morocco and Rio de Oro (now Mauretania).

The unbridled means by which this was accomplished was messy indeed. The rapid shift from informal empire to colonial occupation took the form of a race to acquire territory by the nations of Europe. The instability this

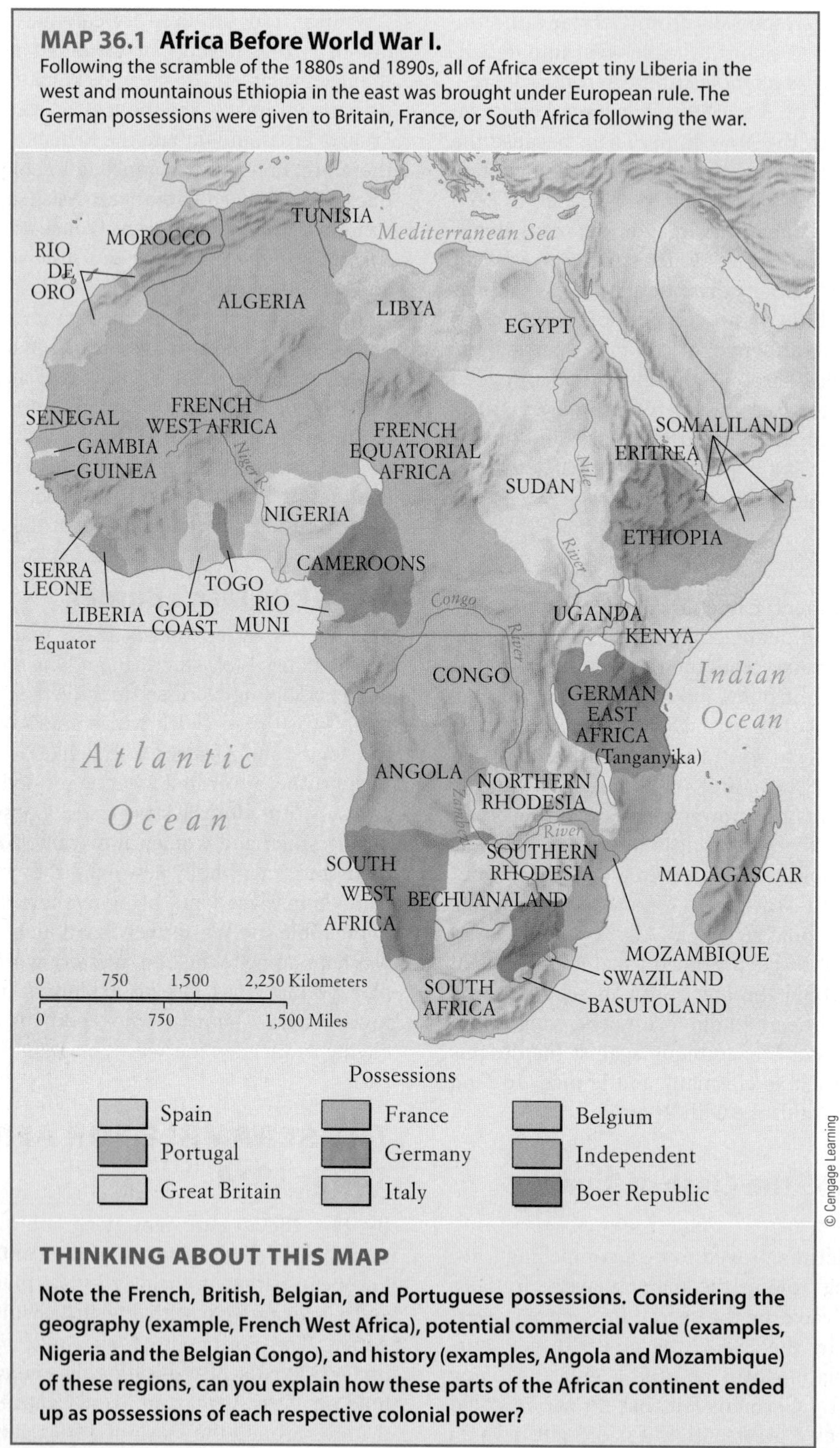

MAP 36.1 Africa Before World War I.
Following the scramble of the 1880s and 1890s, all of Africa except tiny Liberia in the west and mountainous Ethiopia in the east was brought under European rule. The German possessions were given to Britain, France, or South Africa following the war.

THINKING ABOUT THIS MAP

Note the French, British, Belgian, and Portuguese possessions. Considering the geography (example, French West Africa), potential commercial value (examples, Nigeria and the Belgian Congo), and history (examples, Angola and Mozambique) of these regions, can you explain how these parts of the African continent ended up as possessions of each respective colonial power?

brought into the international arena threatened Europe's peace. German Chancellor Bismarck called for a **Berlin Conference** in 1884 to find an agreed-upon formula to regulate the contest among the powers and to temper the most contentious disputes. After negotiations, the conferees ended by defining **"effective occupation"** as the standard for the recognition of territorial claims, a formulation that all-too-frequently resulted in armed force being used against indigenous states and peoples. Essentially effective occupation meant providing proof

"THE ORIGINS OF THE DIVERSE COLONIES." This illustration depicts the negotiations between Germans and Africans, which led to the creation of German East Africa. The Liebig Company, a producer of canned soups and other meat products, produced the card.

that local Africans had formally ceded their sovereignty to the *protecting power*, that is, the Europeans who declared the right to rule. Also, the protecting power had to establish some sort of formal "presence" in the territories they claimed, which usually meant an administrative apparatus to maintain order, interdict slave trading, and govern. More immediately, the new rules of effective occupation set off rounds of treaty making, conquest, and more foot races among competing powers to stake their claims.

By 1900, all of Africa had been allocated to European rule, with the exception of Ethiopia and Liberia (see Map 36.1). No attention whatever was given to local custom or economic relations when the borders of the various colonies were drawn. Whole peoples were split, and teams—sent out from Paris, London, or Berlin to partition the continent—shattered ancient ethnic and social affiliations. That this disregard for African geographic and ecological traditions was an egregious mistake became clear when the colonial system was dismantled after World War II and border disputes occurred all across the continent.

Once in power, one of the first tasks of the new overlords was to train an African constabulary under white officers to break up slaving raids and put down resistance to colonial rule. Another was the establishment of district offices, often staffed by young civil servants fresh from the mother country who were given extraordinary responsibilities in maintaining the peace and establishing European administration. In the British colonies, it was not unusual to see a twenty-seven-year-old, three years out of Cambridge and backed only by his constables, given life-and-death authority over a district population of perhaps thirty thousand individuals. Direct challenges to the new dispensation were rare. Officers could move about freely without fear in the villages, although the nearest European might be a couple hundred miles away. Attacks on the Europeans, when they occurred, were almost always motivated by the whites' breaking of religious taboos, taxation, or repeated cruelties.

REACTIONS TO EUROPEAN DOMINATION

Although terribly outgunned (literally as well as figuratively), Africans did not passively submit to European overlords. Many African leaders sought to check or defeat the Europeans' encroachments throughout the second half of the nineteenth century. Historians of Africa have divided the types of African resistance into two categories. **Primary resistance** involved the initial, violent reaction of individual societies against colonial rule. Its distinguishing characteristic was its relatively small scale, involving the actions of perhaps a few villages from a single ethnic group (or "tribe"). Primary forms of resistance almost never involved planned strikes against outposts or settlements but were more likely to be sudden attacks against colonial representatives performing specific duties associated with their offices. Tax collection (which Africans perceived as simple theft), forcible recruitment of labor, and arrests were the actions most likely to cause such attacks. Almost invariably, these invited retaliation by constabulary forces against villages and farms. Called "hammering" by some, Africans' homes and crops were set afire, livestock confiscated, and resisters killed.

Secondary resistance was a delayed response (sometimes years later) that followed the failure of primary resistance. It took longer to subdue than forms of primary resistance; was far larger in scale; and, most significantly, typically involved thousands of people, drawn from many ethnic groups over a wide region. Its basis was not the defense of a specific, ethnically based way of life, but often took the form of spirit-possession cults, led by prophets who promised immunity from the white man's weapons. In regions that had large numbers of Muslims, Islam served as a basis for resistance to Christian regimes.

In the end, though, with the single exception of the Italians' campaign in Ethiopia, the Europeans' superiority in weaponry and tactics won out, albeit after overcoming resistance that sometimes lasted for years. Against the Maxim guns and exploding artillery, bravery alone was not enough.

Once conquered, the African elites faced two choices: submit and attempt to assume the manners and values of their new masters or withdraw as far as possible from contact with an alien overlord. In the French and British colonies, African leaders generally chose the first way, encouraged by colonial administrators. In the Belgian, Italian, Portuguese, and German colonies, the Africans often chose the second way, because they were given little opportunity to do anything else until after World War II.

In some cases, those who withdrew and remained committed to African tradition retained more prestige in the eyes of their people than those who associated with the conquerors and mimicked their manners.

PATTERNS OF BELIEF

African Spirits Join the Fight against Colonial Encroachment

As Africans groped for ways to cope with the myriads of changes they were facing in the new colonial order, an assortment of popular movements surfaced. Most of these were accommodationist, but some resisted change. One form of resistance was expressed through mass cults that called for disobedience of the colonial powers and promised a new millennium, a return to better, happier times, as a reward.

Millenarian movements—revolutionary movements based on the belief of an imminent spiritual intervention in a world that has gone bad in some way or another—have been a part of history for thousands of years. Charismatic prophets, who claim to possess power from the spiritual realm, have led all of these. Many African societies, at one time or another, also have had their share of prophets, usually individuals who commune specifically with spirits of dead ancestors.

One of the earliest millennial incidents flared up in 1856–1858 as a part of a larger struggle that had been fought by the Xhosa peoples to halt Boer expansion into parts of Natal that they had inhabited for centuries. (See Chapter 25.) This was the "Cattle Killing movement." It began when a Xhosa teenager, Nongquwuse (nohng-koo-WOO-say), started receiving messages from her ancestors that all Xhosa should destroy their cattle herds. In return, the spirits promised that the white man would be driven into the sea; old people would be restored to youth; and the ancestors would return with enough grain, cattle, sheep, goats, and horses to repay all Xhosa who obeyed. At first, few Xhosa did as directed, but when a chief of the Gcaleka Xhosa, Sarhili, slaughtered his animals, more and more followed his example. However, the ancestors failed to return and thousands starved or died of diseases. Ironically, the movement ended with whites gaining in power because many starving Gcaleka Xhosa ended up having to beg for food from the white settlers. The British captured Nongquwuse and imprisoned her on Robben Island. When released, she lived quietly as a farmer and died in 1898.

The more widely known **Maji Maji uprising** (MAH-jee MAH-jee) occurred in German East Africa (later Tanganyika, now Tanzania), in 1905. It was an example of a secondary resistance movement with millenarian aspects. Maji Maji came as a reaction to high taxes, forced labor, orders to grow cotton in place of food crops, and the extraordinarily violent methods that the German governor Karl Peters had used to subdue all resistance. Making matters worse, in 1905 the region was threatened by a drought. A spirit medium, Kinjikitile (kihn-jee-kih-TEE-lay), appeared who averred that a snake spirit, whom he called *Hongo* (gift, tribute), possessed him. Poorly armed with spears and arrows, they had previously fared poorly against German guns. Now, ordered first to destroy cotton plants, Kinjikitile anointed and armed his followers with medicine, made of *maji* (water), castor oil, and millet seed. With the medicine and millet stalk wreaths around their foreheads, his followers marched forth believing the medicine would change bullets into water. They destroyed cotton crops, and attacked German outposts. The movement spread across "tribal" boundaries and inflamed most of southeast Tanganyika before it finally was put down, and Kinjikitile was arrested and hung. Maji Maji and the famine it helped cause produced 100,000–300,000 deaths. Even after Kinjikitile's execution, however, it continued to spread, and was not altogether destroyed until 1907.

ANALYZE AND INTERPRET

What other millenarian-type movements have you read or heard about in your lifetime? What do you know about them? To what extent were they like, or unlike, the two described here?

"THE RHODES COLOSSUS." This contemporary cartoon from Punch magazine depicts the strategic aims of British imperialists in Africa. Cecil Rhodes (1853–1902), famous as the diamond magnate who founded the de Beers monopoly in South Africa, struggled to advance British ambitions to create adjoining British territories in Africa stretching from Cape Town to Cairo.

Having seen the power of the Europeans, however, many believed that the whites' ways were superior and sought to associate themselves with those who provided access to those ways.

Of the three types of Europeans with whom Africans were now in contact—merchants, administrators, and missionaries—the last were perhaps the most important for the evolution of African culture. Missionary efforts at basic education in the local languages were responsible for the creation of a small group of educated Africans who were determined to become like their white mentors. The education offered rarely went beyond the ABCs. By the 1930s, however, the select few who did advance became conscious of the gap between what the European liberals and intellectuals preached and what the governments practiced in their treatment of the colonial peoples. From their ranks in the mid-twentieth century were to come the nationalist leaders of Africa. They saw that the most telling critique of Western colonial practice was to be found in the classic ideals of the West. Like their Asian counterparts, the African intellectuals used the weapons that their Western education delivered to them to free themselves from colonial authorities and to lead their peoples to independence.

CHANGES IN AFRICAN SOCIETIES

By the early twentieth century, the Europeans had completely demolished the traditional division of lands and severely affected commercial and cultural relations among the Africans. The old boundaries based on topography and clan and ethnic associations had given way to European diplomatic agreements and horse trading. In the same fashion, traditional African power relations had been either destroyed or severely altered by the imposition of

European-style officials, police forces, and courts, manned either by whites or by their African pawns.

Personal relations between masters and underlings varied, sometimes even within the same empire. French officials and African subordinates generally got along well in West Africa but poorly in Central Africa because of local variations in the French administration. In some instances, the whites and the African Muslim upper class got on well, but most Africans, who saw them both as exploiters, resented them. In colonies with large numbers of settlers, as in British Kenya and South Africa, the whites generally exploited their African labor and established an impenetrable social "color line," regardless of central government policies.

Undermining of the Old Ways

At the beginning of the twentieth century, although Christianity had already made a slight dent in African traditional religions, the Islamic faith had far more prestige and adherents throughout the northern half of the continent. The burgeoning colonial cities, such as Dakar, Lagos, and Nairobi, increasingly attracted Africans, but the majority continued living in their rural villages. Their standards of living were simple, and illiteracy was nearly universal outside the cities and the few villages with mission schools; but where they were permitted to continue growing their traditional food crops and breeding their livestock, they were not impoverished in any material sense. However, where forced to turn to cash cropping or to wage labor, poverty and social disruption tore asunder the cultural fabric of African societies.

Everywhere in the villages, the old ways of the Africans' culture and institutions lingered on, but subtle changes were under way beneath the surface. The "native rulers" appointed by colonial authorities frequently abused the powers given them by the Europeans. Because these powers usually exceeded traditional authority, their villagers only resented them. People found that the guiding spirits of the ancestors no longer seemed to be effective, so more and more youths sought their futures in the white man's religions, schools, cities, and jobs. The white man's medicine likewise provided an ancillary, and often more effective, source of healing. In these and other fashions, mostly unintended, the Europeans' coming as permanent overlords had a cumulatively erosive effect on the old ways. Many Africans found themselves adrift between the colonialists' preferred models of belief and conduct and the age-old traditions of African life.

Economic Changes

What benefits to the home countries came from the establishment of African colonies? In 1880, the European colonial governments had few if any long-range plans to develop their new territories economically. The chief concern shared among them was to avoid expense or to find ways in which the Africans could be brought to pay for the military and civil expenditures incurred. They had to walk a fine line between excessive expense to the home country taxpayer and excessive coercion or taxation in the colony. A rebellion would be not only distasteful but also expensive to the home government. Ideally, cash cropping and development of African mineral resources would allow a cost-free colony. For most colonial governments, however, this goal proved to be a mirage. Only a few of the colonies (Gold Coast, Nigeria, Senegal, Kenya, and South Africa) with **cash crops**, such as palm oil, peanuts, coffee, tea, and cotton, were better than a break-even proposition for the home nations. The hoped-for large domestic markets for excess European industrial capacity never developed. The Africans' cash incomes were far too small to absorb large quantities of consumer

HIP/Art Resource, NY

A TOBACCO PLANTATION IN COLONIAL RHODESIA (ZIMBABWE). Along with peace and European-style republican governments, the white man's burden meant introducing cash economies to Africa. This colonial-era poster emphasizes this theme, along with colonial paternalism.

goods, and it proved impossible to attract private investments into Africa on any scale comparable to what was going into the Americas or even Asia. Only in one or two situations—notably the copper mines and rubber plantations of the Congo and the diamond and gold mines of the Cape Colony—did the African bonanza materialize. Cecil Rhodes, the British capitalist and greatest of the private empire builders of the nineteenth century, had envisioned a thorough Europeanization of Africa, driven by railroads and mineral wealth. By 1914, it was already clear that this would not happen.

The individual colonies varied sharply in economic aspects. In the center of the continent, the Congo was a royal plantation, held by a private firm in which the Belgian king held a majority share. Originally explored by Henry Stanley (of Stanley and Livingstone fame), the Belgian Congo was a vast area along Africa's second-largest and longest river. It was an important source of several industrial raw materials, especially copper and rubber.

Relatively few Europeans settled permanently here. The main reason for claiming and keeping this kingdom of the west-central rain forest was to exploit its abundant material resources. A great scandal ensued in the early twentieth century when it was gradually revealed how brutal the royal enterprise had been toward its workers and how little had been done to improve the lives of its African peoples. Despite many assertions that European rule was justified by its potential to benefit Africans, the final judgment is spoken by a simple figure: The population declined by half in twenty years (1885–1905) of Belgian royal oversight.

In a few colonies, the economic impact of colonial rule was visible and direct. In British south and east Africa and in Algeria, whole agricultural districts were taken from the Africans to be used exclusively by the whites. Everywhere, new requirements that taxes had to be paid in money forced Africans into providing cheap labor for white businesses and farms. Closely aligned with business interests, for example, colonial governments pressured the *kaffirs* (Boer term for Africans) of South Africa's gold and diamond mines into dangerous and exhausting work.

The three European governments had somewhat different goals for their colonies and administered them in different ways, which were arrived at by necessity and experiment rather than by plan. French possessions were administered from a central office in Dakar and were linked directly with the Paris government. The Africans were given little margin to govern themselves. Through methods of direct rule, called at various times **assimilation and association**, the French exerted strong pressure on the upper-caste Africans to learn French and acquire French manners and values. If they did so, they were paternalistically considered as black Frenchmen and women. They could then enter the colonial bureaucracy and even become French citizens, although few ever did.

The French made considerable effort to convert Africans to Catholicism, but they met with little success until the twentieth century. Very little economic development occurred in these colonies, which were for the most part desert regions deficient in natural resources or rain forest that discouraged exploration. Only in the twentieth century have modern irrigation works made it possible to develop some agriculture in former French colonies such as Mali, Chad, and Mauritania.

The British possessions to the south were more favored by nature and attracted more attention from those seeking profits. A few colonies (Gold Coast and Nigeria) began as the private possessions of monopoly firms similar to the British East India Company in India. Sierra Leone began as a refuge for freed Africans from intercepted slave ships after the maritime slave trade was banned. The British rulers, whether private or governmental, relied heavily on local assistants, whom they appointed to exercise actual day-to-day government under loose supervision. This system of **indirect rule**, which was modeled on the system of governing through local *nawabs* and *rajas* in India (Chapter 35), was implemented partly to reduce administrative costs for the home country and to ease the transition from traditional methods of rule.

As a result of the (sometimes coerced) introduction of commercial crops such as peanuts, palm oil, cotton, cocoa, sisal, tea, and coffee in the late nineteenth century, Europeans' African dominions were gradually integrated into the world market. This proved to be yet another mixed blessing. Before the Great Depression, while prices for commodities remained high, the African colonies prospered. As in the rest of colonial Africa, however, the replacement of food crops by cash crops proved to be a disaster for Africans in the long run. Colonial authorities discouraged industrial development. The manufacturing of finished goods was left to the mother countries, and Africans were permitted only to provide raw materials. So when the prices of their cash crops and other raw materials (including mineral exports) fell, Africans' dependence on the world market proved to be "the mother of poverty." Unable to sell their cash crops at reasonable prices, many went hungry or starved when they could not earn enough to purchase food.

Such methods steadily forced Africans into Western-dominated, capitalist economies of trade and cash. These economic changes undermined centuries-old lifestyles and beliefs that had been rooted in values that traditionally favored family and community ties. In the villages, prestige shifted from those who came from respected lineages or who had religious authority to those who accumulated wealth. The way was being prepared for Africans' belated entry into the world marketplaces, albeit often to their considerable disadvantage.

SOCIETY AND ECONOMY

Women of Colonial Africa

Mary Kingsley: Explorer and Anthropologist

As an explorer and writer, Mary Kingsley greatly influenced European ideas about Africa and African people. She was born in Islington, England, in 1862, the daughter of a doctor and an invalid mother. As a girl, she was housebound to help care for her mother, so she acquired little formal education. Nevertheless, she was exceptionally intelligent and naturally curious, and she made ample use of her father's large library and loved to read and hear stories of foreign lands.

When both of her parents died in 1892, the thirty-year-old Mary was free of family responsibilities and was then able to travel. Her first decision was to visit Africa to begin collecting ethnographic information for a book on the cultures of the peoples of Africa.

She traveled to the Portuguese colony of Angola in 1893 and managed to earn the trust of local people. They taught her the skills that enabled her to survive in the difficult conditions she would encounter in the African wilds. After a short visit home in 1895, she returned to Africa and traveled by canoe up the Ogowe River and spent time studying the Fang peoples of west-central Africa. During a second return to England, she wrote *Travels in West Africa* (1897), for which she achieved instant notoriety. In many ways, Kingsley's writings went against nineteenth-century currents of opinion about Africans and their ways of life. Her criticism of missionaries for trying to change Africans, in particular, created an instant uproar among the Church of England clergy. Both in her books (she wrote a second shortly before her death) and public lectures, Kingsley described and defended many facets of African life that shocked the staid English middle class. She also opposed the common view that Africans were "undeveloped white men" and that their minds were inferior to those of whites.

A true modernist in her opinions, unfortunately Kingley's voice was lost when she died of typhoid in 1900 while working as a nurse among Boer prisoners of the South African War.

Elspeth Huxley and White Settlement of Kenya

Elspeth Huxley (1907–1997) possessed a rare combination of energy, intellect, and sensitivity that served her well through multiple careers in her long life as a successful journalist, writer, and even government advisor. After her birth in Britain, Huxley's parents moved to the new colony of British East Africa—later Kenya—and arrived in Thika, near Nairobi, in 1912 to start new lives as white settlers and coffee planters.

At eighteen, Elspeth left Kenya for England and the United States, but returned in 1929 to her adopted country to take a position as Assistant Press Officer to the Empire Marketing Board. After marriage and the births of three children, she resigned her post in 1932 and began traveling widely and writing. Among her earliest works was *Lord Delamere and the Making of Kenya*, which was an apologetic biography of a famous settler. Later in life, she served as an advisor in the confederation of the two colonies of Southern Rhodesia (now Zimbabwe) and Northern Rhodesia (now Zambia). Throughout these years, Huxley worked and wrote as an advocate and apologist of colonialism in "the Dark Continent." However, in the 1950s, as many of Britain's African possessions began the process of decolonization, she became an advocate for the independence of the colonies.

Huxley is most noted for *Flame Trees of Thika*, an autobiographic account of her early upbringing in Kenya, which poignantly documents the lack of preparation of many European settlers for life in the African "bush"—something that resulted in many failures and bankruptcies. In 1981, it was made into a television miniseries. However, her best work is *Red Strangers*, which details what life had been like for the Kikuyu people before the arrival of colonial government and the white settlers who occupied much of their land. Huxley's book was rare for exhibiting a clear awareness of African life in an age when white colonizers thought Africans to be bereft of histories or civilizations of their own.

ANALYZE AND INTERPRET

Why do you suppose the views and writings of these early colonial women seemed to focus so little on the experiences of (other) Europeans in Africa? Why was Kingsley interested in Africans? Was Huxley?

Photoshot

MARY KINGSLEY ON THE OGOWE RIVER, c. 1896.

SUMMARY

During the Era of the New Imperialism, Europe added almost 9 million square miles—one-fifth of the land area of the globe—to its overseas colonial possessions. Europe's formal holdings now included the entire African continent except Ethiopia and Liberia. Between 1885 and 1914, Britain took nearly 30 percent of Africa's population under its control, compared to 15 percent for France, 9 percent for Germany, 7 percent for Belgium, and only 1 percent for Italy. Nigeria alone contributed 15 million subjects, more than in the whole of French West Africa or the entire German colonial empire. It was paradoxical that Britain, the staunch advocate of free trade, emerged in 1914 with not only the largest overseas empire thanks to its long-standing presence in India, but also the greatest gains in the Scramble for Africa, reflecting its advantageous position at the Scramble's inception. In terms of surface area occupied, the French were the marginal victors, but much of their territory consisted of the sparsely populated Sahara.

Political imperialism followed economic expansion, with the "colonial lobbies" bolstering chauvinism and jingoism at each crisis to legitimize the colonial enterprise. The tensions between the imperial powers led to a succession of crises, which finally exploded in August 1914, when previous rivalries and alliances created a domino situation that drew the major European nations into World War I (Chapter 40).

IDENTIFICATION TERMS

Test your knowledge of this chapter's key concepts by defining the following terms. If you can not recall the meaning of certain terms, refresh your memory by looking up the boldfaced term in the chapter, turning to the Glossary at the end of the book, or accessing the terms on the CourseMate website at **www.cengagebrain.com**.

assimilation and association
Berlin Conference
cash crops
effective occupation
indirect rule
Millenarian movements
New Imperialism
primary resistance
Scramble for Africa
secondary resistance
Maji Maji uprising
white man's burden

FOR FURTHER REFLECTION

1. What changes occurred in European nations during the nineteenth century that led to the scramble for overseas colonies? What changes occurred in Africa?
2. In your opinion, which European nations were *primarily* responsible for the New Imperialism? More specifically, which ones were most to blame for creating the conditions that set off the Scramble for Africa?
3. Once Europeans established their colonial presence in Africa, how did their goals in governing Africa seem to undergo changes?

TEST YOUR KNOWLEDGE

Test your knowledge of this chapter by answering the following questions. Complete answers appear at the end of the book. You may find even more quiz questions on the CourseMate website at **www.cengagebrain.com**.

1. By 1900, the entire African continent had been colonized by Europeans except
   a. Liberia and Zanzibar.
   b. South Africa and Ethiopia.
   c. Kenya and Tanganyika.
   d. Ethiopia and Liberia.
   e. Ethiopia and Egypt.
2. The basic assumption behind the white man's burden was that
   a. It was the duty of Europeans to provide medical assistance to suffering Africans.
   b. Africans were incapable of governing themselves.
   c. God and Christ demanded that Africans be converted to Christianity.
   d. It was the duty of European governments to protect whites from the savagery of Africans.
   e. It was the duty of European governments to protect the health of whites who chose to settle in Africa.
3. Which of the following statements most accurately describes the actions of European countries in Africa?
   a. The British imported their own governors, having no confidence in local Africans to rule adequately.
   b. The French tried very hard to convert their colonial subjects to Catholicism.
   c. French subjects were given great latitude in governing themselves.

d. Most colonial administrators were so fearful of revolt that they almost never left their compounds without being heavily guarded.
e. Most British officers in Africa were seasoned veterans in their forties.

4. The main reason Europeans were interested in the Belgian Congo was a desire to
a. explore the Congo River.
b. maintain a trading center there.
c. extract slaves for the American trade.
d. extract gold.
e. take advantage of its natural resources.

5. Which colonial power in Africa enacted policies intended to allow Africans to elect delegates to the legislature of the mother country?
a. Germany.
b. Britain.
c. France.
d. Portugal.
e. Belgium.

6. German Chancellor von Bismarck convened the Berlin conference to
a. find a formula all the European powers could accept for making claims to overseas possessions.
b. settle outstanding disputes with France over the future of Alsace-Lorraine.
c. create a common-gauge railway system throughout Europe.
d. find a formula for regulating the role of private industry in Africa.
e. find a formula all the European powers could accept for dividing up Africa's mineral resources.

7. To conquer Africa, Europeans
a. relied on European taxpayers to meet the large expenditures new colonial possessions would require.
b. largely depended on Africans to fill the ranks of their armies of conquest.
c. often relied on each other to provide mutual military support.
d. often relied on friendly African kings and chiefs to handle the military responsibilities.
e. essentially had to rely on European recruits for their colonial armies.

8. Generally speaking, European policies on educating Africans during the years of colonial rule
a. were successful in training most Africans to a basic level of literacy.
b. placed the entire cost and responsibility on the colonial administrations.
c. prepared Africans for eventual self-rule.
d. split the responsibilities between the administration and missionary societies.
e. left most Africans with little or no education.

9. Which part(s) of Africa saw few European settlers?
a. East and South Africa
b. Central Africa
c. North Africa
d. West Africa
e. South Africa

10. To involve African leaders in the administration of the colonies, colonial authorities
a. went from using indirect rule to direct rule.
b. promoted commoners over traditional authorities.
c. employed the methods of indirect rule.
d. replaced traditional authorities with Africans who had attended schools and universities.
e. allowed Africans attend universities in Britain and Europe.

CourseMate

Visit the CourseMate website at **www.cengagebrain.com** for additional study tools and review materials for this chapter.

37 China in the Age of Imperialism

Let us ask, where is your conscience?

—LIN ZEXU TO QUEEN VICTORIA CONCERNING THE OPIUM TRADE

1840–1911	Decline of the Qing Dynasty in China
1839–1842	First Opium War
1851–1864	Taiping Rebellion
c. 1861–1894	Self-strengthening movement
1895	First Sino-Japanese War

CHAPTER OUTLINE

The explosive development of Western technology and military prowess in the nineteenth century had an impact on East Asia somewhat later than it did in Western and Central Asia (for comparisons, see Chapters 34 and 35). By the 1850s, China, Japan, and Southeast Asia had all felt the iron hand of the West in their commercial and political relations with the rest of the world.

How did these widely variant nations meet this unexpected challenge to their identities, generated by a Western culture to which none of them had previously paid much attention? As we saw in a previous chapter (Chapter 27), after centuries of resisting foreign influences, Japan quickly but selectively began adopting Western ways that ultimately transformed it into a modern power that could rival Europe (see Chapter 44). China, on the other hand, could hardly have chosen more different ways of dealing with the new situation. Nor could the outcomes have been more different. After a century of resistance to Westernizing ways and internal warfare, by the opening of the twentieth century, China was suffering a collapsing government that attempted to preside over a society torn by unbridgeable gaps. Yet a "self-strengthening" reform movement was taking hold in some quarters. Revolutionary changes lay just over China's horizon, as we shall see in Chapter 44.

THE DECLINE OF THE QING DYNASTY

The Qing Dynasty had originated outside China in Manchuria and had come to China as conquerors, ruling from 1644 onward. This last dynasty of imperial China was notably successful in its early generations (see Chapter 26), but by the mid-nineteenth century, it had weakened considerably. Problems such as overpopulation and famine developed in parts of China, while the almost entirely agrarian and handicraft-based domestic economy stagnated. Declining control over trade by the government and trade disputes with Western powers deepened these crises.

The Opium Wars

China's modern history begins with the **Opium Wars** (1839–1842). In the late eighteenth century, the British East India Company had developed a lucrative trade in Indian opium with south China. The drug had at long last given Westerners an exchange commodity for the teas, silks, and other luxury goods they imported from China, for which they had long been forced to pay with precious gold and silver. Previously little known in China, except for limited application as a medicine, millions of Chinese became addicts, and its illegal trade disrupted the empire's finances. The period from 1816 to 1830 saw a deepening of this predicament as Britain, driven by the ideology of free-market capitalism and her search for new markets, applied heavy pressure on the emperors to open their seaports to trade. For many years, the emperor had confined the opium dealers to Guangzhou (gwahng-choh; British Canton), but now British envoys insisted that other ports be opened to free passage, especially for the odious opium trade.

After some ineffective protests to the East India officials and the British government, the emperor decided to take strong measures to prevent the drug's importation in the 1830s. He appointed an experienced official, Lin Zexu (lihn zeh-shoo), as his imperial commissioner for trade to deal with the problem. Lin Zexu implemented a policy that placed firm restrictions on imports and provided for the rehabilitation of addicts. His efforts to confiscate and destroy opium stores led to a naval war, which was predictably one sided, given the huge differences between British and Chinese weaponry and naval tactics. The outcome was that in 1842, the Beijing government was forced to sign the first of the **unequal treaties** between a weakening China and the Western powers. China, in effect, lost control of some of its territory and its trade patterns to a foreign power. The treaties opened up the previously closed Chinese coastal towns to British consuls, merchants, and missionaries. (This was the beginning of the British colony of Hong Kong.) British residents were now to be subject to British law, not Chinese law. Although not specifically mentioned in the treaty, the opium trade would continue.

The treaty with Britain was followed by others with France and, later, with the United States, Russia, and Germany. All of the treaties were similar. All were extorted from a Chinese government that was still attempting to deal with the West as its ancestors in the sixteenth and seventeenth centuries had dealt with foreigners—as a superior dealing with inferiors. This was by now so far from reality that it became a bad joke among the Europeans. With the exception of some missionaries who were intent on bringing Christ to the Buddhist or Daoist masses, most Europeans in China in the nineteenth and twentieth centuries were there as imperialist fortune seekers. The Chinese resented these Westerners intensely, humiliated by their new inability to protect themselves from the "foreign devils."

The Taiping Rebellion

The region of China that perhaps suffered most from European interference was the south. There, by the 1840s, the lives of hundreds of thousands of the native Hakka (hahk-kah) people were disrupted by the corrosive effects of opium. From the severe social and economic tensions this produced, there arose a prophet-like figure to lead his people out of their misery. Hong Xiu-quan (hung shoh-chwen) began his career as a failed Confucian scholar who later was exposed to Christian missionary teachings. In a dream, he claimed to have been visited by God and Jesus, who revealed that he was Jesus's younger brother sent to create a heavenly kingdom in China. Hong Xiu-quan's anti-Confucian theology formed as his visions continued through the 1840s and 1850s, and the Taiping phase of the movement grew to include millions, many of whom formed a radically egalitarian, socialist utopia in which property was shared and a stern code of sexual behavior was enforced. By the 1850s, they were ready to turn against the ruling dynasty.

Thus, the 1850s through the early 1870s was a period of severe unrest and rebellion as the **Taiping Rebellion** became more widespread and more disastrous. For more than twenty years, during which the Chinese suffered perhaps 20 million deaths, rebel generals led a motley band of poverty-stricken peasants and urban workers against the Qing emperors. The Taipings' success in the early years of the revolt brought them wide support from many educated Chinese, who were sickened by the government's inability to resist the foreigners. The upheaval was encouraged by several factors:

- Discontent with the corruption and incompetence of the government officials.
- The rapidly worsening problems of overpopulation in much of south China.
- The strong appeal of Hong's prophetic visions.
- Hong's promise of a new millenarian order that would follow the overthrow of the Qing rulers and their Confucian elites.
- The total ineffectiveness of the Qing armed forces.

The Taipings extended control over most of southern and central China. From 1854 to 1864, they established the *Heavenly Kingdom of Great Peace* and a countergovernment, with their capital at Nanjing. Hong originally enjoyed sympathy from the West, in part because he seemed to want to imitate Western ways. Some thought he was the would-be founder of a Christian China. But the Taipings also opposed opium smoking and further giveaways of Chinese rights to foreigners. The Western

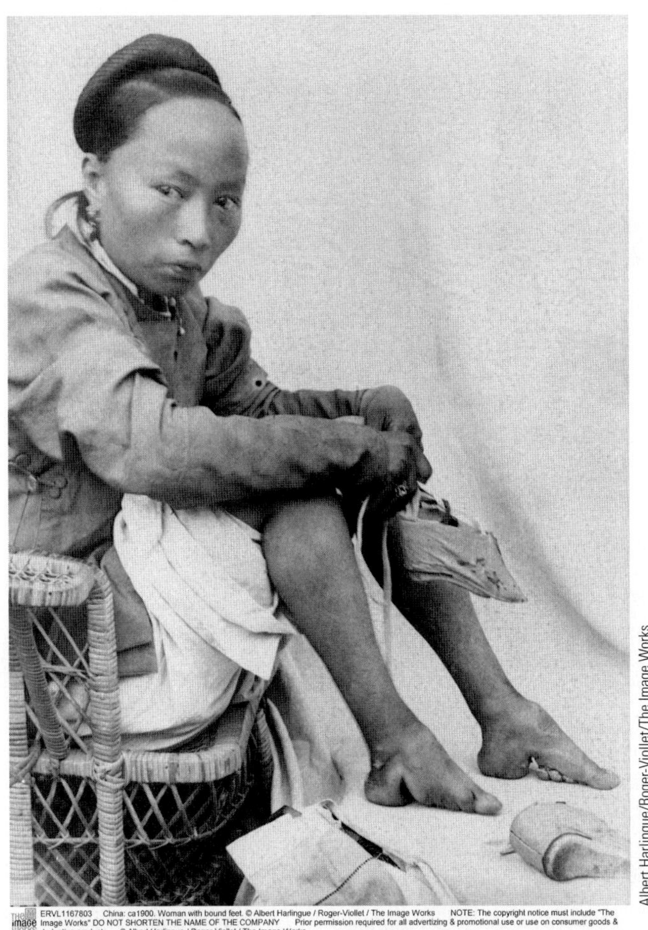

CHINESE WOMAN WITH FEET DEFORMED BY BINDING, C. 1900. In pre-modern China, small feet were considered to be a mark of beauty and status in women. Upper class mothers began the painful process of bending and binding their girls' feet around the age of four when the bones were still soft.

powers thus opted to support the Qing because they knew the government would give them little trouble in the future. At that point, the rebels began to quarrel among themselves; by 1864, they were breaking up. Also, although slow in responding, the Qing eventually defeated the Taipings. Hong was killed and tens of thousands of Taiping rebels were massacred in Nanjing. The defeat saved the ruling dynasty, but in the wake of the rebellion and the Opium War, Chinese leaders began to search for ways of reforming the state.

FAILURE OF THE LATE QING DYNASTY RESTORATION

The government was unexpectedly saved by a group of provincial officials and landlords. They organized regional armies to take the place of the failed central forces. Their effort is known as the *late Manzhou restoration* of the 1870s.

The new governors were reformers, and their **self-strengthening movement** was aimed at restoring vitality to the court and giving China the means to hold its own against the foreign barbarians once more. In the 1870s and 1880s, the movement sought to modernize the Qing state and its army; a modern weapons industry appeared, which included new shipyards and arsenals. In the area of statesmanship, they created an agency for translating Western books. A new ministry was formed for handling the sensitive relations with the Western powers. They addressed the peasants' myriad problems by instituting land-reform measures and encouraging them to grow new crops with more nutritive value. Long-neglected public works programs, such as flood-control projects on the Yellow and Yangzi rivers, were taken in hand with good effect.

Despite these efforts, the foreign powers continued to treat China as an inferior state. Additional military embarrassments piled up. In 1884, the French defeated Chinese forces and established control over Vietnam. Worse, the Chinese were decisively defeated in the first Sino-Japanese war, which China fought with Japan in 1894–1895 over Korea. Japan later annexed Korea and thus announced that it was replacing China as the most powerful Asian nation (a shift that remained in effect until Japan's defeat in World War II).

CHINESE DISINTEGRATION AFTER 1895

The defeat in 1895 was an even ruder shock to the Chinese leaders than the string of humiliations by the Westerners had been. For many centuries, the mandarins had looked on Japan and the Japanese as pitiable imitators of infinitely superior China. Now, modern weapons and armies had been shown to be superior to refined culture and Confucian integrity, even in non-Western hands.

In the wake of the defeat, China again had to submit to a wave of foreign imperialist pressure. Russian, German, and British, as well as Japanese, trade extortions were forced on the Beijing officials, backed by governmental threats. Christian missionaries were granted unprecedented freedoms to attempt the conversion of the mostly unreceptive natives. Coastal enclaves became special spheres of interest for one power or another. The Chinese government conceded that its ancient tributary of Vietnam was now the property of the French colonialists. Control of Korea had been surrendered to Japan (over the heads of the Koreans). Manchuria was all but given to the Russians in the north. (See Map 37.1.)

In 1895, these embarrassments triggered protests and demands for political change. The response was yet another, more determined cycle of reforms. In what is called the *100 Days of Reform*, the emperor issued a series

MAP 37.1 The Partition of China
The European powers never succeeded in making China into a colony, but they partitioned large portions among themselves and Japan.

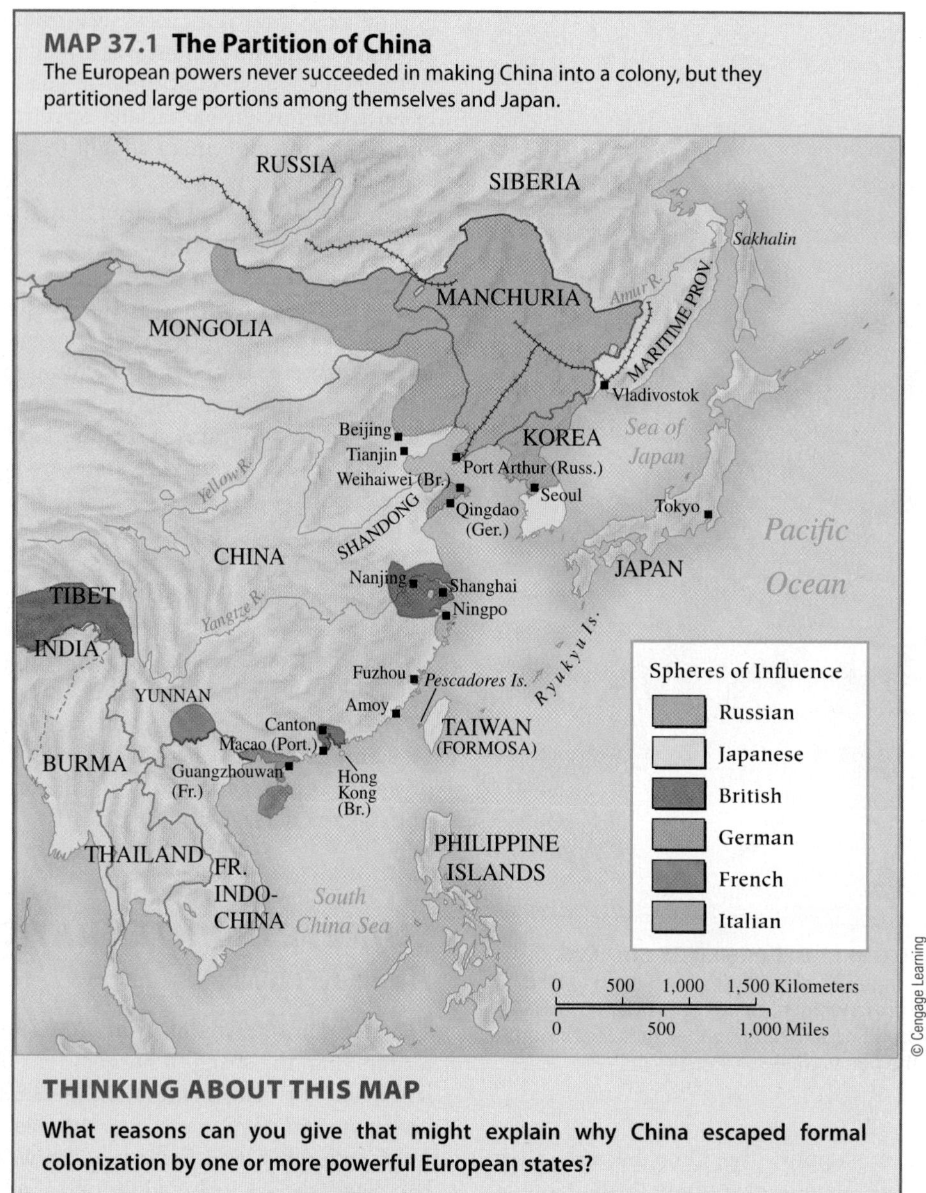

THINKING ABOUT THIS MAP

What reasons can you give that might explain why China escaped formal colonization by one or more powerful European states?

of edicts designed to streamline the government, permit greater public access to officials, and modernize the educational system with the inclusion of Western subjects in the curriculum.

This attempt to blend West and East had only partial success. Reactionary attitudes remained too strong to be overcome among conservative Manzhous and scholar-officials. The **Empress Dowager Cixi**, who managed to hold on to power for almost fifty years (1861–1907), was not opposed to reform in principle, but she was also not in favor of it if it compromised the powers of the Qing dynasty. The only thing that mattered to her was retaining her own position. An expert in political infighting, she was a kind of evil genius of China's government, pulling the strings for many years in the name of her son and her nephew, both powerless child-emperors.

The **Boxer Rebellion** (1900) was an attempted answer to this wave of foreign exploitation. The Boxers were a quasi-religious society who believed that they had nothing to fear from bullets. Rebelling at first against Beijing, they changed their course when the manipulative old empress joined with them in starting a crusade to cleanse China of the foreign devils, but the Boxers had no effective leadership or weaponry. After a few months, an international military force shipped off to China from various European capitals defeated the rebellion and further humiliated the tottering dynasty by demanding cash indemnities. The failure of the Boxers convinced even the most conservative leaders that the old Confucian-based government could no longer be maintained. China had to change or disappear as a state, and a series of radical reform proposals now came forth from various quarters, the subject of which will be taken up in Chapter 44.

Portrait of the Empress Dowager Cixi (1835–1908) (oil on canvas) (see also 209281 for detail), Chinese School, (19th century)/Summer Palace, Beijing, China/The Bridgeman Art Library

EMPRESS CIXI. Dressed in formal court costume, the empress is shown at the height of her powers around the turn of the twentieth century.

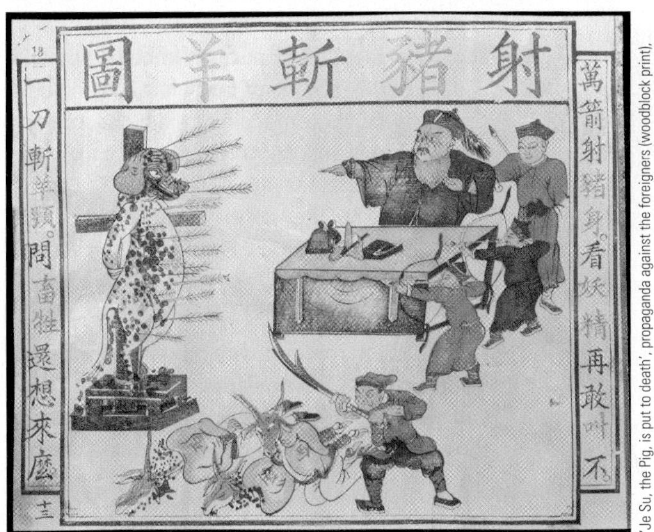

'Je Su, the Pig, is put to death', propaganda against the foreigners (woodblock print), Chinese School, (19th century)/Private Collection/The Bridgeman Art Library

"JE SU, THE PIG, IS PUT TO DEATH." This Chinese print from the time of the Boxer Rebellion depicts rebels executing Christians ("Je Su") and foreigners.

THE BEGINNINGS OF CHINESE NATIONALISM

By the end of the nineteenth century, a small but growing handful of young Chinese had been given a Western-style education, generally through the influence of missionaries who had adopted them. The most important of these was the intellectual Kang Yu-wei (kahng yoo-way; 1858–1927), who argued against the common notion that Confucian philosophy represented an unchanging and unchangeable model of government and society. Kang Yu-wei taught that Confucius was a reformer and that reform was a basic ingredient of his philosophy. Kang believed that history was evolutionary, not static, and that history was moving forward in China—as in the rest of the world—toward democratic government.

Collectively, Kang's ideas were called the *New China Movement*, and they spread widely among educated people in the 1890s. By 1898, the stage was set for an attempt at revolution from above, similar to that carried out by Peter the Great in eighteenth-century Russia. But this attempt was not successful, and its supporters in Beijing were forced to flee for their lives. For a few more years, under the manipulations of the empress, the status quo prevailed. It was clear that if China were to be changed, it would have to be done from below by the exasperated and desperate people.

An important step toward a new China was the abolition of the Confucian examinations for government office in 1905. This move opened the way for aspiring officials with modern ideas, many of whom had been educated in the West or in rapidly Westernizing Japan. The Western-educated liberal **Sun Yat-sen** (soon yaht-sehn; 1866–1925) was the intellectual leader of an antigovernment reform movement that quickly swept the whole country. Sun Yat-sen was trained as a medical doctor in Honolulu and Hong Kong, and on returning to his country, he gradually became convinced that a revolution from below was the only answer to China's many ills. He took up the cause of reform ("Three Principles") among the overtaxed and impoverished peasantry, believing that China could regain political harmony only after a measure of social justice had been established.

The long-awaited revolution against the feeble and incompetent government came in 1911. After Cixi's death three years previously, the dynasty was so weak that few would defend it when it was challenged. Originally, Sun was called to head the new parliamentary government, but to avoid civil war, the head of the army, General Yuan Shikai (yoo-ahn shee-keye), soon replaced him. The Republic of China was formally declared in 1912. The last child-emperor was forced to abdicate and lived long enough to see the installation of Mao's communist government many years later.

For a few years, General Yuan Shikai was master of China and intended to become the next emperor, but his failure to stop the Japanese incursions on the coast during

LAW AND GOVERNMENT

The Father of Modern China

Frequently called the "father of modern China," Sun Yat-sen was instrumental in the overthrow of the Qing monarchy in 1911. When the Republic of China was created in 1912, he was chosen as its first president, and later he helped found the Kuomintang (Nationalist) Party.

Sun Yat-sen was born in 1866 to a peasant family in a village near Macao. In his early years, he was given a traditional Chinese education, but at thirteen he went to live with an older brother in Honolulu, Hawaii. He enrolled in a Christian missionary school, where he was given a Western-style education, learning English among other things. Fearing that Sun would convert to Christianity, his brother sent him back home to China about four years later. But the years he had spent in Hawaii had changed Sun forever; under the influence of his US teachers in Honolulu, he had become disdainful of traditional Chinese religious belief. So, on returning to China, he was disturbed by the relative backwardness of his countrymen. (In later years, Sun acknowledged that the words Abraham Lincoln spoke in his Gettysburg address, that government was "of the people, by the people, and for the people," helped to formulate his own thinking about the role of government, as described in his book, *Three Principles of the People.*)

Within a year, Sun returned to Hawaii to complete the education he had begun. (And he was, in fact, eventually baptized as a Christian.) After several more years of study in Hong Kong, he graduated in 1892 with a degree in medicine. Convinced that the conservative monarchy stood in the way of China's modernization, he soon felt moved to abandon his medical practice to devote himself full-time to the political transformation of his country. Because he had never received training in the classics of Confucian philosophy, it proved impossible for him to be accepted by the country's ideological elites. From that time on, he called for the complete abolition of the monarchy and the social and intellectual leadership that had supported it since the time of the Zhou Dynasty nearly 2,500 years before.

He returned to Hawaii for the second time in 1894 and set about organizing Chinese exiles like himself into a proto-nationalist political society called the *Revive China Society*, with the idea of replacing the monarchy with a government organized along the lines of a modern people's republic. Following a failed coup attempt in 1895, he spent the next sixteen years traveling through Europe, North America, and Japan organizing and raising money to support his cause, using Japan as his principal base. Eventually, he aroused concern in Japan because of the size of his following there, so the Japanese government had to deport him.

Nevertheless, his efforts were rewarded in 1911 when a spontaneous military uprising in China's south ended 3,500 years of imperial rule in his homeland. Although Sun seems to have played no direct part in the rebellion, upon returning home, a meeting of nationalist leaders in Nanjing voted him into office as president pro tem of the newly proclaimed Republic of China. However, China remained divided between the south, which supported the Republic, and the north, which still lay under the control of regional warlords such as the powerful Yuan Shikai. Sun tried unsuccessfully to lead a revolt to unseat Yuan, but once again was forced to flee to Japan, where he began the organization of the Kuomintang.

In 1917, he returned home, seeking safety among his supporters in the south with the express purpose of doing what he could to unify China. At Guangzhou, he established a military academy to begin staffing and organizing an army for a northern expedition to unseat Yuan and the other politicians and warlords who had kept the country divided. (Chiang Kai-shek was its commandant.) To strengthen his hand, he created a strategic alliance with Mao Zedong's Communist Party of China, the CPC-KMT United Front. After 1924, he and the KMT also received assistance from the United States and Japan that enabled them to conquer the north.

Unfortunately, Sun did not live to see the final consolidation of nationalist power in China. He died in 1925 at the relatively young age of fifty-eight, one year before the unification. Many have debated his actual contribution to the history of modern China. Whatever judgment one makes, certain facts speak for themselves: The life he led of continuous struggle, frequent exile, and courageous challenges to imperial authority and the northern warlords made him a key figure in the cause of Chinese modernization. His successes at funding the revolutions of his lifetime kept the movement alive, and his ideological flexibility allowed him to forge large numbers of Chinese of various political stripes into a powerful and effective movement.

ANALYZE AND INTERPRET

How does Sun compare with other modernizers in world history? What similarities and differences do you see, for example, between his struggles and those of Muhammad Ali Pasha or Kemal Ataturk?

SUN YAT-SEN AND CHIANG KAI-SHEK. Sun Yat-sen (*seated*), shown here with the young Chiang Kai-shek, was the founding figure of Chinese nationalism. He helped depose the last Qing emperor and establish the Chinese Republic in 1912.

World War I made him unpopular, and he died in disgrace in 1916. For the next decade, China was in anarchy, ruled by warlords (local strongmen, often ex-bandits) with private armies. More important was the fast growth of fanatical nationalism among the urban classes, particularly the educated youth. Sun was the theoretical leader of this movement, but he was a poor organizer, and the national party he founded, the Kuomintang (kwoh-mihn-dong), split into many factions during the 1920s.

The whole nationalist-reformist phase of China's development in the early twentieth century is called the *May Fourth Movement* because of an incident in 1919 when thousands of Beijing students and youth protested the Versailles Treaty's gift of a part of China to Japan. The movement had no single leader, and its various subgroups went off in many directions. Eventually, the reform ideas it propagated would provide some of the momentum for the communist takeover after World War II. Mao Zedong himself was one of the outraged students who swore that China would no longer be the pawn of foreigners and capitalists who exploited Chinese backwardness.

SUMMARY

What effect did this have on Asians? The large number of converts to Christianity was the most significant cultural change. Reactions to this and the encroachment of foreigners in China produced a series of xenophobic popular uprisings whose failures only served to embolden the colonial powers further. Ultimately, this forced China and many parts of Southeast Asia to implement reforms on one hand, but also helped foster a potent nationalism on the other.

The twentieth century dawned for China much as the old century had ended, with further humiliations suffered at the hands of foreign occupiers, especially the Japanese. The country remained grievously enfeebled by a monarchy that was able to do little to stop the breakup of the Chinese homeland among foreigners and domestic warlords. The Chinese people had responded to the growing crisis with a series of popular, though failed, proto-nationalist rebellions and would-be reformers of various stripes. Both nationalism and reform eventually came together in the formation of the Kuomintang Nationalist Party (KMT), led by Sun Yat-sen. In late 1911, Sun and his followers removed the last emperor and declared the founding of a republic in January 1912.

IDENTIFICATION TERMS

Test your knowledge of this chapter's key concepts by defining the following terms. If you can not recall the meaning of certain terms, refresh your memory by looking up the boldfaced term in the chapter, turning to the Glossary at the end of the book, or accessing the terms on the CourseMate website at **www.cengagebrain.com**.

Boxer Rebellion
Empress Dowager Cixi
Opium Wars
self-strengthening movement
Sun Yat-sen
Taiping Rebellion
unequal treaties

FOR FURTHER REFLECTION

1. The text describes the leader of the Taiping rebellion, Hong Xiu-quan, as having been "prophet-like." What is a prophet? How do you think the term might have been appropriate for Hong? Why do you suppose that this peasant uprising assumed these religious overtones?
2. What other rebellion against foreigners had religious overtones? Did it seem to have a positive agenda, or was it purely a negative expression of popular feelings about change?
3. What seem to be the differences between a reform movement and a revolution? Compare and contrast the self-strengthening movement with the Taiping rebellion in terms of their leadership, social composition, ideology, and aims. Which of these might have been a revolution?
4. In your opinion, would it have been possible for Chinese nationalism to have emerged without the preceding reform and revolutionary movements? Were there nationalist overtones in some of the previous failed campaigns?

TEST YOUR KNOWLEDGE

Test your knowledge of this chapter by answering the following questions. Complete answers appear at the end of the book. You may find even more quiz questions on the CourseMate website at **www.cengagebrain.com**.

1. The principal reason for forcing the sale of opium in China was to
   a. profit the British government.
   b. stir up resentment among Chinese against Qing rule.
   c. serve as payment for Chinese silk, tea, and other luxury exports.
   d. provide increased revenues to the British Crown.
   e. turn Chinese peasants into drug addicts.
2. As a result of the Opium Wars, China's government was forced to accept the first of the so-called
   a. reform treaties.
   b. mercantile treaties.
   c. unequal treaties
   d. opium treaties.
   e. opium memoranda.
3. China's defeats at the hands of Japan and the major European powers resulted in
   a. the end of the Qing dynasty.
   b. the decline of Chinese innovation and productivity.
   c. concessions of port facilities along its rivers and coastlands.
   d. both b and c.
   e. both a and c.
4. The Heavenly Kingdom of Great Peace was established by
   a. the emperor.
   b. the reformer Lin Zexu.
   c. peasant opium consumers.
   d. Sun Yat-sen.
   e. Taiping rebels.
5. The self-strengthening movement for the most part was
   a. a reassertion of power by the Qing emperor.
   b. entirely directed by the Emperor.
   c. belated and failed attempt at modernization by Qing officials.
   d. belated and successful movement of reform and modernization.
   e. an attempt by Court officials to return to past methods of government and warfare.
6. The years that saw the most rapid deterioration of imperial authority in China were
   a. during the Opium Wars.
   b. during the Taiping wars.
   c. the reform years.
   d. during and after World War I.
   e. after 1895.
7. During the reforms (or "self-strengthening") years, the role played by the Empress Dowager was one of
   a. a silent though enthusiastic supporter of needed changes.
   b. total indifference.
   c. a powerful ally of the reformers.
   d. a conservative opponent of reform.
   e. a conservative who advocated only limited reforms.
8. Foreigners and Christian converts had most to fear for their safety from/during the
   a. Opium Wars.
   b. Taiping rebellion.
   c. Boxer rebellion.
   d. unequal treaties.
   e. reforms.
9. The principal reason(s) for Sun Yat-sen's success in leading the nationalist movement was
   a. the lack of leadership from other quarters.
   b. the valuable help he received from Chiang Kai-shek.
   c. his ability to raise funds and to mediate between people adhering to different ideologies.
   d. his strong training in ideology and ability to win people over to it.
   e. his alliance with Mao Zedong.
10. In the waning years of the nineteenth century and the early years of the twentieth century, China endured its greatest humiliations at the hands of
    a. the United States.
    b. Russia.
    c. Korea.
    d. Japan.
    e. Britain.

CourseMate

Visit the CourseMate website at **www.cengagebrain.com** for additional study tools and review materials for this chapter.

38 Latin America from Independence to Dependent States

America is ungovernable. Those who served the revolution have been ploughing the sea. —SIMÓN BOLÍVAR

1810s–1820s	Wars of independence throughout Latin America
1822–1889	Brazil independent under a constitutional monarchy
1830s–1850s	Chaos, military coups, and caudillos
1850s–1900s	National consolidation under oligarchies
1898	Cuba and Puerto Rico break with Spain

CHAPTER OUTLINE

The nineteenth century in Latin America was full of paradoxes and contradictions. The *criollos* of the late colonial period were eager to take power from the *peninsulars,* but their position of dominance over the lower classes depended on the legitimacy of the Crown's authority. In the Spanish colonies, the criollos were forced to declare independence to avoid liberal reforms from Madrid. The protracted wars of independence lasted from 1810 to 1825, but the following thirty years were anything but peaceful. With the monarchy gone (except in Brazil's independent monarchy), the center could not hold, and the criollo factions in most countries—lacking any political experience—could not unite to find a middle ground between the extremes of absolutism and republicanism. A new period of violence and civil wars, punctuated by despotic military regimes proclaiming themselves as saviors of society, lasted until the second half of the century, when the next generation of elites dressed their oligarchies (government by a few) in republican clothing. The booming **monoculture** economies (that is, economies reliant on just one or two cash crops) were based on exporting raw materials, which brought high prices because of growing demand in the industrialized world. As a result, the Latin American economies were dependent on foreign imports and investment, a type of economic colonialism that, in the following century, would lead to debilitating economic and political dependence on more-developed countries. Meanwhile, the masses benefited little from independence; the new elites, following the colonial tradition, ignored the needs of the poor on whose labor they depended. Century's end saw the creation of new, politically aware middle and working classes who would challenge the oligarchies in the twentieth century.

THE INDEPENDENCE MOVEMENTS

The Movement for Independence in Hispanic America

By 1800 in Spanish America, the peninsulars and criollos, although legally equal in status, had actually become two distinct castes with conflicting interests. The criollos had become dissatisfied with rule by Madrid and Lisbon for reasons both commercial and political. Criollo resentment of the Spanish colonial regime was high because, although the Bourbon free-trade reforms had made the colonies more prosperous, they were forced to pay higher taxes, and the Crown still treated the colonies merely as sources of wealth for Spain. To raise revenues, the Spanish king appropriated money from the colonial Catholic Church, which, to meet Spain's demands, had to reclaim all outstanding loans. This move upset both the ruined criollo entrepreneurs and the unpaid priests, who then turned against the mother country. Educated criollos who had been exposed to the Enlightenment ideals of individual liberty and equality and who had been inspired by the French and American revolutions, began to contemplate independence from Spain. Most of all, they aspired to a political revolution so that they might replace the peninsulars in the highest positions—something that had been denied them for centuries. The criollos were not interested in revolutionary social change or in improving the lot of the lower classes. In fact, in many areas, they were outnumbered by the Africans, Indians, and mixed-blood peoples and felt threatened by them. The successful slave revolt in Haiti as well as rebellions by the subjugated groups in Mexico and Peru served as a warning to the criollos to avoid social reforms to protect their own interests.

In the decade between 1810 and 1822, one after another of the Iberian colonies in the Americas declared their independence and escaped from the grip of the mother countries. The revolts against Spain, Portugal, and France were not uprisings of the common people against their masters and landlords. On the contrary, with the single exception of the black slaves in French Haiti, the native-born whites who formed the elite class led all of the revolutions. After the persecution of rebels like the Venezuelan criollo Francisco de Miranda, who in 1806 led a handful of U.S. volunteers in an ill-fated attack against the viceroyalty of New Granada, most criollos limited themselves to discussing their ideas of liberation under cover of the scientific and economic clubs that had been fashionable under the Bourbon kings.

The Napoleonic invasion of Spain and Portugal in 1808 (see Chapter 30) set in motion independence movements throughout the colonies. The Spanish monarchs were taken to France, and Napoleon's brother occupied the throne of Spain. The criollos' first concern was that Napoleon's victory over the Spanish and Portuguese monarchies would result in some type of radical, anti-elite reforms in the colonies. To prevent such reforms, various criollo groups in the Spanish colonies proclaimed that they were severing their colonial ties and taking over political leadership. They summoned the town councils, the one place where criollos had power, to determine their response to the sudden absence of the Spanish king. Would they transfer their obedience to the viceroys until the Spaniards defeated the French and the king was back on his throne? Or would they form their own local governments, to rule in the monarch's name, as occurred in Spain?

From Mexico to Argentina, the councils declared new governments and banished the viceroys on the authentic grounds that the colonies legally belonged to the Spanish crown, not to the Spanish nation. The new criollo governments would ostensibly be stewards of the American colonies until they could be returned to the king. It was not long before the king's representatives, the viceroys, were driven out and independence was declared. After a long struggle, the peninsulars followed the viceroys into exile. Altogether, the wars of independence of the Spanish colonies lasted more than fifteen years, from 1810 to 1825, when the last Spanish soldiers left Peru.

Three of the Latin American warriors for independence were particularly important:

1. *Miguel Hidalgo,* the Mexican priest who started the revolt against Spain in 1810;
2. *José de San Martín,* who liberated Argentina and Chile with his volunteer army; and
3. *Simón Bolívar,* who liberated northern South America and is the best known and most revered of the three. Bolívar, a farsighted and tragic hero, ultimately failed at his self-appointed task of uniting the various regions under a U.S.-style federal constitution. At the end of his life, after seeing one constructive plan after another fail as a result of apathy and greed, a depressed Bolívar declared, "America is ungovernable ... elections are battles, freedom anarchy, and life a torment."

In each colony, other men also contributed to the success of the rebellions: Agustín Morelos in Mexico, Bernardo O'Higgins in Chile and Peru, and Portuguese Prince Pedro in Brazil, among many more. But it should be repeated that, outside of Haiti, the revolts were led and carried out by conservative or wealthy men who had no interest at all in social reforms or political equality.

After Napoleon's eventual defeat, the restored monarchs of Spain and Portugal were far too weak and too preoccupied to interfere with the internal affairs of their colonies. The faint hope of the Madrid government that it could find European support for an overseas expedition to "restore order" was put to rest in 1823 when U.S.

president James Monroe issued the **Monroe Doctrine**, aimed at protecting Latin America from European interference. Within a few years, no less than nine sovereign states had appeared from the wreckage of the former Spanish dominions, and a generation later, this number had reached eighteen. All hope of a large, integrated entity reaching from Texas to Cape Horn soon had to be abandoned because regional and personal quarrels came to the fore.

The great question in the early years of the revolutions in Latin America was whether the new governments should be monarchies or republics. The example of the newly independent United States was well known in Latin America, and many criollos thought that a republic was the only form of government suitable for the new nations (see Map 38.1). But many were fearful of the power of the mob, and especially of the *mestizos* and blacks. They rejected the sharp break with tradition that a republican form of government necessarily represented; instead, they wanted a monarchy. The struggle between the two schools of thought went on throughout the revolutionary decades of the 1810s and 1820s. Except in Brazil, the battle was eventually won by the republicans, who protected the rights of property and the existing social structure by placing supreme powers in a legislature elected through a narrowly drawn franchise. The efforts of some to introduce democratic forms were generally resisted until the twentieth century.

GENERAL SIMÓN BOLÍVAR, INDEPENDENCE HERO. Images and statues of the revered "Liberator" are seen all over South America.

Brazil

The Portuguese colony of Brazil took a more peaceful route to independence. When Napoleon's army reached Portugal, the royal family sought refuge in Brazil, ruling what remained of their empire from their court in Rio de Janeiro. Eventually, when the king and queen returned to Portugal, the Brazilian elites, preferring a monarchy, pressured Prince Dom Pedro to remain in Brazil. After he submitted to their entreaties, Pedro declared independence and led a constitutional monarchy, which ensured the unity of the new nation. By then too weak to do otherwise, the once-great imperial power, Portugal, chose not to make any effort to retain her colony. Thus, the transition to independence was far smoother for Brazil than it was for Spanish Latin America.

Although Brazil faced the same obstacles of regional separatism, conflicts between conservatives and liberals, and questions about the role of the Church, Brazil's constitutional monarch worked with the various factions to resolve the problems of the newborn nation. In 1889, after progressive King Dom Pedro II supported the emancipation of the African slaves, the same elites who had supported him turned against him because their wealth depended on slave labor. Dom Pedro was ousted by an unlikely coalition of these disgruntled elites and liberal factions that for decades had pushed for a democratic republic and the end of the monarchy.

The main outlines of nineteenth-century politics were delineated by the struggle between liberals and conservatives. On the liberal side were those inspired by the French Revolution's original goals: the liberty and fraternity of humankind and the abolition of artificial class distinctions. Mostly from the embryonic middle stratum of society, they regarded Bolívar as their leader and thought the proper form of political organization was a federation, exemplified by the United States. Most of the liberals came from a commercial or professional background and were strong promoters of economic development.

The conservatives were generally either landed gentry or had connections with the powerful Catholic clergy. Like all conservatives, they primarily emphasized stability and protection of property rights. They looked on the Indians and mestizos as wards who could be trained only gradually toward full citizenship but who in the meantime had to be excluded from political and social rights. The conservatives would support a republic only if their traditional preferences were guaranteed; if not, they could be counted on to finance and direct the next "revolution."

38.1 Latin America in the Early Nineteenth Century
s map shows the changes in status after 1804, when Haiti was effectively made independent by a slave rebellion.

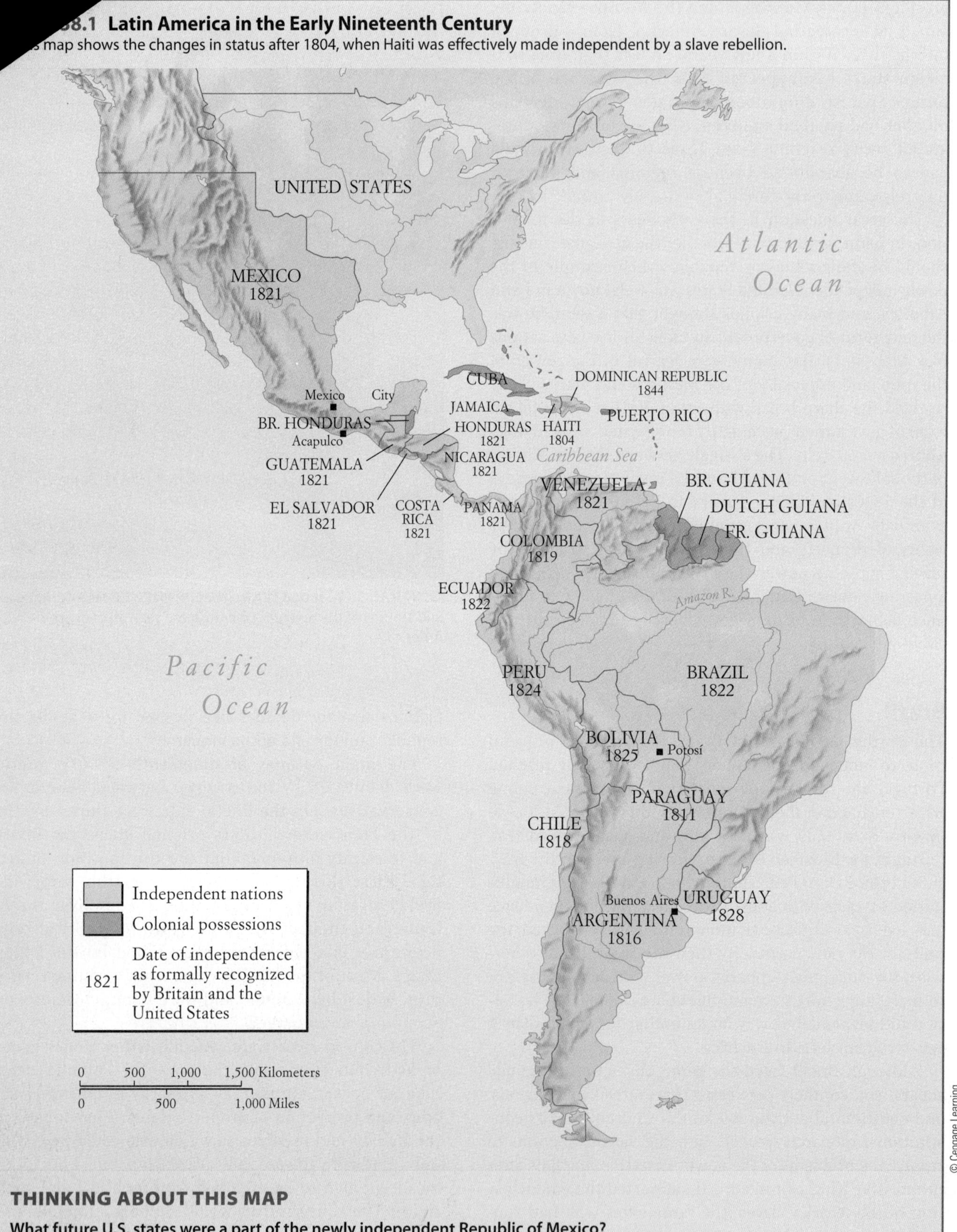

THINKING ABOUT THIS MAP

What future U.S. states were a part of the newly independent Republic of Mexico?

THE AGE OF CHAOS AND CAUDILLOS

Bolívar once said, prophetically, "I fear peace more than war." The thirty years of instability and violence that followed the wars of independence proved that his fears were well founded. Latin America lacked three elements present in the newly independent United States: a middle class with a strong work ethic, experience in self-government, and a fairly homogeneous population. Economic instability also undermined the new regimes. In the 1820s, the new (secular) Mexican and Argentine governments ruined their international credit standing by defaulting on debts to British lenders. Everywhere in Latin America, the civil government operated in the shadow of the military, and the frequent dictators almost always came from the army ranks. A small group of wealthy individuals who were closely linked with the military officer corps tightly controlled government policy. The prestige of the military man was an unfortunate consequence of the battles for independence—unfortunate, that is, for constitutional process and the rule of law.

Few of the Spanish American nations escaped the anarchy and chaos of the 1820s to the 1850s that gave rise to the military strongmen. The frequent "revolutions" and "manifestos" were shadow plays, disguising the raw greed that impelled almost all of the actors. The vacuum of authority, left by the deposed monarchy and a weakened church, resulted in the reassertion of regionalism and the power of the local political bosses, which the colonial regime had just barely been able to contain.

The ***caudillo*** [cow-DEE-yo], the epitome of the military strongman, would rise and assert populist dictatorial rule for a time. He maneuvered for supreme power, using a combination of personal charisma, force of arms, political skills, and patronage. The caudillos who achieved national prominence were the only leaders who had proven capable of quelling the endemic squabbling among the numerous petty regional chieftains. Almost always, these individuals soon made peace with the large landlords and other criollos who had traditionally governed. Social reforms were forgotten for another generation, while the caudillo became corrupt and wealthy. When internal affairs seemed to become too dangerous for their continued survival, many caudillos would find one excuse or another to divert attention by starting a war with their neighbors. For this reason, much of Latin America was at war over pointless territorial disputes throughout most of the nineteenth century.

One of the most infamous examples of such a caudillo is Juan Manuel Rosas, who ruled Buenos Aires, then all of Argentina, from 1828 to 1852. Born a criollo, as a young man, he rejected all things Spanish, acquired a large ranch, and created a successful beef-salting business. He trained himself to be expert at the skills of the *gauchos*, gaining the respect of his gaucho ranch hands and eventually subduing the gaucho chieftains who were ravaging Argentina with their warfare. As governor of the province of Buenos Aires, Rosas aspired to the presidency; however, he did not stage a national coup. Instead, he astutely waited until the civil wars had become so destructive of social order that the Buenos Aires elites begged him to seize control as president with unlimited powers.

Rosas adopted the federalist label while governing as an authoritarian centralist. He called himself "Restorer of the Law," but his opponents called him "Tyrant of the Argentine." His crimes against the people far outweighed the economic improvements he managed to achieve. Rosas's personal police force mercilessly persecuted anyone who opposed him, from peasants to intellectuals. Meanwhile, the elites, who were anxious for peace at any price, looked the other way when the heads of innocent victims appeared on pikes in Buenos Aires. Rosas was finally deposed by a coalition of the gauchos who realized that they had been duped and exiled intellectuals whose writings turned international opinion against the tyrant. Rosas's most constructive legacy was that the movement to oust him unified Argentines of all factions against his despotism.

During the second half of the nineteenth century, liberal leaders such as Domingo F. Sarmiento (sahr-MYEN-toh) in Argentina and Benito Juárez (WAH-rehz) in Mexico—who established the foundations of oligarchic civil republics—replaced the military caudillos. Brazil, Chile, Uruguay, and Costa Rica also achieved constitutional stability based on civil governments. Unfortunately, the lower classes in these republics were excluded once again; in fact, they were considered an obstacle to progress. What is more, in most Hispano-American countries, the authoritarian tradition of the strongman leader predominated during the nineteenth and well into the twentieth century.

BRAZILIANS CHEER THEIR NEW KING. Dom Pedro I liberated Brazil; he and his son, Dom Pedro II, were benign constitutional monarchs.

NATIONAL CONSOLIDATION UNDER OLIGARCHIES

During the second half of the century, a new generation of elites in Argentina, Mexico, Chile, and a few other countries recognized the need for reconstruction after decades of civil war. The political and economic reorganization of the new states took place according to the principles of liberalism: secular government, the protection of individual property rights, free trade, and modernization following European models. The liberal reforms were initially more successful in Argentina than in Mexico.

Argentina's Constitutional Government

After the fall of Rosas, Argentina's civil governments took crucial steps toward modernization and political organization under a new constitution. The southern Indian territories of Patagonia were conquered, and hostile Indians were either subdued or exterminated. After decades of disputes between Buenos Aires and the hinterland, Buenos Aires became a federal district and capital of the country. The infrastructure was developed with the help of the British: Roads and railroads were built, barbed wire sectioned off the Pampas into ranches, and a large-scale livestock industry was developed. Under Sarmiento, the "Schoolmaster President," public schools were created, and primary education was declared free and obligatory. Henceforth, Argentina would have one of the highest literacy rates in the Western Hemisphere. Immigration was encouraged to help populate the empty territories and to "improve" the racial mix. The liberal leaders denigrated Hispanic traditions and the mestizo culture of the gauchos and emulated what they saw as the superior civilizations of the United States and Britain.

The Age of the Caudillos in Mexico

Mexico during the second half of the century, after the overthrow of its most notorious caudillo, Antonio López de Santa Anna, faced more obstacles to national organization than did Argentina. The Catholic Church and its conservative supporters were more entrenched, and the mestizos and Indians more numerous. Benito Juárez, a full-blooded Zapotec Indian who, like his contemporary, Abraham Lincoln, rose from humble origins to become president, is revered as the spirit and soul of his country and protector of its independence.

Juárez was a liberal reformer who also planted the seeds for a whole series of changes in the national consciousness of his country toward the relative importance of criollo and mestizo values. In a society long known for its aristocratic views, he awakened Mexican nationalism and steered his people on the lengthy and rocky path toward political democracy. As minister of justice in the new government that succeeded Santa Anna, Juárez was primarily responsible for the creation of the strongly liberal

Roger-Viollet/The Image Works

BENITO JUÁREZ, FATHER OF MODERN MEXICO. President Juárez is depicted here as a visionary, with the Constitution of 1857 and the reform legislation that he championed. (His gold funeral mask lies in the foreground.)

and reformist Constitution of 1857. All of these activities brought him the solid opposition of the conservative elements, notably the entrenched landowners and the higher churchmen. This opposition led to the War of Reform (1858–1861), in which the liberals were able to beat back the challenge of the reactionary groups and preserve the constitution under Juárez's leadership as acting president.

After the War of the French Intervention (1862–1867)—when Napoleon III tried in vain to make Mexico a French colony—and a final failed attempt by the Mexican conservatives to install a monarchy, Juárez was reelected president. However, the struggle between liberals and conservatives was as fierce as ever and showed no signs of abating after the victory over the French. Like other Latin American reformers, Juárez ended his life painfully aware of the difficulties of getting his fellow Mexicans to agree on even the most basic elements of political and social progress. Mexico was not yet ready for the ideals put forth in the Constitution of 1857. The reaction to the reform came in the forty-year dictatorship under the caudillo Porfirio Díaz. The vision of Juárez and the liberal reformers would be realized only after the Revolution of 1910–1920, when the Constitution of 1917 reintroduced the principles first put forth in 1857, such as secular education and separation of church from state.

By the last quarter of the nineteenth century, members of the once-idle criollo elite class in Argentina, Mexico, and elsewhere had become entrepreneurs in their booming export-based economies. Their prosperity was linked with the Gilded Age in Europe and the United States; in fact, because the Spanish American countries exported raw materials and imported the products they did not yet produce, their wealth came from a kind of economic colonialism. The criollos were interested in pursuing political power to protect their agriculture, livestock, and mining interests. Accordingly, they imposed political control either indirectly through mestizo dictators (like Díaz in Mexico and his peers in Venezuela), or directly through nominally republican oligarchies where elections were fraudulent (in Chile and Peru). The railroads built to carry products to the ports were also used to transport federal troops to quell local uprisings. By ensuring stability, the elites were able to attract foreign investment and, in turn, promote growth of the import-export economy. By the early twentieth century, Latin America had developed some textile and food-processing factories, and the service industries were robust (transportation, government bureaucracy, and commerce, among others). Two results of the growing native enterprises were to have repercussions far into the following century. First, there was the creation of an urban, educated middle sector (professionals, merchants, and small businessmen) that would demand to be included in the power structure. Second, the streams of immigrants who were invited to join working classes (except in Mexico and Cuba, which had large indigenous or African workforces) organized into mutual societies and eventually labor unions, creating demands for better pay and working conditions.

SOCIAL DISTINCTIONS

In the constitutions that were worked out after independence, all legal distinctions among the citizens of the new states were declared void. Slavery was abolished in most of them, but social class distinctions persisted. The Latin society of the colonial period had already evolved a clear scale of prestige: The "pure-blooded" criollos were at the top, various levels of Europeanized mestizos were in the middle, and the Indians, the non-European African-Indian peoples, and black ex-slaves were at the bottom. This order was reinforced by the prevailing nineteenth-century "scientific" theory that the white masters were inherently superior to their workers of color.

States with numerous pure-blooded Indians (most of South and Central America) refused to allow this group to participate as equals in either political or cultural life and made no effort to introduce them into national public affairs for several generations. These restrictions were not necessarily a bad thing: Most of the Indians had neither experience nor interest in government beyond the village levels. Because people were born into their places on the scale, Latin American society is frequently called a "classist society." Status was largely visible at a glance because skin color was an important factor in determining who was who.

Although Latin American society had a distinct social gradient by complexion that was (and is) taken for granted, the system was relatively free of the legal and political prejudice against the dark-skinned population that the people of the United States only partly overcame in the Civil War. Furthermore, blacks and Indians had more opportunity for mobility in Latin America than in North America. Latin American society was willing to consider light-skinned mulattos and mestizos as equivalent to Europeans rather than holding that miscegenation (mixed blood) was an insuperable obstacle to social status. Relative wealth, skills, and education counted for more than blood alone. For example, if an Indian left his village and traditional lifestyle and became Hispanized, in terms of lifestyle and social status, he was no longer considered an Indian. Mexican president Juárez (see previous discussion), who was Indian by birth but criollo by lifestyle, epitomized the social mobility of the fortunate gifted individual of humble origins.

In free Latin America, as under Spain, the towns were the center of everything that was important: politics, administration, cultural events, commerce, and industry. The criollos were disproportionately prominent in the towns. The countryside was inhabited by the bulk of the population: mestizo or Indian small farmers, farm and pastoral laborers, and many hundreds of thousands of people who had no visible means of support. The absentee landlords lived in town, looked toward Europe, and left daily control of the rural plantations to agents and managers.

For the mestizo and Indian masses, life was a losing struggle against poverty; the people lacked good land in rural areas and industrial jobs in the cities. The ruling group lacked the enterprising spirit that would be needed to induce change for the better. Although slavery was forbidden, **peonage** became commonplace on the haciendas. Peonage was a form of coerced labor that served to repay real or alleged debt owed to the employer; it was not much different from slavery for the victim and perhaps even more lucrative for the master.

The universal backwardness of the rural majority was a chief reason for the stagnation of national politics throughout most of the nineteenth century. Illiteracy and desperate poverty were normal; the hierarchy of social classes from colonial days did not change. The Indians, blacks, and their mixed-blood offspring remained mostly outside public life, although they technically became free and equal citizens when slavery was abolished. (Brazil did not abolish slavery until 1888, when it became the last of the Western Hemisphere countries to do so.)

Prosperity and modernization under the oligarchs brought new opportunities for young women, particularly in the cities. Influenced by feminists in Britain and the United States, progressive women questioned the "science" that deemed them intellectually inferior to men.

SOCIETY AND ECONOMY

Women's Voices in Nineteenth-Century Latin America

Equal education was the watchword for nineteenth-century Latin American women activists. Only some privileged women from progressive families received advanced educations (with private tutors). Many of these fortunate women became educators and self-taught journalists, tirelessly advocating education as an indispensable first step toward women's emancipation. Because they invaded traditionally male domains, these women were ridiculed and marginalized. The pioneers discussed here, having been recovered from oblivion by twentieth-century feminist scholars, serve as reminders of the many forgotten women leaders.

The Mexican schoolteacher, writer, and activist, Dolores Jiménez y Muro (hee-MEN-ehz ee MOO-roh; 1848–1925), devoted her life to the liberal republican ideals that she learned in her parents' home during the Juárez presidency. After her parents died, Jiménez learned self-reliance by managing the family estate. She chose to remain single rather than abandon her work as teacher and activist. Jiménez published widely in prose and poetry, but most of her works appeared under pseudonyms and are difficult to identify. She was one of the first Mexican women political journalists, serving as mentor to women writers half her age. Jiménez worked and wrote on behalf of exploited women and children factory workers. During the Díaz dictatorship (1876–1910) and the ensuing Mexican Revolution (1910–1920), Jiménez was an opposition journalist also known for her contributions to composing important rebel documents. Mexicans now revere her as a teacher, revolutionary, and feminist.

Peruvian novelist, journalist, and teacher, Clorinda Matto de Turner (1852–1909), came from a prosperous landowning family. She completed her education at a convent school, married an English businessman, and was widowed before she was thirty years old. Matto de Turner published pseudonymous poems and essays in various journals. She subsequently founded and edited journals in Peru and became well known in intellectual circles. Matto de Turner published controversial novels of social protest that were sympathetic to the exploited Quechua Indians. Matto de Turner fled to Argentina in 1895 after losing her house and printing business in a government coup. Once in Buenos Aires, she contributed to numerous publications and founded a magazine that advocated women's emancipation. She was one of the first Latin American women to develop an international readership.

Narcisa Amália de Campos (1852–1924) was a poet (like her father) and a teacher (like her mother) and became Brazil's first professional woman journalist. While still a teenager, she left her husband—scandalous behavior for a woman of the times. During her twenties, she published her poems to great acclaim and was a famous poet by age thirty. (Romantic or patriotic poetry was the only acceptable genre for women writers.) Campos was a passionate progressive, republican, and abolitionist. She held renowned literary salons during her short-lived second marriage. Campos escaped from her jealous husband, relocating to Rio de Janeiro. There, she took up teaching and founded a bimonthly journal for women; in this and numerous other publications, she advocated the abolition of slavery and defended the rights of women. Critics excoriated her for authoring "unfeminine" political articles, such as her "Emancipation of Women." Campos responded, "some gentlemen of the press ... worry that their wives might heed my call and abandon their stewpots to march for women's liberation." She was already suffering the health problems that made her give up journalism. Campos was blind and paralyzed when she died at age seventy-two.

ANALYZE AND INTERPRET

What similarities do you see among these women's lives? Why do you think women writers published anonymously or pseudonymously? Comment on the other causes, besides education, that these writers championed.

Previously limited to domestic or religious endeavors, unattached women began entering traditionally male fields of endeavor. To meet labor demands, new vocational schools produced the first women secretaries, typesetters, and bookbinders. Women of means and dedication could now become teachers, doctors, lawyers, and journalists. These pioneering professional women led the earliest movements to improve the lives of women and children (see the Society and Economy box). The legal and social restrictions on married women continued into the twentieth century.

LAND AND LABOR

A few families, who often claimed descent from the conquistadores, held land (the source of livelihood for most people) in huge blocks. Sometimes they had land grants from the king to prove it; more often, their ancestors had simply taken over vast tracts from the helpless Indians. Because land was useless without labor, first the Indians and then (in Brazil and the Caribbean) imported blacks were forced to work it as slaves.

Slave agriculture is normally profitable only where monoculture plantations can produce for a large market. For this reason, Latin American agriculture came to be based on one or two export crops in each region—an economically precarious system. Originally, the cash crops were sugar and rice destined for the European or North American markets. Later, bananas, coffee, and citrus in the more tropical lands and cattle and wheat in the more temperate climates became the main exports. Almost all the labor of clearing land, raising and harvesting the crop, and transporting it to market was done by hand. Machinery was practically nonexistent well into the twentieth century, because with labor so cheap, the landholders had no need for machines.

The size of the *latifundios* (lah-tih-FOON-dyos), or huge rural plantations, actually grew after independence. Their owners were practically little kings within the republics. Although these great landowners did not carry formal titles of nobility after independence, they might as well have done so because they comprised an aristocracy in the truest sense. Mostly of European blood, they intermarried with one another exclusively; their sons went into high government office or the army officers' cadres by right of birth. In the nineteenth century, this aristocracy lived very well, in both the material and the intellectual senses, but they inherited the lack of social responsibility that also marked their ancestors. They either could not see or would not recognize that the miserable conditions of the majority of their fellow citizens eventually posed a danger to themselves.

LATIN AMERICAN AND CARIBBEAN CULTURES

The prevalent culture of Latin America owes as much to the European background of its original colonists as does the culture of North America. The two differ, of course. The ideas and values introduced into Latin America were predominantly Spanish or Portuguese, Roman Catholic, and patriarchal rather than British, Protestant, and (relatively) genderless as in the United States and Canada.

Whereas Iberian culture is supreme on the mainland, the Caribbean islands reflect the African origins of their black populations. The native Amerindian populations of the islands were exterminated or fled early and have been entirely supplanted by African ex-slaves and mulattos. Thus, the Caribbean culture is different from the Iberian and is not properly considered a part of Latin America.

From these different roots different societies have developed. As an example, until recently, public life in Latin countries was as much dominated by males as were ancient Greece and the Islamic civilizations. The adoption of the Napoleonic codes of law in these countries contributed to the persistence of the idea that the male is legally and socially responsible for the female. On the contrary, the black ex-slave societies of the Caribbean islands followed the African example of giving females a quasi-equal position in private and—to some degree—public affairs.

The Catholic Church in Latin America

The Catholic Church in Latin America was guaranteed a supervisory role in most aspects of public life and private morals. It was from the start and remained an official church, supported by donations and taxes. It had little competition. Catholicism was the religion of the vast majority of the general population and of the entire ruling group. (As in the European homelands, Latin America has simultaneously had a strong tradition of anticlericalism.) The high clergy were automatically men of influence and did not hesitate to intervene in political affairs when they sensed that the Church or their own family interests were threatened.

In the nineteenth century, the Church was responsible for most educational institutions and practically all social welfare organs. At times, in some places, the Church made a sincere effort at lifting the Amerindians and poor mestizos toward justice and dignity, even when doing so meant breaking with the ruling group from which much of the higher clergy came, but these episodes were the exception. Class ties generally seemed stronger than a sense of obligation to the common people, and the clergy were content to conform to the current ideas of their lay peers.

The Importance of Culture

Cultural stratification is particularly strong in Latin America and has long been an obstacle to national unity. Until the early twentieth century, the landowner–official group who controlled public life regarded themselves as Europeans residing in another continent, rather than as Latin Americans—much as the British colonists regarded themselves as Britons living in Australia or the French settlers regarded themselves as French living in Africa. The elite read European literature, taught their children European languages in European-directed schools, and dressed in current European fashions. When they grew tired of their surroundings, they often spent a year or two in a European capital. Many sent their older children to European schools and universities as a matter of course. When asked about family origins, young men and women would say that they came from some Spanish town, which their ancestors had left (often as poverty-stricken emigrants) 300 years previously! They did not recognize a Latin American culture that was separate and distinct from Iberia. They spent much of their lives attempting to keep up with contemporary European culture and trying to replicate it in their alien environment.

ARTS AND CULTURE

Multicultural Music: Argentina's Tango and Brazil's Samba

After independence, the upper classes tended to emulate European culture, as they had during the colonial period. In contrast, the lower classes (including masses of immigrants) were creatively weaving the indigenous, African, and Spanish cultural traditions into new hybrid forms (especially along the Atlantic coast). Innovative music and dances, such as the tango in Argentina and the samba in Brazil, exemplify the richness of ethnic diversity in Latin America. The Argentine tango emerged in the 1870s in the immigrant areas of Buenos Aires, where rootless people of diverse ethnicities gathered to console themselves with plaintive musical strains drawn from several cultural traditions. The tango blends elements of the African-based candombe (see picture) and the habanera (hah-bahn-AIR-uh) from Cuba. Another strand of tango traces to the gaucho singers of oral traditions and to the indigenous elements of rural folk dances. The last instrument added to the tango ensemble was the small German squeezebox accordion, first brought to Buenos Aires by an Italian immigrant. The tango, with its sensual movements and obscene lyrics, was first rejected as sinful by "decent" society. Over time, a more refined form of the tango has become a symbol of Argentine nationality.

Brazil's samba music and dance also had humble origins and were originally reviled by the upper classes. Afro-Brazilians in the northeastern Bahia region held religious ceremonies where spiritualist priestesses called "aunts" invoked the gods through song and dance accompanied by drums and other percussion instruments. With the abolition of slavery in 1889, there was mass migration to the shantytowns on the hills around Rio de Janeiro. Here, the portly aunts in ample white costumes continued their backyard spiritualist ceremonies. Meanwhile, the samba felt the influence of the city's popular music, including the imported polka and habanera. Neighborhood samba societies formed as a creative outlet for the poor, and these societies (called "schools") would entertain other shantytown neighborhoods during Carnival (the week before Lent). Rio's famous Carnival celebration began in the 1890s and soon incorporated competitive performances by the samba societies. The competitive aspect of samba traces directly to the traditional dance contests that are still held in Africa.

DANCING TO CANDOMBE DRUMS. The Afro-Uruguayan candombe [kahn-DOME-bay] street dance dates from the early 1800s, but its roots are in African ceremonial processions recreated by slaves on the South American coast.

ANALYZE AND INTERPRET

Compare and contrast the origins and development of the tango, the samba, and what you know about U.S. jazz.

A powerful reason for the great difference between Latin and North American social habits and history in this regard was that the whites in Central and South America perceived Amerindian culture as a much greater threat than did the European settlers of North America. The Amerindians of Latin America were far more numerous than their North American cousins. The Spanish and Portuguese conquerors wanted to maintain a sharp distinction between themselves and the natives. This distinction gradually gave way, as a result of the large number of ordinary people who intermarried with the Indians and created the mestizo culture that predominates in many present-day Latin countries. But the ruling class rigorously maintained the distinction, remaining at heart Europeans who lived in Peru, Brazil, or Colombia—not Peruvians, Brazilians, or Colombians. For them, intermarriage was unthinkable.

SUMMARY

We have seen how difficult It was for Latin America to make relatively rapid transitions from colonial states to independent statehood. One should remember this period in the history of the Latin American nations not only for the violence, turmoil, and imperfect results, but also for the extraordinary feat of accomplishing in less than a century a process that took three or four hundred years in other parts of the world.

Criollo resentment against continued foreign rule increased under the late colonial reforms. Armed rebellion against Spain followed on the North American and French models, and by 1825, the colonials had established independent republics that Spain and Portugal could not recapture. Independence proved easier to establish than governing the new nations, however. Military men and local caudillos became the ultimate arbiters of politics, despite grand-sounding manifestos and constitutions. An urban elite of absentee landlords maintained power despite numerous "revolutions."

The agrarian economy became dependent on the exports to western European and North American states. The rural majority lived in agrarian villages or on haciendas in conditions that differed little from serfdom. Little manufacturing could develop because of both the widespread poverty of the internal market and the openness of that market to imports from abroad. By the end of the nineteenth century, Latin America was tied perhaps more closely to foreign economic interests than it had ever been in the colonial era. The newly formed nations could not become truly politically independent because their economic dependence on countries such as the United States and Britain led to interference in their internal political affairs.

The disparities between the governing criollo cliques and the mestizo, black, and Amerindian masses were underlined by cultural orientations. The members of the upper class considered themselves Iberians and Europeans displaced in a Latin American atmosphere.

IDENTIFICATION TERMS

Test your knowledge of this chapter's key concepts by defining the following terms. If you can not recall the meaning of certain terms, refresh your memory by looking up the boldfaced term in the chapter, turning to the Glossary at the end of the book, or accessing the terms on the CourseMate website at **www.cengagebrain.com**.

caudillo
monoculture
Monroe Doctrine
peonage

FOR FURTHER REFLECTION

1. Identify the various socioeconomic classes in Latin American society in the nineteenth century. What effects did independence from Spain have on each class?
2. Spain's first New World colonies, the Caribbean islands of Cuba and Puerto Rico, were the last areas to be lost by Spain (in 1898). What historical factors might explain this seventy-year delay relative to the rest of the Spanish American colonies, which were independent by 1825?
3. A century ago, Argentina and the United States, both rich in natural and human resources, appeared equally capable of becoming strong, stable nations. Compare and contrast the economic development of the two countries from 1850 to 1900.
4. Popular Latin American music, dance, and literature emerged from among the people. Describe the blending of cultures (African, Amerindian, and European) in these forms of artistic expression.

TEST YOUR KNOWLEDGE

Test your knowledge of this chapter by answering the following questions. Complete answers appear at the end of the book. You may find even more quiz questions on the CourseMate website at **www.cengagebrain.com**.

1. The only successful rebellion by slaves in the Western Hemisphere occurred in
   a. Haiti.
   b. Cuba.
   c. Colombia.
   d. Brazil.
   e. Ecuador.

2 Which of the following does *not* describe the conditions under which the Latin Americans gained independence?
   a. In the wake of the Napoleonic invasion of Spain
   b. As a result of the Spanish king's intolerable tyranny
   c. As a counter to a feared movement toward radical democracy
   d. Inspired by the successful North American and French revolutions
   e. The criollos' resentment of being subordinate to the peninsulars
3. Brazil avoided a violent transition from colony to nation because
   a. the plantation slaves, although numerous, were prevented from fighting.
   b. the colonial Brazilians had plenty of experience with self-governance.
   c. Brazil, by choice, operated as a constitutional monarchy for much of the nineteenth century.
   d. the Brazilian criollos were more interested in fiestas than in politics.
   e. the British intervened and stopped the budding revolution.
4. The women writers Jimenez y Muro, Matto de Turner, and Campos all
   a. attended co-educational universities.
   b. wrote exclusively about women's education and emancipation.
   c. were teachers, journalists, and political activists.
   d. had permission from their husbands to pursue writing careers.
   e. adhered strictly to the norms of conduct for Catholic women.
5. The tango of Argentina and the samba of Brazil were both
   a. upper-class entertainments that gradually became popular with the masses.
   b. sensual dance music created by poor people of different ethic backgrounds.
   c. forms of poetry cultivated by pioneering women writers.
   d. traditional Castillian folk music of great prestige.
   e. practiced predominantly on the Pacific coast of Latin America.
6. Presidents Juarez of Mexico and Sarmiento of Argentina both
   a. were military caudillos who ruled as tyrants.
   b. were full-blooded Amerindians who rose to power.
   c. instituted oligarchic governments to replace dictatorships.
   d. regretted the demise of monarchy in the Americas.
   e. relied for support on the Catholic church.
7. The Latin criollos of the independence movement were interested mainly in
   a. obtaining more land for themselves.
   b. keeping U.S. influences out of their homelands.
   c. achieving the installation of popular democratic government.
   d. ousting Europeans from their countries.
   e. maintaining political control against the Indian or mestizo masses to protect their livelihoods.
8. Which of the following is most correct? Racism in the Latin countries has traditionally been
   a. wholly contingent on the economic position of the affected person.
   b. expressed as prejudice but not persecution against the dark skinned.
   c. less overt but more harmful overall to good relations than in North America.
   d. divorced from skin color but reflective of religious prejudices.
   e. harshly practiced and based completely on a person's color.
9. Which was the last country in the Americas to outlaw slavery?
   a. Honduras
   b. Brazil
   c. United States
   d. Mexico
   e. Argentina
10. *Monoculture* and *latifundio* are terms usually associated with
   a. pastoral societies.
   b. self-sufficient farmers.
   c. the growing of garden produce for local consumption.
   d. large-scale forced-labor production for export.
   e. nomadic gauchos.

CourseMate

Visit the CourseMate website at **www.cengagebrain.com** for additional study tools and review materials for this chapter.

39 Modern Science and Its Implications

Discovery consists of seeing what everyone has seen and thinking what no one has thought. —ALBERT SZENT-GYORGI

1859	Charles Darwin, *The Origin of Species*
1871	The Descent of Man
1880s–1920	Marie Curie, Max Planck, Albert Einstein, Sigmund Freud, Carl Jung, Ivan Pavlov
1891	*Rerum novarum*
1895–1920	Émile Durkheim and Max Weber
1920s–1930s	Christian revival

CHAPTER OUTLINE

In the west, the eighty years between 1860 and 1940 proved to be one of the most dazzling periods of innovation and change in intellectual history. In the last years of the nineteenth century, it was still possible for sophisticated persons to hold to a Newtonian view of the universe: The physical world or cosmos was a composition of law-abiding matter, finite in its dimensions and predictable in its actions. Fifty years later, most of the "hard" or natural sciences and especially physics, biology, and astronomy had been radically changed by some new factual data and many new interpretations of old data. The social or "soft" sciences such as psychology, sociology, and economics had undergone a somewhat lesser transformation, although here the novel ideas encountered more resistance because they could not easily be demonstrated as factually correct.

Religion, too, experienced striking changes. Long in retreat before an aggressive secularism, some Western Christians had come to believe that their religion was evolving like other human thought and that the Bible was properly subject to interpretations that would differ sharply in various ages and circumstances. But some fundamentalist denominations moved instead toward an uncompromising insistence on literal interpretation of the Bible as the sole source of God's unchanging truth.

THE PHYSICAL SCIENCES

In the second half of the nineteenth century, the mental frame of reference implied or dictated by rationalism and science became much more commonplace than ever before. By century's end, educated individuals throughout most of the Western world accepted the proposition that empirical science was the main source of accurate and valuable information. Religious revelation, authority, and tradition were not seen as legitimate rivals.

In the first half of the twentieth century, the preponderance of science over competing worldviews became stronger still. Theology and philosophy, which previously had some persuasive claim to presenting a comprehensive explanation of the processes and purpose of human life, became the narrowly defined and exotic preserves of a handful of clerics and academics. In the universities of the West, which became for the first time the recognized intellectual centers of the world, the physical sciences became increasingly specialized while attracting more students. Meanwhile, armies of scientific researchers garnered the lion's share of academic budgets and prestige. Although ever-fewer people were able to understand the intricacies of the new research, the educated public still maintained its belief in the method of science and its handmaiden technology as the most efficacious way of solving human problems. This viewpoint was weakened but survived even the cataclysms of the two world wars.

Biology

The shift from theology to science and hence from spiritual to material causation had begun with the Scientific Revolution of earlier days (see Chapter 29), but certain nineteenth-century ideas hastened its pace greatly. Darwinian biology was perhaps the most important.

In 1859, Englishman **Charles Darwin** published ***The Origin of Species***, a book that did for biology what Adam Smith's *Wealth of Nations* had done for economics. The controversy the book set off roiled European and American society for more than a generation and generated acrid public and private debate. In the end, the Darwinian view generally won out over its detractors.

What did Darwin say? Basically, he argued that through a process of **natural selection**, the individual species of plants and animals (inferentially including humans) evolved slowly from unknown ancestors. The organisms that possessed some marginal advantage in the constant struggle for survival would live long enough to create descendants that also bore those assets in their genes. For example, a flower seed with sufficient "feathers" to float a long distance through the air would more likely find suitable ground to germinate than those with few or none. Slowly over time, that seed type would come to replace others in a given area and survive where others died off.

This is a mechanical explanation of nature's variety and of the evolution of species. It is similar to stating that an automobile moves along a highway because its wheels are propelled by a drive shaft and axles, which are themselves driven by a motor. That is all true, of course, but it leaves out any mention of a person sitting in the driver's seat and turning the ignition key. Darwin carried Isaac Newton's mechanistic explanation of the cosmos into the domain of living things. In so doing, he eliminated the role of an intelligent Creator, or God, who had ordered nature toward a definite purpose and goal: glorifying himself and instructing humans. God was superfluous in Darwinian science and, being superfluous, should be ignored.

Darwin carried this theme forward with his 1871 ***The Descent of Man***, which specifically included humans in the evolutionary process. It treated the morals and ethics they developed as the product of mechanical, naturalistic processes, not of an all-knowing and directing God. If the ability of our thumbs to close on our fingers chiefly distinguishes humans from apes, as some biologists believe, then what some call the human conscience may also be just a product of evolutionary experience, aimed at physical survival rather than justice and obedience to the will of a Creator-Judge.

Contrary to general impressions, Darwin did not explain why natural selection occurs or the factors that cause some variance from the norm (a mutation) that results in the survival of one species and the expiration of others. That task was left to an Austrian monk named Gregor Mendel, who worked out the principles of modern genetics in many years of unrecognized labor with the common pea in his monastery garden. And it should be added that Darwin's work was matched, simultaneously, by the independent research of Alfred Russell Wallace, another English amateur, who never sought or received public notice until after Darwin's work had taken over the stage.

Physics

In physics, the path breakers were Ernst Mach (1838–1916), Wilhelm Roentgen (REHNT-gehn; 1845–1923), Max Planck (plahnk; 1858–1947), and Albert Einstein (1879–1955). The fact that all four were educated in German universities is an indication of the emphasis on scientific research in the German educational system. This model was gradually extended throughout the Western world.

Mach's several publications in the 1880s and 1890s contributed importantly to the underlying concept of all twentieth-century physics: the impossibility of applying philosophical logic to physical matter. Mach believed that scientists could only determine what their intellect and equipment told them about matter, not what matter actually was or did. What a later German physicist would call the "Uncertainty Principle" had replaced the Newtonian world machine and substituted mere probability for law.

Roentgen discovered X-rays, by which solid objects could be penetrated by a form of energy that made their interiors visible. His work, published at the end of the nineteenth century, immediately gave rise to experimentation with subatomic particles, especially in the laboratory of Englishman Ernest Rutherford (1871–1937). Rutherford,

CARTOON OF DARWIN WITH AN APE. Taken from an 1874 edition of *The London Sketch Book*, this caricature mocks Darwin's theory of evolution.

who was a pioneer in the discovery of radioactivity and splitting the atom, is one of the great names of modern science. His work, in turn, was materially helped by the simultaneous research conducted by French scientists Pierre (1859–1906) and Marie Curie (1867–1934), whose laboratory work with radium proved that mass and energy were not separate but could be converted into one another under certain conditions.

Planck headed a major research lab for many years and revolutionized the study of energy with his *quantum theory*, in which energy is discharged in a not-fully predictable series of emissions from its sources, rather than as a smooth and uniform stream. Quantum theory explained otherwise contradictory data about the motion of objects and subatomic matter such as electrons and protons.

Then, in 1905, the young Swiss-German, Albert Einstein, published the most famous paper on physics since Newton—the first of his theories on relativity. Einstein insisted that space and time formed a continuous whole and that measurement of both space and time depended as much on the observer as on the subjects of the measurement themselves. He saw time as a "fourth dimension" of space rather than an independent concept. Eleven years later, Einstein published his ***General Theory of Relativity***, which announced the birth of twentieth-century physics (and the death of the Newtonian model).

How does twentieth-century physics differ from the Newtonian conception? Several fundamental ideas are prominent:

- *Uncertainty.* In dealing with some forms of energy and with subatomic particles, modern science does not assume that cause-and-effect relations are reliable. Strong probability replaces certainty as the best obtainable result. Newtonian laws apply only on levels above that of the atom.
- *Relativity.* The motion and position of the observer affect the object observed, so that no neutral observation is possible.
- *Interchangeability of matter and energy.* Under specified conditions, the Newtonian distinction between matter and energy falls away and one becomes the other.

These mind-bending novelties have been recognized and acted on only by a small handful of specialists—mainly in the universities. They have removed modern physics from the comprehension of most ordinary people, even well educated ones. The assumption—so common in the nineteenth century—that physical science would be the key to a fully comprehensible universe in which matter and energy would be the reliable servants of intellect, was dashed by the physical scientists themselves. Their ever-more-exotic research and its unsettling results widened the previously narrow gap between professional scientists and educated laypeople.

This intellectual divorce between the mass of people and the holders of specialized scientific knowledge has become a subject of concern that continues to the present day. The non-specialists in positions of responsibility are often placed in an intolerable situation when dealing with economic policy, for example. Statesmen and politicians rarely comprehend the scientific background of the internal development policies they are implementing or their possible dangers. For another example, the naïveté of the early proponents of nuclear power plants, who had no understanding of the menace posed by a nuclear meltdown, became a major embarrassment, or worse. The lawmaking and political authorities were forced to rely on scientific advisers who had every professional interest in seeing the plants built. This dilemma of contemporary government is not going to be easily solved.

SCIENCE AND TECHNOLOGY

Joseph Lister, Founder of Modern Surgical Techniques

Sir Joseph Lister (1827–1912) was a pioneer in applying laboratory science to the practice of medicine. He was the first to successfully apply the germ theory to surgery, opening a new chapter in medical history. When Lister began his surgical career in Glasgow, Scotland, in 1853, most physicians simply ignored recent scientific discoveries as irrelevant to their day-to-day practices. He alone had a background in biology, chemistry, and microscopy, as well as in medicine. Lister, born near London to a prosperous Quaker family, attended Quaker schools, which were unusual in their emphasis on science and the scientific languages (French and German). Lister's father, an oculist, invented an improved microscope and taught his son to be an expert microscopist. While a medical resident in London, Lister studied biology, physiology, and chemistry with the foremost scientists of the day. He then went to Glasgow, Scotland, to work with James Syme, the renowned British surgeon.

The young Dr. Lister refused to accept the appallingly high mortality rates in hospital surgeries (really amputation wards). Glasgow was an industrial city, and the hospitals received many injured workers. The main treatment for flesh wounds of the limbs was amputation to prevent the spread of infection. Lister decided to fight the "hospital gangrene" that was killing more than half the amputees. Hospitals were dirty, airless places that reeked of rotting flesh. By 1864, Lister was aware of carbolic acid's use in deodorizing village sewage before it was spread on pastures as fertilizer. Furthermore, the sanitization process eliminated a digestive disorder that had plagued the grazing cattle. In 1865, Lister saved a boy's leg from amputation by mending his compound fracture using a weak carbolic acid solution as an antiseptic. Later, inspired by Louis Pasteur's discovery of microbes that cause spoilage in wine, Lister examined some pus from an infected wound under the microscope and saw the same bacilli that Pasteur had described. Lister concluded that bacteria also caused infection in wounds, and he accepted Pasteur's still-controversial germ theory. Lister continued to refine his antiseptic surgery methods, and mortality rates in his wards dropped sharply.

Lister devised a regime for surgery that is still followed today: hand washing by surgeons with antiseptic solution, clean masks and gloves, sterilization of surgical instruments, sutures that were sterile and absorbable, antiseptic dressings, and drainage tubes for abscesses. Because Lister's procedures have become the norm, it is hard to imagine that, when Lister introduced them, they met with fervent and prolonged opposition. Surgeons prized speed of operation above all and saw Lister's regime as a waste of time. Skeptics of the germ theory criticized the lack of proof linking specific bacteria to specific diseases. Lister avoided the public debates about the validity of the germ theory. He doggedly continued to lecture twice a week on his antiseptic surgical procedures and published his results in the new scientific journals. His ideas were eventually accepted (and improved upon) in France and Germany. By 1900, his procedures had been widely adopted in Britain and the United States.

Even those who opposed his innovative methods respected Lister's irreproachable personal and professional integrity. Lister had a distinguished career as chair of clinical surgery at the universities of Edinburgh and Glasgow, as well as at King's College, London. He had served as a surgeon to Queen Victoria; she knighted him in 1883. Lister is memorialized through the Joseph Lister Institute of Preventive Medicine in London, and the bacterial genus *Listeria* is named after him. Lister's eightieth birthday was celebrated worldwide in 1907. However, by 1927, a mere twenty years after his death, Lister's importance had been mostly forgotten.

Portrait of Joseph Lister (1827–1912), English scientist (oil on canvas) (see 130064-5, 130067), Italian School, (20th century)/Private Collection/The Bridgeman Art Library

PORTRAIT OF JOSEPH LISTER, 1827–1912.

ANALYZE AND INTERPRET

Describe some ways in which Lister applied scientific laboratory discoveries to improve patient care.

THE YOUNG EINSTEIN. This photo was taken about 1902, when Einstein was twenty-three and yet an unknown dabbler in theoretical physics.

Astronomy

In astronomy, the major changes in the scientific paradigm are more recent. The last sixty years have seen fantastic advances and an ongoing debate. The advances have been mainly technological: huge new telescopes and radio devices, space vehicles that venture far into the cosmos to report on distant planets, and spectroscopes that analyze light emitted eons ago from the stars. As a result of this new technology, we know much more about the nature of the universe than before. Space probes have revealed that planets such as Mars and Saturn are physically quite different than previously thought, whereas the moon has become almost familiar territory. The universe is now thought to be much larger than once believed—perhaps infinite—and to contain millions or billions of stars.

Strictly speaking, the debate is not astronomical in character but rather metaphysical ("beyond physics"). It revolves around how the universe was created and how it will develop. The widely supported **Big Bang theory** holds that the universe originated several billion years ago with a cosmic explosion, creating in an instant not just matter and energy, but time, space, dimension, and the very laws by which the universe is regulated. Astrophysicists know that the universe is still expanding, but into what it is expanding is not clear. Some think that the expansion will end with a general cooling and dying off of all life-supporting planets. Others believe that gravity will gradually slow the expansion and bring all of the scattered fragments together again, only to have another big bang and repeat the process.

A third group—creationists—rejects all scientific explanations and holds to the Christian tradition that an intelligent being created the cosmos and all within it in accord with a preconceived plan. In the same way, some respected scientists accept the overwhelming evidence for the slow physical evolution of humans but insist that the separate, instantaneous creation of an immortal soul within *Homo sapiens* by a God is a perfectly possible hypothesis.

THE SOCIAL SCIENCES

The social sciences have human beings, collectively or individually, as their subject matter. They include psychology, sociology, anthropology, economics, and political science. These disciplines were strongly affected by the waves of new ideas and data produced by the physical sciences in the later nineteenth century. Just as the sciences of the seventeenth-century innovators slowly percolated into the consciousness of historians and political philosophers to produce the Enlightenment, so did the innovations and technological breakthroughs of the nineteenth-century physicists and biologists affect the worldviews of the sociologists and psychologists who followed. The effect was probably most spectacular and controversial in psychology.

Psychology

Psychology has been radically altered by the widely held modern conviction that its major purpose should be to heal sick minds, rather than to merely understand how the mind works. In the twentieth century, psychiatry—the healing process—has come to be an important branch of medicine. No one individual has been more crucial to this transformation than Sigmund Freud (SIG-mund froid; 1856–1939), a doctor from Vienna, Austria, who developed a theory of psychiatric treatment called *psychoanalysis.*

Freud believed that the unconscious, not conscious, mind is the controlling factor of the deepest mental life. In effect, he was rejecting the principle of rationality—that is, that men and women are capable and desirous of reasoned acts—on which all previous psychological theory had been built. Psychoanalysis attempts to help the patient first recognize, and then do something about, the distorted impressions of reality that produce social or individual disabilities. Based on Freud's convictions, the sexual drive is the chief motor of the unconscious, childhood events are almost always the source of mental and emotional problems in adult life, and the eternal struggle between the libido (or pleasure principle) and the superego (which might be translated as conscience) will never entirely be resolved within the human mind.

SCIENCE AND TECHNOLOGY

Famous Families of Modern Science: The Curies

The pioneering work on radioactivity carried out by Nobel physicists Pierre and Marie Curie and their daughter and son-in-law, Irene and Frederic Joliot-Curie helped shaped the modern scientific world. Marie Curie was the first woman to win the Nobel Prize, and the first female professor at the famed Sorbonne University in Paris. She remains the only Nobel winner (male or female) in both physics and chemistry. Pierre and Marie's daughter and grandchildren also proved to be outstanding scientists.

A Parisian by birth, Pierre's father educated him, and at just sixteen he earned a university degree in mathematics. Just two years later he received a postgraduate degree. Together, he and his brother Jacques discovered the alpha, beta, and gamma particles.

Marie Sklodowska-Curie was born in Warsaw to a family that had fought for Polish independence. Because of her family's politics and taboos against the roles of women in public, Marie Sklodowska was unable to pursue a career in science in her native Poland. Consequently, she moved to Paris and received a degree in mathematics and physics. She and Pierre married in 1895. Pierre specialized in magnetism and crystals and invented an apparatus for measuring electrical charge. Using Pierre's instrument, Marie was able to investigate the recently discovered phenomenon of radioactivity in uranium. This result was Marie's most important scientific breakthrough: she established that radioactivity was a property of the uranium atom and not the result of chemical processes.

Pierre suspended his own research to work with Marie in a search for more radioactive elements. In 1898 they discovered two new elements—polonium and radium—and in 1902, after years of laboriously processing a ton of pitchblende, they isolated 0.10 gram of radium chloride. For this discovery, the Curies shared the Nobel Prize in physics in 1903. This brought them immediate fame, a Sorbonne professorship and laboratory for Pierre, with Marie as its Research Director.

After Pierre's untimely death in 1906 from a street accident, the Sorbonne awarded his professorship to Marie. Although devastated by Pierre's demise, she continued working to isolate pure radium metal, which she achieved in 1910. She received the Nobel Prize in chemistry in 1911. She founded the Radium Institutes in Paris and Warsaw, both of which still engage in medical research. During World War I, Marie developed mobile X-ray units for military use, facilitating the treatment of battle wounds. She died in 1934 of leukemia caused by exposure to radiation. The Curies' daughter and son-in-law, Irene and Frederic Joliet-Curie, shared the 1935 Nobel Prize in chemistry for their discovery of artificial radioactivity. Their son and daughter also are distinguished French scientists. The Curie family holds the record for the number of Nobel laureates in one family.

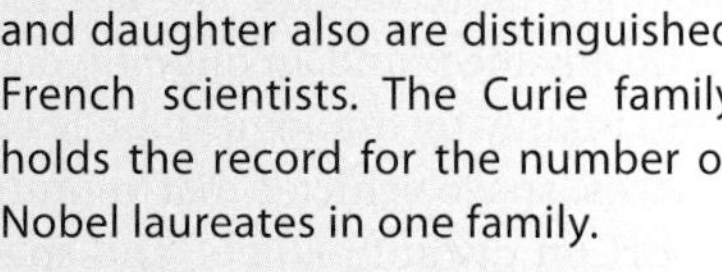

ANALYZE AND INTERPRET

How and why do you think that scientific genius sometimes is found in entire families like the Curies? Do you know of other famous families of modern science?

Historical/CORBIS

PIERRE AND MARIE CURIE WITH THEIR DAUGHTER IRENE, C. 1904

Freud has had several major competitors in explaining the mind's workings and how the sick might be cured. The Swiss Carl Jung (yuhng; 1875–1961) was one of Freud's early collaborators, but he broke with the master (as did many others) and founded his own psychological school that emphasized religious symbolism and archetypal ideas shared by all humans in their unconscious as the bedrock of mental activity.

Ivan Pavlov (ih-VAHN PAV-lof; 1849–1936) is considered the founder of behaviorism, a widely supported theory that insists that the rewards and punishments given to various types of behavior are the controlling factors of individual psychology. Pavlov's work with dogs in his native Russia before World War I made him famous. His work was importantly expanded and supplemented by Americans William James (1842–1910) and B. F. Skinner (1904–1990) in the early and middle decades of the past century.

In recent years, the former sharp division of psychologists into pro- and anti-Freud camps has softened. Although much of Freud's theoretical work is now rejected or discredited from universal application, a good deal more has been accepted as conventional wisdom. When we use terms such as *inferiority complex*, *Freudian slip*, and *Oedipus complex* in everyday speech, we are paying verbal tribute to the Austrian explorer of the mystery of inner space.

Anthropology and Sociology

Both anthropology and sociology treat humans as a species rather than as individuals. These two new sciences flourished greatly in the twentieth century. Anthropology as a scientific discipline is an indirect product of Darwinian biology, although some work was done previously. It is divided into two basic varieties: (1) physical, dealing with humans as an animal species, and (2) cultural, dealing with humans as the constructors of systems of values. Especially since World War II, great advances have been achieved in extending the knowledge of the human species far back into prehistoric time. Combining archaeology with the new subscience of sociobiology, these paleoanthropologists have learned much about the physical and cultural aspects of earlier human life. They have posited several theories and ideas about the nature of humans that sharply contradict the previous traditional concepts and have strongly influenced current anthropological research.

Sociology also came of age in the late nineteenth century. Unlike most fields of science that are the product of many disparate contributors, sociology can trace its basic theory to a small handful of brilliant individuals. First was Auguste Comte (kohmt; 1798–1857), a Frenchman whose philosophical treatise, *The Positive Philosophy*, insisted that laws of social behavior existed and were just as readily knowable as the laws of physical behavior. In this view, humans advance through three stages of ability to perceive knowledge, culminating in the scientific stage just now being entered. Truth could and must be obtained by the application of positivism, by which Comte meant that only empirical, measurable data were reliable and that a philosophy that attempts to identify spiritual, non-materialistic forces or values was falsely conceived and impossible.

Comte's view of sociology as the culmination of all the sciences inspired many imitators. In the last years of the nineteenth century, French sociologist Émile Durkheim (DERK-haym; 1858–1917) and German Max Weber (VAY-ber; 1864–1920) were equally important as formative influences. In his special way, Karl Marx was perhaps the greatest of the nineteenth-century figures who studied the "science of society."

Several Americans were also at the forefront of sociology's development, especially in the early twentieth century when American universities took up the discipline with enthusiasm. The underlying premise of sociology seemed to be particularly appealing to the American mind-set: If one knew enough of the laws of social behavior, then one could alter that behavior in positive and planned ways. This mode of thought fit well with the preeminently American view of society as an instrument that might be tuned by conscious human interventions. But in many minds, this optimism was eventually countered by profound misgivings about the course of human society.

One offshoot of the Darwinian discoveries in biology was a reexamination of human ethics. More specifically, could a code of ethics originate through a particular set of environmental influences? If so, could one type of behavior be promoted over another in some rational manner? Do ethics themselves evolve or does a superior being, as fundamentalist Christians believe, permanently instill them?

Herbert Spencer (1820–1903) was the most noted of the upholders of social Darwinism, a philosophy that held that ethics are evolutionary in nature and that free competition is the main engine of social progress. As among the plants and animals, the fittest will survive, as a ruthless nature demands. Although Spencer did not intend such a result, his philosophy of unbridled social competition made it all too easy for the powerful to justify their own positions as the proper, even the inevitable, reward for their superiority. As for the poor or the unfortunate, their misery was the equally inevitable result of their natural inferiority. Social Darwinism was a temporarily fashionable pseudo-philosophy at the end of the nineteenth century, and its adherents by no means entirely disappeared in the twentieth.

MALAISE IN TWENTIETH-CENTURY SOCIETY

With all of the triumphs scored in understanding the physical universe and the growing acceptance of science as the most certain path to useful knowledge, many people at the nineteenth century's end still felt uneasy about the road ahead. This malaise (apprehensive feeling) became much more tangible and widespread after World War I. What had happened? In unintended ways, psychology has contributed as much to the insecurity and uncertainty that cloud modern lives in the West as the revolution in physics has. Both sciences often leave the observer with the feeling that things are not as they outwardly seem. In psychology, the Freudians insist that the brute instinct is as important as the reason. In physics, matter can suddenly turn into its opposite, non-matter, and the course and nature of such transformations cannot be predicted accurately nor fully understood. Traditional knowledge is no longer applicable or sufficient, and traditional authority has shown itself incompetent to give clear answers to new questions. Freud himself claimed, with a note of ambivalent pride, that his work had finished the destruction of the medieval view of humans begun by the cosmology of Nicolaus Copernicus and continued by the biology of Darwin. Although Copernicus had reduced humankind to residents of a minor planet in a cosmos of many similar planets, Darwin had torn down the precious wall distinguishing beasts and man. Now Freud had shown that these human beings did not and could not fully control their own acts or perceptions.

These new perceptions had widespread consequences. One of the prominent features of the social sciences in the twentieth century was the spread of **cultural relativism**. The nineteenth century's assurance that whatever was the standard in Europe should become the standard of the world's behavior was largely demolished. Recent generations raised in Western culture are much less convinced that there is but one proper way to raise small children, inculcate respect for the aged, assign suitable gender roles, and so forth than was the case a century ago. An appreciation of the variety of ways to solve a generic task—such as instructing the young in what they will need to prosper—has become more common among Western people. It is interesting that this is happening at exactly the time when the rest of the world is voluntarily imitating the West in many respects. This cultural relativism is another face of the general abandonment of traditional ethnocentrism that is an earmark of late twentieth-century thought—in the West especially, but also throughout "the global village" the world has become.

RELIGIOUS THOUGHT AND PRACTICE

During the nineteenth century, the Christian Church came under siege throughout Europe. Both Catholic and Protestant believers found themselves portrayed by numerous opponents as inappropriate, even hateful relics from a forgotten medieval age who were against progress, rationalism, and anything modern.

Churches Under Attack

Attacks came from several quarters. Intellectuals, in particular, rejected the traditional arguments of religion and the clergy's claim to represent a higher order of authority than mere human beings. Liberals rejected the stubborn conservatism of the clergy and the peasants who were the church's most faithful followers. Marxists laughed at the gullibility of the pious believer ("pie in the sky when you die") while agitating against the churches, which they regarded as slavish tools of the bourgeois class, like other institutions of the modern state.

These varied attacks had substantial effect. By the 1890s, much of the middle classes refused to tithe and had little respect for the parish curate, and the European working class had almost entirely ceased to attend church. In France, only a minority of the Catholic peasantry went to hear the priest on occasions other than their wedding days. Like the English and the Germans, the French urban workers were practically strangers to organized religion. In Italy and Spain, where the papal religion was still an established church, anticlericalism was common in all classes, even though most peasants still supported the church as an essential part of their lives.

Positivist science was a strong weapon in the attackers' arsenal. The Darwinians won the intellectual battle over Darwin's biology by century's end, although the topic was still acrimoniously debated in some sectors. The long struggle over lay versus religious control of public education was settled everywhere in the West by the coming of state-supported and state-directed schools in which the religious denominations were excluded or restricted. Religious belief was removed from the qualifications of officeholders, civil servants, and voters. By the 1870s, everywhere but Russia, Jews and atheists were made fully equal with Christians in law if not always in practice. Among the larger part of the educated and influential classes, secularism was taken for granted as the wave of the future in European (and American) civic culture.

The Christian Revival

Meanwhile, the churches everywhere were struggling to renew themselves and regain at least some of the lost ground. In parts of the United States, the fundamentalist Protestant creeds became strong rivals of the Lutherans, Anglicans, and other, less aggressively evangelical churches. The somewhat similar British Nonconformists (those Protestants who did not "conform" to the Anglican credo—Methodists, Presbyterians, Quakers, and Unitarians) showed formidable tenacity in their missionary work and in their foundation of hundreds of schools.

In Germany, Chancellor Otto von Bismarck made a major error in attempting to consolidate support for his government by attacking the Catholic Church. This "Kulturkampf" ended in the 1880s with a rout of the

Bismarck forces. The Church emerged stronger than ever and founded a political party, which was the second largest in the German parliament by 1910. The necessity of meeting the Darwinian challenge and the positivist critics of the Bible made it obligatory for both Catholics and Protestants to reexamine their basis of literal belief. Soon, a school of Christian Bible exegesis on scientific foundations contributed to a revival of intellectually credible research.

In 1891, Leo XIII's major encyclical (papal letter) ***Rerum novarum*** ("about new things") broke the papal tradition of rejecting all that was new. Leo strongly supported the ideals of social justice for the working classes and the poor, while continuing to denounce atheistic socialism. For the next fifty years, *Rerum novarum* provided a guideline for loyal Catholics who wished to create a more liberal, less exploitative economic order. They frequently found themselves opposed by the clergy and their coreligionists in positions of power throughout the Western world.

World War I dealt a heavy blow to all organized religions. Many members of the clergy in all denominations were caught up in the patriotic hysteria of the early weeks of the war and outdid themselves in blessing the troops and the battleships, declaring, "Gott mit uns!" (God's on our side). The ghastly reality of the trenches quickly put an end to such claims. Radical discontent at the endless bloodletting sharpened the critiques. The clergy were denounced as willing pawns of the various governments that controlled their incomes and status. After the 1917 Russian Revolution, Marxist propaganda skillfully intensified these negative feelings both inside and outside of Russia.

A small minority reacted differently. They saw the war and the following period of upheaval as the inevitable results of a godless, mechanistic progressivism that had little of value to offer humans' spiritual nature. In the 1920s and 1930s, both Protestant and Catholic communities in the Western world experienced a perceptible, though limited, revival of Christian belief.

A few intellectuals, too, were ready to risk the contempt of their fellows by taking an overtly religious point of view in the interwar era. Among them were Paul Claudel and Etienne Gilson in France, Karl Jaspers and Reinhold Niebuhr (NEE-buhr) in Germany, T. S. Eliot in Britain, and Dorothy Day in the United States. They were a tiny minority, but that did not deter them from hoping and working for a Christian renaissance out of the blood and terror of the war.

SUMMARY

Advances in the physical sciences multiplied and fed off one another in the second half of the nineteenth century, leading to an explosive ferment in the opening half of the twentieth. Darwinian biology led the parade of theory and data that together profoundly altered the existing concepts of the physical universe and its creatures, including human beings. A new physics pioneered by German researchers overthrew the Newtonian cosmology. Somewhat later, also entering a revolutionary era was theoretical astronomy, which had its own impact on age-old habits of belief.

In the social sciences, the disputed revelations of Freud were equally disturbing to traditionalists. For those who followed the master, irrational forces beyond any awareness overshadowed human consciousness, and the soul was reduced to a biochemical entity—if it existed at all. What was left of traditional morality was ascribed to a psyche entangled in its own irrational fears and follies. Less controversially, sociology and anthropology emerged as accepted academic disciplines and provided new ways of contemplating humans as a community.

Throughout the nineteenth century, self-doubt and persuasive scientific adversaries had assaulted the Christian religion. Much of the population no longer attended or honored the traditional ceremonies. Tardily, both Protestant and Catholic churches took up the challenge. Reaction against positivist science and liberal changes in official church attitudes had assisted a slight recovery by the turn of the century. This limited revival was strengthened in the 1920s and 1930s by the revulsion against World War I.

IDENTIFICATION TERMS

Test your knowledge of this chapter's key concepts by defining the following terms. If you can not recall the meaning of certain terms, refresh your memory by looking up the boldfaced term in the chapter, turning to the Glossary at the end of the book, or accessing the terms on the CourseMate website at **www.cengagebrain.com**.

Big Bang theory
cultural relativism
Charles Darwin
The Descent of Man
General Theory of Relativity
natural selection
The Origin of Species
Rerum novarum

FOR FURTHER REFLECTION

1. Many scholars refer to the breakthroughs of the nineteenth and early twentieth centuries as the Second Scientific Revolution. In what ways did the Second Scientific Revolution build on the discoveries of the First Scientific Revolution?
2. What explanations can you give for the remarkably rapid and broad advances that occurred in the sciences in such a short span of time?
3. In what ways did discoveries in one field help induce and reinforce changes in others during the Second Scientific Revolution?

TEST YOUR KNOWLEDGE

Test your knowledge of this chapter by answering the following questions. Complete answers appear at the end of the book. You may find even more quiz questions on the CourseMate website at **www.cengagebrain.com**.

1. Darwinian biology was ultimately based on
   a. Christian theology.
   b. a mechanical view of the cosmos.
   c. a belief in random change in species.
   d. a belief in a kind of deism much like Newton's.
   e. observation of people.
2. The Uncertainty Principle refers to modern
   a. psychology.
   b. physics.
   c. history.
   d. economics.
   e. sociology.
3. The most clear-cut similarity among later nineteenth-century physicists is their
   a. belief in Christianity.
   b. involvement in an antiwar movement.
   c. reliance on individual research.
   d. unhappy domestic lives.
   e. training in German methodology.
4. Which of the following was not embraced by Freudian psychology?
   a. The superego is engaged in a struggle against the libido.
   b. The sex drive lies at the bottom of much unconscious activity.
   c. Humans are basically seeking rational answers to their difficulties.
   d. Conscious actions are often reflections of unconscious motives.
   e. Unconscious sources of mental anguish could be healed.
5. Freud's theories of psychology
   a. encouraged the belief in rational planning as an answer to misery.
   b. were supported most ardently in his home city of Vienna.
   c. were thought to be insulting by many of his colleagues.
   d. were based on the study of the behavior of animals.
   e. built on Darwin's theories of evolution.
6. Which of the following pairs is *least* logically paired?
   a. Mach and Einstein
   b. Freud and Jung
   c. Marie Curie and Ernest Rutherford
   d. Auguste Comte and Wilhelm Roentgen
   e. Charles Darwin and Alfred Russell Wallace
7. Joseph Lister's discoveries were in what field?
   a. Medicine
   b. Physics
   c. Chemistry
   d. Biology
   e. Theology
8. As a general rule, twentieth-century Christian belief in the Western world
   a. became nearly extinct after World War II.
   b. developed an entirely new view of Christ.
   c. became much stronger as a result of World War I.
   d. recovered some support among intellectuals.
   e. has never recovered from the loss of prestige it suffered because of World War I.
9. Auguste Comte believed that
   a. sociology was less important than psychology.
   b. sociology was the social science that would bring the greatest concrete changes to society.
   c. Karl Marx was the greatest nineteenth-century figure.
   d. truth could not be obtained without using the senses.
   e. sociology was the culmination of all the sciences.
10. In the *Rerum novarum*, Catholics found papal support for being
    a. more liberal.
    b. more conservative.
    c. more militant.
    d. stronger proselytizers.
    e. more socialistic.

CourseMate

Visit the CourseMate website at **www.cengagebrain.com** for additional study tools and review materials for this chapter.

Putting It All Together

1. What is a revolution? How does it differ from ordinary change? We have applied the term *revolution* to several types of sweeping change that have occurred throughout history. Make a list of the types of revolution that took place during the era covered in Part V.
2. Besides those that occurred in Europe, what revolutions took place in the American hemisphere? What spurred those revolutions?
3. How and in what ways were the revolutions of this era linked to developments that had taken place prior to 1600?
4. How are the changes and revolutions that transpired between 1600 and 1914 still affecting life in the modern world? Where are these revolutionary changes occurring today?
5. Imperialism was another hallmark of this period. How and in what ways was European imperialism linked to its revolutions? How did the imperialism of this era differ from that of the previous era, 1400–1600?
6. To what extent were the civilizations of the Americas, Africa, and Asia successful in managing the impact of Europeans on them? In what ways did they do this?

CROSS-CULTURAL CONNECTIONS

Trade and Exchange Networks

Global networks established with faster and more reliable methods of transport. Asia continues to play important role in established Indian Ocean and China Sea networks but forced open to Western trade by eighteenth century despite resistance. Western slave trade replaced by trade in raw materials for manufactured goods. European industrialization damages or destroys economies of Africans, Asians, and Latin Americans because local manufacturing and crafts production lost to cheaper imported goods. Non-Western regions gradually brought into international capitalist system.

Migrations

Europeans: Europeans continue migrations to Western Hemisphere. Smaller numbers settle in Southeast Asia and temperate areas of Africa.
Asians: Larger numbers of Africans imported as slaves in Persian Gulf and western India. Indians and Lebanese immigrate to Africa, Chinese to Southeast Asia. Chinese settle parts of Central Asia.
Africans: Slave trade peaks in nineteenth century; Africans forced to migrate to West and South Asia, Europe, and America. South Asians settle along east coast. West Asians begin settling West Africa. Europeans settle South Africa, Algeria, and Central Africa.
Americans: Native American population continues decline. Overall population grows dramatically through European and African immigration.

Spread of Ideas and Technologies

Europeans: Scientific and Industrial Revolutions spread throughout Europe. New wave of evangelical Christianity directed at new industrial proletariat. Mission societies evangelize among non-Christians of the Third World.
Asians: Christian missions become active in parts of Asia affected by European colonialism. In response, Islamic reformers advocate stricter adherence to Shari'a or selective adoption of aspects of modernity.
Africans: Greater numbers and varieties of Christian missions active, making converts and providing Western-style education for Africans. *Jihads* in Sahara and the Sudan enforce stricter conformity to Shari'a.
Americans: Scientific and Industrial Revolutions spread from Europe. United States begins industrialization. Christian missions active and win converts among Native Americans.

Worldview V

Revolutions and the Age of Empire, 1600–1914

	 LAW AND GOVERNMENT	 SOCIETY AND ECONOMY
EUROPEANS	• After French Revolution, civil law based on secular viewpoint rather than religious authority. Government steadily more sophisticated; bureaucracy universal in advanced societies. Imperialism revives in mid-nineteenth century.	• Industrialization with deep regional variations. By 1920, Northern and Western Europe far more industrial than Eastern and Southern. Mechanized, factory-based modes of production replace handwork after Second Industrial Revolution in later nineteenth century.
ASIANS	• ***East Asians:*** Japan and China encounter Western aggression after 1840. Meiji Restoration in Japan successful, but China's self-strengthening movement fails. In 1911, last emperor replaced by republic. • ***South and Southeast Asians:*** Mughal rule in India declines. British, Dutch, and French appropriate Southeastern Asia and Pacific islands. Spain acquires Philippine Islands. • ***West and Central Asians:*** Muslim regions subordinated to Western imperialism. Middle East Islamic states reduced to satellites or taken over by Europeans. Ottomans helpless to defend interests, empire crumbles. Sultans implement Tanzimat Reforms; Muhammad Ali introduces reforms in Egypt.	• ***East Asians:*** China faces overpopulation early in period; Japan prospers and urbanizes. Urban population and merchants gain prestige, peasantry sinks into further poverty. After 1867, Japan industrializes. China attempts reforms, but progress cannot overcome *traditionalism.* • ***South and Southeast Asians:*** India begins industrial development as British colony. • ***West and Central Asians:*** Economy of West Asia damaged by rise of Atlantic trade and decline of Muslim empires. Industry still unknown at end of period, and technological gap opened between West and Muslim worlds.
AFRICANS	• Western missions and individuals explore African interior. Scramble for Africa completed by World War I.	• Slaving disrupts trade in west, making some coastal states more powerful and undermining others. Agriculture aided by introduction of new crops from Americas and South Asia. Bantu-speaking areas in east and south expand trade with Arab and Portuguese coastal towns.
AMERICANS	• North Americans continue heritage of representative government. South Americans unable to translate republicanism into effective democracy; *criollos* rule over *mestizo* majority.	• North America's industrial economy explodes after the Civil War. By 1920, United States is world's most potent industrial nation. Latin America receives little immigration and capital investment; industry minimal, and agrarian society still dependent on monoculture exports.

 PATTERNS OF BELIEF	 ARTS AND CULTURE	 SCIENCE AND TECHNOLOGY
• Enlightenment and revolutions attack religion and links between state and church. After Darwin, traditional Christianity is seen as antiscientific. Philosophy of progress based on advance of science popular.	• Major achievements attained in plastic and pictorial arts. Neoclassicism followed by Romanticism and Realism. Late nineteenth and early twentieth centuries significant for beginnings of mass culture.	• Spectacular advances in sciences and social sciences. Technological breakthroughs multiply, using new energy sources. Positivism challenged at end of nineteenth century by discrediting of Newtonian physics and antirationalist trends.
• ***East Asians:*** In China and Japan, Buddhism blends with Confucianism, Daoism, and Shintoism. Neo-Confucian philosophy influences Japanese. Christian missionary efforts bring minor returns. • ***South and Southeast Asians:*** Muslims and Hindus contest for allegiance of northern Indians under Mughal rule. • ***West and Central Asians:*** Nadir of Muslim religious and cultural vitality reached. Secularism rejected by traditionalists.	• ***East Asians:*** In China and Japan, later eighteenth century high point in pictorial and literary arts. • ***South and Southeast Asians:*** Mughal arts reach high degree of excellence. • ***West and Central Asians:*** Some fine artisanry produced in Persia, Ottoman Empire, and parts of Africa where Western influences not yet felt.	• ***East Asians:*** Japan behind the West but closes gap in science and technology. China resists Western ways and does not develop scientific outlook. • ***South and Southeast Asians:*** Traditional views hinder India's progress, although upper-caste individuals move toward modern Western viewpoint. • ***West and Central Asians:*** Nadir of Asian science and technology as compared with the West. Modern education blocked by religious fundamentalism and anti-Western feelings.
• African indigenous religions remain dominant in most regions, but Muslims make progress in sub-Saharan areas. Christian societies establish missions and begin proselytizing.	• Despite reduced wealth and sense of impotence, new creative forms accommodate change.	• Most Africans as yet lack basis of modern scientific thought.
• Secularism triumphs in both Americas, although Catholicism remains state religion in Latin America. In United States, separation of church and state generally accepted. United States and Canada debate over place of religion and science. In Latin America, most intellectuals carry anticlericalism to extreme.	• Signs of rebellion against traditional conformism multiply at end of nineteenth century, and early twentieth century sees change toward cultural autonomy.	• In North America in later part of period, physical sciences and technology advance. By 1920, gaps closed in most fields relative to Europe. In Latin America, gaps widen except for tiny minority of educated.

PART VI

Worldview Map VI Poverty in the Contemporary World

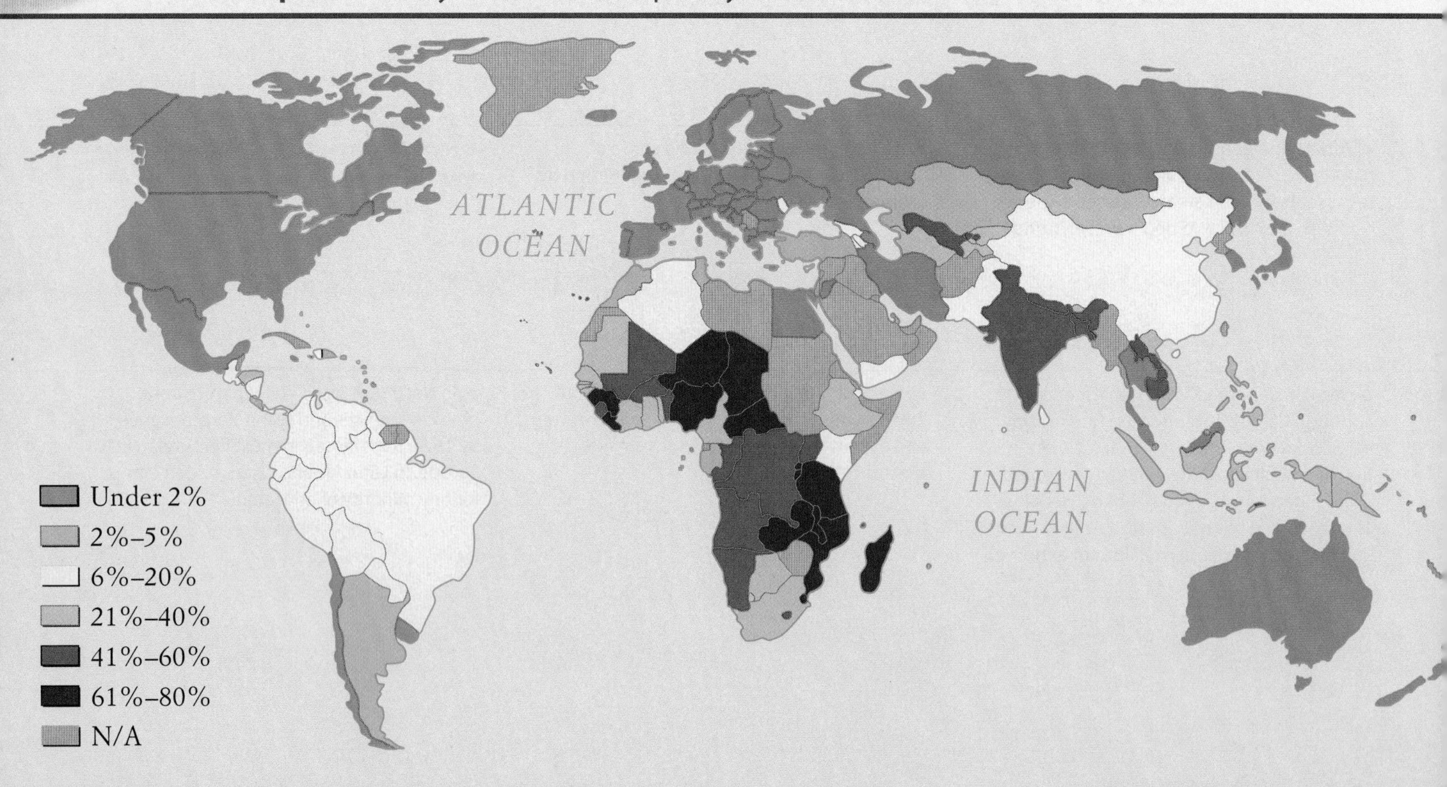

Towards a Globalized World,

1914–Present

Part VI examines the accelerating pace of change over the last century. These years have seen the unilateral military and political authority of the West modified and weakened throughout the non-Western world, while Western cultural forms have expanded into heretofore-untouched regions. New constellations of power, both military and economic, have arisen, sometimes to fall again, as in the case of communist Russia. Asia and Latin America have become major regions of development, and South and Southeast Asia have emerged from the shadow of colonial status with vigor and confidence. For Africa, the story has not been so positive; for many years, Africa remained on the periphery of power and in an essentially dependent relationship with the West. However, with the rapid development of a global economy in recent years, Africa has assumed growing importance. With this has come a greater independence in world affairs and demands to play a bigger role in world bodies.

In the wake of the disastrous World War I, the Central and Eastern European nations generally gravitated into various forms of authoritarian government and bade sour farewell to the classical liberal ideals and presumptions about human nature. Fascism in superficially varied forms won popular support and governmental power in several countries.

Britain, France, Scandinavia, and the United States resisted this trend during the interwar period, but after 1930, it was not the liberal democracies—which seemed helpless and exhausted—that seized the imagination and captured the sympathies of many of the world's less fortunate peoples. They turned instead to the novel socioeconomic experiment mounted by the Bolsheviks after seizing power in a war-prostrate Russia. Under Josef Stalin's brutal aegis, the Five-Year Plans and the Stalinist aberration of Marxism transformed traditional Russia.

Catalyzed by the lust for revenge and the expansionary dreams of Adolf Hitler and his fellow Nazi visionaries, World War II broke out in 1939. The unnatural anti-Nazi partnership of Britain, the United States, and Stalinist Russia fell apart, however, immediately after the common enemy was overwhelmed. The Cold War began and lasted for a long and often-terrifying generation of crises. For a time, the world seemed on the verge of becoming divided into the permanent fiefs of the two atomic superpowers—the United States and the Soviet Union. But Western Europe, which had seemed finished in the ruins of 1945, got back on its economic feet with American aid and by the mid-1950s was showing an astonishing vitality.

In Eastern Europe, the allegedly revolutionary message of communism was revealed to be no more than the ideologically enlarged shadow thrown by a crude Great Power, rather than a new dispensation for humankind. This impression was then demonstrated by the abject collapse of the spiritually bankrupt communist regimes at the beginning of the 1990s.

In those parts of the world that had experienced all the harm and indignities of Western colonialism, the reestablishment of national autonomy went through several stages. In the interwar era, the formation of a critically important local intelligentsia was completed. The two world wars revealed the weaknesses of Western governments and generated much support for national self-determination throughout the world. Either by armed force or by moral suasion, the once-subject colonies became newly sovereign nations and took their place proudly in a United Nations organization that had originally been planned as a club dominated by the Great Powers, namely the United States, the Soviet Union, and Western Europe. Despite that, a kind of cultural and political equilibrium among the members of an increasingly polycentric world was in the process of being painfully and tentatively reasserted. Using the intellectual and moral resources opened to them by Western ideas and ideals, the other three-quarters of humanity were determined to make themselves heard and listened to as the twenty-first century began.

Chapter 40 opens this part by reviewing the attempt to make World War I comprehensible to its survivors. Chapter 41 provides an overview of the postwar decade that saw many changes and presaged the crises of the 1930s. Chapter 42 is the story of the first generation of Soviet Russian government, from Lenin's coup to the enthronement of Stalin. Chapter 43 puts the totalitarian idea—and particularly the Nazi dictatorship—under the spotlight. Chapter 44 examines the momentous events that occurred in East Asia during the half century between 1900 and 1949.

World War II is the subject of Chapter 45, which also looks at the strains that quickly broke down the victorious alliance against the Axis. The Cold War between the United States and the Soviet Union is the focus of Chapter 46. This is followed in Chapter 47 by an examination of the decolonizing phenomenon after the war and the staggering problems of the developing countries since the 1950s.

Chapter 48 reviews the history of the countries on the Pacific's western shores and of South Asia since the end of World War II. Africa is the subject of Chapter 49, which looks at the immense difficulties confronting the sub-Saharan states as they crossed the bridge of independence. In Chapter 50, the same problem-oriented survey is made, this time of the Latin American countries throughout the twentieth century. In Chapter 51, the focal point is the Islamic community, particularly the Middle East. The collapse of the Marxist regimes in Europe is analyzed in Chapter 52. Our final chapter, 53, looks at some aspects of contemporary society, both East and West, and summarizes the immediate challenges of the new millennium.

Worldview Map VI, Poverty in the Contemporary World, illustrates the regions that continue to lag behind the rest of the world in their development. The color code illustrates the percentage of the population in each country living on less than a dollar a day. Which regions seem to be the most impoverished? How do you explain why poverty continues to be problematic in these regions?

40 World War I and Its Disputed Settlement

The lights are going out all over Europe. We shall not see them lit again in our lifetime. —LORD GREY, BRITISH FOREIGN MINISTER

1882	Triple Alliance: Germany, Austria-Hungary, and Italy
1894	Franco-Russian Treaty
1904	Anglo-French Entente
1907	Anglo-Russian Agreement
1914–1918	World War I
1917	United States enters war; Russia withdraws
1919–1920	Paris peace treaties

CHAPTER OUTLINE

In several senses, the nineteenth century and its convictions of inevitable, benevolent progress lasted until 1914, when "the lights went out all over Europe," as one British statesman put it. The twentieth century thus began not in 1900 but in 1918, when by far the bloodiest and most bitter war fought until then finally ended.

World War I was a savage European fratricide and the deathblow to the belief that progress and prosperity were almost automatic. By war's end, much of the youth and the political ideals of the Western world lay in ruins on the battlefields and at home. Disillusionment was rampant, and the stage was set for revolution in several countries. From a war that had no true victors in Europe, the United States and Japan emerged as major powers, whereas the Western imperial image suffered damage in Asia and Africa that never has been repaired.

PREWAR DIPLOMACY

After defeating France in the short Franco-Prussian War of 1870–1871, German chancellor Otto von Bismarck knew that the French would be yearning for revenge. Weakening France to the maximum accordingly made good strategic sense. Thus, Germany seized the two border provinces of Alsace and Lorraine, a move that deprived an industrializing France of its main sources of iron and coal.

The Triple Alliance

To maintain the security of the new Germany, Bismarck also wished to keep France diplomatically isolated, knowing that France alone could not hope to defeat the newly united and powerful Germany. Toward that end, he fanned the flames of international tensions between France and Britain by exacerbating their rivalries in Africa and Asia (Chapter 36) while he also pursued alliances with Austria-Hungary and Russia. These states were engaged in their own strong rivalry over the fate of the weakened Ottoman Empire, and Bismarck intended to bind them together with Germany as the "swing" partners so that neither would join France.

For more than twenty years, Bismarck's system worked well. Germany had what it wanted, and peace was preserved because France was indeed too weak to move alone and, partly because of her imperialist rivalries, could not find allies. When newly unified Italy wanted to play a role in international affairs, Bismarck was able to persuade the Italians that their desires for colonial expansion would have a better hearing in Berlin than in Paris. Italy eventually joined Germany and Austria in the **Triple Alliance** of 1882, which said, in essence, that if any one of the three were attacked, the other two would hasten to its aid.

In 1890, however, the linchpin of the system was removed when the young Kaiser, Wilhelm (or William) II (ruling 1888–1918), dismissed Bismarck, the old master statesman. Wilhelm was not a man to remain willingly in the shadow of another. He was determined to conduct his own foreign policy, and he did so immediately by going out of his way to alienate Russia, allowing a previous treaty of friendship to lapse. As a result, the Russians suddenly showed some interest in negotiating with the French, who had been patiently waiting for just such an opportunity. In 1893–1894, France and Russia signed a defensive military alliance. The pact did not mention a specific antagonist, but it was clearly aimed at Germany.

The Anglo-French Entente and the Anglo-Russian Agreement

The cordial relations between Britain and Prussia-Germany that had prevailed throughout the nineteenth century gave way to unprecedented hostility in the early 1900s for several reasons:

- The damage caused by the calculated role Bismarck assumed in the Scramble for Africa
- The South African War in South Africa (1899–1902) aroused considerable anti-British feeling among the Germans. The British public quickly reciprocated these sentiments, fed by the sensationalist penny press in London.
- Germany's announcement in 1907 that it intended to build a world-class navy was taken as a deliberate provocation that must be answered by British countermeasures.
- The belligerent "sword rattling" in which the impetuous and insecure Kaiser Wilhelm II indulged during the decade before 1914 contributed significantly to the developing tensions. Under Wilhelm II, the German government often gave the impression that it was more interested in throwing its considerable weight about than in solving diplomatic crises peaceably.

By 1904, the British had decided that post-Bismarck Germany was a greater menace to their interests than France, the traditional continental enemy. In that year, Britain and France signed the **Anglo-French Entente** (ahn-TAHNT: understanding). Without being explicit, it was understood that Britain would come to the aid of France in a defensive war. Again, no other power was named in the pact, but its meaning was quite clear.

The final step in the division of Europe into conflicting blocs was the creation of a link between Britain and Russia, which had been on opposite sides of everything since the Napoleonic wars had ended. Here, the French served as middlemen, replicating the previous German role between Russia and Austria-Hungary. In 1907, Britain and Russia signed the **Anglo-Russian Agreement**, which was much like the Anglo-French Entente. Now Germany, Austria, and Italy on the one side faced Britain, France, and Russia on the other. The stage had been set. The action was sure to follow.

CAUSES OF THE WAR

What caused World War I? This question has occupied three generations of historians. Like most wars, World War I had two types of causes: (1) the proximate cause, or the event that actually triggered hostilities, and (2) the more decisive remote causes, or the trail of gunpowder that led to the explosion.

The proximate cause was the **assassination of Archduke Franz Ferdinand**, the heir to the Austrian throne, on June 28, 1914, in the town of Sarajevo in Bosnia, which was at that time an Austrian possession. Bosnia had been transferred from Turkish to Austrian rule by international agreement in 1878, following one of several uprisings. The transfer from one alien overlord to another had not placated the Bosnian Serbs, who wished to join with the independent Serbian kingdom adjoining Bosnia (see Map 40.1). The archduke was murdered by a conspiracy of Serbian nationalist youths who were convinced that the assassination would somehow induce Austria to abandon its Serb-populated possessions. They, of course, were wrong.

The war also had several remote causes:

- *Nationalism.* Extreme nationalist sentiment had been rising steadily, particularly in France, Germany, and among the various small peoples who inhabited the areas of Southeastern Europe that had been held for centuries by the Turks. Some of these peoples were the clients of the Austrians, some were the clients of the Russians, and some had no patron. All were determined to seize as much territory as possible for their

MAP 40.1 The Balkan States, 1914
The intermixing of several ethnic and religious groups in southeastern Europe is a result of many centuries of immigration, conquest, and foreign overlordship. On the eve of World War I, Serbia, Bulgaria, Romania, and Greece were maneuvering for national advantage in the event that the long-awaited collapse of the Ottoman Empire occurred.

THINKING ABOUT THIS MAP

Considering its neighbors, what dangers did the region present for continued peace in 1914?

own nations when the capsizing Ottoman Empire finally sank.

- *International imperialism.* Austria, Russia, Britain, France, Germany, and Italy all shared in the frenzy of the new imperialism of the late nineteenth century, as we discussed in Chapters 35, 36, and 37.
- *Weariness of peace.* A long generation of peace (1871–1914) had allowed Europeans to forget how quickly war can fan the embers of discontent into revolution and anarchy. In addition, some influential persons in public life were convinced that war ennobled the human spirit and that Europe had "suffered" through too many years of peace since 1815. They actually longed for the challenges of war as the ultimate test that would separate the wheat from the chaff among the nations.

After a month's ominous silence, the Austrian government presented the government of independent Serbia (from which the assassins had obtained their weapons and possibly their inspiration) with a forty-eight-hour ultimatum. Acceptance of the conditions would mean, in effect, the surrender of Serbian independence, and refusal meant war. The Serbs chose war.

MILITARY ACTION, 1914–1918

Within a week in early August, all but one of the members of the two blocs formed over the past two decades were also at war. The exception was Italy, which bargained with both sides for the next several months. Austria-Hungary was joined at once by Germany, Turkey, and Bulgaria (in 1915). Joining Serbia were Russia, France, Britain, Italy (in 1915), and Romania (in 1916). The United States and Greece entered the fray in 1917 on the Entente side, or Allied, as it was generally called.

In its military aspect, World War I was almost entirely a European phenomenon, although contingents forcefully recruited from the Allies' colonial possessions came from all continents by the time it was over. The main battlefronts were: (1) the *Western front* in France and Belgium, which was the decisive one (see Map 40.2); (2) the *Eastern or Russian front,* which reached from the Baltic Sea to the Aegean but was always secondary (see Map 40.3); and (3) the *Alpine front,* which involved only Italy and Austria-Hungary and had no major influence on the course of the conflict. In addition, significant fighting took place between the colonial possessions of the respective European powers in Africa. The British joined forces with Arabs who were fighting for their independence from Ottoman rule, and by the end of the war, the Turks had lost all of their Near Eastern provinces to Britain and France (see Chapter 51).

Private Collection/Archives Charmet/The Bridgeman Art Library

THE ASSASSINATION OF ARCHDUKE FRANZ FERDINAND. This event triggered World War I. The assassin, Gavrilo Princip, was later apprehended.

The course of the war was unforeseen. As so often occurs, the military experts were mistaken and the generals were unprepared. This was particularly true on the Western front. The experts had thought that, thanks to railroads, motor vehicles, telephones, and radio communications, as well as the use of much heavier cannons and much larger armies than had been seen before, whichever side got the upper hand in the early days would have a decisive advantage. The offense would also have a big advantage over the defense, thought the experts. The war would be won within a few weeks by the superior attacker, just as in a chess game between experts, in which one player gains the advantage in the opening moves.

Just the opposite happened: The defense proved superior to the offense. Instead of large numbers of motorized troops scoring breakthroughs against the enemy, the war turned out to be endless slogging through muddy trenches and hopeless, cruelly wasteful infantry attacks against machine guns while artillery knocked every living thing to perdition for miles around. Rather than lasting a few weeks, the war lasted four and a quarter ghastly years, with a loss of life far in excess of any other conflict ever yet experienced.

The Bloody Stalemate

Originally, the **Central Powers** (as the German-Austrian allies were called) planned to hold off the Russians with minimal forces while rapidly smashing through neutral Belgium into France and forcing it to surrender. The plan nearly worked. Along the Eastern front, Russian forces at first were successful in driving back big German and Austrian offenses. After enormous artillery barrages and fighting along battle lines that stretched for hundreds of miles, Russian armies soon ran into supply problems. The Germans defeated them in battles at Tanenberg and the Maurian Lakes, driving deeply into Russia before the war bogged down into a bloody stalemate. On the Western front, in late August 1914, the Germans got to within a few miles of Paris, only to be permanently stalled along the river Marne by heroic French resistance. Aided now by a British army that grew rapidly, the French were able to contain one tremendous German attack after another for four years. From the English Channel to Switzerland, the battle lines did not move more than a few miles, as millions of men on both sides met their death.

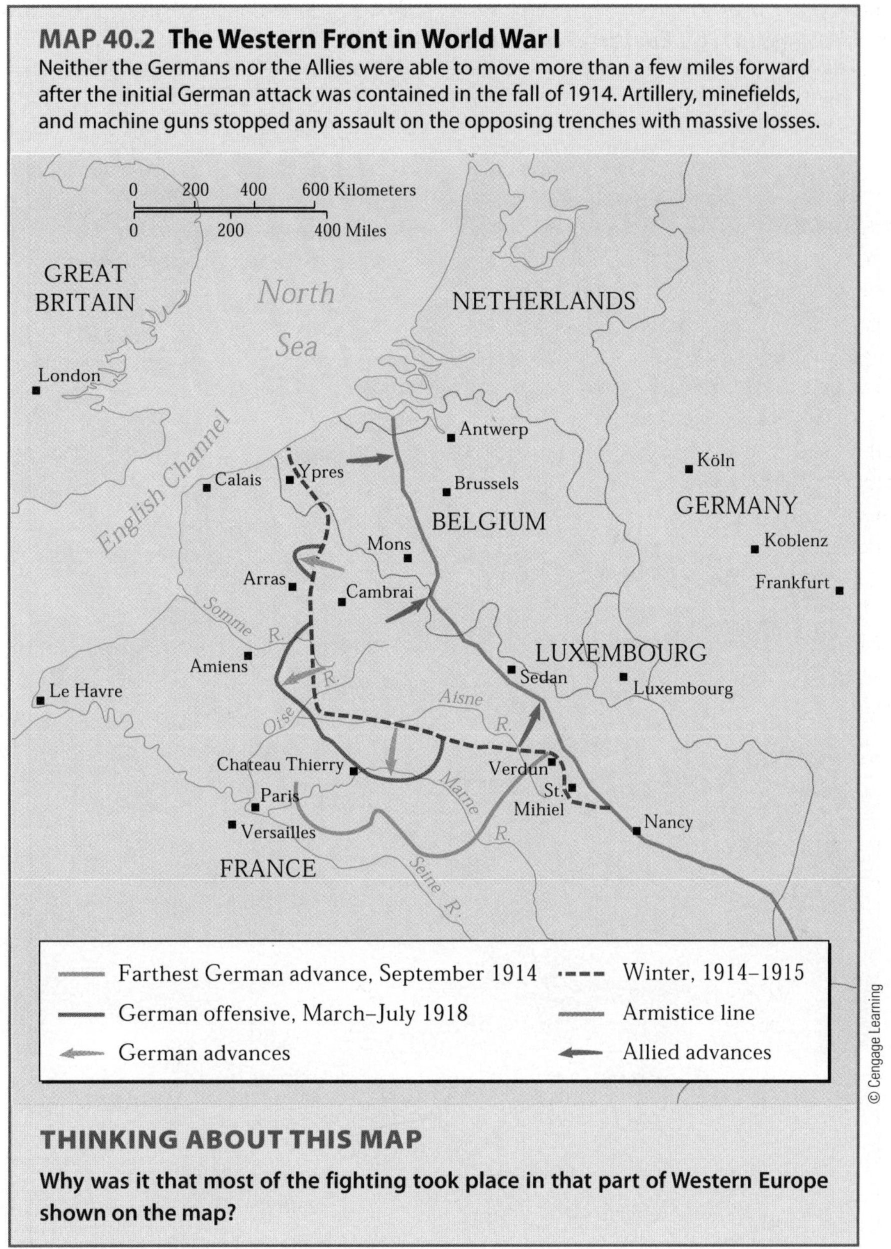

MAP 40.2 The Western Front in World War I

Neither the Germans nor the Allies were able to move more than a few miles forward after the initial German attack was contained in the fall of 1914. Artillery, minefields, and machine guns stopped any assault on the opposing trenches with massive losses.

THINKING ABOUT THIS MAP

Why was it that most of the fighting took place in that part of Western Europe shown on the map?

U.S. Entry and Russian Exit

The entry of the United States into the war in April 1917 was vitally important to the Allies. The U.S. decision was triggered by the resumption of unrestricted submarine war by the German high command. Strong protests after U.S. ships and U.S. lives had been lost to torpedoes had brought a lull in attacks for almost two years, during which time the United States maintained its formal neutral stance. In fact, President Woodrow Wilson and most of his advisers had been sympathetic to the Allied cause from the beginning, yet the public's opinion was sharply divided.

Many Americans were recent immigrants from the lands of the Central Powers and had emotional ties to them. Wilson found it politically inadvisable to intervene in the war until after winning the 1916 presidential election, although some persuasive reason could be found for doing so. In early 1917, several Allied ships carrying U.S. passengers were sunk, giving the pro-Allied party in Washington a dramatic and plausible excuse for intervention.

The U.S. entry into the conflict counterbalanced the collapse of the Russian war effort following the revolutions of 1917 (see Chapter 42) and the terrible losses suffered by the Allies in the Somme River offensive in the summer of 1916. The U.S. war industry and military met the demands placed on them by the exhausted British and French surprisingly rapidly. Men and war supplies

MAP 40.3 The Eastern Front in World War I

The war in Russia was much more fluid than in the West, but until the collapse of the tsarist government in 1917, neither side could deal a fatal blow. The German high command accepted a withdrawal to the Brest-Litovsk treaty line in 1918 only because it fully expected to create a satellite state of Ukraine as its eastern outpost.

Russian advances: 1914–1916

Deepest German penetration, 1918

Separate peace boundary, 1918

(CRIMEA) Regions of national states

THINKING ABOUT THIS MAP

Considering how far into Russia the German-Austrian forces had succeeded in driving, what reasons can you think of that might explain why they would have agreed to a final boundary so far to the west of their lines?

sent from U.S. ports during the winter and spring of 1918 allowed the desperate French to hold on against the final German offensive.

Collapse of the Central Powers

In the fall of 1918, the Central Powers suddenly collapsed. The Austrians asked for peace without conditions in mid-October, by which time the Bulgarians and the Turks had already withdrawn. The German high command now advised the kaiser to accept the armistice conditions that President Wilson had presented some weeks previous, which had been based on the **Fourteen Points** he had enunciated in a speech in January 1918. In summary, the Fourteen Points looked for a "peace without victors," self-determination for the repressed nationalities, disarmament, freedom of the seas for all, and an international body to keep the peace permanently.

Archives Larousse, Paris, France/Giraudon/The Bridgeman Art Library

VERDUN TRENCHES. The first battles of World War I consisted of old-style infantry and cavalry charges out in the open. However, the massive slaughter that ensued soon forced troops on both sides to seek the relative safety of life below ground. Trenches, like these at Verdun, protected lives from bullets and bombs, but more war deaths came from exposure to diseases suffered in the trenches than from battle wounds.

On November 9, 1918, the kaiser handed power to a just-created provisional government. Mainly members of the Social Democratic Party, this government immediately asked for an end to hostilities. On November 11, the long bloodbath came to an end. Everywhere, German troops were still standing on foreign soil, and Germany itself had experienced none of the destruction wrought by war on Allied lands. Those facts were to be important in the future days. They contributed to the impression that Germany had been defeated not by foreign troops or war exhaustion but by the betrayal of some scheming politicians.

THE HOME FRONT DURING THE WAR

After the outburst of manic enthusiasm that overtook all of the belligerent populations in the first weeks of war (and the total failure of the Marxist socialists' hopes for an international general strike), both governments and people came to realize that a long, hard struggle lay ahead. Several steps had to be taken if the demands of this first **total war** were to be met. By 1916, all combatants had acted to ensure that civilians would fully support the battlefronts. Among the most important measures they took were the following:

- *Full mobilization of the civilian population for total war.* Unlike all previous wars, World War I did not allow the unarmed masses to remain neutral. Led by Germany but soon imitated by France and the others, the authorities insisted that everyone had a role to play in attaining victory. The governments made wholesale

Private Collection/Mark Fiennes/The Bridgeman Art Library

FIGHTING AT THE SOMME. This painting depicts the unprecedented savagery of the fighting in World War I. Machine guns, repeater guns, exploding artillery, landmines, hand grenades, and aerial bombardment were all new weapons that raised the casualty levels several degrees higher than had been seen in previous wars.

SOCIETY AND ECONOMY

Home-Front Cookery

World War I was history's first "total war," inasmuch as entire nations, including noncombatants, had to be mobilized, willingly or unwillingly, for but one goal: winning the war with as little cost in blood and treasure as possible. Naturally, this required some privations for the home folks. One area so affected was the kinds of goods available to consumers. Many of these were needed at the front, so people either had to make do without them entirely or find substitutes. These recipes were taken from a wartime cookbook. (Note the author's use of humorous sayings to go with each recipe.)

"Everything has an end except a sausage, which has two." —Danish proverb

Mock Sausages

1 pint pecan meats	1 cup cooked farina or cream of wheat
1 egg	a dash of pepper
½ teaspoonful salt	1 tablespoonful sage

Put the pecans through the meat chopper, add the farina, all the seasonings, and at last the egg beaten. Make into round cakes, place these on paper at the bottom of a baking dish. Bake twenty minutes in a quick oven. Serve on a hot plate with either white or tomato sauce.

"Sma' fish are better than nae fish." —Proverb

Mock Fish

1 pint cooked hominy grits	1 teaspoonful grated onion
½ pint mixed nuts	½ teaspoonful chopped parsley
1 tablespoonful butter	1 teaspoonful salt substitute
2 hardboiled eggs	1 teaspoonful pepper
1 raw egg	

Put the nuts through the meat grinder and add to the grits. Add the seasoning and the hardboiled egg yolks chopped. Oil a piece of paper the shape of a fish. Form the "fish" on it; brush it with the beaten yolk of the raw egg. Dust it with a little celery salt. Take the whites of two hard-boiled eggs, and form the gills and the mouth. Use two good-sized filberts for eyes. If you are without filberts, use peanuts. Cut blanched almonds into quarters lengthwise and arrange them on the back in the imitation of fins. Bake in a moderate oven for twenty minutes.

"Feed sparingly and defy the physician" —Proverb

Mock Tenderloin Steak

1 quart nut meats (English walnuts, peanuts, pine nuts almonds in equal measure)	1 quart bread crumbs
	1 pint of water
	1 tablespoonful salt
	2 spoonfuls pepper

Put the nuts through the meat chopper, mix with crumbs, add the seasoning and the water, pack into tin cans, and steam or boil three hours. Stand in a cold place with the lids off until perfectly cold, then cover and keep them in a refrigerator. When ready for use, turn them out, cut in slices, and heat in the oven or broil quickly. Serve plain or with tomato sauce.

The better way to do [this] is to make a quantity of this, put into cans and cook it then cut it off and broil or heat it when needed. The above ingredients will be sufficient for several meals.

ANALYZE AND INTERPRET

What wartime conditions would seem to have been the causes for this kind of cooking? What explains the frequent use of nuts and eggs? For what were they substitutes? What was used for flavoring?

University of Wisconsin Digital Collections. Recipe for Victory: Food and Cooking in Wartime. http://digital.library.wisc.edu/1711.dl/HumanEcol.WWIHomeCook

Helen W. Moore, *Camouflage cookery; A book of mock dishes*, written and compiled by Helen Watkeys Moore. New York, New York: Duffield & Company, 1918.

use of every type of propaganda available: print media, exhibitions, parades, veterans' speaking tours, and so on. Starting in 1915, they indulged in hate propaganda. Much of it consisted of deliberate lies. All of it was meant to transform the civil population into a productive machine to fight the enemy. (See the Society and Economy box and the Images of the Past box.)

- Food was rationed, and so were fuel and clothing.
- All active males aged seventeen to sixty were considered "soldiers in the war for production" and could be ordered about almost like the troops in battle. Even women were pressed into various kinds of unprecedented service, as will be described.
- *Government control of the economy.* Much more than in any previous war, the governments took command of the entire production system. Labor was allocated by bureaucratic command, and so were raw materials, currency, and imports of all types. New taxes were levied to prevent any excess profit from war contracts. Wage rates, rents, and consumer prices were also controlled by government order. All or almost all of these measures were novelties being tried for the first time.

- *Female labor.* Because millions of men were no longer available to the civil economy after 1914, women were induced to fill their places by various means, including high pay, patriotic appeals, and even coercion. Dozens of occupations that were previously off-limits to women were now opened to them, including jobs involving heavy physical labor or considerable authority. Women worked as police officers, tram drivers, truck drivers, bank tellers, carters, and munitions factory laborers and held a host of civil service jobs that had previously been reserved for men.

In this way, a new world of work opportunity opened for women. After some initial resistance by the labor unions, women were generally accepted as replacements for men and given more or less equal pay. In particular, their ability to do repetitive industrial jobs exceeded male expectations and earned them new respect as productive employees. In every belligerent country, women made up at least 30 percent of the total civilian labor force by war's end—a far higher percentage than in peacetime.

Social Behavior

As in most wars, the insecurity of life and the desire to accommodate the young men going off to fight resulted in a slackening of traditional standards for both sexes, but especially for women. Public demonstrations of affection between the sexes became acceptable even among the respectable classes. Women insisted on access to some form of mechanical birth control because extramarital and premarital sex became more common. Standards of conduct and dress for girls and women became more relaxed. Factory work inspired shorter and less voluminous dresses—it was even possible to show a bit of leg without automatically being considered "fast" by one's peers. Alcohol consumption by both sexes rose sharply despite attempts to discourage it by all governments (which were concerned about worker absenteeism in the war plants).

Unlike previous wars, so many men were involved and the casualty rates suffered by most belligerents were so high that the slackening of moral restraint during the war had a profound and permanent effect on postwar society. Marriageable men were in short supply for years afterward, and the imbalance between men and women aged twenty to thirty-five influenced what was considered acceptable sexual conduct. After the war, it proved impossible to put young men and women back into the tight customary constraints of prewar society.

Additionally, the many millions of conscripts in the armies had been torn out of their accustomed and expected slots in life. For better or worse, many—especially rural youth—never returned to their prewar lifestyles. "How're you gonna keep them down on the farm after they've seen Paree [Paris]?" went a popular song in the United States. That was a relevant question, and not just for Americans.

Psychic Consequences

Perhaps the most significant of all the consequences of World War I was its effect on the collective European psyche. Three effects in particular stand out in retrospect:

1. *Political disillusionment.* Even while the war was being fought, many were disillusioned of its purpose, its justification, and the prospects for meaningful victory, and their mood spread despite intensive propaganda campaigns by all the warring nations. After 1916, the war became one of brutal attrition. Basically, both sides were trying to hold on until the other gave up. As the casualty lists lengthened without any decisive victories for either side, the survivors in the trenches and their loved ones back home came to doubt as never before the wisdom of their political and military leaders. Men were dying by the millions, but what was being fought for remained unclear. When the war ended, disillusionment with the peace was widespread even among the victorious Allies. Some thought it too mild, and others too harsh. Despite Wilson's promises, the losers universally regarded the peace as one of vengeance.

FEMALE WORKERS, WORLD WAR I. The draining off of males to battlefields after 1914 opened the way for millions of women to enter jobs that were previously unknown to them. In this 1917 war poster, the role of women munitions workers is shown.

IMAGES OF HISTORY

Wartime Propaganda

Twentieth-century warfare gave rise to manipulation of the media by the governments of warring states to foment public support for the war effort. In both World Wars, some of the most commonly used media were posters and postcards, as these examples illustrate.

World War I Recruiting Poster with portrait of Field Marshall Earl Kitchener (see also 2987),/Imperial War Museum, London, UK/The Bridgeman Art

"WORLD WAR I RECRUITING POSTER." Portrait of Field Marshall Earl Kitchener. General Kitchener was a military hero for Britons ever since his defeat of the Sudanese Mahdists at the Battle of Omdurman in 1898.

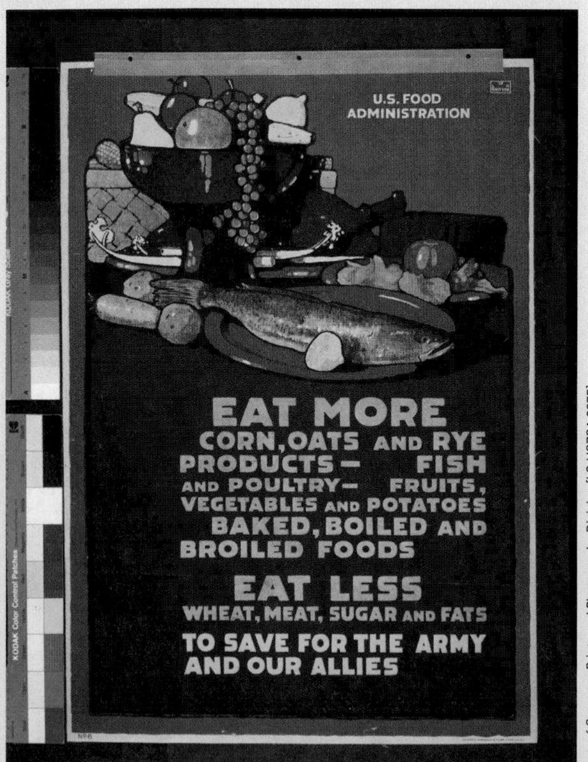

Library of Congress Prints and Photographs Division [LC-USZC4-2975]

"EAT MORE CORN, OATS AND RYE." Compare this with the Society and Economy box.

Library of Congress Prints and Photographs Division [LC-USZC4-2975]

"THE GIRL ON THE LAND SERVES THE NATION'S NEED." World War I YWCA poster. Penfield, Edward (1866–1925).

2. *Skepticism toward authority.* The feelings of betrayal and disappointment were especially common among the veterans who came back from the battlefields. They regarded most military and political leaders as heartless blunderers who had no concern for ordinary people. All authority figures were now suspect: the clergy who had blessed each side's cannons, the diplomats who had not been able to prevent the war, and the teachers and professors who had led the foolish cheering at its outbreak. None of the old guides for right and wrong could be trusted; all of them had acted out of ignorance, cowardice, or self-interest.
3. *An end to the religion of science and progress.* Before 1914, most educated Europeans assumed that the next generation would be able to solve most of the problems that still haunted their own. They believed that material and spiritual progress were inevitable. The war ended that naïve optimism for soldiers and civilians alike. They had seen the mutual slaughter end with no clear achievement for the victors and with chaos for the losers. As the spiritual and economic costs to all sides became apparent, many people began to doubt whether there had even been any victors. The faith of the European bourgeoisie in liberalism, parliamentary government, and the triumph of science looked absurd in 1919, as the smoke of battle cleared and the cemeteries filled. Revolution and a kind of vicious nihilism (belief in nothing), not progress, were on the day's menu.

The dismay was not universal, however. For some, a triumphant new day had dawned after the carnage. In the fine arts, a whole series of new ideas, new perspectives, and challenging new theories emerged during or soon after the war. On the political side, many Eastern and Central European nationalists were initially gratified at the outcome of the war, because the peace negotiations fulfilled many of their dreams of regional dominance and sovereignty. The feminists were pleased because women gained the vote in almost every country, largely as a result of the promises made by desperate politicians during the war emergency. And the Marxist socialists and communists were filled with surging hopes of a Europe-wide proletarian revolution, brought on by the sufferings of the common people during the conflict and the general rejection of the prewar political order. These hopes were ignited by the success of the revolution in November 1917 and the installation of a Marxist socialist regime in Moscow (see Chapter 42).

THE PEACE TREATIES, 1919–1920

The German surrender was based on acceptance of an armistice offered by the Allies in November 1918. A permanent peace arrangement was worked out in Paris during the first months of 1919. The last of five separate treaties with the losing nations (Austria, Hungary, Bulgaria, and Turkey, as well as Germany) was signed in August 1920.

The popular leader of the victorious Allies was clearly American president Wilson. Much of the European public saw him as a knight in shining armor because of his previous proclamation of a peace without victors and his support of "open diplomacy." But Wilson's popularity did not carry into the closed-door negotiations in Paris. The other Allied leaders, convinced that the president's slogans and plans were naïve, soon blocked him. Georges Clemenceau, the French premier, and Vittorio Orlando, the Italian premier, were opposed to a peace without victors, which to them meant political suicide or worse. David Lloyd George, the British prime minister, was originally a bit more sympathetic, but he too turned against Wilson when the president attempted to make his Fourteen Points the basis of the peace. Each of the European leaders had good reasons for rejecting one or more of the points as being inapplicable or foolish, and they united against the American on their mutual behalf. The points, supposedly the basis of the peace, were eventually selectively applied or ignored altogether.

The negotiations were conducted in secret (despite Wilson's previous promises) and involved only the victors. Germany, Austria, Hungary, Bulgaria, and Turkey were each given a piece of paper to sign without further parlays. They were told that if they did not, the war would be resumed. Unwillingly, each signed during 1919–1920. Especially for the Germans, this peace was a bitter pill that would not be forgotten.

Conflicting Principles and Their Compromise

What came out of the Paris negotiations?

Territorially. Germany lost 10 percent of its land and its population to the new states of Poland and Czechoslovakia. Alsace-Lorraine, the "Lost Provinces" of 1870, went back to France (see Map 40.4).

Austria's empire was completely dismantled; a process that had become inevitable during the closing days of the war when each of the major components had declared its independence from Vienna and the last Habsburg ruler had abdicated. The new **Successor states**, as they were called, were Austria, Hungary, Czechoslovakia, Poland, and Yugoslavia. In addition, Romania was greatly enlarged. Bulgaria lost some land to Romania, Yugoslavia, and Greece.

Turkey's empire was also completely dissolved, and its Middle Eastern lands were partitioned among the Allies: Jordan, Palestine, Iraq, Syria, Arabia, and Lebanon became French or British protectorates. The Turkish core area of Anatolia came under a military dictatorship led by ex-officer Mustafa Kemal (later called Ataturk: see Chapter 51).

MAP 40.4 Europe After World War I

The war and the peace treaties carved seven entirely new states out of Russia and the Austro-Hungarian empire: Finland, Latvia, Estonia, Lithuania, Poland, Czechoslovakia, and Yugoslavia. Austria and Hungary were separated, and Romania, Italy, and Greece were enlarged.

THINKING ABOUT THIS MAP

Why do you think the Soviet Union (Russia) would have agreed to the creation of the so-called Successor states between it and Germany?

Ethnically. Some of Wilson's plans for self-determination became a reality, but others were ignored. The old multinational empires had collapsed and were replaced by states in which one ethnic group had at least a majority. But each of the Eastern European Successor states included a large number of minority groups; some represented as much as 30 percent of the total population. Czechoslovakia and Yugoslavia were the most vulnerable in this respect. The Germans living within Czechoslovakia made up close to one-third of the population, and the Magyars, Germans, Albanians, and others in Yugoslavia were a strong counterweight to the dominant Slavs.

Everywhere, the attempts of the peacemakers to draw up ethnically correct borders were frustrated by strategic, economic, geographic, or political considerations. The resulting ethnic map between Germany and the new Soviet Russia and between the Baltic and the Aegean seas looked like a crazy quilt. Protections were formally extended to the minorities by the special treaties that all Successor states were required to sign on entry into the **League of Nations**, a new international organization established to maintain peace and promote amity among nations (discussed later in this chapter). Chauvinist governments were soon ignoring these protections almost without reprimand because there was no mechanism to enforce them. National and religious minorities were often made the objects of systematic prejudice throughout the interwar era.

Politically. Germany was tagged with full responsibility for starting the war (*Paragraph 231 of the Versailles Treaty*), which no German could accept as true. This allowed the European Allies (Wilson would not) to claim reparations for wartime damages from the losers. The amount of damages was to be calculated (solely by the victors) at some future date. It eventually was announced as $33 billion (perhaps eight times that in year 2012 values). The **reparations question** was to be one of the chief bones of contention in international affairs for the next fifteen years. (See Law and Government box for excerpts from the Versailles Treaty.)

LAW AND GOVERNMENT

Terms of the Treaty of Versailles

The Versailles Treaty has been argued over since it was signed, portrayed by supporters as a strict but just limitation on the powers of an aggressive Germany to make war and by its critics as a vindictive act of revenge. Beyond clipping off 10 percent of German prewar territory and population, the treaty's numerous articles went into great detail on topics as widely separate as German citizens' rights in the former African colonies and the supplying of the Allied forces of occupation that were to be stationed temporarily in western Germany.

Some of the articles most pertinent to the status of postwar Germany are cited here:

> Article 119. Germany renounces in favor of the Principal Allied and Associated Powers all her rights and titles over her overseas possessions. [These possessions were mainly in Africa, on the China coast, and in the southern Pacific islands.]
>
> Article 160. By a date which must not be later than March 31, 1920 the German Army must not comprise more than seven divisions of infantry and three divisions of cavalry.
>
> After that date, the total number of effectives … must not exceed one hundred thousand men.…*
>
> The Army shall be devoted exclusively to the maintenance of order within the territory and to the control of the frontiers.
>
> The total effective strength of officers, including staffs, must not exceed four thousand.…
>
> The German General Staff and all similar organizations shall be dissolved and shall not be reconstituted in any form.…
>
> Article 180. All fortified works, fortresses and field works situated in German territory to the west of a line drawn fifty miles to the east of the Rhine shall be disarmed and dissembled.…
>
> Article 198. The armed forces of Germany must not include any military or naval air forces.…
>
> Article 231. The Allied and Associated Governments affirm and Germany accepts the responsibility of Germany and her allies for causing all the loss and damage to which the Allied and Associated Governments and their nationals have been subjected as a consequence of the war imposed upon them by the aggression of Germany and her allies.
>
> Article 233. The amount of the above damage for which compensation is to be made by Germany shall be determined by an Inter-Allied Commission, to be called the Reparation Commission.†

ANALYZE AND INTERPRET

Do you think these peace conditions were reasonable? What were the provisions of the Treaty to enforce them?

* The 100,000-man limit was quickly gotten around, as part of the more or less open defiance of the Versailles armed-force restrictions that took place after 1921 (see Chapter 41).

† The total reparations figure due from Germany was $33 billion in gold, as represented by the Commission in 1921. Of this, about one-third was eventually paid, mainly in goods (see Chapter 45).

Source: Treaty of Peace with Germany.

The defeated states and some of the Successors became republics, having lost their various royal/imperial rulers during the final days of the conflict. The last Habsburg emperor, Charles I, lived out his days in exile. The Hohenzollern kaiser was gone from Berlin (he died in Dutch exile), and the last Romanov tsar was murdered as a hostage of the Bolsheviks in 1918. The Turkish sultan was also gone, deposed by the new, Westernizing government that Mustapha Kemal had installed in place of the moribund Ottoman state.

The new states of Czechoslovakia, Poland, and the three Baltic states were parliamentary republics. Constitutional monarchies (Yugoslavia, Romania, Bulgaria, and Albania) were continued in the Balkans. In all of these entities, democracy was given lip service and little more.

Diplomatically. The Paris treaties created an organ that was new in world history: a League of Nations with universal membership that was to act as a permanent board of mediation when international conflicts arose. The League was Wilson's brainchild, and to obtain it, he had been willing to accept all of the injuries that had been inflicted on his other ideas by the European statesmen.

As it happened, despite his best efforts, Wilson was not able to sell his fellow Americans on the idea of the League. Partly because of concern about involving the United States indefinitely in Europe's tangled affairs and partly because of Wilson's intractability, the U.S. Senate rejected the Paris treaties in 1919. The United States eventually made separate treaties with each of the defeated states, duplicating the Paris treaties with the exception of the League of Nations paragraph.

EVALUATION OF THE TREATIES

Criticism of the peace signed in Paris began as soon as the ink dried, and it came not only from the losing nations but from a good portion of the victors as well. Some of the victors' complaints came from fear that the losers had been left too well-off. Many people in France feared that Germany could and would rise once more despite its partial dismemberment and the extraordinary costs of reparations. But some of these concerns arose from the conviction that the peace had been guided by vengeance and that all of the high-flown principles of the Allied governments had been ignored in the dealings in Paris. After all, the peace negotiated in Paris was not a peace without victors, nor did it guarantee self-determination, nor did it end imperialism or carry through many of the other ideals that the wartime Allies had proclaimed.

The most scathing Allied critique came from young British economist John Maynard Keynes, who believed that the Allies had attempted to impose a "Carthaginian peace" (total destruction) on Germany that could not succeed. Keynes had enormous contempt for Wilson, and his opinions soon became fashionable among influential people in both Britain and the United States. Both groups regarded the French and the Italians as greedy and stupid in their shortsighted fixation on temporary advantage.

The failure of the Versailles Treaty in the U.S. Senate was a major turning point in postwar diplomacy. With no commitment to the League of Nations, the United States could and did turn its attention to Europe only when and how it chose for twenty years. And without the assurance of U.S. support through the League, France was left to face a resurgent Germany by itself in the early postwar era. As a result, the French position became more hard-line than ever and drove France and Britain further apart at a time when close coordination was most necessary.

Perhaps the worst aspect of the peace was that it tried to ignore certain political realities. Russia, now under Bolshevik rule, was not even invited to send a representative to Paris. Confirmed as a pariah nation, it was allowed no access to negotiations that would surely affect its status and future in world affairs. The losing nations, above all Germany, were presented with a fait accompli that was intensely disagreeable to them and that they believed was totally unjust. Neither Germany nor Russia, two of the strongest states in the world, was allowed to join the League of Nations for several years. Germany was commanded to disarm almost entirely, yet no machinery was in place to enforce that unrealistic demand, and none was ever created.

The League was supposed to be not only the enforcer of the Paris treaties but also the keeper of the peace for the indefinite future. Yet the weak secretariat had no armed force at its disposal, and the League members never had any intention of creating one. The League's effectiveness was going to depend on the goodwill of the member governments, and some of those governments were filled with anything but goodwill toward their neighbors.

The 1919 treaties were not as harsh as they have sometimes been painted, but they were a long way from the hopes of the Wilsonians and much of the world's population, who were trying to recover from the "war to end wars." As it turned out, the treaties lasted less than twenty years. What Europe found in 1919 was not peace, but a short armistice between two terribly destructive wars.

SUMMARY

The system erected by Bismarck to keep France isolated and helpless broke down after the impetuous Wilhelm II took over the direction of foreign policy in Berlin. Within a decade, the blocs that would contest World War I had been formed. When a Serbian nationalist youth assassinated the heir to the Austrian throne in 1914, a general war broke out that, contrary to expectations, lasted for more than four years.

The battlefields where huge slaughters took place were matched in importance by the home fronts, where governments intervened in unprecedented ways to spur the civilian war effort. Women in particular were affected because the desperate need for labor impelled politicians in all countries to forget prewar restrictions on female activity.

The war aims of all the combatants were poorly understood and never honestly expressed. As the casualty list soared, a sense of disillusionment and anger toward established authority spread. Even the so-called victors experienced feelings of revulsion at the disparity between the huge sacrifices demanded and the minimal results gained. This disgust was strengthened because it became apparent that the peace without victors was not to be. The social and psychic consequences of the war were enormous and permanent.

The Paris treaties were despised by the losers and satisfied few of the victors with their compromises between the optimistic visions of President Wilson and the hard realities of international and national politics. The former empires of Eastern Europe were dismantled and a group of Successor states established in accord with political and strategic advantage rather than ethnic justice.

IDENTIFICATION TERMS

Test your knowledge of this chapter's key concepts by defining the following terms. If you can not recall the meaning of certain terms, refresh your memory by looking up the boldfaced term in the chapter, turning to the Glossary at the end of the book, or accessing the terms on the CourseMate website at **www.cengagebrain.com**.

Anglo-French Entente
Anglo-Russian Agreement
assassination of Archduke Franz Ferdinand
Central Powers
Fourteen Points
League of Nations
reparations question
Successor states
total war
Triple Alliance

FOR FURTHER REFLECTION

1. For what reason(s) did statesmen create the pre-war alliances? What purposes did they serve: aggressive, defensive, or peaceful? How successful were they? Did they contribute to or help prevent war?
2. Why were the Balkans a danger to peace? Could war have been avoided? What would have to have been done differently? What similar conditions exist in this region today? Are they still a danger to world peace?
3. What conditions in the present-day Near East were results of the defeat of the Ottoman Empire in World War I?
4. How did the outcome of World War I and the Versailles Treaty presage World War II?

TEST YOUR KNOWLEDGE

Test your knowledge of this chapter by answering the following questions. Complete answers appear at the end of the book. You may find even more quiz questions on the CourseMate website at **www.cengagebrain.com**.

1. Bismarck's system of alliances for Germany was meant to
   a. restrain Russia and Austria and to isolate France.
   b. allow Austria to expand to the south and east.
   c. encourage peace with France indefinitely.
   d. force Russia to submit to German eastern expansion.
   e. keep Russia from intervening if Germany invaded Belgium.
2. Britain agreed to the Anglo-French Entente with its traditional enemy, France, because
   a. it had come to see Germany and America as greater threats to its security and economic leadership.
   b. France had become its principal trading partner.
   c. it had come to see Germany as a greater threat to its security.
   d. France had joined the League of Nations, while Germany and America had not.
   e. Germany refused to cooperate with international trade agreements.

3. Which of the following was not a remote cause of World War I?
   a. Aggressive imperialism practiced by several nations
   b. An inclination toward the "supreme test" of war among some leaders
   c. The belligerent nationalism of the Balkan states
   d. Germany's desire for an international "show down" with Britain and France.
   e. Widespread European weariness with peace.
4. Which of the following was true of World War I?
   a. Participants were shocked at the speed with which the Germans seized territory.
   b. Most soldiers spent most of their time waiting to be called to the front.
   c. Infantry attacks were surprisingly successful, given the strength of enemy fortifications.
   d. Machine guns were not as useful as had been hoped, because few recruits received adequate training in their use.
   e. Contrary to what most people had expected, defensive positions were more effective than were offensive maneuvers.
5. In the spring of 1917, two unrelated events changed the course of the war; they were
   a. the failure of the submarine campaign and the entry of Italy into the war.
   b. the success of the socialist revolution in Russia and the first use of conscripts by France.
   c. the toppling of the tsarist government in Russia and the entry of the United States into the war.
   d. the collapse of the French government and the entry of Britain into the war.
   e. the use of submarine warfare and the entry of France into the war.
6. Which of the following did not accompany the wartime use of females in the economy?
   a. A widening of the gap between the wages paid to males and females for their labor
   b. A demonstration of the women's ability to do many physical tasks
   c. Less male restrictiveness toward female public activities
   d. Less distinction between traditionally male and female jobs
   e. A desire among many women to retain their wartime jobs after the war ended
7. World War I is called history's first "total war" because
   a. war profiteers supported it totally.
   b. it pitted two completely different systems of government against each other.
   c. it brought a New World country, the United States, into the war.
   d. of the massive intervention of government into the war economy in all nations.
   e. it pitted two completely different economic systems against each other.
8. Together, the U.S. entry and the Russian exit from the war
   a. offset each other in their effects.
   b. inevitably led to American intervention in Russia.
   c. predisposed Russians to adopt communism.
   d. had few effects.
   e. might have sped up the end of the war.
9. The catastrophic war of 1914 to 1918 is called a "World" War because it
   a. involved both the soldiers fighting on the front as well as the civilian populations.
   b. was fought along fronts in several countries, not just one.
   c. was fought using new, previously untested weapons.
   d. included home militias as well as soldiers fighting in the trenches.
   e. involved many nations outside of Europe for the first time.
10. The most serious complaint against the Paris treaties was that they
    a. failed to punish the losers severely enough to keep them down.
    b. failed to recognize basic international political realities.
    c. did not give enough national self-determination.
    d. ignored ethnic boundaries entirely when redrawing the map.
    e. allowed France to punish Germany too severely.

CourseMate

Visit the CourseMate website at **www.cengagebrain.com** for additional study tools and review materials for this chapter.

41 A Fragile Balance: Europe in the Twenties

I do not worship the masses, that new divinity created by democracy and socialism. . . . History proves that it is always minorities . . . that produce profound changes in human society. —BENITO MUSSOLINI

1919	Weimar Republic established in Germany
1922	Benito Mussolini in power in Italy
1923	France occupies Ruhr; inflation in Germany
1925	Locarno Pact; fascist dictatorship begins in Italy
1926	General strike in Britain
1927–1930	Economic and political stability

CHAPTER OUTLINE

World War I had profound and disturbing effects in every corner of Europe. The 1919 peace treaties were intensely resented by the losers and did not satisfy the winners. Most of the eastern half of the continent was in continuous upheaval for several years. Russia had given birth to the world's first socialist society in 1917 and then attempted to export its Bolshevik revolution by legal and illegal channels. In the immediate postwar era, defeated Germany underwent the world's worst devaluation of money, ruining millions. In supposedly victorious Italy, a brutal new totalitarian style of governing called **fascism** had its violent birth. It was soon after emulated and refined in the irrational philosophy of the German Nazis. For several years, international resentments and rivalries, aggressive Bolshevism, and rampant nationalism made another conflict appear inevitable, but by the late 1920s, Europe seemed more stable and the threat of renewed war was more distant. For a few years after that, it seemed that European society might weather the crisis that 1914 had set off.

POLITICAL AND ECONOMIC BACKDROP

Political Diversity

The United States, and to a lesser degree Europe, saw the rapid democratization of politics, in part because of the extension of the franchise to women and the poorer classes. Political parties had ceased to be defined strictly by class. Some parties began broadening sufficiently to include workers *and* members of the middle class, aristocrats *and* intellectuals. Property alone no longer dictated political affiliation, as it often had in the past. The nineteenth-century division into liberal and conservative made less and less sense as cultural experience, secularization, social philosophy, and other intangibles helped shape the political inclinations of a given individual. The only important exceptions were the Marxists, who claimed a proprietary interest in both progress and the proletariat, and a few ethnic parties in the Successor states of Eastern Europe.

Keynesian Economics

In national economics, the two major innovations of the first half of the twentieth century were (1) the recognition that governments could and probably should intervene to smooth out the roller coaster of the traditional business cycle and (2) the spread and Russianization of Marxist communism.

John Maynard Keynes (1883–1946), the British economist whom we encountered in connection with his harsh critique of the Treaty of Versailles (see Chapter 40), proved to be the most influential economic theorist of the century. He insisted that government had the power and the duty to lessen the violent ups and downs of the business cycle by pumping new money into the credit system in hard times (such as the 1930s). By doing so, the millions of private investors, business owners, and speculators whose collective decisions determined the course of the economy would get the credit they needed to engage in new enterprise. Eventually, the increased tax revenues generated by this stimulus would repay the government for its expenditures and enable it to prevent inflation from accelerating too rapidly. A growth economy with some inflation was both attainable and more desirable than the nineteenth-century boom-and-bust cycles that had caused much misery.

Keynes's ideas did not find many adherents among government leaders before World War II. President Franklin D. Roosevelt instituted some measures along Keynesian lines during the **Great Depression of the 1930s**, but they had relatively little effect. Only after 1945 were Keynes's ideas tried in earnest. Since that time, it has become standard procedure for Western governments to counter the economic cycle by "pump priming" in times of unemployment and stagnation. Essentially, this means pouring new government expenditures into the economy at a time when the government's income (taxes) is declining. Because increasing taxes during a recession is politically difficult, a government that follows Keynes's ideas must either borrow from its own citizens (by issuing bonds or treasury notes) or use its powers to inflate by running the money printing presses a bit faster.

The debate as to whether Keynes's ideas actually work continues. Certainly, it has contributed to long-term inflation, which hits the lower classes hardest. Since the 1970s, free-market theory and practice have experienced a significant revival—not the untrammeled market that the nineteenth-century liberals expounded, but rather a kind of partnership of business and government in the global markets that technology has opened. Recent examples include the economic policies advocated by members of the Republican Party in the United States and by many of the Conservative Party in Britain. Some Southeast Asian nations and the postcommunist governments of Eastern Europe have embraced this modified free-market idea. Such theory rejects the Keynesian view in part and accepts the inevitability of some ups and downs in the national economy.

Marxist Successes and the Soviet Chimera

The other major phenomenon of international economics after World War I was the flourishing of a Leninist version of the Marxist gospel among both workers and intellectuals in much of the world. That the inexperienced and supposedly incompetent "Reds" of revolutionary Russia (see Chapter 42) could turn the new Union of Soviet Socialist Republics (USSR) into an industrial great power by the 1930s seemed to demonstrate the correctness of Karl Marx's analysis of the world's ailments. What had been done in backward, isolated Russia, many reasoned, must and would be done in the rest of the world.

In the early 1920s, new communist parties, inspired and guided by the Russian pioneers, sprang up in every industrial country and many colonies. From the sitting rooms where intellectuals worried that they might be left behind "on the ash heap of history" to the docks and mines where painfully idealistic communist workers labored, various forms of Marxist-Leninist belief spread into all social groups and classes. During the Great Depression of the 1930s, Marxism made substantial progress among not only the miserable unemployed but also the many intellectuals and artists who concluded that capitalism had definitively failed, that its day was done, and that the page had to be turned. Marxists delighted in contrasting the millions of out-of-work, embittered men and women in the Western democracies with the picture (often entirely false) painted by Soviet propaganda of happy workers going off to their tasks of "building socialism in one country" (the Soviet Union) with confidence and dignity.

TOTALITARIAN GOVERNMENT

In Eastern Europe outside the Soviet Union, totalitarian forces were at work. The word *totalitarian* means an attempt—more or less successful—to impose *total* control over the public life and serious intervention into the private lives of a society, and by so doing to create a state in which loyalty to the leader or his political party is the supreme

ARTS AND CULTURE

Modernism and Disillusion in Art

The 1920s and the decades that followed witnessed the flowering of several new trends in literature and art, all of which in one way or another exhibited the widespread disillusion and alienation that ensued from the cataclysm of total war.

THE PERSISTENCE OF MEMORY. The Surrealist school, exemplified in this painting by Salvador Dali (1904–1989), was concerned about the irrationality of human experience. Their works often demonstrated the apparent plasticity of reality—such as time—as well as surprising and absurd placement of the elements of experience.

M.Flynn/Alamy

LAS MENINAS: INFANTA MARGARITA MARIA. Pablo Picasso (1881–1973) was famous as a founder of Cubist art. Cubism often dealt with the multidimensionality of reality. In this portrait, Picasso conveyed this by depicting his subject from several perspectives all at once and through his use of color.

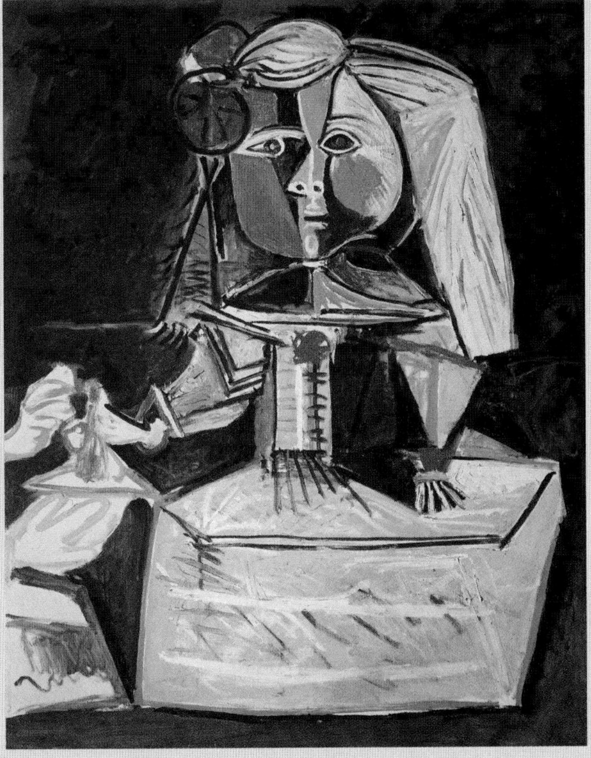

Album/Prisma/Newscom

Mondadori Portfolio/Electa/Art Resource, NY

ATOMIZED LANDSCAPE. Abstract art, such as this work by Enrico Baj (1924–2003), eschews portraiture and artistic narrative altogether. Rather, the artist seeks to create a mood and a highly emotional impression of a person or scene through a mixture of lines and colors.

virtue and all dissent is treason. **Totalitarianism** is a twentieth-century phenomenon that originated in the World War I concept of "total war." The wartime governments had taken full control of the economy, instituting rationing, allocations of labor and materials to industry, wage ceilings, and price controls. Citizens were expected to sacrifice their accustomed personal freedoms for victory. Those who refused were vulnerable to both legal and social retributions. Before then, such an attempt had not been made, in part because it was not technically possible, but largely because religious institutions and the universities strongly resisted the idea.

Six Characteristics

What would a totalitarian state and society mean in practice?

1. An official ideology would play a crucial part in shaping "correct" thinking among the masses. In a communist state, this would include the writings of Marx and Friedrich Engels, as well as the writings, speeches, and sayings of past and current party leaders, such as Vladimir Lenin, Josef Stalin, and Mao Zedong. In fascist regimes, there would be little in the way of a systematic ideology, but rather a number of officially sanctioned attitudes, prejudices, and concepts. Typically these would include ethnic prejudices (e.g. anti-Semitism), notions of a master "race," intolerance of minorities, antirationalism, extreme forms of nationalism, and militarism.
2. The traditional boundaries between the public and private affairs of citizens would be redefined or obliterated. Much that had been considered private would now be declared public and thus a matter for governmental concern and control. Even family relationships and aesthetic values would fall into this category.
3. The state would become an extension of the leader's and his party's will. Government policy would be the implementation of what "the people" truly wanted, as interpreted by the leader.
4. The bond between people and leader would be made concrete and visible by the single allowed party, a mass organization created to form a link between the two. In the cases of fascism and Nazism, the "people" would be understood to include only those belonging to the majority ethnic group (Italians, Germans, or whoever). The others, "aliens," would to one degree or another be considered intruders and have no inherent rights at all.
5. Because the leader and the people would be joined by a mystic bond allowing the leader to be the sole authentic interpreter of the collective will, there would be no need for political competition or discussion. Parliaments and the courts would be subordinated to the leader and his ruling party. Opposing political parties could all be eliminated. They were merely selfish interests seeking to confuse the people and negate their true welfare, which lay in the leader's hands.
6. The collective would be all; the individual, nothing. Individual conscience, affections, and interests would be rigorously subordinated to the needs and demands of the people and the leader, as expressed at various levels through the party.

Antirationalism and Revolutionary Struggle

Totalitarian governments often deliberately turned away from reason and cultivated a kind of *antirationalism* as a philosophy. Instincts were raised above logic—"thinking with the blood," as the Nazis would put it. Such antirationalism was an outgrowth of the late nineteenth century, when a cult of violence appeared among some intellectual fringe groups in Europe. World War I then showed how far civilized humans could descend toward their animal origins. Instead of being revolted by the futile bloodletting of the war, totalitarian theorists often seized on the experiences in the trenches as representing authentic human nature: violent, instinctual, and collective.

Struggle was the key concept for totalitarian states. The struggle of the people and their Leader was never completed. Victory was always conditional and partial because another enemy was always lurking somewhere. The enemies were both domestic and foreign ("international Bolshevism," "Jewish conspiracies," "encircling capitalists"), and it was necessary to be constantly on guard against their tricks and destructive ploys.

Action was also essential, although it often lacked any clear goal. As Benito Mussolini once said, "Act forcefully ... the reason for doing so will appear." In other words, do not worry about why something is done; the act of doing it will produce its own rationale in time. Inevitably, this approach often led to contradictory and illogical policies, but reasonable action was not high on the list of totalitarian priorities.

Italian Fascism

The first example of an attempt at totalitarian government was **fascism** (FASH-ism) in Italy. **Benito Mussolini** (beh-NEE-toh moo-soh-LEE-nee) was the first political figure to see what might be accomplished by blending the techniques of wartime government with an appeal to national sentiment and the resentments of the masses. In his *fascisti*, he brought together traditional underdogs of society and gave them a chance to feel like top dogs. The fascists claimed to be the vanguard of an epoch of national glory, made possible by a radical change in the very nature of social organization and led by a man of destiny—*Il Duce* (il DOO-chay; "the Leader").

After the war ended, Italian workers and peasants became extremely discontented with their liberal parliamentary government. At the Paris peace talks, Italy gained much less than it had hoped for and been promised by France and Britain. The economy was in critical condition because of the sudden end to wartime industrial contracts and the failure to plan for peace. Emigration to the United States, the traditional haven for unemployed Italians, ended when the United States enacted restrictive laws in the early 1920s. The Bolshevik success in Russia was well publicized by the socialists, who soon split into moderates and communists (as did every other European socialist party).

An ex-socialist, Mussolini now came forward as a mercenary strikebreaker and bullyboy in the employ of frightened industrialists and landowners. His party took its name from the ancient Roman symbol of law and order, the *fasces* (a bundle of rods with an ax in the center) carried by the bodyguard of the consul. At first very small, the Fascist Party grew by leaps and bounds in 1921–1922. Fear of communism, a frustrated nationalism, and the accumulated resentments of the lower classes made a potent combination, and Mussolini harnessed and rode that combination into power.

In October 1922, Mussolini pulled off a bloodless coup by inducing the weak King Victor Emmanuel III to appoint him as premier. This was grandiosely termed Mussolini's *March on Rome*. For two years, he ruled by more or less legal and constitutional methods. Then, in 1924, Mussolini rigged elections that returned fascists to a large majority of parliamentary seats. He proceeded to form a one-party state; by the end of 1926, he had forced the other parties to "voluntarily" disband or had driven them underground. Those who protested or attempted resistance were harassed and imprisoned by a brutal secret police. (See the Law and Government box for more on Mussolini.)

Fascist Economic and Social Policies

Fascist economics was a mixture of socialism-without-Marx and *laissez-faire*. Fascist party councils operated at all levels to enforce the government's wishes and distribute government contracts. Organized labor was pressed into becoming an arm of the government. For a few years, this system worked reasonably well and avoided or dampened the class struggles in Italy that were plaguing much of democratically governed Europe during the 1920s and 1930s.

Until the mid-1930s, Mussolini was genuinely popular. Despite his comic-opera strutting and bombast, so long as he did not involve Italy in war, most Italians were fascinated by his undeniable charisma. They believed in his efforts to make Italy a major power for the first time. Drawing freely on his original socialism, he promised action on behalf of the common people, and to some extent he delivered—highways, pregnancy leaves, vacation pay, agricultural credit for the peasants, and the like—but his price was always total control of the nation's politics, enforced by his Black Shirt thugs.

GERMANY IN THE POSTWAR ERA

The new republican government in Berlin came under fire from its first day. It was mainly supported by the Social Democratic Party, which was prepared to accept a parliamentary role. It had the thankless task of attempting to fill the vacuum left by the military and civil collapse at the end of the war. However, the government was forced to accept the hated Versailles Treaty, an act that damned it in the eyes of German nationalists.

Simultaneously, the new government was threatened by Russian-inspired attempts to spread the Bolshevik revolution among the German working classes. In early 1919, German communists attempted to replicate what their Russian colleagues had done in October and November of 1917. However, the German army put down this coup d'état. The conservative generals now chose to go along with the despised Social Democrats rather than risk a communist takeover. In July 1919, the government adopted a new fundamental law, called the *Weimar Constitution* after the town where it was framed. The constitution was a high-minded, liberal, democratic document, but the government it established was already so tarnished in the eyes of many that neither the constitution nor the state it created was considered truly German and legitimate. As long as economic conditions were tolerable and the menace of a communist coup remained, the **Weimar Republic** was not in too much danger from the conservatives, but once these conditions no longer prevailed, the danger was imminent.

Reparations

The most painful part of the Paris peace to Germany was the insistence of the French (less so the Italians and British) that Germany bear the full financial responsibility for war damages and therefore pay reparations. After much delay, the Allies finally presented the full bill in 1921: $33 billion (in 1920 dollars)—approximately the value of Germany's total gross national product for five years! This was supposed to be paid in either gold or goods in annual installments over the next several years.

Paying such sums would have utterly bankrupted Germany, and the government attempted to reason with the French, but the Paris government would not negotiate. In 1921 and 1922, the Germans actually made most of the required payments, but in 1923, they asked for a two-year suspension of payment. The French responded by sending troops to occupy Germany's industrial heartland, the Ruhr area along the lower Rhine. The occupying force was

LAW AND GOVERNMENT

Benito Mussolini (1883–1945)

The totalitarian state was first attempted in Italy. Ceaseless sloganeering and use of every type of modern propaganda carefully promoted its aura of single-minded unity and violence. Coercion of all who resisted was portrayed as the citizen's duty.

The Fascist Party of Italy was the creation of an ex-socialist named Benito Mussolini, the son of a blacksmith, who had obtained an education and become a journalist for socialist newspapers. In 1912, he had become the editor of the major Socialist Party newspaper; from that platform, he called for revolution and regularly denounced all wars in standard Marxist terms as an invention of the capitalists to keep the international proletariat divided and helpless. When World War I broke out, however, Mussolini renounced his pacifism and campaigned for intervention on the side of the Allies; for that, he was kicked out of the Socialist Party, and he proceeded to found a nationalist paper. When Italy entered the war in May 1915, he at once volunteered for frontline duty and in 1917 was wounded in action. He returned to his newspaper, *Il Popolo d'Italia* (The People of Italy), and spent the rest of the war demanding that Italy find its overdue respect and national glory in combat.

The end of the war found an exhausted but supposedly victorious Italy deprived of much of what it had been promised by President Woodrow Wilson's insistence on a peace based on national self-determination. Mussolini rode the ensuing wave of chauvinist reaction and fear of Bolshevism to proclaim himself the patriot who would lead the Italian nation to its just rewards. Appealing cleverly to the whole political spectrum, from the peasants and workers in desperate economic straits to the ultraconservative landlords of the south, the fascist leader appeared to many Italians as the Man of Destiny.

By mid-1922, the fascist black-shirted "squads" were found in every Italian town, composed of disillusioned veterans, unemployed workers, and the flotsam and jetsam of unstable men seeking to find their place in a radically disrupted postwar era. Strengthened by a stream of undercover subsidies from the right-wing parties, the fascists moved into the vacuum in Italian politics left by the bankruptcy of the wartime government's policies.

The 1920s saw the first application of systematic violence, organized and directed from above, against political opponents in a European state. This violence, aimed at obtaining complete conformity of the populace to the wishes of a semi-mythic leader (Il Duce), was promoted by innumerable slogans and distortions of the truth:

> "Mussolini is always right."
>
> "Believe! Obey! Fight!"
>
> "Better to live one day as a lion than a hundred years like a sheep!"
>
> "A minute on the battlefield is worth a lifetime of peace!"
>
> "Nothing has ever been won in history without bloodshed."

ANALYZE AND INTERPRET

Do appeals such as those described here still find resonance in contemporary politics? Can you give some examples?

FoTo PETITTI

BENITO MUSSOLINI. *Il Duce* was nothing if not a showman. He loved to strut around in public in various types of military garb.

instructed to seize everything that was produced—mainly iron and coal. Berlin then encouraged the Ruhr workers to engage in massive nonviolent resistance through strikes that effectively shut down all production.

Inflation and Middle-Class Ruin

The Ruhr occupation and shutdown set off the final spiral of the inflation that had afflicted the German Reich mark since 1919. The inflation ruined many people in Germany's large middle class, which had been the backbone of its productive society for many years. At the height of the inflation, money literally was not worth the paper it was printed on—one U.S. dollar purchased 800 million marks in late 1923. People who lived on fixed incomes, as did much of the middle class, were wiped out. Many were reduced to begging, stealing, and selling family heirlooms to avoid starving.

The inflation was ended by a government loan in U.S. dollars to the German national bank, which reassured people that the paper currency had something of value behind it once more. At the same time, in 1924, the U.S.-sponsored **Dawes Plan** induced the French to leave the Ruhr, forgo some of the reparations payments, and spread the remaining installments over a considerably longer time period if the Germans would resume payments. This agreement held up for a few years (1924–1929), but the psychic and financial damage to the strongest elements of German society could not be made good. The people hated the government that had permitted such things. Many of them began looking for someone who could impose order on a world that had betrayed their legitimate expectations.

Bettmann/Corbis

THE EFFECTS OF INFLATION. Money to burn? This German housewife uses worthless currency to light a fire in her cooking stove. In the early 1920s, the value of the German mark had fallen incredibly.

EASTERN EUROPE

In the Successor states, parliamentary democracy and constitutional government were facing rocky roads after the war. By the mid-1930s, almost all of the Eastern European states had devolved into dictatorships. Czechoslovakia was the only one that retained its democratic and constitutional nature throughout the interwar period. Not coincidentally, it was also by far the most industrially developed, with a vibrant, well-organized working class.

Excessive nationalism was the universal blight of the Eastern Europeans. Every state east of Germany had a large number of minority citizens, most of whom were living unwillingly under alien rule. Many of them (such as the Magyars in Czechoslovakia and Romania, the Germans in the same states and in Poland, and the Austrians in northern Italy) were vulnerable to **irredentism**, the movement to split away from one's present country to unite with a neighboring, ethnically similar state. The fact that Wilson's promise of self-determination was only partially fulfilled at Paris aggravated the condition of those who found themselves left outside of their ethnic state borders. This situation would cause intense political problems throughout the interwar era in Eastern Europe.

The most pressing problem of the Eastern European states was that their economies were still based on subsistence agriculture. Between 60 and 85 percent of the people were either outside the cash economy or derived an erratic and unreliable livelihood from low-paying grain or pastoral agriculture. So long as the world commercial picture was bright and they could export their primary products (grain, hides, lumber), the Eastern Europeans could get along, but when the Great Depression of the 1930s began, this picture quickly changed.

THE WESTERN DEMOCRACIES

The two major European political and social democracies, Britain and France, had several advantages in the 1920s. At least formally, they had been the victors in a war that no European state had really won. Their economies and male labor forces had been hard hit by the war, but not so badly as Germany's, and they had not suffered the destructive inflation of the losing powers.

They had much deeper democratic roots than the other states, and their governments were committed to constitutional processes.

Britain

This does not mean, however, that Britain and France did not have serious problems. For Great Britain, the two most serious issues were economic: (1) unemployment and (2) reduced availability of capital. The British labor force suffered severe and chronic unemployment throughout the entire interwar period for many reasons. During the war, the United States had replaced Britain as the financial center of the world. The British Empire could no longer be relied on to absorb the products of English mines and factories. Wartime losses had dramatically reduced the earnings of the world's largest merchant marine, and British goods and services were now rivaled or overshadowed by several competitors (notably the United States and Japan) in world markets.

Reduced profits and trade opportunities were reflected in the long decline of capital invested by the British in Britain and around the world. Where once the English led all nations by a large margin in profitable investments, they now often lacked the capital to invest. Furthermore, Britain, which had once been the world leader in technology, had slipped behind the United States and Germany in the late nineteenth century and was falling even farther behind now.

These conditions explain the long depression that gripped Britain early and permanently during the interwar period, when millions were "on the dole" (welfare). One result was the sudden rise of the *Labour Party*, a non-Marxist socialist group, to second place in British elections. The new party displaced the Liberals and was even able to elect a Labour government in 1924 over its Conservative opponent. Labour carried great hopes, but it had no more success than the Conservatives and Liberals in curing the nation's ills.

France

In France, on the contrary, economic problems were not apparent in the 1920s. France had a well-balanced national economy, and German reparations and the return of the rich provinces of Alsace and Lorraine after 1918 helped it. But like the other belligerents, France had been seriously weakened by the loss of 1.5 million of its most productive citizens in the war, and German reparations could only slowly make up for the $23 billion in estimated material damage to French property. France's most serious dilemma, however, was of a more psychic or social nature: the fear of a powerful, vengeance-minded Germany on its eastern border and the deeply felt conviction that no cause, not even national survival, was sufficient to justify another such bloodletting as the recent war.

The United States

After the passion aroused by the fight over the League of Nations had subsided, a series of conservative Republican administrations in the United States had been content to preside over a laissez-faire and prospering domestic economy. Foreign policy questions were overshadowed by the general embitterment over the Europeans' "ingratitude" for U.S. contributions to the victory and the Allies' irritating laxity in repaying their war loans. The extensive social reform crusades of the early-twentieth-century Progressives were put aside, and, in President Calvin Coolidge's words, the business of America once again became business.

Fundamental domestic changes were taking place in this decade, although most were unnoticed at the time. The Second Industrial Revolution was now complete. Corporations and the hugely expanded stock market they generated completely dominated both commerce and industry. The consumer economy became much larger thanks to new techniques, such as assembly-line production, retail chain stores, and enormously increased advertising. Suburban living became popular, and the blurring of traditional class divisions that had always been an American characteristic picked up speed. The well-dressed clerk could not be distinguished from the store manager in appearances and tastes; the blue-collar factory hand and the company's stockholders ate the same cornflakes for breakfast and sat in the same grandstand at the baseball game; and the automobile, led by Henry Ford's low-priced and mass-produced creations, swept the country.

The nation as an economic enterprise profited greatly from U.S. involvement in World War I, and the population had suffered little damage compared to the European nations. By the early 1920s, the United States had replaced Britain as the Western Hemisphere's source of technology, trade, and finance and had become the prime creditor nation in world trade. Only a few pessimists were worried about the indiscriminate speculative activity on the New York Stock Exchange.

INTERNATIONAL RELATIONS ON THE EVE OF THE DEPRESSION

The late 1920s saw considerable hope that the lessons of world war had been learned and that war would soon become obsolete. After the failure of the Ruhr occupation and the ensuing economic chaos, the French spirit of vengeance against Germany gave way to a more cooperative stance. In 1925, the two countries signed the

World History Archive/Alamy

THE GREAT CRASH, OCTOBER 24, 1929. As news of the financial catastrophe spread, large panicked crowds converged on the New York Stock Exchange on Wall Street.

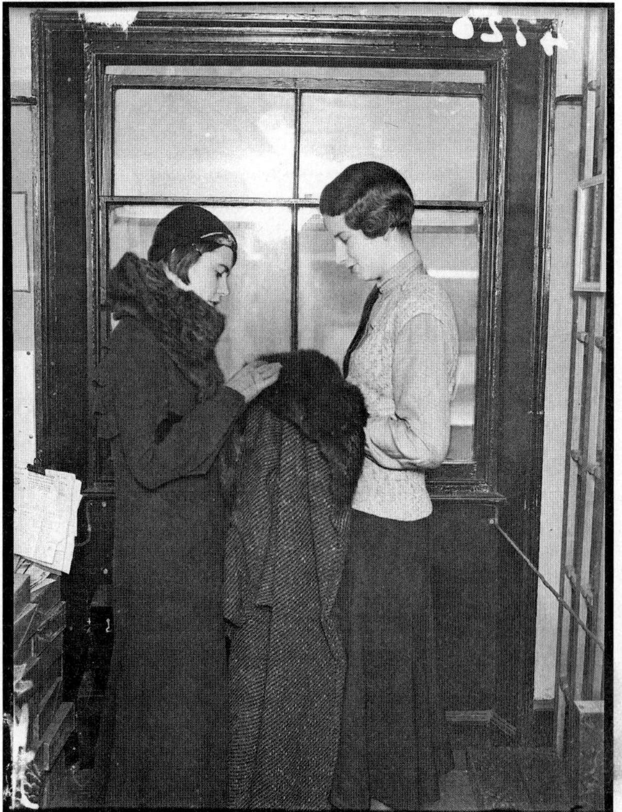
Mary Evans Picture Library/The Image Works

SELLING HER COAT. The Great Depression affected members of all classes. Whereas many protested conditions and went on hunger strikes, middle-class housewives, like this one, sold their personal possessions to help make ends meet.

Locarno Pact, which was to be the high-water mark of interwar diplomacy for peace. Locarno allowed Germany to join the League of Nations in return for its promise to accept its frontier with France and Belgium as permanent. Soon afterward, the Soviet Union was also allowed to join the League. In the same spirit, a series of conferences and agreements were held toward the goal of limiting armaments worldwide.

By this time, the U.S. president was the internationally sophisticated Herbert Hoover—a different individual from his immediate predecessors, Warren Harding and Coolidge, neither of whom had ever set foot in Europe. With Washington's tacit blessings, the flow of investment money from the United States to Europe, particularly Germany, was ever increasing as the profits (on paper) from speculating on the bubbling stock market made many Americans feel rich.

By 1928, Europe appeared to be en route to full recovery from the economic effects of the war. Dollar loans and private investment had helped reestablish German prosperity, and the Germans could thus manage their reduced reparations payments to France and Britain. These countries could then begin to repay the large loans they had received from the United States during the war. For four years, this circular flow of money worked well for all concerned. The Eastern European agricultural products were bought in large quantities by the Western European industrial nations. Except in Britain, unemployment was under control.

Even the West's hostility and fear toward Bolshevism cooled because the Russians ceased to trumpet their confident calls for world revolution and started to behave like reasonable, if somewhat unorthodox, business partners in world trade. It was indicative that by the later 1920s, Soviet diplomats had given up the workers' caps and boots they had donned ten years previously and returned to formal dress of top hat and tails.

The fear that European workers would gravitate en masse toward Bolshevik Russia had proved to be exaggerated. Much communist energy was wasted in fighting the socialists who had refused to join the Communist (Third) International, founded and headquartered in Moscow. Even conservative politicians began to look on the communists, whether in Russia or at home, as a less urgent danger than they had originally appeared to be. In 1929, European international relations seemed to be in a healing mode. The wounds of war were closing, and good economic times allowed old enemies to think of one another as potential partners. Hope was in the air.

SUMMARY

In the immediate postwar years, the political situation was extremely unstable in Central and Eastern Europe, with Russian Bolshevism seeking to expand westward and a series of new states without constitutional stability groping for survival.

The twentieth-century phenomenon of totalitarian government found several homes in Europe after World War I. One experiment occurred in Italy with the fascism of Benito Mussolini, but the German Nazi state under Adolf Hitler would be the most notable and aggressive example. The Weimar Republic of Germany began its history encumbered with the guilt of signing the Versailles Treaty and presiding over a spectacular inflation—two handicaps that it could never overcome in the eyes of many citizens. In Italy, a demagogue named Mussolini bluffed his way to governmental power in 1922 and then proceeded to turn his country into a quasi-totalitarian state.

In the Western democracies, the search for economic recovery seemed to be successful in France, but less so in a subtly weakened Britain. The United States immediately withdrew from its European wartime activity and devoted itself to domestic affairs under conservative Republican administrations. It enjoyed general prosperity, partly as a result of taking the role Britain had vacated in world financial and commercial affairs.

By the end of the decade, international conferences had secured partial successes in disarmament, border guarantees, and pledges of peace. The spread of Bolshevism seemed to have been checked, and the Russians became less threatening. As the decade entered its last year, most signs were hopeful for amity and continued economic progress.

IDENTIFICATION TERMS

Test your knowledge of this chapter's key concepts by defining the following terms. If you can not recall the meaning of certain terms, refresh your memory by looking up the boldfaced term in the chapter, turning to the Glossary at the end of the book, or accessing the terms on the CourseMate website at **www.cengagebrain.com**.

Dawes Plan
fascism
Great Depression of the 1930s
irredentism
John Maynard Keynes
Locarno Pact
Benito Mussolini
totalitarianism
Weimar Republic

FOR FURTHER REFLECTION

1. How did the terms of the Versailles Treaty portend future problems for Europe? What political and economic developments seem to have eased the chances of trouble by the late 1920s?
2. Considering the outcome of World War I for the Western European nations and the United States, how would you explain America's return to more conservative governments and policies in the 1920s? What effects did these have on the behavior of European governments?
3. How do you explain the loosening of social restraints and cultural traditions in Europe and America in the "roaring" 1920s?

TEST YOUR KNOWLEDGE

Test your knowledge of this chapter by answering the following questions. Complete answers appear at the end of the book. You may find even more quiz questions on the CourseMate website at **www.cengagebrain.com**.

1. The necessary prelude to the development of the totalitarian state was
   a. World War I.
   b. the French Revolution.
   c. a decline in the popularity of institutional religion.
   d. the Bolshevik Party charter.
   e. Nazism.
2. Which of the following is not associated with modern totalitarian government?
   a. Continuous striving toward changing goals
   b. The absence of an official ideology
   c. Subordination of the individual to the state
   d. Leadership exercised by a single semisacred individual
   e. A single allowed party
3. Mussolini made his political debut as
   a. a communist organizer in postwar Italy.
   b. a strikebreaker.

c. a military officer.
d. a liberal parliamentary delegate.
e. a writer of scathing editorials against the government.

4. The March on Rome
   a. was a papal visit.
   b. left almost 2,000 people dead.
   c. took place when Hitler visited Mussolini.
   d. was Mussolini's first review of the troops under his command.
   e. brought Mussolini to power.
5. The postwar German state was the product of
   a. a communist coup following Germany's military defeat in the war.
   b. the Allied Powers' intervention and postwar occupation.
   c. a liberal constitution written by the Social Democrats and their allies.
   d. a generals' dictatorship imposed to prevent an attempted communist takeover.
   e. a new republic that worked to enforce the will of the people.
6. The nation that suffered most dramatically from inflation after World War I was
   a. France.
   b. Russia.
   c. Germany.
   d. Britain.
   e. Poland.
7. The Dawes Plan was a
   a. proposal by U.S. financiers to ensure Germany's recovery and payment of reparations.
   b. U.S. government plan to carry out the punishment of Germany.
   c. British-French scheme to ensure German payment of reparations.
   d. U.S. government plan to try to get the country out of the Great Depression.
   e. proposal by the victors of World War I to outlaw war.
8. Easing of post-war French aversion towards Germany resulted in the
   a. occupation of the Ruhr.
   b. creation of the League of Nations.
   c. signing of the Paris Peace Treaty.
   d. American refusal to join the League of Nations.
   e. signing of the Locarno Pact.
9. The nation that had the most deep-rooted unemployment problem in postwar Europe was
   a. Great Britain.
   b. Germany.
   c. France.
   d. Italy.
   e. Belgium.
10. Art in the years after the end of World War II was
    a. characterized by alienation and disillusion.
    b. totally rejected by the public.
    c. unusual for its return to past love of realism.
    d. marked by a desire to understand the causes of the war.
    e. overshadowed by a popular fascination with psychology.

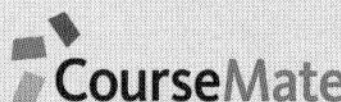

Visit the CourseMate website at **www.cengagebrain.com** for additional study tools and review materials for this chapter.

The Soviet Experiment to World War II

42

It is true that liberty is precious—SO PRECIOUS THAT IT MUST BE RATIONED. —VLADIMIR LENIN

CHAPTER OUTLINE

1917	March/October revolutions
1918	Treaty of Brest-Litovsk; civil war begins
1921	New Economic Policy
1927	Josef Stalin emerges as leader
1928	First Five-Year Plan begins
1936–1938	Great Purge

One of the chief by-products of World War I was a radical experiment in social organization that seized Russia and was destined to last for seventy-five years. In 1917, the Russian Marxists took advantage of the disruptions, resentments, and weaknesses caused by World War I to carry out revolution. The first socialist state, the Union of Soviet Socialist Republics (USSR), was born under the watchful eye of a handful of ambitious, visionary men around Vladimir I. Lenin. Their communist government, which proudly called itself the realization of Marx's "dictatorship of the proletariat," was a frightening phenomenon to most of the rest of the world. But everywhere some men and women were inspired by its example and wished to imitate it in their own countries during the interwar period.

THE MARCH REVOLUTION, 1917

What had set the stage for this radical upheaval? By 1917, the imperial government of Russia had been brought to the point of collapse by the demands of "total war." Twelve years previously, an aborted revolution had finally brought a constitution and the elements of modern parliamentary government to the Russian people. But the broadly democratic aims of the Revolution of 1905 had been frustrated by a combination of force and guile, and the tsar maintained an autocratic grip on the policy-making machinery as the First World War began.

In the opening years of World War I, the Russians suffered huge casualties and lost extensive territory to the Germans and the Austrians. Their generals were the least competent of all the belligerents. The tsar's officials were unable or unwilling to enlist popular support for the conflict.

As the wartime defeats and mistakes piled up, the maintenance of obedience became impossible. By spring 1917, the food supply for the cities was becoming tenuous and bread riots were breaking out. Finally, the demoralized garrison troops refused to obey orders from their superiors. With no prior planning, no bloodshed, and no organization, the **March Revolution (of 1917)** simply came about when the unpopular and confused Tsar Nicholas II suddenly abdicated his throne. A committee of the *Duma* (the parliament), which had been ignored and almost powerless until now, moved into the vacuum thus created and took over the government of Russia. The Duma committee, which called itself the **Provisional Government**, intended to create a new, democratic constitution and hold free elections as soon as possible.

The new government was a weak foundation on which to attempt to build a democratic society, however. It had no mandate from the people but had simply appointed itself. Leadership soon passed into the hands of Alexander Kerensky, a moderate, non-Marxist socialist. The peasants—about 80 percent of the population—were desperately tired of the First World War, whose aims they had never understood and which they hated because it was devouring their sons. If peace were not soon achieved, they would refuse to grow and ship food to the cities, and Russian government of any kind must collapse. But Kerensky thought that Russia dare not make a separate, losing peace despite the ominous tide of discontent. He believed that only a victorious peace would allow the newborn Russian democracy to survive, and he was therefore determined to keep Russia in the war.

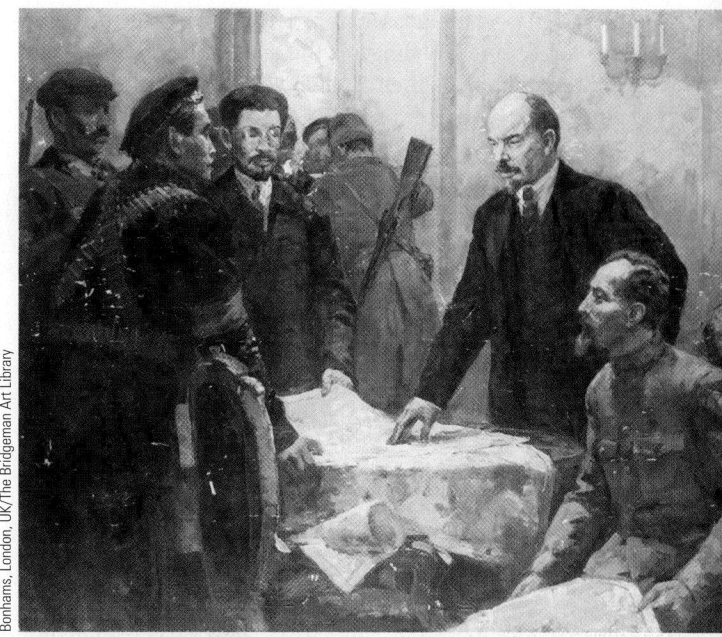

THE COMMUNIST PARTY MEETING. Although a Marxist, Lenin differed from Karl Marx on the importance (as he saw it) of a committed, professionally led party to the success of a workers' revolution. Here he is portrayed with Leon Trotsky (*standing left*) at a meeting of the Bolshevik Party.

THE BOLSHEVIKS

The people's war weariness opened the way for the uncompromising communists, or **Bolsheviks**, led by the brilliant tactician **Vladimir I. Lenin** (1870–1924). Before the spring of 1917, Lenin had been a refugee from his native land, living in Swiss and German exile for twenty years, plotting and propagandizing incessantly for the triumph of the socialist revolution. He was the leader of a movement that had perhaps 100,000 members and sympathizers in the entire Russian imperial population of about 160 million.

Under Lenin's guidance, the Bolsheviks had changed Marx's doctrines a great deal to make them fit with the Russian realities. Lenin insisted on a full-time, professional leadership supervising a conspiratorial, clandestine party. Unlike Marx, he believed that such a party could hasten the coming of the revolution and that the peasantry could be led into revolutionary action. Lenin thought that in a country such as Russia, where the urban workers' class was at most about 5 percent of the population in 1910, only a movement that galvanized peasant discontent stood a chance of success. Lenin was clear that the vague dictatorship of the proletariat that Marx had talked about would quickly become a dictatorship of the Bolsheviks. Within that party, the small group around Lenin, called the Central Committee, would, in fact, rule.

The Bolshevik leader returned to Russia immediately after the March Revolution, when the new government, anxious to display its democratic credentials, allowed total freedom to all political groups. Through the summer of 1917, Lenin and the Provisional Government under Kerensky dueled for power. The chosen arena was the *soviets* (councils) of workers and soldiers, which had formed all over Russia. Chairing the supremely important St. Petersburg soviet was **Leon Trotsky** (1879–1940), Lenin's dynamic second-in-command, who was able to lead the body into the Bolshevik camp.

In the short term, the fate of the country would necessarily be determined by which group could secure the allegiance of the armed forces. The imperial army had been disintegrating since the spring, with mass desertions commonplace. The peasant soldiers hated the war, and a wide cleft had opened between them and their middle- and upper-class officers. Into this rift, Bolshevik pacifist and revolutionary propaganda was pouring and finding a ready audience.

Kerensky decided to accede to the demands of his hard-pressed allies in the West and gamble everything on an ill-prepared summer offensive, which was soon turned into a rout by the Germans' counterattack. By September, the enemy was at the gates of St. Petersburg, and the army was visibly collapsing. The cities were on the point of mass starvation, and the peasants were taking the law into their own hands and dividing up the estates of their helpless landlords, much as their French counterparts had done a century and a quarter previously.

THE OCTOBER REVOLUTION

By mid-October, Lenin had convinced a hesitant central committee that the time for armed revolutionary action was at hand. He insisted that the brilliantly simple Bolshevik slogans of "All power to the Soviets" and "Land, bread, peace" would carry the day despite the tiny number of Bolsheviks.

On the evening of October 26, Old Style (November 6 by the modern calendar), the Bolsheviks used their sympathizers among the workers and soldiers in St. Petersburg to seize government headquarters and take control of the city. The great **October Revolution (of 1917)** of Soviet folklore was in fact a coup d'état that cost only a few hundred lives to topple a government that, as Lenin had insisted, had practically no support left among the people. In the next few weeks, Moscow and other major industrial towns followed St. Petersburg by installing Bolshevik authorities after engaging in varying amounts of armed struggle in the streets. What about the 80 percent of the population outside the cities? For several months, the countryside remained almost untouched by these urban events, with one exception: In the villages, the peasants took advantage of the breakdown of government to seize the land they had long craved from the hands of the nobles and the church. For the peasants, the redistribution of land from absentee landlords to themselves was the beginning and the end of revolution. Of Marxist theory about collectivization of agriculture they knew and wanted to know nothing at all.

Lenin moved swiftly to establish the Bolshevik dictatorship, using both armed force and the massive confusion that had overtaken all levels of Russian government after October. By December, large economic enterprises of all types were being confiscated and put under government supervision. The first version of the dreaded political police, the **Cheka**, had been formed and was being employed against various enemies. The remnants of the imperial army were being bolshevized and turned into a weapon for use against internal opponents.

CIVIL WAR

Against heavy opposition from his own associates, Lenin insisted that Russia must make immediate peace with the Germans and the Austrians. His rationale proved to be correct: A civil war against the many enemies of Bolshevism was bound to come soon, and the party could not afford to still be fighting a foreign foe when it did. In March 1918, the harsh **Treaty of Brest-Litovsk** was signed with the Central Powers. The collapse of the Central Powers eight months later made this treaty a dead letter. By that time, the Bolshevik "Reds" were engaged in a massive and very bloody civil war, which was to last two and a half years and cause about as many Russian deaths as had occurred in World War I.

The Reds won this conflict for several reasons. They were far-better organized and coordinated by a unitary leadership than were their opponent "Whites." Despite his total lack of military experience, Lenin's colleague Trotsky proved to be an inspiring and effective commander-in-chief of the Red Army, which he created in record time. The Reds had a big advantage in that they controlled most of the interior of European Russia, including the major cities of St. Petersburg and Moscow and the rail networks that served them (see Map 42.1). The opposition armies, separated by vast distances from one another, were often at cross-purposes, did not trust one another, and had little coordination in either military or political goals. Moreover, the Whites were decisively defeated in the propaganda battles, in which the Reds played up the White generals' multiple links with both the old regime and the landlords. Personal rivalries also damaged the White leadership.

The intervention of several foreign powers in the civil war also became a Red asset, although it was intended to assist the Whites. In early 1918, fearing that the Bolsheviks would take Russia out of the war and that material meant for the old imperial army would fall into enemy hands, the French and British sent small forces into Russia. Inevitably, these forces clashed with the Reds, and the foreigners (including a small U.S. detachment in the far north) began actively assisting the Whites. Overall, the foreign intervention provided little practical help for the Whites but gave the Leninists an effective propaganda weapon for rallying support among the Russian people.

ECONOMIC REVIVAL AND INTERNAL STRUGGLES

By the summer of 1921, the Bolsheviks were close enough to victory that they abolished their coercive "War Communism"—the label they used for rule at the point of a gun. Lenin had employed this method since 1918 through the Red Army and the Cheka, and it had sustained the Bolshevik rule but only at great costs. Along with terrible famine and the disruptions of civil war, War Communism had instituted state terrorism against many of its own citizens and reduced the Russian gross national product to an estimated 20 percent of what it had been in 1913!

In place of War Communism, Lenin now prescribed the **New Economic Policy (NEP)**, which encouraged small-scale capitalist business and profit seekers, while retaining the "commanding heights" of the national economy firmly in state hands. By this time, state hands meant Bolshevik

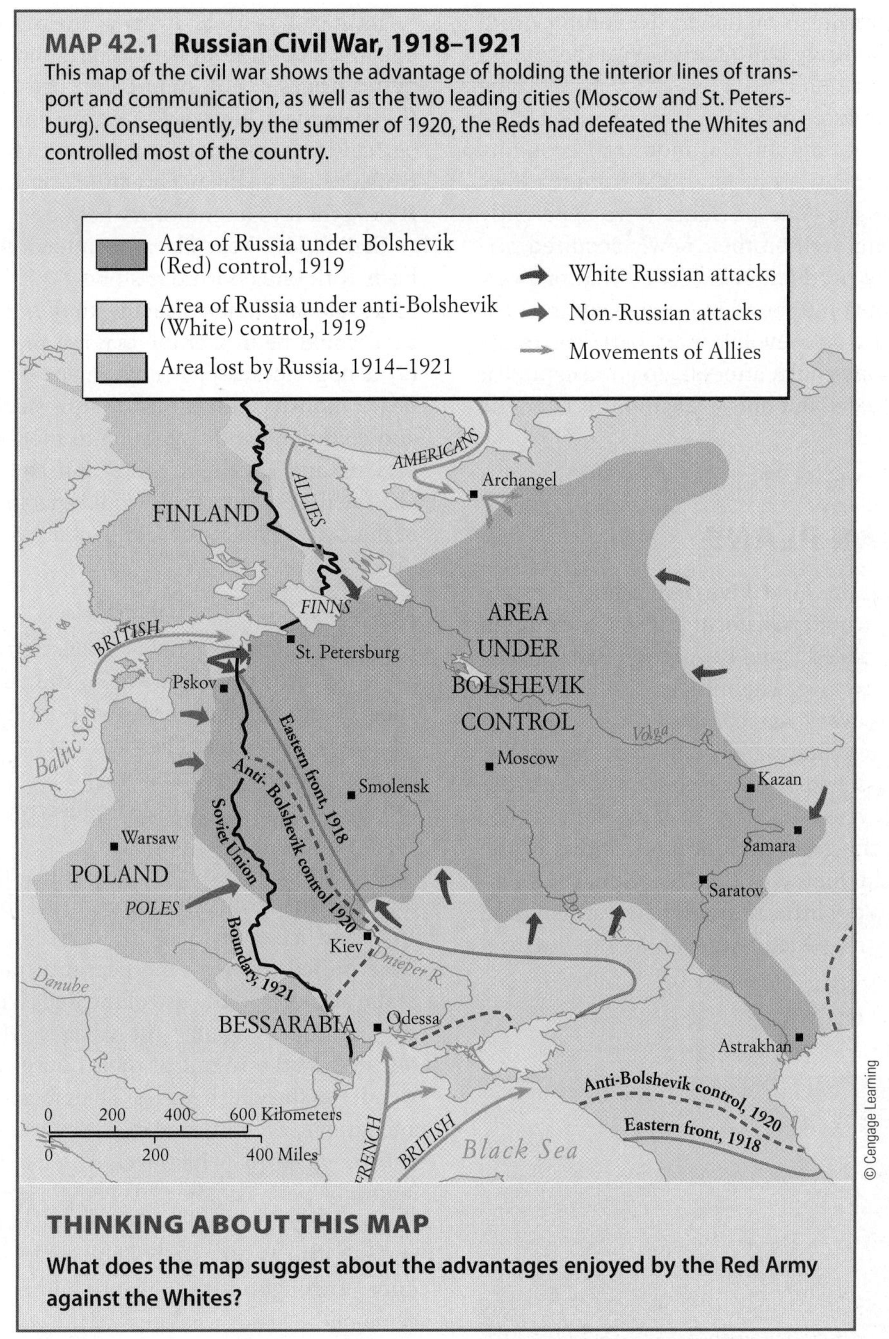

MAP 42.1 Russian Civil War, 1918–1921
This map of the civil war shows the advantage of holding the interior lines of transport and communication, as well as the two leading cities (Moscow and St. Petersburg). Consequently, by the summer of 1920, the Reds had defeated the Whites and controlled most of the country.

THINKING ABOUT THIS MAP

What does the map suggest about the advantages enjoyed by the Red Army against the Whites?

hands. The Communist Party of the Soviet Union (CPSU), headed by Lenin and his colleagues, was in sole control of both economic and political affairs. By 1922, all other parties had been banned, and Russia was fast becoming a totalitarian state.

After being wounded in an attempted assassination, Lenin suffered a series of strokes starting in 1922. Power in everyday affairs was transferred to an inside group of the Central Committee, called the *Politburo* (Political Bureau). This group included Lenin's closest colleagues. Trotsky was the best known and seemed to hold the dominant position within the party's innermost circle, but when Lenin died in January 1924 without naming anyone to succeed him, a power struggle was already under way.

One of Trotsky's rivals was **Josef Stalin** (1879–1953), a tested party worker since early youth. Lenin valued him for his administrative abilities and hard work. At the end of his life, however, Lenin had turned against Stalin because of his "rudeness" and his contempt for others' opinions.

Lenin was too late in reaching this conclusion: Stalin, as the party general secretary (administrator), had already cemented his position. Brilliantly manipulating others, Stalin was able to defeat first Trotsky and then other contestants for Lenin's position by the late 1920s. By 1927, he was the leader of the majority faction in the Politburo and thus of the Communist Party. By 1932, Stalin was becoming dictator of the Soviet Union's entire public life. By 1937, he was the undisputed master of 180 million people. Under the NEP, both the agrarian and the industrial economy had made a stunning recovery by late 1928 from the lows of the early postwar era. The peasants were apparently content and producing well on their newly acquired private farms. Industrial production exceeded that of 1913. To foreign businessmen interested in Russian contracts, it appeared that Bolshevism's revolutionary bark was much worse than its bite. One could, after all, do good capitalist business with the Soviets. But only a few months later, the entire picture changed.

THE FIVE-YEAR PLANS

At Stalin's command, the **First Five-Year Plan** of 1928–1932 was adopted. It would transform the Soviet Union in several ways. The so-called Stalin Revolution had started.

Russia was still an overwhelmingly rural, agrarian society, backward in every way compared with Western Europe or the United States. Throughout the 1920s, some party members had been discontented with the "two steps forward, one step back" concessions of the NEP. In their view, the good proletarian workers in the cities were still at the mercy of the "reactionary" peasants who fed them. Very little additional investment had been made in industry, which was seen as the key to a socialist society.

State K. Savitsky Art Museum, Pensa/The Bridgeman Art Library

REVISING HISTORY: STALIN AT LENIN'S FUNERAL. This painting intentionally features Stalin looking down on Lenin's casket, with no other rivals for the Communist Party leadership in the picture. What does this imply?

In the fall of 1928, many of the more-prosperous peasants decided to hold back their grain until they could get better prices in the state-controlled markets. Stalin used this perceived "betrayal" as a reason to start the drive for agricultural collectivization and rapid industrialization, which would go on at a breathtaking pace until World War II brought it to a temporary halt.

Stalin's Five-Year Plan was intended to kill three major birds with one enormous stone: (1) The age-old resistance of private landholders to any kind of government supervision would be broken by massive pressure to collectivize; (2) a huge increase in investment would be allocated to heavy industry and infrastructure (such as transportation and communication systems) to modernize the backward society; and (3) the organization and efforts required to achieve the first two goals would enable the total integration of the citizenry into the CPSU-controlled political process.

Agrarian Collectivization

In 1929, Stalin began his collectivization campaign as a way to "win the class war in the villages"—that is, the alleged struggle between the poor peasants and those who were better off. The richer peasants (*kulaks*) were to be dispossessed by force; the poorer peasants were to be forced onto newly founded collective farms under party supervision.

As many as 10 million peasants are estimated to have died in the collectivization drive between 1929 and 1933 and most of them in an artificially caused famine. Determined to break the peasants' persistent resistance, Stalin authorized the use of the Red Army as well as armed party militants against the villages. Millions were driven off their land and out of their houses and condemned to wander as starving beggars. Their former lands, machinery, and animals were turned over to the new *collectives*. These enormous farms, which were run like factories with wage labor by party bosses, proved to be inefficient, largely because the peasants heartily disliked their new situation and felt little responsibility and even less incentive to produce. Throughout the Soviet Union's history, agriculture remained a major weakness of the economy.

The collectivization struggle left deep scars, and its costs were still being paid a generation later. Stalin rammed it through because he believed it was essential if the Soviet Union were to survive. The ignorant, conservative peasants must be brought under direct government control and their numbers reduced by forcing them into a new industrial labor force. Both of these goals were eventually reached, but at a price that no rational economist could justify.

Industrial Progress

Stalin's second goal was rapid industrialization. Here again, the costs were very high, but their justification was easier. Soviet gains in industry between 1929 and 1940 were truly impressive. In percentage terms, the growth achieved in several branches of heavy industry and infrastructure was greater than any other country in history has ever achieved in an equivalent period—about 400 percent even by conservative estimates. Whole industrial cities rose up from the Siberian or Central Asian plains, built partly by forced labor and partly by idealists who believed in Stalin and in communism's vision of a new life. Throughout the economy, "fulfilling the plan" became all-important. Untouched by free-market realities and constraints, the Soviet managers plunged ahead in a wild race to raise total production.

The new industry turned out capital goods, not consumer items. Consumer goods such as clothes and baby carriages became more difficult to obtain, and their prices rose ever higher throughout the 1930s. When a suit of clothes could be found, it cost the equivalent of four months' wages for a skilled worker. Items such as refrigerators, automobiles, and washing machines were out of the question. Even basic food had to be rationed for a while because of the drop in production caused by collectivization. It is testimony to the extraordinary capacity of the Russian people to suffer in silence that so much was accomplished at such high costs with so little reward for those doing it.

The dislocations and hardships caused by the industrialization drive in the 1930s were nearly as severe as those caused by collectivization in the countryside. And Stalin's slave laborers performed much of the work on the new mines, canals, logging operations, and other projects. By conservative estimates, fully 10 percent of the 1930s Soviet gross national product was produced by prisoners of the NKVD (one of the several successive names for the Soviet political police).

Hulton-Deutsch Collection/Corbis

LENIN AND STALIN: A FAKED PHOTOGRAPH. This photo of the two leaders, purportedly taken shortly before Lenin's death and used extensively by the Stalinist propaganda machine to show the closeness of their relationship, is known to have been falsified. Stalin's figure was placed into the photo later. Lenin came to distrust Stalin in his last days but took only ineffective measures to warn the party against him.

THE STALINIST DICTATORSHIP

The third goal of the Five-Year Plans was, in effect, a revolution by Stalin and a changed Communist Party against the Soviet peoples. In 1928, Stalin was chief of a CPSU that was still an elite organization. It was relatively small (about 6 percent of the adult population) and difficult to join. The party was tightly disciplined and composed of intellectuals, white-collar personnel, and some workers. It included very few peasants and few women above the lowest ranks. Many members still knew little of Stalin and were totally unaware of the secret high-level struggles for control in the Politburo.

Stalin emerged as the Boss (*vozhd*) on his fiftieth birthday in 1929, when a tremendous fuss was made over his role as Lenin's successor. From this time on, no one else in the Soviet hierarchy was allowed to rival Stalin in press coverage or authority. From the early 1930s, every party member lived in Stalin's shadow. He proved to be a master of Mafia-style politics, never forgetting who had helped and who had hurt him in his climb to power. Absolutely vindictive toward political rivals and enemies (they were the same to him), his character has long fascinated many Russian and foreign analysts.

Stalin cultivated an image of mystery. Unlike his fellow dictators, he had no gift for speech making, and he never indulged in the dramatics that some other dictators constantly employed in their public appearances. After 1935, he was rarely seen in public—and then only under totally controlled circumstances.

Although he was a Georgian by birth, Stalin became a strong Russian nationalist and soon transformed what had truly been a supranational movement under Lenin into a Russian one. He took the international communist organization, called the *Comintern* (Communist International) and based in Moscow, and turned it into an organ of Russian foreign policy. No foreign communists dared to challenge the policies dictated by Stalin's stooges on the governing board of the Comintern, even when, as sometimes happened, those policies were directly opposed to the interests of the Communist Party in the foreigners' country. In the communist world, Moscow alone called the tune.

The Purges: A Terrorized Society

Although Stalin had crushed his high-level opponents by 1933, he still had some opposition in the party. In 1935, he apparently decided that he must crush those opponents too. He proceeded to do so over the next few years in a fashion that shocked and mystified the world.

Between 1936 and late 1938, Moscow was the scene of a series of **show trials**, where leading party members were presented with absurd charges of treason and sabotage. Virtually all of Lenin's surviving comrades had disappeared from public sight by 1939, and Stalin was alone as master. Hundreds of thousands of ordinary citizens were arrested at the same time for alleged crimes against the state and sentenced to prison or to the Siberian labor camps, where most of them eventually died.

To this day, historians do not agree on an explanation of why the purge happened. What is known is that between 1935 and the end of Stalin's life in 1953, perhaps 10 million Soviet citizens were at one time or another banished to prison camps without trial and almost always without proof of violation of Soviet law. Everyone had a close relative or friend who had been spirited away, usually in the night, by the dreaded secret police. These "administrative measures," based on anonymous denunciations, were conducted completely outside the usual court system, and often the prisoners were never told of their crimes, even after serving many years. Some survived their sentences, but many did not. It was commonplace for the camp overseers to extend the original sentences, adding five more years for such "offenses" as trading a bit of bread for a pair of socks.

Stalin never offered an explanation for his actions, then or later. One thing is certain: If Stalin instituted the **Great Purge** to terrorize the party and Soviet society into complete obedience, he succeeded. Until his death, no one in the party, military, or general society dared oppose him openly.

Odessa Fine Arts Museum, Ukraine/The Bridgeman Art Library

VICTORY IN THE FIVE-YEAR PLAN. Soviet propaganda for the "Workers' Paradise" created by Stalin's dictatorship particularly liked to show the alleged enthusiasm of the workers for their new tasks. This view was often the opposite of the truth.

How did Stalin's dictatorship compare with Adolf Hitler's—that other terrifying Western dictatorship of the twentieth century? One major difference should be noted: Stalin posed as the champion of the underdog everywhere, whereas Hitler was the champion only of the Germans. We will see in Chapter 43 that Hitler's narrowly racist ideology had no vision of the beneficial transformation of human society, whereas Stalin's international communism did. Stalin and his assistants were able to fashion that vision so that a significant portion of the world, from China to Cuba, came to believe in it—for a time.

LIFE UNDER THE DICTATORSHIP

Stalin and his associates believed that a "new Soviet man" would emerge after a few years of Soviet rule. In this ideal, they were sadly mistaken. The Soviet people continued to be old-style human beings with all their faults, but a new type of society did emerge in the Soviet Union, and it had both good and bad points.

Possibilities Expanded

On the good side, the forced-draft industrialization and modernization under the Five-Year Plans allowed a large number of human beings to improve their professional prospects dramatically. Mass education of even a rather primitive sort enabled many people to hold jobs and assume responsibilities that they could not have handled or would never have been offered in the old society. Many illiterate peasants saw their sons and daughters obtain degrees in advanced technology, while the new Soviet schools turned out engineers by the millions. For example, Nikita Khrushchev, Stalin's successor as head of the Communist Party, worked as a coal miner in his early years before becoming a full-time communist organizer.

Millions of Russian and Soviet women were emancipated from a life that offered them no real opportunities to use their minds or develop their talents. Despite much propaganda to the contrary, the Soviet leaders did not really believe in equality for women, and the highest positions remained overwhelmingly male until the Soviet Union's collapse, but the leaders *did* believe in additional skilled labor, male or female. By the end of the 1930s, most Soviet women worked outside the home. Living standards were low, and the woman's additional income was crucial for many Soviet families. Still, the door to a more varied, more challenging life had been opened and would not be closed again.

Then, a basic "safety net" was established for all citizens. Medical care was free, all workers received pensions, and education was open and free to all politically reliable people. There were few actual ceilings to talent, provided of course that one was either a sincere communist or paid the necessary lip service to the system and the dictators (see the Arts and Culture box). Aside from such measures,

ARTS AND CULTURE

From Communism to Personality Cult: A Hymn to Stalin

Under both Lenin and Stalin, the relatively benign Marxist notions about socialism and communism had become far more radical, soon evolving into a full-blown personality cult. The Communist Party in the Soviet state became a true instrument of totalitarianism. The party rigorously controlled all thought, all media, and all culture. Survival depended on pleasing the men who controlled the party and the state. This especially became true under Stalin, as the following example evinces:

> Thank you, Stalin. Thank you because I am joyful. Thank you because I am well. No matter how old I become, I shall never forget how we received Stalin two days ago. Centuries will pass, and the generations still to come will regard us as the happiest of mortals, as the most fortunate of men, because we lived in the century of centuries, because we were privileged to see Stalin, our inspired leader. Yes, and we regard ourselves as the happiest of mortals because we are the contemporaries of a man who never had an equal in world history.
>
> The men of all ages will call on thy name, which is strong, beautiful, wise and marvelous. Thy name is engraven on every factory, every machine, every place on the earth, and in the hearts of all men.
>
> Every time I have found myself in his presence I have been subjugated by his strength, his charm, his grandeur. I have experienced a great desire to sing, to cry out, to shout with joy and happiness. And now see me—me!—on the same platform where the Great Stalin stood a year ago. In what country, in what part of the world could such a thing happen?
>
> I write books. I am an author. All thanks to thee, O great educator, Stalin. I love a young woman with a renewed love and shall perpetuate myself in my children—all thanks to thee, great educator, Stalin. I shall be eternally happy and joyous, all thanks to thee, great educator, Stalin. Everything belongs to thee, chief of our great country. And when the woman I love presents me with a child the first word it shall utter will be: Stalin.
>
> O great Stalin, O leader of the peoples,
> Thou who broughtest man to birth.
> Thou who fructifiest the earth,
> Thou who restorest to centuries,
> Thou who makest bloom the spring,
> Thou who makest vibrate the musical chords ...
> Thou, splendour of my spring, O thou,
> Sun reflected by millions of hearts.
> —A. O. Avidenko

ANALYZE AND INTERPRET

How sincere do you think the writer was in his praise for the dictator? Is it possible that he was as sincere in his thoughts and feelings as in his words? Did Stalin and the Communist Party do any good for Russia?

From the *Internet Modern History Sourcebook*, ed. Paul Halsall, 2006.

however, approximately 7 million people died both inside and outside the Soviet labor camps (the infamous *Gulag Archipelago*) from want and from state persecution for their political views.

Liberties Suppressed

On the bad side were all of the drawbacks we have already mentioned as inherent in the Stalinist dictatorship: lack of any political freedom, terror and lawlessness, and low standards of living. There were other disadvantages too: religious persecution, cultural censorship, constant indoctrination with a simplistic and distorted version of Marxism, and constant interference in private lives. For a certain time during the 1920s and early 1930s, many well-meaning people in and outside the Soviet Union were able to rationalize the bad aspects of Soviet life by balancing them against the good. They accepted the Stalinist statement "You can't make an omelet without breaking eggs." They believed that within a few years, Soviet society would be the envy of the capitalists in the West. Then, the glories of developed socialism would be wonderful to behold, and the evils of the transition period would soon be forgotten.

The terror of the purges of the mid-1930s disillusioned many, however, and the continued iron dictatorship after World War II discouraged many more. Even the youths, who had been the most enthusiastic members of the party and the hardest workers, were disappointed that the enormous sacrifices made during World War II seemed to go unappreciated by the leader. The CPSU lost its spirit and its moral authority as the voice of revolutionary ideals. In the postwar years, it came to resemble just another huge bureaucracy, providing a ladder upward for opportunists and manipulators. The only real talent necessary for a successful party career became to pretend to worship Stalin.

MATERIAL AND SOCIAL WELFARE IN THE INTERWAR SOVIET UNION

Material life under Lenin and Stalin generally remained hard, but it gradually began to show improvement. The success of the NEP reversed the near collapse that the Soviet Union's economy had suffered during the civil war years. Radical though they were, Stalin's Five-Year Plans led to considerable improvements in the infrastructure and in the output of basic industries. Living standards remained well below those of Europe and North America; yet overall conditions continued to improve until World War II and the sufferings it brought on the Russian people.

Social problems were sometimes met head-on by government action, and sometimes ignored. The divorce and abortion rates shot up in the 1920s, in line with the communist-supported emancipation of Russian women. In the mid-1930s, Stalin reintroduced tight restrictions on abortion and divorce and rewarded women who bore many children with cash and medals ("Heroine of Socialist Labor"). The underlying reason for this change in policy was the shortage of labor in Soviet industry and agriculture, both of which were extraordinarily inefficient in their use of labor and which suffered from endemic low productivity.

Soviet medical care was supposedly free to all but was spotty in quality, and party membership was a definite advantage. Clinics were established for the first time throughout the countryside, but the problems of poor nutrition, superstition about prenatal and postnatal care, and the large Muslim population's distrust of all Western-style medicine were great handicaps to overcome in lowering the epidemic death rate or infant mortality.

Alcoholism remained what it had always been in Russia: a serious obstacle to labor efficiency and a drain on resources. Repeated government campaigns for sobriety had only limited effects on the peasants and urban workers. Home brew was common despite heavy penalties on its production.

Some common crimes were effectively reduced, at least for a time. (The Soviet government was always reluctant to provide accurate statistics on social problems, especially crime.) Prostitution became rare for a while, partly because the original Bolshevik attitude toward sex was quite liberal: Men and women were equals and should be able to arrange their sexual activities as they saw fit without interference. This changed over time to a much stricter Puritanism. Financial offenses, such as embezzlement and fraud, were almost eliminated because opportunities to commit them were originally almost nonexistent. This, too, was to change radically in later days. Theft, on the other hand, became common, as all classes of people frequently had to resort to it to survive during the civil war; later, the attitude became that stealing from a government-owned shop or enterprise was not really a crime, as all property belonged to "the people," hence to no one. Violence against persons increased in the early Soviet period, when civil war, starving wanderers, and class struggle were commonplace and provided some cover for personal criminal acts. So far as could be seen from statistics, violent crimes then reverted to their original prerevolutionary patterns.

SUMMARY

The Bolshevik revolution of 1917 was one of the milestones of modern history. For a long time, millions of idealists considered it the definitive dawn of a new age. No other modern social or economic movement has convinced so many different people that it was the solution to society's various ills.

Lenin's installation of a dictatorship by the Communist Party immediately after the revolution broke the ground for the Stalinist rule of later date. After a hidden power struggle, Leon Trotsky, the presumed successor to Lenin, was overcome by Josef Stalin, who had mastered the art of closed-group infighting better than any of his competitors. In a few more years, he had made himself the master of his country in unprecedented fashion.

In 1928, the introduction of the First Five-Year Plan was virtually a second (or Stalinist) revolution. Agrarian life was transformed by collectivization of the peasants, and the USSR became a major industrial power. Midway through the 1930s, the Great Purge of both party and people began, claiming millions of innocent victims. Stalinist policies helped the material welfare of large segments of the Soviet populace. These measures improved education, professional opportunities, and medical care and generally allowed the population to live a more modern lifestyle, but the Soviet people paid high prices for these advantages. They gave up all political and economic liberties and suffered through a generation of great hardships under the dictatorial rule of the party and its omnipotent head.

IDENTIFICATION TERMS

Test your knowledge of this chapter's key concepts by defining the following terms. If you can not recall the meaning of certain terms, refresh your memory by looking up the boldfaced term in the chapter, turning to the Glossary at the end of the book, or accessing the terms on the CourseMate website at **www.cengagebrain.com**.

Bolsheviks
Cheka
First Five-Year Plan
Great Purge
Vladimir I. Lenin
March Revolution (of 1917)
New Economic Policy (NEP)
October Revolution (of 1917)
Provisional Government
show trials
Josef Stalin
Treaty of Brest-Litovsk
Leon Trotsky

FOR FURTHER REFLECTION

1. In what ways does it appear that Lenin and the Bolsheviks differed in their ideas about "communism" from Marx?
2. To what extent was Lenin's and Trotsky's success in bringing the Bolshevik (or Communist) Party to power in Russia in 1917 the result of chance?
3. What efforts did Soviet leaders make to export the communist revolution to other parts of the world? To what extent were they successful? Why would conditions during the 1930s have been especially favorable to the spread of communism? What might be the appeal of communism (or at least Marxism) to countries with extremely high levels of poverty?
4. To what extent did Lenin and Stalin solve the major problems of Russia once they came to power?

TEST YOUR KNOWLEDGE

Test your knowledge of this chapter by answering the following questions. Complete answers appear at the end of the book. You may find even more quiz questions on the CourseMate website at **www.cengagebrain.com**.

1. The March, 1917 Revolution in Russia resulted in
   a. the abdication of Nicholas II and the crowning of a new Tsar.
   b. new leadership under the Duma and a Provisional Government.
   c. the surrender of Russia to Germany.
   d. new leadership under the Duma.
   e. the murder of Alexander Kerensky and his associates.
2. In the early 1920s, Lenin's closest associate and apparent successor as leader of the Soviet Party and state was
   a. Stalin.
   b. Trotsky.
   c. Khrushchev.
   d. Romanov.
   e. Kerensky.
3. The October Revolution began in the city of
   a. Leningrad.
   b. Moscow.
   c. St. Petersburg.
   d. Kiev.
   e. Stalingrad.
4. By 1921 in Russia,
   a. a large part of the population was taking up arms against communism.
   b. the majority of Russians had become communists.
   c. a civil war had greatly worsened the damage sustained during World War I.
   d. the economy had almost recovered from wartime damages.
   e. the White Russians were on the verge of winning the civil war.
5. During the Five-Year Plans, the peasants were
   a. finally liberated from dependence on the government.
   b. ignored by the authorities, who were concentrating on industry.
   c. deprived of most of their private property.
   d. given a major boost in productivity by government action.
   e. relegated to the fringes of society but left in charge of their own lands.
6. The Five-Year Plans called for
   a. subordination of the Communist Party to the government.
   b. rapid, forced industrialization.
   c. distribution of the farmlands to the peasants.
   d. war on the Western democracies.
   e. the occupation of Russia's Eastern European neighbors.
7. War communism was enforced by
   a. Lenin and Stalin.
   b. Bolshevik Party members.
   c. Lenin's personal bodyguard.
   d. the White Army.
   e. the Cheka and the Red Army.

8. The Great Purges started
   a. after an assassination attempt on Stalin.
   b. after evidence of a foreign spy ring within the Communist Party was uncovered.
   c. because of a rebellion of party leaders against the Five-Year Plans.
   d. because of Stalin's suspicions about his associates' loyalty.
   e. after Stalin became concerned about the growing strength of Leon Trotsky.

9. One of the chief rewards for the workers in the new Soviet Union of the 1930s was
   a. improved and expanded housing.
   b. mass educational facilities.
   c. a decisive voice in public affairs.
   d. security of life and property against the state.
   e. improvements in their working conditions.

10. To revive Russia's economy following the civil war, Lenin and Trotsky implemented
    a. war communism.
    b. forced collectivization of the peasants.
    c. the Treaty of Brest-Litovsk.
    d. the New Economic Policy.
    e. collectivization of all industries.

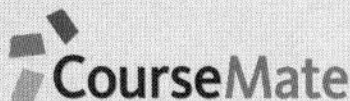

Visit the CourseMate website at **www.cengagebrain.com** for additional study tools and review materials for this chapter.

43 Totalitarianism Refined: The Nazi State

One does not establish a dictatorship in order to make a revolution; one makes a revolution in order to establish a dictatorship.

—GEORGE ORWELL, *1984*

1920	Adolf Hitler takes charge of NSDAP
1923	Munich *putsch* fails
1924	*Mein Kampf*
1930–1932	Great Depression in Germany
1933	Hitler becomes chancellor; Enabling Act
1935	Nuremberg Laws on race
1936–1939	Nazi preparation for war
1938	*Kristallnacht*; harassment of Jews intensifies
1942	Wannsee Conference: the "Final Solution" for Jewish extermination implemented

CHAPTER OUTLINE

In the twentieth century, a new form of state organization came into the world—a savage form called *totalitarianism* (see Chapter 41). It was an unprecedented denial of the traditional freedom of the individual citizen to glorify and strengthen the powers of the state. Was totalitarianism the result of some peculiar, temporary combination of circumstances in the political-economic spectrum of the 1920s and 1930s? Or was what occurred in those years in several European countries the result of the inevitable stresses generated by the modern nation-state and therefore the possible harbinger of worse things still to come? Experts continue to argue about these questions.

Totalitarian states were necessarily always ruled by dictators, but not all dictatorships were necessarily totalitarian. The interwar years (1919–1939) saw the rise of several dictatorships in various parts of the world. Most of these regimes were not totalitarian in character. In this chapter, we concentrate on the most aggressive and militant of totalitarian states: that erected by Adolf Hitler, the leader of Nazi Germany from 1933 until his death at the end of World War II. Hitler took some of his strategies and tactics from the Italian fascist pioneers, but he soon refined and systematized them to an extent not approached by the followers of Benito Mussolini.

HITLER AND THE THOUSAND-YEAR REICH

The "honor" of creating the most ruthless totalitarian system was divided between the communist dictatorship of Josef Stalin in Russia (see Chapter 42) and the Nazi dictatorship of Adolf Hitler in Germany. We have seen that Stalin attained tremendous power by cynically manipulating an idealistic movement aimed at bringing first Russia and then the world into a new era of equality and freedom. The German dictator had no such visions, however.

Hitler's Early Career

Adolf Hitler was born an Austrian citizen in 1889. He was the only child of a strict father and a loving mother who spoiled him in every way her limited resources allowed. When he was seventeen, he went off to Vienna in hopes of an art career. Rejected as having no talent, he survived for the next few years on the fringes of urban society, living hand to mouth on money from home. He fully absorbed the anti-Semitism prevalent in Vienna at that time, and his constant reading convinced him of the falsity of typical "bourgeois" values and politics. But he despised Marxism, which was the most common hope and refuge of social outsiders like himself. When World War I broke out, Hitler was a young malcontent of twenty-five, still searching for some philosophy that would make sense of a world that had rejected him.

Enlisting immediately, Hitler distinguished himself for bravery under fire, receiving the Iron Cross. The wartime experience gave him his first idea of his life's purpose. With millions of other demobilized men, he spent the first months of the postwar era in a state of shock and despair, seeing the socialist government that had replaced the kaiser and accepted the Versailles Treaty as the betrayers of the nation. As time passed, he became determined to join those who were aiming to overturn the government.

In 1920, Hitler took over a tiny group of would-be reformers and renamed them the National Socialist German Workers' Party (NSDAP), or "Nazis" for short. Devoting his fanatical energy to the party, he rapidly attracted new members in the Munich area, where he had been living since before the war. In 1923, Hitler, supported by a few discontented army officers, attempted a ***putsch*** (coup d'état) in Munich, but it failed miserably. Arrested for treason, he used the trial to gain national notoriety. He was sentenced to five years in prison by a sympathetic judge and used the year he actually served to write his autobiography and call to arms: ***Mein Kampf*** (*My Struggle*).

The Nazi Program

In wild and ranting prose, *Mein Kampf* laid out what Hitler saw as Germany's problems and their solutions. It insisted on all of the following:

- ***Anti-Semitism.*** Jews were declared born enemies of all proper German values and traitors to the nation.
- *Rejection of the Versailles Treaty and German war guilt.* Hitler called the treaty the most unfair in world history, dictated by a (temporarily) strong France against a helpless, tricked Germany.
- *Confiscation of illicit war profits.* This measure was aimed mainly at Jews but also at non-Jewish German industrialists. This point reflected the Nazis' claim to be socialists (though anti-Marxist).
- *Protection of the middle classes from ruinous competition.* The Nazis made a special show of paying attention to the growing concerns of the shopkeepers and white-collar workers who feared that they were being forced downward on the economic ladder by big business.
- *Land redistribution for the peasants.* With this pseudo-socialist measure, Hitler claimed to be protecting the peasants who were being squeezed out by large landholders.

The basic tenor of *Mein Kampf* and of Nazi speeches and literature in the 1920s was consistent: hatred for the existing situation in Germany and the determination to change it radically. The "Marxist-Zionist" government that had accepted the Versailles Treaty had given a "stab in the back" to the brave German Army in 1918. Germany must be reborn and once again gain its rightful place! Whatever means were necessary to do this were justified because only the strong would survive in a jungle world of competing nations. In later years, Hitler and the Nazis developed and defined notions of a "pure-blooded Aryan" (i.e., German) master race who were destined for world domination of all "inferior" races (non-"Aryans"). This meant that groups in addition to the Jews were targeted for imprisonment, enslavement, and annihilation to free Germany of "impurities" they brought into the blood of the master race. The list included racial minorities, gypsies, homosexuals, Slavs, and those born with mental and physical handicaps. After the failure of the Munich *putsch*, Hitler swore that he would come to power by constitutional, legal means. No one could later say that he had acted against the will of his people. From the moment that he was released from jail, he devoted himself tirelessly to organizing, speech making, and electioneering from one end of the country to the other.

Hitler was an extremely gifted rabble-rouser who quickly learned how to appeal to various groups in language they could not forget. His targets were always the same: Jews, the signers of the Versailles Treaty, the communists, and the clique of businessmen and bureaucrats who supposedly pulled the strings behind the scenes. (For more about Hitler's life and his appeal, see the Law and Government box.)

Between 1925 and 1929, which were prosperous years for Weimar Germany, the Nazis made little headway among the masses of industrial workers, who remained

LAW AND GOVERNMENT

Adolf Hitler (1889–1945): The Puzzle of His Rise to Power

Despite many tries, no one has been able to satisfactorily explain why Hitler's political and social doctrines were so attractive to most German people. During the 1930s, few Germans were disturbed by his anti-Semitic and antiforeigner slogans, his manic nationalism, or his crude and violent ideas for renovating the German nation.

True, the plight of the Germans after World War I and the struggle for survival during the first years of the Great Depression contributed to their acceptance of Hitler's views. The orderly and progressive world of Kaiser Wilhelm II had crumbled before their eyes. Germany was forced to yield to a partial Allied occupation and to give up most of its much-honored army and its equipment. Most irritating of all, Germany was forced to accept a peace treaty that branded it as the sole culprit for causing the ruinous war and was required to pay many billions of dollars as compensation to the victors.

The punishment was far greater than most had anticipated, and the common people suffered the consequences. Inflation, unemployment, and political turmoil spread. The fear of communism was acute among the middle classes, while the laborers and intellectuals struggled to make their voices heard. The old system was thoroughly discredited, and Germans looked for a new architect of morals. In 1923, a candidate appeared who had not yet found his proper voice. His name was Adolf Hitler.

From 1924 on, the Nazi movement slowly gained strength. Hitler became an ever-more skilled manipulator of political propaganda and gathered around him a mixed band of dreamers, brutes, ambitious climbers, and opportunists. Some of them firmly believed in the *Führer* and his self-proclaimed mission to save Germany and bring a New Order to Europe. Others hitched their wagons to his star without necessarily believing the wild rantings in *Mein Kampf*. Few took his promises to exterminate Jews and communists as anything more than a rabble-rouser's empty words.

Hitler's personality was a collection of contradictions. He despised organized religion and proclaimed himself untrammeled by common morality, yet he lived a life of ascetic restraint. A strict vegetarian and teetotaler, he frowned on the more boisterous and indulgent lifestyle of some of his followers (such as that of the fat hedonist Göring). He was fascinated by the power of the intellect and will, yet held intellectuals in contempt. He would work thirty-six hours at a stretch, yet went into nervous collapse and secluded himself from his officials in several political crises. He was a notorious charmer of susceptible women, yet abstained from all sexual relations and was probably impotent.

He was perhaps the most murderous power holder of the twentieth century, committing endless atrocities against Germans and other human beings, yet he had a deep reverence for the arts and considerable artistic talent. Perhaps a hint of the truth lies in his artistic personality: When his paintings were exhibited after the war, critics were impressed by his talent for rendering structural accuracy but noted his inability to sketch the human form.

ANALYZE AND INTERPRET

Why do you think Hitler seized on the Jews as the German people's most dangerous enemy? Is it unusual for a political leader to hold sharply contradictory views of moral standards for himself versus for the mass of people?

Lordprice Collection/Alamy

NURENBERG NAZI RALLY, 1938. The massive display of strength and unity so dear to the Nazis was nowhere better on view than at the regular rallies held in the Bavarian town of Nuremberg. In this photo, Hitler exchanges salutes with party officials.

Mary Evans Picture Library/The Image Works

NAZI TOTALITARIANISM AND THE MEDIA. "The whole of Germany hears the *Führer* with the people's radio." This illustrates the critical importance to totalitarian regimes of controlling the national media.

loyal to either the Social Democrats or the large, legal German Communist Party. But the Nazis did pick up voters among the members of the middle classes who had been ruined in the great inflation and among the numerous white-collar workers who saw their relative status slipping in postwar Germany. As late as the elections of 1928, the Nazis received only 2.6 percent of the vote and 12 seats in the *Reichstag* (German parliament). In comparison, the Communists had 77 seats, and the Social Democrats had 156. Moderate or conservative parties that regarded Hitler as a loose cannon who might possibly be useful against the socialists held the rest of the Reichstag's 500 seats.

The Great Depression's Effects

The collapse of the German (and world) economy in 1930–1931 set the stage for Nazi political success. In late 1929, the New York Stock Exchange went into a tailspin that soon had effects on every aspect of finance in the Western world. Germany was particularly affected because for years German industrialists and municipalities had been relying on American investment and loans. Suddenly, this credit was cut off because loans were called in on short notice. Instead of new investment, international finance and trade shrank steadily as each nation attempted to protect itself from external competition by raising tariffs and limiting imports.

The results for Germany were horrendous: The number of unemployed rose from 2.25 million in early 1930 to more than 6 million two years later (about 25 percent of the total labor force), and this figure does not count involuntary, part-time workers or the many women who withdrew from the labor market permanently. In no other country, not even the United States, was the industrial economy so hard hit.

The governing coalition of Social Democrats and moderate conservatives fell apart under this strain. In the frequent elections necessitated by the collapse of the coalition, the middle-of-the-road parties steadily lost seats to the extremes on right and left: the Nazis and the Communists. In an election for the Reichstag in mid-1930, the Nazis won a total of 107 seats, second only to the weakening Social Democrats.

As the economy continued downhill, Hitler promised immediate, decisive action to aid the unemployed and the farmers. In another national election in early 1932, the Nazis won 14.5 million votes of a total of about 35 million. The Nazis were now the largest single party but still lacked a majority. Their attacks on the government and the other parties intensified both verbally and, increasingly, in the streets.

The Seizure of Power

Finally, in a move aimed at moderating Hitler by putting him into a position where he had to take responsibility rather than just criticize, the conservative advisers of the old president, Paul von Hindenburg, appointed Hitler chancellor on January 30, 1933. Within eight weeks, Hitler had transformed the government into a Nazi dictatorship, and technically he had accomplished this seizure of power by constitutional procedures, as he had promised.

How did this transformation occur? It involved two complementary processes: the capture of legal authority for the Nazis and the elimination of competing political groups. First, the Nazis whipped up hysteria over an alleged communist revolutionary plot. Under the constitution's emergency provision, Hitler as chancellor introduced the equivalent of martial law and used it to round up tens of thousands of his opponents in the next weeks.

After the election that Hitler called for in March (in which the Nazis still failed to gain a simple majority), all Communist and some Social Democratic delegates to the Reichstag were arrested as traitors. Finally, in late March, the Nazi-dominated rump parliament enacted the so-called **Enabling Act**, giving Hitler's government the power to rule by decree until the emergency had passed. It did not pass for the next twelve years, until Hitler was dead in the ruins of Berlin.

Private Collection/Archives Charmet/The Bridgeman Art Library

AN ALL-GERMAN PARTY RALLY. A major reason for the Nazi success was the masterly touch of drama accompanying the party's functions. Slogans and banners that proclaimed the party's strength in every part of the homeland fostered the impression of overwhelming force.

The German Communist Party was immediately outlawed, and the Social Democrats were banned a few weeks later. One by one, the centrist and moderate parties disappeared, either by dissolving themselves or by being abolished by Nazi decree. In mid-1933, the Nazis were the only legal political organization left in Germany. In its various subgroups for women, youths, professional associations, farmers, and others, all patriotic Germans could find their place.

Hitler completed the process of consolidating power with a purge within the party itself. This was the infamous *Night of the Long Knives* in June 1934, when the paramilitary **Storm Troopers (SA)**, who had been important to the Nazi movement as bullyboys, were cut down to size. Using another of his suborganizations, the new **Blackshirts (SS)**, Hitler murdered several hundred of the SA leaders. By doing so, he both rid himself of potentially serious rivals and placated the German Army generals, who rightly saw in the brown-shirted SA a menace to their own position as the nation's military leaders.

THE NAZI DOMESTIC REGIME

When the Nazis took power, the NSDAP had an active membership of about 1 million and probably twice that many supporters who could be counted on to show up for major party affairs or contribute some money. By 1934, about 15 percent of the total population had joined the Nazi Party. The numbers rose steadily thereafter. By the middle of the war, about one-fifth of adult Germans belonged, although many joined under severe pressure and contributed nothing except mandatory dues.

Rank-and-file party members were drawn from all elements of the population, but the leaders were normally young men from the working and lower-middle classes. Like the Russian communists, the Nazis were a party of young men who were in a hurry and had no patience with negotiation or gradual reform. Unlike the Communists, they saw themselves not so much as implementing a revolution but as restoring proud Germanic traditions that had been allowed to decay.

As under the Bismarck and Weimar governments, Prussia was the most important region in Germany. The brilliant and unscrupulous propagandist, Joseph Goebbels (1897–1945), was Hitler's deputy here. Another member of Hitler's small circle of intimates was Hermann Göring (1893–1946), the rotund, wisecracking, and entirely cynical pilot-hero of World War I who was generally seen as the number-two man in the hierarchy.

The party was represented in all parts of Germany, which were now reorganized into *Gaue*, or districts under the command of a *Gauleiter* (a district party boss). Special organizations oversaw the explanation and practice of party doctrine for different parts of the population. But there was remarkably little philosophy in Nazism; the emotional rantings of *Mein Kampf* and the babblings of racist ideologue Alfred Rosenberg's brochures—which no one could render intelligible—were the official credos of the movement. In the end, the Nazi phenomenon depended on an extreme form of German nationalism and resentments of the peace treaty and the Jews.

From his release from the Munich jail, Hitler's policies were designed to make Germany into a totalitarian state, and they did so considerably more thoroughly and more rapidly than Mussolini was able to accomplish in Italy. His right arm in this process was **Heinrich Himmler** (1900–1945), the head of the SS and of the *Gestapo (Geh-STAH-poh)*, or political police. Himmler was Hitler's most loyal colleague, and he was charged with overseeing the internal security of the Nazi regime. Himmler's SS operated the concentration camps that opened as early as 1934 within Germany (and later in the conquered territories); a branch of the SS conducted the Holocaust of the Jews, setting up the slave labor camps and installing a reign of terror against all possible resistance.

HITLER YOUTH. At the annual mass rally of Nazi organizations in Nuremburg, the uniformed Hitler Youth were always given a prominent place to salute the Führer's carefully staged arrival. Membership was all but mandatory; those who did not join were singled out for social ostracism.

THE DEHUMANIZING OF THE JEWS. The Nazis viewed Jewish–Christian sexual relations as pollution of German blood. The woman's sign reads, "I am the biggest pig in the place and get involved only with Jews." The Jewish man's placard says, "As a Jewish fellow, I take only German girls to my room." The public humiliation of such couples began immediately after the Nazis came to power in 1933.

The "Jewish Question"

The most horrible of the Nazi policies was the genocide against the Jews, Slavs, gypsies, and other minorities deemed unfit for the future Nazi state. For the first time in modern history, a systematic, cold-blooded war of extermination was practiced against noncombatant peoples, solely on the basis of ethnicity. Of these, it was the Jews who were persecuted the most, followed by Slavic peoples. The war against the Jews went through four distinct phases in the twelve years of Nazi rule between 1933 and 1945:

1. From March 1933 to 1935, German Jews were publicly humiliated and excluded from government jobs.
2. In September 1935, the **Nuremberg Laws** prohibiting social contacts between Jews and "Aryans" (defined as persons with no Jewish blood for two generations on both sides of their family) made Jews into noncitizens. The government began to constantly harass Jews and push them either to emigrate or enter urban ghettos for easier surveillance.
3. In November 1938, new policies made it almost impossible for Jews to engage in public life and business and forbade emigration unless they surrendered all their property in Germany and went as paupers. By this time, many thousands of "antistate" Jews (Communists, Social Democrats, anti-Nazis) had been consigned to the camps.
4. At the **Wannsee Conference** in Berlin in 1942, the **Final Solution** for the "Jewish problem" was approved by Hitler. The Jews were rounded up from the ghettos throughout Germany and occupied Europe and sent to the death camps in Poland. The Holocaust had begun and would not end until Germany's defeat in 1945. By then, some 6 million Jews from all over Central and Eastern Europe had been murdered, starved to death, or had otherwise fallen victim to Himmler's henchmen. Of the more than 2 million Jews living in Germany in 1933, only a few tens of thousands had survived at the close of the war, overlooked or hidden by sympathetic neighbors.

Nazi Economic Policy

Economic policy in the Nazi state was a peculiar mixture of a fake "socialism" and an accommodation of the big businesses and cartels that had dominated Germany for a generation. As in Mussolini's Italy, the government's economic policies generated some measure of social reform. Workers and farmers were idealized in propaganda as the true Aryan Germans, but private property remained untouched, and the capitalist process was subjected to only sporadic and selective interference by the government. The labor unions, like every other type of public association, were fully subordinated to the party and became arms of the Nazi octopus. Strikes were illegal, and the Marxist idea of class conflict was officially declared nonexistent among Germans.

Hitler had come to power partly on the strength of his promises to end the unemployment problem. From 1933 to 1936, he instituted measures that were effective at providing jobs. The huge road construction and public works programs he began in 1934 absorbed a large portion of the pool of unemployed. With rearmament, the military was greatly enlarged, and munitions factories and their suppliers received government orders. Raw materials were rapidly stockpiled. Synthetic substitutes for the vital raw materials that Germany lacked (petroleum, rubber,

SOCIETY AND ECONOMY

The Nuremburg Race Laws and Pseudo-Scientific Racism

Fascist and Nazi notions about other ethnic groups (so-called races) were based on false scientific understandings of genetics, what often is called pseudo-scientific racism. Many of these ideas were current throughout Europe and America during the nineteenth and early twentieth centuries. Laws were passed that openly discriminated against Jews and other so-called inferior races in all of the fascist states in the 1920s and 1930s, but it was only the Nazis who took pseudo-scientific racism to such horrific ends. Codes such as *The Laws for the Protection of German Blood and German Honor* were based on widespread beliefs that whites were superior to dark-complexioned peoples, and that blond, blue-eyed so-called Aryans were a master race among all peoples. Hence these laws were passed to eschew racial "mixing" and to encourage racial "purity."

The Laws for the Protection of German Blood and German Honor

(15 September 1935) Moved by the understanding that the purity of German blood is essential to the further existence of the German people, and inspired by the uncompromising determination to safeguard the future of the German nation, the Reichstag has unanimously resolved upon the following law, which is promulgated herewith:

Section 1

Marriages between Jews and citizens of German or kindred blood are forbidden. Marriages concluded in defiance of this law are void, even if, for the purpose of evading this law, they were concluded abroad.

Proceedings for annulment may be initiated only by the Public Prosecutor.

Section 2

Extramarital sexual intercourse between Jews and subjects of the state of Germany or related blood is forbidden.

Section 3

Jews will not be permitted to employ female citizens under the age of 45, of German or kindred blood, as domestic workers.

Section 4

Jews are forbidden to display the Reich and national flag or the national colours.

On the other hand they are permitted to display the Jewish colours. The exercise of this right is protected by the State.

Section 5

A person who acts contrary to the prohibition of Section 1 will be punished with hard labour.

A person who acts contrary to the prohibition of Section 2 will be punished with imprisonment or with hard labour.

A person who acts contrary to the provisions of Sections 3 or 4 will be punished with imprisonment up to a year and with a fine, or with one of these penalties.

Section 6

The Reich Minister of the Interior in agreement with the Deputy Führer and the Reich Minister of Justice will issue the legal and administrative regulations required for the enforcement and supplementing of this law.

Section 7

The law will become effective on the day after its promulgation; Section 3, however, not until 1 January 1936.

Two months after the Nuremburg Laws were passed, its provisions were extended to include peoples who possessed "racially alien blood," namely gypsies, Africans, peoples of African descent, and even Germans who were mentally retarded or who suffered from physical defects.

Sources: Jeremy Noakes, and Geoffrey Pridham. *Documents on Nazism 1919–1945*. New York, 1974, pp. 463–467.

ANALYZE AND INTERPRET

Were such ideas really new in history? What other peoples throughout history have suffered from discrimination and persecution? From what pre-20th century ideas do you think these false notions of so-called racial inferiority had their roots? What forms of discrimination exist in today's world?

tin, and many other exotic minerals) were invented in government-supported laboratories and produced in new factories.

Already by 1936, Hitler was putting Germany on a war footing. Labor was allocated according to government priorities. Government ministries decided what would be imported and exported. In the western border region, a huge "West Wall" was being erected. This system of fortifications would mirror the fortified French Maginot Line across the frontier. The *autobahns*

MAP 43.1 Europe in 1939, on Eve of World War II

Most of Europe was under dictatorial rule of various types by the end of the 1930s. The impact of the Great Depression pushed some of the former parliamentary democracies into the dictatorship column during the middle of the 1930s.

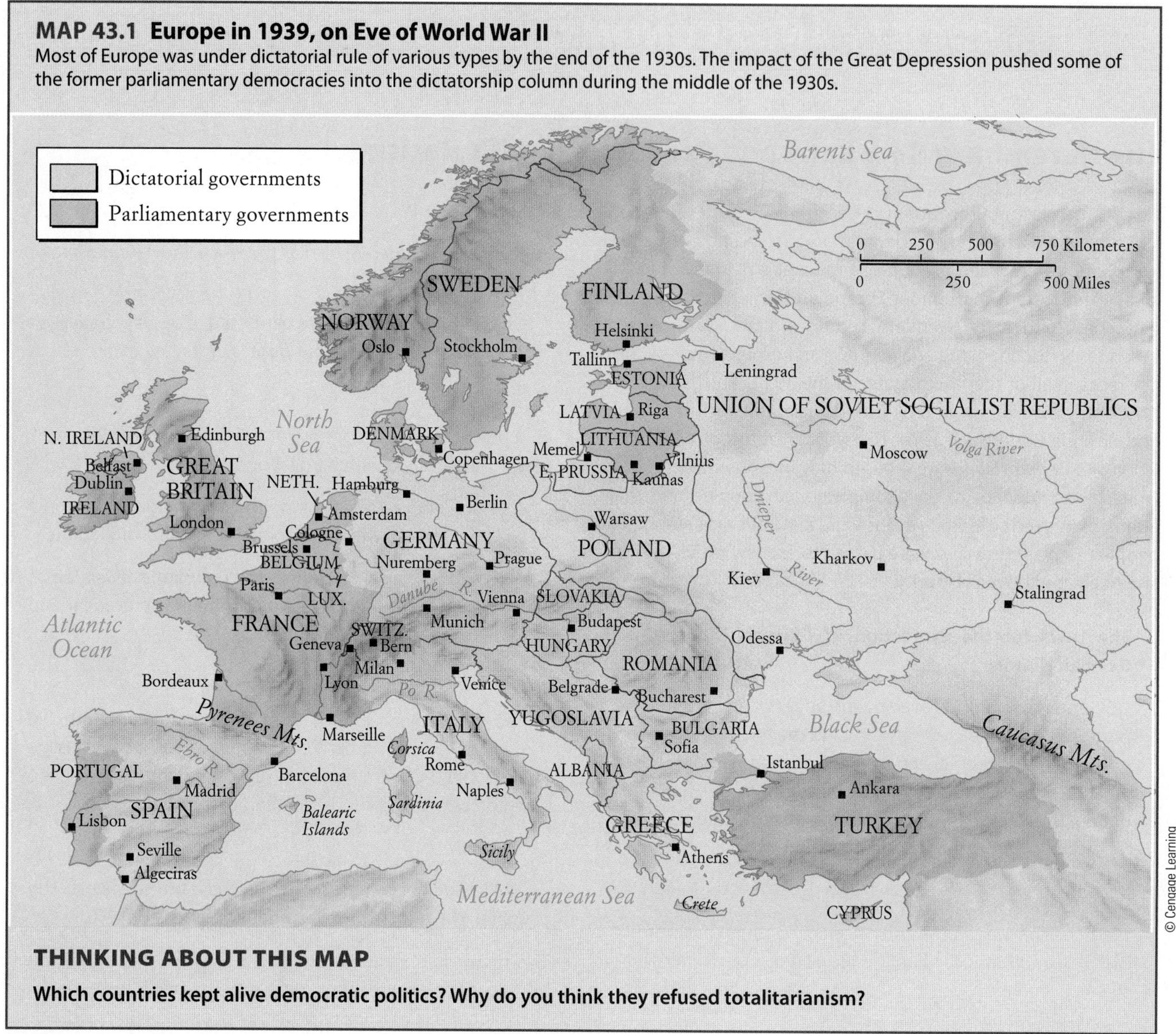

THINKING ABOUT THIS MAP

Which countries kept alive democratic politics? Why do you think they refused totalitarianism?

(expressways) were built to crisscross the country, creating a system that could move men and material quickly in case of war.

By 1937, the number of unemployed was down to 400,000 (from 6 million), and a labor shortage was developing. Unmarried women and youths were put into more or less compulsory organizations to relieve the shortfall. In every German village and town, Nazi Youth organizations gave boys and girls ages seven to twenty-one a place to get together with their peers for both work and fun while imbibing the Nazi viewpoints. The nation was prosperous, the Great Depression became a dim memory, and many millions of Germans were proud of their government and their ***Führer*** (FYOO-rer).

SUMMARY

The defeat in 1918, the runaway inflation of the early 1920s, and the weak and unpopular socialist government combined to exert a devastating effect on German national morale. Millions of voters lost faith in liberal democracy and the parliamentary process. So long as the economic situation remained favorable, this political weakness was manageable, but the onset of the world depression brought on a crisis from which the gifted demagogue, Adolf Hitler, and his Nazi Party emerged triumphant in 1933. The Nazis could soon boast that the Führer made good on his promises to his people. He had obtained government power legally, and an intimidated legislature gave him dictatorial authority soon thereafter.

By the mid-1930s, rearmament and a vigorous social investment policy had restored German prosperity. Most Germans were content with Hitler's guidance. His ranting anti-Semitism and brutal harassment of all opposition elements did not overly disturb the majority, who had found prosperity, security, and a sense of national purpose that had been sorely lacking since 1918.

IDENTIFICATION TERMS

Test your knowledge of this chapter's key concepts by defining the following terms. If you can not recall the meaning of certain terms, refresh your memory by looking up the boldfaced term in the chapter, turning to the Glossary at the end of the book, or accessing the terms on the CourseMate website at **www.cengagebrain.com**.

anti-Semitism
Blackshirts (SS)
Enabling Act
Final Solution
Der Führer
Heinrich Himmler
Mein Kampf
Nuremberg Laws
putsch
Storm Troopers (SA)
Wannsee Conference

FOR FURTHER REFLECTION

1. What conditions in Germany during the 1920s and 1930s help explain the rise of Adolf Hitler and the NSDAP? How did these conditions compare with those in Russia in the years before the Bolshevik revolution?
2. Compare Hitler to other dictators who rose to power during the interwar years (Vladimir Lenin, Josef Stalin, and Benito Mussolini). What similarities were there, if any, in their personalities and political ideologies?
3. How do Marxist Leninism, fascism, and Nazism compare with each other? Is it possible that Germany could have experienced a Marxist-Leninist revolution instead of a fascist-style seizure of power? Why did it not?

TEST YOUR KNOWLEDGE

Test your knowledge of this chapter by answering the following questions. Complete answers appear at the end of the book. You may find even more quiz questions on the CourseMate website at **www.cengagebrain.com**.

1. Hitler's major political ideas were formed
   a. during his early manhood in Vienna.
   b. as a reaction to the Great Depression.
   c. during his boyhood in rural Austria.
   d. after he formed the Nazi Party in the postwar era.
   e. during his incarceration after the 1923 putsch.
2. Which of the following was *not* a part of Hitler's call to arms in *Mein Kampf*?
   a. Protection of the middle classes
   b. Rejection of the Versailles Treaty
   c. Land redistribution
   d. Confiscation of money and goods gained as a result of World War I
   e. Government ownership of all property
3. Which of the following did *not* help Hitler in his bid for political power?
   a. His sympathy for Marxist theory and practice
   b. His gift for influencing the masses
   c. The ineptitude of the democratic leaders in meeting the economic crisis
   d. Massive economic hardship
   e. His personal charisma
4. The most complete legal embodiment of Nazi pseudoscientific racism was the
   a. Paris Treaty
   b. Dawes Pact
   c. Nuremburg Laws
   d. Munich Beer Hall Putsch
   e. Enabling Act

5. The German chancellorship came to Hitler in 1933 through
   a. legal appointment.
   b. a conspiracy.
   c. an overwhelming electoral victory.
   d. armed force.
   e. a military takeover.
6. The Enabling Act
   a. made Hitler chancellor of Germany.
   b. gave Nazis in the Reichstag absolute power.
   c. outlawed the Communist Party.
   d. gave Hitler's government the right to rule by decree.
   e. banned the Social Democratic Party.
7. The Night of the Long Knives was
   a. Hitler's seizure of power from von Hindenburg.
   b. Hitler's purge of the Nazi party.
   c. the SS purge of the SA Storm Troopers.
   d. the German reoccupation of the Ruhr and the Rhineland.
   e. the Night of Hitler's appointment as Chancellor.
8. Hitler's head of the SS and the Gestapo was
   a. Goebbels.
   b. Himmler.
   c. Göring.
   d. Gauleiter.
   e. Bismarck.
9. The Nuremberg Laws
   a. outlawed the German Communist Party.
   b. laid out the details of the Nazi dictatorship in Germany.
   c. detailed who was Jewish and what that meant.
   d. were the formal rejection of the reparations bill from World War I.
   e. expelled all Jews from Germany.
10. Hitler partly succeeded politically through
    a. a comprehensive program of socialism.
    b. his policy of nationalizing German industries.
    c. his seizure of Jewish owned businesses.
    d. his ability to provide unemployed Germans with jobs in the government and armaments industries.
    e. forcing companies to hire the unemployed.

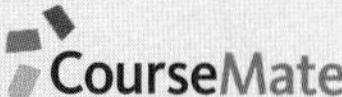

Visit the CourseMate website at **www.cengagebrain.com** for additional study tools and review materials for this chapter.

44 East Asia in a Century of Change

The art of government is the organization of idolatry.

—GEORGE BERNARD SHAW

1867–1900	Meiji reforms in Japan
1904–1905	Russo-Japanese War
1910	Japan annexes Korea
1912	Founding of Chinese Republic
1937	Beginning of Second Sino-Japanese War
1941–1945	Pacific Allies' War against Japan
1947–1949	Civil War in China

As was seen in Chapter 37, almost 4,000 years of imperial rule in China ended when Sun Yat-sen and others overthrew the last Qing emperor and declared a republic. However, the declaration of the republic did not end China's tribulations. A temporary coalition between the **Kuomintang** (Nationalist Party) and the Communist Party of China in the 1920s and the 1930s helped to carry on a struggle against Japanese occupation. But the ideological differences between the two groups led to an inevitable showdown that resulted in a victory for the communists in 1948. The remnants of the Kuomintang were forced to flee to the nearby island of Taiwan.

In contrast, Japan had undergone one of the most remarkable self-willed transformations known to history. An aggressive imperialism brought Japan into conflict with a struggling China in the 1930s and later with the West.

Elsewhere, almost all of Southeast Asia were European colonies, and by the early twentieth century, this region was experiencing a buildup of frustrated nationalism among both intellectuals and ordinary folk. This became even truer after the Asians witnessed the humiliation of Russia by Japan in 1905 and the mutual slaughter of Europeans in World War I. In retrospect, the late nineteenth and early twentieth centuries were the high point of European domination of Asia. After World War II, the tide would turn toward a closer balance in East–West relations.

CHINA

By the third decade of the twentieth century, China had undergone the early stages of a revolution. Nationalism, the force that more than any other had driven change throughout the world in the nineteenth century, had spread to Western Asia and had now reached the Far East. Chapter 37 briefly discussed how, after thirty-five centuries of dynastic imperial rule, those who followed Sun Yat-sen (the leading thinker of Chinese nationalism) deposed the last emperor and established a republican form of government in China.

Chiang Kai-shek's Regime

Sun Yat-sen's most able and aggressive lieutenant was **Chiang Kai-shek** (chung keye shehk), who headed the Kuomintang's military branch. After the founder's death in 1925, Chiang moved quickly to take over leadership, while maintaining the liaison with the tiny **Chinese Communist Party (CCP)** that Sun had established in the early 1920s to assist in modernizing the state. In 1926, Chiang felt strong enough to go after the warlords who had made themselves into petty kings in the north and northeast and bring them under effective central control. This Northern Expedition was a success, and several provinces were recovered. Strengthened by this and by the increasing support of Chinese financial circles, Chiang decided to finish off the communists who had displayed disturbingly little support in Shanghai and a few other coastal cities. In 1927, he conducted a sweeping blood purge of all suspected communists, killing tens of thousands before it was over. The CCP appeared to have suffered an irremediable defeat. Chiang was clearly in control and established himself as the president of a national Kuomintang government in Beijing a few months later.

The Kuomintang government under Chiang (1928–1975) was a barely disguised dictatorship, led by a man who believed in force as the ultimate political argument. He had married a Westernized Chinese plutocrat, who successfully acted as his intermediary when dealing with Western governments throughout his long career. Chiang believed that the obstacles to making China into a sovereign, respected state were first the Japanese and then the communists. As time passed, however, that order began to reverse. Under new leaders, the CCP had staged a quick recovery from the events of 1927 and, within a few years, had established a strong base among the peasants in south China. Knowing that he did not as yet have the strength to challenge the superior weaponry and training of the Japanese, Chiang threw his 700,000-man army against the communists.

Following their leader, **Mao Zedong** (mau tseh-duhng), the communists were driven from their rural strongholds and forced into the famous **Long March of 1934**. At the start of this migration, Mao's followers numbered perhaps 100,000 poorly armed peasants. Their epic journey lasted more than a year and covered more than 6,000 miles through western China. Out of those who started, only 10,000 or so survived starvation and

John Dominis/Time & Life Pictures/Getty Images

CHIANG KAI-SHEK AND MADAME CHIANG. The newsweekly *Time* selected Chiang and his spouse as "Man and Wife of the Year, 1937." Madame Chiang handled much of China's diplomacy with the Western powers in this epoch.

Private Collection/Archives Charmet/The Bridgeman Art Library

THE LONG MARCH. Once the Chinese Communist Party was in power, it created a totalitarian state in which myth and propaganda played major roles. These posters, created after the fact, contributed to raising the Long March virtually to the level of legend in modern Chinese history. In the top one, Mao Zedong is depicted leading the march, and in the bottom, he is shown instructing his followers.

combat and finally managed to barricade themselves in Shensi in the far northwest near the Mongolian border. Here, during the remainder of the 1930s, they preached the Marxist gospel to the desperately poor peasants around them.

By these actions, they were following Mao's new precept: The Chinese peasants are a true revolutionary force, and no revolution will succeed without them. Mao pursued peasant support in clever and concrete ways. He never spoke of collectivization but only of justice, lower interest rates, and fair distribution of land. The members of the CCP became village teachers—the first ever in Shensi Province—and made sure that the communist army did not behave like previous Chinese armies and "liberate" what they needed and wanted from the helpless farmers. Soon the locals were sufficiently impressed with Mao's forces that they began to join them.

The Sino-Japanese War and the Maoist Challenge

Americans sometimes forget that for four years before Pearl Harbor, the Japanese and the Chinese were engaged in a bloody war. This conflict had actually begun with the Japanese aggression in Manchuria in 1931, but it had been sporadic until a minor incident in the summer of 1937 gave the Japanese commanders the pretext they had long sought to begin war. After a few months of unequal fighting, the two major cities of Beijing and Nanjing had fallen, and much of coastal China was under Japanese control.

EVIDENCE OF THE PAST

Japan's "Rape of Nanjing"

One of the most notorious incidents of Japanese brutality with captives before and during World War II was the "Rape of Nanjing" in 1937. Even today, the Chinese memory of these events remains a sensitive issue that clouds diplomatic relations between China and Japan. The following are excerpts from an account given by one observer:

Aboard the U.S.S. *Oahu* at Shanghai, Dec. 17 [1937]

The killing of civilians was widespread. Foreigners who traveled widely through the city Wednesday found civilian dead on every street. Some of the victims were aged men, women and children.

Policemen and firemen were special objects of attack. Many victims were bayoneted and some of the wounds were barbarously cruel.

Any person who ran because of fear or excitement was likely to be killed on the spot as was any one caught by roving patrols in streets or alleys after dark. Many slayings were witnessed by foreigners.

The Japanese looting amounted almost to plundering of the entire city. Nearly every building was entered by Japanese soldiers, often under the eyes of their officers, and the men took whatever they wanted. The Japanese soldiers often impressed Chinese to carry their loot....

The mass executions of war prisoners added to the horrors the Japanese brought to Nanking. After killing the Chinese soldiers who threw down their arms and surrendered, the Japanese combed the city for men in civilian garb who were suspected of being former soldiers.

Just before boarding the ship for Shanghai the writer watched the execution of 200 men on the Bund [dike]. The killings took ten minutes. The men were lined against a wall and shot. Then a number of Japanese, armed with pistols, trod nonchalantly around the crumpled bodies, pumping bullets into any that were still kicking.

Keren Su/China Span/Getty Images

MEMORIAL TO THE "RAPE OF NANJING." The Japanese invasion of Nanjing in 1937 was notorious for its brutality. Most estimates of the civilian death toll are in the range of 100,000 to 200,000.

(Continued)

The army men performing the gruesome job had invited navy men from the warships anchored off the Bund to view the scene. A large group of military spectators apparently greatly enjoyed the spectacle.

When the first column of Japanese troops marched from the South Gate up Chungshan Road toward the city's Big Circle, small knots of Chinese civilians broke into scattering cheers, so great was their relief that the siege was over and so high were their hopes that the Japanese would restore peace and order. There are no cheers in Nanking now for the Japanese.

The flight of the many Chinese soldiers was possible by only a few exits. Instead of sticking by their men to hold the invaders at bay with a few strategically placed units while the others withdrew, many army leaders deserted, causing panic among the rank and file.

Those who failed to escape through the gate leading to Hsiakwan and from there across the Yangtze were caught and executed.... Civilian casualties also were heavy, amounting to thousands. The only hospital open was the American-managed University Hospital and its facilities were inadequate for even a fraction of those hurt.

The capture of Hsiakwan Gate by the Japanese was accompanied by the mass killing of the defenders, who were piled up among the sandbags, forming a mound six feet high. Late Wednesday the Japanese had not removed the dead, and two days of heavy military traffic had been passing through, grinding over the remains of men, dogs and horses.

The Japanese appear to want the horrors to remain as long as possible, to impress on the Chinese the terrible results of resisting Japan.

From F. Tillman, "All Captives Slain," *The New York Times*, December 18, 1937, 1, 10. Copied from "The Internet East Asian History Sourcebook," ed. Paul Halsall.

ANALYZE AND INTERPRET

Who is the writer of the account? What was he doing in Nanjing, and from where did he observe the events he recounts? Does it appear that he personally witnessed everything he reports? What else besides personal observation might have influenced his account?

Assuming the accuracy of the account and aside from the obvious brutality of the Japanese soldiers, what purposes do the actions of the Japanese seem to have served?

Besides the attacks on the Chinese soldiers, what other actions by the Japanese made this a war crime?

Instead of submitting and becoming a Japanese puppet as expected, Chiang elected to move his government many hundreds of miles west and attempt to hold out until he could find allies. The move inland meant, however, that Chiang was isolated from his main areas of support. Furthermore, the Kuomintang army and officials appeared to the local people around the new command city of Chongqing (chun-king) as a swarm of devouring locusts. Famine was endemic in this poverty-stricken region, and official corruption in the army and civil government was widespread.

Morale deteriorated steadily under these conditions, especially because Chiang refused to actively fight the Japanese invader. After the attack on Pearl Harbor, he had decided that the Americans would eventually defeat Tokyo and that the communists under Mao were China's real enemy. Protected in his mountainous refuge, he wanted to husband his forces. When World War II ended in 1945, Chiang was the commander of a large but poorly equipped and demoralized garrison army that had no combat experience and was living parasitically on its own people.

The Maoists, on the other hand, made steady progress in winning over the anti-Japanese elements among the people, especially the peasants. They claimed to be nationalists and patriots as well as reformers, and they fought the invader at every opportunity from their bases in the northwest. Mao set up a local government system that was far more just and more respectful of the peasants than the Kuomintang had been. He introduced democratic practices that won the communists the support of many of the intellectuals and the workers. Mao's armed force grew by large numbers during the war years to a total of almost 1 million men in organized units, plus many thousands of guerrilla fighters behind the Japanese lines. The CCP set up mass organizations with branches in every village for women, youth, educators, and others.

The Communist Victory

At the Pacific war's end, Chiang's army was about three times the size of Mao's, and now that the Americans had disposed of the Japanese, he was confident of victory over the internal rivals. The civil war broke out soon after the Japanese surrendered. The United States at first backed Chiang with supplies and money but could not counter the effects of years of corrupt Kuomintang rule, inaction, and failure on Chiang's part to appreciate what China's peasant masses wanted. While the Kuomintang armies deserted, the communist forces enjoyed wide and growing support. The superior fighting spirit and military tactics of the Maoists decisively turned the tide in 1948, when Beijing and the big port cities fell into their hands.

By October 1949, all of China was under Mao's control, and Chiang with several hundred thousand Kuomintang men were refugees on the Chinese offshore island of Taiwan. Here, they set up a regime that called itself the Republic of China and was recognized as the legitimate government of China by the anticommunist world for some time to come. But "Red" China (properly the People's Republic of China, or PRC), with the world's largest population, was now presumably a devoted Cold War ally of the Soviet Union under the ruthless communist Mao and aiming at world revolution side by side with the Soviets.

JAPAN

In the mid-nineteenth century, Japan's two centuries of seclusion under the Tokugawa shoguns ended, and the country began its twenty-year transformation into a modern nation.

The Emergence of Modern Japan

The trigger for Japan's modernization was the forceful "opening of Japan" by U.S. commodore Matthew Perry in 1853 and 1854 (see Chapter 27). In the name of international commerce, Perry extorted a treaty from the *shogun* that allowed U.S. ships to dock and do business in Japanese ports. This treaty was soon followed by similar agreements with the European trading nations. With the country divided over whether to allow the "pale-faced barbarians" into the ports, a brief conflict broke out among the *daimyo* lords for the shogun's power, and a few resident foreigners were molested. In 1863, a retaliatory attack by Western naval forces revealed how far Japan had fallen behind in the arts of war.

Japan seemed on the brink of being reduced to yet another helpless victim of Western imperialism, but guided by China's negative example, some of the daimyo and samurai faced the causes and consequences of Japanese impotence squarely: They decided to imitate the West as rapidly as possible. These men engineered the revolt against the shogunate in 1867—termed the **Meiji Restoration** (may-JEE) because, in a formal sense, the emperor was restored to the center of political-governmental life and the shogunate was abolished. It was not the teenaged emperor who was in control, however, but the powerful daimyo, who had seen that the semi-feudal shogunate was obsolete and now replaced it with a new style of government.

Starting in 1871, one major reform after another came out of the imperial capital in Tokyo (formerly Edo). All were modeled on the West. Unlike their neighbors across the China Sea, the Japanese leaders were willing and able to add up the pluses and minuses of accepting Western ideas and come to definite, consensual decisions about them. Then they systematically carried out reforms, even at the expense of some cherished traditions. (See the Society and Economy box.)

The Meiji Reforms

The major reforms of the Meiji Restoration included the following:

- *Administrative.* Daimyo domains were abolished in 1871 and replaced by prefectures under government-appointed officials.
- *Military.* The daimyo-samurai feudal forces were removed in favor of a conscript army with a modern organization, modern weaponry, and professional discipline.
- *Social.* The governing oligarchy proclaimed equal status for all classes and abolished the traditional social hierarchy and samurai privileges. People were free to choose their occupations and to move about freely. Prefectures administered by government-appointed officials replaced daimyo domains.
- *Educational.* A national education system was created in 1872 to support growth of a modern Japanese state. By 1900, the government provided six years of free education for nearly everyone.
- *Financial.* A new national tax system and a new national bank and currency were established; credit facilities and corporations on the Western model were introduced.
- *Agrarian.* Land was redistributed, quasi-feudal dues were abolished, and ownership was established clearly and securely by survey.
- *Constitutional.* In 1889, a group of notables framed an entirely new constitution. It gave the parliamentary vote to a small electorate and allowed the emperor considerable (but not supreme) power over the government elected by the parliament.

By no means did all Japanese support these reforms. The samurai majority were so discontented by their total loss of status (even their precious swords were taken from them in 1876) that they attempted to rebel several times, only to be crushed by the new army. The new tax system, which required money payments to the government rather than service to the daimyo, reduced many peasants from landowners to tenants and was unpopular, but after twenty years, the reform element in Tokyo was unshakably entrenched.

Students were sent abroad by the hundreds annually to study Western science and Western government. For a time, everything Western was highly fashionable in Japan—from pocket watches to Darwinian biology. As elsewhere, the most potent of all the Western influences was the modern sense of nationalism, which struck Japanese youth just as strongly as it had Chinese. New political parties sprang up and vigorously contested the seats in the lower house of the *Diet* (parliament), even though only about 5 percent of the male population had the franchise. The constitution of 1889 was modeled after the German constitution authored by Otto von Bismarck and reserved

SOCIETY AND ECONOMY

Fukuzawa Yukichi (1835–1901): From Lowly Samurai to Revered Meiji Leader

Fukuzawa Yukichi's life is emblematic of Japan's transformation from feudalism to modernity during the Restoration of the Meiji Emperor. As one of the first samurai who worked for Japan's selective Westernization, Fukuzawa is still revered as the father of modern Japan. Most Japanese see his portrait daily because he is the only Meiji leader whose image appears on the paper currency.

As a young man looking for freedom from traditional society, Fukuzawa was eager to learn about Western science and technology by reading European books. His hard-won expertise in European languages made him indispensable, first to the Tokugawa shogunate lords, and later to the Meiji emperor's advisors. He shed his samurai title without regret when feudalism was abolished in 1868. Fukuzawa went on to become an influential educator, author, publisher, and entrepreneur during the Meiji period.

Fukuzawa lived his first eighteen years chafing against the Tokugawa system. As the youngest son of a low-level samurai, Fukuzawa felt trapped in his family's obscure castle town with its rigid social hierarchy. A man of his low rank had to suffer continual humiliations under the arrogant upper-level samurai. Fortunately for Fukuzawa, the old shogunate began to crumble just as he was plotting to escape its restrictions.

The Japanese were in a hurry to catch up with Western military technology in time to defend against a dreaded Western invasion. Thanks to this campaign to modernize, the nineteen-year-old Fukuzawa was able to secure a government stipend to study Western subjects for three years in the relatively cosmopolitan port cities of Nagasaki and Osaka. Fukuzawa began to teach Western studies in 1856 in the schools of his samurai domain. Later, he cannily used his knowledge of Dutch and English to join government fact-finding missions to the United States (1859, 1862) and Europe (1867).

When Fukuzawa returned to Japan from these fact-finding missions, he wrote his ten-volume work, *Conditions in the West* (published between 1867 and 1870), to describe what he had seen during his foreign travels. Fukazawa's innovative, colloquial style of writing helped make this work a bestseller. The newly wealthy Fukuzawa decided to become a publisher as well as an author, with the mission to educate his people about new ideas in science, technology, economics, and business so they could stand firmly against imperialism. Eventually, he wrote or translated (and published) more than one hundred books about the United States and Europe, volumes that made their author rich as they helped shape modern Japan.

Fukuzawa realized that the ideals of freedom, equality, and individual improvement were essential to successful modernization. However, Japanese tradition had emphasized self-effacement and subservience to the class-based hierarchy. Therefore, Fukuzawa invented new Japanese words when he introduced such alien concepts as competition, debate, or parliament. He became the foremost proponent of educational reforms in Meiji Japan, insisting that schools should emphasize practical knowledge and rational thinking, rather than the traditional Confucian poetry-based curriculum. In 1868, the year the emperor was restored, Fukuzawa established the Western-style Keio College to teach economics, public finance, and accounting. The graduates of his school (currently the prestigious Keio University) became the business and government elites of Meiji Japan. Fukuzawa's protégés headed most of Japan's large banks and were prominent in such firms as Mitsubishi.

Fukuzawa had refused any official appointments because he knew such duties would restrict his independence and his income; he preferred to exert his considerable influence from behind the scenes. Fukuzawa's expertise in Western affairs meant that his views were often sought on aspects of Japan's transition. He voiced his opinions in his newspaper, books, and speeches. Once a lowly and impoverished samurai, he had become a wealthy entrepreneur, a capitalist who invested in the businesses of his friends and former pupils.

Toward the end of his life, Fukuzawa grew more conservative and nationalistic. Many criticized him for supporting some of Japan's expansionist policies. He concluded that, in international conflicts, military force would trump the ideals of diplomacy.

ANALYZE AND INTERPRET

How did the milestones of Fukuzawa's life parallel the events in a changing Japan?

decisive powers to wealthy voters and imperial ministers. The emperor was sovereign, not the people. He was also commander-in-chief of the armed forces, and the ministers answered solely to him, not to the parliament.

At the same time, the Meiji leaders made sure that the ancient regime and the traditional values of the people were held in high esteem. The reformers strongly supported the Shinto faith, which revered the emperor as the quasi-divine leader of his country. The constitution (which remained in force until 1945) explicitly stated that "the empire of Japan shall be governed by a line of emperors unbroken forever." The Meiji reformers made no attempt to throw out what they thought of as truly Japanese. Rather, the reform consciously—and successfully—aimed at making Japanese of all classes into good patriot-citizens.

Industrial development received much attention from the outset. Government funds were directed to railroad construction, shipyards, mines, and munitions under the supervision of foreign technicians. Later, in the 1890s, many of these costly enterprises were sold at bargain rates to combinations of individual investors. Thus began the peculiar Japanese form of government-assisted large corporations called ***zaibatsu*** (zeye-BAH-tsoo), which came to dominate the nation's economy.

New banks were founded to provide credit for entrepreneurs, and the internal transport of people and goods was greatly eased by the construction of a dense network of railways. Mountainous terrain and the island geography had physically isolated much of Japan's population until the early twentieth century, but the railroads changed that.

Agriculture became more productive because taxes were paid in fixed amounts of money rather than produce, and peasants were able for the first time to freely buy, mortgage, and sell land. Silk—in demand everywhere in the industrial world—was the big money crop, rising from 2.3 million pounds in 1870 to 93 million in 1929. Japan's mechanization of silk production practically blew the Chinese out of the world market they had previously dominated. Rice production—the key Japanese commodity—also rose sharply, more than doubling in tonnage produced in one generation's time.

JAPAN'S FIRST RAILWAY. In 1872, the Tokyo–Yokohama rail line was opened, only a few years after the Meiji reform era began. Built under the direction of Western engineers, the line fascinated the Japanese, who portrayed it in this early print of the Shimbashi Station in Tokyo.

Foreign Successes

The foreign policy of Meiji Japan was aggressive and grew more so as time went on. The challenge to "big brother" China in 1895 was a great success. Another success was the gradual elimination of the unequal treaties signed with the Western powers in the 1850s and 1860s. As in China, Japanese authorities had at first agreed to a series of treaties that allowed Westerners to enjoy extraterritoriality. Persistent negotiations reversed this situation by the end of the nineteenth century, and Japan became the first Asian power in modern times to trade with Europeans as equals.

But the big breakthrough for Japanese prestige in foreign eyes was the Russo-Japanese War of 1904–1905. This war—the first between an Asian and a European nation that ended in victory for the Asians—announced to the world that Japan had arrived as a major power. The formal annexation of occupied Korea was a major result of the war, and the Japanese nationalists felt cheated that they had not obtained still more reparation from the beaten Russians. They would have their chance a few years later, when the Bolshevik revolution and civil war made Russia temporarily helpless. After nominally participating on the Allied side in World War I, Japan attempted to seize eastern Siberia as its reward from the Soviets. Pressured mainly by the United States, the Japanese reluctantly agreed to evacuate in 1922 but kept their eyes firmly on the huge border province of Manchuria as a possible field for imperial expansion.

Between the World Wars

The foundation of civil government in Japan was aided substantially by the fact that economic prosperity for the upper and middle classes continued without setback for the entire reign of the Meiji emperor (1868–1912). World War I armament production then gave the entire economy a boost but also created severe inflation, which caused serious rioting in 1918. The 1920s and 1930s saw a strengthening of the army in politics, a factor that Japan had not previously experienced. Career officers often resented their diminished position in Japanese life compared to what the samurai had once had. Considering themselves to be the samurai descendants and the most devoted and reliable exponents of all that was good in Japanese culture, the officers came to hold parliamentary politicians in contempt.

In the early and most difficult years of the Great Depression, the officers' ambitions were particularly attracted to resource-rich Manchuria. In 1931, they in effect rebelled against the Tokyo civil government and seized the province from the weak hands of China. From this point onward, Japan's army was engaged in an undeclared war against China and also against its own government in Tokyo. The Chinese war became an open struggle only after 1937, but the war against the civil government was already won in 1932. From that year, the military was in effective command of Japan's domestic and foreign policies. Any civilians who opposed the aggressive and self-confident generals and admirals were soon silenced.

In 1936, Japan, whose military shared the usual contempt for Marxism among army men, joined the Hitler-sponsored Anti-Comintern Pact. By 1937, Japan was formally at war with Chiang Kai-shek's government and had close to 1 million men in China. The alliance with Adolf Hitler (and Benito Mussolini) was supposedly strengthened by the signing of the 1940 Tripartite (three-sided) Pact, but the Japanese resented not being informed of Hitler's decision to go to war against the West in 1939. When Germany decided to attack Russia in 1941, the Japanese were again not informed, and they decided to remain neutral despite the provisions of the pact and inciting German anger. The Japanese had, in fact, little to do with their supposed ally throughout World War II. The war in the Pacific was almost entirely distinct from the European conflict in timing, motivation, and contestants.

The Japanese attacked Pearl Harbor, Hawaii, in December 1941 because the Tokyo military command was convinced that war was inevitable if the United States would not go along with Japan's plans for imperialist expansion in Asia. Because the U.S. government showed no signs of changing its expressed resistance after long negotiations, the Tokyo general staff wished to strike first and hoped that greater willpower would overcome greater resources (see Chapter 45).

For about eight months, it seemed that the Japanese might be correct. Then, with the great naval battles of the mid-Pacific in the summer of 1942, the tides of war changed. From that point on, it was apparent to most observers (including many of Japan's leaders) that the best Japan could hope for was a negotiated peace that would leave it the dominant power in the western Pacific. Those hopes steadily diminished and were finally dashed with the explosions over Hiroshima and Nagasaki in August 1945.

SOUTHEAST ASIA

Although China and Japan managed to maintain their formal independence from the Europeans, the Asians in the southeast of the continent and in the Pacific islands were not so fortunate. In the nineteenth century, all those who had not already become part of a European empire fell under one or another of the great powers, except Thailand, which played off various rivals and thereby retained independence (see Chapter 35).

In the middle of the nineteenth century, the kingdom of Burma, which had been independent for many centuries, fell under British rule through imperialist war and was united with British India. At the same time, the British colonial fiefs in Malaya and especially Singapore (the port at its tip) began to experience a great economic upsurge. The tin mines and rubber plantations that sprang forth in interior Malaya attracted much British capital and Chinese labor. By the end of the century, Singapore was a large city serving shipping from around the industrial world as well as East Asia. The political leadership was entirely British, but the Chinese dominated trade and commerce, and their business acumen enabled them to maintain equality with the resident Europeans in all except political matters.

The French presence centered on **Indochina**—or Vietnam, Laos, and Cambodia, as they are now called. The French had seized Indochina by stages, starting in the 1850s. They were aided by the same invulnerable naïveté that impeded an effective Chinese response to European aggression: The mandarins simply could not believe that their superior culture was endangered. In 1859, France used a pretext to seize Saigon and, a few years later, Cambodia. Following a brief war with China in 1885, the French then took over all of Vietnam and Laos.

In time, tens of thousands of French came to Indochina to make their careers or fortunes as officials, teachers, rubber-plantation owners, and adventurers of all sorts. Like the British in Malaya, the French introduced some beneficial changes into the economy and society, making southern Vietnam, for example, into an enormously fertile rice bowl that exported its product throughout East Asia. They opened village schools, ended the practical slavery of women, forbade the marriages of children, and introduced new cash crops (rubber and coffee). But as happened everywhere else in colonial Asia, these improvements in social and economic possibilities benefited mainly the small minority of alien middlemen (mainly immigrant Chinese) and native landlords, and they were outweighed in nationalist eyes by the humiliations suffered at the hands of the European conquerors and overlords.

In the major maritime colonies of Dutch Indonesia and the Spanish Philippine Islands, the Europeans had a much longer presence, dating to the seventeenth century. The Indonesian islands had been placed under a limited (in the geographic sense) Dutch rule in the 1600s, when bold Hollanders had driven out their Portuguese rivals for the rich spice export trade. Since then, little had changed until the mid-nineteenth century. At that juncture, the nature of colonial controls had tightened, and their impact expanded with the introduction of the "culture system" of coerced cropping of specific commodities. Dutch overlords gradually conquered and replaced native leaders, and a small group controlled large estates that produced coffee and sugar at high profits. Despite efforts to assist them after 1870, the Indonesian peasants suffered as massive population growth turned many of them into landless semi-serfs for Dutch and Chinese landlords.

Alone among the Asian lands taken over by European rule, the Philippines became a nation in which the majority was Christian. This fact heightened the Filipinos' resentment when Spain continued to deny them political and social rights. The southern half of the Philippine archipelago was never brought under European rule, and here the Muslim faith was paramount among an aggregation of sultanates. A rebellion against the stagnant and faltering Spanish rule broke out in the northern islands in the late 1890s. It was still going on when the Americans became embroiled in war with Spain and captured the islands (1899–1900).

Because the United States was originally no more inclined to give the Filipinos their independence than the Spaniards had been, the rebellion turned against the Americans and persisted for two more years before it was finally extinguished. What had been promoted as "liberation" became an occupation. Even though American policy became steadily more benevolent and advantageous to the Filipinos and independence was promised in the 1930s, the Philippines had to wait another decade before attaining sovereignty immediately after World War II.

SUMMARY

China and Japan met the overwhelming challenge of Western intervention in vastly different ways. Like the *ulama* and *mullahs* in the Islamic lands with regard to their traditions, the Chinese mandarins were unwilling to leave the false security that Confucian philosophy and many centuries of assured superiority gave them. They went down a blind alley of hopeless resistance and denial until they were pushed aside by rebellion and revolution at the beginning of the twentieth century. In contrast, the Japanese upper classes soon recognized the advantages to be gained by selectively adopting Western ways and used them to their own highly nationalistic ends during the Meiji Restoration of the late nineteenth century.

China's halfhearted and confused experiment with a democratic republic came to an end in World War II, when the corrupt Chiang Kai-shek regime was unable to rally nationalist support against either the Japanese or Mao's communists. After two years of civil war, Mao took Chinese fate in his confident hands. Japan's civil government was much more stable and successful than China's until the 1930s, when a restive and ambitious military establishment pushed it aside and put the country on a wartime footing with an invasion of China. Then, in 1941, Japan entered World War II with the attack on Pearl Harbor.

Elsewhere, almost all nations of Southeast Asia were European colonies, and by the early twentieth century, this region was experiencing a buildup of frustrated nationalism among both intellectuals and ordinary folk. This became even truer after the Asians witnessed the humiliation of Russia by Japan in 1905 and the mutual slaughter of Europeans in World War I. In retrospect, the late nineteenth and early twentieth centuries were the high point of European domination of Asia. After World War II, the tide would turn toward a closer balance in East–West relations.

IDENTIFICATION TERMS

Test your knowledge of this chapter's key concepts by defining the following terms. If you can not recall the meaning of certain terms, refresh your memory by looking up the boldfaced term in the chapter, turning to the Glossary at the end of the book, or accessing the terms on the CourseMate website at **www.cengagebrain.com**.

Chiang Kai-shek
Chinese Communist Party (CCP)
Indochina
Kuomintang
Long March of 1934
Mao Zedong
Meiji Restoration
zaibatsu

FOR FURTHER REFLECTION

1. Why did the Kuomintang fail to hold on to power in China?
2. Why did Japan succeed in adopting Western technology so easily, whereas China did not?
3. Why did neither country become a democracy?

TEST YOUR KNOWLEDGE

Test your knowledge of this chapter by answering the following questions. Complete answers appear at the end of the book. You may find even more quiz questions on the CourseMate website at **www.cengagebrain.com**.

1. Mao's famous Long March resulted in
   a. a victory of the communists over the Nationalists.
   b. an increase in the number of his followers of about 100,000.
   c. the loss of about 90 percent of his followers.
   d. a victory over the Japanese occupying forces.
   e. an alliance with the Nationalist forces led by Chiang Kai-shek.
2. The text describes Chiang Kai-shek's Kuomingtang government as a/an
   a. dictatorship.
   b. republic.
   c. oligarchy of warlords.
   d. pure democracy.
   e. plutocracy of wealthy landlords.
3. The main reason for the victory of the Chinese Communist Party over the Kuomintang in 1947 was
   a. the brilliant escape from the clutches of Chiang's army during the Long March.
   b. the extensive military assistance the Soviets gave Mao and the CCP.
   c. the extensive support rendered by the old mandarin elites.
   d. Mao's successful appeal to the peasants.
   e. Mao's ability to fuse the ideas of Marx and Lenin with traditional Confucian teachings.
4. At times the Kuomintang and the Chinese Communist Party cooperated with each other because they
   a. shared many of the same leaders.
   b. shared a common ideology.
   c. both admired the achievements of the Bolsheviks in Russia.
   d. were both opposed to capitalism.
   e. both desired to see China modernized and foreigners evicted.
5. Unlike Karl Marx, Mao Zedong based his revolution on
   a. the failure of the Boxer Rebellion.
   b. World War II and the damages it did to China's cities.
   c. the New China Movement.
   d. the Opium Wars.
   e. winning over the peasants.
6. One of the main reasons for the success of Mao Zedong's communist forces in China's civil war was
   a. the fact that his army was about three times the size of the Nationalist forces.
   b. his strength among the country's intellectuals.
   c. the lack of a will to fight among Nationalist forces.
   d. the resentment among many Chinese toward American support for the Nationalists.
   e. the peasants' resentment of Chiang Kai-shek's corruption and inaction.
7. The Meiji Restoration in Japan saw
   a. the return of the emperor to supreme governing power.
   b. a turning away from the West to a renewed isolation.
   c. the reinstallation of the samurai and daimyo to power.
   d. the adoption of Western techniques and ideas by Japan's rulers.
   e. the construction of a new capital city for the shogun at Tokyo.
8. Which of the following does *not* describe Fukuzawa Yukichi?
   a. He was a successful capitalist.
   b. He founded an important school.
   c. He was a government official.
   d. He was an author and translator.
   e. He was a world traveler.
9. Which of the following places was *not* made into a European colony?
   a. Thailand
   b. Indonesia
   c. Malaya
   d. Burma
   e. Vietnam
10. In the 1800s, the only Southeast Asian nation whose dominant faith was Christianity was
    a. Thailand.
    b. the Philippines.
    c. Indonesia.
    d. Cambodia.
    e. Malaya.

CourseMate

Visit the CourseMate website at **www.cengagebrain.com** for additional study tools and review materials for this chapter.

45 World War II

I have been actuated by love and loyalty to my people in all my thoughts, acts, and life. They gave me the strength to make the most difficult decisions which have ever confronted mortal man.

—*ADOLF HITLER*

1931	Japanese seizure of Manchuria
1935	Ethiopian War
1936–1939	Spanish Civil War
1938	*Anschluss* of Austria; Munich conference
1939–1945	War in Europe
1941–1945	War in Pacific
1945	Yalta and Potsdam conferences among Allies
1945–1948	Eastern Europe comes under Soviet control; Cold War begins

CHAPTER OUTLINE

For the first fifteen years after the end of World War I, the peace held together. Despite the bitter complaints of the losers, especially the Germans, the Paris treaties were backed up by French diplomacy and the potential application of military force by France and Britain. For a brief period in the late 1920s, the Germans voluntarily adopted a policy of "fulfillment," adhering to the provisions of the treaties. But with the worldwide economic collapse and the coming of Adolf Hitler to power in the early 1930s, the treaties were unilaterally rejected and an atmosphere of international hostility resumed. The impotence of the League of Nations was quickly evident, and Hitler successfully bluffed his way forward until he felt himself in an invulnerable position to undertake a war of vengeance and conquest.

THE RISE AND FALL OF COLLECTIVE SECURITY

When the French saw the U.S. Senate reject Woodrow Wilson's League of Nations and realized that the British were having second thoughts about continuing their wartime alliance, they hurriedly took independent steps to protect France from potential German revenge. To this end, France signed a military alliance with Poland, Czechoslovakia, and Romania—three of Germany's eastern neighbors. This *Little Entente* stated that if Germany attacked any of the signatories, the others would give assistance. Also, France stayed on good terms with fascist Italy throughout the 1920s, and the French consistently argued that the League must take unified action against any potential aggressor nation; an attack on one was an attack against all.

Even before Hitler's seizure of power, however, the Paris-inspired policy of "collective security" against a resurgent Germany was under severe strain. For one thing, the aggressive stirring of international revolutionary hopes by the Bolsheviks meant that Soviet Russia was an outcast (see Chapter 42). For years, it was not invited to join the League of Nations, and even after a reluctant invitation was extended, Russia was not considered a suitable ally by the capitalist democracies. For another, Japan, a member of the League, totally disregarded the League's disapproval of its invasion of Manchuria in 1931 and got away without penalty. The League could only express its moral condemnation.

The League's powerlessness was revealed even more clearly in 1935 in a case that was much closer to European affairs. Hoping to revive his sagging popularity with the Italian people, Benito Mussolini started a blatantly imperialistic war with Ethiopia. The Ethiopians appealed to the League and obtained a vote that clearly branded Italy as an aggressor nation. But neither Paris nor London would take decisive measures, such as banning oil shipments to Italy, which had no oil of its own. In the end, the triumphant invaders were not even threatened in their occupation of Ethiopia. The League of Nations had been shown to have no teeth. Collective security had been struck a hard, but not yet lethal blow.

The Spanish Civil War

All hope for collective security was finished off by the Spanish Civil War, which broke out in the summer of 1936. Spain in the 1930s was a sharply divided nation. Its liberals had recently forced out an ineffectual monarch and declared a republic, but the public remained divided among every variety of leftist group, moderate democrats, and fascists. Like most of the Spanish upper classes, many army commanders were afraid that Spain might soon come under a communist government if current trends were not checked. To prevent such a takeover, they entered into a military revolt, supported by the Catholic Church, much of the peasantry, and most of the middle classes.

Despite open support for the rebel forces from both Mussolini and Hitler, the Western democracies refused to take sides and declared an embargo on shipments of arms and matériel to both contestants. In the circumstances, this was the same as assisting the rebels led by General Francisco Franco against the legitimate Spanish government.

Josef Stalin decided early on that the Spanish conflict was a golden opportunity. It might allow the Soviet Union to gain popularity among the many Western antifascists who as yet could not sympathize with communism. The Comintern orchestrated an international campaign to assist the outnumbered and outgunned Spanish Loyalists in the name of a **Popular Front** against fascism. For two years, the Soviets abandoned their previous vicious propaganda against the democratic socialists in all countries. In some instances, Popular Front tactics were quite successful. Much Soviet military aid was sent to Spain, and some tens of thousands of volunteers from all over the world (including the United States) went to fight with the Loyalists.

Hitler's and Mussolini's arms and advisers were more numerous and more effective in the long run, however. In the spring of 1939, the Loyalists surrendered, and Franco established himself as the military dictator of his country for the next generation. Although friendly to the fascist dictators, he stubbornly defended his freedom of action and never allowed himself to be their tool. Like Sweden, Switzerland, and Portugal, Spain sat out World War II as a neutral party.

HITLER'S MARCH TO WAR, 1935–1939

Since 1922, the fascist Mussolini had made no effort to conceal his contempt for the Western democracies, but Germany, much more than Italy, represented the real danger to the Paris treaties. Even before gaining power, Hitler had sworn to overturn the Versailles Treaty, and he proceeded to take Germany out of the League of Nations almost immediately—in 1933.

Did Hitler intend a major war from the outset of his dictatorship? This question is still much debated. Historians generally agree that he realized that the program of German hegemony described in *Mein Kampf* could only be made reality through war because it entailed a major expansion of German territory eastward into Slavic lands (Poland and Russia). But he seems to have had no concrete plans for war until about 1936, when he instructed the General Staff to prepare them.

In 1935, Hitler had formally renounced the provisions of the Versailles Treaty that limited German armaments. This move had symbolic rather than practical importance because the treaty limitations had been ignored even during the Weimar era. A few months later, he started conscription for a much larger army and the creation of a large *Luftwaffe* (air force). Neither France nor Britain reacted beyond a few words of diplomatic dismay and disapproval.

The Reoccupation of the Rhineland

In 1936, Hitler sent a small force into the Rhineland, the area of Germany west of the Rhine on the French borders. Under both the Versailles and Locarno agreements, the Rhineland was supposed to be permanently demilitarized. To the French, stationing German troops there was a direct threat to France's security, but in the moment of decision, France said that it did not want to act alone, and Britain said it would not support France in an offensive action. What the British and French did not know was that the German army was more frightened of the consequences of the Rhineland adventure than they were. The General Staff strongly opposed the action, advising Hitler not to try this ploy because the army was as yet in no condition to resist Allied attacks. Hitler insisted on proceeding with his bluff and scored a great psychic and diplomatic triumph over his own generals as well as the French. From this point, the quite erroneous legend of Hitler as the master strategist was born.

From 1936 on, Germany was rapidly rearming, whereas France and Britain were paralyzed by defeatism or pacifism among both the general public and the government officials. In Britain, where the English Channel still gave a false feeling of security, many members of the Conservative government leaned toward appeasement of *der Führer* and were ready to abandon France. Much of the party leadership was more fearful of a Bolshevik revolution than of a fascist or Nazi society. Some hoped that a Hitler-like figure would rise in Britain and put "order" back into the depression-wracked country. The French, for their part, put all of their hopes into the huge line of defensive fortifications—the so-called Maginot Line, built during the 1920s along their eastern borders—and their allies in Eastern Europe.

Also in 1936, Hitler and Mussolini reached a close understanding, the Rome-Berlin **Axis Pact**, which made them allies in case of war. This agreement eliminated any hopes the French might have had that Mussolini would side with France and against Germany.

Anschluss in Austria

In 1938, the pace of events picked up. Hitler, an Austrian by birth, had always intended to bring about the "natural union" of his birthplace with Germany. The Versailles Treaty explicitly forbade the ***Anschluss*** ("joining"), but by this time, that was a dead letter. In Austria, the Nazis had strong support. Most Austrians were German by blood, and they regarded the enforced separation from the Reich as an act of vengeance by the Allies. A previous attempt at a Nazi coup in 1934 had failed because of Mussolini's resistance. Now in 1938, Mussolini was Hitler's ally, and the Anschluss could go forward. It was completed in March by a bloodless occupation of the small country on Germany's southern borders, and Nazi rule was thus extended to another 7 million people.

Next to fall was the Successor state of Czechoslovakia, a country created by the Versailles Treaty that Hitler had always hated. Linked militarily with France, it contained within its borders 3.5 million Germans, the Sudetenlander minority who were strongly pro-Hitler. Under the direction of Berlin, the Sudeten Germans agitated against the democratic, pro-Western government in Prague. Concessions were made, but the Germans always demanded more. After the Anschluss in Austria, it appeared to be only a matter of time before the Germans acted. The attitude of the British government was key. If Britain supported Czech armed resistance, the French promised to honor their Little Entente treaty obligation and move against Germany.

Munich, 1938

In September 1938, Hitler brought British Prime Minister Neville Chamberlain and French Premier Edouard Daladier to a conference at Munich, where Mussolini joined them. After several days of threats and negotiations, Hitler succeeded in extracting the **Munich Agreements** from the democratic leaders. The Czechs were sacrificed entirely, although Hitler had to wait a few months before taking the final slice. Chamberlain returned to Britain waving a piece of paper that he claimed guaranteed "peace in our time." One year later, Britain and Germany were at war.

Almost before the ink was dry on the Munich Agreements, Hitler started pressuring Poland about its treatment of its German minority. These Germans lived in solid blocs on the borders with Germany and in

Arthur Ackermann Ltd., London/The Bridgeman Art Library

WINSTON CHURCHILL. Statesman, soldier, historian, journalist, and artist, Churchill was an extraordinary man in extraordinary times. After the failure of the policy of appeasement, Churchill was elected as prime minister. His strong leadership and the close working relationship he formed with President Franklin D. Roosevelt provided a crucial spark that enabled Britain to defeat German invasion plans.

MAP 45.1 World War II in Europe
In contrast to World War I (1914–1918), World War II was decided militarily as much or more on the Eastern fronts as in the West. Until the war's end, the largest part of Nazi forces was deployed in Russia and occupied Eastern Europe. Civilian and military casualties far outstripped those of World War I, again mainly in the East, where slave labor was extensively recruited and the extermination camps were located.

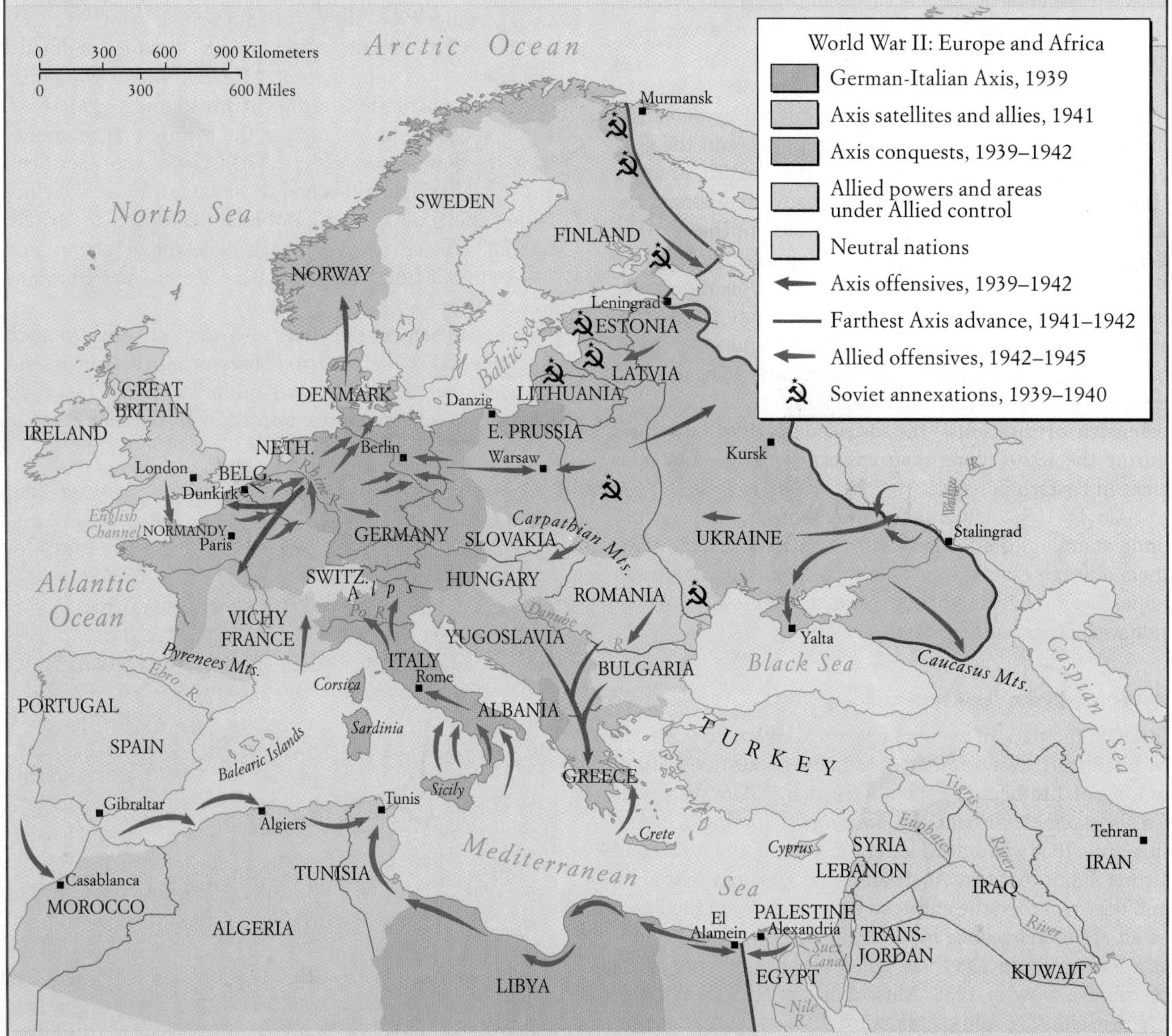

THINKING ABOUT THIS MAP

In addition to the obvious need to defeat Hitler, what other strategic objective do you think Stalin had in mind in his race with the British and the Americans to Berlin?

the so-called Free City of Danzig (Gdansk) in the Polish Corridor to the sea between Germany and its province of East Prussia (see Map 45.1).

Prodded by British public opinion and the speeches of Churchill in Parliament, Chamberlain now at last moved firmly. In March 1939, he signed a pact with Poland, guaranteeing British (and French) aid if Germany attacked. Hitler did not take this threat seriously because he knew that the Allies could aid Poland only by attacking Germany in the west and that the French, having put their military in an entirely defensive orientation behind the Maginot Line, were not prepared to go on the offensive. Of more concern to Hitler was the attitude of the other nearby great power, the Soviet Union.

The Nazi-Soviet Nonaggression Pact

At this point, the only convincing threat to Hitler's war plans was the possibility of having to face the Soviet Union in the east and the Allies in the west simultaneously—the two-front war that had proved disastrous in 1914–1918. But even at this stage, neither Chamberlain or Daladier nor their conservative advisers could bring themselves to ask the communist Stalin to enter an alliance. In fact, the Russians were equally as suspicious of the West's motives as Paris and London were of Moscow. Stalin had not forgotten that the Soviet Union had been excluded from the postwar arrangements and treaties. Nor had he overlooked the fact that when the chips were down, Britain and France had sacrificed their ally Czechoslovakia rather than coordinate action with the Soviet Union, as Stalin had offered to do through Czech intermediaries.

Even so, it was a terrific shock to communists and to all antifascists everywhere to hear, on August 23, 1939, that Stalin and Hitler had signed a **Nonaggression Pact of 1939**. By its terms, the Soviet Union agreed to remain neutral in a war involving Germany. In return, Hitler agreed that the Russians could occupy the three small Baltic states (Estonia, Latvia, and Lithuania), eastern Poland, and a slice of Romania. These areas had once belonged to imperial Russia and were still claimed by the Soviets. Both sides affirmed their "friendship." Hitler no longer had to worry about what Russia might do if he attacked Poland, and the Allies came to the Poles' aid as they had promised. The Nonaggression Pact made war certain.

For communists all over the world, the pact represented a 180-degree turn in the party line, and they were entirely unprepared. Hitler was now the head of a friendly government. The Popular Front against fascism died overnight. Many members of the Communist Party outside the Soviet Union dropped out, unable to swallow this latest subordination of truth and others' national interests to the momentary advantage of the Soviets. But Stalin had gained some time. The Soviet Union did not enter World War II for almost two more years. Whether or not he used the time well to prepare for war is a topic of debate to the present day.

WORLD WAR II

World War II can be divided into three major chronological periods and two geographic areas, or theaters. Chronologically, the first phase of the conflict saw the German and later the Japanese victories and expansion from 1939 to late 1942. The second phase was the Allied counterattack from late 1942 through 1943, which checked and contained both enemies. The third phase was the steady Allied advance in 1944 and 1945, bringing final victory in August 1945.

The European Theater

Geographically, the European theater (including North Africa) was the focus of Allied efforts until the German surrender in May 1945. Then, the emphasis shifted to the Pacific, but the anti-Japanese campaign was unexpectedly shortened by the atomic bombs and Japan's ensuing surrender. The United States, alone among the belligerents, played an important role on both fronts. The Pacific theater was fundamentally a conflict between Japan and the United States. The Soviet Union was drawn into the European war in mid-1941 but maintained neutrality with Germany's ally Japan until the final three weeks. (We will consider the Pacific war as an adjunct of the European theater, as indeed it was for all combatants except Japan and China.)

Phase 1: Axis Blitzkrieg

The German *blitzkrieg* ("lightning war") machine smashed into Poland on September 1, 1939 (see Map 45.1). Britain and France retaliated by declaring war on Germany two days later. Italy remained neutral for the time being (the Axis Pact did not demand immediate assistance to the other partner), and so did Germany's other ally, Japan, and the United States, Spain, the Scandinavian countries, and the Balkan countries. The Soviet Union remained neutral as well, but it moved quickly to occupy the promised segments of Eastern Europe in accord with the Nonaggression Pact.

Poland fell almost at once to the well-trained, well-armed Germans despite brave resistance. Soviet forces occupied the eastern half of the country. For several months, all was quiet. Then, in the spring of 1940, Hitler struck. France fell to the German tanks (now assisted by the Italians) within a few weeks. Denmark, the Netherlands, Belgium, and Norway had been overwhelmed before France. By July, Britain stood alone against a Nazi regime that controlled Europe from the Russian border to the Pyrenees.

For the next several months, the *Luftwaffe* attempted to bomb England into submission—as many experts feared would be possible with the huge new planes and their large bomb loads. But the Battle of Britain, fought entirely in the air, ended with a clear victory for the defenders. The British still controlled the English Channel, and Hitler's plans for an invasion—like those of Napoleon a century and a half previous—had to be abandoned. Just before the fall of France, Churchill had replaced Chamberlain as head of the British government, and he personified the "British bulldog" that never would give up. His magnificent speeches and leadership rallied the British people, cemented the growing Anglo-American sympathies, and played a key role in the Allies' eventual victory.

The high point of the war for the Nazis came in 1941, when attacks on Yugoslavia (April), Greece (May), and the Soviet Union (June) were all successful. The Germans gained huge new territories and turned all of Eastern Europe into either a Nazi satellite (Romania, Bulgaria, and Hungary) or an occupied land (the Ukraine, Poland, and western Russia).

IMAGES OF HISTORY

Identifying Jews

In 1934, the Nazis began issuing special identity cards to Jews. Later, all German Jews and Jews of occupied Europe were required to wear a yellow Star of David sewn to their clothing.

Star of David patch printed with "Juif" (French for "Jew"), c. 1942.

Private Collection/Archives Charmet/The Bridgeman Art Library

German Identity cards for Jews, 1939.

Paris, France/Archives Charmet/The Bridgeman Art Library

Operation Barbarossa, the code name for the attack on Russia, got off to a tremendous start because Stalin's government was caught entirely by surprise despite repeated warnings from spies and Allied sources. In the first two days alone, some two thousand Russian planes were destroyed on the ground, and a half-million men were taken prisoner by the end of the first month. The Red Army, which was still recovering from a massive purge of its officers during the Great Purge of the 1930s, looked as though it had been all but knocked out of the war (see Chapter 42). At this critical point, Hitler overruled his generals and insisted on diverting many of his forces southward, toward the grain and oil of Ukraine and the Black Sea area, rather than heading straight for Moscow. As a consequence, the Germans were struck by the numbing cold of an early winter before they could take the capital, and Stalin was given precious time to rally and reinforce. For all practical purposes, the Germans had already lost their chance for a quick, decisive victory on the Eastern front in the fall of 1941.

Phase 2: Allied Counterattack

In December 1941, the attack on Pearl Harbor brought the United States into the war against Japan and its allies, Germany and Italy. In many ways, the U.S. entry into World War II and its later decisive role were similar to what had occurred in World War I. As the U.S. public became aware of the oppressive nature of Germany's occupation regime in Europe, opinion began running strongly in support of London and against Berlin. Thus, the attack on Pearl Harbor only accelerated a process that was already under way toward the entry of the United States into the conflict.

Although the U.S. peacetime military was very small and poorly equipped, U.S. industrial resources were immense and played the same important role they had in

SOCIETY AND ECONOMY

"Rosie the Riveter" and the U.S. Home Front in World War II

World War II, like World War I, was total war, waged by soldiers and civilians alike. The U.S. Office of War Mobilization directed the conversion of most factory production from consumer goods to war materials. Everyone was expected or required to contribute to the war effort and to put the needs of the soldiers first. For the first time, women and minorities worked side by side in jobs vacated by soldiers. One of these working women (called "Rosie the Riveter") was Oklahoman Kate Grant, who related her wartime experiences in a 2003 interview, excerpted here:

> "It was the first time that ... we worked, the blacks and the whites together. It was quite a change, but everybody needed the money and the government needed us all to work.... In World War II we didn't think of ourselves as being anything special. We felt like it was our duty.... I felt like the boys and the men who went to war were the ones that should be honored....
>
> "... I went to work in the Richmond [California] shipyards in the middle of '43 ... They gave me two weeks' training.... They gave me the leather pants and jacket, goggles, hood, gloves, steel-toed shoes.... So after training they put me 40 feet down in the bottom of the Liberty Ships to be a tack welder on the seams on the big steel they brought in ... I would lay the beads of hot lead on top of each other for a little strip down, then I would take a steel brush and brush it down.... Then the welders came along and they would weld a whole seam to make it strong so it could take the high winds, deep waters, and heavy weights.... [After my night shift] ... I'd go home in the morning, ... help [my sister] get the work done, take care of the baby, then I'd lay down and go to sleep, then get up and do some more, then sleep some more, until midnight when I went to work.... I was taught to work [as a farm child], but this was a different work, alright."

http://www.rose.edu/EOCRHC.htm accessed 10 March 2009.

John Parrot/Stocktrek Images/Alamy Limited

ANALYZE AND INTERPRET

How might women's lives have changed after the war, with the soldiers' return? During World War II, women and men of different races worked together in unprecedented numbers. How do you think this experience would have affected the postwar society? Kate Grant also stated that today "we need to all pull together more," as during World War II. Do you agree with her? Compare our home front society during the wars in Iraq and Afghanistan with the situation during World War II.

1917–1918. Neither Japan nor Germany had the wherewithal to hold out indefinitely against this power. In an economic sense, the outcome of the war was decided as early as December 1941, but the Allies' eventual victory was far from clear at the time. The Germans had been checked in Russia but not defeated. Their Italian ally was not much help but did contribute to the takeover of North Africa and the Balkans and the blockade of the British forces in Egypt. German submarines threatened Britain's supply lines from the United States for the next two years and were defeated (by the convoy system) only after heavy losses.

In the summer of 1942, the Russians were again pushed back hundreds of miles by superior German armor and aircraft. Stalin then ordered a "not one step backward" defense of the strategic city of **Stalingrad** on the Volga. Historians agree that the ensuing battle in the fall and winter of 1942 was the turning point of the war in Europe. The Nazis lost an entire army, which was surrounded and captured, and from

AMERICAN WAR POSTERS, 1944. As was the case in the War of 1914–1918, World War II was a "total war," fought on the home fronts as much as on the battlefields.

this point on, they were defending more than attacking. At the same time, the Western Allies were at last counterattacking. By the summer of 1943, the Germans and Italians had been driven from Africa, and the Allies landed in southern Italy. After a few months, Nazi puppet Mussolini fell and was discredited, but his German allies rescued him and restored him to power in northern Italy. Despite these political maneuvers, Italy capitulated in September.

Phase 3: Allied Victory

In Europe, the tide had turned decisively in 1943. An Allied army landed in the south of France and started pushing northward. In the Balkans, the German occupiers were under heavy attack by partisans (guerrillas) supplied by the Allies. By late 1944, Greece, Yugoslavia, Bulgaria, and Albania had been cleared of Axis forces, but the main theater of the war in Europe was on the Russian front, where the Germans had the bulk of their forces. Here, too, the Nazis were forced steadily back, and by the fall of 1944, they were again on German soil. Poland, Hungary, and Romania had all been freed of the occupiers. The Red Army became entrenched in those countries while it pursued the retreating Germans.

The human losses on the Eastern front were immense. The Nazis had treated the occupied areas with great brutality, taking millions for slave labor in German factories and mines. Millions more starved to death. The large Jewish populations of Poland, Hungary, and Romania, as well as the western Soviet Union were systematically exterminated in the gas chambers of Auschwitz, Bergen-Belsen, Maidenek, and the other death camps set up by the SS.

Stalin's repeated calls for a **Second Front** in the West were finally answered by the June 1944 invasion across the English Channel by British, American, and Canadian forces; the invasion began on June 6, or **D-day**. For the next several months, fighting raged in northern France and Belgium without a decision, but by the winter of 1944–1945, Allied troops were on Germany's western border. The next spring, the fighting was carried deep into Germany from both east and west.

On May 1, 1945, a half-mad Hitler committed suicide in the smoking ruins of his Berlin bunker as the Russians entered the city. Several of his closest associates chose the same death, but others fled and were hunted down for trial at Nuremberg as war criminals. Germany's formal surrender—unconditionally this time—took place on May 8. In accordance with previous agreements, the Russians occupied eastern Germany, including East Berlin. The British and Americans controlled the western part of the country.

The Pacific Theater

In the Pacific theater, naval battles in 1942 checked what had been a rapid Japanese advance (see Map 45.2). All of Southeast Asia and many Pacific islands had fallen to the flag of the Rising Sun, and the Japanese were threatening Australia and India by the middle of that year. But by the end of 1942, it was clear that the United States was recovering from Pearl Harbor. The **Battle of the Coral Sea** had nullified the Japanese threat to Australia, and British India proved ready to defend itself rather than passively submit, as Tokyo had hoped.

Even with the bulk of the U.S. war effort going toward Europe and the Russians remaining neutral, the Japanese did not have the raw materials or the manpower to keep up with the demands of prolonged conflict over so wide an area. (The Japanese high command knew this. They had counted heavily on the attack on Pearl Harbor to "knock out" American power in the Pacific or at least to make the United States amenable to a negotiated peace that would leave Japan in control of the western Pacific.) The turning point came at the **Battle of Midway Island**. There, an American force succeeded in ambushing the Japanese Pacific fleet, destroying four of their aircraft carriers, which then put the Americans on the offensive for the remainder of the war.

In 1943–1944, the United States rolled back the Japanese, taking one Pacific island chain after another in bloody fighting. The Philippines were liberated from Tokyo's forces in late 1944 in a campaign led by American

MAP 45.2 World War II in Asia and the Pacific

The failure of the Japanese to deal the U.S. Navy a lethal blow in the first months of the Pacific war meant that the war could not end in victory for them because it would only be a matter of time until Washington could summon its far greater resources and drive the Japanese back. From 1943 onward, the best Tokyo realists could hope for was a negotiated peace that gave Japan some favored position in China.

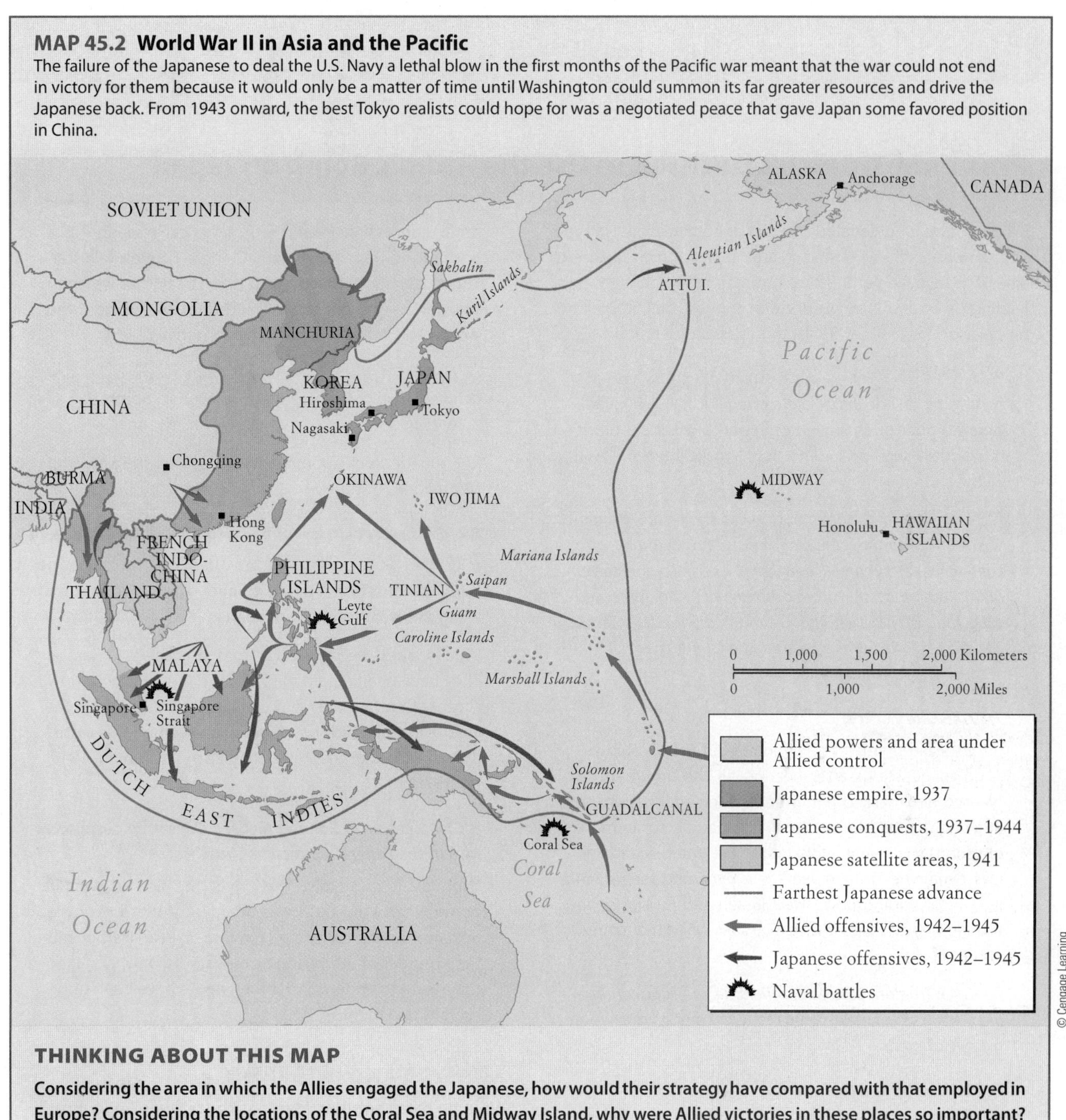

THINKING ABOUT THIS MAP

Considering the area in which the Allies engaged the Japanese, how would their strategy have compared with that employed in Europe? Considering the locations of the Coral Sea and Midway Island, why were Allied victories in these places so important?

commanders General Douglas MacArthur and Admiral Chester Nimitz, the chief architects of the victory in the Pacific. The Japanese homelands were pummeled by constant bombing from these newly captured island bases.

Japanese Defeat and Surrender

The end of the Pacific war came quickly after the Nazi capitulation. During 1944–1945, the Japanese occupation forces had gradually been forced from maritime Southeast Asia. Burma and Indochina had been cleared when the Japanese withdrew to return to their homeland. The long war between Japan and China was also now swinging in favor of the communist army under Mao Zedong (see Chapter 44).

The closer American and Allied forces got to the Japanese mainland, the stiffer the Japanese resisted and the higher the numbers of casualties both sides suffered. After absorbing huge losses in the assault on Iwo Jima Island, the Americans were preparing for massive

EVIDENCE OF THE PAST

President Truman's Decision to Use the Atomic Bomb on Japan

Scholars have long debated whether or not President Harry S. Truman was justified in using an atomic weapon on Japanese cities. The following entries from Truman's diary on the weeks leading up to and after his decision suggest that, in making his decision, he took several factors into consideration.

6/17/45 Diary entry:

"I have to decide Japanese strategy—shall we invade Japan proper or shall we bomb and blockade? That is my hardest decision to date. But I'll make it when I have all the facts."

[7/16/45: The first atomic bomb was successfully tested. That night, Truman, who was in Potsdam, Germany, at a conference with Churchill and Stalin, received a brief secret notification that the atomic bomb test had "exceeded expectations." It's likely that Truman's diary reference on 7/17/45 to his "dynamite" refers to the A-bomb news of July 16th, of which he had not told Stalin.]

7/17/45 Diary entry:

"I told Stalin that I am no diplomat but usually said yes & no to questions after hearing all the argument. It pleased him. I asked him if he had the agenda for the meeting. He said he had and that he had some more questions to present. I told him to fire away. He did and it is dynamite—but I have some dynamite too which I'm not exploding now." "He'll [Stalin and Russia] be in the Jap War on August 15th. Fini Japs when that comes about."

[7/18/45: Truman received another brief message confirming the success of the a-bomb test. Later that day he wrote his wife a letter.]

7/18/45 Letter to Bess Truman:

"... I've gotten what I came for—Stalin goes to war [against Japan] August 15 with no strings on it. He wanted a Chinese settlement [in return for entering the Pacific war, China would give Russia some land and other concessions]—and it is practically made—in a better form than I expected. [Chinese Foreign Minister] Soong did better than I asked him. I'll say that we'll end the war a year sooner now, and think of the kids who won't be killed! That is the important thing."

[7/21/45: On this afternoon, Truman received his first detailed report of the successful atomic bomb test of 7/16/45.]

[8/6/45: An atomic bomb was dropped on the people of Hiroshima.]

8/6/45 Excerpt from public statement by President Truman:

[This was the first time he publicly gave a reason for using the atomic bomb on Japan.]

"The Japanese began the war from the air at Pearl Harbor. They have been repaid many fold.... If they do not now accept our terms, they may expect a rain of ruin from the air, the like of which has never been seen on this earth." (Public Papers of the Presidents, Harry S. Truman, 1945, pp. 197, 199.)

8/11/45 Letter to Samuel McCrea Cavert, general secretary of the Federal Council of Churches:

"Nobody is more disturbed over the use of Atomic bombs than I am but I was greatly disturbed over the unwarranted attack by the Japanese on Pearl Harbor and their murder of our prisoners of war. The only language they seem to understand is the one we have been using to bombard them."

ANALYZE AND INTERPRET

What do these entries suggest as the reasons uppermost in the President's mind in making his decision? In your opinion, was he justified? How did he himself feel about it afterwards?

Source: excerpts from the diaries of President Truman.

casualties in a planned invasion of the Japanese islands. At that point, American president Harry S. Truman ordered that atomic bombs be dropped on Hiroshima and Nagasaki in August 1945. Within a few days, the Japanese government indicated its readiness to surrender, and the formal act was completed on August 15, 1945. The sole condition was that Emperor Hirohito be allowed to remain on his throne.

Should the atomic bombs have been used? This issue has remained profoundly acrimonious. Critics say that the bombing of the two Japanese cities was admittedly aimed against civilians rather than military targets and cite the

Private Collection/Peter Newark American Pictures/The Bridgeman Art Library

JAPANESE SURRENDER. These Japanese officials and senior military officers are shown aboard the battleship *USS Missouri* in Tokyo Bay on September 2, 1945, preparing to surrender.

huge loss of civilian life in Hiroshima (more than 70,000 of a population of about 200,000). This was entirely unnecessary, they say, because Japan would soon have surrendered to overwhelming Allied forces in any case. Another school of criticism thinks that the real reason for the bombing was that the U.S. government was looking ahead to the postwar era and wished to intimidate the Soviets.

On the other side, the defenders of President Truman and the U.S. high command point out that the Japanese had shown fanatical determination to resist and would have stalwartly defended their home islands. Some estimates at the time allegedly thought that more than a million U.S. casualties and countless more Japanese might have been expected before the fighting was over. To avoid such massive casualties, the atomic attack was entirely justified in their view. In any case, the sight of the enormous mushroom cloud of the atomic explosion would hover like some ghastly phantom over the entire postwar era. The knowledge that humans now had the power to entirely destroy themselves was the most fearsome insight to come out of World War II.

The other balance sheets of the war were almost as terrible. More people died in World War II than in any other disaster in recorded history. The final count will never be known for certain, but it is thought that about 30 million people died as a direct result of hostilities around the world. The Jews of Europe, followed by the Russians and the Germans, suffered the most devastating casualties. In material categories, much of Central and Eastern Europe was reduced to shambles by ground or air war, and many parts of Italy and France also suffered severe damage. Many Japanese and Chinese districts were in bad shape from bombings and (in China) years of ground war. Everywhere, the survivors stood on the edge of an abyss. Starvation, cold, epidemic disease, family disintegration, and psychic disorientation posed distinct threats to human life in much of the world.

THE ONSET OF THE COLD WAR

During the conflict, the Allies had not been able to agree on their postwar aims. Between the Western Allies and the Soviets stood a wall of mistrust that had been veiled temporarily but had by no means been dismantled. As soon as the victory over the Axis powers was secured, the dimensions of this wall were again visible for all to see.

Wartime Alliance and Continuing Mistrust

The so-called Cold War between the Soviet Union and the West began as early as 1945. During the war against the Axis, three Allied summit conferences (Tehran in 1943, Yalta and Potsdam in 1945) had been held. The main concrete results of these meetings were to assure the Soviets of political-military dominion over Eastern Europe after the war, to assign parts of conquered Germany to Allied armies of occupation, and to move Germany's eastern border a hundred miles to the west. Moving Germany's border would allow the Soviet border with Poland to be moved west a similar distance, fulfilling an old demand of the Soviets dating back to 1919.

The immediate trigger for inter-Allied suspicion was the Soviets' clear disregard for their commitments in Eastern Europe and Germany. At the **Yalta conference** in February 1945, the participants had agreed that free elections would be held as soon as wartime conditions permitted, even though all of these nations fell under what was conceded to be a Soviet "sphere of interest." Already at the Potsdam conference in July 1945, it was apparent that major problems were arising. From Stalin's point of view (the only one of the Big Three still in power), the assurance of freedom in any real sense for these nations was an unjustified presumption on the West's part. Since 1918, the nations of Eastern Europe had consistently been hostile to the Soviet Union and would undoubtedly continue to be so, given the chance. Therefore, the only freedom for them that the Soviets would agree to was the freedom to choose between various types of Soviet dominance. The Eastern Europeans could install their own native communist party dictatorship or they could accept the Soviet one—in either case, backed up by the Red Army already on the scene.

From the Western point of view (which increasingly meant the U.S. perspective), Stalin's government was violating the plain meaning of the promises it had made about Eastern Europe and eastern Germany. Also, the tiny communist parties were being falsely portrayed as the voices of the majority of Poles, Hungarians, and others in a like situation by Soviet media; governments composed of party members were being imposed on anticommunist majorities through rigged elections and political terror.

The almost inevitable rivalry between the United States and the Soviet Union in the contest for postwar leadership was the basic reason for the Cold War. Only those who have a doctrinal commitment either to Marxism or to its capitalist opponents can easily say which side was indeed the more culpable for the fifteen years of extreme tension that followed. The following assertions seem in order now.

Until Stalin's death in 1953, the Soviets were certainly trying to expand their direct and indirect controls over Europe. The large communist parties of France and Italy (which consistently obtained more than 25 percent of the vote in postwar elections) were regarded as Trojan horses by all other democratic leaders, and rightly so. These parties had shown themselves to be the slavish followers of Moscow's commands, and if they had obtained power, they would have attempted to turn those democracies into imitations of the Soviet Union. World revolution was still seen as a desirable and attainable goal by some communists—possibly including Stalin. The progress of the Maoist rebellion against the Chinese government in the late 1940s certainly buoyed these hopes, while greatly alarming American opinion.

On the other hand, the U.S. military and some U.S. political leaders were almost paranoid in their fears of communism. They were prone to see Muscovite plots everywhere and to think that all communists shared a monolithic commitment to Moscow's version of Marx, employing the same goals and methods. Like the most fanatical communists, they could not imagine a world where communists and capitalists might coexist. They viewed the exclusively U.S.-controlled atomic bomb as the ultimate "persuader" for a proper world order.

Private Collection/Peter Newark American Pictures/The Bridgeman Art Library

THE BIG THREE AT YALTA, FEBRUARY 1945. This final summit meeting among the three Allied leaders—Churchill, Roosevelt, and Stalin—came a few months before the German surrender. It was devoted to arranging the Soviet Union's entry into the Pacific war against Japan and the fate of postwar Eastern Europe.

The Original Issues

During the immediate postwar years, several specific issues concerning Germany and Eastern Europe brought the two superpowers—the United States and the Soviet Union—into a permanently hostile stance:

- *Reparations in Germany.* The Soviet Union claimed, more or less accurately, that the Allies soon reneged on their promises to give the Russians a certain amount of West German goods and materials, as reparations for war damage.
- *"Denazification" of German government and industry.* Again, the Russians were correct in accusing the West of not pursuing the Nazi element vigorously as soon as the Cold War frictions began. By 1949, the Western powers had dropped denazification altogether, seeing it as an unwelcome diversion from the main issue of strengthening Germany as a barrier to the spread of communism.
- *The creation of a new currency for the Allied sectors of Germany in 1948.* Without consulting its increasingly difficult Russian occupation "partner," the West put through a new currency (the deutsche mark), which split the supposed unity of the occupation zones in economic and financial affairs.
- *The Berlin government and the Berlin blockade in 1948–1949.* The Russians showed no interest in maintaining the agreed-on Allied Control Council (where they could always be outvoted) and made East Berlin and East Germany practically a separate administration as early as 1946. In 1948, Stalin attempted to bluff the Western allies out of Berlin altogether by imposing a blockade on all ground access. The Allies defeated the **Berlin blockade** by airlifting food and vital supplies for eleven months, and Stalin eventually lifted it (see Chapter 46).
- *The country-by-country Soviet takeover of Eastern Europe between 1945 and 1948.* From the moment the Red Army arrived, terror of every kind was freely applied against anticommunists. For a brief time after the war's end, the communist parties attempted service to democratic ideals by forming political coalitions with non-communists who had not been compromised during the Nazi occupation. Under Moscow's guidance, these coalitions were turned into "fronts" in which the non-communists were either powerless or

stooges. Protests by Western observers were ignored or denounced. The communists then took the leading positions in all of the provisional governments and used their powers to prepare for "free" elections. The elections were held at some point between 1945 and 1947 and returned a predictable overwhelming majority for the communist parties. Stalinist constitutions were adopted, the "protecting" Red Army was invited to remain for an indefinite period, and the satellite regime was complete.

Many other factors could be mentioned, but the general picture should already be clear: The wartime alliance was only a weak marriage of convenience against Hitler and was bound to collapse as soon as the mutual enemy was gone. After 1946 at the latest, neither side had any real interest in cooperating to establish world peace except on terms it could dictate. For an entire generation, the world and especially Europe would lie in the shadow thrown by the atomic mushroom, with the paralyzing knowledge that a struggle between the two superpowers meant the third, and final, world war.

SUMMARY

World War II came about through a series of aggressive steps taken by the fascist and Nazi dictatorships in the later 1930s against the defeatist and indecisive democratic states of Western Europe. Hitler quickly recognized the weakness of his opponents and rode his support by most Germans to a position of seeming invincibility in foreign affairs. The remilitarization of the Rhineland was followed by the annexation of Austria and Czechoslovakia, and finally the assault against Poland in September 1939, which began the general war.

In the first three years of war, the battles were mainly decided in favor of the Axis powers led by Germany, but the Battle of Stalingrad and the defeat of the Axis in North Africa marked a definite military turning point in the fall of 1942. In a long-range sense, the entry of the United States into the war following the Japanese attack on Hawaii was the turning point, even though it took a full year for the Americans to make much difference on the fighting fronts.

By late 1944, the writing was clearly on the wall for both the Germans and the Japanese, and attention turned to the postwar settlement with the Soviet ally. Despite some attempts, this settlement had not been spelled out in detail during the war because of the continuing mistrust between East and West. As soon as the fighting had stopped (May 1945 in Europe, August 1945 in the Pacific), the papered-over cracks in the wartime alliance became plain and soon produced a cold war atmosphere. The political fate of Eastern Europe and the administration of defeated Germany were the two focal points of what proved to be a generation of conflict between the West, led by the United States, and the communist world, headed by Soviet Russia.

IDENTIFICATION TERMS

Test your knowledge of this chapter's key concepts by defining the following terms. If you can not recall the meaning of certain terms, refresh your memory by looking up the boldfaced term in the chapter, turning to the Glossary at the end of the book, or accessing the terms on the CourseMate website at **www.cengagebrain.com**.

Anschluss
Axis Pact
Battle of the Coral Sea
Battle of Midway Island
Berlin blockade
D-day
Munich Agreements
Nonaggression Pact of 1939
Operation Barbarossa
Popular Front
Second Front
Stalingrad
Yalta conference

FOR FURTHER REFLECTION

1. In your opinion, what actions might have prevented the outbreak of the Second World War? Why did these not occur, or how did they fail to stop the war? Considering this, do you believe that another world war is possible today? How is the present world a more complicated one than in 1939?
2. In what ways was the Second World War a war that, even more than the First, truly involved much of the world? If another world war could occur, what nations most likely would be involved?
3. How do you explain the ability of Russia, after crushing initial defeats, to turn the tables on the Germans and to take the offensive? How do you explain the relative tardiness of the Americans and the British to reinvade Europe and to create the Second Front against Germany and Italy?
4. How did the war in the Pacific differ from the European theater of war?
5. Why did the United States and Russia emerge from World War II as the world's two strongest nations?

TEST YOUR KNOWLEDGE

Test your knowledge of this chapter by answering the following questions. Complete answers appear at the end of the book. You may find even more quiz questions on the CourseMate website at **www.cengagebrain.com**.

1. One ostensible reason for the Spanish Civil War was the military's fear of
   a. the country's new republic.
   b. a fascist takeover.
   c. communism.
   d. Mussolini.
   e. a return to monarchy.
2. Germany's fears of Russia prior to their invasion of Poland were offset by
   a. Stalin's promise not to invade Germany.
   b. a nonaggression agreement with Russia.
   c. Britain's promise to intervene if Russia invaded Germany.
   d. the Spanish civil war.
   e. the *Anschluss.*
3. A chief reason for Britain's prolonged appeasement of Hitler was that
   a. the British government wanted a counterweight to France on the continent.
   b. he was seen by some leaders as an anticommunist bulwark.
   c. the British government of the late 1930s was strongly pro-German.
   d. he was seen as a way to tame the Eastern European troublemakers.
   e. the United States urged Britain to stay out of any dangerous situations.
4. At the Munich conference in 1938,
   a. Austria was sacrificed to a Nazi invasion.
   b. Czechoslovakia was abandoned by its Western allies.
   c. Soviet Russia was invited to join the League of Nations.
   d. Hitler and Mussolini decided on war.
   e. Neville Chamberlain first began to understand the true evil of Adolf Hitler.
5. World War II was started by the Nazi invasion of
   a. France.
   b. Austria.
   c. Poland.
   d. Czechoslovakia.
   e. Belgium.
6. Which of these did *not* occur during the first phase of World War II?
   a. The German blitzkrieg against Denmark and Norway
   b. The D-day invasion of France
   c. The occupation and neutralization of France by Germany
   d. The invasion of Russia
   e. The conquest by Germany of the Balkans
7. Winston Churchill was elected as Britain's Prime Minister
   a. because of his successful reorganization of Britain's military.
   b. when the King made him the Lord of the Admiralty.
   c. after Chamberlain's policy of appeasing Hitler failed to produce a lasting peace.
   d. because of his successful record as Britain's Air Marshall during World War I.
   e. when Chamberlain chose him as his successor.
8. The event that brought the United States into World War II was the
   a. Japanese sneak attack on Pearl Harbor.
   b. German invasion of Poland.
   c. Italian invasion of Ethiopia.
   d. German bombing of London.
   e. Japanese invasion of Manchuria.
9. Stalin's principal reason for denying freedom to the Eastern European nation's after World War II was
   a. his fear that they might ally themselves with the West.
   b. the military buildup that was taking place in Eastern Europe in 1945.
   c. Eastern European leaders' expressed desire to join their nations to the NATO alliance.
   d. Eastern European nations' pre-war hostility to Russia
   e. his desire to spread communism in Eastern Europe.
10. The focal point of the Yalta conference among the Allied leaders in 1945 was
    a. the future of Japan.
    b. the postwar political arrangements in Eastern Europe.
    c. the details of a peace treaty with Germany.
    d. the signing of a peace treaty with Italy.
    e. a plan to liberate the Jews in occupied Poland.

CourseMate

Visit the CourseMate website at **www.cengagebrain.com** for additional study tools and review materials for this chapter.

46 The Cold World War

We are eyeball to eyeball … and I think the other fellow just blinked. *—U.S. SECRETARY OF STATE DEAN RUSK, OCTOBER 1962*

1947	Marshall Plan and Truman Doctrine
1948–1949	Blockade of Berlin; North Atlantic Treaty Organization (NATO) and Warsaw Pact
1950s	Western European economic recovery; Stalinization of Eastern Europe
1950–1953	Korean War
1957	Treaty of Rome establishes European Economic Community (EEC)
1961	Berlin Wall
1962	Cuban Missile Crisis
1970s	Détente in Cold War
1979	Soviet invasion of Afghanistan

CHAPTER OUTLINE

As World War II ended, the two great victorious powers were becoming increasingly suspicious of each other's intentions. Leadership in the Western world was passing to the United States from Britain and France for the indefinite future. In the East, Josef Stalin's Union of Soviet Socialist Republics (USSR) was the engine of a drive to make the world over according to Marx. The two superpowers would have to find a way to settle their differences peaceably or plunge the world into an atomic conflict that would leave all in smoking ruins. For the two decades after 1945, the question of atomic war overshadowed everything else in world affairs and dictated the terms of all international settlements.

The so-called **Cold War** became the stage on which the other vast drama of postwar diplomacy was played: the ending, forcible or peaceable, of the colonial system in the non-Western world. The links between the two struggles were many. In those same decades (1945–1965), Europe staged a remarkable recovery from both the material and the spiritual damages of war. Although many had almost written off Europe as a loss, the nations in the noncommunist two-thirds of Europe were exceeding prewar levels of production as early as 1950. Over the next thirty years, they succeeded in progressing far down the road to economic unity, and the ancient hopes of political unification looked increasingly attainable.

CONFLICT IN THE POSTWAR GENERATION

The hostility between the United States and the Soviet Union had both proximate and remote causes. We briefly reviewed the immediate causes in Chapter 45: the Soviets' insistence on "friendly" regimes along the western borders of their country and the arguments over the treatment of postwar Germany and the defeated Nazis. But these disputes were only specific reflections of the broader, more remote causes: the friction between two militarily powerful states, each of which had a tradition of strong nationalism and was convinced that its politics and social organization were based on an exclusive truth. The Russian communists (who were at all times the directing force within the Soviet Union) believed that in Stalin's version of Marxism they had found the ultimate answers to the problem of making humans happy on earth. The Americans thought their forebears had produced, and they themselves had maintained, a political and economic system that reflected the justified aspirations of all right-thinking people everywhere. The war against fascism had briefly brought these two nations into the same political bed. Now that the war was won, their latent ideological antagonism must inevitably make itself apparent. (See the Law and Government box on "The Iron Curtain")

The Division of Europe

Both superpowers realized that control of Germany meant control of most of Europe. The focus of conflict soon shifted from the elections and governments of the Eastern European countries (which were clearly within the Russian zone of dominion) to defeated Germany. Germany was originally divided into three and then four occupation zones: Russian, American, British, and French. By 1946, arguments over industrial reparations from Germany had already broken out. The Russians confiscated everything movable in their zone, shipping it back to the badly wounded USSR, and the Americans, British, and French soon decided that stripping Germany of its industrial capacity would only bring on political and social chaos and possibly a communist revolution.

To counter the menace of Soviet expansion and to speed up the still-slow recovery, in the summer of 1947, U.S. secretary of state General George Marshall put forth the **Marshall Plan** for reconstruction of the European economy. It proved to be one of the most successful foreign policy initiatives ever undertaken and was largely responsible for the beginning of the European recovery.

The **Truman Doctrine** was also announced in 1947. Named for the then-president, it committed the United States to defend governments throughout the world when they were threatened by communist-inspired subversion. This policy was a historic departure from the traditional U.S. position of refusing the "entangling alliances" warned against by George Washington long ago. The acceptance of the policy by the U.S. Congress and the public indicated that a decisive change in attitude had taken place since Woodrow Wilson's League of Nations was rejected in 1919. The United States was now prepared, however reluctantly, to shoulder the burdens of what was soon termed "free world" leadership.

The Soviet blockade of Berlin in 1948 (Chapter 45) was decisive in showing that there was no hope of reviving the wartime alliance and that Stalin was committed to expanding communism into the European

Private Collection/The Bridgeman Art Library

THE NUREMBERG TRIAL, 1946. Shortly after the German surrender, the Allies put several leading Nazis on trial for "crimes against humanity." The months-long trial was presided over by judges from Russia, the United States, Britain, and France. It resulted in convictions and sentences varying from prison terms to death for all but three of the defendants. Hermann Göring, the number-two Nazi (*far left*, first row), cheated the hangman by taking cyanide.

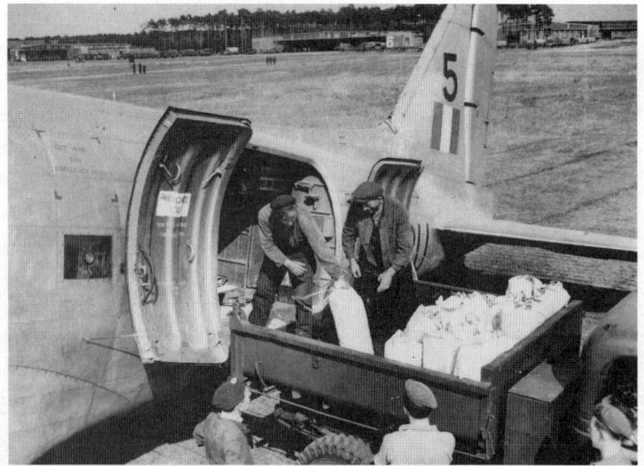

Popperfoto/Getty Images

THE BERLIN AIRLIFT. After Stalin blocked all surface routes into West Berlin, the Allies responded by starting an airlift of supplies from their occupation zones in western Germany into the isolated city. Beginning in June 1948, the airlift continued for eleven months until the Soviets allowed overland access again, tacitly admitting defeat.

LAW AND GOVERNMENT

The Iron Curtain

In the spring of 1946, Winston Churchill, just retired by the voters from his job as British wartime prime minister, visited the United States as a guest of President Harry Truman. In Westminster, Missouri, he gave a speech that caught the attention of the whole world and gave the phrase "Iron Curtain" to the language. His purposes were to alert the U.S. government and public to what was happening in Soviet-controlled Eastern Europe and to assure a united stand against it.

> A shadow has fallen upon the scenes so lately lighted by the Allied victory. Nobody knows what Soviet Russia and its Communist international organization intends to do in the immediate future, or what are the limits, if any, to their expansionist and proselytizing tendencies.... From Stettin in the Baltic to Trieste in the Adriatic,* an iron curtain has descended across the Continent. Behind that line lie all the capitals of the ancient states of Central and Eastern Europe. Warsaw, Berlin, Prague, Vienna, Budapest, Belgrade, Bucharest and Sofia, all these famous cities and the populations around them lie in what I must call the Soviet sphere, and all are subject in one form or another, not only to Soviet influence but to a very high and, in many cases, increasing measure of control from Moscow....The Communist parties, which were very small in all these Eastern States of Europe, have been raised to pre-eminence and power far beyond their numbers and are seeking everywhere to obtain totalitarian control....
>
> I do not believe that Soviet Russia desires war. What they desire are the fruits of war and the indefinite expansion of their power and doctrines....Our difficulties and dangers will not be removed by closing our eyes to them. They will not be removed by mere waiting to see what happens; nor will they be removed by a policy of appeasement. What is needed is a settlement, and the longer this is delayed, the more difficult it will be and the greater our dangers will become.

ANALYZE AND INTERPRET

How might the situation described by Churchill have been expected? To what extent might the United States and Britain have been complicit in the division of Europe?

*A line drawn between these two cities would enclose to its east the areas of Europe recently taken by the Red Army and made into Soviet satellites.

heartland. The key to containment of this threat was a West-oriented Germany. Conjured from the three western zones in September 1949, West Germany (*Bundesrepublik Deutschland*) was larger and more powerful than its Russian-created counterpart, the *Deutsche Demokratische Republik*, or East Germany, which came into existence a few weeks later.

The **North Atlantic Treaty Organization** (NATO) was similarly an outgrowth of the East–West struggle. Created in April 1949, it was Washington's solution to the need for an international military organ dedicated to stopping the spread of communism. It originally counted twelve Western European and North American members—later increased to fifteen—who pledged to come to the aid of one another if attacked. The Soviet answer quickly came with the **Warsaw Pact**, which made the communist governments of Eastern Europe military allies. The pact merely formalized what had been true since the series of Russian takeovers in 1945–1948.

Not only Germany but now all of Europe was thus divided into two enemy blocs, along with a handful of militarily insignificant neutrals (Austria, Finland, Spain, Sweden, and Switzerland). (See Map 46.1.) The situation whereby the European continent was more or less at the military mercy of two non-European powers, Russia and the United States, was a definite novelty in history. In the late 1940s and through the 1950s, it appeared that whatever the Europeans might be able to do about their own prosperity, they would remain the junior partners of outside powers in military affairs and diplomacy.

Grudging Coexistence

In 1950, the **Korean War** broke out when South Korea, a U.S. satellite, was invaded by North Korea, a Soviet satellite. Within a year, the conflict had become an international war, with the United States providing the leadership in the South and the Chinese (not the Soviets) coming to the aid of their hard-pressed North Korean allies. The fighting ended in deadlock, and a truce was finally signed in 1953.

Stalin also died that year, and with him died the most aggressive phase of the Cold War. His successors, however fanatical their communist belief, were never so given to paranoia as Stalin had been in his later years. After a behind-the-scenes power struggle, Nikita Khrushchev (1894–1971) emerged as Stalin's successor and chief of the Communist Party and the government.

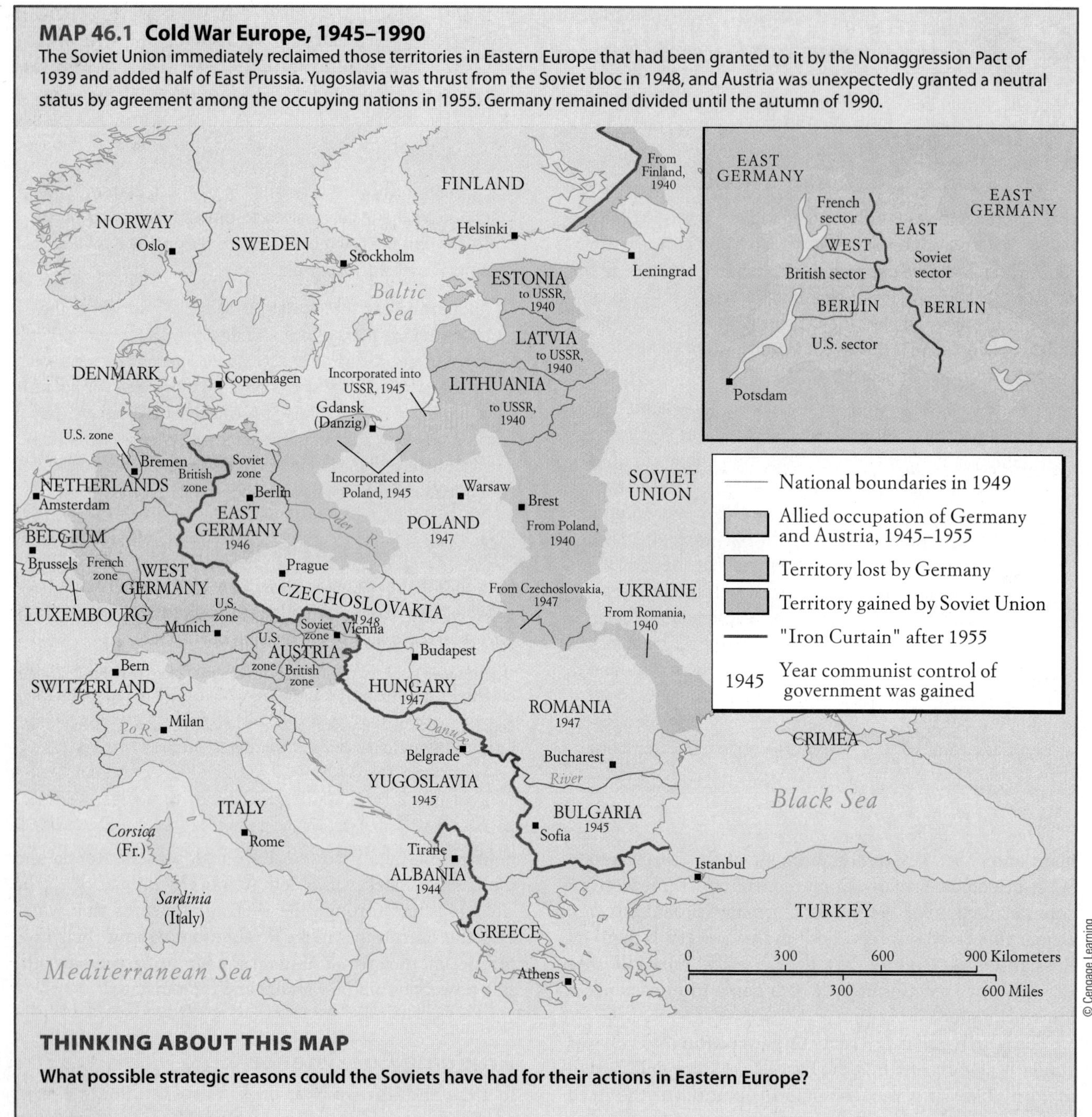

MAP 46.1 Cold War Europe, 1945–1990

The Soviet Union immediately reclaimed those territories in Eastern Europe that had been granted to it by the Nonaggression Pact of 1939 and added half of East Prussia. Yugoslavia was thrust from the Soviet bloc in 1948, and Austria was unexpectedly granted a neutral status by agreement among the occupying nations in 1955. Germany remained divided until the autumn of 1990.

THINKING ABOUT THIS MAP

What possible strategic reasons could the Soviets have had for their actions in Eastern Europe?

Khrushchev, the son of peasants, was different from the secretive, mysterious Stalin. Although just as convinced that Marxism must inevitably triumph in the whole world, he was generally more open in his dealings with the West and less menacing. He said he believed in peaceful coexistence with the West, and he challenged the West to engage in economic rather than military competition—a challenge that would turn into a bad joke for the Russians later.

However, Khrushchev was not about to give up what World War II had brought to the Soviet Union or to release the Eastern Europeans from their bonds to communism. In 1956, when the Hungarians rose up in revolt against their highly unpopular satellite government, he sent Soviet tanks to restore order and keep Hungary firmly within the Soviet orbit. The failure of the NATO powers to take any action made it clear that the West had accepted the Soviet-style regimes in Eastern Europe, however much it might denounce their illegality and repression. Since 1949, the Russians possessed their own atomic weaponry, and in the shadow of the mushroom cloud, the *Pax Sovietica* (Soviet peace) was deemed acceptable.

From Cuban Missiles to NATO's Decline

The Cold War was sharpened with the sudden erection of the **Berlin Wall** in 1961 by the East Germans to prevent the steady outflow of political refugees. The success of this unparalleled division of a city and a nation perhaps inspired Khrushchev to make an unexpected gamble in an attempt to help his Cuban Marxist ally, Fidel Castro, in 1962. Three years previously, Castro had conquered Cuba with a motley army of insurgents, kicked out the corrupt government, and then declared his allegiance to Marxism. An abortive, U.S.-sponsored invasion at the Bay of Pigs had been a total failure. Fearing another attempt, Castro asked the Russians for military help. Khrushchev decided to install intermediate-range rockets with nuclear warheads, and the project was well under way when it was discovered by U.S. aerial surveillance over Cuba.

After a few days of extreme tension, the Soviets backed down and removed their weapons when presented with an ultimatum by President John F. Kennedy. Kennedy allowed Khrushchev some room for maneuver by making some concessions on U.S. bases in Asia, along with a promise not to attempt another invasion. Both sides could thus claim to have achieved their goals when the missiles were withdrawn.

The world fright over the **Cuban Missile Crisis** stimulated the nuclear powers to make more serious efforts to reduce the level of hostility (see the Law and Government box on this topic). In 1963, they signed the **Nuclear Test Ban**, limiting the testing of atomic weapons in the atmosphere. Under the new leadership of Willy Brandt, the West German government moved to recognize the postwar borders to its east after years of resistance and thus to establish better relations with its communist neighbors and with the Soviet Union. This German ***Ostpolitik*** (Eastern policy) was a key point in reducing tensions in Europe.

AP Photos/Marty Lederhandler

NIKITA KHRUSHSHEV AND FIDEL CASTRO EMBRACING. With NATO bases encircling them, the Soviet Union and its allies felt they were in constant threat of invasion or nuclear annihilation. Russian Premier Nikita Khrushchev looked to the Cuban revolution and the rise of Fidel Castro as an opportunity for Russia to get a "foothold" in the Western hemisphere.

By the mid-1960s, then, the Cold War was less confrontational. The ideology of communist revolution had become a minor part of the Soviets' baggage in international affairs; it had been replaced by the predictable, selfish interest of a great power with imperialist motives. The Soviet Union was becoming a conservative state—a stable factor in world politics—despite its revolutionary slogans. The best evidence of this shift was the failure of the Soviets to provide military support for the communist side in the Vietnam conflict during the later 1960s (see Chapter 48).

The progress of ***détente*** (relaxation) between the Soviet Union and the West was marred but not derailed by the Soviet invasion of Czechoslovakia in 1968, when that nation attempted to oust its Stalinist overlords through a peaceful revolution. The United States was again not inclined to involve NATO in this "internal matter," and communist rule was reimposed without bloodshed. Coming in a year when many Western nations experienced explosive internal frictions between government and citizens, the Czechs' misfortunes were soon forgotten in the West.

The NATO alliance was not so close knit by this time. Under war hero General Charles de Gaulle, France had no sympathy for what it considered the American obsession about the Soviets. The bombastic Khrushchev had been replaced in 1964 by a tight group of *apparatchiks* (Communist Party bureaucrats) headed by Leonid Brezhnev (1906–1982), who showed little commitment to any type of revolution or foreign policy gambles. De Gaulle and many others thought Western Europe was no longer seriously threatened by violent communist intervention, and France withdrew its military from NATO command in 1962.

The decline of NATO reflected the shift from foreign policy issues to those of domestic policy that preoccupied European leaders in the 1960s. Originally generated by student discontent with the outmoded educational and cultural institutions carried over from the prewar era, protests of every type (the "youth revolt") soon erupted

Jandke/Caro/Alamy Limited

VOLKSWAGEN ASSEMBLY LINE. This plant, a frequent target of Allied bombers during World War II, led the way to mass production of cheap automotive transport for millions of European consumers.

LAW AND GOVERNMENT

Cuban Missiles in 1962

In the fall of 1962, the stunning discovery that the Soviets had secretly deployed nuclear-tipped intermediate-range missiles in Castro's Cuba ignited the most dangerous incident in the generation-long Cold War. Aerial photography of the island during September and October gradually confirmed that Russian engineers were building missile launch sites and bringing in a large number of missiles by ship. If fired, the missiles already transported could destroy much of the eastern United States.

Faced with the cruelest dilemma of any postwar presidency, John F. Kennedy had to frame a response that was absolutely firm yet restrained and not provocative. A nuclear war might well have been the price of miscalculation. After the Soviets were quietly put on notice that Washington was aware of what was going on and they had not responded, Kennedy decided it was necessary to "go public" with the news. For some days, the White House continued the agonizing search for the most unambiguous wording, designed to put maximum pressure on Soviet leader Nikita Khrushchev while giving him an opportunity to retreat without losing face. On October 22, Kennedy made a televised address to a nervous nation and world:

> Good evening, my fellow citizens.
>
> This government, as promised, has maintained the closest surveillance of the Soviet military build-up on the island of Cuba. Within the past week, unmistakable evidence has established the fact that a series of offensive missile sites are now in preparation on that imprisoned island....
>
> This secret, swift, and extraordinary build-up of communist missiles—in an area well known to have a special and historical relationship with the United States and the nations of the Western hemisphere—in violation of Soviet assurances, and in defiance of American and hemispheric policy—this sudden, clandestine decision to station strategic weapons for the first time outside Soviet soil is a deliberately provocative and unjustified change in the status quo which cannot be accepted by this country if our courage and our commitments are ever to be trusted again by either friend or foe.
>
> ...All ships of any kind bound for Cuba from whatever nation or port will, if found to contain cargoes of offensive weapons, be turned back.
>
> ...It shall be the policy of this nation to regard any nuclear missile launched from Cuba against any nation in the Western hemisphere as an attack by the Soviet Union on the United States, requiring a full retaliatory response upon the Soviet Union.
>
> ...I call upon Chairman Khrushchev to halt and eliminate this clandestine, reckless, and provocative threat to world peace, and to stable relations between the two nations....

After a few horribly tense days, the Russians agreed to dismantle and withdraw their missiles in return for a face-saving pledge on Kennedy's part that the United States would not attempt another invasion of Castro's island. The crisis was over.

ANALYZE AND INTERPRET

What factors might have prompted Soviet Premier Nikita Khrushchev to arm Cuba this way? Do you think it was a deliberate provocation? How might Khrushchev have viewed the situation?

Source: Elie Abel, *The Cuban Missile Crisis* (Philadelphia: Lippincott, 1966).

against the policies and politics of governments and other forms of traditional authority. These protests—often violent—reached a peak in 1968, when European disaffection with NATO support of the U.S. war in Vietnam and with the continuing arms race between the East and West reached tidal-wave proportions. Not only was the defense against a fading Marxism becoming superfluous, but to European minds, there were far more urgent and profitable areas for their governments to pursue.

EUROPE'S ECONOMIC RECOVERY

Cast into the shadows by the disasters of the first half of the century, Europe had reemerged by the last quarter of the twentieth century as the most important locale of technical, financial, and commercial power in the world. The word *renaissance* is not too strong to use in describing the developments in Western Europe since 1945. In that year, the continent was for the most part an economic ruin, and two external powers were contesting for supremacy over what was left intact. By 1965, the Western European countries had surpassed every measure of prewar prosperity and were rapidly regaining independence of action in politics.

Factors Promoting Prosperity

What had happened to encourage this rebirth? Five factors in particular can be identified:

1. *Marshall Plan aid* was remarkably successful in restarting the stalled economies of both the former enemies

and the allies. For five years (1947–1951), Austria, West Germany, France, Britain, Italy, and others benefited from this fund of U.S. dollars available for loan. The conditions imposed by supervisory agencies ensured a new spirit of collaboration not only between governments but also between governments and employers for the benefit of the general public.

2. *Social reforms* were enacted immediately after the war to provide benefits for ordinary citizens that they had long sought. Pensions for all, universal medical insurance, family allowances, paid vacations, paid schooling, and other changes all gave the working classes a new sense of being part of the process. Now they felt they had a stake in the success of their countries.
3. *Effective national planning* provided intelligent direction for the economy without eliminating individual enterprise and its profit reward. The "mixed economy"—with some industries and financial institutions directly controlled by the government, some totally private, and many in between—came to be the rule from Scandinavia to Portugal.
4. *A large, willing labor pool* in most countries allowed employers and entrepreneurs to expand at will when they saw opportunities. The unions, which had generally opposed employers as a matter of principle in the prewar era, now cooperated because socially conscious politicians protected and expanded their rights to a point where they now had an important voice in management.
5. *Free trade was made general.* The tariff, quota, and license barriers of the 1930s were gradually junked among the NATO countries; the various national currencies were made easily convertible and transferable; and international investment—much from the United States—was simplified and directly encouraged.

For these reasons, the growth of the Western European economies was little short of sensational after the immediate postwar years. West Germany led the way in these "economic miracles" of the 1950s, but France, Italy, and the Benelux nations (Belgium, Luxembourg, and the Netherlands) were close behind. Only Britain did not do well because of an overly tradition-bound mentality and the breakup of the Commonwealth trading bloc that had long given British industry a false sense of security from competition. The average rate of growth in Western European gross national product during 1948–1972 was approximately 4.5 *percent per annum*—an unbelievable achievement over a full quarter century. Some nations did much better, and no recessions or business crises occurred.

The United States promoted much of this economic development by pouring in new capital first through the Marshall Plan and then much more through private investment by U.S. companies. By the 1960s, many Europeans were becoming concerned that their economies were being tied too closely to the United States or that Europe had become a kind of voluntary satellite to the colossus across the Atlantic.

In retrospect, it is clear that the early 1960s represented the apex of American economic influence and political power in Europe. Subsequently, the intervention in Vietnam combined with the erosion of the dollar's value to weaken U.S. moral and financial prestige. President Richard M. Nixon's reluctant decision to allow the dollar to find its own level in the international gold market (1971) immediately demonstrated that the U.S. currency had become overvalued, and the Swiss franc and the German mark began to rise steadily against it. This financial event dramatized the more general economic changes that had been taking place under the surface, bringing Europe collectively back into a status of balance with the United States (and far overshadowing the Soviet Union).

European Unity

As the economies of the various Western European states recovered and then boomed in the 1950s, the old dream of supranational union quickly took on new life. For a couple of generations, some Europeans had looked to the day when the nations would give way to some kind of federation (with or without a powerful central organ). Now at the end of a gruesome war that had been caused, at least in part, by German and French enmity, these visionaries saw their best opportunity ever. With the strong backing of the United States—a successful federation—they would turn Europe into a new and peaceable political organism.

The main actors in this movement were the leaders of the Christian Democratic parties in Italy, France, Belgium, and West Germany. These middle-of-the-road Catholic parties had become the leading political forces in their countries immediately after the war. Their leaders in the early 1950s were gifted men such as Alcide de Gasperi in Italy, Konrad Adenauer in West Germany, and Robert Schuman in France. They shared a consensus on future politics for the European continent. They believed that inter-European wars were an absolute disaster and must be avoided through political controls over each nation by some type of international group. Being realists, they thought that the best way to form this political association was to create economic ties among the potential members that would grow so strong and all-embracing that an individual government could not logically consider waging war against its partners. First would come the economic bonds, then the social, and eventually the political ones.

In chronological order, the most important steps in this process of unifying Western Europe (communist Europe was for obvious reasons a hostile bystander until the 1990s) were the following:

- 1947: The founding of the Organization for European Economic Cooperation (OEEC). The OEEC was the supervisory arm of the Marshall Plan aid to Europe.
- 1951: The founding of the European Coal and Steel Community. France, West Germany, the Benelux nations, and Italy agreed to subordinate their individual needs in coal and steel to a supranational council.

The system worked splendidly, and the six countries formed the nucleus of the Common Market of Europe.

- 1957: The **Treaty of Rome**, the founding charter of the **European Economic Community (EEC)**. The EEC has been the fundamental organ for European unity for the last fifty years, and the current European Union evolved from it. The EEC is responsible for the Common Market, which now embraces most of Europe's countries in a single, nondiscriminatory trading system. The EEC was meant to become the vehicle by which Europe would be drawn into social as well as economic integration. It has largely achieved these aims for its original twelve members and has now expanded to twenty-seven.
- 1992: The **Maastricht Treaty**. This treaty gave extensive powers to the European Parliament (created in 1957 by the Treaty of Rome) and facilitated economic and financial intercourse among the member states.

The name of the organization (headquartered in Brussels) that supervises these affairs is now simply the European Union (EU). By 1998, labor, money, credit, raw materials and manufactures, communications, and personal travel flowed across the national boundaries of fifteen European states with few, if any, restrictions. In 2002, a single, unified currency, the euro, went into effect for most EU members. All European states, except traditionally neutral Switzerland, have joined or are candidates to join the EU. Several of the former communist states have applied for membership. Ten countries joined on May 1, 2004: Cyprus, Czech Republic, Estonia, Hungary, Latvia, Lithuania, Malta, Poland, Slovakia, and Slovenia. Even without those states awaiting membership and the former Soviet Union, the EU now contains the largest, richest single market in the world—more than 400 million consumers.

The global financial crisis that began in 2008 has challenged the EU to improve its economic policies to benefit all member nations, rich and poor. Nevertheless, this has caused significant strains between the richer, largely northern European states, and the poorer southern nations.

THE COMMUNIST BLOC, 1947–1980

Eastern Europe (that is, Poland, Hungary, the Czech and Slovak Republics, Romania, former Yugoslavia, Bulgaria, and Albania), where the communists took over after World War II, developed very differently. Here, the orthodox Marxist program was put into effect, following the lead of the Soviet Union. For several years, the development of heavy industry and transportation was the number-one priority. Labor and capital were placed into heavy industry at the expense of agriculture and all consumer goods.

This Stalinist phase lasted from the late 1940s to the mid-1950s. As in the Soviet Union, it resulted in a huge increase in industrial capacities and the partial industrialization of previously peasant-based economies. Urban areas in particular grew by leaps and bounds as the abundant excess labor of the rural areas was siphoned off by the demand for workers in new industries. As in Soviet Central Asia a generation previously, whole new towns sprouted out of the fields, built around the new steel plant or the new chemical complex. Agriculture was collectivized and then relegated to permanent stepchild status in the budget.

After Stalin's death in 1953, somewhat more attention was paid to consumer needs, although the standard of living in communist Europe lagged far behind that in Western Europe at all times. Khrushchev, Stalin's successor, summed up the period between 1955 and 1970 when he called it "goulash communism"—communism that would put some meat in the pot. By the early 1960s, it was possible for people with professions or skills—and perhaps with good Communist Party connections—to live fairly comfortably and to hope for a still better future for their children.

Salaries and wages were low by Western standards, but medical care and education at all levels were free, and rents and food prices were low. In this way, the communist governments more or less satisfied a large proportion of their subjects economically, especially those who had been on the lower end of the social ladder in pre-communist days.

In the 1970s, however, in one communist-ruled country after another, the economic advance halted and went into reverse as far as most consumers were concerned. The Marxist "command economy," which was always struggling with major defects, now showed increasing signs of breaking down altogether. Workers' discontents radically increased, and the governments' attempts to placate them with concessions backfired. As periodicals and television reception from the West were legalized and Western tourism increased, Eastern Europeans had a better opportunity to see how miserably they fared in contrast to their Western counterparts.

The "technology gap" was growing more rapidly than ever before, to the huge disadvantage of the communists, not only in international economics but also at home. The average man in Warsaw, Budapest, or Moscow recognized how far behind his society was and how hopeless its chances of catching up. And the average working woman was rapidly tiring of the dubious benefits that communism had given her: a double task inside and outside the home, lower pay than males and "glass ceilings" in her work, declining health care, and other handicaps in both public and private life. In the face of this rising wave of discontent, the rigid old men who were in charge of the Communist Party and government in all of the Eastern European communist lands were paralyzed. They simply did not know what to do, short of abandoning the system to which they had devoted their lives and that had treated them, at least, quite well. As the 1970s became the 1980s, all of the European communist countries drifted and stagnated at the top, while the steam was building up below. And, of course, the safety valve of protest—democratic politics and free elections—did not exist. We take up subsequent developments in Chapter 52.

SUMMARY

The field of ruins that was Europe in 1945 gave birth to new economic and political life in a surprisingly short time. With U.S. aid, but mainly by their own determination and energy, the Western Europeans came back strongly and created a stable, prosperous economy by the 1960s. Progress in economic unity gave great encouragement to hopes of an eventual sociopolitical integration of the European heartland.

During the same two postwar decades, the Cold War waxed and waned in accord with U.S. and Soviet initiatives and gambles such as the Berlin blockade. So long as Josef Stalin lived, it seemed impossible to find an accommodation that would take the world out from under the atomic mushroom cloud. His successor, Nikita Khrushchev, proved more flexible, despite erecting the Berlin Wall in 1961 and the missile adventure in Cuba in 1962. Peaceful coexistence became the slogan of the day, leading to a considerable relaxation in East–West relations by the mid-1960s.

Internally, the Eastern European communist states went through a Stalinist phase of heavy industrial development that transformed these peasant economies into modern, urban-based ones. But the industrial development was not matched by an increase in living standards, and the previous gap between East and West in this respect grew steadily larger in the 1970s. By the early 1980s, the slowdown in the chase for prosperity was noticeable everywhere in the Soviet bloc, and discontent was rising.

IDENTIFICATION TERMS

Test your knowledge of this chapter's key concepts by defining the following terms. If you can not recall the meaning of certain terms, refresh your memory by looking up the boldfaced term in the chapter, turning to the Glossary at the end of the book, or accessing the terms on the CourseMate website at **www.cengagebrain.com**.

Berlin Wall
Cold War
Cuban Missile Crisis
détente
European Economic Community (EEC)
Korean War
Maastricht Treaty
Marshall Plan
North Atlantic Treaty Organization (NATO)
Nuclear Test Ban
Ostpolitik
Treaty of Rome
Truman Doctrine
Warsaw Pact

FOR FURTHER REFLECTION

1. Aside from his suspicions about the Western Allies, how do you explain Stalin's reluctance to allow Eastern Europeans their freedom in the years after World War II? Was he motivated by ideology? Was he motivated by strategic or by military concerns?
2. How did the Soviets enforce their control over the Warsaw Pact nations?
3. Why were President Truman and General Marshall right in their fears that Europe was in danger of electing communist governments in those early years of the Cold War? Why was the Marshall Plan a good strategy to prevent that from happening?
4. Is it likely that the European nations would have recovered without the American aid?

TEST YOUR KNOWLEDGE

Test your knowledge of this chapter by answering the following questions. Complete answers appear at the end of the book. You may find even more quiz questions on the CourseMate website at **www.cengagebrain.com**.

1. The most dangerous phase of the Cold War's early period (1946–1950) was
   a. the Soviet attempt to blockade access to West Berlin.
   b. the Soviet decision to assist North Korea's invasion of South Korea.
   c. the arguments over proper operation of the military government in Berlin.
   d. the Western Allies' attempt to get a democratic government in Poland.
   e. the Soviet construction of the Berlin Wall.
2. Khrushchev emerged as successor to Stalin in the Soviet Union
   a. from the public election held in 1954.
   b. after much backstage maneuvering.
   c. on a platform of anti-Stalinism and more democracy in the Communist Party of the Soviet Union.
   d. because of his wide popular appeal to Russians.
   e. because there was no one who could provide a viable alternative to him.

3. The success of the Berlin Wall may have
   a. led to the Soviet blockade of Berlin.
   b. caused Benito Mussolini to invade Ethiopia.
   c. led to the communist revolution in China.
   d. inspired Fidel Castro to ally Cuba with the Soviet Union.
   e. inspired Soviet Premier Khrushchev to place nuclear missiles in Cuba.
4. What is the correct chronology of these events?
   a. Berlin Wall erection, Berlin blockade, Cuban Missile Crisis, Korean War
   b. Berlin blockade, Korean War, Berlin Wall erection, Cuban Missile Crisis
   c. Korean War, Berlin blockade, Berlin Wall erection, Cuban Missile Crisis
   d. Korean War, Cuban Missile Crisis, Berlin blockade, Berlin Wall erection
   e. Berlin blockade, Cuban Missile Crisis, Berlin Wall erection, Korean War
5. Generally speaking, tensions between the Soviet- and American-led blocks lessened
   a. during Stalin's last years in power.
   b. during the Premiership of Nikita Khrushchev.
   c. with the rise of communism in Cuba and parts of Latin America.
   d. after the death of Nikita Khrushchev.
   e. as a result of the success of the Soviet economy under communism.
6. The economic "miracle" of West Germany during the 1950s was founded on
   a. a mixed state and private economy.
   b. free-market capitalism with few restrictions.
   c. the decision to create a model welfare state.
   d. extensive imports from Britain and the United States.
   e. a tremendous amount of financial donations from the United States and neighboring Western European countries.
7. Early postwar leadership in Western Europe was generally held by
   a. socialist parties that severed ties with the communists.
   b. coalitions of communists and socialists.
   c. moderate conservatives in the Christian Democratic parties.
   d. strong conservatives rejecting all aspects of socialism.
   e. strong coalitions between conservatives and labor groups.
8. The Common Market in Europe was originated by
   a. the Treaty of Versailles in 1919.
   b. the wartime Alliance of the United States, Britain, and the Soviet Union.
   c. the NATO treaty in 1949.
   d. the Treaty of Rome in 1957.
   e. the union of Europe's steel and coal companies.
9. During the early years of communism in Eastern Europe, the economic emphasis was on
   a. consumer goods.
   b. a military buildup.
   c. the development of transportation networks and heavy industry.
   d. teaching the citizenry about the virtues of communism.
   e. the development of countermeasures to the Marshall Plan.
10. Which description of communist Europe's economic progress is most correct?
    a. Much industrial progress from 1945 to 1955, then tapering off to stagnation in the 1970s
    b. Poor results until Stalin's death, then rapid improvement until the 1970s
    c. Gradual change from agrarian to industrial economy during the 1950s and 1960s, with a switch to consumer products successfully undertaken in the 1970s and 1980s
    d. A continuous disaster of poor planning and lack of expertise
    e. Moderate economic success in countries such as Yugoslavia and East Germany

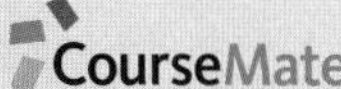

Visit the CourseMate website at **www.cengagebrain.com** for additional study tools and review materials for this chapter.

47 Decolonization of the Non-Western World

The moment the slave resolves that he will no longer be a slave, his fetters fall. Freedom and slavery are mental states. —MOHANDAS GANDHI

1945–1975	End of Western colonies
1946–1947	Philippines, India, and Pakistan become independent
1949	Indonesia attains independence
1954	French rule ends in Indochina
1957	Ghana becomes first sub-Saharan colony to attain independence
1960s	Most British, French, and Belgian colonies become independent
1970s	Portuguese driven from African colonies
1989–1991	Soviet empire collapses
1994	Majority democratic rule in South Africa
2011–2112	Arab spring; many Western-supported dictatorships fall in North Africa and the Middle East.

CHAPTER OUTLINE

The fifty years after World War II saw the end of the colonial empires that had been built up since 1500 by the European powers. In the Western colonies, the end came soon after the war. In 1945, many hundreds of millions of Asians, Africans, Polynesians, and others were governed by Europeans from distant capitals. By the end of the 1970s, practically none were.

In the late 1980s, the last of the colonial powers, the Soviet Union, confessed its inability to coerce continued obedience from its Eastern European and Asian satellites and released them from imposed communist rule. A short time later, the collapse of the Soviet Union allowed the emergence of several new independent states from its ruins (see Chapter 52).

Decolonization, or the "retreat from empire," as it has frequently been called, was a major turning point in world history. Europe (with North America and Japan) continues to exercise great power over non-Europeans, but today this influence is subtler; it is basically economic rather than political and military in nature. Until the U.S. military intervention in Iraq in 2003, it was inconceivable that a Western country would attempt to install an openly colonial regime in any non-Western land, if only for fear of the penalties it would suffer from its own neighbors. Since the collapse of the Soviet system in the early 1990s, the same can be said of the Russians. For most of the world, colonialism as an overt political relationship is "history."

DECOLONIZATION'S CAUSES

What brought about this unexpectedly rapid end to a story that dated back to sixteenth-century Western expansion? The movement toward decolonization had several major causes. In certain instances, such as India, Vietnam, and the Philippines, the rise to independent, sovereign status was the culmination of a generation or more of struggle—sometimes with gun in hand. In other cases, such as French-speaking West and Central Africa, Libya, and Iraq, independence came as a more or less sudden "gift" from the home country, sometimes to populations that were only partly ready for the event. Whatever the individual circumstances, all of the independence-seeking colonies profited from some general developments that had occurred during the immediate postwar years.

American Photographer, (20th century)/Private Collection/ Peter Newark American Pictures/The Bridgeman Art Library

ROOSEVELT AND CHURCHILL AT THE ATLANTIC CHARTER CONFERENCE, 1941. President Franklin D. Roosevelt opposed colonialism. In August 1941, he and Winston Churchill held a conference aboard the HMS *Prince of Wales*, where they signed the Atlantic Charter, which stipulated that all nations had the right of self-determination.

Rising Nationalism in Asia and Africa

National pride and a burning resentment of Western dominion were in all cases the driving forces of decolonization. European rule had sown the seed of its own dissolution in the colonies by creating a small but vitally important intelligentsia among subject peoples. Frequently the products of European missionary schools, these individuals sometimes had obtained higher education in the colonial mother country. There they had learned not only academic subjects but also to reject the inferior status they suffered under colonial rule at home. They also absorbed Western ideas about the dignity and civil rights of all members of the human race, Western nationalism, and Western techniques of political organization. In a few cases, such as Vietnamese **Ho Chi Minh** (1890–1969) in France, the intelligentsia encountered and adopted Marxism as a path to successful revolution. The Asian militants' efforts to build a popular following were aided by the repeated humiliations Japan inflicted on European/American armies and navies early in World War II, which revealed that the colonial powers were not invincible.

Loss of European Moral Authority

In the nineteenth and early twentieth centuries, most Europeans looked on their colonies with the sense that in ruling them they were doing the right thing—that is, meeting their duties as carriers of the "white man's burden." By the 1950s, the conviction that they were destined to rule others had been much weakened by the experiences of the two world wars and by the postwar spirit of egalitarian democracy. The façade of moral and cultural superiority that lay behind the largely mythical white man's burden was stripped away by the contradictions and hypocrisies of colonial rule. Moreover, having suffered from two highly destructive "civil" wars (World Wars I and II), Europeans' self-assurance about their own fitness to govern foreign peoples had evaporated.

Temporary Prostration of Europe

After the war, until about 1960, Europe's six overseas colonial powers (Belgium, Britain, France, Italy, the Netherlands, and Portugal) were absorbed with repairing the damage caused by the war or reforming the low-tech economies, social antagonisms, and obsolete educational systems they had carried over from the 1930s. The public had no interest in supervising "difficult" colonials or pouring badly needed capital and labor into colonial projects that, like many previous ones, might never work out. The postwar elections of socialist-leaning governments in Europe, such as that of Britain's Labour Party, also introduced a new spirit that was more critical of imperial responsibilities, especially in light of the difficulties being faced by their populations in recovering from the effects of the wars.

Opposition to the Continuation of Colonies in Both Allied War Aims and U.S. Policy

The stated aims of the United Nations, founded at the end of World War II by the Western powers, were clearly anticolonial, and the United States, which played such a major role in postwar Europe, always felt uneasy about holding colonies, even its own. (It acknowledged Philippine independence as early as 1946.) In August 1941, President Roosevelt and Prime Minister Winston Churchill met to establish a vision for the post–World War II world. They negotiated the **Atlantic Charter**, which included eight basic freedoms; prominent among these was the right of self-determination for all peoples and nations. This charter proved to be an important step toward the formation of the United Nations, and the right of self-determination became a cornerstone of the United Nations Charter.

In light of these facts, the Western countries' release of their colonies between 1946 and 1974 becomes more understandable, especially when one considers the tremendous costs visited on the colonial powers when and where they tried to stop the march toward independence in Southeast Asia and parts of Africa. By the 1970s, only the Soviet Union was still an important colonial country, holding Eastern Europeans as unwilling satellites and suppliers.

DISMANTLING OF WESTERN COLONIES

How did decolonization proceed? Britain led the way by making good on the Labour Party's wartime promise to release India from the British Commonwealth. For many years, British Conservative governments had steadfastly opposed the peaceable but unrelenting movement for independence led by the Hindu Congress Party and its founder, **Mohandas Gandhi** (1869–1948). Gandhi's magnificent ability to reveal the moral inconsistencies in the British position made him an unbeatable opponent, however, and the Labour Party had been gradually won over to his point of view. (See the Law and Government box on Gandhi.)

In 1945, Labour won the first postwar election, and negotiations with Gandhi and his associate Jawaharlal Nehru were begun. It soon became clear that the Hindu leaders could not speak for the large Muslim minority, which demanded separate statehood. The British government, immersed in severe postwar problems at home, tried in vain to resolve this dilemma. In 1947, independence was granted to India on a ready-or-not basis.

The immediate result was a bloody civil war, fought by Hindus and Muslims over the corpse, so to speak, of Gandhi, who had been assassinated by a fanatic. From this war came two new states, India and Pakistan (and eventually Bangladesh, the former East Pakistan), which remain hostile to this day and engage in mutual misunderstandings. (Frequent border disputes also erupt, such as the current antagonisms over Kashmir that brought both nations to the brink of possible nuclear war in 2003.) It was a shaky beginning to the decolonization movement.

Elsewhere, however, the British generally managed things more adroitly. Myanmar (Burma) and Sri Lanka (Ceylon) gained their independence peaceably by mutual agreement in the late 1940s. The British colony of Gold Coast became the first colony in sub-Saharan Africa to be granted self-government. Naming itself Ghana, after the ancient empire of the same name, it was then recognized as a sovereign member of the voluntary association called the *British Commonwealth* in 1957. Almost the entire list of British colonies, from Malaysia to Belize (British Honduras) in Central America, quickly followed. By the mid-1960s, even such minor holdings as the islands of the South Pacific (Fiji, the Solomon Islands) and the Bahamas were granted either self-government under the British Crown or full independence.

In France, the attitude of the public and the government toward retaining the colonial empire underwent a sharp shift around 1960. This reversal was generated by France's defeats in its colonial wars in Vietnam (1945–1954) and Algeria (1958–1961). Both of these proved lost causes that led to many thousands of French casualties and much discontent at home. In 1958, war hero General Charles de Gaulle became president of France and almost immediately began to change course on the colonial question. Within four years, most of the former possessions had been granted independence and membership in a French version of the British Commonwealth.

The members of this community remain closely linked with France in economics and culture but go their individual ways in international affairs. With some bitter exceptions, the French were successful, as were the British, in retaining a position of privilege and influence in their former colonies. Despite strong nationalism among the former subjects, the ties generated by common languages and education often survived the political scissions.

The Belgians, Dutch, and Portuguese, on the other hand, were all forced from their Asian and African possessions by a combination of uprisings and international pressure exerted in the United Nations. These small European countries had relatively more prestige and wealth invested in their colonies and gave them up only reluctantly. The Belgians were compelled to grant self-rule in the huge African Congo by threatened rebellion in 1961. The Dutch

IDENTITY CARD PHOTO OF AN ALGERIAN WOMAN, 1960. During the Algerian War of Independence, French authorities took photos of Algerians to issue identity cards for closer monitoring. Muslim women were required to violate the rules of purdah for their pictures, as shown in this example.

LAW AND GOVERNMENT

Mohandas Gandhi (1869–1948)

Mohandas Gandhi's masterful and charismatic leadership united both Indian elites and the poor masses in their resistance to British rule. His followers, or "peace soldiers," called him *Bapu* (Father) and *Mahatma* (Great Soul). Gandhi was from a privileged family in Gujarat, India. After obtaining a law degree in London, he first worked in South Africa on behalf of the persecuted Indian community. There, inspired by Henry David Thoreau's writings and by Hindu and Christian concepts, he developed the program of peaceful resistance to oppression that he later used successfully in India. Gandhi described one strategy, civil disobedience, in these words: "[It] involves self-sacrifice.... When we do not like certain laws, we do not break the heads of lawgivers but we suffer [arrest, beatings] and do not submit to the laws." The key was to peacefully provoke arrest; the ensuing mass arrests and abuses revealed British brutality while inspiring support for independence. An excellent example of civil disobedience is Gandhi's 1930 Salt March to protest the British monopoly and tax on salt from the Indian coast. Gandhi and his closest followers walked 240 miles in 24 days, from his inland home to the seacoast salt fields. Along the way, Gandhi spoke to large crowds, and thousands of people joined the march. Once at the sea, Gandhi picked up a lump of natural salt, cueing his followers to break the salt laws. During the following week, Gandhi and some sixty thousand of his "peace soldiers" were arrested. The Salt March forced the British to negotiate with Gandhi, and it united the nation behind the independence movement. The following passage is from Gandhi's speech on the eve of the Salt March.

> From what I have seen and heard during the last fortnight, I am inclined to believe that the stream of civil resisters will flow unbroken [to the sea]. But let there be not a semblance of breach of peace even after all of us have been arrested. We have resolved to utilize all our resources in the pursuit of an exclusively nonviolent struggle. Let no one commit a wrong in anger. This is my hope and prayer.... These [salt] laws can be violated in three ways [by manufacturing, possessing, or trading in contraband salt]...
>
> I have faith in the righteousness of our cause and the purity of our weapons.... A [peace soldier], whether free or incarcerated, is ever victorious. He is vanquished only when he forsakes truth and nonviolence and turns a deaf ear to the inner voice ... God bless you all and keep off all obstacles in the path of the struggle that begins tomorrow.

Gandhi always promoted the unity of Indian Muslims and Hindus and opposed the partition of India. He was an early critic of Western modernity and technological progress, which he deemed ruinous to Indian traditional values. Inevitably, independent India chose the path to Westernization that Gandhi had rejected. Since his assassination, Gandhi's philosophy has had less influence within India than beyond its borders.

MOHANDAS GANDHI AND MOHAMED ALI JINNAH. Gandhi (*right*) and Jinnah (*left*) were united in the cause of throwing off British rule. Jinnah and his Muslim followers, however, split with Gandhi and India once their goal was achieved, and Jinnah went on to found Pakistan as the homeland for Muslims of largely Indian descent.

ANALYZE AND INTERPRET

What similarities do you see between Gandhi and Martin Luther King, Jr.? What other examples of civil disobedience do you know of? What are some advantages and disadvantages to nonviolent resistance?

(The Selected Works of Mahatma Gandhi, Volume 6: The Voice of Truth, pp. 25–28, Ahmedabad: Navajivan Publishing House, 1997)

let go of their Indonesian empire only after prolonged and vain fighting against the nationalists in the late 1940s. The Portuguese gave up their outposts in Africa also under severe pressure from guerrilla wars and after a military *coup* deposed Portugal's longstanding fascist government in 1974.

PROBLEMS OF THE NON-WESTERN WORLD

Until the mid-twentieth century, the writing of history in the United States or any other Western country was largely concerned with the acts of a relatively small minority of the world's peoples: namely, the inhabitants of Europe and North America. But the largest part of the world's population has always been located primarily in Asia and Africa. The majority live in the non-Western World (formerly known as the *Third World*)—that is, of neither the American nor the Soviet side of the Cold War—of poor and predominately rural countries such as Egypt, Togo, and Bolivia. In these countries, the *per capita* cash income is perhaps one-twentieth of the West's, and this material poverty is reflected by a basically different set of cultural values and fewer opportunities in a world that is still dominated by Western capitalism.

In fact, about three-fourths of the 7 billion people inhabiting the world in 2012 lived in the poorer countries. This majority in numbers has not yet been translated into economic opportunity, but with the global village beckoning in the twenty-first century, we in the West had better prepare to encounter and assist these people if we intend to live in peace. What is a non-Western society? The rapid economic and social development of some non-Western nations in recent years makes it imperative to distinguish among countries that used to be lumped together under that term. Thus, the following description applies only to the least-developed nations of the world, some of which are in the Americas but most of which are located in Asia and Africa.

Economically speaking, it is a society in which poverty frequently is the rule and the production of basic raw materials still makes up a high proportion of the gross national product. Unskilled labor is predominant in both town and country; for most, there remain few opportunities for higher education and economic advancement; and the industrial and larger commercial enterprises are commonly controlled by foreign capital and remain dependent on world markets. Policies imposed on these subject peoples during the colonial era encouraged the production of commodities and raw materials (and labor during the era of the slave trade; see Chapters 35 and 36) for Europe's and America's factories but also discouraged the development of local forms of manufacturing. Many non-Western nations, although now free of colonial rule, remain underdeveloped as a result of high tariffs that Western nations continue to impose on finished products from poor non-Western nations. Such disadvantageous and discriminatory practices are usually called **neocolonialism**.

Politically speaking, a non-Western society is one in which a small elite, often derived from the bureaucracy of the colonial era, controls access to power and wealth. Again, their roots go back to the privileged few of the colonial era who were favored by their former colonial masters with Western-style educations. (Perhaps the most egregious hypocrisy of colonialism was the claim to a "civilizing" role in Africa, even though no effort was made to extend education to the overwhelming majority of subject peoples.) One political party or the army controls public life, often with dictatorial power. Large landholders are dominant in the countryside, overshadowing or intimidating the more numerous and disadvantaged small farmers and landless laborers.

Socially speaking, it is a society in which the overpopulation problem is severe and is worsening each year. Males still exercise control over females within the family and have far more rights and prestige outside it. Education is highly desired and prestigious but is often still beyond the means of too many people and ill designed for the present tasks. The clan or the extended family is far more important than in developed countries. Upward mobility is still possible but is becoming more difficult to achieve as the gap between the rich and the poor widens and as opportunities for the many become ever more meager. An unhealthy imbalance between burgeoning town and stagnant country life is steadily more apparent.

Internationally speaking, a non-Western country is one that in most ways is still dependent on the more developed countries—sometimes as much so as when it was a colony. Once it achieved independence in the days of the Cold War, both the West and the former Soviet bloc treated it basically as a pawn in their foreign policy designs. Since the Cold War ended, its weak bargaining powers have almost always been reduced even further.

Since the collapse of the Soviet bloc and the discrediting of Marxist economics (see Chapter 52), the tension between the rival ideologies of communism and capitalism can no longer be turned to third-party advantage in the competition for political and economic power. Attitudes of cultural superiority and even racism continue to bedevil the thoughts and behaviors of many Westerners toward non-Europeans. In the post–Cold War world, the needs of even some of the poorest and most helpless African, Asian, and Latin peoples remain tragically ignored.

For some nations, the standard of living has actually declined since they attained independence. Africa is a particularly tragic case. The famines and banditry afflicting much of the **Sahel** (Somalia, Ethiopia, and Dar Fur in the Sudan), Guinea, Liberia, Sierra Leone, Uganda, and the eastern Congo in recent years are manifestations of this decline. So are the dictatorships that continue to be the rule in many African governments. Where dictators are absent, it is often only because social antagonisms (Somalia, Rwanda), religious warfare (Sudan), or a combination of these (Democratic Republic of Congo) have prevented a single individual or party from seizing power. Almost everywhere, the root causes of these evils are a population that is too large for the available resources, continuing Western policies, misapplied technology, and an unequal distribution of power and wealth. (For more information about Africa, see also Chapter 49.)

The Population of the Earth

A book appeared in the 1970s with the arresting title *The Population Bomb.* Written by a respected biologist, Paul Ehrlich, at an American university, it warned that a time was rapidly approaching when the earth would face massive, prolonged famine. The rate of population growth in the less-developed countries, it said, threatened to overwhelm the earth's capacity to grow food.

Professor Ehrlich's prognosis of early famine proved erroneous. The Green Revolution, plus a series of good crop years around the globe, actually increased the ratio of available food to mouths, but many believe that Ehrlich's basic argument is still valid: Inevitably, starvation will come. They point to the examples of the African Sahel, Bangladesh since independence, and many of the Andean populations in South America, to assert that the number of consumers is exceeding the available resources. It is just a matter of time, they argue, until the well fed will be using lethal weapons to hold off the starving hordes.

Other observers, however, argue that Ehrlich and similar doomsayers are not taking the so-called **demographic transition** into account. This transition occurs when parents stop viewing many children as a familial and economic necessity and instead produce a smaller number of better-cared-for children. Historically, this has occurred when a society becomes industrialized and urbanized. Children then become less economically necessary to the family, and a lower mortality rate means that most will live to maturity. Hence, parents no longer need to have many children to ensure that some will survive to care for them in their old age. Because the three continents where the large majority of nonindustrial peoples live (Africa, Asia, and South America) are rapidly developing urban and industrialized societies, it was hoped that birthrates would drop substantially within a generation, but this has not happened.

In Latin America, parts of Asia, and much of Africa, birthrates have remained at levels that are double or triple Western rates. The "gap" between the present-day medical and technological capacities to preserve and prolong life and the cultural demands to have children early and frequently so that some will survive into adulthood has not closed as swiftly as was hoped. Efforts to lower the birthrate by artificial means have worked in some places (China, for instance) but failed in most others. Yet, some means of controlling the hugely increasing demands of the world's population on every type of natural resource (including privacy, quietude, and undisturbed contemplation) must be found soon, presumably. The human inhabitants of Spaceship Earth are increasing in geometric fashion. The earth's first half-billion inhabitants took perhaps 50,000 years to appear, and the second half billion appeared over 500 years (1300–1800), but nearly 2 billion people out of the 2012 total of 7 billion came aboard in a period of twenty years! Most of this proportion lives in the less-developed countries, where the rate of natural increase—births over deaths without counting migration—is two to four times that of the industrial world.

Misapplied Technology

The developed countries' postwar attempts to assist the former colonies and the Latin American states sometimes compounded the difficulties those nations were already experiencing. In nations with a superabundance of labor, where the economy could not supply more than a few months' paid labor for many citizens, the World Bank and other international agencies frequently promoted industrial projects that actually lessened job opportunities. Instead of encouraging the continued use of shovels and baskets or other straightforward but economically productive means of moving earth, for example, well-meaning agencies shipped in bulldozers and large dump trucks to construct a new dam or mine. In agriculture, modern heavy equipment was substituted for plows or hoes, sometimes with devastating consequences for thin topsoils and delicate biosystems. Moreover, the small farmers and other laborers thus thrust out of work only contributed to the problems of the poverty-stricken villages or the overcrowded city slums.

The Aswan Dam project in Egypt is a good example. Built with Soviet aid in the 1950s, the huge dam and the lake it created radically altered the ecology of the Lower Nile River. Although the lake (despite tremendous loss from evaporation) supplied tens of thousands of acres with water for irrigation, downstream from the dam, the changes were entirely for the worse. A variety of snail that had previously not lived in the Lower Nile waters began to flourish there, causing a massive outbreak of epidemic disease. The schools of Mediterranean fish that had previously been fed from the flooding Nile delta disappeared; with them went the food supply of many Egyptians and the livelihood of many more who had netted the fish and sold them. The new upstream lands now under irrigation from Lake Nasser could not make up the deficit for the hungry Egyptian peasants, because almost all of these lands were devoted to cotton or other industrial crops for export.

All told, the efforts of the non-Western nations to achieve industrial or agrarian development in the thirty years following World War II were unsuccessful in raising living standards for the masses of people. Some groups did prosper and some regions did much better than others—notably the western rim of the Pacific Ocean—but in much of Africa and Latin America, the few rich got richer, the many poor stayed poor, and those in between did not multiply as hoped. The uneven distribution of wealth is best displayed by some comparative figures. In the industrialized Western nations, the personal income of the uppermost 10 percent of society was about five times the income of the bottom 10 percent. In comparatively well-off Mexico, the disparity in income grew over the past decades, until the upper 10 percent were receiving twenty-seven times as much as the bottom 10 percent by the 2001.

SUMMARY

Decolonization came in the first quarter century after World War II, as the colonial powers realized that economic exhaustion and anticolonial sentiment made it impossible to retain their former possessions in Asia and Africa. Beginning with the difficult and bloody severance of India and Pakistan from the British Empire, the colonial structures were dismantled or toppled by armed revolts between 1947 and 1974. The British gave their remaining subjects uncontested self-government and then sovereignty in the 1960s, but the French were at first less pliant. First in Vietnam and then in North Africa, they engaged in extended warfare that eventually resulted in defeat and withdrawal. Only then, under Charles de Gaulle, did they achieve a workable postcolonial relationship. The Dutch, the Belgians, and the Portuguese mirrored the mistakes of the French, and nationalist rebellions in the 1940s and 1950s defeated each in its turn. In the Soviet instance, the attempt to retain satellites persisted into the 1980s.

The non-Western World that emerged from the postcolonial settlements was a hodgepodge of different states and societies, but to some degree all suffered from generic handicaps in dealing with the West and the communist states. Poor management in the distribution of national wealth, misapplication of technological assets, and the overwhelming growth of population were three of the worst problems.

IDENTIFICATION TERMS

Test your knowledge of this chapter's key concepts by defining the following terms. If you can not recall the meaning of certain terms, refresh your memory by looking up the boldfaced term in the chapter, turning to the Glossary at the end of the book, or accessing the terms on the CourseMate website at **www.cengagebrain.com**.

Atlantic Charter
decolonization
demographic transition
Ho Chi Minh
Mohandas Gandhi
neocolonialism
Sahel

FOR FURTHER REFLECTION

1. What role, if any, did the United States play in the decolonization of Europe's overseas colonies?
2. Why do you suppose that the European colonizers were more willing to give up their control of some colonies than they were of others? Please provide examples to support your answer.
3. How have the former colonial powers continued to dominate their former colonies? Which Europeans powers, in particular, seem to have been guilty of neocolonialism?
4. How did the Cold War aggravate the problems of neocolonialism?

TEST YOUR KNOWLEDGE

Test your knowledge of this chapter by answering the following questions. Complete answers appear at the end of the book. You may find even more quiz questions on the CourseMate website at **www.cengagebrain.com**.

1. The weakness of most colonial powers' economies
   a. helped spread communism in the colonies.
   b. induced America to censure the colonial nations.
   c. led to a slow recovery of Western colonial nations.
   d. helped speed up decolonization.
   e. had little or no impact on decolonization.
2. Which of the following African countries fought a long war against a colonial power and eventually won its independence?
   a. Nigeria
   b. Egypt
   c. Algeria
   d. South Africa
   e. The former Belgian Congo
3. The decolonization process generally went ahead with the least violence in
   a. Southeast Asia.
   b. French North Africa.
   c. the Middle East.
   d. Portuguese Africa.
   e. British Africa.

4. The last surviving major colonial power was
   a. Portugal.
   b. China.
   c. the United States.
   d. France.
   e. Belgium.
5. Mohandas Gandhi's principal tactics in winning India's independence involved
   a. violent confrontations of colonial officials and police.
   b. peaceful confrontation and civil disobedience.
   c. civil disobedience and passive resistance.
   d. demonstrations, peaceful and violent.
   e. ignoring colonialist directives and refusing to buy imported cloth.
6. One of the prominent identifying factors for a non-Western society is
   a. a prospering rural and agrarian economy.
   b. the problem of overpopulation.
   c. a reluctance to accept foreign aid.
   d. equal status for young males and females.
   e. a steady drain of population into the cities.
7. Which of the following was not a factor in the West's lessening attention to the problems of the non-Western World in recent years?
   a. The collapse of the communist hopes of revolution
   b. The diversion of foreign aid to the former communist lands of Europe
   c. The inability of non-Western nations to collaborate effectively in international negotiations
   d. The slowing rate of population growth in most ex-colonial countries
   e. The effects of continuing attitudes of racial and cultural superiority among some Western leaders
8. For most non-Western nations, the process of decolonization took place
   a. in the decade following the end of World War I.
   b. during the years of the run-up to World War II.
   c. prior to World War I, almost immediately after colonialism had established itself.
   d. in the two decades following the end of World War II.
   e. from about 1960 to 2000.
9. Political and economic inequality in many non-Western nations has its roots in
   a. colonial policies.
   b. racial discrimination.
   c. religious strife.
   d. ethnic rivalries.
   e. constitutions that favor military or dictatorial rule.
10. Colonial policies that discouraged industrialization have
   a. had little or no long-term impact on the economic development of non-Western nations.
   b. contributed to the development of both the Western and non-Western nations.
   c. played little part in the development of Western nations.
   d. contributed significantly to the underdevelopment of non-Western countries.
   e. sped up the development of Asian nations, but not Africa.

CourseMate

Visit the CourseMate website at **www.cengagebrain.com** for additional study tools and review materials for this chapter.

48 The New Asia

A revolution is not a dinner party. —MAO ZEDONG

1945–1952	U.S. occupation of Japan
1949–1976	Mao Zedong leads China
1950–1953	Korean War
1950–1990	Japanese economic success
1955–1973	U.S. involvement in Vietnam War
1958–1959	Great leap forward in China
1966–1976	Great Proletarian Cultural Revolution in China
1975	Vietnam reunified under communist government
1976–1997	China under Deng Xiaoping
1984	Assassination of Indira Gandhi
1989	Tiananmen Square massacre
1990–present	Japanese economic recession
2002	China admitted to the World Trade Organization
2011	Terrorist leader Osama bin Laden killed in Pakistan
2012	Myanmar (Burma) holds second free elections in fifty years
2008–present	Global recession poses challenges to the new Asia

CHAPTER OUTLINE

The two leading Asian powers had both suffered greatly during the war and were temporarily restricted in their international roles while recovering. China and Japan continued to take sharply differing paths to establishing modern societies. China chose the path of revolution and became the world's largest Marxist state. Japan adapted Western ideas and technology to fit its own culture and became for a time the world's exemplary economic success.

Whereas World War I had brought relatively minor change to these areas, World War II proved to be the wellspring of major transformations. Many areas in eastern and southern Asia had been Western colonies and were intent on gaining full independence as soon as the war was concluded. The U.S.-held Philippines were the first to succeed, followed by India and the European possessions in Southeast Asia and the Pacific islands. By the end of the twentieth century, several newly independent states had attained international significance by taking full advantage of a rapidly changing global economy.

MAO'S CHINA, 1949–1976

A triumphant Mao Zedong proclaimed the People's Republic of China (PRC) in the fall of 1949. China entered into a formal alliance with the Soviet Union a few months later. Government and all social institutions were reorganized on Soviet communist lines, and for the first ten years, the Soviets were both its helpers and its mentors.

The conquest of the world's largest population had essentially been the work of one man—Chairman Mao Zedong (of the Chinese Communist Party's [CCP's] Central Committee)—with the help of some brilliant assistants, especially Zhou Enlai. Although Mao had profited from some Soviet arms and economic support and guidance since the 1930s, in its fundamentals Chinese communism was his creation. No one else, not even Josef Stalin, had played much of a role besides him in Chinese eyes. This was to be a critical factor in the years to come.

Mao was convinced that in an agrarian society such as China's (about 90 percent of the population were peasants), the correct path to socialism could only lie through a revolutionary peasantry. Thus, at all times during his rule, keeping the peasants with him was his chief concern. What the urbanites thought and did was of secondary importance. Mao's long and fruitful contacts with the rural folk also seem to have made him increasingly distrustful of intellectuals—an untraditional attitude for a Chinese leader and one that would have horrendous effects in the Cultural Revolution of the 1960s.

In its first three years (1949–1952), the regime instituted the basic policies it would employ to ensure political and social control indefinitely. In the countryside, land was expropriated from the landlords, and many—perhaps millions—of them were killed or imprisoned. The land was first redistributed to the peasants and then in 1955–1957 collectivized as the Soviets had done in their Five-Year Plan. Although millions more than in Russia were killed or allowed to starve in the great famines of 1960–1962, the peasants did not resist as fiercely as in the Soviet Union. Why not? In part, because of the ancient Chinese tradition of regarding the central government as the legitimate source of authority and in part because so many desperately poor peasants ardently supported the new arrangements.

The new social organ called the *commune* was made the basis of rural production and of government, with disastrous effects for both the agricultural and the industrial economies. The communes were so large (about 25,000 persons) and their responsibilities so unclear that they could not function. As a result of poor planning and low incentives, food production barely matched the rapidly increasing population, even in good years. When bad harvests came after 1960, mass famine was inevitable. To keep the industrial plant functioning at all, grain was mercilessly confiscated from the communes, and the peasants starved just as they had in Russia previously under war communism and during the Five-Year Plans. Eventually, the communes were abolished, and smaller units were created that resembled the traditional villages except that land and work were collectivized.

The Chinese pursued industrial expansion in the same fashion as the Soviets had previously, emphasizing heavy industry at the expense of consumer goods. A Stalinist Five-Year Plan instituted in 1953 produced substantial results in metals, coal, and other basic goods for industry, but Mao had become impatient with Soviet models and plans. In 1958, he personally introduced the **Great Leap Forward**. This attempt at overnight mass industrialization was an enormously costly failure (the infamous "backyard steelmaking," for example). It accelerated the growing gap between the Chinese and their Russian mentors, especially between Mao and Nikita Khrushchev.

The Russians criticized Mao for foolishly attempting the impossible and also for allowing himself to be made into the sort of Great Father in China that Stalin had been in Russia. In 1956, Khrushchev had just finished revealing Stalin's true nature to a shocked communist world, and he had no intention of allowing Mao to step up onto the vacant pedestal. On his side, a confident Mao made it clear that although he was no great admirer of Stalin or any other foreigner, he believed that true revolutions demanded a nearly supernatural leader, with whom the ignorant masses might identify—something that Khrushchev never pretended to be or was capable of being.

Furthermore, Mao told the Russians that they had been diverted from the authentic revolutionary path by their fears of losing what they had in a war with capitalism and that he intended to take their place as spokesman of the oppressed masses. By 1960, the barely concealed **Sino-Soviet conflict** was splitting the communist ranks. The rift became fully public at the time of the Cuban Missile Crisis, when the Maoists derided the Soviets' fear of U.S. "paper tigers," and Moscow denounced Beijing's readiness to plunge the world into atomic war.

Mao had long been convinced that the Soviet revolution had been suffocated by bureaucratization, and he was determined that China would not share this fate. In 1965, he suddenly called for the **Great Proletarian Cultural Revolution**. This extraordinary upheaval was meant to—and did—turn Chinese society on its head for many years. Like Stalin's "second revolution" of 1929, Mao's plan went far beyond political rearrangement. He wished to create a truly new relationship among party, people, and the exercise of revolutionary power. The attack was aimed primarily at the intellectuals, particularly those in the CCP's cadres of officials.

To achieve his main end, Mao was prepared to undertake what seemed an impossible task: to rid the Chinese people of their reverence for tradition. He called on the youthful **Red Guards**—mainly students—to make war on the older generation and its "empty formalisms." Mao was a profoundly skeptical spirit who distrusted all systems, even those he had created. He wished to introduce the permanent, self-perpetuating revolution that he thought the Russians had given up in return for peace and a pseudo-Marxist society.

For the next three or four years, China experienced barely controlled, officially inspired anarchy. Professors were publicly humiliated, learned doctors were made to scrub the floors in their hospitals, scholars were abused for having foreign language books in their libraries, and Communist Party secretaries were accused of sabotage. Factional fighting in the party was allowed and encouraged, sometimes in the streets. The economy, only now recovering from the Great Leap Forward's mistakes, again suffered severe damage. Managers and skilled personnel were sent as outcasts to the villages to "learn the revolution's lessons" as barnyard sweepers or potato diggers. For a time, the only qualification for getting a responsible post was to have memorized the *Thought of Chairman Mao*, immortalized in the **little red book** that tens of millions of Chinese waved daily like an amulet against unknown evils. In 1969, the anarchy had become so bad that Mao had to call off the Red Guards and put the army in charge of everyday affairs. (For a sampling of the *Thought of Chairman Mao*, see the Law and Government box.)

The tensions between China and the Soviet Union had erupted in the **Amur River War**, as troops stationed on both sides of the frontier sporadically fired on each other. The military chiefs told Mao they could not guarantee what might happen if Russia attacked while the unrest continued. Still, until Mao's death in 1976, the spirit of the Cultural Revolution lived on, especially among the millions of radical, barely literate youth who thought the demolition of the Communist Party's apparatus and the government's disarray presented a once-in-a-lifetime chance for them to get ahead.

Within weeks of Mao's death, the inevitable reaction set in. The Cultural Revolution was first partially and then entirely condemned as a mistake. A collective leadership of party officials moved cautiously but steadily to put Mao's contributions into perspective. In 1980, his portraits, formerly everywhere, were silently removed from all public places. The era of the godlike chairman and his omnipresent little red book was definitely over.

RECENT CHINA

Under **Deng Xiaoping** (dung shau-ping; 1904–1997), an elderly but vigorous pragmatist, the CCP groped its way forward into the vacuum left by Mao's demise. A prisoner of the Cultural Revolution, Deng was determined to return China to "normal" socialism. He got rid of his enemies, put his supporters in key positions, and allowed greater freedom of expression. His most important achievement was to allow free-market incentives to gradually replace China's old economy, which had been tightly controlled under a system of state ownership. In Deng's words, China would remain socialist in spirit, regardless of the semi-capitalist economic system it seemed to be adopting. During the 1980s and 1990s, prosperity gradually spread

LAW AND GOVERNMENT

Chairman Mao's Thought

The founder and master of the Chinese Communist Party, Mao Zedong, had a peculiarly un-Chinese contempt for the traditional scholar-official (mandarin) class. His feelings were frequently expressed in his many speeches and writings during his long tenure of the party chairmanship:

> Intellectuals and Workers (1942)
>
> I began life as a student and at school acquired the ways of a student.... At that time I felt that the intellectuals were the only clean people in the world, while in comparison workers and peasants were dirty.... But after I became a revolutionary and lived with the workers and the peasants and with soldiers of the revolutionary army, I gradually came to know them well, and they came gradually to know me well, too.... I came to feel that, compared with the workers and the peasants, the unremolded intellectuals were not clean, and that, in the last analysis, the workers and peasants were the cleanest people, and even though their hands were soiled and their feet smeared with cow dung, they were really cleaner than the bourgeois and petty-bourgeois intellectuals.

ANALYZE AND INTERPRET

To what do you attribute Mao's attitudes toward intellectuals? What did this "thought" by the man who became the unchallenged leader of China for many years portend about the place of intellectuals in Mao's China?

Source: Selected Works of Mao Tse-tung: Talks at the Yenan Forum on Literature and Art, May 1942, from http://www.marxists.org/reference/archive/mao/selected-works/volume-3/mswv3_08.htm

into China's hinterlands from the thriving coastal cities of Hong Kong and Shanghai. Deng, who had long been associated with the moderate wing of the party, was particularly interested in establishing better relations with foreign capitalists who might help China recover from Mao's mistakes.

Recent years have seen the dramatic rise of China as an important economic power. Since the 1990s, the economic numbers it has produced have been reminiscent of what Japan's were in previous decades. Over the two decades from 1984 to 2008, its gross domestic product (GDP) increased at an annual average of nearly 9 percent, making it the fastest-growing economy among the major nations of the world. While once having been among the poorest of nations, its GDP has climbed to being ranked the world's sixth highest. Yet this has generated its own set of problems for China's leaders: Like other fast-growing countries throughout history, there are vast disparities in the levels of income among Chinese, particularly between its urban dwellers and its rural peasants. Civil servants and many professional people (teachers and physicians, for example) also chafe from being grossly underpaid in relation to those who work in the private sector. Corruption among officials at the middle and upper levels of government has become a persistent vexation because these differences cause resentment and people seek additional income by whatever means they have.

Spurred by President Richard M. Nixon's surprise visit to Beijing in 1972, the China-U.S. relationship had grown somewhat warmer since the ending of the U.S. presence in Vietnam. The Soviet invasion of Afghanistan (1979) increased Chinese interest in coming to a better understanding with the other superpower. Hence, in the 1980s, with U.S. encouragement, considerable progress was made in opening the country to foreigners and democratizing the secretive Communist Party and its iron controls over the political life of the populace. But in 1989, the rapid spread of freedom of thought and expression among university students again frightened the leaders, and when student demonstrators erected a "Goddess of Democracy" statue in Beijing, the leaders reasserted party control in the infamous **massacre in Tiananmen Square**. Hundreds, perhaps thousands, of young people died fleeing the guns of their own army.

Since that time, Deng's most recent successor, Hu Jintao, and China's government have been walking a fine line between diplomatic isolation and a partial acceptance of Western demands for relaxation of its repressive political measures. Relations with the United States especially have remained ambivalent. Simmering resentment over American military alliances with Japan, South Korea, and the nations of Southeast Asia in what it considers its own "sphere of influence" has sometimes made China hypersensitive to any perceived slights. A particular sore spot has been Taiwan, an island about one hundred miles from the mainland, to which China has laid claim since 1947. American trade, military assistance, and support for democratic elections on Taiwan have further complicated relations between the two nations. Tensions were worsened in April 2001, when a U.S. Navy EP-3 Aries II reconnaissance plane collided with a Chinese F-8 fighter plane, forcing the navy plane to land at a Chinese base on Hainan Island. Despite this incident, both sides realized the importance of maintaining cooperative relations. The United States supported China's application to become a member of the World Trade Organization, and in 2002 it became a full-fledged member, further opening its 1.25 billion people (now 1.35 billion) to the regulations and advantages of the world marketplace.

CHINESE YOUTH DEFIES TANKS. The never-identified youth stood alone to stop the tanks heading to Tiananmen Square in May 1989. After a brief hesitation, the vehicles rolled around him and continued to another destination.

Following the al-Qaida attacks on New York's World Trade Center and the Pentagon in Washington, D.C., in September 2001, both nations also found common ground in fighting worldwide terrorist attacks by extremist Muslims and those who give them aid. China's spectacular industrial expansion has forced its leaders to launch an aggressive international search for raw materials. They have ignored world opinion and continued to turn a blind eye to the actions of international pariahs such as Iran and the Sudan in exchange for their reserves of oil. The United Nations' inability to curb Iran's nuclear ambitions or Sudan's genocidal actions has been as a result of the reluctance of China (and Russia) to impose sufficiently strong sanctions on regimes such as these.

However, North Korea's unexpected test of a low-grade nuclear weapon in 2006 stirred world condemnation and severely embarrassed its patrons in Beijing. Since then, China has allied itself with the United States, Japan, and Russia in exerting pressure on Korea to halt its development of nuclear bombs. Nevertheless, these efforts have had no lasting success, as Korea's "Dear Leader," Kim Jong Il, has continued to order the stockpiling of atomic weapons and the testing of ballistic missiles with ever-increasing range. His son and successor, Kim Jong Un, propped up by his father's generals, has continued these policies, which have heightened tensions with South Korea, Japan, and the United States. Still worse, North Korea unilaterally has repudiated the armistice that ended the Korean War in 1953.

POSTWAR JAPAN TO 1952

The defeat and occupation of the Japanese islands by a foreign force (for the first time in history) was a tremendous shock, but it soon proved to be a constructive shock, unleashing a great deal of new energy and innovative thinking. Despite heavy war damage and loss of life, both military and civilian, Japan's economy rebounded with unexpected speed and then proceeded to shoot far ahead of anything it had achieved before.

The government of occupied Japan was an American-supervised affair under General Douglas MacArthur. Unlike the situation in occupied Germany after its defeat, a native civilian government was allowed to function, but it was limited to carrying out the directives of MacArthur's staff. The Japanese accepted all of MacArthur's many reform decrees in politics and social matters almost without criticism. Spiritually and materially exhausted by war and defeat, they were in a mood of self-questioning, which was unusual for this proudly nationalist and confident nation. As happened during the Meiji era, they seemed ready to accept a new basis for their social and political organization, and their willingness to change made the American occupation a great success.

In the first two years of his regime, MacArthur's office initiated radical changes in the traditional Japanese system, culminating in an entirely new constitution that established a government similar to that of the British. The parliament (Diet) was declared the most important branch of government, with sovereignty residing in the Japanese people. The emperor remained (and remains) in place, but only as a symbol. Japan "forever renounces war as a sovereign right of the nation," maintaining only a small self-defense force.

The war in Korea (1950–1953) was key in elevating the United States from conqueror to protector. The active support given to the North Korean communist army by Mao's China after 1951 made the U.S. armed forces in South Korea and elsewhere in the western Pacific an indispensable guardian for disarmed Japan. Japanese of all persuasions generally recognized the need for U.S. military protection, even though some were disturbed by the U.S.-instigated transformations in their social relations and political culture.

INDEPENDENT JAPAN

In 1952, the occupation ended and Japan again became a sovereign state. It signed a treaty of alliance with the United States that extended the U.S. nuclear umbrella over Japan in any future war. In return, the United States was guaranteed the right to have naval and military bases on Japanese soil for the indefinite future. Although minimally opposed at the time, this treaty caused tensions later, when the socialist and communist parties denounced the treaty as a tool of U.S. imperialism. By then, however, it was clear that Japanese politics tended toward the conservative and that an anti-U.S. position had little appeal. A homogeneous people who value tradition and group approval, the Japanese have never shown much interest in social experimentation or political radicalism.

For the first few years, the Liberal Party was the leading force in independent postwar politics. The Liberals merged with their closest rivals in 1955 and became the Liberal Democratic Party (LDP). For almost forty years, the LDP formed every Japanese government. Despite the name, it was a conservative party, dominated by the big business interests that have always worked closely with government in Japan. The LDP finally went down to defeat in 1993, when it was the culprit in a series of political corruption scandals that rocked the country and the business establishment. Always more an aggregation of financial and economic interests than a political unit, the LDP split into factions and lost out to a coalition of opponents. In most recent years, the LDP's factions have become almost separate parties, fighting one another in the Diet and allowing socialists and other groups to effectively contest the national leadership. Japan has become a fully democratic state, with governments that reflect both the strengths and weaknesses of that condition.

Economic Progress

The economic success of postwar Japan was admired throughout the world and was even considered as a possible model by the older industrialized states of the West. What explains this success? A combination of external and internal factors contributed to Japan's prosperity from the 1950s through the 1980s.

Externally, Japan benefited from several developments. When the United States assumed the burden of Japan's defense, the budgetary expenditures that would have gone into nonproductive weaponry, housing, and pensions for the military were saved and could be invested in the civilian economy. The Korean War stimulated Japanese industry in many different ways. Also, Japan is entirely dependent on imported oil, and oil was cheap during the initial postwar decades. International credit institutions such as the World Bank and the International Monetary Fund were eager to lend money for investment and the acquisition of technology. Japan soon showed itself to be a willing student and a highly reliable credit risk.

Internally, Japan had the world's highest personal savings rate, and the banks reinvested the savings in new industry. The Japanese labor force was disciplined and skilled and had been well educated in one of the world's most effective primary and secondary school systems. The Japanese population rose throughout the postwar era, providing a large labor pool as well as a growing internal market. Under strong government urging, labor continued to work with employers rather than take an adversarial position. Unions were rewarded with extensive powers in the workplace.

Most of all, in the opinion of many, Japan's postwar surge was the result of the consistent support of business by the government, which made large sums available for ongoing research and development and aggressively promoted business interests in its diplomacy. Business and manufacturing combines (called *zaibatsu*), which had originally been broken up by the Americans, were allowed to reconstitute themselves in a slightly different fashion and with even more political and financial clout. New industrial giants such as Sony and Honda were the product of bold entrepreneurs. Industry and government directed a major effort toward expanding foreign trade, and Japanese trade with almost every noncommunist country rose without interruption during the postwar decades. Japanese goods—including electronic products, automobiles, watches, and cameras—conquered the consumer markets of the globe. The "Made in Japan" label, which had been synonymous with cheap imitations in the prewar era, became a symbol of advanced design and the world's best quality.

All of these factors combined to give Japan the highest rate of growth in GDP (about 10 percent per annum) in the world during the quarter century between 1950 and 1975. Since then, the rate of growth has slowed because of several factors: Other Asian countries began to compete effectively in the global markets; unsound credit extension saddled banks with enormous loan defaults; and widespread corruption in government–business relations weakened Japan's capacities and self-confidence. In the 1990s, the country slipped into a recession that is not yet overcome, although it showed the first stirrings of a recovery in 2006.

In recent years, Japan has taken a more active role in world affairs, especially in those of Asia. With China showing an obvious desire to assume a position of leadership, Japan's change of attitude can be seen as the natural response of a long-time rival. From the 1890s through World War II, Japan was an occupier and aggressor toward its neighbors, so it is natural that China considers itself as having turned the tables and is reluctant to share with an old enemy its new standing as a world power. To date, this competition has remained peaceful—even cooperative. Each country is the other's second-biggest trading partner, but there remain unsettled disputes over oil rights in the East China Sea that have elicited threats from China. The Chinese still suffer painful memories of incidents like the "Rape of Nanjing" and the sexual enslavement of Chinese women in World War II (see Chapter 44), facts that many Japanese remain disinclined to acknowledge. Moreover, China is already—while Japan is capable of being—a nuclear power. Also, each nation has an active and sophisticated space program.

SOUTH AND SOUTHEAST ASIA SINCE INDEPENDENCE

The Indian subcontinent emerged from the colonial era divided between antagonistic Hindu and Muslim segments. This eventually yielded the major separate states of India, which is predominantly Hindu, and Pakistan and Bangladesh, which are mostly Muslim.

India

Today India's social and economic problems are severe, but its adherence to constitutional and political means to devise solutions is an inspiration to democrats throughout the world. Shortly after India gained its independence, Mohandas Gandhi's assassination left the Hindu masses in confusion and sorrow but did not interfere with the erection of the new India. As leader of the majority Congress Party, Gandhi's close associate and designated heir, Jawaharlal Nehru (1889–1964), sprang into the breach. Unlike Gandhi, Nehru believed that Western-style industrialization was absolutely necessary to avoid social chaos in India, and he set the country firmly on that path during his fifteen years at the government's head. He also believed that India could best live with neighboring Muslim Pakistan by showing it a strong hand. In practice, this policy meant that India and Pakistan were on a quasi-war footing for the next three decades, largely over the ownership of the rich border province of **Kashmir**, where Muslims predominated but India ruled.

Nehru led India toward a moderate democratic socialism that owed little to Marx and much to the British Labour Party. A mix of state ownership and free enterprise was worked out that has been relatively successful. For many tens of millions of Indians, living standards have risen in the past seventy years, but for perhaps 60 percent of the total of 1.3 billion, there has been discouragingly little change from the poverty of pre-independence days. The most acute challenge to Indian prosperity, as in so many other developing nations, remains the high rate of population growth. Various governmental campaigns for fewer births have not been successful in the traditionalist villages where most Indians live.

In 1966, Nehru's daughter Indira Gandhi (no relation to the Mahatma) became the first female prime minister of an Asian state and continued her father's vision of a modern, industrial India. Her increasingly dictatorial style created conflicts with many Congress Party leaders, however, and she was turned out of office in the 1975 general election, only to return in 1980. These peaceable electoral transitions were evidence of the maturity that India—the world's largest democracy—had achieved in its government only a generation after colonial subordination. It was an impressive and heartening performance.

The picture of stability and political consensus has been rudely marred in recent years by increased ethnic and religious friction. Above all, this has been fueled by the rise of religious intolerance among Hindus and Muslims. Hindu nationalists have attacked and destroyed mosques on one hand, while on the other, the Kashmir problem has become the focus of Muslim terrorist attacks and exchanges of gunfire between soldiers of the Indian and Pakistani armies. During an especially tense period in 2002, both nations threatened nuclear war. Fortunately, the situation has cooled down, and in 2003 and 2004, these two nations were content to satisfy their rivalries on the soccer field. In the northwest, the Sikh minority is demanding autonomy for their Punjabi province. Its denial by the government of Indira Gandhi was the trigger for her assassination by Sikh extremists in 1984. In the far south, Tamils and Sinhalese fought one another in a long-drawn-out, nasty, but little-publicized guerrilla war (that ended in 2009). Outraged by what he thought was the government's favoritism of the Sinhalese, a Tamil fanatic killed Indira Gandhi's son and successor, Rajiv Gandhi, in 1991, and in the last several years, recurrent riots between militant Hindus and the Muslim minority have sharpened interfaith mistrust.

INDIRA GANDHI. The first Asian female prime minister proved herself an adept politician. However, the intense maneuvering required to unite the many factions of the Congress Party became too much for her patience, and her increasingly authoritarian stance caused the defeat of her party in national elections in 1975. She returned to power a few years later and was assassinated in 1984 by Sikh fanatics.

Given these deep-seated animosities, it is all the more remarkable that Indian democratic government has held together almost without lapse. The Congress Party (formerly the Indian National Congress, see Chapter 35), which formerly held the allegiance of a large majority, has found itself in increasing electoral difficulty as nationalist parties and regional groups have become prominent. From 1998 to 2004, the Hindu nationalist Bharatiya Janata Party (BJP) was in power, after which the Congress Party retook control of Parliament and the Prime Ministry. India maintains the third-largest military force in the world, and so far it has not meddled in politics, nor have any civilian adventurers attempted to gain power by using the military.

In recent years, India has seen economic expansion on a stupendous scale. Between 1997 and 2010, its GDP grew at an average of 7.8 percent a year. India has shown considerable foresight in the investments it has made in high-quality technical and professional training for its best minds. This has begun to bear fruit as more and more companies in the West have outsourced many jobs in information technology and other skilled areas to well-trained Indians willing to work at a fraction of the wages and benefits required for American and European employees. India, however, faces two hurdles to its continued expansion: difficulties its technical institutes face in keeping up with the demand for highly trained graduates and an electrical grid that is vulnerable to frequent shutdowns. The years since 2010 have seen some slowing of India's growth as a result of the global economic crisis, political corruption, and an inadequate infrastructure.

Pakistan and Bangladesh

When the British withdrew from the subcontinent in 1947, the large Muslim minority demanded separate and sovereign status in a state of its own. The widespread distribution of the Muslim population made it impossible to create this state as a single unit, so West and East Pakistan came into existence. All Muslims not already within their borders were encouraged to migrate to those areas. Together, the two Pakistans included about one-fourth of the former British colony's population but considerably less than one-fourth of its human and material resources. These new states suffered from severe handicaps: Their economies were undeveloped, and they had no infrastructure and few potential leaders. Under the leadership of the devout Mohammed Ali Jinnah, the two Pakistans were committed from the outset to the supremacy of Islam in public life. This religious emphasis contributed to Pakistan's alienation from, and suspicions of, Nehru's determinedly secular India.

The geographically widely separated states soon discovered that they had nothing in common except Islam, and that was simply not enough to hold them together. With India's assistance, East Pakistan became the independent nation of Bangladesh in 1971. As measured by gross national product per capita, the overpopulated and flood-prone Bangladesh is among the poorest countries in the world. Pakistan is not much farther up the ladder, despite a generation of rival Chinese and American foreign aid programs. Even before the 2001 Afghani conflict, the burden of caring for 3 to 4 million Afghani refugees from the lengthy civil war in that country added to Pakistan's difficulties. Since the U.S.-led invasion of Afghanistan in 2002, the difficulties the ruling military government under General Musharaf and his successor, Asif Ali Zardari, have faced in trying to exert control over the mountainous northern parts that border on Afghanistan have complicated Pakistan's long-standing alliance with the United States. Almost impossible to control, with its warlike and fiercely independent tribes people, this part of the country has been a hotbed of Islamic extremism. Under the control of fundamentalist shaykhs, its religious training institutes (*madrasas*) have been breeding grounds that have spawned the notorious **Taliban** (literally, "students"), whom the Americans expelled from Afghanistan in 2002.

Osama bin Laden succeeded in eluding capture by American and Pakistani forces largely because these tribesmen supported his cause and provided shelter to him and his followers (see Chapter 51). Bin Laden's final refuge was in Abbottabad, northern Pakistan, where American Navy SEALs killed him in 2011. Since the operation was undertaken without the knowledge of Pakistan's powerful military and intelligence services, it placed additional strains on an already troubled relationship between the United States and Pakistan, which have not yet been rectified.

Southeast Asia Since World War II

Stark contrasts are found in the postwar history of mainland and offshore Southeast Asia. During the middle decades of this century, some areas of the region may have experienced more violence than any other place on earth, whereas others developed peaceably. Since the expulsion of the Japanese invaders in World War II, insurgents of one stripe or another have challenged the governments of Southeast Asia in several guerrilla campaigns (see Map 48.1). In former French Indochina (that is, Cambodia, Laos, and Vietnam), these insurgencies produced communist governments after long struggles. In Malaya (Malaysia) and the Philippines, leftist guerrillas brought unsuccessful challenges in the later 1940s, while in the Dutch East Indies (Indonesia), the campaign for national independence was triumphant. Both Thailand and Burma (Myanmar) withstood significant minority rebellions, but these uprisings were more tribal than revolutionary in nature.

The War in Vietnam

The lengthy war in Vietnam began as a nationalist rebellion against the French colonial overlord in the immediate postwar years. Under the Marxist-nationalist Ho Chi Minh, the Viet Minh guerrillas were at last able to drive the French army from the field and install a communist regime in the northern half of the country in 1954. At this point, the U.S. government under President Dwight D. Eisenhower took over the French role in the south, installed an American-funded puppet, and agreed to hold free elections for a national Vietnamese government. But the Americans became convinced that Ho would successfully manipulate any elections, and as a result, none were ever held. In the ensuing John F. Kennedy administration in the early 1960s, the decision was made to "save" the client government in Saigon from a communist takeover by countering increasing guerrilla activity in the south with U.S. ground and air power. Then President Lyndon B. Johnson, who found that he had inherited a small-scale war, determined to bring it to a successful conclusion. He believed that he could do so without crippling the simultaneous War on Poverty in the United States or his effective support for civil rights for blacks.

He was wrong on both counts. By 1968, half a million U.S. troops were on the ground in Vietnam. The entire nation was debating the wisdom and the morality of engaging in this faraway, bloody, and apparently unending conflict that appeared on television screens nightly. The War on Poverty had been curtailed by both budgetary and political constraints. The campaign for civil rights had run into black resentments, and there was a sharp decline of white liberal support for a president who continued to slog through the morass of Vietnam.

Johnson in effect resigned the presidency by deciding not to seek reelection in 1968, and his Republican successor, Richard M. Nixon, eventually opted to withdraw U.S. forces in the early 1970s under cover of a supposed "Vietnamization" of the conflict. A patched-together peace was signed with North Vietnam's government in 1973 after a year of negotiations, and the South Vietnamese took over their own defense. By 1975, the corrupt and demoralized Saigon authorities had fallen to their communist opponents, and North and South Vietnam were reunited on standard communist political and economic principles.

Until recently, both West and East relegated the country to a diplomatic limbo. The failure of the Soviets to assist their fellow communists in Vietnam fully brought to light the change in the Cold War and the conclusive nature of the break between the Soviet Union and China. In contrast

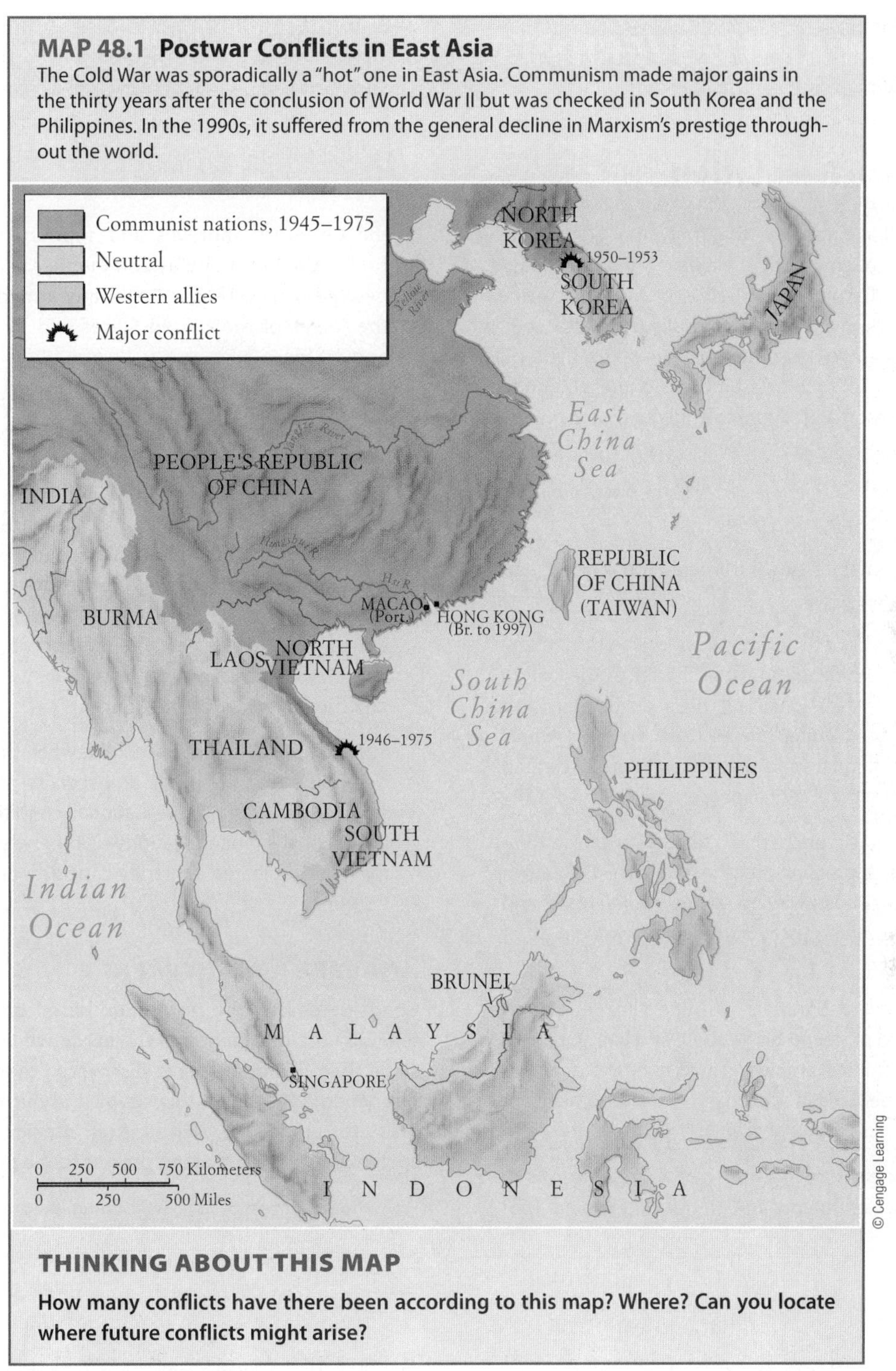

MAP 48.1 Postwar Conflicts in East Asia
The Cold War was sporadically a "hot" one in East Asia. Communism made major gains in the thirty years after the conclusion of World War II but was checked in South Korea and the Philippines. In the 1990s, it suffered from the general decline in Marxism's prestige throughout the world.

THINKING ABOUT THIS MAP

How many conflicts have there been according to this map? Where? Can you locate where future conflicts might arise?

to 1962, when Khrushchev was willing to gamble in Cuba, the Soviet government under Leonid Brezhnev preferred to forgo a foothold in South Asia and a propaganda advantage in the Third World rather than risk a war where Soviet security was not at stake. For its part, China was an active supplier of the guerrillas but carefully avoided placing its full resources behind the North Vietnamese. After the communist reunification, frictions between the supposed allies reached the point where the Chinese briefly invaded Vietnam and withdrew only after giving a lesson to the recalcitrants in Hanoi. Relations between the two countries continue to be strained as Vietnam's commitment to Marxism weakens and the fear of a recurring Chinese dominance is reawakened. In most recent times, the still-communist regime in Hanoi has sought ties with all sources of potential aid for its lagging economy, and thus seems to be following the same path in its economic policies as its large neighbor to the north.

LAW AND GOVERNMENT

Gulf of Tonkin Resolution

The U.S. Constitution stipulates that only the Congress can declare war on an enemy nation. However, Congress passed the "Gulf of Tonkin Resolution" in 1964, following an incident in which a North Vietnamese gunboat allegedly attacked an American naval vessel. No declaration of war was ever voted on, and based on the Gulf of Tonkin Resolution, Congress authorized the presidents (Johnson and Nixon) to engage in what, in effect, became a war.

Joint Resolution of U.S. Congress: Public Law 88-408, August 7, 1964, Approved on August 10, 1964

To promote the maintenance of international peace and security in southeast Asia.

Whereas naval units of the Communist regime in Vietnam, in violation of the principles of the Charter of the United Nations and of international law, have deliberately and repeatedly attacked United States naval vessels lawfully present in international waters, and have thereby created a serious threat to international peace; and

Whereas these attacks are part of a deliberate and systematic campaign of aggression that the Communist regime in North Vietnam has been waging against its neighbors and the nations joined with them in the collective defense of their freedom; and

Whereas the United States is assisting the peoples of southeast Asia to protect their freedom and has no territorial, military or political ambitions in that area, but desires only that these peoples should be left in peace to work out their own destinies in their own way: Now, therefore, be it

Resolved by the Senate and House of Representatives of the United States of America in Congress assembled, That the Congress approves and supports the determination of the President, as Commander in Chief, to take all necessary measures to repel any armed attack against the forces of the United States and to prevent further aggression.

Sec. 2. The United States regards as vital to its national interest and to world peace the maintenance of international peace and security in southeast Asia. Consonant with the Constitution of the United States and the Charter of the United Nations and in accordance with its obligations under the Southeast Asia Collective Defense Treaty, the United States is, therefore, prepared, as the President determines, to take all necessary steps, including the use of armed force, to assist any member or protocol state of the South-east Asia Collective Defense Treaty requesting assistance in defense of its freedom.

Sec. 3. This resolution shall expire when the President shall determine that the peace and security of the area is reasonably assured by international conditions created by action of the United Nations or otherwise, except that it may be terminated earlier by concurrent resolution of the Congress.

ANALYZE AND INTERPRET

Congress passed the resolution, based on information provided by the president and the executive branch. In the years since then, historians have discovered that the attack never happened. What does this suggest about the need for Congress to require more and better intelligence before giving such extensive war-making powers to the president?

From *The Department of State Bulletin* (August 24, 1964), 268.

Important though the Vietnam conflict was in international affairs, its most striking consequences were probably within the United States. Many Americans now older than age fifty-five formed their views of government, the duty of citizens, and public affairs in general as a result of some type of personal involvement with the issues of the Vietnam War. The 1960s' upheavals generated by war protest movements and resistance to what many saw as a wrong-headed and arrogant Washington were second only to the black civil rights movement as a milestone in the domestic affairs of the United States in the second half of the twentieth century. With the U.S. invasion of Iraq in 2003, these issues continue to resonate among those Americans who experienced the 1960s. To many of this generation, events appear to have repeated themselves in both Iraq and Afghanistan.

Progress and Future Prospects

Other nations of Southeast Asia have been much more successful than unfortunate Vietnam in escaping from poverty and technological backwardness. Although handicapped by rapid population growth and a still-heavy dependence on agriculture and exports of raw materials in

IMAGES OF HISTORY

Remembering Vietnam

A VETERAN OF THE VIETNAM WAR. A veteran searches for names among the 58,226 American dead whose names are engraved on the wall.

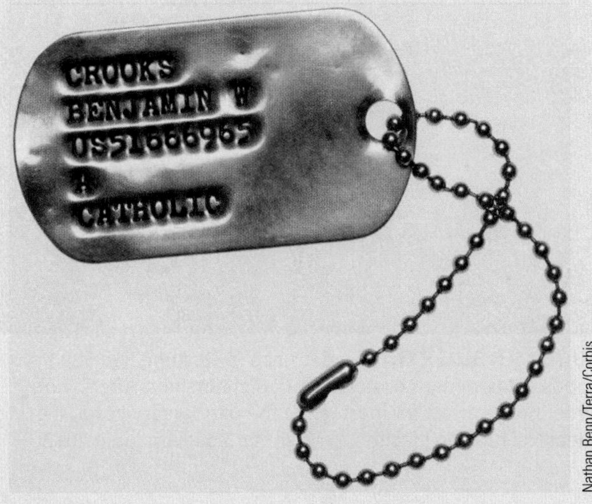

Nathan Benn/Terra/Corbis

GI "DOG TAGS." Identity card worn by Vietnam-era soldiers. This set was left at the National Vietnam War Memorial.

Steve Raymer/Terra/Corbis

a high-tech world, they are overcoming these obstacles to prosperity.

The **"four little tigers"** of the Pacific Rim—South Korea, Taiwan, Singapore, and Hong Kong—have followed the course plotted by the Japanese. Until recently, they maintained superior growth rates in the drive to establish an electronically driven, information-based economy. They are being joined by Malaysia, and just behind these five are Thailand and Indonesia. Throughout the western Pacific, fomenting rapid economic growth based on a modified free market has become the first priority for government, whether Marxist or capitalist in formal ideology. From a backwater status in the early part of this century, industrialized East Asia and Southeast Asia have become a vital part of a mutually dependent global interchange.

With relatively abundant resources, high literacy rates, stable village agriculture, and few border conflicts, much of Southeast Asia stands a good chance of making the difficult transition from a premodern to a modern economy and society within another generation. (The financial misalignments and speculative bubbles that burst in 1998 in several nations put a severe, but probably short-lived, ripple in this picture of progress.) The major long-term danger is still excessive population growth and the pressures it puts on the social fabric, but this threat is not as acute as elsewhere and is partly countered by steady growth in industrial development, which has drained off the excess rural population in constructive fashion.

The most successful exemplars are Hong Kong and Singapore, two city-states with entrepreneurial business

Tibor Bognar/Alamy Limited

GINZA SHOPPING DISTRICT. Postwar Japan has undergone another of its rapid adaptations to Western influences—this time to the global marketplace introduced to the country by the American occupation regime. Here, the Ginza shopping district in downtown Tokyo reflects the new consumer economy of the 1970s.

EdStock2/iStockphoto.com

AUNG SAN SUU KYI. A leader since 1988, Aung San Suu Kyi opposed Myanmar's brutal military dictatorships. After being under house arrest for fourteen of the past twenty years, she was released and won election to Myanmar's parliament in 2012.

as their driving force. Both have found profitable niches in the evolving global interchange of goods and services. (How well Hong Kong can retain this special position after its reannexation to mainland China in 1997 is an open question. Efforts by the Chinese government to blunt demands by pro-democracy demonstrators for universal suffrage have created a political standoff that remains unresolved.)

Next come South Korea, Taiwan, and Malaysia, where skilled and politically ruthless leaders encouraged the growth of modern economies. The authoritarian rule that was the norm between 1950 and 1980 is now being replaced by more open and truly democratic arrangements, as the prosperity created for the rich under previous generation filters down and widens choices and horizons. Indonesia, Cambodia, the Philippines, Thailand, and Vietnam come next on the ladder of prosperity, whereas the isolated Burma (Myanmar) remains on the bottom rung under the thumb of a brutal military dictatorship, the so-called Peace and Development Council (SPDC) until 2011, when the generals loosened some restrictions and allowed free elections to a national parliament.

SUMMARY

In the second half of the twentieth century, East Asia saw two world powers arise: communist China and capitalist Japan. Taking sharply divergent paths since they contested one another for predominance in World War II, both nations have come to play important roles in world affairs. In China, this role has primarily been military and political. In the case of Japan, it has been entirely economic and commercial up to the present.

As founder of the Chinese Communist Party, Mao Zedong had tremendous influence after his victory in the civil war in the 1940s. His break with his Soviet mentors ten years later divided communism into hostile camps. It also allowed Mao to follow his own path into a communism that focused on the peasants and the necessity of continual revolution. After his death in 1976, his successors soon rejected this path, and the present leaders are experimenting with an unstable mix of socialism in politics and capitalism in the economy. Under this strange mixture China has prospered, enjoying more than a decade of double-digit growth. China has invested much of its wealth in upgrading and modernizing its military services and is playing a more forceful part in regional affairs that have produced tensions with Japan, South Korea, and even Vietnam over claims to offshore islands and undersea oil fields to which all lay claim.

In Japan, the economy and society were modernized and Westernized under the American occupation. The American-sponsored constitution allowed a new political culture to take shape that found a wide and positive response in a nation ready to accept change. A sustained partnership between government and business encouraged an unprecedented surge in productivity that was undisturbed by social or political discontents until very recently. Now one of the world's great economic powerhouses, Japan stands on the verge of having to make a decision about its role in international politics and diplomacy, especially now that it faces the prospects of having a more assertive China as its neighbor.

The Indian subcontinent emerged from the colonial era divided between antagonistic Hindu and Muslim segments. India has shown admirable maturity in retaining democratic politics despite the heavy pressures exerted by ethnic and religious frictions among its several peoples and inadequate, though substantial, economic development. Pakistan faces intimidating problems generated by retarded civic development, by the commitment to hostility with neighboring India, and by its involvement with the Taliban.

In Southeast Asia, the picture has brightened in recent years after more than thirty years of violence and wars. Worst of these was the Vietnam conflict, which also had serious internal repercussions on the United States. Several of the former colonies of Southeast Asia are making a successful transition to the high-tech global economy.

IDENTIFICATION TERMS

Test your knowledge of this chapter's key concepts by defining the following terms. If you can not recall the meaning of certain terms, refresh your memory by looking up the boldfaced term in the chapter, turning to the Glossary at the end of the book, or accessing the terms on the CourseMate website at **www.cengagebrain.com**.

Amur River War
Deng Xiaoping
"four little tigers"
Great Leap Forward
Great Proletarian Cultural Revolution
Kashmir
little red book
massacre in Tiananmen Square
Red Guards
Sino-Soviet conflict
Taliban

FOR FURTHER REFLECTION

1. Name at least four world ideologies that have exercised the greatest influence over Asia since World War II. Which of these predate the modern era? Which have developed in the past five centuries?
2. Why have both capitalism and communism failed to entirely win over Asian nations? Why and how has communism had to make compromises to survive as the official state ideology of China and Vietnam?

TEST YOUR KNOWLEDGE

Test your knowledge of this chapter by answering the following questions. Complete answers appear at the end of the book. You may find even more quiz questions on the CourseMate website at **www.cengagebrain.com**.

1. The Great Leap Forward was
   a. the final communist victory over Nationalist forces.
   b. Mao's attempt at reengaging with the West.
   c. an effort at making wholesale changes in Chinese culture.
   d. The first successful Five-Year Plan.
   e. China's attempt in the 1960s to make itself industrially independent.
2. What major change in international affairs became fully apparent in the early 1960s?
   a. China and the United States joined forces against the Soviet Union.
   b. China and Japan became allies.
   c. China and the Soviet Union became allies for the first time.
   d. China and the Soviet Union became hostile toward each other.
   e. China and Japan renewed their hostilities toward each other.
3. Mao started the Great Proletarian Cultural Revolution because he
   a. believed that China was in danger of imminent attack.
   b. thought that it was the proper time to introduce political democracy.
   c. believed that all revolutions should be constantly renewed.
   d. wanted to forestall the Soviets' move toward coexistence.
   e. thought he could thereby control the peasants.
4. Which Asian nation developed the highest sustained growth in gross national product in the fist four decades after World War II?
   a. the Philippines
   b. Burma (Myanmar)
   c. Malaysia
   d. Japan
   e. South Korea
5. Japan's postwar political scene has been mainly controlled by the
   a. Socialist Party.
   b. Liberal Democratic Party.
   c. emperor through his political allies.
   d. labor unions.
   e. democratically elected Diet.
6. Since independence from Great Britain, except for a brief period from 1998 to 2004, India has been governed by the
   a. Bharatiya Janata Party.
   b. Indian National Congress
   c. Sinhalese
   d. Tamil Tiger Party
   e. Congress Party.
7. Since attaining independence, which Asian nation has established itself as the world's largest democracy?
   a. China
   b. India
   c. South Korea
   d. Pakistan
   e. Malaysia
8. What Southeast Asian nation combined nationalism and communism in its fight to free itself from French and American domination?
   a. Malaysia
   b. Burma
   c. North Vietnam (later Vietnam)
   d. Thailand
   e. Cambodia
9. Since the 1990s, China's relationship with the United States can best be described as
   a. wary.
   b. open-handed and warm.
   c. frequently hostile.
   d. largely conditioned by internal politics.
   e. resentful.
10. Pakistan's and India's relations with each other have been colored primarily by
    a. fundamental differences in their ruling philosophy.
    b. religious differences.
    c. rival imperialist ambitions in the region.
    d. rivalries and personality conflicts between their leaders.
    e. their growing strength in nuclear weapons.

CourseMate

Visit the CourseMate website at **www.cengagebrain.com** for additional study tools and review materials for this chapter.

49 Africa's Decolonization and Independence

The African woman does not need to be liberated. She has been liberated for many thousands of years. —LEOPOLD S. SENGHOR, FORMER PRESIDENT OF SENEGAL

1960–1965	Decolonization of most of Africa
1963	Organization of African Unity founded
1973	OPEC oil boycott, collapse of commodity prices
1970s–1990s	Trend toward dictatorship and one-party states; Cold War interventions by United States, Soviet Union, and China
1970s–1980s	Dependence on world markets spreads poverty; droughts, overpopulation, and AIDS wrack the continent
1994	South Africa achieves majority rule; entire continent free of colonialism
1990–Present	More stable, open governments appear in several states; Islamism gains in the northern tier
2011	Arab Spring; toppling of dictatorships in North Africa and Egypt

CHAPTER OUTLINE

Many of the factors that powered Africa's decolonization were linked to global trends. Calls for self-determination, the founding of the United Nations, American opposition to colonialism, the international labor movement, and successful independence movements in Asia provided a backdrop to events in Africa. At the same time, Africa had its own internal dynamics that helped set in motion the rapid changes following World War II and led to independence: the injustices of colonial rule; white racism; the development of African nationalism; a new set of leaders who had benefited from Western-style educations; and not least of all, the yearning for freedom. Conditions within individual colonies helped determine the speed and ease with which freedom was achieved and would help shape their future.

After the initial euphoria of independence, many African nations found themselves faced with a host of problems: maintaining national unity, stability, prosperity, and even survival in the face of pandemics and natural disasters. Continual interference by foreign powers during the Cold War years only added to the difficulties many nations faced. The results of independence so far have been mixed, at best. Millions have died needlessly from famine, civil wars, and political terror. Millions of others have been reduced

"IT'S HARD TO SAY GOODBYE!" This cartoon pokes fun at the real reasons for Europe's decolonization of Africa.

to misery as refugees. Nevertheless, the last two decades have produced reasons for guarded hope: the freeing of the last "colony," South Africa; the generosity most Africans have shown toward their former colonizers and occupiers; the spirit of reconciliation that has arisen in areas worst affected by ethnic conflict; a gradual winding down of civil wars; somewhat better leadership; movements toward democracy; and even a return to prosperity in some nations.

DECOLONIZATION: THE RUN-UP TO INDEPENDENCE

In 1950, few people would have guessed that hardly a decade later more than half of Africa's colonies would become independent nations. Decolonization proceeded rapidly (and unexpectedly peacefully, for the most part) between 1950 and 1965 (see Map 49.1). About thirty-five states derived from the former European colonies emerged in that decade and a half. Since then, independence has been obtained through armed action in the Portuguese colonies in 1975, in the British settler colony of Rhodesia in 1980, in Eritrea in 1993, and finally in South Africa in 1994.

Many factors influenced this process. First, there were those that were external to the continent:

- With the signing of the Atlantic Charter in 1941, Britain and the United States pledged themselves to the principle of self-determination (Chapter 47).
- The United Nations was pledged to the principle of self-determination and an end to colonialism and acted to end it whenever and wherever it could.
- The appearance of nationalist movements in Asia pressured colonial powers to allow self-determination there and in Africa. India's independence in 1947, the successes of the nationalists in reasserting control over China, and the forced decolonization of French colonies in Syria, Lebanon, and Indochina helped spur Africans to demand their own independence.
- The international labor movement helped to organize African protests for fair treatment and wages that occasionally resulted in strikes. The successes of the latter fueled African militancy and a realization that European colonialism could be defeated.
- **Pan-Africanism** was a movement that actually began in the United States and the Caribbean islands in the early twentieth century, but by World War II it had become more international in scope, with Africans and African Americans reaching across the Atlantic and providing mutually supportive ideas associated with "blackness" and Negritude. Occasional Pan-African Congresses reinforced this sense of racial unity and strength and helped raise many future African leaders' political "awareness." (See the Society and Economy box.)

African nationalism originated during the years prior to World War II among the small numbers of educated Africans—usually employed as teachers, clerks, lawyers, and clergymen—whose primary focus was on African modernization. For the most part, they still believed that Africa's future lay with what the Europeans could bring to Africa, rather than what Africans could do for themselves. They were aware of some of the injustices of colonialism—the racist "color bar," forced labor and other forms of exploitation, unequal opportunities for Africans, and sometimes actual physical abuses—but they confined their protests to peaceful forms of expression: delegations, letters to newspapers, and petitions for the most part. In most respects, it was as ineffective as it was elitist.

Following the Second World War, new leaders emerged. They came from varied backgrounds, but most were union leaders, soldiers who had fought in the war, and university students returning home from America and Europe. Like the generation before them, they shared the vision of a better Africa, but above all an "Africa for Africans." They were more politically active than their predecessors, skillful at organizing and channeling the sense of grievance many ordinary laborers and farmers had accumulated over half a century of colonial rule. By

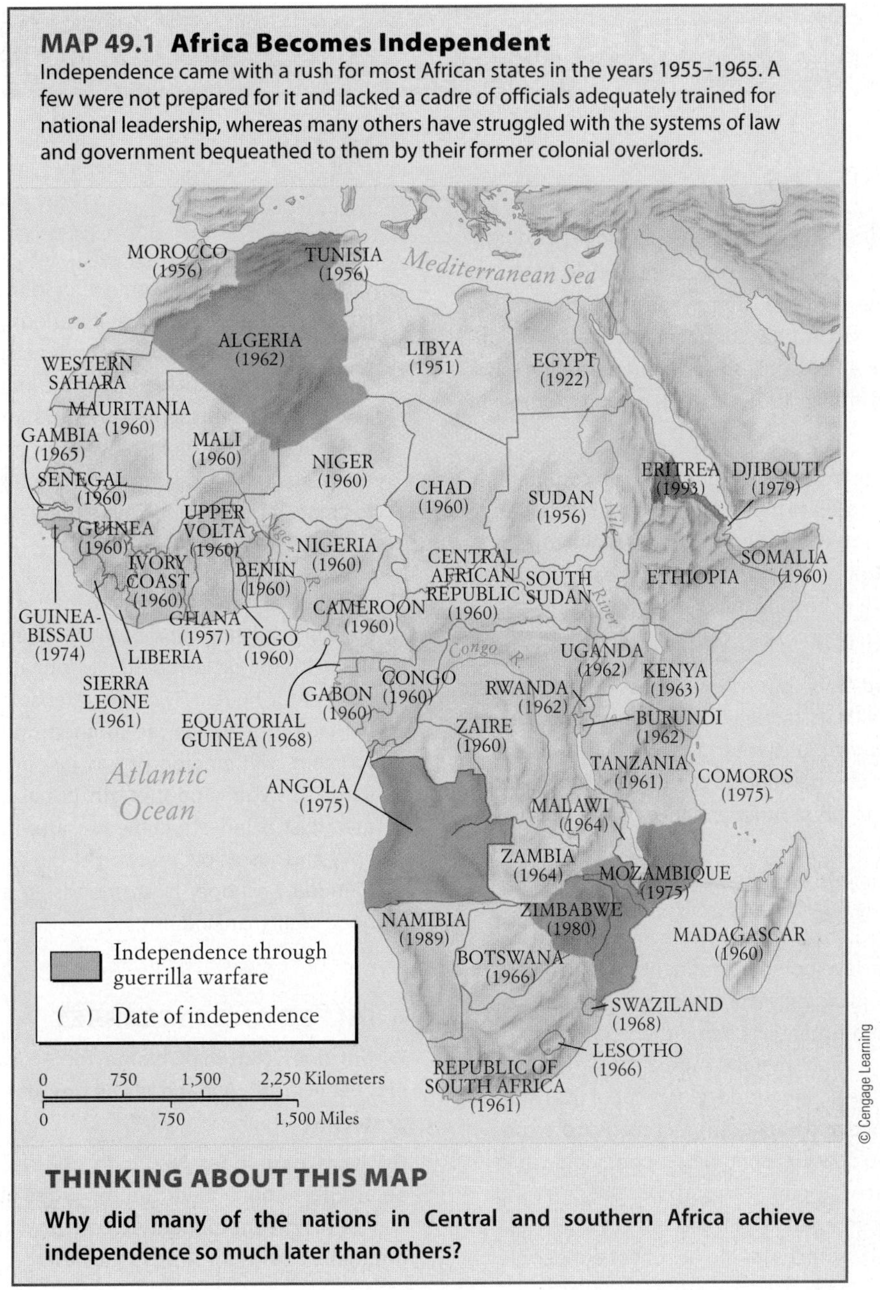

MAP 49.1 Africa Becomes Independent
Independence came with a rush for most African states in the years 1955–1965. A few were not prepared for it and lacked a cadre of officials adequately trained for national leadership, whereas many others have struggled with the systems of law and government bequeathed to them by their former colonial overlords.

THINKING ABOUT THIS MAP

Why did many of the nations in Central and southern Africa achieve independence so much later than others?

the 1950s, some colonies experienced for the first time the phenomenon of mass nationalism and the successful organization of national political parties under this new generation of leaders such as Leopold Senghor (sehn-GOHR) of Senegal, Nnamdi Azikiwe (NAHM-dee ah-ZEE-kih-way) of Nigeria, Kwame Nkrumah (KWAH-may ng-KROO-mah) of the Gold Coast, Jomo Kenyatta of Kenya, Julius Nyerere (nyeh-REH-ray) of Tanganyika, Kenneth Kaunda (kah-OON-dah) of Northern Rhodesia, and many others.

Until about the middle of the 1950s, all of the colonial powers resisted African demands for representation in their governments or outright independence. By the second half of that decade, though, Britain and France began to reconsider their positions. A combination of factors—including the international events already listed and the distaste many of their own citizens had developed in the years following the war about their lingering imperialism—moved the two biggest colonial powers to contemplate granting some degree of autonomy if not outright independence to their possessions. Once this decision had been made, the only questions that remained were how and when this transfer of power should be effected.

Thereafter, the courses that the individual African colonies followed in achieving their independence went in two different directions. For most, it was accomplished in an orderly way and with a minimum of violence.

SOCIETY AND ECONOMY

Pan-Africanism

Under the leadership of Kwame Nkrumah (1909–1972), the British colony of Gold Coast achieved independence in 1957 and assumed the new name of Ghana, after the ancient African kingdom. Until he was deposed in 1966, Nkrumah was a major proponent of Pan-Africanism and a spokesman for modern Africa. The following speech, delivered in 1961, provides a good example of his thinking.

> For centuries, Europeans dominated the African continent. The white man arrogated to himself the right to rule and to be obeyed by the non-white; his mission, he claimed, was to "civilise" Africa. Under this cloak, the Europeans robbed the continent of vast riches and inflicted unimaginable suffering on the African people.
>
> All this makes a sad story, but now we must be prepared to bury the past with its unpleasant memories and look to the future. All we ask of the former colonial powers is their goodwill and co-operation to remedy past mistakes and injustices and to grant independence to the colonies in Africa . . .
>
> . . . .
>
> Never before have a people had within their grasp so great an opportunity for developing a continent endowed with so much wealth. Individually, the independent states of Africa, some of them potentially rich, others poor, can do little for their people. Together, by mutual help, they can achieve much. But the economic development of the continent must be planned and pursued as a whole. A loose confederation designed only for economic co-operation would not provide the necessary unity of purpose. Only a strong political union can bring about full and effective development of our natural resources for the benefit of our people.
>
> . . . .
>
> Critics of African unity often refer to the wide differences in culture, language and ideas in various parts of Africa. This is true, but the essential fact remains that we are all Africans, and have a common interest in the independence of Africa. The difficulties presented by questions of language, culture and different political systems are not insuperable. If the need for political union is agreed by us all, then the will to create it is born; and where there's a will there's a way.
>
> . . . .
>
> We have to prove that greatness is not to be measured in stockpiles of atom bombs. I believe strongly and sincerely that with the deep-rooted wisdom and dignity, the innate respect for human lives, the intense humanity that is our heritage, the African race, united under one federal government, will emerge not as just another world bloc to flaunt its wealth and strength, but as a Great Power whose greatness is indestructible because it is built not on fear, envy and suspicion, nor won at the expense of others, but founded on hope, trust, friendship and directed to the good of all mankind.
>
> . . . .

ANALYZE AND INTERPRET

Whom does Nkrumah blame for Africa's disunity and poverty? Specifically, what does he propose as a solution to these problems?

On what basis does Nkrumah believe Africa's (then) newly emerging nations could unite? What obstacles stood in the way of his dream of a united Africa? What organization came out of his visions for Africa's future?

From Kwame Nkrumah, *I Speak of Freedom: A Statement of African Ideology* (London: William Heinemann Ltd., 1961), xi–xiv.

Kwame Nkrumah (1909–1972) led the way in the Gold Coast. In 1957, the Gold Coast became the first African nation to win its freedom, and it immediately took the name *Ghana*. In 1958, the French President, Charles de Gaulle, allowed the colonies of French West Africa and French Equatorial Africa to vote on a referendum that granted them self-rule within the framework of the French Empire. All but Guinea voted to refuse the offer. Two years later, largely because of the successful refusal to compromise taken by Guinea's Ahmed Sékou Touré (SEE-koo too-RAY), France granted independence to all of its African possessions. The year 1960 was a "miraculous year" for Africa because more than half of the continent became independent. More new states followed in the next four years (see Map 49.1).

For some colonies, however, the transition to independence was delayed and violent. Why? These were the **white settler colonies**: Algeria, Kenya, (Southern) Rhodesia, Mozambique, Angola, Southwest Africa, and South Africa. What distinguished them from the rest of Africa was the presence in each of a significant minority of Europeans who had immigrated after both world wars, hoping to improve their lives. For most, this was

Bettmann/Corbis

FIGHTING "MAU MAU." The so-called Mau Mau rebellion was actually an uprising of the Kikuyu people of central Kenya, seeking a return of lands taken from them by the colonial government of Kenya to give to white settlers. This picture, *c.* 1954, shows British soldiers and police rounding up suspected rebels.

accomplished. The way of life they enjoyed in the colonies was substantially better than they could have had in their home countries: large houses surrounded by verandahs and gardens; big, productive farms to leave their descendants; plenty of cheap African labor to work as servants and as laborers; and most significantly, colonial governments that favored their interests over those of the indigenous Africans. In Kenya, Africans who had been denied the use of their own lands in the colony's central highlands in favor of white settlers took up arms in 1952 to fight back. They called themselves the "Land and Freedom Army," but the whites knew them by another name—the "Mau Mau." These rebels directed their attacks primarily against other Africans they saw as collaborators. A few (thirty-two) white farmers were also attacked and killed, panicking the settlers and the colonial government. Many suspected "Mau Mau" were rounded up and put into camps where they were brutalized.

However, when word of the camps leaked back to Britain, many were outraged. Soon there was a major change of heart, and the government in Whitehall decided that the only reasonable course was to grant the colony its freedom. Kenya became independent in 1963 under its first president, Jomo Kenyatta.

The course followed in the other white settler colonies was much the same: years of conflict between the settlers (Rhodesia and South Africa) or between colonial government forces (Algeria, Angola, Mozambique, and Southwest Africa) and rebel armies determined to throw off minority rule and colonial subjugation. One by one, however, these colonies won their freedom. South Africa held out the longest—until the Afrikaner-supported government of F. W. de Klerk allowed the African majority the right to vote in 1994. Nelson Mandela was then elected the country's first president.

THE IMMEDIATE POSTINDEPENDENCE YEARS

Aside from resurrecting some African names from the precolonial era (Mali, Ghana, and Benin, among others), the new states showed remarkably little inclination to try to wipe out the two generations of European presence. The various kingdoms and empires that had been established as recently as the mid-nineteenth century by African rulers were not reestablished, nor was a serious effort made to do so. Instead, the colonial borders were maintained without change. Where they were challenged by secession—as in the Congo, Nigeria, and Ethiopia—they were defended (not always successfully) by armed force. It soon became clear that, despite the severe obstacles to true national unity that the colonial-era borders imposed, the new leaders were determined to keep them. If they acceded to a neighboring state's dismantling, they saw that they were inviting the same misfortune in their own.

The first years of independence saw a wave of optimism about Africa's prospects—specifically about the intentions

Marion Kaplan/Alamy Limited

JOMO KENYATTA. Born into Kenya's Kikuyu people, Kenyatta traveled to Britain in the 1930s and became an outspoken advocate for African rights in Britain's colonies. Following World War II, he returned to Kenya and was arrested for his alleged participation in the "Mau Mau" rebellion. From Kenya's independence in 1963 until his death in 1978, Kenyatta served as Kenya's first president.

and abilities of African leaders to maintain the democratic parliamentary governments they had inherited. In most of the newly independent sub-Saharan states, leadership was drawn almost entirely from among Africans who were Christian converts and who had been educated in Europe or America. Some, such as Kwame Nkrumah, Jomo Kenyatta, and others, had resided for many years abroad. These men were thoroughly familiar with Western forms of government and liberal values.

By the 1970s, however, democratic multiparty systems inherited from the departing colonial powers were replaced by an all-embracing (and completely artificial) "people's union" or "national assembly" single party. Once again, it was Ghana that led the way. The Western-educated Nkrumah was a popularly elected president in 1957. In 1960, he pushed through a new constitution that effectively made him the sole authority, and he banned the opposing politicians and made Ghana a one-party state in 1964. He reigned over it as a dictator until he was deposed in 1966 by an army rebellion. In other parts of the continent, similar moves came much later, and sometimes for understandably better reasons.

First, like Eastern Europe, pre-independence Africa had no tradition of Western-style political institutions and customs associated with parliamentary give and take. In the colonial era, only the British and the French had attempted to prepare their colonies for self-government along such lines, and the process had barely begun before World War II. When the war ended, the combination of circumstances mentioned in Chapter 47 brought the government of the colonies into a semblance of parliamentary politics with a rush. In most, the "Westminster model," based on British precedents, was adopted under European inspiration. But this type of government, based on the interplay of a majority party and a loyal opposition whose voice must be permitted to be heard, was alien to Africa.

On the contrary, in many parts of Africa there was a strongly rooted tradition of personal leadership and loyalty to a lineage or kin group. However, in precolonial Africa, the process by which political decisions had been made in most communities was not only by and large universally participatory, but inclined toward seeking community *consensus* rather than political *opposition* and a simple "rule of the majority." The case that many postindependence leaders made, therefore, was that the multiparty systems they inherited were alien and unworkable in Africa.

In addition, foreign interests sometimes promoted the removal of a democratically elected regime and its replacement by a group, civil or military, which favored the foreigners. This pattern was most visible in nations that were caught up in the Cold War struggles among Russia, China, and the West for control of various parts of the continent. Ethiopia, Somalia, Angola, and Mozambique are examples.

The breakdown of democratic parliamentary government often resulted in the establishment of a military dictatorship. The first in sub-Saharan Africa appeared in Ghana in 1966, but such dictatorships were soon endemic from Nigeria to Somalia and from Algeria to Angola. Some of the generals have come into power with a vision of what they wished to accomplish, but too many have simply wanted power and its accompanying opportunities to get rich. Worst of all have been those who combine the worst features of African regionalism and European terror: the repulsive Jean-Bedel Bokassa in the Central African Republic, Idi Amin in Uganda, Joseph Mobutu (Sese Seko) in Zaire (now the Democratic Republic of Congo), and more recently, Robert Mugabe of Zimbabwe, Charles Taylor of Liberia, and Omar al-Bashir of Sudan.

Yet some signs indicate that a better day is dawning. Some of the vicious repressors have been forced out. Popular protests against several of the one-party dictatorships have been increasing, and since the 1990s, they have succeeded in winning the right to establish legal opposition. Most promising of all, this trend has continued into the first two decades of the twenty-first century.

THE AFRICAN ECONOMY

Postindependence economies in Africa were naturally the outgrowths of colonial-era policies. In the interwar years, all of the European powers had encouraged the rise of **monoeconomies**—that is to say, based narrowly on producing single crops such as cacao, rubber, coffee, and palm oil or on one or two minerals such as copper or bauxite for export to the developed world. Whatever their specific characteristics, these operations were owned and developed by Westerners, but the laborers who were sometimes forced to work on the plantations or in the mines were African.

Domestic manufactures were relatively scarce because the home countries, which exported goods to the colonies, discouraged them. African enterprises tended to turn out substitutes for imports. For example, a factory might make simple consumable goods like soap and beverages that would otherwise be imported but virtually never manufactured consumer goods that required assembly lines and advanced technology.

The final epoch of the colonial era had changed African economics in several ways. Migratory labor, for example, became more prominent all over the continent. Some went to a new area because of money wages or the demands of coerced labor in lieu of taxes. The cash economy introduced along the new railway and river steamship routes made it necessary for people who had never seen cash before to earn it—if they wished to buy the new goods introduced by the Europeans. The emphasis on export crops in most colonies meant that gradually many Africans who had previously produced all of their own food from their gardens and by gathering now had to purchase it, as they would any other commodity.

With the coming of World War II, the international market for raw materials of all kinds quickly expanded, prices rose, and African producers enjoyed a long period of prosperity that continued into the mid-1970s. This prosperity was a major reason why Africans and non-Africans alike were optimistic about the prospects for the new states in the years leading up to and following independence. For more than a decade, Africa continued to enjoy the fruits of this prosperity. Gross national products (GNPs) continued to rise modestly, jobs were to be had, store shelves were full, and many towns and villages took particular pride in their newly built schools. Every newly independent nation soon had its own university. Most tellingly, many of Africa's new leaders remained popular because it appeared to many that they had delivered on the promises they had made to improve people's lives.

This prosperity, however, was a house built on sand. The 1970s saw reversals and mistakes made that still have not been remedied. The immediate cause was the oil shock generated by the Organization of Petroleum Exporting Countries (OPEC). Suddenly, supplies were tight, and almost overnight the price of oil doubled, tripled, then quadrupled, sending shockwaves through world economies. The Western nations quickly raised interest rates to head off inflation, and their economies contracted. Demand dropped for the raw materials on which Africa's fragile economies depended. Prices quickly followed, and with the cost of oil suddenly so high, African states found themselves slipping rapidly backward.

Except for Nigeria and Angola, few oil wells existed south of the Sahara, and the quadrupling of oil prices in 1973 hit the developing industries and the general citizenry hard. Inflation quickly got out of hand. The governments attempted to meet the crisis by redoubling their exports, in effect running harder just to stay in place. By the end of the decade, several formerly self-sufficient countries were having to grow more cash crops and found themselves having to import part of their food. Nigeria, for example, chose to use a good chunk of its increased oil revenues to pay a subsidy to importers of food, thus keeping food prices low for consumers but putting local farmers out of business. When the oil bubble burst in the 1980s, Nigeria faced sharply reduced revenues from petroleum and far fewer farms to feed its increased population.

The true dimensions of the problem became visible only in the 1980s. Several events coincided to bring this about: the diminishing domestic food stocks; the prolonged drought in Ethiopia, Somalia, and the Sudan; civil wars in the Sudan, Chad, Angola, Mozambique, and Ethiopia; and the sharp reduction in foreign aid flowing into Africa from international bodies and Cold War opponents. The injurious effects of all of these problems were magnified by the continuing rapid increase in population, which was partly offset by the equally rapid spread of AIDS in several countries.

Through the 1980s and much of the 1990s, the record continued to worsen. The small farmers and herdsmen who make up a majority in every country in tropical Africa suffered most from the overpowering changes as a result of a collapse in prices for commodities in the mid-seventies. Farm output barely increased in most countries, while fertility rates and population growth remained the highest in the world. More than one-quarter of sub-Saharan Africans lived—and continue to do so—in what the **World Bank** calls "chronic food insecurity." That is, they are hungry.

Since achieving independence, much of the continent has witnessed the abandonment of traditional diets and work patterns in the villages, which has driven people to seek work in the exploding cities. Increasingly, labor is flowing from the countryside to the towns, which almost never have adequate employment opportunities. Unable to find regular employment, people are driven into the streets, as in India or Latin America, where they live by hawking bric-a-brac, cooked food, Coca-Cola, or plastic toys. Prior to colonialism, theft was almost unknown in African society, but it has now become common, as has street violence in the cities. Hunger and deprivation are the reasons.

THE POPULATION BOMB

The economic and social problems enumerated here are largely the result of one overwhelmingly important fact: Africa is producing too many people for the means available to satisfy their rising expectations. As yet, no African country has made a serious effort to control its surplus population. Several governments still maintain that there is no overpopulation problem, only a resource availability problem, but this position cannot be sustained in the face of any serious investigation of the facts of African ecology.

Only about 10 percent of African surface soil is suitable for any type of crop cultivation. Much of the farming is carried out on marginal land that is subject to repeated droughts, which come in long cycles. Africa only has 8 million hectares (each hectare equals 2.47 acres) of irrigated land, versus Asia's 135 million. Just as in the Amazon basin, the tropical rain forest—one of Africa's most valuable resources—is being rapidly diminished. Once the big trees (mahogany, above all) are cut down, the nutrient-poor land they have shaded becomes useless for agriculture and is poor even for pasturage. But the lumber has immediate export value, and that has been a sufficient inducement for governments desperate for revenues and private owners greedy for cash.

The concentration on export crops and timber has seriously disrupted the African ecological balance, and the explosive growth of population has increased the pressures. Nomadic herders in the Sahel, for example, have had to increase their flocks of camels, goats, and cattle because in a drought cycle—such as was experienced in the 1970s and early 1980s—the animals cannot prosper and grow sufficient meat for human consumption. But these increased numbers put even more stress on the vegetation they graze on, magnifying the effects of the drought. As a result, in this area, the Sahara is rapidly expanding southward as the natural vegetation is eliminated.

The popular image of Africa as a vast expanse of jungles and plains filled with lions and elephants is wildly distorted and always has been. Although the herds are dwindling rapidly, big game is left in Africa in certain regions, and the tourist money that it attracts is a major generator of income for some African nations (Kenya, Tanzania, and South Africa lead the list). As the population has grown in those countries, however, large regions where lions previously roamed have had to be opened to human habitation. The upshot, predictably, is a conflict between human and animal uses of the land, which, again predictably, the animals always lose. That in turn harms the tourist trade, reducing the money available to the governments to assist the excess population in the struggle to stay alive.

The current surge in African population numbers has produced several vicious circles of this sort. The "population bomb" that the ecologists in the 1970s feared would threaten the livability of the entire planet proved to be exaggerated, *except* in tropical Africa where, in some senses, it has exploded. Recall the dire predictions of Paul Ehrlich and his associates cited in Chapter 47. A prime reason why they have not come true—thus far, at least—was the **Green Revolution** in agriculture. Through a combination of fertilizers and new hybrids, yields of corn, rice, and wheat were greatly increased in much of Asia and Latin America. But this outcome did not occur in Africa, where yields have remained low throughout the postindependence period and probably cannot be raised much more than current levels.

PROSPECTS FOR THE TWENTY-FIRST CENTURY

What does the twenty-first century hold in store for Africa? If one were to listen to the daily news bulletins as the sole source of information, it would be easy to predict a future of chaos, famine, and brutality. These have been a depressingly large part of Africa's fate in the recent past, but there are some hopeful indications that things might be improving. The continent still has most of the world's poorest people (see Worldview Map VI), but at 5.0 percent, Africa lagged only behind Asia in the growth rate of its gross domestic product (GDP) in 2012. At the same time, five African nations (Libya, Angola, Niger, Ethiopia, and Rwanda) were among the world's ten fastest growers of their GDP in the world. In recent studies, it was found that the *per capita* GDP was \$180 for Zimbabwe, \$390 for Ethiopia, \$810 for Kenya, \$1310 for Cameroon, and \$1570 for Nigeria. In the same year (2012), it was estimated that U.S. per capita GDP was \$49,340. Life expectancies for males and females were 41.2 and 44.3 years in Angola; 41.7 and 42.4 in Mozambique; and 39.8 and 39.4 in Swaziland (perhaps the world's lowest). For the United States, they were 75.7 and 79.9.

Sierra Leone had one physician for every 35,133 residents in 2008. The infant mortality rate in sub-Saharan Africa averages about 100 per 1,000. In the United States, it is about 7 per 1,000. The adult literacy rate in many countries of Africa is below 50 percent overall and far lower among village dwellers. Higher education (postsecondary) is still a rarity, and most higher degrees are issued for the traditional specialties such as law, the humanities, foreign literature, and education. Relatively few students are interested in the applied sciences, engineering, or health specialties, which are precisely the disciplines most needed in their countries. These curricula lack prestige unless they can be studied at a foreign university, a dream that is open to few Africans.

One of the more gloomy and recalcitrant situations is the huge menace of the acquired immune deficiency syndrome (AIDS) epidemic, which started in Africa and has hit that continent much harder than any other part of the world. According to reliable estimates, in parts of tropical Africa, about 30 percent of the population is infected with the human immunodeficiency virus (HIV), and already far more people have died from the disease in Africa than in the rest of the world combined. Until recently, official countermeasures to fight the disease

Ahmed Jallanzo/EPA/Corbis

TWO AFRICAN PRESIDENTS. After years of civil war and brutal misgovernment under Charles Taylor, Nigerian soldiers restored order. In 2006, Liberians elected Ellen Johnson-Sirleaf as Africa's first woman head of state. Here she is shown at her inauguration, accompanied by President Olusegun Obasanjo of Nigeria.

ZUMA Wire Service/Alamy Limited

WANGARIA MAATHAI: AFRICAN WOMAN AND NOBEL LAUREATE. In 1977, Kenyan Wangari Maathai founded the Green Belt Movement, a grassroots environmental organization whose mission is to help prevent soil erosion by planting new trees. A member of Kenya's Parliament, she was awarded the Nobel Peace Prize in 2004 for "her contribution to sustainable development, democracy and peace."

have been weak and ineffective. Strapped by scarce funding and an absence of basic public health facilities, most African governments are relying on the international health authorities to find a solution and bring it to Africa. In South Africa, until voted out of office, the government itself became a major obstacle to treatment for its citizens. Believing the widespread presence of the disease in their country to be an embarrassment, the recent government of President Thabo Mbeki denied that there was a connection between HIV and AIDS, making any therapy program difficult to implement. Fortunately, South Africa is proving to be the exception; drugs are becoming available and more African governments are actively encouraging programs of public education. With Mbeki forced to resign his office in late 2008, South Africa's new president, Jacob Zuma, has abandoned his predecessor's misguided policies and has renewed efforts to address the AIDS menace.

In a different arena, the internal and international conflicts afflicting Africa have been frightening. Besides the strengthening challenges of the Islamic fundamentalists in the north, for a while in the 1990s it seemed that Africa's future was one of unending rebellion. As late as 2002, major rebellions were occurring in at least seven countries. Riots and street demonstrations against the current regimes were taking place in another half dozen. Since then, however, there is solid evidence of a new harmony. (See Nelson Mandela's words in the Law and Government box.) The **Organization of African Unity (OAU)**, founded in the wake of the independence surge in the 1960s as both a sounding board and a peacekeeper for the continent, has shown itself willing to take on the latter role. Peacekeepers from neighboring countries have intervened in the vicious bloodlettings in Liberia, Sierra Leone, Congo-Kinshasa (the former Belgian Congo), and elsewhere. Although the record is not perfect, peace has returned to Liberia, but new violence has appeared elsewhere in West and East Africa. Islamic religious warfare has reduced Somalia, Mali, and northern Nigeria to chaos. The official government in Mogadishu exercises little control outside of Mogadishu, while fighting between Muslims and Christians in northern Nigeria has become a common occurrence. Jihadists in Mali have imposed Shari'a law and control part of the country, forcing many refugees to flee the country. In some cases, civil wars have given way to national elections (see the picture and caption about Ellen Johnson-Sirleaf), but the threat of religious militancy remains a growing problem in West and East Africa.

Economically, all of the African states are more or less deeply in debt to the World Bank and a series of private international banks from which they borrowed large sums in the late 1960s and the 1970s. Because the possibility that these monies will ever be returned has disappeared, lenders now insist on internal economic reform in

AP Photo/Sunday Alamba

JIHADIST ATTACKS IN NORTHERN NIGERIA Women walk past the ruins of a market outside the state police headquarters in Kano, Nigeria, January 2012. More than 185 people died in the attacks. Calling themselves *Boko Haram*, jihadists have imposed strict Islamic law in northern Nigeria.

LAW AND GOVERNMENT

Inaugural Address by Nelson Mandela

The rise of Nelson Mandela to the presidency of the Republic of South Africa must be one of the more amazing events of recent African history. Imprisoned for twenty-five years as a subversive by the white South African government, Mandela remained the rallying point for all those who believed that the day of apartheid must finally pass.

Raised the son and heir of a thoroughly traditional African chief, Mandela broke with his family and culture to gain a legal education in the city. As a thirty-six-year-old black lawyer, he entered the still-subterranean world of African politics and rapidly rose to prominence before his career was cut off by imprisonment.

For his mainly black followers in the African National Congress, Mandela's convincing majority in the first universal balloting ever permitted in South Africa was an event of great elation and a satisfying end to an "extraordinary human disaster." But the white and colored minorities were naturally nervous about what the future might hold. Would Mandela allow his more passionate black adherents to take revenge for their long exclusion from power and from human dignity? Would he remember the humiliations he had suffered both before and during his long imprisonment at the hands of the dominant Afrikaner whites? Or would he attempt to calm the waters stirred by a bloody electoral campaign and look into the future rather than back at the past? His inaugural address of May 10, 1994, was eagerly awaited.

> Today, all of us by our presence here ... confer glory and hope to newborn liberty. Out of the experience of an extraordinary human disaster which lasted too long must be born a society of which all humanity will be proud.
>
> Our daily deeds as South Africans must produce an actual South African reality that will reinforce humanity's belief in justice, strengthen its confidence in nobility of the human soul, and sustain all our hopes for a glorious life for all.
>
> The time for the healing of the wounds has come. The moment to bridge the chasms that divide us has come. The time to build is upon us....
>
> We have triumphed in the effort to implant hope in the breasts of the millions of our people. We enter into a covenant that we shall build the society in which all South Africans, both black and white, will be able to walk tall, without any fear in their hearts, assured of their inalienable right to human dignity—a rainbow nation at peace with itself and the world....
>
> We dedicate this day to all the heroes and heroines in this country and the rest of the world who sacrificed in so many ways and surrendered their lives so that we could be free. Their dreams have become reality. Freedom is their reward. We understand ... that there is no easy road to freedom. We know it well that none of us acting alone can achieve success. We must therefore act together as a united people, for national reconciliation, for nation building, for the birth of a new world.
>
> Let there be justice for all. Let there be peace for all. Let there be work, bread, water, and salt for all. Let each know that for each the body, the mind, and the soul have been freed to fulfill themselves....
>
> Let freedom reign! God bless Africa! —Nelson Mandela

ANALYZE AND INTERPRET

See what additional information you can find about Mandela's presidency. To what extent and in what ways did it fulfill the high tone of his inaugural address?

the guise of so-called **Structural Adjustment Programs (SAPs)**. It is hoped that SAPs will help restart stalled African economies and allow increased export earnings, but the SAP goals are contingent on painful governmental measures to reduce chronic inflation, reduce social programs on which the poorest people often depend, reduce subsidies to exporters and importers, or put in place other measures that cause a disproportionate share of the suffering to be borne by impoverished citizens. Fortunately, however, meetings of the "Big Twelve," leaders of the twelve largest economies in the world, and of the European Union have produced agreements to forgive many of the loans acquired in the 1960s and 1970s. With all of these economic and political negatives, is it still possible to look at the first years of African independence as a learning experience that may produce much of value for the continent's peoples? In several instances, a ray of light has entered the political and economic darkness that engulfed Africa during the last thirty years of the twentieth century. Here are some examples:

- Several of the one-party autocracies established in the 1970s have been forced to surrender power or loosen their grip on it. Malawi, Botswana, Kenya, and Mozambique, among others, have to some extent democratized their politics, thanks to popular protest or armed rebellion.

- The end of the Cold War competition for allies has allowed a measure of sanity to creep back into relations between the First and Second Worlds and the African Third World. Fantasts, tyrants, and **kleptocracies** (governments made up of thieves) are no longer supported on the grounds that "if we don't, they will."
- International lenders are no longer willing to put up money for grandiose projects, which over the years have too often proven to be ineffective, if not completely wasteful. New projects must now be rationally justified and suited to the real needs of the country. Mini-grants to enterprising individuals and small groups, especially to women, have replaced the big programs of the past. So far, these have produced much better results.
- After many unhappy experiences, African governments have toned down their exclusive emphasis on cash export crops and have focused more on family farming, hoping to meet the constantly growing domestic food demand.
- Several African governments and political parties have displayed a change in attitude toward women and their roles in society. Women are receiving active support and being encouraged to make their voices heard not only in politics but also in the working economy and in public affairs generally.
- Finally, the new millennium has brought improved prospects for the economies of many African nations. More than anything, the rise of China and other Asian nations as industrial powers have provided new hope for Africa. China's seemingly unquenchable thirst for raw materials has boosted demand and raised prices for the commodities produced in Africa and Latin America; therefore, for the first time since the early 1970s, exports have exceeded imports in some African nations. Furthermore, China has invested very heavily throughout the continent, bringing in precious capital, technological expertise, and badly needed improvements to long-decayed infrastructures.

Africa's future as a part of human society is impossible to predict. This rich continent, with its immense variety in both natural phenomena and human activities, may continue to suffer from a welter of civil wars, tyrannical politics, and economic hardship internally and peripheral status internationally. But it could be that the first generation or two of freedom was a period of growing pains and that the twenty-first century will see a recovery from past internal mistakes, followed by a steady rise from neocolonialism to equality in the world community. "Out of Africa, always something new," said the Roman sage Pliny in 65 C.E., and his words remain true today.

SUMMARY

Africa's decolonization occurred with unexpected rapidity. Even before World War II, there was an emerging, educated leadership that advocated African improvement and lobbied for better treatment of Africans. After the war, this coalesced around increasing strident—and sometimes violent—protests aimed at achieving African equality, opportunity, and participation in their own governments.

Since independence, the second-largest continent has seen some evil days, especially in the 1970s through the mid-1990s. Whereas the 1960s saw generally tolerant leaders in most countries and steady economic growth in Africa's export-oriented economies, about 1975, things took a turn for the worse. As prices for the exports of African nations declined, poverty spread and growing criticism of governments drove many African leaders to more autocratic methods of governing. Democracy yielded to single-party or outright dictatorial regimes. Where guerrilla wars had been necessary to attain independence, the warrior leaders often imposed themselves on their country in the guise of united fronts or similar vehicles of personal power. In other cases, free elections produced the rule of a dominant ethnic or "tribal" group. In still others, the military reacted to civilian squabbles by brushing them aside. Corruption became endemic and was stimulated by foreign aid and trade arrangements.

In the economy, the new states continued the colonial era's emphasis on cultivating export crops and mining but added a new dependency on international credits for often ill-conceived "prestige" projects. When combined, these factors made Africa vulnerable to conditions no government could control: famine in the wake of droughts, low raw material prices on the world market, and rising food imports to feed an exploding population. In most African countries, the economy stumbled severely and often there were actual losses in GNP. The early years of the first decade of the twenty-first century have seen encouraging signs of a shift toward economic growth and political toleration. Beginning around 1998 and until the worldwide recession began in 2008, the demand for Africa's primary products rose dramatically, prices rose, and Africans began to prosper in ways they had not since the 1960s. As of this writing, Africa's future prosperity hinges on a return to worldwide prosperity and attacking the overpopulation problem. Another hopeful sign has been the willingness shown by the developed nations to forgive many of the debts African governments accumulated over the years. What the future holds in both politics and living conditions is impossible to know, but there is reason for hope, and Africa will need both luck and assistance from the developed world to overcome the tragic decline of the last three decades of the old century.

IDENTIFICATION TERMS

Test your knowledge of this chapter's key concepts by defining the following terms. If you can not recall the meaning of certain terms, refresh your memory by looking up the boldfaced term in the chapter, turning to the Glossary at the end of the book, or accessing the terms on the CourseMate website at **www.cengagebrain.com**.

Green Revolution
kleptocracies
monoeconomies
Kwame Nkrumah
Organization of African Unity (OAU)
Pan-Africanism
Structural Adjustment Programs (SAPs)
white settler colonies
World Bank

FOR FURTHER REFLECTION

1. Why were white settlers concentrated primarily in the eastern and southern parts of the continent?
2. Why did the transition to independence go more smoothly in the colonies that were *not* white settler colonies? Can you name some of these?
3. After years of relatively low levels of violence, how might one account for the rise in genocidal civil wars in Africa in the last two decades?
4. What seem to be the principal legacies that colonialism bestowed on Africa that have endured? Generally speaking, have these been positive or negative?

TEST YOUR KNOWLEDGE

Test your knowledge of this chapter by answering the following questions. Complete answers appear at the end of the book. You may find even more quiz questions on the CourseMate website at **www.cengagebrain.com**.

1. Which colonial power did the worst job of preparing its African possessions for self-government?
   a. Spai
   b. Belgium
   c. Germany
   d. Britain
   e. France
2. The first decade of independence
   a. were years of relative growth.
   b. saw the almost-immediate rise of autocratic governments.
   c. saw the growing influence of the OAU.
   d. saw many secession movements across the continent.
   e. were years of wholesale decline.
3. The former colonial powers have
   a. largely ignored Africa.
   b. actually increased their presence in their former African colonies.
   c. largely refrained from interfering in Africa.
   d. seated and unseated one dictator after another.
   e. continued to exercise limited control in Africa through neocolonialism.
4. Which of the following statements about African nations is *false*?
   a. They all have primarily rural populations.
   b. They have fewer schools since achieving independence.
   c. They are all aware of their impoverished status in contrast to the West.
   d. They have almost all experienced a colonial past.
   e. Most of them in the twenty-first century are experiencing problems related to epidemics.
5. From the 1970s until recently, the general trend of government in Africa has been toward
   a. one-party dictatorships.
   b. monarchies.
   c. socialist states.
   d. parliamentary democracies.
   e. democratically elected presidencies.
6. In Africa, since independence, the most common population movement has been from
   a. the cities to the rural areas.
   b. the inland cities to the coastal areas.
   c. the nomadic life to the farm villages.
   d. the farm villages to the cities.
   e. the nomadic life to the cities.
7. Which of the following have endured the worst violence from jihadist Islam?
   a. Nigeria and South Africa
   b. Mali and Somalia
   c. Liberia and Sierra Leone
   d. Somalia and Kenya
   e. Tanzania and Congo

8. The 1970s event that contributed most to the decline of Africa's economies was the
   a. rise of dictatorships.
   b. end of the Cold War.
   c. OPEC oil embargo.
   d. American and Soviet intervention in Africa's internal affairs.
   e. invention of new synthetic fibers and plastics to replace African commodity exports.
9. The last African country to throw off minority (colonial) rule was
   a. Mozambique.
   b. Botswana.
   c. Eritrea.
   d. South Africa.
   e. Tanganyika.
10. Which recent developments have provided hope for Africa's economic development recently?
   a. The forgiveness of some African nations' loans by the developed nations of the world.
   b. The rise of China and Asian nations as industrial powers.
   c. a and b.
   d. Renewed interest in Africa's development by the former colonial powers.
   e. The end of civil wars throughout the continent and a return to peace.

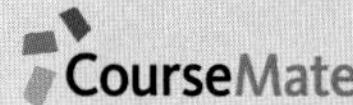

Visit the CourseMate website at **www.cengagebrain.com** for additional study tools and review materials for this chapter.

Latin America in the Twentieth Century 50

Those who make peaceful revolution impossible will make violent revolution inevitable. —JOHN F. KENNEDY

CHAPTER OUTLINE

1900–1933	Repeated forceful intervention in Caribbean affairs by the United States
1910–1920	Mexican Revolution
1930s	Lázaro Cárdenas presidency in Mexico
1933	President Franklin D. Roosevelt begins Good Neighbor Policy
1940s–1955	Juan Perón in Argentina
1948	Organization of American States founded
1959	Fidel Castro seizes control in Cuba
1961	Bay of Pigs invasion of Cuba
1970s	Military governments established in most of Latin America
1980s–early1990s	U.S. intervention in Grenada, Nicaragua, Panama, and Haiti
1983–1990	Reestablishment of constitutional governments in most of American continent
1992	Mexico, United States, and Canada form the North American Free Trade Association (NAFTA)
1994–2002	Economic meltdown in Mexico, Argentina, and Brazil
1999–2013	Venezuela's neo-populist president, Hugo Chavez, is pro-Cuba, anti-U.S.
2004	Creation of the South American Community of Nations, a ten-nation, free trade association
2006–2007	Twelve Latin American countries elect moderate and democratic presidents
2006–present	Mexican drug wars cause surge in violence
2008	Cuba's Castro cedes power to Raúl Castro
2011	Brazil is world's sixth largest economy

In the twentieth century, the histories of the twenty countries making up Latin America varied sharply in detail but were generally similar. In all cases, the politics and international relationships of the Latin countries were fundamentally influenced by the economic and social problems they faced—problems that were roughly alike from Mexico to Argentina. Militarism, authoritarianism, and corruption (practices inherited from the nineteenth century) were persistent obstacles to stability. All of the countries also had to come to terms with the United States, the dominant power in the Americas with the ability—repeatedly demonstrated—to intervene at will in hemispheric affairs. The Mexican Revolution of 1910–1920 successfully overthrew a U.S.-backed regime and achieved some redistribution of wealth. Mexico's revolution inspired numerous rebellions throughout Latin America, but the next true revolution did not occur until 1959, in Cuba.

The worldwide Great Depression of the 1930s was a turning point for the Latin Americans in an economic sense because some of the larger countries attempted to recover from their loss of export markets by developing the neglected domestic markets and adopting economic nationalism. Although not completely successful, they did manage a partial escape from the neocolonialism to which they had formerly acquiesced. Since the end of World War II, other attempts have been made to introduce more or less radical changes in both the political and economic structures, but with the exception of a faltering and controversial Marxism in Cuba, these efforts have not been sustained for more than a few years. Deep class divisions have continued, and social problems—especially those generated by population pressure and abject poverty—still await alleviation.

PERSISTENT DEPENDENCY

Because of its economic difficulties, Latin America remained dependent on the United States and Europe throughout the nineteenth and early twentieth centuries (many would say until the present). This did not mean merely that Latin America was dependent on outside areas for imports of goods and services it did not produce, but also that Latin America was increasingly dependent on foreign capital—and therefore foreign political approval—for domestic investment of all types.

Latin America did not lack export markets. On the contrary, throughout the nineteenth century, demand in the Western world was rising for its raw materials: Bolivian tin, Brazilian coffee and rubber, Chilean copper and fertilizer, Mexican silver and oil, and Argentine meat and grain. Instead of providing a general stimulus to the Latin economies, the benefits derived from these exports were limited to a mere handful of wealthy families or to foreigners. The elite families sent the profits abroad, used them for their own extraordinarily wasteful lifestyles, or squandered them on poorly considered schemes. Little was invested in rational, farsighted ways by either the governments or the rich. No attempt was made to strengthen the social fabric by encouraging the poor and the unskilled to become educated and thus qualify themselves to participate in the political process.

In many cases, the real beneficiaries of the exploitation of Latin America's raw materials were the foreign investors who supplied the necessary capital to get production under way: American mining corporations, European coffee plantation owners, and British shipping firms. None of their profits went into the pockets of any of the citizenry, let alone the workers, and to ensure the continuance of this arrangement, corruption in government was endemic.

The rising disparities between the rich handful and the poor majority created an atmosphere of social unrest in much of the continent. At times in the nineteenth century, the disenchanted and the desperate were able to find a popular leader who frightened the wealthy with his threats to install democratic reform (as in Guatemala in the 1830s). In every case, either the ruling group was able to bribe and co-opt the leader or another army-led "revolution" forcibly removed him. In some cases, when the traditional ruling group did not remove the disturber swiftly enough, the United States acted instead, beginning with the Mexican War of the 1840s. Examples of U.S. intervention became more numerous after the Spanish-American War of 1898 and brought the North Americans more directly into the Latin world.

National economic policy throughout modern Latin America has aimed at escaping from the basic pattern of impoverishment: exporting cheap raw materials and importing expensive manufactured goods and technical expertise. A few countries made significant progress in the middle years of the twentieth century, usually in combination with a radicalization of internal politics. For example, in Argentina in the 1940s, the lower classes enthusiastically supported dictator Juan Perón (pair-OWN) when he attacked both domestic class privileges and Argentina's import dependency on the United States. In the 1930s under President Lázaro Cárdenas (CAR-duh-nuhs), the Mexicans went further; they actually expropriated U.S. oil firms (with compensation) and withstood the wrath of the Giant to the North until a negotiated agreement was reached. The most recent example of a populist caudillo, Venezuela's president Hugo Chávez (CHAH-vehz), was also an anti-imperialist, who denounced the U.S. role in Venezuela's petroleum industry.

In general, however, the economy of the southern continent (and of its Caribbean outliers) continued nearly as much under the control of external forces as it had since colonial days. Until well into the twentieth century, the majority of the South American and all of the Central American states remained agrarian societies. They exported raw materials such as coffee, grain, beef, timber, petroleum, and copper ore. They imported the vital elements of industry and personal consumption such as machinery, steel, automobiles, transformers, and telephone wire. In such an equation, the raw material exporters are always at a disadvantage in the marketplace because their products can almost always be found elsewhere or be replaced by new technologies.

NEW AND OLD SOCIAL PROBLEMS

By the mid-twentieth century, the Latin American countries were divided into two major groups: the more industrialized and urban societies, which included Argentina, Brazil, and Chile (the ABC countries) and with reservations, Mexico; and the majority, which remained agrarian and rural. In the first group, the migration of much of the population into the handful of major towns accompanied industrialization, accentuating the accustomed isolation of the countryside from the highly centralized government. The peasants in their adobe villages or the laborers in the mine and ranch country saw the capital city as a distant seat of invisible (and parasitic) powers, rather than as the source of leadership in addressing national problems.

In the cities, the industrial working class was growing rapidly and began to play a new role in national affairs in the 1930s and 1940s, under the guidance of populist politicians. During this time, women organized to secure voting rights, and by mid-century most Latin American countries had universal suffrage. Primary education allowed a few workers to rise in the social scale and even join the thin ranks of an ethnically diverse middle class, but in the nonindustrial majority of countries, the people at large remained as isolated from the government as they had always been and continued their traditional political passivity. The illiterate mestizo, mulatto, and Amerindian peasants remained in abject conditions, dominated in every sense by the (often absentee) landowners and with no hope of the social and economic mobility that the cities offered to some degree.

The social and political complexion of a given Latin American country depended largely on the number of its immigrants between about 1890 and 1930. In a select group consisting of the ABC countries plus Uruguay and Costa Rica, immigration from Spain and Italy in particular was large enough to establish and maintain a European culture in the cities and extinguish whatever Amerindian culture the countryside may have once possessed. At first glance, these countries seemed to have favorable prospects for extensive and intensive development. With the exception of Brazil, they had little or no history of slavery and its accompanying social distinctions. Basic natural resources were generally adequate to abundant, and good farmland was in sufficient supply. In short, these countries seemed to have enough actual and potential wealth to meet their growing populations' needs for a long time to come *if* no human-made obstructions to the exploitation and distribution of that wealth were imposed.

It was precisely such obstructions that caused much of the social tension in Latin America in the twentieth century. In the ABC countries (less so in Uruguay and Costa Rica), the Creole large landholders and their caudillo partners in government prevented the land from being subdivided for the immigrant latecomers in the nineteenth and twentieth centuries. Settling the vast and underdeveloped countryside thus could not relieve social discontent in the cities. Mineral wealth such as Chile's copper or Venezuela's oil remained in a few, mainly foreign, hands. Industry and commerce were almost as tightly controlled as the fertile lands by the lack of available credit. In the absence of a vibrant economy that would act as the rising tide that lifts all ships, these nations attempted to find answers to their problems in political doctrine. After 1920 or so, the proffered solutions ranged from a demagogic nationalist populism to total dependency on foreign (meaning mostly U.S.) interests and investment.

Until recently, Latin America's most intractable social problems were in countries such as Colombia, Peru, and Bolivia, where a large Amerindian or mestizo population continued to rival the Iberian culture of the dominant Creoles. As late as the 1940s, the Creoles normally responded to the perceived menace by attempting to exclude the indigenous and mestizo peoples completely from national affairs. Only in recent years has the uppermost class accepted the impossibility of continued political segregation between themselves and the masses.

Now, the ancient chasms between the landowning class and their peon laborers and between the Creole elites and the masses have been further complicated by the widening gap between urbanites and rural dwellers. In the last forty years or so, the demographic picture has changed markedly everywhere in Latin America. Propelled by high birthrates as well as migration, the cities are growing at an incredible rate. Rural migrants must endure overcrowding, unsanitary makeshift accommodations, and the absence of even elementary public services (schools, police, pure water, and the like). In the meantime, the villages and small towns have become even less important in the affairs of the nation than before. Always a disproportionately urban-based economy, Latin America is becoming a series of huge heads (Mexico City now has an estimated population around 20 million) weakly supported by anemic bodies.

Unemployment, both urban and rural, is endemic and constant. No reliable figures are kept because it is impossible to do so, but perhaps one-third of the adults in the cities work in the informal economy. Income distribution is now as bad as or worse than it has ever been. Even by the standards of the developing world, Latin America has the most skewed distribution of cash income imaginable. A very small group of industrialists, large landowners, and import-export business owners are rewarded handsomely, while a very large number of unskilled urban and agricultural workers have next to nothing. In the middle, the number of professionals, white-collar employees, managers, and small business owners is increasing, but they are usually still too few, too unorganized, and insufficiently independent to play an important role in civic affairs.

ECONOMIC NATIONALISM

One result of acute social stratification and continuing economic dependency on foreigners has been the wave-like rise of radical reform movements with strongly nationalist overtones. Interestingly, the leaders of such protests have often been military men. The widespread foreign perception of Latin American military leaders as reactionaries who automatically uphold the status quo has become increasingly erroneous. Depending on the circumstances, they have frequently been at the forefront of economic nationalism, often sacrificing human rights to achieve their production goals.

Seeking to avoid a radical socialism that ran contrary to Latin individualism and would invite the active disapproval of the United States, the reform leaders of the past century were often strongly influenced by the idea of a corporate state in which all sectors of the population would supposedly find adequate representation. The most popular of these broad-based movements appeared in Mexico under leftist President Cárdenas in the 1930s and in Argentina a decade later under rightist Perón. In both cases, the labor union leadership became increasingly radical, causing backlashes against the populist regimes. In Argentina, the military ousted Perón and remained in control for thirty years. In contrast, Mexico's military has been subordinate to the civilian government since 1940.

Mexico Under Cárdenas

The spasmodic and multisourced revolution that took place in Mexico between 1910 and 1920 was, as has been mentioned, the only genuine social and political change in the first half of the twentieth century. The women who fought in the Mexican Revolution later led successful movements for women's equal rights. Out of the revolution finally came a single-party government committed to social equalization and redistribution of both wealth and power. In this mestizo country, where a small number of large landowners had held all power for generations, such goals were unprecedented—and unfulfillable. In the 1920s, the governing party (later termed the Institutional Revolutionary Party, or PRI), despite much talk, did little to advance social causes. But under the impact of the Great Depression and the Marxist experiment in Russia, President Cárdenas (governing 1934–1940) tried to give substance to some of the revolution's ideals. He confiscated and redistributed enough land to Amerindians and peasants to destroy the repressive hacienda system in southeastern Mexico. Cárdenas was the first Mexican president to visit the poverty-stricken state of Chiapas, where he met with Mayan villagers to hear their hopes and complaints. When Cárdenas expropriated seventeen U.S., British, and Dutch petroleum firms, the Mexican people celebrated their economic emancipation from foreign interests. However, agricultural and petroleum production declined as a result of his policies. The communist tendencies of the powerful labor unions triggered a reaction to the Cárdenas government, and most presidents since 1940 have been conservative. By insisting on sovereignty in all things, Cárdenas set the nationalistic pattern known as "Mexico for the Mexicans" that most of his successors in office have followed. His efforts to achieve security and a political voice for the lower classes, however, have generally not been followed, and the gap between the haves and the have-nots in Mexico remains vast. In 1992, the Mexican Congress officially ended the land redistribution program and signed the **North American Free Trade Association (NAFTA)** with Canada and the United States. The landless peasants of southern Mexico rebelled against the government's retraction of promises made during the revolution. However, their rebellion was quelled, and U.S. factories moved to Mexico in the 1990s, offering new jobs to the unemployed. Unfortunately for Mexico, many of these factories have since moved to Asian countries like China, where labor costs are even lower than in Mexico. Critics of NAFTA contend that neoliberalism has led Mexico to a contemporary version of the prerevolutionary dictatorship. To date, Mexico's national economy is still far from realizing its productive potential.

In the political arena, the PRI had long since become an intricate web of established social powers ranging from labor leaders to intellectuals, all of whom expected—and got—a calculated payoff for their support. Despite undoubted abuses, particularly corruption at the top, the Mexican system has recently allowed an increasing pluralism in politics. The old allocation of political powers solely to a few recognized groups broke down, and scandal plus incompetence has ended the PRI's former grip on high-level affairs. National elections in 2000 brought the leading opposition party to power, with promises yet unfulfilled of major structural reform. In the early twenty-first century, global recession, violent narcotics cartels, and low economic productivity threaten Mexico's stability and thwart the country's prospects for emerging from neocolonial status into a more democratic era. The PRI recaptured the presidency in 2012.

Argentina Under Perón

In Argentina in the 1940s, Perón and his military and industrialist backers were ardent nationalists who dreamed of making Argentina the dominant power in Latin America—a status for which it seemed destined by its size, natural resources, and human diversity. Colonel Perón was one of a group of officers who threw out the elected government in 1943. He soon made himself its leader, a charismatic caudillo reminiscent of Juan Manuel Rosas, the nineteenth-century dictator (see Chapter 38). Perón's pro-German sympathies guaranteed that the United States would condemn him, which all but ensured his election in 1946 on a vehemently nationalist platform. His wife Eva (the "Evita" of song and story) was a product of the slums who knew her people intimately. She was always at his side in public; her personal charisma and undoubtedly sincere concern for the Argentine working classes made her an idol whose popularity among the populace exceeded the colonel's. In terms of political impact, she was the most important woman in twentieth-century American politics, North or South. Her early death in 1952 was in a sense the beginning of the decline of the movement her husband headed.

Perón (or Evita) understood something that eluded most Latin American reformers: To overcome the apathy of the rural dwellers and the tradition of leaving government in the hands of a few, it was necessary to appeal to people in a way that they could respond to, directly and with passion. Such an appeal must concentrate on their many economic and social discontents, not on their political ideals. Perón played on this theme effectively, organizing huge rallies of the lower classes and making inflammatory speeches against the foreign and domestic "exploiters" while simultaneously, though quietly, assuring the entrepreneurs and big business of government contracts and concessions of unprecedented size. It was a fine balancing act between encouraging the egalitarian desires of the *descamisados* (dehs-cah-mee-SAH-dohs; "shirtless ones") and reassuring the rich that nothing unbearable was in store. Perón's new constitution put the federal government in charge of the national financial structure and economy. He nationalized foreign-owned transportation and communications companies at enormous cost to the nation. The unionized workers and the military sector enjoyed rising wages and lavish fringe benefits, while the agricultural sector languished under state-imposed price controls. Perón's misguided drive to rapid industrialization drew impoverished peasants to the cities in search of nonexistent jobs. Meanwhile, after World War II, worldwide demand declined for Argentine grain and meat, the nation's main source of income. The political and economic ineptitude of **Peronismo** had bankrupted Argentina.

Bettmann/Corbis

JUAN AND EVITA PERÓN. This 1951 photo shows the couple acceding to the "demand" of the Argentine people that they run for reelection.

By 1954, however, Perón was confronted by a gradually strengthening democratic opposition. Attempting to keep his popularity among the workers, he allowed the radical socialist wing of the *Peronistas* more prominence, which alienated his industrial and business support. In that year, he also made the mistake of taking on the Catholic Church—which had originally been mildly favorable toward Peronismo—by attacking its conservative higher clergy. In 1955, the military drove Perón into exile.

During the ensuing decades, the military or its puppets again ruled Argentina, brutally crushing any dissenters and giving way to civil rule only in 1982 after the self-incurred disaster of the brief Falkland Islands War with Britain. Only in the early 1990s did this potentially rich country stabilize politically and find its way—briefly—out of the social conflicts and mismanagement of the economy that mark its history. Like all of Latin America, its economic well-being and social harmony still largely depend on events and processes in which it is essentially a bystander, as the national bankruptcy of the 1990s again demonstrated.

The appeal of nationalism remains strong and will become stronger as the Latin Americans gradually come into contact with the world beyond their neighborhoods by means of international trade arrangements, such as NAFTA and the South American Community of Nations (CSN). It remains to be seen whether globalization will bring tangible benefit to the masses of the poor or just be a modern variant on the neocolonialism of previous times. The neoliberal tenets of privatization, free trade, and foreign investment may hold more promise for Latin America's rich than for its poor. Free trade pacts

Micheline Pelletier/Sygma/Corbis

MOTHERS OF THE MISSING: DEMONSTRATION BY ARGENTINA'S MOTHERS OF THE PLAZA OF MAYO. Weekly since 1977, mothers and grandmothers of offspring kidnapped in the 1980s by the secret police have gathered in Buenos Aires' main square outside the presidential palace to demand, "Where are they? What have you done to them?" The women wear white headscarves bearing their lost children's names. Their constant vigil brought international attention to the atrocities committed by the military junta during the "dirty war" waged against the people. Fewer than one hundred of the thousands of kidnapped innocents have been found alive. In Argentina and in Chile, after the fall of the military regimes, the Mothers of the Missing continued to gather, demanding punishment for the perpetrators of these crimes.

do not necessarily lead to fair trade at fair prices for peasants and workers. In any case, those who clamor for political power in the name of "the people" will always find a ready audience in this sadly unbalanced society. What Mexican peasants saw in Cárdenas and Argentine descamisados in Perón was a leader who, whatever his faults, claimed to stand on *their* side of the social and economic barricades, and that was a rarity they appreciated. Beginning in 2000 and until his death in 2013, Venezuela's caustically anti-U.S. president, Hugo Chávez, spearheaded a new populist movement in South America. Chávez aimed to counteract U.S. domination of the region by allying himself with Cuba's Castro and other socialist neighbors.

RELATIONS WITH THE UNITED STATES

What about the powerful neighbor to the north? During the first two-thirds of the twentieth century, Uncle Sam repeatedly played a heavy-handed and frankly conservative role in Latin American international affairs. There is no doubt that in ways both open and covert, Washington was the court of final appeal in Latin foreign relations and, in some cases, not just foreign relations.

The United States first began to pay close attention to Latin America during the Spanish-American War (1898–1900), which was fought, in part, over the rights of the Cuban people to independence. In the ensuing thirty years, Washington intervened at will in Latin and Caribbean affairs. Incidents ranged from Theodore Roosevelt's creation of Panama as a suitable place to build his desired canal, to the sending of armed forces against Mexico and Haiti, and the use of the Marines to squelch the rebels of General Augusto César Sandino—the original *Sandinistas*—in Nicaragua.

After World War I, U.S. capital and finance rushed in to replace European investors. The dependence of some of the Central American **banana republics** on the plantations of the United Fruit Company was merely the most notorious example of the economic imperialism that was practiced throughout Latin America. Cuba's huge sugarcane farms and mills were 80 percent owned by U.S. investors; U.S. firms using U.S. engineers brought in the big oil strikes in Venezuela; Mexico's original petroleum fields were dependencies of U.S. firms until nationalization; and 20 percent of the land surface of Mexico's border states was owned or leased by foreign investors in the 1920s—to name only a few examples. Mexicans lamented being "so close to the U.S. and so far from God."

But the story of Latin dependency on the United States has another side. Had it not been for U.S. investment and commerce, the countries to the south would have been even less developed economically and would have sunk deeper into their obsolete system of production and consumption. Until World War II, it is largely true that the Caribbean and northern Latin America (with the exception of Cárdenas's Mexico) were U.S. colonies in everything but name. The question remains: What would have been the region's fate in this period in the absence of the United States? Through their own efforts and expertise, they probably would not have achieved reasonable living standards for even a small segment of their peoples during the first half of the past century (and perhaps not in the second, either). If the U.S. capitalists had not been involved, would Latin Americans have found more benevolent and selfless sources of help outside the Americas? It seems doubtful. (See the box on Arts and Culture for a different perspective on this issue.)

In Franklin D. Roosevelt's presidency (1933–1945), the United States embarked on a **Good Neighbor Policy**, treating the Latins more as sovereign nations than as colonies. For many years, no troops were landed to ensure a "stability" acceptable to the United States, but still no one had any doubt where true sovereignty

Arts and Culture

The Solitude of Latin America: Nobel Lecture by Gabriel García Márquez in 1982

Colombian novelist Gabriel García Márquez (1927) captured the stranger-than-fiction reality of Latin America by narrating legends, fantasy, and historical facts as equally true elements of the Latin American identity. He is best known for his novel, *One Hundred Years of Solitude* (1967), which vividly describes the effects of the United Fruit Company on a coastal Colombian town. García Márquez belonged to the first generation of Spanish-American writers who achieved international acclaim, beginning in the 1960s. He received the Nobel Prize for Literature in 1982, when military dictatorships still dominated Latin America. His Nobel Lecture in Uppsala, Sweden, described Latin America's problems and its creative potential, as well as denouncing misguided foreign interference during the Cold War. The following segment is from the last half of the speech.

> [Between 1970 and 1982], the Europeans... have been struck, with ever greater force, by the unearthly tidings of Latin America.... We have not had a moment's rest.... There have been five wars and seventeen military *coups*, there emerged a diabolic dictator who is carrying out, in God's name, the first Latin American ethnocide of our time. In the meantime, twenty million Latin American children died before the age of one—more than have been born in Europe since 1970. Those missing because of repression number nearly 120 000, which is as if no one could account for all the inhabitants of Uppsala [Sweden].... Numerous women arrested while pregnant have given birth in Argentine prisons, yet nobody knows the whereabouts and identity of their children who were furtively adopted or sent to an orphanage by order of the military authorities. Because they tried to change this state of things, nearly 200,000 men and women have died throughout the continent, and over 100,000 lost their lives in three small and ill-fated countries of Central America: Nicaragua, El Salvador and Guatemala. If this had happened in the United States, the corresponding figure would be that of 1,600,000 violent deaths in four years.
>
> And if these difficulties, whose essence we share, hinder us, it is understandable that the rational talents on this side of the world [in Europe], exalted in the contemplation of their own cultures, should have found themselves without valid means to interpret us.... Venerable Europe would perhaps be more perceptive if it tried to see us in its own past. If only it recalled that London took three hundred years to build its first city wall... ; that Rome labored in a gloom of uncertainty for twenty centuries....
>
> Latin America neither wants, nor has any reason, to be a pawn without a will of its own.... Why is the originality so readily granted us in literature so mistrustfully denied us in our difficult attempts at social change? Why think that the social justice sought by progressive Europeans for their own countries cannot also be a goal for Latin America, with different methods for dissimilar conditions? No: the immeasurable violence and pain of our history are the result of age-old inequities and untold bitterness, and not a conspiracy plotted three thousand leagues from our home. But many European leaders and thinkers have thought so, ... as if it were impossible to find another destiny than to live at the mercy of the two great masters of the world. This, my friends, is the very scale of our solitude....

ANALYZE AND INTERPRET

What does this selection convey about the Western World's perception of Latin America? What historical events are highlighted? What comparisons does the author make between Latin America as contrasted with Europe and the United States? During the Cold War, how were Latin American countries "pawns" of the super-powers?

lay in the Western Hemisphere. With World War II and the coming of the Cold War, Washington became more concerned about the political allegiance of the Latin states. In treaties signed immediately after the war, the United States pledged political and economic assistance to the other Latin American signatories. In 1948, the **Organization of American States (OAS)** was founded under American auspices and served several useful commercial, cultural, and legal purposes besides its primary one of assuring democratic and pro-Western governments in the hemisphere.

But the real catalyst for U.S. activity was the coming of **Fidel Castro** (fee-DELL CAST-roh) to revolutionary power in Cuba with a radical program of reform. Originally the organizer of a hopelessly outnumbered band of idealists, Castro rather surprisingly overturned the corrupt and unpopular, but U.S.-backed, Fulgencio Batista government at the beginning of 1959. After a year of increasing tension, he declared himself a Marxist and began systematically persecuting those who openly disagreed with that philosophy, while denouncing the United States as the oppressor

LAW AND GOVERNMENT

Fidel Castro's Manifesto

Fidel Castro attempted to begin a revolutionary movement in Cuba in 1956, three years before a second attempt was successful. The attack on the Moncada Barracks was a failure, and Castro was captured, but he was given an opportunity by the trial judges to broadcast his appeal to the Cuban people. His summation in his own defense is titled *History Will Absolve Me.* Cuban revolutionaries regard it as the fundamental statement of Castro's beliefs:

> When we speak of the people we do not mean the comfortable ones, the conservative elements of the nation, who welcome any regime of oppression, any dictatorship, any despotism, prostrating themselves before the master of the moment.... When we speak of struggle, the people means the vast unredeemed masses to whom all make promises and whom all deceive; we mean the people who yearn for a better, more dignified and more just nation...
>
> Seven hundred thousand Cubans without work....
>
> Five hundred thousand farm laborers, inhabiting miserable shacks, who work four months of the year and starve the rest....
>
> Four hundred thousand industrial laborers and stevedores whose retirement funds have been embezzled, whose benefits are being taken away... whose salaries pass from the hands of the boss to the moneylender....
>
> One hundred thousand small farmers who live and die working on land that is not theirs, looking at it in sadness as Moses looked at the Promised Land, to die without ever owning it....
>
> Thirty thousand teachers and professors who are so devoted, dedicated and necessary to the better destiny of future generations and who are so badly treated and paid....
>
> Twenty thousand small business men, weighted down by debt ... and harangued by a plague of grafting and venal officials.
>
> Ten thousand young professionals...who come forth from school with their degrees, anxious to work and full of hope only to find themselves at a dead end with all doors closed....
>
> These are the people, the ones who know misfortune and, therefore, are capable of fighting with limitless courage!
>
> To the people whose desperate roads through life have been paved with the bricks of betrayal and false promises, we were not going to say: "We will eventually give you what you need," but rather—"Here you have it, fight for it with all your might, so that liberty and happiness can be yours!"

Popperfoto/Getty Images

FIDEL CASTRO IN HAVANA. The Cuban revolutionary leader enjoys his victorious entry into Havana after chasing out the corrupt Batista regime in 1959. In 2008 the ailing Castro ceded power to his brother Raúl, who has begun Cuba's transition to a more open economy.

ANALYZE AND INTERPRET

How closely did Castro's actions follow his words when he did manage to secure power in Cuba? Should it have been such an unpleasant surprise to the U.S. government of Dwight Eisenhower when Castro proceeded to nationalize all U.S. industrial properties? Do Castro's statements affect your own understanding of how he has been able to retain power in Cuba for more than forty years?

Source: Fidel Castro, *History Will Absolve* Me (London: Cape, 1968).

of freedom-loving Latin Americans. After he nationalized the extensive U.S. business interests in Cuba, a state of near-war existed between the two countries, culminating in the abortive Bay of Pigs invasion by U.S.-financed anti-Castroites in 1961. A year later, the placement of long-range missiles on the island by the Soviets brought the world to the brink of nuclear war (see Chapter 46).

Since then, relations between the Castro government and Washington have remained frigid. The Cuban revolution, despite some real achievements for the people of the island (literacy, public health, technical education, housing), has proved unable to guarantee a decent material life, especially because Castro's original Soviet and Chinese supporters have collapsed or withdrawn their aid. The revolution has also proved unsuitable for export to the rest of the continent, as Castro had once intended. No other Latin state ever "went communist," although a few Marxist-leaning governments have been elected—notably, those of Salvador Allende (ah-YEHN-day) in Chile in 1971 and of the Sandinistas (sahn-dee-NEES-tahs) in Nicaragua in the 1980s. All of these have been overtly and covertly undermined by the United States, as have the attempts by Marxist-led guerrillas or terrorists to seize power. The fiasco of Marxist theory and practice in Eastern Europe (see Chapter 52) and the manifest disinterest of the Chinese in political intervention have all but eliminated this threat to capitalist and democratic governments in the continent. The termination of the Cold War has had a beneficial effect on U.S.–Latin American relations because the United States no longer worries that some type of hostile Soviet puppet regime will be installed in these near neighbors. On the other hand, since the 1990s, the United States has missed opportunities to provide leadership in hemispheric trade agreements; meanwhile, Brazil, Chile, and Venezuela have increased trade with Asia and Europe. Finally, time will tell whether the United States will again take the lead in controlling immigration and in fighting drug trafficking.

The U.S. Role in Recent Latin Affairs

In the early days of the John F. Kennedy administration (1961–1963), under the emblem of anti-Castro action, the United States entered into an **Alliance for Progress** with the Latin American states. More than $10 billion was set aside for economic development loans and credits, more than twice the money allocated to postwar Europe under the Marshall Plan. But as so often happens with government programs that are intended to make a quick impression on the electorate, much of the money went to make the rich richer or wound up in the wrong pockets. The single most effective, externally funded program for Latin American development was the quiet work on improving crop yields, done mainly in Mexico during the 1950s and 1960s. This botanical laboratory project gave a tremendous boost to world food grain production, resulting in some places in the Green Revolution that we have mentioned previously. Its success in greatly stimulating rice, wheat, and other food grain production is a main reason why the threatened world famine has thus far been confined to regions of Africa and has not menaced Latin America and the entire developing world.

In the last decades of the twentieth century, U.S. involvement with the Caribbean nations again became openly interventionist and reactionary, but generally within dimensions that the OAS as a whole was willing to approve. Presidents Ronald Reagan (Grenada, Nicaragua), George H. W. Bush (Panama), and Bill Clinton (Haiti) acted forcefully to protect what they perceived to be U.S. strategic, political, or economic interests in the area. Ongoing efforts funded and guided by the North Americans to control narcotic drug smuggling from several Latin states into the United States have drawn further U.S. intervention, but a return to the pre-1930 system of "gunboat diplomacy" by the United States is hardly possible, even were it desirable. A major voluntary change in the levers of control occurred in 2000 when the U.S.-built-and-managed Panama Canal became part of the sovereign territory of Panama. Pending political questions in the Caribbean basin include possible independence for Puerto Rico (a U.S. territory for the past century) and the fate of Cuba after the inevitable demise of Fidel Castro and his brother, Raúl, who now rules in his place.

CURRENT ISSUES AND PROBLEMS

In Latin America as elsewhere, economic and social issues are linked together and have had numerous direct political repercussions. In Latin America as a whole, just as in Africa, probably the highest-priority long-term social problem is controlling a rate of population growth (2.9 percent) that is too high for the available resources. As in Africa, several governments would contest this assessment, saying that faulty or nonexistent access to resources, both domestic and foreign, generates most social frictions in their countries. There is, in fact, something to be said for this argument. In the eyes of many Latin Americans, the developed world, and especially the United States, has taken unfair and shortsighted advantage of the underdeveloped world during the past century and continues to do so in the following ways:

1. The terms of foreign trade—that is, the rate at which raw materials are exchanged for manufactures, consumer goods, and necessary services—are loaded in favor of the developed countries.
2. Financial credits have been extended to the underdeveloped American nations with unrealistically high interest and short terms, which nearly guarantees that the loans cannot and will not be repaid on time, if at all. This condition then becomes the basis of demanding still-harsher terms for the next loan.
3. Currently, the underdeveloped nations are being pressed to avoid using the main resources they possess—what nature has given them—to ensure a more secure future for the developed minority. Environmental concerns are being used to justify

interference in internal affairs such as how many trees are cut down, or where beef cattle should graze, or how many fish should be caught.

What are we to make of these complaints? First, there can be little doubt that Latin America, like the rest of the developing world, has been forced to accept consistently disadvantageous trade conditions while getting only an occasional and undependable sop in the form of World Bank or bilateral loans and grants. Since World War II, a ton of wheat, a bag of coffee, or a container of bananas purchases less and less of the electrical machinery, office equipment, or insurance policies that the developed countries sell to the underdeveloped nations.

Whether the second accusation is true is debatable. Much of the waste, corruption, or misuse of international credits was indisputably the work of recipients in the developing countries, who had little fear of ever being held personally responsible. At the same time, the international lending community has rarely if ever "pulled" loans that were clearly being diverted to the illicit benefit of individuals. In any case, the terms of the international loans extended to the Latin countries in the past have been notably more severe than those granted to Africa and Asia. The efforts to repay have handicapped Latin America's domestic investment and contributed to the fragile condition of the current Latin economies.

The third charge has a complex background but demands a decisive answer because it will affect us all in a powerful fashion. The Latin Americans (and others) are saying in essence, "You, the developed industrial societies, have now awakened to the dangers of pollution and abuse of the environment but want us, the less developed, to pay the price of implementing rational policies while you enjoy the short-term benefits of irrationality." It was all right, in other words, for nineteenth-century American timber companies to cut down every tree over a foot thick in Michigan, but it is not all right for twentieth-century Brazilian timber companies to cut down mature mahogany in the Amazon basin. Multiply this example by hundreds, and you will have the position adopted by the Latin Americans and most other leaders of developing countries in response to the environmental concerns of the developed world. Interestingly, organized indigenous groups in the Amazon basin are demanding a voice in planning for sustainable use of the rain forests in the future.

The flight to the cities we have already mentioned in connection with modern Africa is equally strong in Latin America. Towns such as Lima or Bogotá, which were still slumbering in the early twentieth century, have been overwhelmed with peasant migrants in the last forty years. The majority live in unfinished, do-it-yourself neighborhoods that spring up in an ever-widening circle around the older city. Many of the inhabitants of these barrios have established a settled, even secure life, but many others are living on a tightrope, balancing petty and sporadic income against the constant demands of food and fuel. Much of the urban population seems to be "living on air," hustling up unskilled work on a day-to-day basis or depending on networks of kin and friends to see them through until they can return the favor. (See the Society and Economy box for more about urban migration.)

Rich and Poor

The chasm between rich and poor is deeper and more apparent in Latin American countries than anywhere else. Africa has relatively few rich and not many people who are well-to-do. In most of Asia, wealth is fairly evenly distributed except in one or two cities in each country. But in South America, the extremes are growing, while the number of those in the middle is more or less stagnant. There are a great many poor and a very small but growing number of rich—and the contrast between them is a powder keg in most Latin American countries.

So visible and disturbing is the polarization of Latin American society that the Catholic Church, long the main bastion of conservatism and reaction, has taken the lead in country after country as a voice for the poor. **Liberation theology**, an unusual combination of Marxist social theory and Catholic humanitarianism, has come to life in several countries, notably Brazil, to speak for the common people against a social and economic system that has exploited them for many generations.

Hundreds of priests, nuns, and higher officials of the church were imprisoned or even murdered by military and civilian reactionaries. Archbishop Oscar Romero (roh-MEH-roh) of El Salvador was shot down while saying mass in his own cathedral because he spoke out against the bloody excesses of the military in the civil war in El Salvador in the 1980s. The Romeros of two generations before would have been blessing the army's guns.

Changing Styles in Government

Latin America since 1930 has thus tried several different styles of government—including socialism, corporatism, and nationalist populism—in an effort to achieve greater social justice and economic prosperity. Most of these have quickly degenerated into dictatorship. All have proved either ineffective or corrupt or were unable to retain their momentum. Castro's Cuba remains the one experiment with scientific socialism, and even its defenders acknowledge that it has failed its people economically in the last twenty years.

In the 1960s, it appeared quite possible that Latin American Marxists, inspired by Castro's success, would attempt to seize power in several countries. Economic nationalism was faltering, and little social reform had

SOCIETY AND ECONOMY

The Human Face of Modern Urbanization: Pascuala's Story

Megacities from Mexico City to Santiago, Chile, and Rio de Janeiro, Brazil, are the result of massive, uncontrollable migrations from impoverished and strife-ridden rural Latin America during the second half of the last century. The thousands of newcomers who arrive daily depend at first on the hospitality of family or friends who preceded them to the city. Then they scrabble to find (or invent) jobs as "informals" in the dynamic, unofficial informal economy (whose productivity equals that of the official economy that is reflected in the statistics). Next, they join others to build temporary huts on unoccupied lands in remote outskirts of the city. After ten or twenty years of persistent political activism and unrelenting toil, the shantytown eventually becomes a settlement of owner-built houses incorporated by the city, provided with water and utilities, and linked to the urban public transportation system. The inhabitants must cobble together two or three jobs as construction workers, street vendors or performers, or domestic servants in the faraway city centers, commuting hours each way. Because they are officially invisible, they have no benefits or employment guarantees. They spend their scant leisure time thinking of new ways to earn money at home. The transition from rural village to megacity is wrenching: Family structures and traditional lifeways often disintegrate. Yet this precarious and often-dangerous life is preferable to starving in their villages of origin, where the small plots of rocky soil cannot sustain families.

One of urban migration's rare success stories is that of Pascuala (pahs-KWAH-lah), a single mother and informal worker living on the outskirts of Lima, Peru, in the 1980s. Pascuala came from an Aymara Indian village in the mountains of Peru, where she left school after first grade to shepherd her father's animals. As a young girl, she began working as a maid for a fashion-conscious wealthy woman in Lima. Pascuala convinced her mistress to send her to seamstress school, where she excelled. When her middle-class boyfriend abandoned her and their baby and she lost her job as a domestic, Pascuala was determined to support herself by sewing. Her business, at first piecework done at home, expanded to a small market stall where she befriended a helpful older woman vendor who helped her get a vendor's license. Eventually, Pascuala rented space in a shopping mall, where she employed several seamstresses, also Aymara Indian migrants to Lima. Pascuala now has a small house and drives her shiny new car when she visits her family in the village.

ANALYZE AND INTERPRET

Comment on the obstacles that Pascuala overcame as she advanced. Conversely, what factors helped her to establish her business? In your opinion, what type of government would be best for urban poor people?

Source for Pascuala's story: "Simply Pascuala" by José María Salcedo, pages 452–455 in *The Peru Reader* (Durham, N.C.: Duke University Press, 1995).

been achieved. Terrorist activity became a menace to the upper classes in Argentina and Brazil, where urban guerrillas operated. The military establishment in country after country pushed aside the ineffectual politicians and governed directly on a platform of law and order. Encouraged by government policy makers, Western banks loaned huge sums to the Latin American nations. Foreign debt increased by more than twelve times in the 1970s, to a point where, due to the slightest economic reversal, the Latin American nations could not pay even the interest on time. A wild inflation was the main enemy of reform plans. At one time, the value of the Argentine peso against the U.S. dollar was dropping at the rate of 10 percent per day.

The 1970s were the low point for constitutional government. At one point in that decade, only three of the twenty Latin American nations had elected governments. Everywhere else, the military attempted to meet the increasing demands for economic reform by going outside the political process and ignoring opponents' civil rights. In **Operation Condor**, military dictators of South America agreed clandestinely to cooperate in capturing and eliminating any dissidents—particularly the younger generation, which was automatically suspect. The secret police of Argentina, Brazil, and Chile kidnapped untold thousands of innocent young people, most of whom disappeared forever. The mothers of the missing (desaparecidos) relentlessly protested against the repressive regimes and demanded that justice be done. (See previous section "Argentina under Perón")

In the 1980s, with Argentina and Brazil again leading the way, the pendulum swung back to civilian rule; by the end of that decade, only a few countries were still ruled by men in uniform. The military in Buenos Aires stepped down in disgrace after foolishly provoking a war with Britain over the Falkland Islands, and a few years later, the Brazilian generals gave up power to the first duly elected government in a quarter century.

The emergence from a century and a half of neocolonialism is a painfully slow process that will continue well

Julio Etchart / Alamy Limited

RIGOBERTA MENCHÚ. This Guatemalan activist of Mayan descent won the Nobel Peace Prize in 1992 for speaking out on behalf of the downtrodden Amerindian masses. Latin American women activists of all classes, from peasants to professionals, now participate in politics.

into the twenty-first century even in the most hopeful scenarios. Democratic, constitutional government is still a fragile flower in most of the continent, but it made some strong gains in the 1980s and 1990s. Even in the most precarious new democracies, there are more freedoms and an unprecedented inclusion of ethnic and racial minorities in politics at all levels. Will democracy take root in Latin America, or will authoritarianism and militarism emerge once again? The outcome will depend largely on whether and how socioeconomic discontent is resolved. In the early twenty-first century, several newly elected Latin American presidents are moderate social democrats who support helping the poor while pursuing economically conservative policies (and rejecting the neopopulist movement of Chávez). One of these leaders was Chile's Michelle Bachelet (bah-che-LET), the first woman elected president of a South American country (in 2006).

SUMMARY

The twenty nations in Latin and Caribbean America have overriding similarities, despite some differences. Everywhere, policy makers are concerned with the question of economic development—how to achieve it and how to manage it. Everywhere, the relationship between the United States and the others is vital to the future stability and prosperity of the continent. Various types of economic nationalism, sometimes introduced by the military, have been the Latin Americans' response to their status as poor relations of the more developed nations of the world. Cárdenas in Mexico and Perón in Argentina were perhaps the most noted examples in the last eighty years, but many others have appeared and will continue to do so. Sixty years ago, Castro offered a Marxist response to neocolonial status in Cuba, but Marxism has had minimal appeal outside that country, despite initial efforts to spread it. Its future is dim.

Social problems, especially the unequal distribution of wealth and the pressures generated by a high birthrate, haunt the continent south of the Rio Grande. One of the most striking manifestations of these problems is the uncontrollable growth of the cities and their shantytown surroundings. Another is the widespread street crime and law evasion. Despite repeated populist promises of thoroughgoing reform, political solutions have been sporadic and partial at best. Foreign aid has been both sparse and undependable over the longer term. Nevertheless, after the failure of the military regimes of the 1970s, there has been a vigorous recovery in parliamentary government, with increasing numbers of women and ethnic minority participants. Since the 1990s, some hopeful signs have indicated that constitutional democracy and self-determination will triumph permanently if the overbearing socioeconomic and environmental crises can be mastered. Currently, continent-wide initiatives exist to develop scientific investigation, democratize technologies of communication and information, and develop sustainable tourism that boosts economies and preserves the environment.

IDENTIFICATION TERMS

Test your knowledge of this chapter's key concepts by defining the following terms. If you can not recall the meaning of certain terms, refresh your memory by looking up the boldfaced term in the chapter, turning to the Glossary at the end of the book, or accessing the terms on the CourseMate website at **www.cengagebrain.com.**

Alliance for Progress
banana republics
Fidel Castro
Good Neighbor Policy
Liberation theology
North American Free Trade Association (NAFTA)
Operation Condor
Organization of American States (OAS)
Peronismo

FOR FURTHER REFLECTION

1. Briefly describe the main styles of government attempted in twentieth-century Latin America. Generally speaking, what were the benefits and drawbacks in each case?
2. Trace the development of relations between the United States and Latin America in the twentieth century. What role do you think the United States should play in Latin America in the future?

TEST YOUR KNOWLEDGE

Test your knowledge of this chapter by answering the following questions. Complete answers appear at the end of the book. You may find even more quiz questions on the CourseMate website at **www.cengagebrain.com**.

1. After the Great Depression of the 1930s began, the larger Latin American states
   a. became totally dependent on imported goods.
   b. carried out long-delayed agrarian reforms to favor the peons.
   c. started on a program of economic nationalism.
   d. suffered economic collapse.
   e. joined the Pan American Union and became economically successful.
2. Mexican President Lázaro Cárdenas was
   a. very socially conscious.
   b. a ruthless dictator.
   c. a communist in league with Soviet Russia.
   d. a fascist, closely allied to Italy and Germany.
   e. concerned about maintaining good relations with the United States.
3. The most widely recognized female in twentieth-century Latin American history was probably
   a. St. Theresa.
   b. Eva Perón.
   c. Carmen Miranda.
   d. Madonna.
   e. Michelle Bachelet.
4. Juan Perón was forced from power in 1955 by
   a. a mass uprising.
   b. a free election.
   c. U.S. intervention.
   d. a military plot.
   e. ill health.
5. The most successful Latin American revolutions of the twentieth century were in
   a. Nicaragua and Venezuela.
   b. Guatemala and Mexico.
   c. Mexico and Cuba.
   d. Mexico and Bolivia.
   e. Haiti and Cuba.
6. President Franklin D. Roosevelt is responsible for implementing
   a. the Good Neighbor Policy.
   b. Dollar Diplomacy.
   c. the United Fruit Company.
   d. the Panama Canal treaty.
   e. the Alliance for Progress.
7. Latin Americans would most accurately be described as viewing U.S. concerns for the environment of Central and South America as
   a. compassionate.
   b. unnecessary.
   c. misguided.
   d. arbitrary.
   e. hypocritical.
8. The strongest voice for the poor in many Latin American countries has been
   a. military strongmen.
   b. the wives of government leaders.
   c. intellectuals.
   d. democratically elected representatives.
   e. the Catholic church.
9. In the 1970s, the government and politics of most Latin American countries experienced
   a. a swing toward the Marxist left.
   b. intervention by military-based dictatorships.
   c. a swing toward social welfare programs.
   d. a renewal of clerical influence.
   e. a process of democratization.
10. In the later 1980s and 1990s, Latin America experienced a strong movement toward
    a. democratically elected governments.
    b. military takeovers.
    c. Marxist dictatorships.
    d. fascist governments.
    e. state capitalism.

CourseMate

Visit the CourseMate website at **www.cengagebrain.com** for additional study tools and review materials for this chapter.

51 The Reemergence of the Muslim World

The people [of the Muslim world] sometimes make much more history than they consume locally. —SAKI (H. H. MUNRO)

1915	McMahon Letter
1916	Sykes-Picot Agreement
1917	Balfour Declaration on Palestine
1920s	Ataturk leads Turkey; Saudi Arabia united by Ibn Saud
1946–1948	Mandate territories become independent states
1948	Israel founded; Israeli-Arab War begins
1956	Suez Canal nationalized by Egypt
1964	Palestine Liberation Organization (PLO) founded to fight Israel
1967	Six-Day War
1973	Organization of Petroleum Exporting Countries (OPEC) oil boycott
1979	Iranian Revolution; Soviet intervention in Afghanistan; Camp David Accords end warfare between Egypt and Israel
1980–1988	Iraq-Iran War
1985	Soviet withdrawal from Afghanistan
1991	Gulf War against Iraq
1993	Peace Agreement between Israel and PLO
1999	Renewed Israeli–Palestinian confrontation
2001	al-Qaida attack on World Trade Center
2002	U.S. occupation of Afghanistan and Iraq
2011	Osama bin Laden killed
2011–2012	Arab Spring

CHAPTER OUTLINE

For the first time in centuries, the Muslim peoples are at the center of world events and are playing major roles in international affairs. The term *Muslim world* refers to far more than the Middle East or the Arab countries. Muslims now number about one-sixth of humanity, and Islam is the dominant religion in thirty-eight countries reaching from Southeast Asia to the Atlantic coast of Africa. The 148 million Arabs are mostly Muslims, but a great many of the 1 billion Muslims are not Arabs. In this chapter, however, we will focus on the Arab Middle East because that is where the major events and processes defining the Muslim relationship with the world have taken place in the last century.

One of the most important factors in Middle Eastern history over the last seventy years has been geology. By far the largest known oilfields in the world are located under Saudi Arabia and the other Persian Gulf Muslim countries. Their development was the key to the massive change in relations between Muslims and non-Muslims in the later twentieth century, particularly after the oil boycott of 1973.

Another major component of modern Middle East history, Arab nationalism, was originally directed against the Turkish overlords, and it had become so strong by the time of World War I that the British found the Arabs willing allies in the fight against their fellow Muslims. The Arabs' reward was supposed to be an independent state, reaching from Egypt to Iraq and headed by the Hashimite family of *shaykhs* in Arabia, who had been among the most prominent of the British allies during the war.

Contradictory wartime diplomatic deals made by the French, British, and Italians in 1916–1917 ended the Arabs' dream of a large, independent state, however. In effect, Turkish prewar imperial rule was replaced by European rule. The postwar Near Eastern Arab lands were converted into **mandates**, which were made the legal responsibility of the League of Nations but placed under the direct administrative rule of the British and French until such time as the Arabs proved their ability to act as responsible sovereign powers. Syria and Lebanon were French mandates from 1919 to 1946, and Jordan, Palestine, and Iraq were British mandates. When the Hashimite-led nationalists protested and rebelled, they were put down with decisive military action. Egypt, where the British had had an occupation force since 1882, got a slightly better arrangement. There, nationalism was strong enough to induce the British to grant the Egyptians pro-forma independence in 1922. British troops remained, however, and real independence was withheld until the 1950s because of British concerns about the Suez Canal and their "lifeline to India."

During the 1920s and 1930s, the small gains effected by individual Arab groups gave momentum to nationalist pan-Arabism, a movement that tried to get Arabs everywhere to submerge their differences and unite under one political center. The example of Saudi Arabia was held up as a possible model. Under conservative shaykh Ibn Saud, most of the Arabian Peninsula was unified in the 1920s by conquest and voluntary association and turned into a poverty-ridden but sovereign state. But the pan-Arabists could show few other gains by the time World War II broke out. The colonial grip on individual regions was too strong, and the disunity and jealousies that had plagued Arab politics for a long time showed no sign of abating.

THE TURKISH REPUBLIC

The exception to the continued subordination of the Muslim states or societies was the new Republic of Turkey. In the aftermath of its defeat as Germany's ally in World War I, the sultan's government had lost all credibility in Turkish eyes. Backed by Great Britain, the Greek government attempted in 1919 to realize the "Great Idea" of restoring the former Byzantine Empire and making the interior of Turkey (Anatolia) once more a Greek colony. A Greek army landed on the Turkish coast and began to move inland.

At this critical point, a leader emerged who almost single-handedly brought his people back from the edge of legal annihilation. This was Mustafa Kemal, called **Ataturk** (father of Turkey). Kemal had been a colonel in the Ottoman army. In 1919–1921, he organized the national resistance to the invaders and won a decisive victory against the poorly led Greeks. Among the defeated in World War I, Turkey alone was able to secure an eventual revision of the original peace. The new treaty recognized the full sovereignty of the Turkish state within the borders it now has. The former Arab provinces were abandoned to the Western mandates.

But this was no longer Ottoman Turkey. Kemal was elected the first president (with near-dictatorial powers) of the new parliamentary republic. Until his death in 1938, Kemal retained the presidency as he drove Turkey and the Turks to a systematic break with the past. Modernization and Westernization were the twin pillars of Kemal's policies as he focused on separating Turkish civil society from Islamic culture.

In every visible and invisible way Kemal could devise, the citizens of modern Turkey were distinguished from their Islamic ancestors. Western-style dress was introduced and even made mandatory for government workers. The veil was abolished. The Latin alphabet replaced the revered Arabic script. Women were made legally equal to men and could divorce their husbands. Polygamy was forbidden. Western schooling was introduced and made compulsory for both sexes. A new legal code was introduced, based on Western models and allowing no preference for Muslims. The capital was moved from the ethnically half-Greek Istanbul to the more-Turkish Ankara.

By the time of his death, Kemal had kept his promise to do for the Turks what Peter the Great had attempted to do for the Russians: to thrust them forward several generations through the abandonment of their Islamic base and through bringing them more into line with twentieth-century Western civilization. Despite intense resistance from conservative Muslim circles, Kemal had managed to turn his people into a superficially secular society in less than twenty years. He had also provided a model that was emulated by other, like-minded reformers all over the non-Western world.

PALESTINE/ISRAEL

The thorniest of all problems in the Middle East after World War I was the fate of the British mandate of Palestine (later, Israel). Hoping to draw the Arabs into the war against the Turks, the British government began negotiations with one of the principal leaders of

LAW AND GOVERNMENT

The McMahon Letter to the Sharif of Mecca, 1915, and the Balfour Declaration, 1917

Sir Henry McMahon was the British High Commissioner in Egypt and Husayn ibn Ali al-Hashimi was the Sharif of Mecca when the following letter was written in October 1915. In 1915 and 1916, McMahon wrote Husayn to ask for Arab support against the Ottoman Empire, which was fighting on the side of Germany and Austria against the Allied nations. To get this assistance, Britain had to promise its support for an independent Arab state at the end of the war.

> As for those regions lying within those frontiers wherein Great Britain is free to act without detriment to the interests of her ally, France, I am empowered in the name of the Government of Great Britain to give the following assurances and make the following reply to your letter:
>
> 1. Subject to the above modifications, Great Britain is prepared to recognise and support the independence of the Arabs in all the regions within the limits demanded by the Sherif of Mecca.
> 2. Great Britain will guarantee the Holy Places against all external aggression and will recognise their inviolability.
> 3. When the situation admits, Great Britain will give to the Arabs her advice and will assist them to establish what may appear to be the most suitable forms of government in those various territories.
> 4. On the other hand, it is understood that the Arabs have decided to seek the advice and guidance of Great Britain only, and that such European advisers and officials as may be required for the formation of a sound form of administration will be British.
> 5. With regard to the vilayets [Ottoman provinces] of Bagdad and Basra, the Arabs will recognise that the established position and interests of Great Britain necessitate special administrative arrangements in order to secure these territories from foreign aggression, to promote the welfare of the local populations and to safeguard our mutual economic interests.
>
> I am convinced that this declaration will assure you beyond all possible doubt of the sympathy of Great Britain towards the aspirations of her friends the Arabs and will result in a firm and lasting alliance, the immediate results of which will be the expulsion of the Turks from the Arab countries and the freeing of the Arab peoples from the Turkish yoke, which for so many years has pressed heavily upon them.

Source: Great Britain, *Parliamentary Papers*, 1939, Misc. No. 3, Cmd. 5957.

This letter from the British Foreign Secretary to Lord Rothschild was intended to curry Jewish support for the Allies in the First World War:

> Foreign Office
> November 2nd, 1917
> Dear Lord Rothschild:
>
> I have much pleasure in conveying to you, on behalf of His Majesty's Government, the following declaration of sympathy with Jewish Zionist aspirations which has been submitted to, and approved by, the Cabinet:
>
> His Majesty's Government view with favor the establishment in Palestine of a national home for the Jewish people, and will use their best endeavors to facilitate the achievement of this object, it being clearly understood that nothing shall be done which may prejudice the civil and religious rights of existing non-Jewish communities in Palestine, or the rights and political status enjoyed by Jews in any other country. I should be grateful if you would bring this declaration to the knowledge of the Zionist Federation.
>
> Yours,
> Arthur James Balfour

ANALYZE AND INTERPRET

If you were an Arab, how might you have interpreted the first and third paragraphs of the McMahon Letter? To what extent did the Balfour Declaration conflict with the promises the British had made to the Arab leaders? Why do you suppose the British made these conflicting agreements?

Source: *The Times of London*, November 1917. Taken from the Internet Modern History Sourcebook. The Sourcebook is a collection of public domain and copy-permitted texts for introductory-level classes in modern European and World history.

the pan-Arab movement, the Sharif of Mecca, Husayn ibn Ali al-Hashimi (the Hashimites were the clan of the Prophet Muhammad). In 1915, the British High Commissioner of Egypt, Sir Henry McMahon, acting on behalf of his government, wrote Husayn the **McMahon Letter**, in which he promised British support for the creation of an Arab homeland in the region between Iraq and Egypt in return for Arab support. In exchange for this promise, and led by Husayn's son, "Prince" Faisal, and a British advisor, Col. T. E. Lawrence, Husayn and Arab tribesmen fought a successful guerilla war to expel the Turks from Arabia, Palestine, Syria, and Iraq. Meanwhile, in 1917, realizing the political influence of wealthy Jews such as Lord Rothschild and seeking support for an American entry into the war, Britain also made promises to the **Zionists**, Jewish nationalists who claimed to represent most European and American Jews. In the **Balfour Declaration**, the British agreed to support a "Jewish national homeland," but this could be achieved only at the expense of Husayn, Faisal, and the Arabs to whom they had promised support in the region for the creation of an Arab state. The Arabs had shared Palestine with the biblical Jews and had been the majority people there for nearly 1,800 years. To the Arabs of post–World War I, then, the British promise of a "national homeland" sounded like a Jewish-controlled state in which they would only be a tolerated group, and they felt that they had been "double-crossed" (see the Law and Government box).

Jewish immigration into Palestine had begun in a minor way as early as the 1880s but had taken on potentially important dimensions only after the founding of the international Zionist movement by journalist Theodor Herzl at the turn of the twentieth century. Under the well-meaning but muddled British colonial government, Arabs and Jews began to take up hostile positions in Palestinian politics during the 1920s. Soon, this hostility was taking the form of bloody riots, suppressed only with difficulty by the British police. The situation was considerably worsened by the dramatic increase in the number of Jews who immigrated into Palestine immediately after the Balfour Declaration was made public. The British mandate authority did nothing to alleviate the situation until 1939, when belated promises were made to limit immigration. By then, however, the situation was beyond its control. Throughout the 1930s, Jewish immigrants had been pouring into Palestine from Hitler's Germany and Eastern Europe, where vicious anti-Semitism had become commonplace. At the outbreak of World War II, perhaps 30 percent of Palestine's inhabitants were Jews.

Jack Picone/Alamy Limited

THE PALESTINIAN *INTIFADA*: BOYS THROWING STONES AT ISRAELI SOLDIERS. Beginning in 1989 under Palestine Liberation Organization (PLO) leadership, the Palestinian Arabs in the Gaza Strip and the West Bank/occupied territories challenged Israeli claims to these areas. Rock-throwing youth rioted in the streets in a persistent *intifada*, or uprising, which forced Israeli countermeasures and gave the Tel Aviv government a black eye in the world press. A second intifada began after the breakdown of the 1993 agreement, the Oslo Accord.

At the end of the war, the British in Palestine, as elsewhere, were at the end of their strength, and they wished to turn over the troublesome Middle East mandates as soon as possible to the United Nations. The pitiful remnants of the Jews of Nazi Europe now defied British attempts to keep them from settling illegally in Palestine. Attempts to get Arabs and Jews to sit down at the negotiating table failed, and the frustrated British announced that they would unilaterally abandon Palestine on May 14, 1948. Faced with this ultimatum, the United Nations eventually (November 1947) came out with a proposal for partitioning the mandate into a Jewish state and an Arab state—a compromise that, needless to say, satisfied neither side. By the time the United Nations proposal was put forth, fighting between irregular Arab and Jewish militias was already under way. Zionist leaders in Palestine immediately proclaimed the creation of the nation of Israel upon British withdrawal in May 1948.

The results of the 1948 war—the first of six armed conflicts in the last sixty-five years between Israel and its Arab neighbors—were strongly favorable to the new Jewish state. Unexpectedly, it held its own and more against its several enemies. But the triumphant Israelis then expelled many hundreds of thousands of Palestinian Arabs from their ancestral lands, creating a reservoir of bitterness that guaranteed hostility for decades to come, with both Palestinian Arabs and Jews making mutually contradictory claims to a "Right of Return."

In 1964, after fifteen years of intra-Arab dissension about how best to deal with the Israeli presence, Arab leaders formed the **Palestine Liberation Organization (PLO)**, whose single goal was the destruction of the state of Israel. Both sides pursued their respective goals with bloodshed and intolerance for each other for almost thirty years until 1993. In this effort the PLO was assisted by most of the Arab states, which saw Israel as an enemy that could not be tolerated in their midst. For its part, as a besieged state, Israel used its well-disciplined and largely American-equipped armed forces to repay violence with violence and to continue occupying Palestinian lands. This enmity, like all other conflicts during the Cold War era, became caught up in the general hostility between the United States and the Soviet Union, with the former siding strongly with the Israelis and the latter with the Arabs (see Map 51.1).

THE RISE OF ISLAMISM

Westerners have always misunderstood the nature of Islam and have tried to equate it with Christianity in Europe, with unfortunate results. Islam is much more

MAP 51.1 Israel and Its Arab Neighbors, 1947–2007

The extraordinary complexity of the conflict between Jews and Arabs stems in large part from the many years of peaceable intermixing of populations, making it impossible to separate them and to place them under separate governments without coercion. As in the Balkan states, the success and duration of the past domination of the region by Muslims have made the current conflict more savage.

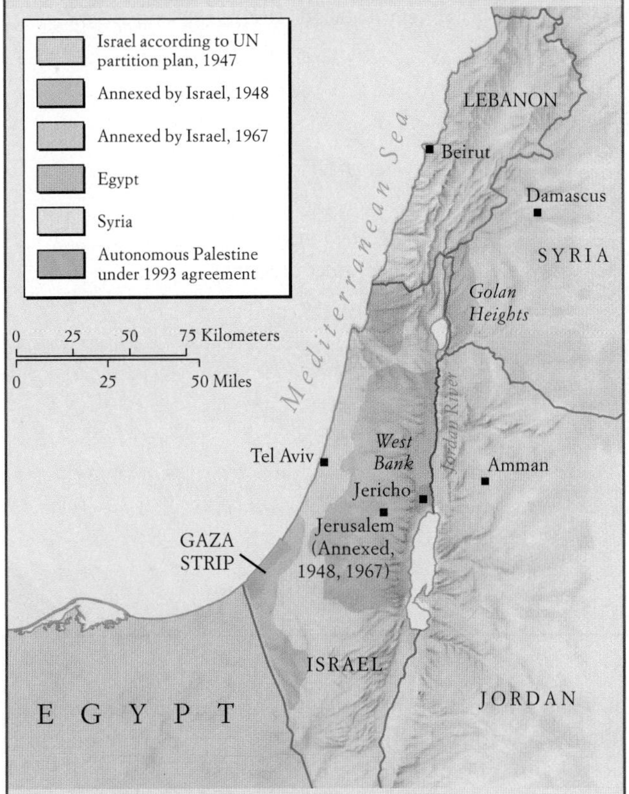

THINKING ABOUT THIS MAP

Note the dates of Israel's "annexation" of Palestinian lands. What specific events enabled Israel to annex these lands?

than a religion as the West understands that term and is certainly not limited to the private sphere as Christianity has been since the French Revolution. Islamic law, especially, does not recognize the separation of church and state nor of religious belief and civil practice. Rather, for the good Muslim, these concepts are a unity and always have been. They can no more be separated than can the human personality from the body it inhabits. Muslims have always felt a higher identity embracing them than the mere fact of being Syrian or Egyptian. For many, "The Fatherland of a Muslim is wherever the Holy Law of Islam prevails."

This feeling is not new. Explosive movements of renewal and reform (frequently oversimplified as "fundamentalist") have a long history in Islamic lands. Whenever and wherever they have appeared, excesses committed by brutal rulers—such as the illegal taxation and even enslavement of their subjects—have provided the spark that set off cries demanding a return to the time-honored wellsprings of justice embodied in holy law, the *Shari'a*. Always these calls have issued first from the mouths of the religious leaders of the masses—the *ulama*, the *mullahs*, and the Sufi shaykhs. From time to time, these purgative movements have taken the form of *jihad*, or holy war (Chapters 34 and 35). In the 1890s, the *Salafi* movement began as a movement of reform that sought to accommodate modernism. However, this campaign took a more militant turn in the 1920s when Salafi Muslims in Egypt formed the *Muslim Brotherhood*. It was this organization that employed violence for the first time, such as assassinations against "infidel" occupying powers including the British. Even at the high point of secular nationalism in the Middle East—during the years before and after World War II when the Turkey of Kemal Ataturk, the Iran of Reza Shah, and the Egypt of Gamal Abdel Nasser were blazing new paths—there was a strong undercurrent of religiously based patriotic feeling that rejected secularism as an ideology that had been imposed on Muslim peoples by the West (see Chapter 35 and discussion in this chapter). When some of these secular regimes (notably Egypt's) were discredited by the humiliation suffered in the 1967 **Six-Day War** and by their failures to raise Muslim lands out of poverty, Muslims abandoned even popular leaders such as Nasser. They turned en masse to **Islamism**, Islamic principles, as a powerfully creative force to guide them through the difficulties of life in a world that had grown beyond their understanding, much less control. When governments like Egypt's responded with imprisonment and executions to stifle Islamist dissent, some came to regard leaders such as Anwar Sadat and Hosni Mubarak themselves as infidels, subject to jihad.

But only in recent decades have Islamists come into the spotlight in world affairs. In several countries—Afghanistan, Egypt, Pakistan, Jordan, the Sudan, Yemen, and Algeria—they enjoy widespread and vociferous public support to the point of dominating public life and intimidating their civic rivals. In some others—Saudi Arabia and Syria—they are a minority but seem to be gaining ground against the secularists who still control the governments. In still others—Indonesia, Morocco, and Algeria—the balance is neatly held and can shift momentarily. But overall it is evident that militant forms of Islam are a potentially major factor in international affairs in the twenty-first century. In recent years, the emergence of **al-Qaida**—the network of Muslim terrorists headed by the now dead Arab, **Osama bin Laden**, and presumed to be responsible for the September 11, 2001, attacks on the World Trade Center and the Pentagon—has put a different and much more immediately menacing face on the Islamist movement (for more, see Chapter 53).

IMAGES OF HISTORY

Islamic Royalty

"PRINCE" FAISAL AND DELEGATION, 1919. Faisal was the son of the Sharif of Mecca, Husayn ibn Ali al-Hashimi. Here he is shown attending the Versailles Peace Conference in 1919. Also in the photograph is Col. T. E. Lawrence (Lawrence of Arabia). The British briefly installed Faisal as the king of Syria, then later of Iraq.

THE IRANIAN REVOLUTION

Three outstanding events or processes in the twentieth century have together defined many of the spiritual and material bases of the Muslim universe. The first was the establishment of the secular Republic of Turkey by Ataturk. The second was the oil boycott of 1973–1974, organized and implemented by the Arab members of the **Organization of Petroleum Exporting Countries (OPEC)**. The third was the Iranian Revolution of 1979, led by the Ayatollah Khomeini.

The modern state of Iran is the successor to the great Persian empires of ancient times. Its inhabitants, who are not Arabs, have been Muslims almost without exception since the Arab conquest in the 640s. In many epochs, the Iranians have been among Islam's most distinguished leaders. Nevertheless, they are separated from the majority of Muslims in one decisive way: They are Shi'ite Muslims.

Modern Iran came into being in the aftermath of World War I, when a military officer named Reza Shah Pahlavi (ruling 1925–1941) seized power from a discredited traditional dynasty and established an authoritarian regime modeled on that of his Turkish neighbor. His son, Muhammad Reza Shah Pahlavi (ruling 1941–1979), continued his Westernizing and secularizing policies. By the 1970s, considerable progress had been made in the cities at least. The nation had a substantial middle class, technically advanced industry (especially connected with petroleum engineering), an extensive Western educational system, and mechanized agriculture. Its immense oil deposits generated sufficient income to pay for large-scale government projects of every sort, and these proved profitable for a select few contractors and their friends in the bureaucracy.

But the shah had neglected to see to the well-being of much of the urban and most of the rural population. Government corruption was universal, the army and police were all-powerful, and the ruling clique held traditional religious values in more or less open contempt. On top of that, many people viewed the shah and his advisers as slavish puppets of the West, who had neither understanding of nor respect for the greatness of Islamic Persia.

The upshot was a massive swell of protest, inspired and led by the exiled Ayatollah (Shi'ite theologian) Ruhollah Khomeini. Under the banners of "Back to the *Qur'an*" and "Iran for the Iranians," Khomeini skillfully led his people into revolution and then returned in 1979 to take the helm of the government that succeeded the bewildered shah. For the next decade, the Ayatollah implemented what he had promised Iran from afar: a thoroughly Islamic, uncompromisingly anti-Western, antisecular government. Resistance to this course was brushed aside by his

AN IRANIAN WOMAN CONSULTS WITH HER MULLAH. With the Ayatollah Khomeini's establishment of a mullah-led government in 1979, Iranian women have been forced to wear the traditional *hijab*. While public humiliation is the sentence for defying the codes the religious leaders have issued, many Muslims, women included, have accepted these conservative measures as necessary for a life based on Islamic values, called *Islamism*.

authoritarian attitude that allowed no concessions. The atheistic Soviets were denounced almost as heartily as the Americans, whose long-standing support for the shah as a Cold War counter against the Soviets had earned Khomeini's especial contempt.

In the Ayatollah's Iran, militant Islamism found its most dramatic and forceful exponent so far. But it was by no means a necessarily attractive scenario for other secular Muslim states, and within a year of the Ayatollah's return, Iran was at war with a Muslim neighbor. In 1980, Iraq attempted to take advantage of the upheaval next door to seize some disputed oil-bearing territory from Iran. The eight-year conflict that followed was one of the bloodiest in recent history, claiming at least 1 million lives (mainly Iranian) and dealing both countries blows from which they have not yet recovered.

With its much smaller population, Iraq would have been defeated early in the war had it not been for the active financial support and armaments supplied by other states. Led by the Saudis, many Arab leaders thought that the Ayatollah's radical brand of Shi'ite Islam posed a serious threat to all of them and wished to see it contained or defeated. The militant anti-Western positions embraced by Khomeini (notably, the holding of U.S. hostages in 1979–1980) also induced the Western states to support Iraq in various covert ways—actions that they would soon come to regret.

THE OIL WEAPON

What was the number-one history-making event or series of events in the 1970s in retrospect? Most would now say that it was not the Cold War between the United States and the Soviet Union or the American adventure in Vietnam or even the rapid steps being taken toward European unity, but rather the worldwide economic crisis precipitated by the OPEC oil boycott. In 1973, the favoritism shown by the West, and especially the United States, toward Israel was answered during that year's brief Arab-Israeli conflict (sometimes known as the **Yom Kippur War** because it began on that Jewish holiday) by the Arabs' decision to withhold all oil shipments to the United States and its NATO allies. Because the Middle East had long been the dominant supplier of world petroleum markets, the impact was immediate and catastrophic. Prices of crude oil quadrupled within a few months. The economies of the Western nations and Japan were put under great strain. Even the United States, which came closest to oil self-sufficiency of all the affected nations, faced shortages.

A major recession, the worst since the 1930s, with unemployment rates zooming to 13 percent in Western Europe, was one of the results. Soaring energy costs caused consumer prices for practically every necessity of life to spiral upward even as demand decreased. As mass unemployment was accompanied by double-digit inflation in the mid- and late 1970s, a new word came into the vocabulary—*stagflation*. This unlovely compound referred to the worst of all economic worlds: the combination of stagnation and inflation.

The postwar boom, which had lasted a quarter of a century, had definitely ended, and most of the West remained in a painful business recession well into the 1980s. Some countries have never entirely recovered from the great oil shock. Their labor markets have been permanently altered by the disappearance of many blue-collar production jobs that depended on cheap energy. (The 1973 shock was later reinforced by events in Iran. Beginning in 1979–1980, international oil prices again quadrupled for several years because of fears of a supply pinch following the Iranian Revolution and the outbreak of the Iran-Iraq War.)

This windfall in Arab oil profits did not last more than a decade, and the OPEC nations were eventually forced to adjust their prices to a diminished world demand. But the brief havoc exacted in oil supplies—which the West had always thought were shielded from producer-country influence—established a new respect for Arab political potency. What Western consumers knew after 1973 was that a handful of heretofore peripheral and insignificant Middle Eastern and North African kingdoms had risen on a tide of crude oil to become at least transitory major players in world politics. The surge in price made some of the major producers (notably, the largest of all, Saudi Arabia) immensely rich in dollars, and money here, as elsewhere, spelled both economic and political power. No longer could any industrial nation afford to ignore what OPEC was doing or planning. For the first time in at least two centuries, the Muslim East had attained importance through its own initiatives, rather than merely because of what one or another alien group was doing there.

THE GULF WAR AND THE INVASION OF IRAQ

In 1990, the ambitious and bloodstained Iraqi dictator, Saddam Hussein, victor in the just-concluded conflict with Iran, believed the time was ripe for a settlement of accounts with Kuwait, his oil-rich neighbor at the head of the Persian Gulf. In an undisguised grab for additional oil revenues, Saddam invaded the tiny country and declared it annexed, thinking that he would present the world with an accomplished fact backed up by a large and well-armed army.

To his surprise, the West reacted violently and was soon joined by most of the non-Western world, including the Soviet Union and most Arabs. The majority of the United Nations presented Saddam with the most unified front that organization had seen since its inception. The Iraqi dictator refused to back down, however. It took a powerful air and ground attack led by the United States on his forces in 1991 to induce him to withdraw with heavy losses (the Gulf War).

Although a treaty was forced on Saddam that required him to destroy his stockpiles of chemical, biological, and nuclear weapons (weapons of mass destruction), his defiance of his enemies and his efforts to frustrate the work of weapons inspectors caused tensions to continue through the 1990s. Urgings by President George H. W. Bush that Iraqis remove him from power had only tragic consequences when his administration failed to back up promises of support to Shi'ites in the south of Iraq and Kurds in the north when they rose up against Saddam in 1991–1992. Thousands were killed in gas attacks and air assaults, resulting in further distrust of the United States.

When many of President Bush's advisers returned to power in 2001 under the administration of his son, George W. Bush, the "hawks" among them urged the new president to resume the war against Saddam. When Bush and his advisers claimed that Saddam was allied to al-Qaida and was still hiding weapons of mass destruction, the United States invaded Iraq, despite broad international opposition that claimed that the invasion was blatant aggression. In ways reminiscent of the Vietnam War, the United States found itself bogged down again in a war that has proven difficult to justify, steadily losing international standing. The invasion succeeded in removing Saddam Hussein from power, but at the price of breeding more Arab hatred of the United States than ever before. Perhaps most ironically, Iraq temporarily became a recruiting ground for new legions of Islamist zealots bent on destroying the West in the name of Allah. Sovereignty has been returned to an elected Iraqi president and prime minister. It now appears likely that Iraq will manage to hold together in the face of radical forms of political Islam, ethnic and sectarian rivalries, and opposition from elements of the old regime that remain opposed to democracy. American forces withdrew from Iraq in 2011, however, and sectarian violence, in the form of public bombings, once more has been on the rise.

Yet the military intervention of American and Allied forces in the region is not yet over. After being driven from Afghanistan, many refugees found refuge in the mountains of northern Pakistan. From the protection of bases in Pakistan's mountainous north and with help from local Pashtun (pahsh-TOON) tribesmen, the Taliban have retaken control of approximately 50 percent of Afghanistan's rural areas. Afghan units have assumed more and more of the fighting and policing, and the NATO nations have set a timetable for the withdrawal of the remaining foreign forces by 2014.

THE MUSLIM NATIONS TODAY

The relative importance of the Muslim nations in today's world can be viewed from sharply differing perspectives. Some observers, who focus on the continuing weakness of the domestic political infrastructure and the technological dependency of most Muslim societies on Western nations, tend to dismiss the twentieth-century resurgence as a temporary "blip" that will have no permanent effects on the overall picture of Western world domination.

Others, focusing on such disparate phenomena as the shocking capabilities and determination of the Islamist terrorists and the sophisticated financial initiatives of the Saudi Arabian government to protect its oil revenues, are of the contrary opinion. They believe that the Muslims have placed themselves firmly and permanently on the world stage. In this view, the West would be making a huge mistake to leave the Islamic peoples out of its calculations on any important international issue. It appears that the latter view is becoming generally accepted. However, the lesson of the Iraqi and Afghani invasions and more than a century of Western imperialism is that responsibility for the future of all Non-Western states must remain primarily with their own citizens.

The Arabs

It is difficult to generalize accurately about the Arab nations. The various Middle East countries inhabited by Arabs are commonly known by their control over much of the world's oil and their enmity with Israel and, because of its support for Israel and the invasion of Iraq, with the United States. But even these supposedly basic facts are subject to sharp variances both over time and between countries. The oil trade has become much less confrontational and less politicized, but the Arab-Israel hostility seems resistant to any solution. Even the extraordinary diplomatic efforts of U.S. President Bill Clinton in the early 1990s, like those of President Jimmy Carter before him, produced only a mirage of peace rather than its actuality. In 1993, Clinton was able to persuade the government of Israel and the PLO to sign a "path to peace" agreement. But in the first years of the new millennium, this so-called Oslo Accord has repeatedly been tossed aside by hardliners on both sides, and the bloodshed has resumed. At times it has appeared that the ongoing conflict is needed by some of the Arab leadership to divert popular attention from their domestic economic problems, which have persisted despite both oil profit windfalls and international aid. At other times, the Jewish leadership has been deliberately provocative in its assertions of control over Palestinian people and places and in its support of new Israeli settlements in east Jerusalem and the West Bank.

Egypt, with the largest population of the Arab world, is in an especially difficult position. With few resources beyond the fields of the Nile Valley, it has become entirely dependent on U.S. and World Bank assistance and migration to rich Saudi Arabia to maintain an even minimal living standard for its people. Economic desperation—especially in contrast to the oil wealth of the Saudis, Iranians, and others—has added fuel to other resentments, which have given rise to a militant Islamic fundamentalism in Egypt and other nations. This has resulted in the election of the first president in the nation's history who is a member of the Muslim Brotherhood. At the time of this writing, the future of agreements entered into between Egypt and Israel at Camp David has become a question mark.

The region remains fraught with problems. Will the villagers continue to support the urban politicians who have promised them a better life but have delivered on that promise only partially and sporadically since 1945? The secularists include such different past and present personalities as Nasser and Anwar Sadat in Egypt, Hussein in Iraq, Ahmad Ben Bella in Algeria, King Husayn in Jordan, and Hafiz al-Assad in Syria. All of them have wanted to lead their nations into a Westernized technology and economy, while giving perhaps only lip service to Western-style political and civil rights.

On the other side of the equation are the Islamists of various stripes, led by the former Islamist associates of Khomeini in Iran, the members of the al-Qaida terrorist network established under bin Laden, and the leaders of the Muslim Brotherhood, Islamic Jihad, and the Shi'ite **Hizbullah**, as well as many others whose names are as yet unknown to the world. They are willing to accept most of the modern world's material and technical achievements, but only if the power of selection remains securely in their own hands and as long as it is understood that the society using these achievements must be fully in tune with the words of the *Qur'an* as interpreted by themselves.

For America and its allies, the extremes to which bin Laden and his al-Qaida followers were willing to go to free the Middle East from America and other "Crusading" states was demonstrated on September 11, 2001. After having failed to destroy the World Trade Center in the early 1990s, al-Qaida terrorists under bin Laden's orders hijacked four American airliners, two of which were flown into the World Trade Center, one into the Pentagon, and one crashing in Pennsylvania, costing thousands of innocent lives. Demands by the United States that the Taliban rulers of Afghanistan turn bin Laden and his lieutenants over to the United States for trial were refused. In an effort to destroy the terrorist network and its Taliban allies, the president and Congress allied themselves with dissident Afghani tribes, under a loose confederation of warlords called the "Northern Alliance." Their goals were capturing or killing bin Laden, destroying his organization, and toppling the Taliban.

As of 2012, the first of these objectives was achieved. U.S. Navy SEALs killed bin Laden in 2011 and his network has been seriously crippled, although it has found new recruits around the world among those whose hatred of the United States has been fueled by American actions in Iraq. However, as explained previously, the Taliban has held on in Afghanistan, and the future of Western objectives in the region remains clouded.

Since 2010, much of the so-called Arab world has produced some hopeful signs of better times ahead. Called the **Arab Spring**, a broad movement for reform has spread from Morocco to Iraq with several regional tyrants overthrown and many nations experiencing the return of democracy for the first time in many years. (See the Society and Economy box.)

The Non-Arabic Nations

The Muslim countries of Africa and Asia have thus far shown only limited and scattered interest in coordinating their activity, foreign or domestic, with the Arabs, despite extensive aid to these nations from Saudi Arabia and Iran. This attitude is partly a result of the circumstances in which Islam was introduced and grew in these parts of the globe. The offspring of converts who continue to be strongly rooted in their indigenous cultures, the African and Asian Muslims have not been quite as single-minded and exclusive as their Arab fellows in religious affairs.

Since attaining independence in 1949, Indonesia, the largest Muslim state and boasting the fourth-largest population in the world, has felt its way forward by the technique of "guided democracy." The country was originally guided by the charismatic leader of the anticolonial struggle, Sukarno, and then until 1998 by the secularist General Suharto. (Guided democracy claims to be more authentic in representing the popular will than are Western parliamentary governments. It purports to reconcile clashing points of view by the benign guidance of a single leader.) Preoccupied with ethnic-religious conflicts and the problems created by a burgeoning population with limited resources (rich oil deposits are by far the most important), the government has shown no interest

SOCIETY AND ECONOMY

The Arab Spring

The so-called Arab Spring is a recent term that has been applied to a wave of demonstrations, rebellions, and revolutionary movements that has occurred across North Africa and the Near and Middle East. In certain respects, they have been the most significant development in the so-called Arab world since the founding of Israel in 1947. The rebellions started in Tunisia in December 2010 when a street merchant, Sidi Bouzid (SEE-dee BOO-zeed), set himself afire to protest police corruption and violence against the citizenry. Bouzid's act of defiance spread rapidly throughout Tunisia in the months that followed, and led to the overthrow of the dictatorial President Zayn al-Abidin bin Ali in January 2011. The success of the Tunisian movement set off additional uprisings in neighboring Algeria, as well as Jordan, Egypt, and Yemen, and then spread further to other countries. (See Map 51.2.)

However, these rebellions have differed in their character, intensity, and outcomes. In some instances, demonstrations have led to civil wars and, in some cases, the unseating of local dictators. In Egypt, massive protests in Cairo ended in February 2011 with the resignation of the long-time president Hosni Mubarak. With the aid of air support provided by NATO, rebels overthrew the Libyan leader Muammar Gaddafi in August 2011. A National Transitional Council (NTC) took control, and the hated dictator was murdered in his hometown of Sirte. Rebels in Yemen coerced President Ali Abd-Allah Salih to agree to a national election, and a successor, Abd ar-Rab Mansur al-Hadi, replaced him in February 2012. Several other heads-of-state also have announced their intentions to step down from office at the end of their current terms. Among these are the Sudanese President Umar al-Bashar (who also is wanted by the International Criminal Court for human rights abuses) and Iraqi President Nuri al-Maliki.

Protests also have erupted in Bahrain, Kuwait, Morocco, Lebanon, Mauretania, Oman, Saudi Arabia, and Western Sahara. In some cases, the uprisings have had Islamist components. In Mali, Tuareg (Berber) fighters returning from Libya's civil war rebelled against the government in Bamako, seeking independence for the northern half of the country. They in turn have been driven into Mauretania by al-Qaida fighters who have seized the north, including Timbuktu, and have imposed strict Shari'a law and attacked many symbols of Mali's ancient culture. Elsewhere, in elections held in June 2012, Egyptians elected Mohammad Mursi (or Morsi), a member of Egypt's Muslim Brotherhood, to the presidency. Despite his background, however, Mursi has taken care to invite non-Islamists into his cabinet, including a Coptic Christian.

By far the most violent rebellions have been in Syria. There, after forty-two years of Ba'ath Party rule under the brutal Hafiz al-Assad and his son, Bashar al-Assad, rebels in Homs and other cities took up arms. Assad's army has committed atrocities, often murdering civilians as well as opposition fighters indiscriminately. The outcome is still in doubt, but in August 2012, the Deputy Prime Minister has stated that the government is prepared to discuss the resignation of the President. To date, this has not occurred.

ANALYZE AND INTERPRET

Despite the differences, what common elements and aspirations seem to be common to many of these rebellions? What possible hopes and concerns might they raise?

in forming associations even with nearby Muslim states. In this melting pot of religions, Islamic fundamentalism has produced several movements that seek either the establishment of an Islamic state under Shari'a law or total separation.

Pakistan and Bangladesh are the next-largest Muslim states. Throughout its short history, Pakistan has been entirely occupied with its recurrently dangerous quarrel with India over Kashmir. Both countries now possess nuclear weapons; both have large populations of minorities who have little identification with the governing groups. In most recent times, the chaos in neighboring Afghanistan has made Pakistan more important in Western eyes, balancing the former tilt toward India. Internally, a series of military takeovers and deep internal divisions have prevented any real commitment to democratic politics, which is perhaps impossible given the huge political and economic problems created by events over which the government has comparatively little control (see Chapter 48). The assassinations and bombings visited upon the country by Islamist militants has added appreciably to its precarious state.

On its side, Bangladesh has been struggling since its creation with abject poverty in an economy that ranks as one of the world's poorest. Lacking any notable human, mineral, or energy resources, Pakistan and Bangladesh have remained on the periphery of both Muslim and world affairs and are heavily dependent on aid from foreign sources ranging from China (Pakistan) to the United States (both). Neither has shown any interest in making common policy with other Muslim countries. (They could not even get along with one another in an earlier joint

MAP 51.2 The Arab Spring

The Arab Spring has had differing levels of impact and have assumed broadly different natures and outcomes across the Near and Middle East, as shown in this map.

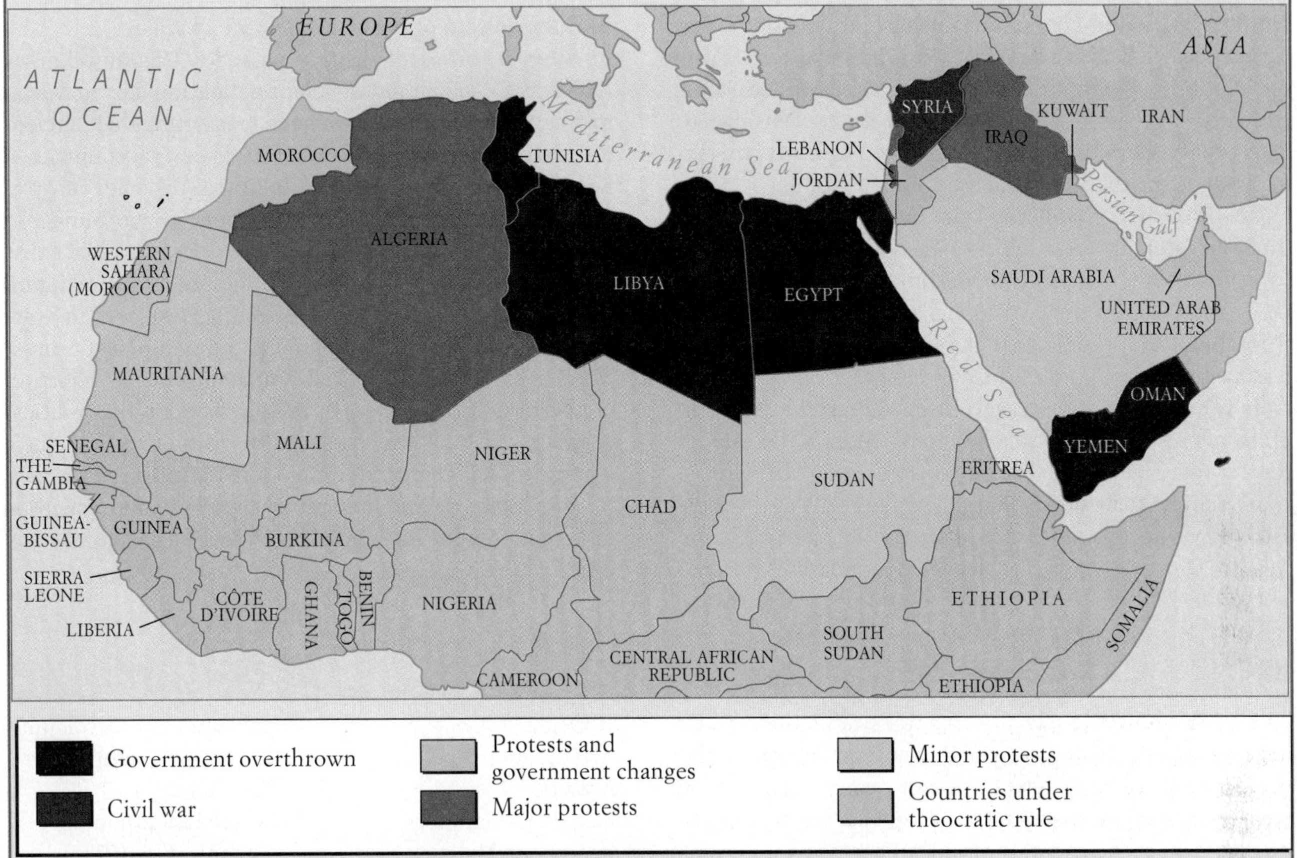

Government overthrown
Civil war
Protests and government changes
Major protests
Minor protests
Countries under theocratic rule

THINKING ABOUT THIS MAP

Which countries have seen the greatest changes? Which ones the least? Why do you think the revolutions we call the Arab Spring were of greater or less severity in different nations?

state.) Secularist generals or their civilian accomplices and puppets have ruled both most of the time since their creation. Radical Islamism is as yet only weakly represented in Bangladesh.

As a summary labeling, the politics and governments of most Muslim states appear to have begun a transition to democracy. Until recently, monopolistic party with an authority figure at its head was the rule (as random examples, Mubarak in Egypt, Saddam Hussein in Iraq, and Qaddafi in Libya). The central authorities treated ethnic minorities or religious "deviants" roughly if they showed the slightest resistance. Civil wars, declared and undeclared, raged in several nations, both between competing sections of the Muslim populace and between Muslims and their religious and cultural rivals (Iraq, Sudan, Algeria). Whole regions containing groups unfriendly to the regime were systematically punished—sometimes by armed force, as in Turkey and Iraq. The Arab Spring has changed much of this, but many issues remain unresolved.

The domestic economic condition varied from reasonably stable (the oil-blessed Middle East) to very shaky (most of North and Northeast Africa). Indonesia and Malaysia were so badly shaken by recent fiscal and economic miseries as to bring down entrenched dictators, governments, and parties. Even rich Saudi Arabia proved not immune from the worldwide recession of 2001–2002. In most countries, connections with the bureaucracy were usually necessary for successful enterprise, corruption was rampant, and necessary government investments in infrastructure (roads, airports, sewer lines, and the like) were still conspicuous by their absence. All in all, the reentry of Islam into a prominent place in the modern world has not been easy, and the ride ahead promises to be perhaps even rougher—not only for the countries concerned but also for their non-Muslim neighbors.

SUMMARY

The Muslim World has returned to an important role in world politics and economics during the twentieth century, after two or three centuries of insignificance. Making up about one-sixth of the globe's population, Muslims from West Africa to Southeast Asia have been able to insert themselves back into Western consciousness, especially since the oil boycott of the 1970s.

The first real change was the creation of the secular Turkish republic after World War I. This state served as a model for many other Muslim thinkers and politicians and fostered the creation of nationalist associations throughout the Middle East and North Africa. The Arab-Israeli struggle over Palestine has been a galvanizing force from the 1920s to the present. It was followed by the creation of the Arab-sponsored Organization of Petroleum Exporting Countries, the oil boycott, and the rise of more-radical forms of Islamism in the 1970s and 1980s. Fueled by a decade of extraordinary profits from oil, some Muslim countries have experienced a tremendous burst of modernization. Others, lacking oil, have remained at or near the bottom of the world prosperity scale.

After centuries of relative passivity, Islamic religious leaders (the ulama among Sunnis, the mullahs and ayatollahs among Shi'ites) have been reasserting their ancient claims to leadership of the Muslims in several countries—notably since the revolution in Iran. Although all previous pan-Arabic and pan-Islamic appeals have foundered amid sectarian and national rivalries, it is possible that the present surge of Islamism could erect and maintain such an alliance should these movements succeed in overthrowing the secular governments now in place in most Middle Eastern lands. Their uncompromising rejection of Western ideals—such as religious toleration, political equality, and popular sovereignty—combined with their appeal to an alienated underclass in poverty-stricken Muslim countries, makes them a potentially dangerous force not only for their secular rivals at home but also for international peace.

IDENTIFICATION TERMS

Test your knowledge of this chapter's key concepts by defining the following terms. If you can not recall the meaning of certain terms, refresh your memory by looking up the boldfaced term in the chapter, turning to the Glossary at the end of the book, or accessing the terms on the CourseMate website at **www.cengagebrain.com**.

al-Qaida
Arab Spring
Ataturk
Balfour Declaration
Osama bin Laden
Hizbullah
Islamism
mandates
McMahon Letter
Organization of Petroleum Exporting Countries (OPEC)
Palestine Liberation Organization (PLO)
Six-Day War
Yom Kippur War
Zionists

FOR FURTHER REFLECTION

1. Explain how British promises to the Arabs and to the Jews during World War I would have caused resentment among the Arabs. What does this suggest about the later conflicts in the region between Arab and Jewish nationalists?
2. What seem to be the reasons why Muslims have shifted away from modern secular leadership and government to Islamism? Are these reasons new, or have they existed in past centuries?
3. In your opinion, do most Muslims seem to favor a return to Islamist-style leadership and governments? Be sure to provide reasons and facts to support your answers. What recent events suggest otherwise?
4. Some people believe that the presence of Israel and its actions are at the root of many problems in the Near and Middle East. Is this a fair and accurate assessment? Again, state the reasons for your position.
5. What outcomes have occurred as results of the Arab Spring? Have they been uniformly good? Who have been the beneficiaries and who the losers?

TEST YOUR KNOWLEDGE

Test your knowledge of this chapter by answering the following questions. Complete answers appear at the end of the book. You may find even more quiz questions on the CourseMate website at **www.cengagebrain.com**.

1. The British promise to recognize a Jewish homeland in Palestine was made in the
   a. Camp David Accords.
   b. Balfour declaration.
   c. McMahon letter.
   d. Intifada agreements
   e. Paris Peace Treaty.
2. The historical movement to unite all Arabs under a single political leadership is
   a. Arabs First!
   b. pan-Arabism.
   c. the Arab Awakening.
   d. Arab Unity.
   e. the Arab Brotherhood.
3. Kemal Ataturk believed that Turks
   a. must remain Muslim to retain a national identity.
   b. must expand beyond their old borders to solve their national woes.
   c. had an obligation to liberate their Muslim comrades in Europe.
   d. must adopt a Western lifestyle.
   e. had a duty to convert all of their surrounding neighbors to Islam.
4. The McMahon Letter promised
   a. British support for an Arab state in the Middle East.
   b. Allied support for an Arab state in Palestine.
   c. British support for a Jewish homeland in Palestine.
   d. British support for the division of Turkish territories into colonial-like mandates.
   e. Allied support for a mandate in Palestine.
5. At the time of the Balfour Declaration on Palestine, that country's population
   a. was in its majority Arab.
   b. was about half Arab and half Jew.
   c. was almost zero.
   d. was polled on its preferences for the postwar era.
   e. had seen an influx of Muslims in recent years.
6. The state of Israel traces its creation to
   a. an Arab-Jewish pact in World War II.
   b. a United Nations decision to create two states from British Palestine in 1947.
   c. U.S. military intervention after World War II.
   d. a war against Egypt and Syria in 1963.
   e. the success of its Jewish residents in the Yom Kippur War.
7. Perhaps the greatest irritant to Palestinians during the immediate postwar period was
   a. Zionist statements that they desired the creation of a Jewish state in Palestine.
   b. unchecked Jewish immigration into Palestine.
   c. the division of Middle East lands into mandated territories.
   d. the failure of the British to deliver on the promises made in the McMahon Letter.
   e. the strong support given to the Zionists by outside groups.
8. The Iranian Revolution in 1979 was aimed against
   a. the shah of Iran and his Soviet backers.
   b. the shah and his U.S. backers.
   c. the communists who had seized power.
   d. the Sunni Muslims who had captured the shah.
   e. the shah's inability to deal effectively with the country of Iraq.
9. The goal of all radical Islamists is the
   a. creation of a Turkish style secular state.
   b. overthrow of the United States government.
   c. restoration of strict Shari'a law in all Muslim lands.
   d. murder of secular rulers in all Muslim lands.
   e. creation of a new Islamic state under a Caliph.
10. The Arab Spring
    a. has been largely confined to North Africa.
    b. is the latest form of Islamic jihadism.
    c. began in Iran.
    d. has been most effective in Mali and Indonesia.
    e. has forced several dictators to relinquish power.

CourseMate

Visit the CourseMate website at **www.cengagebrain.com** for additional study tools and review materials for this chapter.

Collapse and Reemergence in Communist Europe 52

Communism fit Poland like a horse's saddle on a pig. —LECH WALESA

CHAPTER OUTLINE

1945–1948	Eastern Europe comes under Soviet domination
1948–1960	Stalinist phase in Eastern European economies
1953	Josef Stalin dies
1955–1964	Khrushchev era
1956	Hungarian revolt suppressed
1964	Nikita Khrushchev replaced by Leonid Brezhnev
1979–1989	Afghani invasion by Soviet Union
1985–1991	Gorbachev era
1989–1990	Eastern Europeans reject communist governments
1991	Dissolution of Soviet Union; Boris Yeltsin elected president of newly created Commonwealth of Independent States (CIS)
2002–2009	Renewed tensions between CIS and Western nations
2009	Russia invades Georgia

In 1989, an astounded world watched the spectacle of the impossible happening in Eastern Europe: the rapid and complete collapse of the forty-five-year-old communist system. A year later, the doubly impossible happened in the Soviet Union: the peaceable abolition of the Communist Party's control of government. One year after that, the Soviet Union dissolved, and its component ethnic regions became independent states.

Rarely, if ever, has such a totally unexpected and complete reversal of the existing state of international political affairs occurred in such a brief span. The Cold War—which had defined all other international arrangements for a long generation—was abruptly terminated. And an integrated system of political and military controls, governing an economic apparatus that had ruled from fifty to seventy-five years over 300 million people, was simply thrown into the trashcan and the table swept clean. The most memorable Revolution of the Proletariat, so vehemently proclaimed by the followers of Karl Marx, turned out to be the revolution that ended the reign of Soviet-style Marxism.

THE IMMEDIATE POSTWAR ERA

As we saw previously, the Soviet government under Josef Stalin emerged triumphant from the "Great Patriotic War." The Red Army stood in the center of Europe, hailed by some at least as the liberator from the Nazi yoke. While the impatient Americans quickly demobilized their forces, Stalin proceeded to reap the fruits of his costly victory over the Nazi enemy.

The Communization of Eastern Europe

Under the Allies' Yalta Agreement of 1945, the Russians were to carry through free, democratic national elections in the Eastern European countries as soon as conditions permitted. The divisions among the Big Three (Britain, the Soviet Union, and the United States), which became evident at the war's end, made it impossible to specify more exactly when and how the elections should be held. The Yalta Agreement was in fact a tacit acknowledgment by the West that Stalin and his Red Army would be in control east of the Elbe for at least the immediate postwar years. The best that Washington and London could hope for was the election of governments that would be Soviet-friendly without being outright puppets.

But Stalin, whose suspicion of the Western "capitalist encirclers" had not diminished during the wartime years, was not inclined to accommodate himself to any type of pro-Western or even independent leadership among the Eastern Europeans. But the vital test case of whether the West would accept Stalin's long-term plans for Eastern Europe was Poland. During the war, the Polish government-in-exile had been promised the firm support of the Allies in recovering its country. Many Poles fought bravely in the British Royal Air Force (RAF) and distinguished themselves in the Allied Italian and French campaigns. In 1944, Stalin broke with the Polish exile government over the question of who was responsible for the massacre in the Katyn Forest (thousands of Polish army officers had been murdered in Soviet-occupied Poland in 1940) and then put together a group of Polish communists to act as his cat's-paw in liberated Poland. Despite Western protests, the pro-Soviet group, backed by the Red Army, gradually made political life impossible for their opponents. After a series of highly predictable elections under Soviet "supervision," Poland's decidedly anticommunist and anti-Russian population was forced in 1947 to accept a Soviet satellite regime. The Baltic countries of Estonia, Latvia, and Lithuania received even less consideration. The advancing Red Army simply treated them as recovered provinces of Soviet Russia.

Thus, throughout Eastern Europe, a total of about 110 million people from the Baltic to the Adriatic had been forced under Stalinist rule by Soviet puppets. If truly free elections had been held in the area, it is thought that the Communist Party would have received perhaps 10 to 20 percent of the vote, but in the circumstances, that fact was irrelevant.

The Stalinist Regime

The Soviet Union recovered rapidly from the horrendous damage caused by the Nazi invasion, thanks partly to stripping the Soviet Zone of occupied Germany of all industrial goods and also to the forced "cooperation" of the Eastern European satellites. For the first several years, the postwar economic policy was a continuation of already-familiar Soviet goals and methods. The lion's share of investment went into either new construction or reconstruction of war-ravaged heavy industry and transportation. The first postwar Five-Year Plan reached its goals in considerably less time than planned. By 1950, the Soviet Union was an industrial superpower as well as a military one. It surpassed faltering Britain and still overshadowed recovering Germany, France, and Italy. New Soviet oilfields in central Asia, new metallurgical combines in the Ural Mountains, and new Siberian gas and precious metal deposits were coming on stream constantly.

But in basic consumer goods, the postwar era was even worse than the deprived 1930s. The housing shortage reached crisis proportions in the cities. To have a private bath and kitchen, one had to be either a high party official or an artistic/literary favorite of the day. Personal consumption was held down artificially by every means available to a totalitarian government: low wages, deliberate scarcity, diversion of investment to heavy industry, and constant propaganda stressing the necessity of sacrificing to "build a socialist tomorrow."

In the Eastern European communist states, the backward agrarian economies of the prewar era were changed by the same methods employed in the Soviet Union in the 1930s: coercion of the peasantry, forced (and wildly inefficient) industrialization, and the absolute control of the national budget and all public affairs by the single party. The Eastern European communist parties and their leaders were more or less exact replicas of the Soviet Communist Party and Stalin from the late 1940s until at least the late 1950s. The positive and negative results they obtained resembled those obtained in the Soviet Union fifteen to twenty years previously, with one important exception: Unlike Stalin, who transformed himself into a Russian nationalist when it suited him, the Soviet puppets in Eastern Europe were never able during Stalin's lifetime or for years thereafter to appeal for loyalty to the deep-seated nationalism of their own peoples. On the contrary, they bore the burden of being in the general public's eye what they were in fact: minions of a foreign state.

In 1948, Stalin declared Yugoslav leader Marshal Tito an enemy of communism and undertook a campaign against him that embraced everything but actual war. Tito's crime was that he had objected to the complete subordination of his party and his country to Soviet goals—a process that was well under way everywhere else in Eastern Europe. After a period of hesitation, the United States decided to assist Tito with economic aid. By so doing, Washington allowed the Yugoslav renegade to escape almost certain catastrophe for his country and himself. Tito, still a stalwart Marxist, responded by changing his foreign policies from unquestioning support of the Soviet Union to a prickly neutrality. By 1956, Yugoslavia was busily experimenting with its own brand of social engineering, a peculiar hybrid of capitalism and socialism that for a time seemed to work well enough to attract considerable interest among many African and Asian nations.

FROM STALIN TO BREZHNEV

Tito's heresy was the beginning of the slow breakup of international communism into two competing and even hostile camps. The phases of the breakup can best be marked by looking at the Soviet leadership and its policies after the death of Stalin (by a stroke, supposedly) in 1953.

Goulash Communism

Nikita Khrushchev (1894–1974), a longtime member of the Politburo, succeeded to the leadership first of the Communist Party and then of the Soviet state by gradual steps between 1953 and 1955. A son of peasants, Khrushchev was a different sort of individual than Stalin. Having suffered in fear through the 1930s Stalinist purges himself, Khrushchev was determined that the party, and not the secret police, would be the seat of final power. By 1957, the dreaded KGB had been put back into its cage, and Khrushchev, after a couple of close calls, had succeeded in breaking the Stalinist wing of the party. That wing considered him to be the heedless and ignorant underminer of the system it believed was indefinitely necessary.

Khrushchev's difficulties within the hierarchy of the Communist Party of the Soviet Union (CPSU) sometimes revolved around his crude and volatile personality, but substantive frictions occurred over foreign and domestic policy as well. In foreign policy, Khrushchev allowed the tensions with the Maoist Chinese party to reach a complete break in 1959, splitting the vaunted unity of the world communist movement. In 1961, despite his proclamation of **peaceful coexistence**, he challenged the West and particularly the new U.S. president, John F. Kennedy, by allowing the Soviets' East German satellite to build the **Berlin Wall** in defiance of existing access agreements. Finally, Khrushchev took and lost the huge gamble of the Cuban Missile Crisis of 1962. To save Fidel Castro's vulnerable communist regime in Cuba, the Soviets tried to introduce atomic missiles within ninety miles of Florida (see Chapter 46) and were forced by the United States to give way. All of these initiatives ended in erosion of the Soviet Union's prestige in the Third World—that large group of ex-colonies and neutral nations that sought to avoid being enmeshed in the Cold War.

But Khrushchev was ultimately brought down more by his domestic political innovations than by his foreign policy. Most important by far was his attack on Stalin at the Twentieth Congress of the Party in February 1956. At this highest party meeting, Khrushchev gave a long, supposedly **secret speech** in which he detailed some (although by no means all) of the sins of the dead idol, whom a generation of Russians had been trained to think of as a genius and incomparable savior. Khrushchev's denunciation, which immediately became known outside as well as inside Russia, marked a turning point in international communism. Never again would Stalin occupy the same position in the communist pantheon, and never again would a European communist leader be looked on as a demigod.

Foreign reactions soon followed. In the autumn of 1956, first the Poles and then the Hungarians attempted to act on Khrushchev's revelations about Stalin by shaking off Soviet political and military controls. Both were unsuccessful, but the Soviet Party would never again have the same iron control over its satellites. Grudgingly, the CPSU had to admit that there were "many roads to socialism" and that each communist party should be allowed to find its own way there.

Secondarily, Khrushchev's "harebrained" attempts to change the structure of the CPSU and to install a mistaken agrarian policy contributed to his political demise. Party leaders came to see him more as a debit than an asset to Russian power and prestige, and in 1964, Khrushchev was unceremoniously ushered into premature retirement by his enemies within the Politburo. Khrushchev confidently expected the Soviet system to out produce the capitalists in the near future and devoted much effort to improving the lot of the Soviet and Eastern European consumers during his ten years in office. He coined the telling phrase "goulash communism" to explain what he wanted: a system that put meat in the pot for every table. Some progress was made in this respect in the 1950s and 1960s when consumption of goods and services rose substantially. The tight censorship over the arts and literature imposed by Stalin was also loosened temporarily, but the Khrushchev era was by no means a breakthrough into market economics or political democracy. It was an advance only in comparison to what went before.

Stagnation

Leonid Brezhnev (BREZH-nef: 1906–1982), an *apparatchik* (Communist Party boss) who had climbed the party ladder by sailing close to the prevailing winds, replaced Khrushchev. Worried about the long-term effects of the denunciation of Stalin, Brezhnev and his associates presided over a degree of re-Stalinization of Russian life. He cracked down hard on writers who did not follow party guidelines and on the small but important number of dissidents who attempted to evade censorship by *samizdat* (self-publishing). At the same time, he endorsed Khrushchev's policy of increasing consumption. In the 1970s, the living standards of ordinary Russians finally reached upward to levels that had been current in Western Europe in the Great Depression of the 1930s.

The hallmark of Brezhnev's foreign policy was a determination to retain what had been gained for world communism without taking excessive or unnecessary risks. The best example of this attitude was the so-called Brezhnev Doctrine, applied in Czechoslovakia in 1968. Several months previously, Alexander Dubcek (DOOB-chek), a reformer, had been voted into the leadership of the still-Stalinist Czech Communist Party and proceeded to attempt to give his country "socialism with a human face." The Soviet leadership watched this loosening of the reins with intense and increasing concern. The generals warned that Czechoslovakia must not be allowed to escape its satellite status.

In August 1968, Brezhnev acted: Soviet and Eastern European army units poured into Czechoslovakia in overwhelming numbers. The Czechs had no alternative but to surrender. Dubcek was forced out, and a faithful puppet was installed in his place. Despite verbal denunciations, the Western countries accepted this resolution of the issue without lifting a hand. As in Hungary twelve years previously, it was clear that the NATO nations were not prepared to risk a world war on behalf of the freedom of Eastern Europeans. Anticommunists in the satellite nations realized that their freedom to act independently could come about only if (1) the Soviet Union gave them leave or (2) the Soviet Union itself radically changed its system of government. Neither prospect seemed likely within a lifetime in 1968.

Brezhnev remained in power (1964–1982) longer than any Soviet leader except Stalin, but his effect on the Soviet state was in no way comparable. Where Stalin had turned the Soviet Union on its head, Brezhnev was intensely conservative. His eighteen years as chief of the state and the party were marked by a general loss of morale and momentum in every aspect of Soviet life except the military. Opportunists and career seekers completely dominated the CPSU. Corruption in its top ranks (starting with Brezhnev's own son-in-law) was rampant and went unpunished. Using party connections to obtain personal privileges, such as the rights to buy in special stores and permission for foreign travel, was taken for granted. Intellectuals and artists had once considered it an honor to join the party, but now its prestige had degenerated to the point that authentically creative people refused to join.

For a time, the increased emphasis on consumer goods in the 1970s masked what was happening to the **command economy**: The overall productivity of Soviet labor was declining while government investments were being misapplied. Pushed by his generals, Brezhnev went along with a huge increase in the military budget to match the U.S. atomic weaponry. Two forces thus converged to squeeze Soviet consumers from about 1975 onward: increased unproductive investment in military hardware and personnel, and declining civilian gross national product.

The *era of stagnation*, as it was later dubbed, made itself apparent in daily life in different ways. For many people, the most depressing was that Soviet living standards continued to lag far behind those of the West. Instead of catching up by 1980 as Khrushchev had once rashly predicted, the gap was increasing. After sixty-five years of communist promises, Soviet consumers still faced long lines outside shops selling inferior goods; unexplained shortages of meat, produce, and even bread in the cities; a housing shortage that never seemed to improve; and five-year waits to buy the very expensive but poor-quality domestic automobiles.

The Soviet Union was actually slipping backward, not just compared with the United States and Western Europe but also relative to Japan, South Korea, and Taiwan. In fact, the Soviet Union was rapidly becoming a Third World country in every way except military technology and power. The entire postwar communications revolution had bypassed Eastern Europe. Even a private telephone was a rarity for all but the higher party ranks and a few favored urbanites. Computers and their electronic spin-offs were few in number and obsolete compared with those in the West. The efficiency and productivity of communist industry and agriculture in both the Soviet Union and the satellites were far below world standards. They showed no signs of improvement as the ailing Brezhnev wheezed on into the 1980s. Had it not been for recently opened Siberian gas and oil resources, the U.S. Central Intelligence Agency estimated that Soviet domestic product would have actually *diminished* in the last years of Brezhnev's era.

THE END OF COMMUNIST RULE

The problems were not limited to the Soviet Union. By the 1980s, the gerontocracies (rule of the aged) of Eastern Europe were also beginning to show signs of doom. Poland, the largest of the Soviet satellites, was the catalyst. The Polish leaders had failed to provide sufficient consumer goods for years, and in 1989–1991 a nationwide peaceable protest, led by shipyard electrician Lech Walesa (vah-LEH-sah) and called the **Solidarity movement**, almost succeeded in ousting them from power. In retaliation, a communist general imposed martial law for the next several years and tried to repress Solidarity against massive popular resistance. Although Poland was the most dramatic example, by the mid-1980s, all of the Eastern European states were experiencing a rising tide of popular rage at the inability of the leaders to provide a decent standard of living. Yet the leaders insisted on clinging to their obsolete and discredited communist ideology while attacking their critics as misinformed or subversive.

In 1985, **Mikhail Gorbachev** (GOHR-bah-chuf: b. 1931) rose to the leadership of the Soviet Union, promising to reform both the sputtering economy and the CPSU itself.

He pushed his program of ***perestroika*** (peh-rehs-TROY-kah: restructuring) and ***glasnost*** (GLAZ-nohst: openness) slowly, however, as it became apparent that both the party and much of the populace were fearful of a future in which the old rules might not hold anymore. Two full generations of Soviet citizens had accustomed themselves to "the system," and they had learned that reforms and reformers tended to disappear in disgrace while the system went on.

Nevertheless, it became clear that economic restructuring and the regeneration of the tired party could not proceed without basic political reforms that allowed free criticism and initiative. In 1987–1988, Gorbachev took the plunge in this direction, spurred by heroic Soviet dissidents such as physicist Andrei Sakharov, by his own convictions, and by the necessity of reducing the tremendously costly arms race with the United States. As long as that race went on, the money necessary for productive economic investment would not be available, and the communist world would fall further behind the West.

Gorbachev therefore initiated a rapid winding down of the Cold War, meeting several times with President Ronald Reagan of the United States to sign agreements on arms control and troop reductions in divided Europe. Gorbachev also made gestures of reconciliation to China, and in 1989, he withdrew Russian troops from Afghanistan. They had been engaged there in a highly unpopular war—the Soviet Vietnam—on behalf of Soviet puppet rulers since 1979, while the United States supported the opposing guerrilla forces. Afghanistan proved to be the last of the surrogate wars fought between the two rival systems all over the globe since 1946.

Diane-Lu Hovasse/AFP/Getty Images

BORIS YELTSIN DEFIES THE ATTEMPTED COUP. In August 1991, Yeltsin, the president of the Russian Republic, mounted a tank drawn up before the Parliament Building to read out his refusal to surrender governmental powers to the hard-liners. At this time, coup participants were holding Gorbachev under arrest.

The most remarkable of Gorbachev's domestic initiatives was his drive to separate the Communist Party from the government of the Soviet Union. Between 1988 and 1991, the CPSU First Secretary presided over a series of moves that transformed the Soviet state. He initiated a true multiparty democracy with a parliament and a radically revised constitution. The CPSU's seventy-year monopoly on political life was abolished. A Congress of People's Deputies and a Supreme Soviet (a standing parliament) were elected and took office in 1989. Immediately, bitter conflicts arose between the worried communist hard-liners in the parliament and its sizable noncommunist minority.

Gorbachev's cautious moves toward democracy had greatly upset the old-guard CPSU activists and bureaucrats, but they had not gone nearly far or fast enough to satisfy the growing numbers of anticommunists and the supporters of thoroughgoing reform. A convinced believer in the possibilities of Marxism, the Soviet Union's last president also knew that real reforms were necessary. Gorbachev was a classic case of the moderate who is criticized by both extremes and cannot bring himself to join either one for survival. The result was his political death in the summer of 1991. The reformers led by Boris Yeltsin (YEL-tzihn) foiled an attempted coup by CPSU hard-liners, but it simultaneously revealed how naïve Gorbachev had been about his friends and his enemies. He was discredited and was soon pushed aside by Yeltsin.

The failed coup had undermined not only Gorbachev's prestige but also the authority of the Communist Party. Yeltsin had already demonstratively resigned from it, and he was now joined by millions of others. Within a few months, the party was declared illegal in Russia (although this decree was later reversed by court action), and its ranks faded to a few hundreds of thousands of embittered and demoralized members. To use Leon Trotsky's cruel words to the anti-Bolsheviks in 1917, it had been "thrown on the ash heap of history." Its enormous property and financial resources were either taken over by the government of Yeltsin or offered to private hands, in line with a vast "privatization" campaign that was introduced spasmodically, and with great difficulty, into the industrial and consumer economy as a whole. The dismantling of communism in the economic sphere, in fact, was going to prove as challenging as its introduction had been.

THE BREAKUP OF THE SOVIET UNION

Gorbachev had failed to recognize the depth of discontent in the Soviet Union. Above all, the fires of nationalism were finding steady fuel from the possibility—for the first time in a century of tsarist and communist rule—of expressing ethnic discontents openly. Indeed, glasnost proved to be a tremendous boost to the many peoples in this truly multiethnic union who wished to end their connection with Russia as well as with communism. Among them were Turkic and Mongol Asians who were second-class citizens in their own countries, Muslim fundamentalists who rejected Russia and communism with equal passion, and Ukrainian and Baltic nationals who had never accepted their coerced incorporation into the Soviet Union (see Chapter 42).

Once the reins were loosened, all of the western and southwestern borderlands of the Soviet Union were potential breakaways. Within two years of the initiation of glasnost, Armenians and Azeris were fighting one another over ancient disputes in the far Caucasus Mountains; wrathful Kazakhs in the new Kazakhstan were hunting down Russian immigrants; and the three Baltic republics of Latvia, Estonia, and Lithuania were demanding total independence. Ukraine, Georgia, Moldova, and some of the Muslim provinces along the southern borders of Siberia soon joined them. By mid-1991, the Soviet political structure of a federation dominated by the huge Russian Republic was in a state of collapse. The final straw came in August with the bungled coup, whose conspirators claimed that their goal was to reestablish the Union, although their first concern was to restore the rule of the Communist Party.

What eventually emerged from the events of 1991 was the **Commonwealth of Independent States (CIS)**, whose name reflects the difficulty of finding some common ground among its varied members once the lid of Russian communist rule was blown off. Eleven of the fifteen Soviet republics opted to join the commonwealth, whereas four (the Baltic states and Georgia) refused. The CIS was always a weak confederation—the smaller members would not agree to anything else—and was politically, economically,

MAP 52.1 Eastern Europe and the Former Soviet Union

Although in Eastern Europe only Yugoslavian borders were changed as an immediate result of the dissolution of the communist regimes, the borders of the Soviet Union were radically rearranged into four independent states and eleven members of a Commonwealth of Independent States (CIS). The Russian Republic is by far the most prominent of these, followed by Ukraine and Kazakhstan.

THINKING ABOUT THIS MAP

What were the political and economic reasons for the breakup of the old Russian empire?

and territorially dominated by the Russian Republic. In recent years, the CIS has become all but meaningless, replaced by bilateral agreements between sovereign states of the former Soviet empire (see Map 52.1).

Russia, led by Yeltsin's successors, Vladimir Putin (POO-tin) and Dmitry Medvedev (MEHD-veh-dehf), has remained a politically and economically fragile entity. During their terms as president, both men have managed to walk a fine line between intimidation or outright repression of political dissenters and the introduction of modern democratic civil life. The economy has been particularly vulnerable to corruption of every type, derived in large part from the too-rapid and helter-skelter distribution of state-owned resources to private parties in the Yeltsin years. Yet on balance, foreign observers agree that Russia has made a successful transition into a mainly—though not altogether—free-market economy. Agriculture and the isolation of the rural villages have remained what they had been under communism: the weakest points of the nation's economic and social life. The long-lived, bloody, repressive campaign against the breakaway Chechen terrorists in the far south has also been a major debit factor in both men's performance in both domestic and foreign eyes.

EASTERN EUROPE'S REVOLUTION OF 1989

In the fantastic fall of 1989, the communist governments of Czechoslovakia, East Germany, Bulgaria, and Romania were thrown out by peaceful protests or more violent means. Previously, the Hungarian communists had saved themselves temporarily only by agreeing to radical changes, and the Polish Communist Party had in desperation agreed to share political power with Walesa's Solidarity. A bit later, in 1990, the Yugoslav and the Albanian communist parties were cast aside. Thus, Soviet-style communism was decisively rejected by all who had had the misfortune to live under it for a long generation in Eastern Europe.

As in the Soviet Union, the primary cause of the Eastern European **Revolution of 1989** was the failure of the system to deliver on its promises of economic progress. This failure reinforced the nationalist resistance to Russian dominion, which most Eastern Europeans traditionally felt but which had been temporarily silenced in the postwar years. When Gorbachev showed that he believed in democratic ideas and was not inclined to keep Eastern Europe under communist control by force as his Soviet predecessors had, the cork came flying out of the bottle of discontent. (See the Evidence of the Past box.)

How did the Eastern Europeans go about ridding their nations of communism? The means varied from the massive, peaceful protests mounted by the East Germans and the Czechs (the "Velvet Revolution" in Prague), to the more gradual pressures brought by a wide spectrum of anti-Marxists in Bulgaria and Albania, to the lethal street fighting in Romania. In all of these countries, the communist party attempted to retain some support by renaming itself and participating as a legal party in the free elections held throughout post-communist Europe in 1990 and 1991. As in Russia, the frictions and disappointments of the transition to a free-market economy and a democratic polity allowed some former party leaders a second chance. Some "reform communists" were able to vindicate themselves in the eyes of their fellow citizens and retained or regained important posts in the Baltics, Hungary, Romania, and other states.

Generally speaking, the discredited old leaders were allowed to retire without being subjected to witch hunts. There was no attempt to bring any but a handful of the most hated to trial. In the name of the future, the most respected of the anticommunist leaders, including Walesa of Poland and Vaclav Havel (VAH-clauf HAH-vehl) of the Czech Republic, were inclined to put the past behind them as rapidly as possible and to forgive and forget those who had harassed and imprisoned them.

PROBLEMS OF THE POST-COMMUNIST ERA

The immediate economic problems of the new governments of Eastern Europe and the former Soviet Union were immense. They had to cope with a backward, collectivized agriculture that required far too much of their available labor and produced too little. Markedly inadequate consumer distribution networks and services had been the rule for forty years. Communication and information technology were decades behind current Western practice. The interest payments on the foreign debt accumulated by communist governments seeking popularity in the 1970s were eating up an intolerable percentage of the gross national product. Above all, the industrial sector, packed with superfluous workers by a standard communist policy of maintaining full employment through artificial means, was performing miserably. Most large companies were actually bankrupt, a fact masked by government ownership and subsidies. The biggest plants were almost always antiquated in technology, pollution ridden, and inefficient. Their low-quality output could not be sold in hard-currency markets and had to be forced on the domestic market or other communist countries.

The post-communist democratic governments had to make the difficult choice between adopting free-market capitalism in one sudden sink-or-swim shift or attempting to achieve a mixed economy less traumatically through a gradual transition from state to private

EVIDENCE OF THE PAST

The End of the Berlin Wall

The ultimate symbol of the Cold War between East and West came to be the ten-foot-high concrete line of the Berlin Wall. Erected by the East German government with Soviet approval and assistance in August 1961, it ran along the boundary between East and West Berlin in an attempt to stem the increasing numbers of East Germans who sought asylum in the free and economically prospering West Germany. The "death zones" on the eastern side of the wall were just that: Hundreds of people lost their lives attempting to sneak or burst their way across the barrier in the 1960s and 1970s. President John F. Kennedy's "*Ich bin ein Berliner*" speech at the wall in 1963 committed the Western alliance to the defense of the West Berliners and the eventual removal of the hated barrier to German unity.

The abrupt decision of the tottering East German government in November 1989 to allow free passage across the Berlin boundary signaled the end of the wall and of the Cold War. It heralded the demise of communism in Eastern Europe and, a little later, the Soviet Union. On November 9, 1989, the demoralized East German border guards gave up their defense of a collapsing state. American historian Robert Darnton gives his eyewitness account:

> The destruction of the Wall began in the early evening of Thursday, November 9th, soon after the first wave of East Berliners... burst upon the West. A young man with a knapsack on his back somehow hoisted himself upon the Wall... he sauntered along the top of it, swinging his arms casually at his sides, a perfect target for bullets that had felled many other Wall jumpers... border guards took aim, and fired, but only with power water hoses and without much conviction. The conqueror of the Wall continued his promenade, soaked to the skin, until at last the guards gave up....
>
> A few minutes later hundreds of people... were on the Wall, embracing, dancing, exchanging flowers, drinking wine... and chipping away at the Wall itself.

Another view comes from an East Berlin woman:

> I was performing with my cabaret group in Cottbus, about three hours' drive away from Berlin, when someone said they'd heard on the radio that the Wall had been opened. We all dismissed that as rumor. But you didn't know what to believe, there were so many rumors going around. About an hour after the performance, we were driving back and heard it on the radio ourselves. When we arrived in Berlin, we immediately drove across into the West....The city center, on Ku'damm, was one big party. After an hour we came back, and my friend dropped me off at my home.
>
> Bert, my husband, was away on a business trip and the kids were already asleep. Thirty minutes later, my friend called me back and said he couldn't sleep. I couldn't, either, so we decided to go back again. It was something like two or three in the morning....I didn't come back till it was time for my kids to get up.
>
> The next weekend Bert and I and the kids went off on a trip to West Germany. People were passing out drinks along the autobahn. There were huge lines. I took a glass of something and thought: what kind of funny lemonade is this? It was champagne!
>
> That first week people were marvelous. There was an openness, a new spirit.

ANALYZE AND INTERPRET

Where else besides Berlin has a physical barrier been erected to separate people for purely political/ideological reasons? Do you think such separation could be effective in creating permanent ethnic divisions? What was the German experience?

Source: Robert Darnton, *Berlin Journal, 1989–1990* (New York: Norton, 1991), 75.

Pictorial Press/Pictorial Press Ltd/Alamy Limited

THE WALL COMES DOWN. A horde of willing volunteers turned up on November 9, 1989, and every succeeding day for a month to help smash down the hated wall that had divided Berlin and the Berliners for almost three decades. Here, East German border guards look on from above at the Brandenburg Gate on November 11.

Bernd Heinz/vario images GmbH & Co.KG/Alamy Limited

VACLAV HAVEL (1936–2011). After an irresistible wave of public protests brought down the former regime, playwright and political dissident Vaclav Havel was inaugurated as the first post-communist president of the Czech Republic in 1990. Because no lives were lost during the uprising, the Czech revolt against the communist government is known as the "Velvet Revolution."

ownership. With the exception of Poland, which introduced basically free markets all at once, the governments opted for the gradual or partial approach. Some, like the Russians and Romanians, have tried to introduce free or freer markets, only to have to back off when they ran into popular resistance.

At the time of this writing, the Poles appear to have been more successful, but all of the countries have had severe difficulties in satisfying the justified demands of their citizenry for decent living standards and a better life. The first fruits of the post-communist economic order were rapid inflation, endemic corruption, large-scale unemployment at bankrupt state-owned enterprises, and the highly visible division of the new free-market society into haves and have-nots. For many farmers, unskilled workers, and pensioners, the new situation could not be coped with and was a definite worsening of their material status. Although these evils have abated in the past decade, they and similar problems of transition from the communist command economy remain strong enough to generate many negative estimates.

Many citizens, especially the older generation, were embittered at the initially surging crime rates, the appearance of a "mafia" of newly rich and corrupt *biznezmeni* (bizh-NEHZ-meh-nee: business elite), and other unsavory phenomena of a disoriented and dislocated society. The prolonged inability of the Yeltsin government in Russia (1992–2000) to attain fiscal stability and organize its revenues had injurious repercussions throughout all of Eastern Europe, frightening off much potential Western investment that was badly needed.

These economic facts have of course been reflected in the internal political sphere. Russia and most of the Eastern European states (Romania was an exception) quickly installed complete personal freedom, honest elections, a free press, and effective justice and security, but these changes were not enough to ward off a certain disillusionment. It should be remembered that the Eastern Europeans are laboring under a special handicap: They have never had a prolonged period of political freedom and constitutional government. In most of their countries, the years of parliamentary democracy could be measured on the fingers of both hands (see Chapter 42). The postwar communist repression of the educated and the middle classes and its artificially imposed "class solidarity" have made the necessary consensus for parliamentary give-and-take even more difficult to achieve. Worst of all, the violent, negative nationalism that was the curse of the early twentieth century was lying just below the surface in communist nations, as the spectacular and tragic disintegration of the former Yugoslavia has demonstrated. The eruption in Kosovo between Serbs and Albanians and the bloody repression of the Chechen rebellion in Russia were other severe blows to hopes for an easy transition from communist coercion to democratic cooperation.

Clearly, the tasks of establishing effective, responsive, and just government in these multiethnic countries have been enormous and will not be solved for many years, if at all. Besides the former Yugoslavia, ethnic rivalries and split loyalties have caused the breakup of Czechoslovakia. In Russia, Putin and Medvedev (Putin's temporary successor as president) have steadily rolled back many of the civil rights their citizens had enjoyed through the 1990s. Many Russian companies have been harassed or driven out of business, while the Russian press has found itself no longer free to criticize the government. In the international arena, the outlook has also become clouded. On one hand, Russia under Putin and Medvedev has shown itself committed to maintaining reasonable relations with the West, even to the point of tolerating some of its former satellites joining the European Union (see Chapter 46). Russia has also had to accept the permanent and authentic sovereignty of the Eastern European states, although an invasion and occupation of Georgia's northern provinces in 2008, occasioned by unresolved border issues, demonstrated the limits of that acceptance.

The twenty-first century has been good for Russia. Its fortunes have improved dramatically with the discovery and export of oil, gas, and other valuable industrial materials from its vast resource base. For Russians, this has produced a gradual improvement in their standards of living. For the Russian leadership, it has meant freedom from the embarrassment of having to accept aid from its erstwhile enemies and has enabled Putin and Medvedev to reassert an independent Russian voice in world affairs.

In recent years, Russia has resumed interfering in the internal politics of former Soviet member states, including an occupation of northern Georgia; resumed (albeit muted) saber-rattling over American plans to deploy an antimissile system in Eastern Europe; and allied itself with China in opposing stronger international sanctions designed to curb gross human rights abuses in the Sudan and to prevent the spread of nuclear weapons to Iran. Furthermore, Russia provided Venezuela with tanks and aircraft to counter American military and political power in the Caribbean basin and Latin America. The election of President Barak Obama, however, helped to reverse some of these worrisome trends. A diplomatic effort by the President and former Secretary of State Hillary Clinton improved relations to some extent, including an agreement to further reduce nuclear weapons by both nations.

SUMMARY

The astonishingly rapid collapse of the Soviet political and economic dominion in the years 1989–1990 came as a surprise to even the most perspicacious observer. An accumulating discontent with the multiple failures of the communist system to provide freedom or a decent material life for its citizenry joined with the long-standing resentments of non-Russian nationalists under Soviet rule to bring down the Marxist-Leninist regimes like falling dominos. The collapse of the Soviet Union immediately brought forth a series of claims to independence by the peoples along the western and southern borders of the traditional Russian state, claims that had to be recognized, however reluctantly, by the former masters in Moscow. The former Soviet satellites in Eastern Europe broke entirely free and began a sometimes painful and halting reintegration into the general European community. Both they and the new Russia found their way into the new millennium laden with inherited difficulties in their economies and in political issues—particularly a rampant nationalism that had survived the communist era.

IDENTIFICATION TERMS

Test your knowledge of this chapter's key concepts by defining the following terms. If you can not recall the meaning of certain terms, refresh your memory by looking up the boldfaced term in the chapter, turning to the Glossary at the end of the book, or accessing the terms on the CourseMate website at **www.cengagebrain.com**.

Berlin Wall
command economy
Commonwealth of Independent States (CIS)
glasnost
Mikhail Gorbachev
Nikita Khrushchev
peaceful coexistence
perestroika
Revolution of 1989
Secret Speech
Solidarity movement

FOR FURTHER REFLECTION

1. Politicians and historians sometimes assert that the fall of communism in Russia and Eastern Europe was a sudden event brought on by policies enacted by President Ronald Reagan. Based on material presented in this chapter (and previous ones), evaluate the accuracy of this claim.
2. What specific causes brought about the demise of communism in Europe? Why has it persisted in Cuba and eastern Asia?
3. What problems have Russia and Eastern Europe faced in maintaining systems based on democracy, individual rights, and free-market capitalism since 1989?

TEST YOUR KNOWLEDGE

Test your knowledge of this chapter by answering the following questions. Complete answers appear at the end of the book. You may find even more quiz questions on the CourseMate website at **www.cengagebrain.com**.

1. Stalin's main objective in Eastern Europe in the immediate postwar era was to
   a. hunt down and punish Nazis and their sympathizers.
   b. secure military assistance against a possible Western attack.
   c. generate a better supply of consumer goods.
   d. repair war damage to the Soviet Union and assure communist control.
   e. help Eastern European countries become stronger than those in Western Europe.

2. Which Eastern European country proved that the Western Allies were no longer willing to fight Stalin for control in that region?
   a. Czechoslovakia
   b. Poland
   c. Hungary
   d. Yugoslavia
   e. Germany
3. The Soviet Union controlled the communist governments in every Eastern European state except
   a. Yugoslavia.
   b. Romania.
   c. Czechoslovakia.
   d. Bulgaria.
   e. Poland.
4. The major reason for Khrushchev's sudden expulsion from leadership of the CPSU in 1964 was his
   a. submission to the Maoists.
   b. embarrassment over the attempt to place missiles in Cuba.
   c. disregard of the mounting pressure for consumer goods.
   d. efforts to emulate Stalin too closely.
   e. attempts to restructure the CPSU and to implement a new farm policy.
5. The creator of the term *goulash communism* was
   a. Gorbachev.
   b. Khrushchev.
   c. Stalin.
   d. Yeltsin.
   e. Tito.
6. A revolt in 1956 that challenged Soviet control occurred in
   a. Poland.
   b. Berlin.
   c. East Germany.
   d. Hungary.
   e. Yugoslavia.
7. The only aspect of Soviet life that did not lose momentum under the leadership of Leonid Brezhnev was
   a. religion.
   b. consumer spending.
   c. technology.
   d. the arts.
   e. the military.
8. As the head of the Communist Party in the late 1980s, Gorbachev's fundamental problem
   a. was his inability to see the need for change.
   b. came from foreign affairs such as the Afghan war.
   c. was his indecision about the extent of necessary reforms.
   d. was his continuing belief in the probability of war against the United States.
   e. developed from his need to make friends with Ronald Reagan.
9. Following the end of the era of Soviet domination and the Cold War, the biggest problem facing Russia and some Eastern European nations has been
   a. little sense of national identity and cohesion.
   b. the return of communism.
   c. the return to autocratic government.
   d. excessive nationalism.
   e. weak governments.
10. Under the leadership of Putin and Medvedev, Russia has experienced
    a. a return to a centrally controlled, command economy.
    b. the creation of a two-tiered society.
    c. a significant loss of individual civil rights that had been won in the 1990s.
    d. the revival of Russia's military power.
    e. the return to Russian control over her former Eastern European satellites.

CourseMate

Visit the CourseMate website at **www.cengagebrain.com** for additional study tools and review materials for this chapter.

53 A New Millennium

If you educate a woman, you educate a nation. —GHANAIAN PROVERB

1945	United Nations founded
1948–1973	Economic boom in West
1950s–1960s	End of Colonial Era
1963	Nuclear Atmospheric Test Ban
1970	Widespread recognition of environmental crisis begins
1970s–1980s	Female economic equality drive
1986	Chernobyl nuclear plant meltdown
1991	Atmospheric pollution documented over Antarctica
1990s	Global warming demonstrated
2000	United Nations Millennium Declaration to address issues of development
2001	Attack on World Trade Center
2008–2012	Global economic downturn
2011–2012	Arab Spring revolutions
2012	World Population reaches 7 billion

CHAPTER OUTLINE

A SHORT AND VIOLENT CENTURY BEHIND US

The end of the first decade of the new millennium is a good point for making a brief survey of current trends in the world that readers of this book are inheriting. One of the most urgent demands for attention is the sharpening of ethnic, religious, and national hostilities around the world. Simultaneously, the global Cold War between the two great power blocks that defined the second half of the old century has faded into relative unimportance. A noteworthy book[1] by the historian John Lukacs claims that what we call the *twentieth century* really lasted only the seventy-five years between the outbreak of world war in 1914 and the collapse of communism in Europe in 1989. According to Professor Lukacs, these two landmarks defined the last century—the first

[1] John Lukacs, *The End of the Twentieth Century and the End of the Modern Age* (New York: Ticknor & Fields, 1993).

announcing its commencement, the second its end. For many who lived through a century that was dominated by colonialism, two world wars, and the Cold War (when Western Powers for the most part shaped those events), Lukacs's view of the world had some appeal. From the perspective of the current century, however, we know that his thesis was an oversimplification of history that failed to take into consideration emerging technologies, globalization, and the importance of the non-Western world. Many of these changes do not bode well for a new day of world harmony.

TECHNOLOGY AND POLITICAL CULTURE

It is a shopworn cliché to say that our globe has shrunk incredibly in the last two generations. Mass communications and instantaneous transfer of data and ideas from one corner of the earth to the others have worked a transformation that contemporary human beings have not yet fully grasped. We only dimly understand the dimensions of the problems that have arisen, let alone their solutions. (See the Science and Technology box.)

A chief difficulty is that our technology has far outrun our ethics, our ways of thinking, and our political culture. We can do things that have tremendous power for good or evil in the lives of human beings—our own and those in the future—but we do not know how to determine "good" or "evil" in a consensual fashion. In a world that has become immensely more interdependent, rivals of all types are still pursuing the old chimera of "I win, so you lose." This is as true in economic development and environmental protection as it is in international wars and ethnic conflicts. The results are often chaotic and sometimes fatal for whole groups.

One of the noteworthy contradictions of the contemporary world is the fact that, as advances in electronics are making physical distance almost irrelevant to communication, economic and social factors are splitting the human community into pieces that seem to have little to communicate to one another. The wealthy nations abound in previously unheard-of personal luxuries and social resources of every type, whereas the poor nations possess few resources and are unable to produce them sufficiently to meet the growing demand. Several countries have already experienced a Third Industrial (or Postindustrial) Revolution, but it has not begun in many others. Some of these nations have even remained largely untouched by the first two industrial revolutions.

Contemporary society is a kaleidoscope of significant differences, often concealed beneath a thin veneer of similarities that are generated in the West and then adopted worldwide: Women apply much the same cosmetics, for exactly the same reasons, throughout the modern world; from Kenyan villages to New York apartments, children play with plastic toys mass-produced in Chinese factories; Afghan heroin finds its dark path into Russian seaports as well as Houston nightclubs. But these superficial uniformities of cultural behavior are deceptive. A better acquaintance or the arrival of a crisis lays bare the lasting differences. Many of them are direct reflections of the extreme variations in the economies of the most- and least-developed nations in the world of the twenty-first century.

THE RICH AND THE POOR: CONTRASTS

Despite the best efforts of well-meaning individuals in powerful positions, the personal-income gradient from the heights of developed countries to the lower slopes of the underdeveloped remains as steep as ever. In the 1990s, the enrichment of the already prosperous was steadily matched by the impoverishment of the already poor. According to the World Bank, in 1950, the average per capita gross domestic product—a commonly used measure of individual wealth—of the world's "advanced economies" was ten times that of the least advanced ones. In 2007, that gap had increased to nearly seventeen times. Gross domestic production per capita in Burundi, the poorest nation in the world, was slightly more than 1/400th of that in the United States ($120 versus $43,730 according to statistics from *The Economist*). And there are a few countries—namely Norway, Sweden, Switzerland, Denmark, and Luxembourg—in which the per capita GDP exceeds that of the United States.

Both social interventionists and supporters of the unrestricted free market have advanced various schemes for improving the living standards of the poor, but in the most poverty-stricken economies, these attempts have failed. Africa, in particular, has experienced meager improvement. Despite the current deep recession, most of the West and Asia has been experiencing the *longest-sustained economic advance in modern history*—nearly a quarter century of burgeoning prosperity for both the owning and the laboring classes—which has resulted in important social, political, and cultural changes by the present decade. The failure of most of the less-developed nations, particularly in Africa and Latin America, to provide anything like a comparable living standard for their citizens has created a dangerous gap between the two worlds of rich and poor. Neither the doctrinaire prescriptions of the communists nor the "unseen hand" of the free marketers has forestalled this sharpening division between haves and have-nots. And despite the hopes of some, the consequences of the increased globalization of world trading patterns continues to show many debatable or downright-debilitating features for the have-nots.

SCIENCE AND TECHNOLOGY

The Future of the Internet

Since its inception, the Internet has expanded exponentially. Combined with wireless technology, the Internet had 2 billion users by 2010. By the year 2020, there could be 5 billion individuals throughout the world interacting in this global brain and nervous system.

It is probably impossible to predict the future ramifications of information technology. Some computer scientists foresee a world thick with intelligent cyber-devices and seamless interfacing between humans and technology. The new emphasis will be on the *quality*, not the *quantity* of data. Time, not space, will be the preoccupation of technological humanity. In addition, a future evolution of the Internet could expand our horizons, instead of reinforcing our preconceived notions.

Recommendations from the Millennium Project's 2011 "State of the Future" report include the challenge to make technology accessible and functional for everyone in the world. Quoting from the report, "[This challenge] will have been addressed seriously when Internet access and basic tele-education are free and available universally and when basic tele-medicine is commonplace everywhere."

"New forms of civilization will emerge from [the] convergence of minds, information, and technology worldwide.... The race is on to complete the global nervous system.... Collaborative systems, social networks, and collective intelligences are self-organizing into new forms of transnational democracies that address issues and opportunities.... "

"It is hard to imagine how the world can work for all without reliable tele-education, tele-medicine, and tele-everything. Internet bases with wireless transmission are being constructed in remote villages; cell phones with Internet access are being designed for educational and business access by the lowest-income groups, and innovative programs are being created to connect the poorest 2 billion people to the evolving nervous system of civilization.... Social networking spurs the growth of political consciousness and popular power, as in the "Arab Spring."

"Developing countries and foreign aid should have broadband access as national priorities, to make it easier to use the Internet to connect developing country professionals overseas with the development processes back home....

"Humanity, the built environment, and ubiquitous computing are becoming a continuum of consciousness and technology reflecting the full range of human behavior...." The Millennium Project report warns that there are also problems to be dealt with so that the potential can be reached: "Low-cost computers are replacing high-cost weapons as instruments of power in asymmetrical warfare. Cyberspace is also a new medium for disinformation,... and is a battleground between cybercriminals and law enforcement.... We have to learn how to counter future forms of

CAIDA/Science Source/Photo Researchers, Inc.

MAP OF GLOBAL INTERNET TRAFFIC. Computer graphic of global Internet traffic. Each line represents the path of sample data sent out to one of 20,000 preselected locations using a system called Skitter. The lines are color-coded to show the nationality of that part of the Internet, for example: United States (pink), United Kingdom (dark blue), Italy (light blue), Sweden (light green), and white (unknown). The Internet is a global computer network through which information can be shared. Maps like this will make moving around the Internet easier, as well as showing when and where data jams occur. Made by the Cooperative Association for Internet Data Analysis, University of California, USA.

information warfare that otherwise could lead to the distrust of all forms of information in cyberspace." Other important matters include: increasing the bandwidth to ensure the reliability of the Net, privacy issues arising from cloud-computing, and the question of net neutrality to ensure equal access to all.

ANALYZE AND INTERPRET

What are the present-day Internet's advantages and disadvantages for you as an individual and for global society? Do you think it likely that the poorest two billion people will attain access to the Internet, as suggested by the Millennium Project? Are you optimistic or pessimistic about relying on technological innovations to address the world's problems? What threats might future communications technology pose to the civil rights of individuals?

The Millennium Project; Global Futures Studies & Research, "Global Challenges for Humanity, 2011," by Jerome C. Glenn, Theodore Gordon, and Elizabeth Florescu. www.millennium-project.org/millennium/challenges Accessed 9/21/2011.

APPROACHES TO SOCIAL REFORM

The collapse of the Soviet communist bloc in 1989–1991 was the unforeseen end of a system of economics and politics that had haunted the Western democracies for seventy years. In the interwar years and immediately after World War II, communism seemed likely to spread throughout the world either by revolution or by parliamentary procedure. In the underdeveloped lands, many millions saw it as the best hope at a decent material life for them and their children. In some countries such as China and Cuba, communism did bring an initial surge of social and economic justice to the masses and earned the support of many. They were willing to pay for their better economic prospects by giving up the political and social freedoms they had only minimally and imperfectly enjoyed under the previous colonial or capitalist system.

But this was not true of the Western countries, including Eastern Europe. Here, when the people had a choice, they firmly rejected the political, economic, and intellectual sacrifices demanded by communism. The Western socialist parties severed all connections with Soviet communism during the 1950s and even distanced themselves from many of the long-treasured ideas of Karl Marx. Other forms of socialism, such as evolution and gradualism, rather than radical change became the order of the day among the social democrats.

What had previously been considered a peculiarly American viewpoint—that the secret of social harmony was in making a bigger pie rather than rearranging the slices—came to prevail in all Western nations. Furthermore, although never clearly admitted, this view came to be the new Soviet orthodoxy after Josef Stalin's death. Revolution in the eyes of Leonid Brezhnev or even Nikita Khrushchev was reserved for developing countries, where any other means of effecting change was out of the question, and such a revolution was desirable only where it served Soviet foreign policy. By the 1970s, it was fair to say that only Fidel Castro in Cuba, Mao Zedong in China, and the leaders of a few newly independent African and Southeast Asian states gave more than lip service to Marx's original doctrines of social and economic egalitarianism. The Marxist dream of the proletariat achieving a universal earthly heaven had been put on the shelf indefinitely.

Prosperity in the Developed Societies

So long as the economic boom in the West lasted, social changes *did* come as both a reflection and a cause of vast improvement in the workers' living and working conditions. These improvements were what finally nullified the appeal of communism, as the Soviet system proved unable to generate anything like them.

In the 1980s, Western workers (extending "Western" to mean Japan) worked about one-fourth fewer hours weekly to earn wages that purchased about two and a half times as much in real terms as in 1950. They had guarantees of job security, wage or salary increases, vacation and sick time, insurance against accidents and ill health, extended unemployment pay, family leave, and other benefits that would have astounded workers of the 1940s. Under the impact of the higher energy costs after the OPEC oil boycott, increased competitive pressures in world markets since globalization, and the loss of jobs to low-wage countries, some of these gains have been curtailed by businesses or diluted by governments.

Higher education is vastly more accessible, with state scholarships or stipends for student living expenses the rule in all countries. Material living conditions have also vastly improved. In the United States, most salaried and about half of the wage-earning people own their homes. In Europe and Japan, where rentals are the urban standard, working-class families can afford more space, and private automobiles have been commonplace for many years even among manual workers. Upward mobility out of the working classes into the technical or professional groups has been extensive everywhere. In these real senses, social and material progress in the West has been consistent and effective since 1945, although the severe recession of 2007–2009 has brought serious hardships for millions, and as of this writing it remains to be seen if previous levels of prosperity will be regained in the near future.

Losing Ground in the Developing Countries

The developing world has unfortunately often shown a contrary pattern. The shift from manual to mental white-collar work and from agriculture to technological pursuits has been slow and halting, at best. Productivity has in some places and job types actually declined, as in much of sub-Saharan family farms. Social mobility has increased, but only a small proportion of people with access to higher education and connections have moved upward. In absolute numbers, *downward mobility* has probably been more common than upward in Africa and Latin America, where large groups of previously independent small landowners have been forced out of their traditional niches or impoverished by demographic pressures and overdependence on market-oriented agriculture. The near-total absence of organizations such as independent trade unions or farmers' associations leaves these people vulnerable to changes imposed by the vicissitudes of world markets, with no one to help defend their interests. The small Latin American farmer and African mine worker can rarely improve their economic or social prospects except by migration to the city, with its attendant dangers and frequent failure.

THE GENDER GAP

Since the middle of the twentieth century, women have been slowly closing the gap between them and men in the social and economic arenas of the Western world. In 1964, a French wife and mother had to obtain the written permission of her husband to open a bank account in her own name. Ten years later, after a ferocious verbal battle, the French parliament legalized abortion upon the request of the pregnant woman. Twenty years after that, women outnumbered men in the parliament. These three facts are useful to symbolize the changes in the status of women brought about by the struggle for **women's liberation** in the last several decades.

Many if not most countries now have laws (sometimes unenforced) that prohibit paying women less than men for the same work, discriminating on the basis of gender for promotions or entry into a profession, refusing credit to women, denying them contractual rights, denying women custody of minors, and so on. However, in the United States, women's pay is still about three-fourths that of men doing the same work, and few corporations promote women beyond middle management. In graduate schools of law, medicine, and education, the number of women students equals or exceeds the number of men. But men still vastly outnumber women in the fields of business and science. Change is not limited to the economic and labor sectors. The formerly normal status of marriage for young women has been radically questioned. In the United States, one-third of all babies are born to single women—up from about 8 percent forty years previously. Similar or higher numbers are found in countries ranging from Scandinavia to South Asia.

In the non-Western world, where women's empowerment will be a vital resource for improving the lot of poverty-stricken humanity, unfortunately women continue to be the poorest of the poor. Women comprise two-thirds of the world's one billion people living in extreme poverty, and two-thirds of the illiterate population. Generally speaking, women work twice the hours that men do, earn only 10 percent of the world's income, and own less than 1 percent of the property. Violence is the second leading cause of death among women, after cancer. According to World Vision's president, "When a girl is educated, her income potential increases, maternal and infant mortality is reduced, her children are more likely to be immunized, the birth rate decreases, and HIV infection rates... are lowered. She is more likely to acquire skills to improve her family's economic stability, and... to ensure that her daughters also receive an education. Educating girls pays dividend after dividend to the whole community."[2]

FAMILY AND THE INDIVIDUAL

The dramatic changes in family life over the past generation are evident in several ways. The two-parent two-generation male breadwinner and female-housewife model, which had been the ideal for Western urban families since the mid-nineteenth century, has clearly become but one of several *alternative* lifestyles. This change will presumably have wide-ranging but as-yet-unknowable effects on the importance and permanence of the nuclear family.

The increasing numbers of female-headed households and economically independent females in all Western and some non-Western countries have put women into a position of potential political power that has been unparalleled in recent history. But to the dismay of more aggressive feminists, so far this potential has not been realized. Despite the occasional emergence of charismatic political leaders such as Indira Gandhi, Benazir Bhutto, and Golda Meir and a steady upward trend for females in legislative and administrative bodies worldwide, women have shown themselves generally unmoved by appeals to feminism as a political—as distinct from a socioeconomic—force. One cogent reason is that informal living together supplants formal marriage, and abandonment by the male grows easier and more common, while enforcing legal responsibility for maintenance of spouse or children is difficult, if not impossible. Annually, many millions of women, from the villages of Africa to the ghettos of U.S. cities, find themselves thrown into permanent poverty by the breakup of their living arrangements with a man. Grappling with acute problems of survival, poor women have had little interest or energy to organize for longer-term political goals. The United Nations is working to ensure that women's human rights are not restricted in the name of religious or cultural traditions. (See the Law and Government box.)

A third phenomenon in recent familial history is that the social identification that individuals in the past received from their families has largely become superfluous or is consciously rejected. The individual, not the family or the clan, exercises choice, creates opportunity, accepts responsibility, and generally makes his or her own personal mark in the Western world (and, increasingly,

[2] R.E Sterns, "Thank Heaven for Little Girls? Much of the World Doesn't," World Vision Magazine, Vol. 10, No. 3 [Spring, 2007], p. 4.

LAW AND GOVERNMENT

2010 United Nations Millennium Development Goals: A Progress Report

In 2000 the United Nations member nations pledged to free the world's inhabitants from poverty, hunger, disease, and illiteracy. The world's major development institutions joined with the nations to formulate, implement, and track the Millennium Development Goals (MDGs) for 2015. This project has been more successful in some areas (reduction in child mortality) than in others (gender equality). The following selection from a recent annual report provides some details.

> Many countries are moving forward, including some of the poorest, demonstrating that setting bold, collective goals in the fight against poverty yield results.... But unmet commitments, inadequate resources, lack of focus and accountability, and insufficient dedication to sustainable development have created shortfalls ... [which] were aggravated by the global food and economic and financial crises....
>
> Gender equality and the empowerment of women are at the heart of the MDGs and are preconditions for overcoming poverty, hunger and disease. But progress has been sluggish on all fronts—from education to access to political decision-making.
>
> **Building on successes**
>
> Progress on poverty reduction is still being made, despite significant setbacks due to the 2008-2009 economic downturn, and food and energy crises.... The overall poverty rate is still expected to fall to 15 per cent by 2015 [half the rate in 1990].
>
> Major advances have been made in getting children into school in many of the poorest countries, most of them in sub-Saharan Africa.
>
> Remarkable improvements in key interventions—for malaria and HIV control, and measles immunization, for example—have cut child deaths [by about one-third].
>
> The rate of deforestation, though still alarmingly high, appears to have slowed, due to tree-planting schemes combined with the natural expansion of forests.
>
> Increased use of improved water sources in rural areas has narrowed the large gap with urban areas.... However, the safety of water supplies remains a challenge and urgently needs to be addressed.
>
> Mobile telephony continues to expand in the developing world and is increasingly being used for m-banking, disaster management and other non-voice applications for development....
>
> **Bridging the gaps**
>
> Though progress has been made, it is uneven. And without a major push forward, ... [old] and new challenges threaten to further slow progress in some areas or even undo successes achieved so far. Vulnerable populations who have contributed least to the problem are feeling the most severe impact of climate change. The risk of death or disability and economic loss due to natural disasters is increasing globally and is concentrated in poorer countries.
>
> Armed conflict remains a major threat to human security and to hard-won gains. Large populations of refugees remain in camps with limited opportunities to improve their lives, ... four-fifths of them in developing countries.
>
> The number of people who are undernourished has continued to grow, while slow progress in reducing the prevalence of hunger stalled ... in some regions ... About one in four children under the age of five are underweight, mainly due to lack of ... quality food, inadequate water, sanitation and health services, and poor care and feeding practices.
>
> An estimated 1.4 billion people were still living in extreme poverty in 2005 [and in 2010]. Moreover, the effects of the global financial crisis are likely to persist: poverty rates will be slightly higher in 2015 and even beyond, to 2020, than they would have been had the world economy grown steadily at its pre-crisis pace....

ANALYZE AND INTERPRET

Explain how gender equality and the empowerment of women would be critical to reducing world poverty. Have you learned of (or contributed to) any specific projects that address issues mentioned? What additional global problems could be cited?

(Source: "Overview" By Sha Zukang, U.N. Under-Secretary-General for Economic and Social Affairs at http://www.un.org/milleniumgoals, pp. 4–5.)

everywhere else). Although this may be seen as a further large step toward democracy and fair play, it also has certain detrimental aspects for both individuals and society. One, the feeling of alienation from others, is highly stressful. It has been most apparent in those locales where the traditional family has become weakest: the urban, mobile, wealthy West where the individual is an atom among atoms rather than a link in a chain. The degree to which this has become true can easily be demonstrated by a simple question to the reader of these lines: Do you know where you are going to be buried? Probably, you have no idea where this traditionally most sacred rite will be carried out or who will do it—an unthinkable thing to confess until recently in human history.

LOOMING PROBLEMS

The United Nations and National Sovereignty

One of the touchiest of all topics in the current political discourse has been the degree to which national sovereignty must or should be surrendered to a supranational organization. The United Nations (UN) was founded in 1945 by the victorious Allies to do what its predecessor, the League of Nations, was unable to do: guarantee international peace. Unlike the League, the UN has a potentially powerful executive organ in the Security Council. The council has wide authority, including the power to take air, sea, and land military action against aggression.

The UN General Assembly has no such powers and can only debate issues and recommend action to the Security Council. All states of the world have an equal vote in the General Assembly, which in effect means that the developing countries have a large voice in the UN's nonmilitary aspects, such as labor, cultural affairs, and public health—through the International Labor Organization (ILO); the United Nations Educational, Scientific, and Cultural Organization (UNESCO); and the World Health Organization (WHO), respectively. These organs have played an important and positive role in world affairs for the last fifty years, even while the political and military performances of the UN were disappointing to many sympathetic observers.

The reason for their disappointment was that ultimate powers were retained by the sovereign states and not by the UN Secretariat (executive office). When a major state saw that its interests were being threatened by UN intervention of some type, it either exercised its veto in the Security Council or ensured by other means that there would be no effective interference. Throughout the Cold War era, the UN was able to intervene effectively only on the few occasions when both blocs could agree that a given conflict was intolerably dangerous (namely, the Israeli-Arab contest) or when one side chose to boycott the proceedings (for example, the UN decision to defend South Korea in the 1950s). The smaller powers, on the other hand, were frequently forced to conform to Security Council resolutions aimed at controlling their political and military inclinations and initiatives. Thus, the UN's guardianship of the peace was applied on two levels: one for the powerful, when it was dismissible, and the other for the less so, when it was sometimes effective.

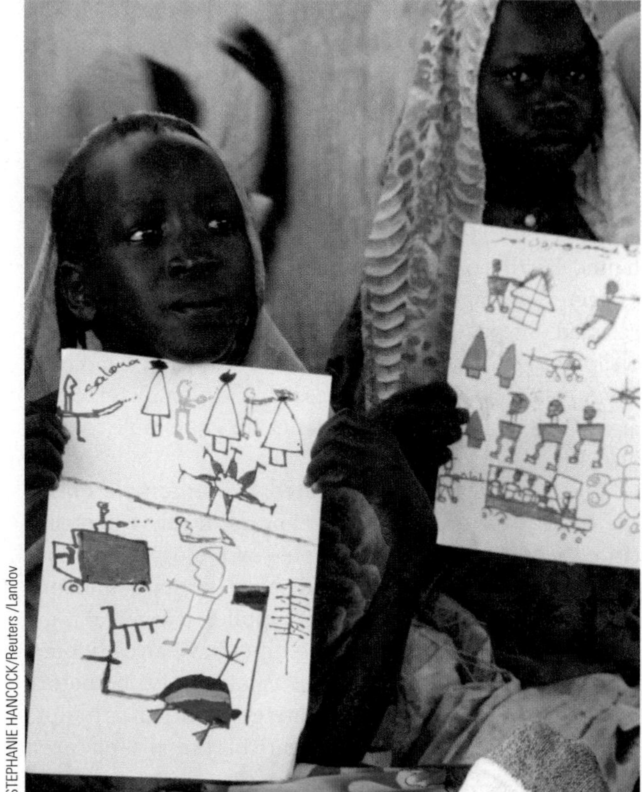

STEPHANIE HANCOCK/Reuters /Landov

REFUGEE GIRLS HOLD UP DRAWINGS OF JANJAWEED ATTACKS. Children's art starkly illustrates attacks on refugee camps. This particular one occurred in eastern Chad in 2007.

In most recent times, the relative collaboration between the United States and Russia in international affairs has given the UN an unprecedented freedom of action in maintaining peace and redressing injustice that might lead to war. The successful coalition against Iraq in the Gulf War of 1991 was an outstanding example of what can be done. Other examples were the universal condemnation of the terrorist acts of the al-Qaida group in 2001 and the support for the antiterrorist campaign in Afghanistan that followed. The limits of such collaboration among the world powers was, however, clearly shown in the international quarrels that marked the U.S. unilateral campaign to remove Iraqi dictator Saddam Hussein shortly thereafter. The fact that Cold War maneuvering has ended by no means has proved sufficient to bring international harmony. Instead, the blunders and frustrations that marked the attempted interventions by NATO and the UN to establish peace in the Yugoslav, Somali, and Rwandan civil wars of the 1990s, and in recent years in Dar Fur, may be the rule.

Control of Weapons of Mass Destruction

Another pressing problem awaiting solution is the proliferation of nuclear and other weaponry. So long as only the United States, the Soviet Union, Britain, and France had atomic weapons, the "deadly secret" of creating them could be contained. But in the late 1960s, the Chinese under Mao went ahead with their own research effort, and by the mid-1970s, they had cracked the atomic code. The Israelis and South Africans were next, followed closely by the Indians and Pakistanis, and in 2006, by the North Koreans. The mushroom cloud is spreading over wider territories and can be set off by more and more hands. Furthermore, the Iranian government is suspected of secret attempts to develop atomic weaponry and has resisted international efforts to end its refinement of weapons-grade uranium. Many also fear that Cold War weapons stocks might be accessed or stolen by terrorists and also that nuclear power plants are vulnerable to their attacks.

The same fears are generated by contemplation of the deadly use of so-called **weapons of mass destruction (WMDs)**—as, for example, in biological warfare through release of epidemic disease germs or poisons into the atmosphere or water supplies (chemical warfare). It is certain that such attempts have already been made. Many think that it is just a matter of time before some terrorist band or desperate government attempts chemical, biological, or nuclear blackmail—or even annihilation.

Terrorism

For centuries, people of all religions have debated the circumstances under which it is permissible to engage in "holy war" against followers of other faiths. For Muslims, *jihad* is meant to be employed against "unbelievers"—essentially non-Muslims. Although this seems clear enough in most situations (for example, where someone has declared himself to be a Christian), it becomes thorny when one has to judge who qualifies as an unbeliever. Muslims, for example, have long debated what makes a Muslim a Muslim. Does the fact that a person *declares* that he or she is Muslim, or does his *behavior* decide the question? In recent years, the world has seen the appearance of violent groups of religious extremists—such as Islamic Jihad and al-Qaida—who advocate not just a simple reassertion of Islamic values (Chapter 51), but holy war against governments and entire populations whom they judge to be heretics, including even civilians and (putatively) Muslim states. Called ***takfiri*** (from *takfir*: to accuse someone of being an unbeliever) Muslims, they employ terrorist methods to carry out what they see as their sacred duty to fight unbelief, including martyrdom in carrying out bombings.

From the perspective of Westerners, and Americans in particular, the entire question of terror employed for political or military ends came into focus with the airborne attacks on New York City and Washington, D.C. by the worldwide al-Qaida network headed by Saudi Arabian renegade Osama bin Laden on September 11, 2001. It was a day of mass death from enemy action, the first time that the United States had ever suffered such an event on its own soil. Whether others will follow it, as al-Qaida has repeatedly stated, cannot be known at this time. In the twelve years since the 2001 attacks, international surveillance and police collaboration have been able to intercept and render harmless many different plots to destroy lives and property. But al-Qaida and similar takfiri organizations have succeeded in several other attempts against governments and innocent bystanders, ranging the world from Spain to Indonesia.

Yet it must be said that it would be an egregious injustice to allege that only Muslims have engaged in such acts and to brand their beliefs as being inherently violent, as some have done. World history is replete with episodes of mass carnage carried out in the name of God, gods, saints, or prophets. Followers of all three of the monotheistic religions—Christianity, Judaism,

Scott Kemper/Alamy

WORLD TRADE CENTER ATTACK. Volunteers from all over the country converged on "ground zero" of the World Trade Center to clean up the debris of the attack of September 11, 2001. Hijacked airplanes were used as the instruments of destruction by terrorists of the al-Qaida international network of Islamic extremists.

and Islam—and Hinduism have made followers of other faiths the targets of attacks. Polytheists and Jews persecuted early Christians; in their conquests, Muslims attacked Christians and carried out frightful slaughters of Hindus and Buddhists; medieval Christians perpetrated atrocities in their Crusades against Muslims and repeatedly made Jews scapegoats for their (Christians') assorted sufferings. This pattern of conduct has continued right into the past century, which bore witness to systematic genocide against Jews (the Holocaust); attacks on Christians in Armenia, the Middle East, and Africa; instances of genocide against Muslims in Palestine and India; and murderous attacks on Hindus during the partition of India and Pakistan. So our world is left with an ancient stain that has yet to be blotted out—namely, that one person's holy war is another one's terrorism.

Cliff LeSergent/Alamy Limited

ONE ANSWER TO GLOBAL WARMING. The contribution of greenhouse gases to global warming, as well as dependence on imported oil, has been moderated by some communities that use alternative sources of energy such as these giant wind turbines near the Rocky Mountain foothills in Alberta, Canada.

Environmental Deterioration

We have all heard so much about the environmental threats to the continued survival of the human race that we may be tempted to throw up our hands and trust to good luck or hope that another habitable planet is found before this one becomes unlivable. Nevertheless, certain environmental dangers are both real and can be addressed effectively, if only we have the will to do so. The most urgent near-term problems facing us in the new millennium seem to be the following:

- *Excessive and unbalanced consumption of nonrenewable energy.* Each year, the average U.S. citizen consumes roughly thirty-five times as much energy (fossil fuel, water, electric) as a person in India and about three times as much as an individual in Italy or France. The tremendous difference between the rich nations and the poor in global affairs is nowhere more apparent than in energy consumption. The less-developed countries, with about 60 percent of world population, consume only 12 percent of the energy produced in the world; the developed countries consume the rest. And if per capita use remains the same in 2030 as it is today, the world will need to produce 50 percent more energy just to keep pace with population growth.
- *Global warming.* In the past fifteen years, what the world's scientific communities had looked upon as a possibility or a probability has become a certainty: the Earth's temperature is going upward at a rate unprecedented in historical times—**global warming** is a reality. Debate continues about the rate of increase, and some still question the nature of the causes. However, no serious scientists any longer question the basic fact, and a large majority attributes it to **greenhouse gases** produced by hydrocarbon fuel-burning power plants and automobiles. If the speed of change approximates the higher ranges now foreseen for the next ten years, the world's climate, vegetation, and sea levels will see massive alteration. Some predict that sea levels could rise as much as twenty feet, inundating large portions of the world's coastlands, while water shortages and droughts—already a major problem in many places—will become even more frequent and longer in duration. Already in short supply as a result of pollution, sources of fresh, potable water are plummeting as another result of global warming. Some foresee a future world of wars and mass migrations as competition for this most precious of resources continues to escalate.
- *Food production in Africa.* As a result of the sharply rising populations dependent on severely limited (and shrinking) reserves of arable land and the continued misuse of farmland to raise cash crops, African nations have been facing dwindling food supplies. Growing numbers of them now are permanently dependent on imported food and have become beggars in the world economy. Massive starvation on a periodic scale is the probable future of these nations without a coordinated

international attempt to assist them in feeding themselves. One result will be an explosion of civil wars such as the one currently being instigated by the North Sudanese government against its Dar Fur region and against South Sudan.

- *Pollution and radioactive wastes.* Many developing countries are almost entirely ignorant of or choose to disregard the most elementary pollution-control measures. Their industries and mines—frequently controlled by owners in the developed countries—poison the earth, air, and water on a large scale. The meltdown at the Chernobyl nuclear plant in Ukraine more than twenty-five years ago was the most spectacular example of the dangers posed by inadequate or nonexistent policing and protection. Many others might be cited. These potential catastrophes have no respect whatever for national borders, and the long-term, slow effects of pollution may be worse than the occasional explosive event such as Chernobyl.

This list is by no means comprehensive and deals only with what the authors of this book believe to be the problems with the most immediate global repercussions. During the life spans of students reading these lines, the developed world (the United States foremost) will either master the most urgent of these problems or substantially change the hitherto-known environment of human beings from a life with nature to a life *against* or *outside* nature. Whether this latter style of life is possible and at the same time humane is an open question.

SUMMARY

We earthlings live on a small planet, which is only a minor part of an eight-planet solar system, itself one of perhaps many thousands within a still-expanding cosmos. We will soon either succeed (temporarily) or fail (permanently) in our attempt to keep Earth livable for creatures like ourselves. We have seen that it is possible for humans to damage their habitat so drastically that it will no longer be a fit place for the species. What will be done in these regards in the next decades is largely up to people like yourselves, the educated men and women of a powerful country.

At bottom, there are only two rational approaches to the solution of basic environmental problems: *conservation*, which is the attempt to retain (conserve) existing systems, and *technology*, which is the attempt to discover (develop) superior replacements. The conservationists argue that the Earth's natural systems are the results of eons of slow evolution; that of all earthly beings, humans alone rebel against those systems rather than live with them; and that this rebellion, although it may be successful in the short run, spells ruin in the longer term. The technicians argue that evolution is only one path to an acceptable, sustainable system and that humans can and must try to find other paths when the natural one proves inadequate or has been blocked. The choices that must be made between these differing approaches will largely determine the quality and character of your lives.

Choices of every kind lie before you, as they have before all of your predecessors. Like them, you will often not be sure of what must be or should be done. Like them, you will have to seek guidance from many sources: religion, science, parents, and the study of history. The answers from history especially will often be unclear or cryptic; they may have sections missing or lend themselves to more than one interpretation. But the historical answer will usually be most applicable and most comprehensive: This is what humans, in all their variety, have done successfully to meet and overcome problems somewhat like those you currently encounter. And, like all of your predecessors on this earth, you will have to hope that you have understood correctly and have taken a constructive, viable path as you join the long parade of men and women moving forward into the infinite future.

IDENTIFICATION TERMS

Test your knowledge of this chapter's key concepts by defining the following terms. If you can not recall the meaning of certain terms, refresh your memory by looking up the boldfaced term in the chapter, turning to the Glossary at the end of the book, or accessing the terms on the CourseMate website at **www.cengagebrain.com**.

global warming
greenhouse gases
takfiri
weapons of mass destruction (WMDs)
women's liberation

FOR FURTHER REFLECTION

1. Do an online search for the latest information concerning actions by the United Nations and its various agencies to address the issues of peace, global inequalities, social reform (especially the rights of women and children), weapons control, terrorism, and global warming. What seem to be the major obstacles preventing these actions?

2. What do you think the planet Earth will be like in fifty years, compared with its current ecological, social, and economic state? Comment on the present and future gaps between the rich and the poor, on the main sources of energy now and then, on lifestyle changes worldwide, and on allocation of water and other natural resources. Reflect on how an understanding of historical events can help your generation make constructive decisions about these issues.

TEST YOUR KNOWLEDGE

Test your knowledge of this chapter by answering the following questions. Complete answers appear at the end of the book. You may find even more quiz questions on the CourseMate website at **www.cengagebrain.com**.

1. One of the chief problems of today's world is that ethics and the political culture have been outpaced by
   a. education.
   b. longevity.
   c. ambition.
   d. national aspirations.
   e. technology.
2. As of your textbook's printing, the poorest nation in the world was
   a. Burundi.
   b. Bangladesh.
   c. Rwanda.
   d. Djibouti.
   e. Eritrea.
3. The social democrats found their greatest strength in which of the following places?
   a. Cuba
   b. Soviet Union
   c. Eastern Europe
   d. Western Europe
   e. China
4. In Africa and Latin America, "downward mobility" has often been the lot of
   a. dictators.
   b. those who rejected Christianity.
   c. independent small landowners.
   d. former aristocrats.
   e. almost everyone.
5. Two conflicting approaches to solving environmental problems are
   a. conservation vs. technology.
   b. solar energy vs. fossil fuels.
   c. electric cars vs. high-speed railways.
   d. denial vs. acceptance.
   e. WDGs vs. WMDs.
6. Which of these United Nations development goals have had the most success?
   a. education of women and girls
   b. defeating world-wide terrorism
   c. reducing extreme poverty
   d. e-medicine via smart phones
   e. the ouster of Cuba's dictator
7. One of the touchiest subjects for the United Nations has been
   a. an international currency.
   b. national sovereignty.
   c. nuclear proliferation.
   d. poverty eradication.
   e. African dictatorships.
8. The United Nations Security Council voted to defend South Korea in 1950 because of
   a. a unanimous vote by all its members.
   b. the strong support by the United States.
   c. the leadership of U Thant.
   d. the strong fear of communism.
   e. a boycott by one of the council's members.
9. The world's developed countries, with about 40 percent of the earth's population, consume about what percentage of the energy produced?
   a. 40
   b. 62
   c. 25
   d. 88
   e. 95

10. Most of the world's poorest countries are in
    a. Southeast Asia.
    b. South America.
    c. Middle East.
    d. Africa.
    e. East Asia.

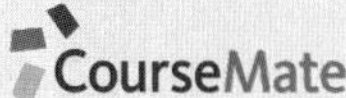

Visit the CourseMate website at **www.cengagebrain.com** for additional study tools and review materials for this chapter.

Putting It All Together

1. What changes occurred in the twentieth century that had global ramifications?
2. To what extent were World Wars I and II and the Cold War global phenomena? Explain your answer.
3. What important changes in the world did decolonization entail? What were the characteristics of these transformations?
4. Because decolonization became a major theme in world affairs, what ideologies emerged that had global significance? When these new ideologies spread around the world, how were they adapted to fit local traditions and values? To what new problems did their emergence give rise?
5. What further global changes have occurred in recent decades that have resulted (at least partly) from decolonization?

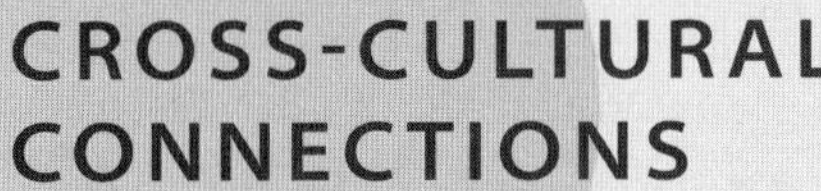

CROSS-CULTURAL CONNECTIONS

Trade and Exchange Networks

- Opening of Panama Canal (1914) facilitates international shipping; after World War II, jet airplanes speed up global trade connections.
- The Information Revolution is the culmination of century-long increase in communication capability and speed that began with radio and telegraph and culminated in communications satellites, computers, and the Internet. Information exchange on scale and speed unimaginable even twenty-five years before.
- Creation of regional trade zones began with European Common Market (1957; after 1970, expanded to become the European Union). In Americas, North American Free Trade Agreement (NAFTA; 1994) in North America, CACUM (1960; renewed 1986) in Central America, and Mercado Comun del Sur (MERCOSUR; 1991) in southern South America free-trade zones.
- Other organizations promoting international trade and development are Pacific Economic Cooperation Forum (APEC), which connects Pacific-rim countries of both hemispheres; Southern African Development Community (SADC); and Economic Community of West African States (ECOWAS). The Organization of Petroleum Exporting Countries (OPEC) unites petroleum-producing countries in the developing world.
- International institutions and agreements established to address problems of global scale: League of Nations, succeeded by United Nations; Kyoto Protocol (1997); International Criminal Court (2002) to prosecute crimes against humanity; a variety of nongovernmental organizations (NGOs) to promote human rights (Amnesty International, Doctors Without Borders); General Agreement on Tariffs and Trade (GATT; 1948), supplanted by World Trade Organization (WTO; 1996); World Bank and International Monetary Fund (IMF; 1945).
- Recent emphasis on micro-loans from private sources encourages small-scale entrepreneurs, particularly women, in impoverished areas.
- Rise of multinational corporations, largest of which wield power and influence comparable to that of richest countries. Export processing zones established in developing countries; favor multinational corporations with low taxes and pools of low-wage (mostly female) workers.
- Growth of service and information-exchange industries in developed countries, accompanied by outsourcing of factory jobs to underdeveloped countries.

Migrations and Population Changes

- Decline in infant mortality rates due to post-World War I emphasis on domestic hygiene ("cult to cleanliness") in West; spreads to developing world. Biological technologies increase life expectancy. Continuing population growth in developing countries; diminishing birthrates in developed world. Population growth and global interdependency result in need for foreign aid, development projects, outsourcing of menial jobs, and international solutions.
- Legal and illegal immigration to developed countries; increases cultural diversity and creates problems of assimilation and resentment by native citizens.
- Revolutions, civil wars, repressive regimes, genocides, poverty, and famine decimate populations and make refugees of millions of the survivors. Economic refugees outnumber political refugees at century's end.
- Rural people flood the cities. First waves of internal migrants build better lives in the cities; subsequent waves overwhelm megalopolises such as Rio de Janeiro, Brazil, and Lagos, Nigeria, where millions barely survive on fringes and in landfills of established societies.

Spread of Ideas and Technologies

- *Foods:* Government planning to prevent commercial (market-driven) famines for the first time. International efforts create high-yield strains of rice and wheat combine with mechanized farming implements to increase crop yields in developing world. Global commerce provides year-round access to seasonal produce, for a price.
- *Diseases:* Elimination or diminishment of diseases, but cholera, malaria, AIDS, and others persist. Spread of contagious diseases such as the Spanish influenza, Asian flu, AIDS, and severe acute respiratory syndrome (SARS), and the threat of new ones such as avian and West Nile flu, facilitated by improved and speeded-up international travel.
- *Ideas:* Beginning with the transistor radio in the 1960s, modern ideas and electronic communications technology reach isolated areas of Latin America, Africa, and Asia. Spread of democracy, free press, and personal freedoms after World War II. Conflicts can be resolved peacefully through elective process.
- Universal acceptance and adoption of Western scientific methods.
- Spread of the concept of universal human rights; however, century-long problem of terrorism a global phenomenon.
- Decrease in the number of spoken languages as national languages replace regional ones; English, French, and Spanish emerge as predominant languages of global exchanges.
- Political movements of transnational scope: 1968 youth protests, women's rights movement, and Amnesty International. In Information Age, human rights abuses difficult to hide. Public pressure decreases abuses of women, children, and political prisoners.
- Increased political participation and leadership by minorities and women. Women win suffrage rights in democratic countries and now serve at all levels of government, including as presidents of numerous countries.
- Spread of global religions (Buddhism, Christianity, and Judaism) along with diminished numbers of local religions.
- Emergence of global culture transcending national cultures, perceived by many as either threatening to traditional cultures or source of new choices in adapting to a changing world.

Worldview VI

Towards a Globalized World, 1914–Present

	 LAW AND GOVERNMENT	 SOCIETY AND ECONOMY
WESTERNERS*	• Rise of mass democracy creates new-style party government where money plays important role. Law increasingly reflects popular attitudes. Property rights under attack; civil rights advance. Totalitarian governments in some nations after World War I and Great Depression. After World War II, long economic boom allows democratic recovery and stability in West. Soviet communism expands for a generation, then collapses.	• 1920–1945 sees decline and near collapse of free market in West and impoverishment of middle classes and agriculturalists; 1945–present a long boom, interrupted by oil crisis of the 1970s. Japan emerges as financial power in 1980s. European Community becomes economic reality, whereas Soviet bloc stagnates and collapses. Global economy forming under Western dominance.
ASIANS	• ***South and East Asians:*** Former British possessions generally retained Western outlook on law and government. French and Dutch territories less committed to these ideals. In several nations, Marxist socialism combines nationalism with radical reform. Governments range from liberal democratic constitutionalism to dictatorships. China's mutated Marxism in a category of its own, combining political censorship with economic and social freedoms. • ***West Asians:*** Minority attempts to introduce modern Western law, education, and politics made after World War I with moderate success, except for Turkey. After World War II, forms of Islamic revival develop, led most recently by Iran. Governments range from limited Western constitutionalism to undisguised theocracy. Nationalism and Islam powerful forces throughout Africa and Asia.	• ***South and East Asians:*** South and East Asia a mixed picture of progress. In Bangladesh, Sri Lanka, and Burma, traditional agrarian and poverty-stricken economy barely changed or worsened as result of rapid population increases. South Korea, Taiwan, and Malaysia move toward modern industry and services in last thirty years. Japan's successful free-market example influential, but China remains unknown quantity in Asia's economic picture • ***West Asians:*** Middle East oil the major export, generating dependence. Effort was exerted to avoid this by using oil funds for domestic investments. Arab states and Indonesia relatively successful, but oil production remains key to prosperity. Poor Muslim countries unstable and still not integrated into world economy.
AFRICANS	• "Scramble" for Africa completed by early 1900s. Law and government continue on colonial lines until after World War II. Decolonization brings mixture of African traditional law and political structures with European models. Western forms often at odds with precolonial content. Postindependence problems encourage authoritarian governments. Regionalism, ethnic rivalries, and corruption major problems.	• Emphasis on export crops and mining converts some areas to food-deficit regions. Little manufacturing, even after end of colonialism. International aid provided in attempt to overcome declining agricultural productivity and dependency on world markets and imports. Because of large population increases, many national economies in crisis by 1990s.
LATIN AMERICANS	• Fundamental laws European, and governmental structures resemble those of West. Social gap between rich and poor frustrates intent of constitution and makes segregated legal procedure inevitable. Government represents only uppermost minority, although changing.	• Westernized urban lifestyle supported for minority by modern industrial economies. In most of continent, however, agrarian and deprived mestizo/mulatto population has made little progress. Rapid population increase prevents substantial or permanent gains from international investments and loans. Most of Latin America continues dependent on Western nations.

*It seems appropriate to replace Europeans of previous Parts with Westerners in Part VI, given the fact that by the modern era Europeans had spread through much of the Western hemisphere.

 PATTERNS OF BELIEF	 ARTS AND CULTURE	 SCIENCE AND TECHNOLOGY
• In the "post-Christian era," secularism elevated to formal doctrine in most countries, assisted by influence of Marxism through 1960s. Failure of Marxism in 1980s underlines sterility of Western philosophical ideas. Western interest in Eastern religion and philosophies rises sharply.	• Art becomes fragmented. No models or authority recognized. Influence from non-Western sources. Abstraction in pictorial arts matched by rejection of traditional models in other arts among avant-garde. Literature and philosophy either "serious" or popular; no middle ground. Mass cultural forms often dictated by commercial considerations. Sub-Saharan pictorial and plastic arts widely recognized for first time.	• Science the defining reference for knowledge and truth. Social sciences rise to prominence. Technology makes enormous strides, removing physical labor as obstacle to almost any task and enabling "information revolution" through computers and electronic apparatus.
• ***South and East Asians:*** Asians retained religious and cultural independence from West, even during colonial era. Buddhism still the most popular of mass cults; Islam and Taoism competitors in southeast and China. India remains Hindu, while secularism accepted among educated. • ***West Asians:*** Secularism of some intellectuals and reformers opposed by traditionalists. After World War II religious revivalists and fundamentalists learn how to propagandize effectively with nationalist appeal. Islam combined with strong rejection of West's values.	• ***South and East Asians:*** Cultural autonomy expressed in arts, as always. Non-Western approach manifested through regional variations in fine arts, folklore, and artisanry. Literature and philosophy deeply affected by Western influences in last generation but remain distinct. Higher education resembles that in West. • ***West Asians:*** Increased literacy results in revival or first appearance of literature in several Muslim states. Oil wealth of 1970s provides governmental arts patronage in Arab states. Nationalism reflected in art forms and revived interest in folk art.	• ***South and East Asians:*** Formerly huge gap between sciences in South and East Asia and the West almost closed. Technology lags as result of shortages of investment funds. • ***West Asians:*** Physical and life sciences dependent on Western training and goal setting. Situation rapidly changed to autonomous science in much of Muslim world since 1970. Emphasis on science and technology in higher education accepted by fundamentalist Muslims as modern necessity.
• Christian missions make inroads into traditional religions in central and southern regions. Islam dominates north, west, and eastern coasts. Most Africans blend one or other formal doctrines with local beliefs. Education for masses begins after 1950 and increases after decolonization.	• Modern artists blend Western training with native motifs and media. Independence brings greater opportunities, domestically and internationally. Literature continues mainly in Western languages, hence limited audience at home, where oral folklore still the main way of transmitting cultural values.	• Labor-rich and slow-developing economy has only slight connection with technology. Sciences and technology heavily dependent on Western models and direction. Higher education slow in reorienting itself toward modern curriculum, while mainly foreign-owned companies not research oriented.
• Catholicism split into reform-minded and traditionalist party within clergy as it loses automatic acceptance among the masses, which have been touched by modern secularism and Protestant evangelism. Formal link between state and church nearly gone. Education unmet need in mestizo and Indian countries; literacy rates still low.	• In fiction and poetry, Latin American authors have won world acclaim, and the fine arts have prospered in last century. Formal culture still restricted to wealthy and urban middle class, however.	• Physical and social scientists few in number and depend on foreign sources for training, financing, and direction. Higher educational facilities oriented toward nonscientific programs and degrees. Technology imported from West and Japan sometimes has devastating impact.

Glossary

Abbasid Dynasty (ah-BAH-sihd) The dynasty of caliphs who governed the Islamic Empire from the 750 until 1258 C.E.

Abduh, Shaykh Muhammad (1849–1905) Egyptian jurist and rector of the Azhar Mosque University in Cairo. Founder of the Salafi movement.

Abolition, Act of Law passed in 1829 by governor-general of British East India Company, which banned certain Hindu practices, such a *sati*.

Act of Supremacy of 1534 A law enacted by the English Parliament, making the monarch the head of the Church of England.

Actium, Battle of The decisive 31 B.C.E. battle in the struggle between Octavian Caesar and Mark Antony, in which Octavian's victory paved the way for the Principate.

Adena culture One of the Native American Woodland civilizations that thrived *c.* 1000 B.C.E.–200 C.E.

Afghanistan Wars (1839–1842, 1878–1881, 1919) Fearing a possible invasion of India through Afghanistan, the East India Company fought these wars to occupy Afghanistan.

Afro-Asiatic speakers People who speak a language that is a member of the Afro-Asiatic language family.

Agincourt (AH-zhin-cohr) The great victory of the English over the French in 1415, during the Hundred Years' War.

agrarian civilizations Civilizations that are based primarily on peasant farming.

Ain Jalut (AYN jah-LOOT) A decisive battle in 1260 during which an Egyptian Mamluk army turned back the Mongols and prevented them from invading North Africa.

Akbar the Great (ACK-bar) Best known of the shahs of the Mughal Empire of India (r. 1556–1605). He was most famous for his policy of cooperation with his Hindu subjects.

Akhnaton (ahk-NAH-tun) Name of a fourteenth-century B.C.E. Egyptian ruler who attempted to introduce monotheistic religious practice.

Alexander the Great (356–323 B.C.E.) Son of King Philip II of Macedon. Remembered for his conquest of the Persian Empire and most of the Near East, 336–323 B.C.E., from which the Hellenistic era began.

Allah (ahl-LAH) Arabic title of the one God.

Alliance for Progress The program proposed by U.S. president John F. Kennedy in 1961 for large-scale economic assistance to Latin America.

Alliance of 1778 A diplomatic treaty under which France aided the American revolutionaries in their war against Britain.

al-Qaida A militant Islamist organization, formed by Osama bin Laden in the 1990s, that has adopted *takfiri* doctrines and declared *jihad* against all Westerners and their Muslim supporters.

Amerindians Short for (Native) American Indians.

Amun-Ra (AH-mun-RAH) Originally, the Egyptian god of air and life, later he came to represent the sun and creation.

Amur River War Sporadic shooting between Soviet and Chinese troops stationed along the Amur River in 1976 following tensions that arose upon the death of Mao Zedong.

Anabaptists Radical Protestant reformers who were condemned by both Lutherans and Catholics.

The Analects Book of Confucius's sayings collected by his students.

anarchism A political theory that sees all large-scale government as inherently evil and embraces small, self-governing communities.

Anasazi (ah-nah-SAH-zee) Term sometimes used to refer to Ancestral Puebloans.

Ancestral Puebloans These are the people native to the Four Corners area of the present United States. They built the Chaco Great Houses and cliff dwellings at Mesa Verde.

Anghor Wat (ANG-ghohr WAHT) A great Buddhist temple in central Cambodia, dating to the twelfth-century C.E. Khmer Empire.

Anglican Church The official Protestant Church of England, with the monarch as its official head.

Anglo-French Entente The diplomatic agreement of 1904 that ended British-French enmity and was meant as a warning to Germany.

Anglo-Russian Agreement The equivalent to the Anglo-French Entente between Britain and Russia; signed in 1907.

anschluss (AHN-shluhs) The German term for the 1938 takeover of Austria by Nazi Germany.

anthropology The study of humankind as a particular species.

anthropomorphic gods Gods that have a human form.

Antigonid Kingdom (an-TIH-goh-nihd) One of the Hellenistic successor kingdoms to Alexander the Great's empire. Included most of Greece and Asia Minor.

Antikythera mechanism. First-century Greek device used to calculate the movements of the sun, the planets, and the moon.

anti-Semitism Literally, opposition or hatred of Semitic peoples (Arabs, Jews, and Lebanese, for example), but specifically Jews in most modern contexts.

anti-Slavery Movement Faction among mostly British evangelical Christians, which, beginning in the 1790s, was able to pressure Parliament with increasing effectiveness to ban slavery and the slave trade in Britain and throughout the British Empire.

Arab Spring A series of protests and revolutions that have occurred across North Africa and the Middle East that began in 2010 and resulted in significant reforms in the many dictatorial governments in the region.

Arabian Nights, The Also known as *The 1001 Nights*. Medieval collection of tales from the Islamic Middle East that greatly reflect life at the time of the Abbasid caliphs of Baghdad.

archaeology The study of cultures through the examination of artifacts.

Archaic Period 8000–2000 B.C.E. in Native American history. Period when gathering slowly replaced large-game (megafauna) hunting.

Archduke Franz Ferdinand *See* Assassination of Archduke Franz Ferdinand.

aristocracy A social governing class based on birth.

Aristotle (384–322 B.C.E.) One of the three greatest philosophers of classical Greece. A student of Plato and teacher of Alexander the Great.

Aryans A nomadic pastoral people from central Asia who invaded the Indus Valley in about 1500 B.C.E.

Ashikaga clan (ah-shih-KAH-gah) A noble Japanese family that controlled political power as shoguns from the 1330s to the late 1500s.

Ashoka (ah-SHOH-kah) Greatest of the kings of ancient India. He greatly expanded the Mauryan kingdom through conquest. Later converted to Buddhism and encouraged its spread.

Askia Muhammad the Great Sultan of the Songhay Empire, 1493–1528. Famous for promoting Islamic scholarship and Islamic scholars at Timbuktu during his reign.

assassination of Archduke Franz Ferdinand Archduke Franz Ferdinand, the heir to the throne of the Austro-Hungarian Empire, was assassinated on June 28, 1914, in the town of Sarajevo in Bosnia. This event touched off World War I.

assimilation and association French administrative policies applied to their colonies in Africa and Southeast Asia, whose objective was to acculturate their colonial subjects to French language, history, and civilization.

Assur The chief god of the Assyrian people.

Ataturk Mustafa Kemal Ataturk, known simply as Ataturk. The "father of the Turks"; a World War I officer who led Turkey into the modern age and replaced the sultanate in the 1920s.

Atlantic Charter An agreement co-signed in 1941 by President Franklin D. Roosevelt and Prime Minister Winston Churchill outlining eight basic freedoms, which they proposed as essential for reconstructing the post-World War II world. It included the right of self-determination as one of those principles.

atlatls Throwing stick used in place of a bow for propelling a dart at high velocity.

Austronesians Linguistic group of Southeast Asians. Populated islands of the Pacific Ocean, Madagascar, and much of modern Indonesia and Malaysia.

Austro-Prussian War The conflict for mastery of the German national drive for political unification, won by the Otto von Bismarck-led Prussian Kingdom in 1866.

Avicenna (ah-vih-SEHN-nah) *See* Ibn Sina.

Axis Pact The treaty establishing a military alliance between the governments of Adolf Hitler and Benito Mussolini, signed in 1936.

Axum (AX-uhm) The center of the ancient Ethiopian Kingdom.

ayllu (eye-YOO) Quechua name for the clan organization of the Peruvian Indians.

Ayuthaya The capital of the Thai Kingdom of early modern southeastern Asia.

Aztec Latest of a series of Indian masters of central Mexico before the arrival of the Spanish; developers of the great city of Tenochtitlan (Mexico City).

Babylon Most important of the later Mesopotamian urban centers.

Babylonian Captivity The transportation of many Jews to exile in Babylon as hostages for the good behavior of the remainder; occurred in the sixth century B.C.E.

Babylonian Captivity of the papacy *See* Great Schism.

Bactria Ancient Central Asian region comprised of parts of eastern Iran and modern Afghanistan and Pakistan. After the Islamic conquest in the seventh century C.E., it was known as Transoxiana.

Baghdad (bag-DAD) Capital of the Islamic Empire under the Abbasid Dynasty. Built by Caliph al-Mansur, *c.* 763.

bakufu (bah-KOO-foo) The military-style government of the Japanese shogun.

Balfour Declaration The 1917 public statement that Britain was committed to the formation of a "Jewish homeland" in Palestine after World War I.

banana republics A dismissive term referring to small Latin American states.

Bantu (BAN-too) Related peoples who speak languages that are part of the African language group called Bantu, which is a subgroup of the Niger-Congo language family. They are spread through most of subequatorial Africa.

Bantu speakers People who speak one of the member languages of the Bantu language family (See above).

Battle of the Nations Decisive defeat of the army of Napoleon by combined forces of Prussia, Austria, and Russia in October 1813 at Leipzig in eastern Germany.

Benedictine Rule The rules of conduct given to his monastic followers by the sixth-century Christian saint Benedict.

Bengal Renaissance A social reform movement during the nineteenth and early twentieth centuries in the Indian province of Bengal.

Benin Ancient West African forest kingdom located in present-day Nigeria.

Benin bronzes Bronze castings associated with court ritual and political power in the Benin kingdom. Most date from the fifteenth century and afterward.

Berbers Indigenous people of North Africa and the Sahara Desert.

Beringia (beh-RIHN-jee-ah) A land mass in the region of the Bering Strait over which Ancestral Native Americans migrated to the Western Hemisphere, *c.* 30,000 to 10,000 B.C.E.

Berlin blockade The 1948–1949 attempt by the Soviet Union to squeeze the Western allies out of occupied Berlin; it failed because of the successful Berlin Airlift of food and supplies.

Berlin Conference of 1884–1885 A conference called by Otto von Bismarck of all the major European powers to find a formula for adjudicating competing claims to foreign territory and to temper potential conflicts.

Berlin Wall The ten-foot-high concrete wall and "death zone" erected by the communist East Germans in 1961 to prevent further illegal emigration to the West.

"Bhagavad-Gita" (BAH-gah-vahd-GEE-tah) The best-known part of the "Mahabharata," detailing the proper relations between the castes and the triumph of the spirit over material creation.

Bhakti Hinduism A more-popular form of Hinduism that emerged in India near the end of the first millennium B.C.E. The opposite of Brahmanism, it emphasizes individual spiritual devotion to a particular god, for example Shiva, Vishnu, or Krishna.

big bang theory The theory that the cosmos was created by an enormous explosion of gases billions of years ago.

Bill of Rights of 1689 A law enacted by Parliament that established certain limits of royal powers and the specific rights of English citizens.

Bismarck, Otto von Chancellor of Prussia, then Germany under Kaiser William I. Unified Germany and built the Triple Alliance.

Black Death An epidemic of bubonic plague that ravaged most of Europe in the mid-fourteenth century.

Blackshirts (SS) Adolf Hitler's bodyguard; later enlarged to be a subsidiary army and to provide the concentration camp guards.

Bodhisattva Avalokitesvara A saint-like figure whom Buddhists believe to be the protector of travelers, merchants, and seamen.

Boer War South African war between the Boers (people of Dutch descent) and Great Britain. Fought 1899–1902.

Boers (bohrs) The Dutch colonists who had been the initial European settlers of South Africa.

Bolsheviks (BOHL-sheh-vihks) The minority of Russian Marxists led by Vladimir Lenin who seized dictatorial power in the October Revolution of 1917.

Bornu West African Islamic kingdom found to the west of Lake Chad. Active in the international trade of the central Sudan.

bourgeoisie (BOOZH-wah-zee) The urban upper middle class; usually commercial or professional.

Boxer Rebellion A desperate revolt by superstitious peasants against the European "foreign devils" who were carving up China in the new imperialism of the 1890s; quickly suppressed.

Brahman (BRAH-muhn) The title of the impersonal spirit responsible for all creation in Hindu theology.

Brahmanism The earliest form of Hinduism. Its practices and doctrines were restricted to the priests, or Brahmins.

Brahmin (BRAH-mihn) The caste of priests, originally limited to the Aryans and later allowed to the Indians, with whom they intermarried.

British East India Company Company originally chartered in 1600 by Queen Elizabeth I to trade with the East Indies. However, driven out of the Indies by the Dutch, they concentrated on mainland India, Afghanistan, and Burma.

British Reform Act of 1832 *See* Reform Act of 1832, British

Bronze Age The period when bronze tools and weapons replaced stone among a given people; generally about 3000–1000 B.C.E.

Buganda East African kingdom that appeared in the sixteenth century. Located west of Lake Victoria Nyanza.

Bunyoro-Kitara Another kingdom, like Buganda and others, that appeared as a result of mixing Nilotic religio-political traditions with Bantu agricultural production and urban traditions. It was the most powerful of the Great Lakes region until the late eighteenth century.

burning of the books China's Legalist first emperor attempted to eliminate Confucian ethic by destroying the Confucian writings and prohibiting its teaching.

bushido (boo-shee-DOH) The code of honor among the samurai.

Byzantine Empire The continuation of the Roman imperium in its eastern provinces until its fall to the Muslim Turks in 1453.

Caesaro-Papism A concept that applies when the supreme power of government is combined with supreme leadership of the Christian Church.

Cahokia (cah-HOH-kee-ah) Large Native American settlement near East St. Louis, Illinois, *c.* 600–1300 C.E. Noteworthy for its enormous ceremonial mounds.

caliph (kah-LEEF) Arabic (*Khalifa*) for *deputy* to the Prophet Muhammad; leader of Islamic community.

calpulli Aztec kinship groups.

Calvin, John (1509–1564) French theologian who developed the system of Christian theology called Calvinism, as delineated in his text, *The Institutes of the Christian Religion.*

Cardinal Richelieu *See* Richelieu.

Carthage Rival in the Mediterranean basin to Rome in the last centuries B.C.E. before ultimate defeat.

cash crops Crops that are grown for sale rather than for consumption.

caste A socioeconomic group to which a person belongs by reason of birth.

Castro, Fidel (b. 1926) Revolutionary who seized control of Cuba in 1959 and established a communist dictatorship.

caudillo (cow-DEE-yoh) A regional chieftain and usurping strongman who achieves national power in Latin America.

Cavour, Camillo (1810–1861) Prime minister of Sardinia after 1852, he brought about the unification of the Italian states into the united Italy.

censors Officials with great powers of surveillance during the Roman republic.

Central Powers The alliance of Germany, the Austro-Hungarian Empire, the Ottoman Empire, and Bulgaria that fought the Allied Powers (Britain, France, and Russia) in World War I.

Chaco Canyon Canyon located in present-day northwestern New Mexico that was the center of the Chaco phenomenon.

Chaco phenomenon (CHA-coh) Ancestral Puebloan civilization that centered on the Great Houses of Chaco Canyon, *c.* 800–1150 B.C.E.

Charlemagne (SHAR-luh-mane, 742–814 C.E.) King of the Franks (ruled 768–814) and the first Holy Roman Emperor (800–814). Promoted the so-called Carolingian Renaissance.

Chartists/Chartist Movement A British working-class movement of the 1840s that attempted to obtain labor and political reform.

Chavín (chah-VEEN)/**Chavín** civilization (900–200 B.C.E.) The earliest and one of the most developed civilizations of the South American Andes Mountains.

Cheka An abbreviation for the first version of the Soviet secret police.

Chiang Kai-shek (chung keye-shehk; 1887–1975) Early colleague of Sun Yat-sen, who succeeded Sun as the leader of the Kuomintang. Opposed the rise of the Chinese Communist Party, but was defeated in 1949 and forced to flee to Taiwan.

Chichén Itzá (chee-CHEHN ee-TSAH) Site in the Yucatán of Mayan urban development in the tenth to thirteenth centuries.

Chinese Communist Party (CCP) Communist party established in 1920s. In 1947, they defeated the Kuomintang and drove Chiang Kai-shek and his followers to flee to Taiwan.

Chinghis Khan (JENG-guhs KAHN) Mongol conqueror, 1167–1227.

Chola Powerful Tamil kingdom of southeastern India that thrived *c.* 800–1200 C.E. Very active in the Indian trade with Cambodia and Sumatra.

city-states States or societies that are dominated by a single city.

Civil Code of 1804 Napoleonic law code reforming and centralizing French legal theory and procedures.

Cleisthenes (CLEYES-theh-nees) A sixth-century B.C.E. Athenian tyrant who laid the foundations of polis democracy.

cliché (klih-SHAY) A common saying, name, or stock phrase, often repeated in a society and found in oral traditions, which can symbolize past events and people.

Clive, Robert (1725–1784) Employee, soldier, and later governor of the British East India Company in India. Also known as Clive of India, he established the military and political supremacy of the East India Company in southern India and Bengal.

Clovis culture (CLOH-vihs) The earliest Native American "culture" known to archaeologists. Dated *c.* 9500–8900 B.C.E., it was largely based on hunting very large game.

Cold War Term for the rivalry that existed between the North Atlantic Treaty Organization and communist bloc nations from 1945 until 1992.

Coloureds South Africans of mixed European and African descent.

Columbian Exchange A term for the global changes in the resources, habits, and values of Amerindians, Europeans, Africans, and Asians that followed the "discovery" and settlement of the Americas by Europeans and Africans.

command economy The name given to economic planning of the communist party in the Soviet version after 1929.

Committee of Public Safety The executive body of the Reign of Terror during the French Revolution.

Common Sense A pamphlet by Thomas Paine that was influential in hastening the American war of independence against Britain.

Commonwealth of Independent States (CIS) The loose confederation of eleven of the fifteen former Soviet republics that was formed after the breakup of the Soviet Union in 1991.

Communist Manifesto The 1948 pamphlet by Karl Marx and Friedrich Engels that announced the formation of a revolutionary party of the proletariat.

community of discourse A group of people who share a common set of beliefs, symbols, and values.

Conciliar Movement The attempt to substitute councils of church leaders for papal authority in late medieval Christianity.

Confederation of Northern German States A confederation forged by Otto von Bismarck following the Prussian victory in the Austro-Prussian War of 1866.

Confucius (cuhn-FYOO-shuhs) The fifth-century B.C.E. philosopher whose doctrines were permanently influential in Chinese education and culture.

conquistadores (cahn-KEES-tah-dohrs) Title given to sixteenth-century Spanish explorers/colonizers in the Americas.

conservatism The political and economic position that opposes change and holds to past and present values and attitudes.

Constance, Council of The fifteenth-century C.E. assembly of Christian officials called to settle the controversy over the papacy and to review and revise the basic doctrines of the church for the first time in a millennium.

Constantine the Great (272–337 C.E.) Emperor of Rome, 324–337, best known for issuing the Edict of Milan that reversed Diocletian's persecution of the Christians and proclaimed religious toleration throughout the Roman Empire.

Constantinople Greek colony that became the official residence of Constantine and remained the capital of the Eastern Roman and Byzantine Empires.

consuls Chief executives of the Roman republic; chosen annually.

Copernicus, Nicholas (1473–1543) Early figure of the European Scientific Revolution who introduced the idea that the universe is heliocentric.

Coral Sea, Battle of the Naval engagement in the southwest Pacific during World War II, resulting in the removal of a Japanese invasion threat to Australia.

corporation A company that the law bestows with the rights and liabilities of an individual. Generally, these are larger than partnerships and are highly capitalized through shares that are sold to the public.

corpus iuris (COHR-puhs YOO-rihs) *Body of the law*; the Roman law code, produced under the emperor Justinian in the mid-500s C.E.

Cortés, Hernán (cohr-TEHZ) Spanish conquistador of the Aztec Empire, 1518–1521.

Council of Nicaea *See* Nicaea, Council of

Counter-Reformation Series of measures that the Catholic Church took in the 1540s to counterattack against the Protestants, including a thorough examination of doctrines and practices and an emphasis on instruction of the young and of all Christians.

Crecy (cray-SEE) Battle in the Hundred Years' War won by the English in 1346.

Crimean War Conflict fought in the Crimea between Russia and Britain, France, and Turkey from 1853 to 1856; ended by the Peace of Paris with a severe loss in Russian prestige.

criollos (cree-OH-yohs) Creole; term used to refer to whites born in Latin America.

Crusades Medieval European wars waged principally to recover the Holy Lands (and Spain and Portugal) from Muslim control beginning in 1096.

Cuban Missile Crisis 1962 crisis created when Soviet premier Nikita Khrushchev placed nuclear armed missiles in Cuba. The United States imposed a naval blockade, and a settlement was reached when the missiles were withdrawn in exchange for a U.S. agreement to remove missiles from Turkey.

cultural relativism A belief common in the late twentieth-century West that there are no absolute values to measure contrasting cultures.

culture system Dutch method of extracting wealth from Indonesian peasants by paying fixed (and often unfair) prices for their crops.

cuneiform (KYOO-nih-form) Mesopotamian wedge-shaped writing begun by the Sumerians.

Cuzco (COOS-coh) Capital city of the Inca Empire.

cynicism A Hellenistic philosophy stressing poverty and simplicity.

da Gama, Vasco (duh GAH-mah, VAHS-coh; 1469–1524) First Portuguese to sail directly from Portugal to India and back, 1497–1499.

daimyo (DEYE-myoh) Japanese nobles who controlled feudal domains under the shogun.

Damascus Ancient city located in present-day Syria. It served as the capital of the Islamic Empire during the Umayyad caliphate (661–750).

Dao de Jing (DOW deh CHING) (*Book of Changes*) Daoism's major scripture; attributed to Lao Zi.

Daoism (DOW-ism) (Taoism) A nature-oriented philosophy/religion of China.

Charles Darwin English naturalist who discovered natural selection and the modern theory of evolution. Author of *Descent of Man*.

Dawes Plan A plan for a dollar loan and refinancing of post–World War I reparation payments that enabled recovery of the German economy.

D-day The invasion of France from the English Channel by combined British and American forces on June 6, 1944.

Declaration of the Rights of Man and Citizen The epoch-making manifesto issued by the French Third Estate delegates at Versailles in 1789.

decolonization The process by which Europeans withdrew from their colonies in Africa and Asia and restored self-rule.

deductive reasoning Arriving at truth by applying a general law or proposition to a specific case.

de las Casas, Bartolomé (day lahs CAH-sahs, bahr-toh-loh-MAY) Spanish Dominican friar who wrote a scathing report in 1522 describing the devastation experienced by Native Americans at the hands of the Spanish.

Delhi sultanate (DEH-lee) The government and state erected by the conquering Afghani Muslims after 1500 in North India; immediate predecessor to the Mughal Empire.

demesne The arable land on a manor that belonged directly to the lord.

democracy A system of government in which the majority of voters decides issues and policy.

demographic transition The passage of a large group of people from traditional high birthrates to lower ones, induced by changing economic conditions and better survival chances of the children.

Deng Xiaoping (dung shau-ping; 1904–1997) Chairman of the Chinese Communist Party (CCP) after the death of Mao Zedong; began the relaxation of CCP antipathy to capitalism, allowing limited free enterprise under liberalized CCP oversight.

dervish (DER-vihsh) A Turkish term for a *Sufi*. *See* Sufi.

Descartes, René (1596–1650) Mathematician and logician of the European Enlightenment. He believed that the material world could be understood with the aid of mathematical formulas.

Descent of Man, The The 1871 publication by Charles Darwin that applied selective evolution theory to mankind.

détente (lit.) (day-TAHNT) Relaxation; the term used for the toning down of diplomatic tensions between nations—specifically, the Cold War between the United States and the Soviet Union.

devshirme (duv-SHEER-muh) Ottoman system of recruiting young Christian boys of the Balkan villages for the Janissary corps.

dharma (DAHR-mah) A code of morals and conduct prescribed for one's caste in Hinduism.

dhimmis (THIHM-mees) *People of the Book*: Christians, Jews, and Zoroastrians living under Muslim rule and receiving privileged treatment over other non-Muslims.

The Diaspora The scattering of the Jews from ancient Palestine.

Diocletian Roman Emperor, 284–305 C.E., known for his conquests and for establishing the tetrarchy, the political division of the Roman Empire into western and eastern halves.

Directory The five-member executive organ that governed France from 1795 to 1799 after the overthrow of the Jacobins.

divan (dih-VAHN) A Turkish form of the Arabic word, *diwan*, meaning a Royal Council which advises the ruler.

Domesday Book A complete census of landholdings in England ordained by William the Conqueror.

Dream of the Red Chamber, The The best known of the eighteenth-century Chinese novels.

Dupleix, Joseph François Governor-general of French possessions in India, 1742–1754.

Dutch East India Company A commercial company founded with government backing to trade with the East and Southeast Asians. The Dutch, English, and French governments sponsored such companies starting in the early seventeenth century.

Edict of Milan The Roman Emperor Constantine promulgated the Edict of Milan in 313 C.E., establishing religious toleration throughout the Roman Empire.

Edict of Nantes Edict issued in 1598 by King Henry IV of France, which guaranteed freedom of worship to his French subjects.

Edo (EH-do) Name of Tokyo before the eighteenth-century

Effective Occupation One of the principles established during the Berlin Conference of 1884 for recognizing colonial claims. Essentially, it required that for a claim to be made, an effective administrative and police presence had to be established in the territory in question.

Eightfold Path The Buddha's teachings on attaining perfection.

ekklesia (ehk-KLAY-zee-yah) The general assembly of citizens in ancient Athens.

Elect, The A doctrine made famous by John Calvin that posits the notion that only a small minority (i.e., the "Elect") of the human race is predestined for salvation.

Elizabeth I, Queen Last monarch of the Tudor dynasty, the daughter of Henry VIII and Anne Boleyn. She ruled England in 1558–1603. A political genius, she united Britons and managed to settle the quarrels between Protestants and Catholics in her realm.

empirical method Using empirical data to establish scientific truth.

empiricist A school of Hellenistic Greek medical researchers.

Empress Dowager Cixi (1830–1908) Concubine of Qing emperor Xianfeng, she became the regent for her son, the emperor Tongxi. Exercising power for nearly fifty years, she encouraged the Taiping Rebellion and opposed badly needed reforms.

Enabling Act A law the German Reichstag passed in 1933 giving Adolf Hitler dictatorial power.

encomienda (en-koh-MYEN-dah) The right to organize unpaid native labor by the earliest Spanish colonists in Latin America; revoked in 1565.

***Encyclopédie,* The** The first encyclopedia; produced in mid-eighteenth-century France by the philosophe Diderot.

Enlightenment The intellectual reform movement in eighteenth-century Europe that challenged traditional ideas and policies in many areas of theory and practice.

Epicureanism A Hellenistic philosophy advocating the pursuit of pleasure (mental) and avoidance of pain as the supreme good.

Era of the Warring States The period of Chinese history between *c.* 500 and 220 B.C.E.; characterized by the breakdown of the central government and feudal war.

Essay Concerning Human Understanding An important philosophical essay by John Locke that underpinned Enlightenment optimism.

Estates General The parliament of France; composed of delegates from three social orders: clergy, nobility, and commoners.

Etruscans (ee-TRUHNS-cuns) The pre-Roman rulers of most of northern and central Italy and cultural models for early Roman civilization.

European Economic Community An association of Western European nations founded in 1957; now called the European Union, it embraces fifteen countries, with several more in candidate status.

Exodus The Hebrews' flight from the wrath of the Egyptian pharaoh in *c.* 1250 B.C.E.

extended family Parents and children plus several other kin-group members such as in-laws, cousins, uncles, and aunts.

factories Fortified trading posts that Europeans established along the coast of (mostly West) Africa during the Age of Informal Empire.

Factory Acts Laws passed by Parliament in 1819 and 1833 that began the regulation of hours and working conditions in Britain.

factory system Massing of labor and material under one roof with a single proprietorship and management of production.

fallow Land left uncultivated for a period to recover fertility.

fascism A political movement in the twentieth century that embraced totalitarian government policies to achieve a unity of people and leader; first experienced in Benito Mussolini's Italy.

Fertile Crescent A belt of civilized settlements reaching from Lower Mesopotamia across Syria, Lebanon, and Israel and into Egypt.

Fidel Castro *See* Castro, Fidel.

fief The grant of a privilege, right, or manor by a suzerain to his or her vassal in return for the vassal's promise of loyalty and service.

Final Solution Name given by the Nazis to the wartime massacres of European Jews.

First Emperor (Shih Huang-di) The founder of the short-lived Qin Dynasty (221–205 B.C.E.) and creator of China as an imperial state.

First Estate The Roman Catholic Church clergy in France during the pre-revolutionary era.

First Five-Year Plan Introduced in 1929 at Josef Stalin's command to collectivize agriculture and industrialize the economy of the Soviet Union.

First Industrial Revolution The initial introduction of machine-powered production; began in late eighteenth-century Britain.

First International Title of original association of Marxists and other socialists in 1860s Europe.

Five Great Relationships Confucius's scheme of the five forms of hierarchical human relationships that govern family and community life.

Five Pillars of Islam Popular term for the basic tenets of Muslim faith. Includes the profession of faith (*shahada*), prayer, fasting, pilgrimage, and giving alms.

Forbidden City The center of Ming and Qing government in Beijing; entry was forbidden to ordinary citizens.

Four Corners region Region located near the point where the contemporary U.S. states of Utah, Colorado, New Mexico, and Arizona meet.

four little tigers Singapore, Taiwan, South Korea, and Hong Kong in the 1960s–1980s economic upsurge.

Four Noble Truths The Buddha's doctrine on human fate.

Fourteen Points The outline for a just peace proposed by Woodrow Wilson in 1918.

Franco-Prussian War The 1870–1871 conflict between these two powers resulting in German unification under Prussian leadership.

Fujiwara clan (foo-jee-WAH-rah) *Daimyo* noble clan controlling the shogunate in ninth- to twelfth-century Japan.

Galileo, Galilei (1564–1642) One of the Scientific Revolution's most imposing figures, he was an important contributor to the development of the scientific method.

Gandhi, Mohandas (GAHN-dee, moh-HAHN-dahs; 1869–1948) Advocate of nonviolent protest against British rule and one of the founders of the modern state of India.

gaucho An Argentine "cowboy."

General Theory of Relativity Albert Einstein's theory that introduced the modern era of physics in 1916.

geocentric *Earth centered*; theory of the cosmos that erroneously held the Earth to be its center.

Ghana (GAH-nah) The earliest of the extensive empires in the western Sudan; also a modern West African country formed from the colony of Gold Coast when it won independence from Great Britain in 1957.

Ghazis (GAH-zees) Muslim "crusaders," or holy warriors, who fought against unbelievers.

ghetto Italian name for the quarter restricted to Jews.

Gilgamesh, Epic of (GIHL-gah-mesh) One of the earliest epics in world literature, originating in prehistoric Mesopotamia.

glasnost (GLAS-nohnst) The Russian term for *openness*; along with *perestroika*, employed to describe the reforms instituted by Mikhail Gorbachev in the late 1980s.

global warming The steady warming trend of the planet's temperature in the past century.

Glorious Revolution of 1688 The English revolt against the unpopular Catholic king James II and the subsequent introduction of certain civil rights restricting monarchic powers.

Golden Horde The Russia-based segment of the Mongol world empire.

golden mean Greek concept of avoiding the extremes; "truth lies in the middle."

Good Neighbor Policy President Franklin D. Roosevelt's attempt to reform previous U.S. policy and honor Latin American sovereignty.

Gorbachev, Mikhail (b. 1931) Soviet leader at the time of the Revolution of 1989.

Gothic style An artistic style, found notably in architecture, that came into general European usage during the thirteenth century.

Grand Canal Chinese canal whose construction began as early as the fifth century B.C.E. Its purpose was to link southern

China with northern China, enabling the transport of rice into the agriculturally less-productive North.

Grand Vizier (vih-ZEER) Title of the Turkish prime minister during the Ottoman era.

Great Depression of the 1930s A depression that began in 1929 when the New York Stock Exchange collapsed, causing a severe crisis for banks and securities firms that spread around the world and created high levels of unemployment.

Great Elector Frederick William of Prussia (1640–1688); one of the princes who elected the Holy Roman Emperor.

The Great Exhibition International trade fair organized in 1851 by Britain's Prince Albert to showcase World's social and industrial progress. Its centerpiece was the Crystal Palace, built entirely of glass on an iron framework by Joseph Paxton.

"Great Game," The Refers to nineteenth- and twentieth-century competition by Britain and Russia for influence and control in western and southern Asia.

Great Houses Large multistoried structures associated with the Ancestral Puebloan civilization. Most were built *c.* 800–1150 C.E. and appear to have had a ceremonial function.

Great Indian Mutiny (1857) Sometimes shortened to the Great Mutiny. Mutiny of Indian soldiers (*sepoys*) of the East India Company army caused by cultural insensitivity of Company officers.

Great Leap Forward Mao Zedong's misguided attempt in 1958–1960 to provide China with an instantaneous industrial base rivaling that of more advanced nations.

Great Proletarian Cultural Revolution The period from 1966 to 1976 when Mao Zedong inspired Chinese youth to rebel against all authority except his own; caused great damage to the Chinese economy and culture.

Great Purge The arrest and banishment of millions of Soviet Communist Party members and ordinary citizens at Josef Stalin's orders in the mid-1930s for fictitious "crimes against the State and Party."

(Russia's) Great Reforms Decrees affecting several areas of life issued by Tsar Alexander II between 1859 and 1874.

Great Schism A division in the Roman Catholic Church between 1378 and 1417, when two (and for a brief period, three) popes competed for the allegiance of European Christians; a consequence of the Babylonian Captivity of the papacy in Avignon, southern France.

Great Trek The march of the Boers, beginning in 1836, into the northeastern interior of South Africa where they founded the so-called Boer Republics.

Great Zimbabwe (zim-BOB-way) The leading civilization of early southern Africa and exporter of gold to the East African coast.

Green Revolution The increased agricultural output in many Third World nations during the 1960s and 1970s that came from introducing high-yield crops and pesticides.

greenhouse gases Gases, such as carbon dioxide, that trap light radiation in the earth's atmosphere and produce a warming, greenhouse-like effect on world temperatures.

gross domestic product (GDP) A measurement used by economists of the total wealth being produced by a country.

guilds Medieval urban organizations that controlled the production and sale prices of many goods and services.

Gupta Dynasty (GUHP-tah) The rulers of most of India in the 300–400s C.E.; the last native dynasty to unify the country. They ruled over a "golden age" in the cultural history of the subcontinent, when Hinduism was revived and Sanskrit literature thrived.

Habsburg Dynasty The family that controlled the Holy Roman Empire after the thirteenth century; based in Vienna, they ruled Austria until 1918.

hacienda (hah-SYEHN-dah) A Spanish-owned plantation in Latin America that used native or slave labor to produce export crops.

Hagia Sophia (HAH-gee-yah soh-FEE-yah) Greek name (*Holy Wisdom*) of the cathedral in Constantinople, later made into a mosque by Ottoman Turkish conquerors.

haiku (HEYE-koo) A type of Japanese poetry always three lines in length. The lines always have five, seven, and five syllables.

hajj (HAHJ) The pilgrimage to the sacred places of Islam.

Hammurabi (ham-moo-RAH-bee; *c.* 1810–1750 B.C.E.) Sixth king of Babylon.

Hammurabi's Law Code History's first known law code, it was written by King Hammurabi in the eighteenth century B.C.E.

Han Dynasty The dynasty that ruled China from *c.* 200 B.C.E. to 221 C.E.

Han synthesis Ideology of the Han state that blended elements from Confucianism, Daoism, and Legalism.

Hanoverian Dynasty The dynasty of British monarchs after 1714; from the German duchy of Hanover.

Hausa West African people found north of the confluence of the Niger and Benue rivers in present-day Nigeria. Noted for their extensive trade networks and craft skills, they organized themselves in city-states.

Hebrews The followers of Abraham, Isaac, and Moses who settled in the land of Canaan and who were governed by God's laws, the Tanakh. More commonly known as the Jews.

Heinrich, Himmler (1900–1945) Prominent member of the NSDAP, or Nazi Party, and head of Hitler's SS and the Gestapo.

heliocentrism Opposite of geocentrism; recognizes sun as center of solar system.

Hellenistic kingdoms Kingdoms carved out of the empire conquered by Alexander the Great. Blended Greek and Asiatic cultures; extant in the Mediterranean basin and Middle East between 300 B.C.E. and *c.* 200 C.E.

Henry VIII, King (1491–1547) King of England, 1509 until his death in 1547, Henry was a strong ruler and an important figure of the Protestant Reformation. He defied the pope by signing the Act of Supremacy, which established the monarch as the supreme head of the Church of England.

Henry the Navigator, Prince (1394–1460) The third son of King João (John) I of Portugal, Henry played an important part in the early Portuguese exploration of the eastern Atlantic and the West African coast.

heresies Wrong beliefs in religious doctrines.

hieroglyphics (high-roh-GLIH-fiks) Egyptian pictographs, beginning as far back as 3000 B.C.E., that could convey either an idea or a phonetic sound.

hijra (HIHJ-rah) Literally, *flight*; Muhammad's forced flight from Mecca in 622 C.E.; it marks the first year of the Muslim calendar.

Hinayana Buddhism (hih-nah-YAH-nah) A stricter monastic form of Buddhism, claiming closer link with the Buddha's teaching; often called Theravada. Headquartered in Sri Lanka and strong in Southeast Asia.

historical linguistics The scholarly discipline of reconstructing the relative chronology, as well as the changes in grammar, sounds, and methods of expressing ideas, in languages and families of languages.

historiography The writing of history so as to interpret it.

history Human actions in past time, as recorded and remembered.

Hittites (HIHT-tites) An Indo-European people who were prominent in the Near East around 1200 B.C.E.

Hizbullah Literally, *The Party of God*, a radical Shi'ite guerilla organization formed to resist Israel's occupation of Lebanon; allied to Iran.

Ho Chi Minh (hoh chee MIHN; 1890–1969) Communist and nationalist leader in French Indochina who fought against the Japanese in World War II. One of the principal founders of the modern nation of Vietnam, he fought to free his country from French rule, then from American invasion.

Hohokam Native American civilization of the Sonora desert region, located in modern southern Arizona, c. 500-1300 C.E.

Holocene Era The period in archeology and climatology that came after *c.* 10,000 B.C.E. and the last Ice Age.

Homer Legendary author of the two epic poems of ancient Greece, the *Iliad* and the *Odyssey.*

hominid (HAH-mih-nihd) A humanlike creature.

Homo ergaster The earliest *Homo Sapiens,* dated to around 150,000 B.C.E.

Homo sapiens (HOH-moh SAY-pee-yehns) *Thinking man*; modern human beings.

Horus (HOH-ruhs) The falcon-headed god whose earthly, visible form was the reigning pharaoh in ancient Egypt.

hubris (HYOO-brihs) An unjustified confidence in one's abilities or powers, leading to a tragic end.

humanism The intellectual movement that sees humans as the sole valid arbiter of their values and purpose.

humanistic An adjective meaning something that emphasizes human qualities.

Hundred Schools Period The period of cultural and intellectual creativity that occurred in the last centuries of the Zhou Dynasty in China, *c.* 550–221 B.C.E.

Hussein, Saddam Iraqi dictator; an American invasion of Iraq in 2003 led to the overthrow of his government and widespread chaos.

Hyksos (HIHK-sohs) A people who invaded the Nile Delta in Egypt and ruled it during the Second Intermediate Period (*c.* 1650–1570 B.C.E.).

Ibn Sina (ih-bihn SEE-nah) Well-known Islamic philosopher and physician (980–1037).

Ibn Taymiyya, Taqi al-Din (ih-bihn tie-MEE-yah) (1263–1328) Ultra-conservative Hanbali legal scholar whose writings are the foundation of the fundamentalist Wahhabi movement.

Ifè West African forest kingdom of the Yoruba people whose date of origin is uncertain.

Ignatius of Loyola (1491–1556) Major figure of the Catholic Counter-Reformation who founded the Society of Jesus, or Jesuits.

Il Khans (il KHAHNS) One of the four major dynasties established from the empire of Chinghis Khan. Founded by Hulegu, Chinghis's grandson, after he destroyed Abbasid rule in Baghdad.

Iliad The first of the two epics supposedly written by Homer in eighth-century Greece.

Inca Title of the emperor of the Quechuan-speaking peoples of Peru before arrival of the Spanish.

Indian National Congress Political party formed in India in 1885. Eventually led the Indian Independence Movement.

indirect rule The British policy of governing their overseas colonies through native rulers.

Indochina *See* Indochina, Union of.

Indochina, Union of Official term for the French colonies in Indochina until their dissolution in the 1950s.

Indo-European A large family of languages that includes most of the modern languages of Europe, Iran (Persia), and India. A subgroup are the Indo-Iranians.

inductive reasoning Arriving at truth by reasoning from specific cases to a general law or proposition.

Indus Valley civilization Earliest known civilization of India; flourished *c.* 3000–1500 B.C.E. Largely known from archaeological discoveries at Mohenjo Daro and Harappa.

Informal Empire The era in African history that lasted from the 1400s to about 1880, when Europeans remained content to restrict their dealings with Africa primarily to trade.

Inquisition Roman Catholic agency that was responsible for censorship of doctrines and books; mainly active in Iberian lands in the fifteenth through seventeenth centuries.

Institutes of the Christian Religion, The John Calvin's major work that established the theology and doctrine of the Calvinist churches; first published in 1536.

intendants (ahn-tahn-DAHNTS) The traveling officials appointed originally by Cardinal Richelieu to monitor the honesty and efficiency of provincial French authorities.

Investiture Controversy A dispute between the Holy Roman Emperor and the pope in the eleventh and early twelfth centuries about which authority should appoint German bishops.

Iranians Another name for Persians. Indo-European pastoral nomads who settled the Iranian Plateau and unified *c.* 850 B.C.E. and formed a powerful kingdom, which played a crucial part in the history of the ancient Near East. Closely related to the Aryans of India.

irredentism The attempt by members of a nation living outside the national state to link themselves to it politically and/or territorially.

Islamism The modern, militant reassertion of basic Islamic values and principles by many Muslims.

ius gentium (YOOS GEHN-tee-yum) *Law of peoples*; Roman law governing relations between Romans and others.

Ivan the Terrible (Ivan IV: 1530–1584) The first ruler of Russia to assume the title of tsar. He overcame Mongol resistance to extend the Russian empire into Siberia.

Jacobins Radical revolutionaries during the French Revolution; organized in clubs headquartered in Paris.

Jacquerie (ZHAH-cuh-ree) A French peasant rebellion against noble landlords during the fourteenth century.

Janissaries (JA-nih-sayrees) From Turkish *yeni cheri,* meaning *new troops*; an elite troop in the Ottoman army consisting of Christian boys from the Balkans.

Jesuit Order Also called the Society of Jesus, a Catholic religious order founded in 1547 to combat Protestantism.

Jesus of Nazareth. Jewish *rabbi* and prophet believed by his followers, the Christians, to have been the Messiah.

Jewish War A rebellion of Jewish Zealots against Rome in 66–70 C.E.

jihad (jee-HAHD) Holy war on behalf of the Muslim faith.

Julius Caesar (100–44 B.C.E.) Roman patrician who formed the First Triumvirate and who was the victor in Rome's second civil war.

July Monarchy The reign of King Louis Philippe in France (1830–1848); so called because he came to power in July 1830.

justification by faith Doctrine held by Martin Luther whereby Christian faith alone, and not good works, could be the path to salvation.

ka (kah) The immortal soul in the religion of ancient Egypt.

Ka'ba (KAH-bah) The original shrine of pagan Arabic religion in Mecca containing the Black Stone; now one of the holiest places of Islam.

Kabuki (kah-BOO-kee) A type of popular Japanese drama depicting heroic and romantic themes and stories.

Kalidasa (kah-lih-DAH-sah) Hindu philosopher and playwright of the Gupta period; influenced the development of Sanskrit literature.

Kamakura shogunate (kah-mah-KOO-rah) Government by members of a noble Japanese family from the late twelfth to the mid-fourteenth century in the name of the emperor, who was their puppet.

Kampuchea (kahm-poo-CHEE-yah) Native name of Cambodia, a state of Southeast Asia bordered by Thailand and Vietnam.

Kanishka the Great A powerful ruler who presided over the Kushan empire, *c.* 78–125 C.E. He expanded Kushan control over the western oases of the Silk Road trade routes and was notable for his religious tolerance and sponsorship of Mahayana Buddhism.

Karlowitz, Treaty of (1699) Treaty in which, for the first time, the Ottoman Empire had to cede territory in the Balkans to its Austrian opponent.

karma (KAHR-mah) In Hindu belief, the balance of good and evil done in a given incarnation.

Kashmir (kazh-MEER) A province in northwestern India, largely populated by Muslims, that Pakistan also claims.

Kepler, Johannes (1571–1630) A major contributor to the European Scientific Revolution. He discovered the three laws of celestial mechanics that governed planetary motion around the sun.

Kerma One of the earliest capitals of ancient Nubia, or Kush; located in northern Sudan.

Keynes, John Maynard (1883–1946) English economist who believed it was the duty of government to lessen the effects of the business cycle by pumping new money into the credit system in hard times.

KGB An abbreviation for the Soviet secret police; used after Cheka and NKVD had been discarded.

Khanate of the Golden Horde Sub-khanate of the Mongol Empire located in eastern and central Russia.

khans Supreme rulers over the Turko-Mongolian tribes of Central Asia.

Kharijites (KHAH-rih-jites) Like Shi'ites, they are one of the two religious minorities in Islam. Basically, they reject the caliphate and believe that leadership of the Umma (q.v.) rightfully belongs to the most pious and that authority comes from the community itself.

Khmers (kuh-MARES) The inhabitants of Cambodia; founders of a large empire in ancient Southeast Asia.

Khoisan One of the four language families of Africa. At one time Khoisan-speakers were found throughout much of subequatorial Africa, but they now are confined to the deserts of southwestern Africa.

Khomeini, Ayatollah Ruholla (1900–1989) Iranian Shi'ite cleric who led the 1979 Iranian revolt against the shah.

Khrushchev, Nikita Succeeded Stalin as First Secretary of the Soviet Communist Party, 1955–1964. Utterly convinced of the eventual triumph of communism in the world, he followed policies that generally were more conciliatory towards the West.

Kilwa (KILL-wah) A Swahili city-state that dominated the gold and ivory trade from East Africa, *c.* 1300–1450 C.E.

kivas (KEE-vahs) Underground ceremonial chambers among Puebloan Native Americans.

kleptocracies Governments staffed by thieves.

Korean War War between United Nations (led by the United States) and North Korea from 1950 to 1953; precipitated by the invasion of South Korea.

Kubilai Khan (KOOB-lay KHAHN) Mongol Great Khan and founder of the Yuan Dynasty of China.

Kuomintang (KMT) The political movement headed by Chiang Kai-shek during the 1930s and 1940s in China.

Kush (kuhsh) Kingdom in northeast Africa that had close relations with Egypt for several centuries in the pre-Christian epoch.

Kushan Empire Originally, the Kushan were a tribal group that migrated from the east into the region that included much of northeastern India. By the second century C.E., they succeeded in establishing control over a region that included much of today's Afghanistan, Pakistan, and northwestern India. Their rule preceded that of the Guptas.

Kwame Nkrumah (KWAH-may Ng-KROO-mah; 1909–1972) In 1957, led the Gold Coast—renamed Ghana—as the first nation among the colonial states of Africa to achieve independence. Fierce advocate of African socialism and Pan-Africanism.

Kyoto (KEE-oh-to) Ancient capital of the Japanese Empire and seat of the emperor.

Labour Party Political party founded in 1906 by British labor unions and others for representation of the working classes.

l'ancien régime (LAHN-syahn ray-ZHEEM) *The old government*; the pre-Revolutionary style of government and society in eighteenth-century France.

language families Groups of languages that share common or similar vocabularies, grammars, and ways of expressing ideas. Language families develop over time from a common language.

Lao Zi (lau-TSUH) Mythical author of the *Dao de Jing*, or *Book of Changes*, which has served as the text for various versions of Daoist folklore and philosophy for many centuries in China.

Lapita culture Neolithic maritime and farming culture in Near Oceania with distinctive pottery (*c.* 1500–*c.*1000 B.C.E.) found at hundreds of sites between Island New Guinea and Samoa.

Laws of Manu A section of the Hindu Vedas, which provides instruction in the rules of living for the various classes of society. The text is written as if the philosopher Manu were speaking the lines.

League of Nations An international organization founded after World War I to maintain peace and promote amity among nations; the United States did not join.

Legalism A Chinese philosophy of government emphasizing strong authority.

Lenin, Vladimir (1870–1924) Founder of the Bolshevik Party and leader of the October 1917 Revolution in Russia.

Levantine Corridor Region that included most of present-day Israel-Palestine, Lebanon, Syria, and northern Iraq. Archaeologists have discovered the earliest evidence of agriculture here.

levée en masse (leh-VAY ahn-MAHS) General conscription for the army; first occurred in 1793 during the French Revolution.

Liberation theology Unofficial Roman Catholic doctrine that blends Marxism and Catholic theology in defense of Latin America's poor.

lineage (LIHN-ee-age) A technical term for family or clan association.

Little Ice Age A period of global cooling that lasted from the late thirteenth century to the seventeenth century.

little red book Contained the thoughts of Chairman Mao Zedong on various topics; used as a talisman during the Cultural Revolution by young Chinese.

llama A wooly pack animal commonly found in the Andes Mountains of South America and in Argentina. It is related to the camel but has no humps. Besides transport, llamas provide meat, wool, and hides.

Locarno Pact An agreement between France and Germany in 1925.

Lollards Name of unknown origin given to the English religious rebels of the 1380s who later protested against the privileges of the clergy and were vigorously persecuted.

Long March of 1934 The six thousand-mile fighting retreat of the Chinese communists under Mao Zedong to Shensi province in 1934–1935.

Louis XIV, King King of France 1643–1715, famous as the leading Bourbon practitioner of royal absolutism and the builder of the royal *chateau* at Versailles.

L'Ouverture, Toussaint (1743–1803) Leader who led the struggle for the independence of African and Afro-Haitian slaves from French colonial rule.

Luther, Martin (1483–1546) Began the Protestant Reformation with his famous Ninety-Five Theses. Also noted for his translation of the Bible into German.

Maastricht Treaty (MAHS-trict) Signed in 1991 by members of the European Community; committed them to closer political-economic ties.

Maat (MAHT) Egyptian goddess of universal order and balance.

Machu Picchu (MAH-choo PEE-choo) Incan city in the high Andes Mountains.

Maenads Female followers of the Greek god of the grape and wine, Bacchus.

Magellan, Ferdinand (mah-JEL-lan) First man to sail completely around the world, 1519–1522.

Mahayana Buddhism (mah-hah-YAH-nah) A more liberal, looser form of Buddhism; originating soon after the Buddha's death, it deemphasized the monastic life and abstruse philosophy in favor of prayer to the eternal Buddha and the bodhisattvas who succeeded him.

Mahdi, The (MAH-dee) A charismatic Islamic mystic, Muhammad Ahmad, who led a serious rebellion against Egyptian rule in the Sudan, 1881–1885.

maize/maize cultivation Known to North Americans as corn, maize was cultivated as one of the staple foods of American Indian civilizations, along with beans and squash.

Majapahit (mah-JAH-pah-hit) The main town of a maritime empire in fourteenth-century Indonesia.

Maji Maji uprising (MAH-jee MAH-jee) A millenarian movement and secondary uprising against German colonial authority in Tanganyika, *c.* 1905–1907.

Mali (MAH-lee) The West African empire that was the successor to Ghana in the 1300s and 1400s.

Manchuria Large province of northeastern China, seized in the nineteenth century by Russia and Japan before being retaken by the Maoist government.

mandarins (MAN-dah-rihns) Chinese scholar-officials who had been trained in Confucian principles. Usually associated with the landed elite.

mandate of Heaven A theory of rule originated by the Zhou Dynasty in China, emphasizing the connection between imperial government's rectitude and its right to govern.

mandates Britain and France governed several Asian and African peoples after World War I, supposedly as agents of the League of Nations.

manor An agricultural estate of varying size, normally owned by a noble or the clergy and worked by free and unfree peasants/serfs.

Mansa Musa (MAHN-sah MOO-sah) King of Mali, early fourteenth century.

Manu (MAH-noo) Legendary lawgiver in India.

Manzhou (man-CHOO) Originally, nomadic tribes living in Manchuria who eventually overcame Ming resistance and established the Qing Dynasty in seventeenth-century China.

Mao Zedong (mau tseh-duhng; 1893–1976) Joined the Communist Party in the 1920s and became its principal leader. Later defeated the Kuomintang, and, as Chairman of the Chinese Communist Party, ruled China until his death in 1976.

marabout (MAH-rah-boot) A leader of a radical Sufi brotherhood in North Africa and the Sahara Desert.

Marathon The battle in 490 B.C.E. in which the Greeks defeated the Persians, ending the first Persian War.

March Revolution of 1917 The abdication of Tsar Nicholas II and the establishment of the Provisional Government in Russia.

Maritime Expeditions (China's) Early fifteenth-century explorations of the Indian and South Pacific oceans ordered by the Chinese emperor.

Marshall Plan A program proposed by U.S. Secretary of State George Marshall and implemented from 1947 to 1951 to aid Western Europe's recovery from World War II.

Marx, Karl (1818–1883) Seminal early socialist historian, philosopher, and social theoretician who, in collaboration with Friedrich Engels, wrote *The Communist Manifesto* and *Das Kapital* (*Capital*) and founded the International movement.

Massacre on Tiananmen Square *See* Tiananmen Square, Massacre on.

matriarchy A society in which females are dominant socially and politically.

matrilineal descent Attribution of name and inheritance to children via the maternal line.

Mauryan dynasty The first great dynasty of rulers of India that reigned from 322 to 185 B.C.E.

Maya The most advanced of the Amerindian peoples, who lived in southern Mexico and Guatemala and created a high urban civilization in the pre-Columbian era.

McMahon Letter British correspondence in 1916 that promised support for the creation of an Arab state in the Middle East in exchange for an Arab alliance in driving Turkey out of the region.

Mehmed the Conqueror (1432–1481) Also known as Mehmed II. Ottoman Sultan who besieged and conquered Constantinople in 1453, thereafter renaming it Istanbul.

Meiji Restoration (mei-JEE) The overthrow of the Tokugawa shogunate and restoration of the emperor to nominal power in Japan in 1867.

Mein Kampf (mine KAHMF) *My Struggle*; Hitler's credo, written while serving a prison term in 1924.

mercantilism A theory of national economics popular in the seventeenth and eighteenth centuries; aimed at establishing a favorable trade balance through government control of exports and imports as well as domestic industry.

meritocracy The rule of the meritorious (usually determined by examinations).

Meroe Last capital of the ancient African kingdom of Kush. Location of extensive iron smelting, *c.* 500 B.C.E.

Mesopotamia Literally, *the land between the rivers*; the fertile lands between the Tigris and Euphrates rivers where the earliest known civilizations appeared in the fourth millennium B.C.E.

Messenian Wars Conflicts between the neighbors Sparta and Messenia that resulted in Messenia's conquest by Sparta in about 600 B.C.E.

messiah A savior-king who would someday lead the Jews to glory.

mestizo (mes-TEE-so) A person of mixed Amerindian and European blood.

Mexican Revolution The armed struggle that occurred in Mexico between 1910 and 1920 to install a more socially progressive and populist government.

Middle Kingdom The period in Egyptian history from 2100 to 1600 B.C.E.; followed the First Intermediate Period.

Midway Island, Battle of (1942) Naval victory won by the Americans that put them on the offensive in the Pacific war against the Japanese.

Milan, Edict of A decree issued by the emperor Constantine in 313 C.E. that legalized Christianity and made it the favored religion in the Roman Empire.

Millenarian movements Mass movements, led by prophets, who promise the coming of a millennium in return for following the dictates of a spirit or god, with whom (s)he claims to be in contact.

Ming Dynasty Ruling dynasty of China, 1368 to 1644.

Minoan (mih-NOH-wan) An ancient civilization that was centered on Crete between *c.* 2000 and *c.* 1400 B.C.E.

missi dominici (MEE-see doh-MEH-nih-chee) Agents of Charlemagne in the provinces of his empire.

modernism A philosophy of art of the late nineteenth and early twentieth centuries that rejected classical models and values and sought new expressions and aesthetics.

Mohenjo-Daro (moh-HEHN-joh DAH-roh) Site of one of the two chief towns of the ancient Indus Valley civilization.

moksha (MOHK-shah) The final liberation from bodily existence and reincarnation in Hinduism.

monarchy Rule by a single individual, who often claims divine inspiration and protection.

Mongols Name for collection of nomadic, savage warriors of central Asia who conquered most of Eurasia in the thirteenth century.

Monks Mound The largest of the earthen ceremonial mounds found at Cahokia.

monoculture Overreliance on one or two crops in a region; an economically precarious system.

monoeconomies Economies very narrowly based on just one commodity (or a very few) produced for export.

monotheism A religion having only one god.

Monroe Doctrine The announcement in 1823 by U.S. president James Monroe that no European interference in Latin America would be tolerated.

Mughals (MOO-guls) A corruption of *Mongol*; refers to the period of Muslim rule in India.

Muhammad (moo-HAH-mahd) The Prophet of Islam.

Muhammad Ali Pasha (1769–1849) Viceroy of Egypt, 1803–1849, he introduced important reforms to reorganize Egypt and its army and navy along European lines.

mulatto (muh-LOT-to) A person of mixed African and European blood.

Munich Agreements The 1938 meetings between Adolf Hitler and the British and French prime ministers that allowed Germany to take much of Czechoslovakia; the agreement confirmed Hitler's belief that the democratic governments would not fight German aggression.

municipia (myoo-nih-KIH-pee-yah) The basic unit of Roman local government; similar to a present-day municipality.

Mussolini, Benito Fascist dictator of Italy during the 1920s and 1930s. One of the three Axis allies during World War II.

Mycenaean (meye-seh-NEE-yan) Referring to the history and culture of the earliest known Indo-European inhabitants of the Greek peninsula, between *c.* 1600 and *c.* 1100 B.C.E.

mystery religions Various Hellenistic cults promising immortal salvation of the individual.

Nantes, Edict of A law granting toleration to French Calvinists that was issued in 1598 by King Henry IV to end the religious civil war.

Napoleonic Settlement A collective name for the decrees and actions by Napoleon between 1800 and 1808 that legalized and systematized many elements of the French Revolution.

nationalism A form of allegiance in which people owe their loyalty and devotion to the state or nation in which they live.

Natufians The earliest settlers of the Levantine Corridor, they founded the first known settled communities.

natural selection The Darwinian doctrine in biology that change in species derives from mechanistic changes induced by the environment.

Navigation Acts Laws regulating commerce with the British colonies in North America in favor of Britain.

nawab Provincial rulers of the Indian Mughal Empire and the *Raj.*

Nazism The German variant of fascism created by Hitler.

Neanderthal Man A species of *Homo sapiens* flourishing between 100,000 and 300,000 years ago that mysteriously died out; the name comes from the German valley where the first remains were found.

neocolonialism Literally, *new* colonialism, meaning the control—primarily economic—that the former colonial powers continue to exert over their former colonies in Asia, Africa, and Latin America.

Neo-Confucianism An eleventh- and twelfth-century C.E. revival of Confucian thought with special emphasis on love and responsibility toward others.

Neolithic Age The time when humans went from being nomadic food hunters and gatherers to producing food for themselves by domesticating wild plants and animals, *c.* 10,000–2,000 B.C.E.

Neolithic (food-producing) Revolution (*c.* 10,000-3000 B.C.E.) The substitution of farming for hunting-gathering as the primary source of food by a given people.

New Economic Policy (NEP) A policy introduced at the conclusion of the civil war that allowed for limited capitalism and private enterprise in the Soviet Union.

New Imperialism, the The late nineteenth-century worldwide colonialism of European powers interested in strategic and market advantage.

New Kingdom or Empire The period from *c.* 1550 to 700 B.C.E. in Egyptian history; followed the Second Intermediate Period. The period from 1550 to *c.* 1200 B.C.E. was the Empire.

Newton, Isaac (1642–1727) Giant of the European Scientific Revolution and considered by many to have been the greatest scientific thinker of the last three centuries of world history. His most imposing work was the *Principia Mathematica*, in which he summarized his theories concerning the nature of matter, gravity, and motion.

Nicaea, Council of (neye-SEE-yah) (325 C.E.) The first general council of the Christian Church. The Emperor Constantine convened the council at the Greek city of Nicaea to address the heresy of Arianism and to promote doctrinal unity in the Church.

Niger-Congo language family One of the four major language groups found in Africa. Originally found in woodlands north of the West African rain forest. Today, the Niger-Congo languages are spoken throughout most of subequatorial Africa.

Niger-Congo speakers People who speak one of the member languages of the Niger-Congo language family.

1001 Nights, The *See Arabian Nights, The.*

Nilo-Saharan language family One of the four major groups of languages spoken in Africa. Largely spoken throughout northern and eastern Africa.

Nilo-Saharan speakers People who speak one of the languages that are members of the Nilo-Saharan language family.

Ninety-Five Theses The challenge to church authority publicized by Martin Luther, October 31, 1517.

Nineveh (NIH-neh-vay) The main city and later capital of the Assyrian Empire.

nirvana (ner-VAH-nah) The Buddhist equivalent of the Hindu moksha; the final liberation from suffering and reincarnation.

Nonaggression Pact of 1939 The treaty between Adolf Hitler and Josef Stalin in which each agreed to maintain neutrality in any forthcoming war involving the other party.

North American Free Trade Agreement (NAFTA) An agreement signed by the United States, Canada, and Mexico in 1993 that provides for much liberalized trade among these nations.

North Atlantic Treaty Organization (NATO) An organization founded in 1949 under U.S. aegis as a defense against threatened communist aggression in Europe.

Nubia Region of Africa south of Egypt, located roughly in today's Sudan. It was where the ancient African kingdoms of Kush and Meroe were found.

nuclear family Composed of parents and children only.

Nuclear Test Ban The voluntary cessation of aboveground testing of nuclear weapons by the United States and the Soviet Union; in existence from 1963 to the present.

Nuremberg Laws Laws defining racial identity that were aimed against Jews; adopted in 1935 by the German government.

Ôba King of the African state of Benin.

October Revolution of 1917 The Bolshevik coup d'état in St. Petersburg that ousted the Provisional Government and established a communist state in Russia.

Odyssey (AH-dehs-see) Second of the two Homeric epic poems, detailing the adventures of the homeward-bound Ulysses coming from the siege of Troy; see also *Iliad*.

Old Kingdom The period of Egyptian history from 3100 to 2200 B.C.E.

oligarchy Rule by a few.

Olmec civilization (*c.* 1500-500 B.C.E.) The earliest Amerindian civilization in Mexico.

Olympe de Gouges Author of the "Declaration of the Rights of Woman and the Female Citizen" (1791), which demanded the same rights for women as those that had been granted to men by the French National Assembly in 1789.

Omani Arabs Imamate, and later sultanate, located in southeastern Arabia.

Operation Barbarossa Code name for German invasion of the Soviet Union in 1941.

Operation Condor Secret agreement entered into by South American dictators during the 1970s to round up and imprison political dissidents.

Opium Wars Conflicts that occurred in 1840–1842 on the Chinese coast between the British and the Chinese over the importation of opium into China. The Chinese defeat began eighty years of subordination to foreigners.

Organization of African Unity (OAU) The association of sub-Saharan African nations founded in 1963 for mutual aid and, it was hoped, eventually the creation of a "United States of Africa."

Organization of American States (OAS) An organization founded in 1948 under U.S. auspices to provide mutual defense and aid; now embraces all countries on the American continents except Cuba.

Organization of Petroleum Exporting Countries (OPEC) Oil cartel founded in 1961 by Arab governments and later expanded to include several Latin American and African members.

Origin of Species, The Charles Darwin's book that first enunciated the evolutionary theory in biology; published in 1859.

Osama bin Laden (oh-SAH-mah bihn LAH-dihn; 1957–2011) Saudi-born Arab who organized the al-Qaida terrorist organization to wage Islamic *jihad* against the Western nations.

ostpolitik (OHST-poh-lih-tihk) German term for Chancellor Willy Brandt's 1960s policy of pursuing normalized relations with West Germany's neighbors to the east.

Oyo West African kingdom of the Yoruba people. Considered to be one of the "daughter" states of Ifè.

Pagan Ancient capital of the Burmese Kingdom in southeastern Asia. Destroyed by the invading Mongol army in the thirteenth century C.E.

Paleoindian/Paleoindian Period 9500–8900 B.C.E. in Native American history. A period when American Indians used Clovis spearheads to hunt large mammals like the wooly mammoth and giant bison.

Paleolithic Age The period from the earliest appearance of *Homo sapiens* to *c.* 10,000 B.C.E., though exact dates vary by area; the Old Stone Age.

Palestine Liberation Organization (PLO) An organization founded in the 1960s by Palestinians expelled from Israel; until 1994, it aimed at destruction of the state of Israel by any means. Superseded by the autonomous Palestinian Authority created in 1997.

Pan-Africanism Movement begun in the early twentieth century among African and Caribbean Americans to create unity among black people around the world. In the 1960s, became a movement to create a politically unified Africa.

Paris Commune of 1871 A leftist revolt against the national government after France was defeated by Prussia in 1871; crushed by the conservatives with much bloodshed.

Parthenon The classic Greek temple to Athena on the Acropolis in Athens's center.

Parthian Empire Persian Empire that lasted 247 B.C.E.–224 C.E.

pastoral civilization A civilization that is based primarily on pastoralism and pastoral ways of living.

pastoralism Relying at least partially on domestic livestock as sources of basic necessities like food, clothing, and shelter.

pastoral nomadism A way of life prevalent in most steppe lands. Characterized by nomadism and dependence on livestock breeding rather than on agriculture.

patents of nobility Royal documents conferring nobility.

patria potestas (PAH-tree-yah poh-TEHS-tahs) The power of the father over his family in ancient Rome.

patriarchy A society in which males have social and political dominance.

patricians (patres) The upper governing class in ancient Rome.

patrilineal descent Attribution of name and inheritance to children via the paternal line.

Pax Mongolica (PAHKS mon-GOH-lih-cah) The *Mongol peace*; between *c.* 1250 and *c.* 1350 in most of Eurasia.

Pax Romana (PAHKS roh-MAH-nah) The *Roman peace*; the era of Roman control over the Mediterranean basin and much of Europe between *c.* 31 B.C.E. and 180 C.E. or later.

Peace of Augsburg Pact ending the German religious wars in 1555, dividing the country between Lutheran and Catholic hegemony.

peaceful coexistence The declared policy of Soviet leader Nikita Khrushchev in dealing with the capitalist West after 1956.

Peloponnesian War (pehl-luh-puh-NEE-zhan) The great civil war between Athens and Sparta and their respective allies in ancient Greece; fought between 429 and 404 B.C.E. and eventually won by Sparta.

peonage (PEE-on-ihj) In Latin America, a type of serfdom that tied peasant workers to a hacienda through alleged debts owed to the employer.

perestroika (payr-rihs-TROY-kah) The Russian term for *restructuring,* which, with *glasnost,* was used to describe the reforms instituted by Mikhail Gorbachev in the Soviet Union in the late 1980s.

Pericles (PAYR-rih-clees) The Athenian democratic leader and spokesman who died in the midst of the Peloponnesian War in the fifth century B.C.E.

Peronismo Term used for the economic policies of Argentine dictator Juan Perón that bankrupted that nation's economy in the 1940s.

Persian Wars The conflict between the Greeks and the Persian Empire in the fifth century B.C.E., fought in two installments and ending with Greek victory.

Persians An early Indo-European tribe that, along with the Medes, settled in Iran.

Peruvian textiles Pattern cloth woven from alpaca wool and cotton by the ancient Andean peoples. They were used to convey religious symbols and meaning.

Peter the Great, Ruler of Russia (1682–1725) Peter I is noteworthy for his absolutist style of rule and as a great innovator who tried to modernize his country along European lines.

Petrine Succession The doctrine of the Roman Catholic Church by which the pope, the bishop of Rome, is the direct successor of St. Peter.

pharaoh (FAYR-roh) The title of the god-king of ancient Egypt.

philosophes A French term used to refer to the writers and activist intellectuals during the Enlightenment.

philosophy A Greek term meaning *love of knowledge.*

Phoenicians (*c.* 3000–1000 B.C.E.). The peoples of ancient Phoenicia, a region that approximately includes modern Lebanon. They were noted sailors, merchants, and colonizers of the ancient Mediterranean Sea.

phonetic alphabet A system of writing that matches signs with the sounds of the oral language.

pit houses A type of dwelling found in some Neolithic civilizations. Early farmers dug oval-shaped or rectangular pits into the ground over which they erected walls and roofs from tree branches and twigs, animal bones, animal hides, and mud.

Plassey, Battle of (1757) Battle fought between French-sponsored army of Siraj ad-Dawla and East India Company forces led by Robert Clive. Clive's victory reduced French and Dutch influence in India.

Plato (427–347 B.C.E.) Student of Socrates and teacher of Aristotle. Recorded Socrates' dialogues. Wrote the *Metaphor of the Cave* and *The Republic.*

plebeians (plebs) The common people of ancient Rome.

Pleistocene Age In archeology, the age of repeated glaciations (Ice Ages) that occurred *c.* 2.5 million–10,000 B.C.E.

polis (PAH-lihs) The political and social community of citizens in ancient Greece.

polytheism A religion having many gods.

pope, the The Bishop of Rome and the acknowledged pastoral head of the Roman Catholic Church.

Popular Front The coordinated policy of all antifascist parties; inspired by the Soviets in the mid-1930s against Adolf Hitler.

Praetorian Guard (pree-TOH-ree-yan) The imperial bodyguard in the Roman Empire and the only armed force in Italy.

pre-Socratics The Greek philosophers of the seventh and sixth centuries who came before the Classical philosophers, Socrates, Plato, and Aristotle, who focused on the nature of the material world.

primary resistance A term applied by some historians for the initial, largely local form of resistance that usually followed soon after European occupation of territory in Africa.

Princeps (PRIHN-keps) *The First* or *the Leader* in Latin; title taken by Augustus Caesar.

Principality of Kiev The first Russian state; flourished from *c.* 800 to 1240, when it fell to Mongols.

Principate The reign of Augustus Caesar from 27 B.C.E. to 14 C.E.

Principia Mathematica Newton's seminal publication in which he summarized his revolutionary ideas about the nature of matter, gravity, and motion.

proconsuls Provincial governors and military commanders in ancient Rome.

proletariat Poverty-stricken people without skills; also, a Marxist term for the propertyless working classes.

Provisional Government A self-appointed parliamentary group exercising power in republican Russia from March to October 1917.

Ptah (pu-TAH) Egyptian god of rebirth, renewal.

Ptolemaic Kingdom of Egypt (tah-luh-MAY-ihk) Egyptian state created by Ptolemy, one of Alexander the Great's generals, in the Hellenistic era.

Pueblo culture (PWEH-bloh) Name given to the Native American culture that has flourished in the Four Corners region of the United States, *c.* 400–present.

Punic Wars (PYOO-nihk) The three conflicts between Rome and Carthage that ended with the destruction of the Carthaginian Empire and the extension of Roman control throughout the western Mediterranean.

Punt To ancient Egyptians, the lands that probably included southwest Arabia and the Horn of Africa.

purdah (PURR-dah) The segregation of females in Hindu and Muslim society.

Puritans The English Calvinists who were dissatisfied by the theology of the Church of England and wished to "purify" it.

putsch A coup d'état, the overthrow of an existing government.

putting-out system An economic arrangement between individuals or small producers for production of handwork at home and payment by the piece; it was replaced by the factory beginning in late eighteenth-century Britain.

Qadis (KAA-dee) Islamic judges, learned in Islamic theology and law.

Queen Elizabeth I *See* Elizabeth I, Queen.

Qin Dynasty (221–202 B.C.E.) Chinese dynasty (of only two rulers) founded in 221 B.C.E. by Shih Huangdi, the "First Emperor."

Qing Dynasty (ching) The last Chinese dynasty, which ruled from 1644 until 1911; established by Manzhou invaders after they defeated the Ming rulers.

Qur'an (koor-AHN) The holy scripture of Islam, thought to be (lit.) the word of God.

Raffles, Sir Thomas (1781–1826) British statesman known for his founding of Singapore. Also important for helping to drive French and Dutch from Java (Indonesia), contributing to the expansion of the British Empire into Southeast Asia.

raison d'état (RAY-zohn day-TAH) The idea that the welfare of the state should be supreme in government policy.

The Raj Shorthand for the British *Raj*, a term that refers to the period of British rule in India.

Ramadan One of the twelve months of the Muslim calendar, it is the month set aside for the ritual fasting.

Realpolitik (ree-AL-poh-lih-tik) Political policies that are based on practical considerations rather than on ideology.

Red Guards The youthful militants who carried out the Cultural Revolution in China during the 1960s.

Reform Act of 1832, British Brought about a reform of British parliamentary voting and representation that strengthened the middle class and the urbanites.

Reformation The sixteenth-century upheaval led by Martin Luther and John Calvin that modified or in some cases rejected altogether some Catholic doctrine and practices; led to the establishment of Protestant churches.

Reign of Terror The period (1793–1794) of extreme Jacobin radicalism during the French Revolution.

Renaissance The social, artistic, and cultural "rebirth" that arose in Europe in the fourteenth century.

reparations question Money and goods that Germany was to pay to the victorious Allies after World War I under the Versailles Treaty.

republican government A form of governing that imitates the Roman *res publica* in its rejection of monarchy.

Rerum novarum (REHR-rum noh-VAHR-rum) An encyclical issued by Pope Leo XIII in 1890 that committed the Roman Catholic Church to attempting to achieve social justice for the poor.

Restoration (English) The period of the 1660s–1680s when Charles II was called by Parliament to take his throne and was thus restored to power.

revisionism (Marxism) The late-nineteenth-century adaptation of Marxist socialism that aimed to introduce basic reform through parliamentary acts rather than through revolution.

Revolution of 1989 The throwing out of the communist governments in Eastern Europe by popular demand or armed uprising.

Richelieu, Cardinal (1585–1642) Secretary of state to King Louis XIII and principal architect of royal absolutism in France that was created under the Bourbon monarchy.

Rigveda (rihg-VAY-dah) The most ancient of the four Vedas, or Hindi religious epics, brought into India by the Aryans.

Robespierre, Maximilien Leading theoretical thinker of the Reign of Terror during the French Revolution and member of the notorious Committee of Public Safety.

Romanesque style The style of European public and church architecture that was popular through the twelfth century. Characterized by rounded arches, thick walls, and relatively little glass in external walls.

Romanov Dynasty (ROH-mah-noff) Ruled Russia from 1613 until 1917.

Romantic movement The generic name for the trend in literature and the arts of early nineteenth-century Europe, away from rationalism and social improvement and toward a celebration of the emotions and individualistic views.

Rome, Treaty of The pact signed by six Western European nations in 1957 that is the founding document of the European Union.

Rose Chamber Rescript of 1839 A major component of the Tanzimat; it called for the full equality of all Ottoman subjects, regardless of religion or ethnicity.

Rousseau, Jean-Jacques (1712–1778) *Philosophe* of the French Enlightenment noted for his liberal ideas concerning children's education.

Roy, Ram Mohun (1774–1833) One of the most important figures in the nineteenth-century Indian social reform movement known as the Bengal Renaissance.

Rubaiyat (roo-BAY-yaht) The verses attributed to the twelfth-century Persian poet Omar Khayyam.

Safavid Empire (SAH-fah-vihd) The dynasty of Shi'ite Muslims that ruled Persia from the 1500s to the 1700s.

Sahel The arid belt extending across Africa south of the Sahara; also called the Sudan.

Sayyid Sa'id (SAHY-yihd sah-EED) bin Sultan al-Busaidi (1797–1856) Prince of the ruling family of Oman, eastern Arabia. Became Sultan of Oman and Muscat in 1804, founded the Zanzibar Sultanate in East Africa in 1832, and relocated his capital to Zanzibar in East Africa in 1840.

sakoku (sah-KOH-koo) Japan's self-imposed isolation from the outer world that lasted two centuries, until 1854.

Salafi movement (SAH-lah-fee) Intellectual movement begun by Muhammad Abduh to try to modernize Islamic law. More recently, the term has come to be associated with Islamism and a repudiation of the West.

samurai (sa-muh-REYE) Japanese warrior-aristocrats of medieval and early modern times.

sanga/sangha A Buddhist monastery. *Sanghas* often served as havens for travelers, especially for those on a religious pilgrimage.

Sanskrit The sacred language of ancient India; came originally from the Aryans.

Sardinia-Piedmont The north Italian kingdom that led the unification of Italy in the mid-nineteenth century.

Sassanian Empire Persian Empire that followed the Parthian Empire and lasted 224 C.E.–651 C.E.

sati (sah-TEE) In India, the practice in which a widow committed ritual suicide at the death of her husband.

satrapy (SA-tra-pee) A province under a governor or *satrap* in the ancient Persian Empire.

savanna The semiarid grasslands where most African civilizations developed.

scientific method The method of observation and experiment by which the physical sciences proceed to new knowledge.

Scramble for Africa The sudden race for colonies in Africa among the major European nations that occurred between about 1882 and 1914.

Second Estate The members of the French nobility during the *l'ancien regime*.

Second Front The reopening of a war front in the west against the Axis powers in World War II; eventually accomplished by the invasion of Normandy in June 1944.

Second Industrial Revolution The second phase of industrialization that occurred in the late 1800s after the introduction of electric power and the internal combustion engine.

Second International Association of socialist parties founded in 1889; after the Russian Revolution in 1917, the Second International split into democratic and communist segments.

secondary resistance A term some historians apply to the more delayed, regional, and supra-ethnic forms of armed resistance that occurred after European occupation of territories in Africa during the first few decades of the colonial era.

secret speech Premier Nikita Khrushchev of the Soviet Union gave an account in February 1956 of the crimes of Josef Stalin against his own people that was supposed to remain secret but was soon known internationally.

secularism The rejection of supernatural religion as the arbiter of earthly action; emphasis on worldly and humanistic affairs.

Seleucid Kingdom of Persia One of the three Hellenistic Kingdoms. The successor state to the empire of Alexander the Great in most of the Middle East.

Self-strengthening movement The late nineteenth-century attempt by Chinese officials to bring China into the modern world by instituting reforms; failed to achieve its goal.

Selim III, Sultan (seh-LEEM) Ottoman sultan, 1792–1807. He introduced the first reforms of the Ottoman Empire, which later became the Tanzimat.

Seljuks (sel-JUCKS) Turkish converts to Islam who seized the Baghdad government from the Abbasids in the eleventh century.

Semitic Adjective describing a person or language belonging to one of the most widespread of the western Asian groups; among many others, it embraces Hebrew and Arabic.

sepoys Term applied to rank-and-file Indian soldiers of the East Africa Company and British Indian Army.

serfdom Restriction of personal and economic freedoms associated with medieval-European agricultural society.

serfs A term for the peasant farmers who lived on rural manors and worked the land in various degrees and types of servitude throughout medieval Europe.

Seven Years' War Fought between France and England, with their allies, around the world, 1756–1763; won by England, with major accessions of territory to the British Empire.

Seventeen Point Constitution A list assembled by Prince Shotoku in 604 of the proper relationship between a government and its citizens.

Shah Abbas the Great (SHAH ahb-BAHS) Greatest of the Safavid shahs of Persia (r. 1587–1629). He extended the boundaries of the Safavid Empire to their greatest extent.

Shaka (SHAH-kah) King of the Zulu people of South Africa. During the 1810s, he united the Zulu into a powerful, militaristic state in the region of Natal.

Shang Dynasty The first historical rulers of China; ruled from *c.* 1500 to *c.* 1100 B.C.E.

Shari'a (shah-REE-yah) The sacred law of Islam; based on the *Qur'an* and the oral traditions (Sunna) of the Prophet Muhammad.

shaykh (shake) An Arabic honorific form of address for a respected elder, leader, or a scholar.

Shaykh al-Islam (shake al-is-LAHM) Highest religious official of the Ottoman Empire.

Shi'ites (SHEE-ites) A minority sect of Islam; adherents believe that kinship with Muhammad is necessary to qualify for the caliphate.

Shinto (SHIHN-toh) Native Japanese animism.

Shiva (SHEE-vah) A member of the high trinity of Hindu gods; lord of destruction but also of procreation; often pictured dancing.

shoen (SHOH-ehn) Parcels of land in Japan with *shiki* (rights) attached to them; could take many forms and have various possessors.

shogunate (SHOH-guh-nate) The government of medieval Japan in which the shogun, a military and civil regent, served as the actual leader, while the emperor was the symbolic head of the state and religion.

Silk Road One of the two most important trade routes of the premodern world. It and the Indian Ocean sea trade were the commercial backbones that brought together the trade of the Old World Eurasian and African continents. Actually comprised of several major trunk routes, the so-called Silk Road connected the ancient Mediterranean world with Iran, India, and China.

Shotoku, Prince A member of the Japanese royal family who assembled the Seventeen Point Constitution.

show trials First used for the staged trials of alleged traitors to the Soviet system in 1936–1937; generically, political trials in which the conviction of the accused is a foregone conclusion.

Siddhartha Gautama (sih-DAHR-thah gau-TAH-mah) The proper name of the Buddha.

Sikhs (SEEKS) Members of a cult founded in the sixteenth century C.E. who seek a middle way between Islam and Hindu belief; centered on the Punjab region in northern India.

Sino-Soviet conflict Differences in the interpretation of Marxism that were accentuated by conflict over proper policy vis-à-vis the United States in the 1950s and 1960s in Moscow and Beijing.

Sino-Tibetan languages The family of languages spoken by the Chinese and Tibetan peoples.

Six-Day War War briefly fought in six days in 1967, during which Israel occupied the Golan Heights (in southwest Syria), Jerusalem, the Left Bank, the Golan strip, and the entire Sinai Peninsula to the Suez Canal.

Smith, Adam (1723–1790) Enlightenment-era author of the *Wealth of Nations*, in which he theorized about the need for free trade and free markets.

Socialism An economic position that advocates that all property, production, and distribution of wealth should be regulated by the entire community.

Socrates (470–399 B.C.E.) First of the three great philosophers of the Greek Classical Age. Questioned the nature of knowledge and ethical conduct. Athenian court tried and executed him for "corrupting" the youth of the city.

Solidarity movement The umbrella organization founded by Lech Walesa and other anticommunist Poles in 1981 to recover Polish freedom; triumphed with new government in 1989.

Song Dynasty (sung) The dynasty that ruled China from *c.* 1127 until 1279, when the last ruler was overthrown by the Mongol invaders.

Songhay Empire (song-GEYE) A West African state, centered on the bend of the Niger River, which reached its fullest extent in the sixteenth century before collapsing.

Spirit of the Laws One of the basic tracts of the eighteenth-century Enlightenment, written by Baron Montesquieu and adopted by many reformers of government throughout Europe.

Sri Vijaya Great maritime and commercial empire of Southeast Asia, greatly influenced by India. Seated in Sumatra, it extended its control over much of the Malayan trade between the seventh and thirteenth centuries.

Stalin, Josef (1879–1953) Minor figure in the October Revolution of 1917 in Russia, but followed Vladimir Lenin as the chairman of the Communist Party. Soviet dictator from 1928 until his death in 1953.

Stalingrad The battle in 1942 that marked the turning point of World War II in Europe.

state The term for a territorial, sovereign entity of government.

steppes/steppe land In physical geography, steppes and steppe lands generally are characterized by relatively low levels of rainfall and growth of short grasses. Usually suitable only for livestock.

sternpost rudder Ship's rudder mounted on a post on or behind the poop deck.

Stoicism A Hellenistic philosophy that emphasized human brotherhood and natural law as guiding principles.

Storm Troopers (SA) The street-fighting "bully boys" of the Nazi Party; suppressed after 1934 by Hitler's orders.

Structural Adjustment Programs (SAPs) Programs designed by the World Bank to achieve economic improvement in developing countries; frequently failures.

Sublime Porte A term that came to be applied to the Chancery and diplomatic corps of the Ottoman bureaucracy.

Successor states Usual term for the several eastern European states that emerged from the Paris treaties of 1919 as successors to the Russian, German, and Austro-Hungarian Empires.

Sudan (soo-DAN) Literally, Arabic for *blacks*, from the *Bilad al-Sudan*, the *Land of the Blacks*, in the arid belt extending across Africa south of the Sahara.

Sudanic kingship A form of ritual kingship that evolved in the Saharan-Sudanic region of precolonial Africa, in which the king plays a crucial role in the spiritual and material well-being of his country.

Sufi (SOO-fee) Arabic term for a popular form of Islam that emphasizes emotional union with God and mystical powers.

Sui Dynasty (soo-wee) Ruled China from *c.* 580 to *c.* 620 C.E.; ended the disintegration of central government that had existed for the previous 130 years.

sui iuris (SOO-wee YOO-rihs) *Of his own law*; Roman term for an individual, especially a female, who was not restricted by the usual laws or customs.

Suleiman the Magnificent (SOO-lay-man) Ottoman sultan, 1520–1566 C.E. Greatest of the Ottoman sultans, his long reign was the high-water mark of the Ottoman Empire.

Sumeria The earliest known civilization, based on city-states located in southern Iraq along the Tigris and Euphrates rivers.

Sumerians The creators of Mesopotamian urban civilization.

Sun Yat-sen (soon yaht-sehn; 1866–1925) Educated in Western schools, Sun helped overthrow the Qing monarchy and became one of the founders of the Kuomintang Party and of the Chinese Republic.

Sunna (SOO-nah) Literally, the *way* or example set by the Prophet Muhammad. It is the oral tradition that Muslim legal scholars rely upon to supplement the *Qur'an* as another source of the Shari'a.

Sunnis (SOO-nees) The majority group in Islam; adherents believe that the caliphate should go to the most qualified individual and should not necessarily pass to the kin of Muhammad.

suzerain The superior of a vassal to whom the vassal owed feudal duties.

Swahili (swah-HEE-lee) A hybrid language based on Bantu and Arabic; used extensively in East Africa. Often used to refer to the people and civilization of the East African coast.

syncretism The intermeshing of two different things, for example two different religions.

syndicalism A doctrine of government that advocates a society organized on the basis of syndicates or unions.

Taiping Rebellion Rebellion that occurred in China in the 1860s that opposed the Qing government and foreign opium vendors.

Taj Mahal (TAHJ mah-HAL) The beautiful tomb built by the seventeenth-century Mughal emperor Jahan for his wife.

takfiri A radically Islamist doctrine that declares all moderate Muslims who refuse to engage in jihad against the West to be themselves unbelievers and therefore under a sentence of death.

Tale of Genji (GEHN-jee) First known novel in Asian, if not world, history; authored by a female courtier about life in the Japanese medieval court.

Taliban (students) Islamic fundamentalist militants who came to power in Afghanistan in 1995 and were expelled from the country a few years later by American and native forces.

Tanakh The Hebrew Bible, or Old Testament, as it is known to Christians.

Tang Dynasty Ruled China from *c.* 620 to *c.* 900 C.E. and began the great age of Chinese artistic and technical advances.

Tanzimat reforms (TAN-zih-maht) Literally, "New Order" in Turkish. The state-directed reforms of the Ottoman Empire that lasted from 1839 to 1876.

tariqa (tah-REE-kah) Muslim Sufi (popular mystic) brotherhoods, generally all-male.

Taxila Central Asian city, along with Balkh and Peshawar, which was a western linchpin of the famed Silk Road trade routes connecting Iran, India, and China.

Temujin The birth name of Chinghis Khan.

Tenochtitlan (teh-noch-tiht-LAHN) Chief city of the Aztec civilization. It was probably built *c.* 1325 and was conquered by Cortés in 1521. It was renamed Mexico City and served as the capital of colonial Mexico.

Teotihuacan (TAY-oh-tee-WAH-kahn) One of the Classical Native American civilizations of Mexico, dated 300 B.C.E. to 800 C.E.

Tetrarchy "Rule of four"; a system of monarchic rule established by Roman emperor Diocletian at the end of the third century C.E.; failed to achieve its goals.

theocracy The rule by gods or their priests.

Theravada Buddhism (thayr-rah-VAH-dah) A strict monastic form of Buddhism entrenched in Southeast Asia; same as Hinayana Buddhism.

Third Estate The great majority of Frenchmen: those neither clerical nor noble.

Third International An association of Marxist parties in many nations; inspired by Russian communists and headquartered in Moscow until its dissolution in 1943.

Third Republic of France The government of France after the exile of Emperor Napoleon III; lasted from 1871 until 1940.

Third Rome A Russian myth that Moscow was ordained to succeed Rome and Constantinople as the center of true Christianity.

Tian The Chinese name for a heavenly force that governed the entire universe.

Tiananmen Square, Massacre on The shooting down of perhaps thousands of Chinese who were peacefully demonstrating for relaxation of political censorship by the communist leaders; occurred in 1989 in Beijing.

Tokugawa leyasu (toh-koo-GAH-wah ee-eh-YAH-soo) Founded the Tokugawa Shogunate in Japan, 1603–1616.

Toltec (TOHL-tehc) An Amerindian civilization centered in the Valley of Mexico; succeeded by the Aztecs.

Torah (TOH-rah) The first five books of the Old Testament; the Jews' fundamental law code.

Tories A nickname for British nineteenth-century conservatives; opposite of Whigs.

total war The modern form of warfare that first appeared in the twentieth century that involved the recruitment of entire civilian populations, in addition to the troops in the field, in support of the war effort.

totalitarianism The attempt by a dictatorial government to achieve total control over a society's life and ideas.

Trafalgar, Battle of Naval battle in which the English fleet, under Admiral Lord Nelson, defeated the combined French and Spanish fleets in 1805, permanently forestalling French plans to invade England.

trans-Saharan trade Ancient trade between Mediterranean and Red Sea regions and sub-Saharan regions of Africa; primarily linked the Maghrib with the western and central Sudan.

Treaty of Brest-Litovsk (1918) The separate peace between the Central Powers and Lenin's government in Russia.

Trekboers (TREHK-bohrs) South African Boer "pioneers" who trekked away from Cape Colony and British rule to settle deep inland on the South African frontier. Eventually founded the two Boer republics: the Orange Free State and the Transvaal.

tribunes The chief representatives of the plebeians during the Roman republic.

Triple Alliance A pact concluded in 1882 that united Germany, Austria-Hungary, and Italy against possible attackers; the members were called the Central Powers.

Triumvirate "Three-man rule"; the First Triumvirate existed during the 50s B.C.E. and the Second in the 30s B.C.E., during the last decades of the Roman Republic.

Trotsky, Leon (1879–1940) Vladimir Lenin's coconspirator and primary instrument in planning and executing the October 1917 communist revolution in Russia. Succeeded as commissar of the Red Army during the Soviet civil war (1918–1923) and was the chief planner of the New Economic Policy.

Truman Doctrine The commitment of the U.S. government in 1947 to defend any noncommunist state against attempted communist takeover; proposed by President Harry Truman.

Tumen A unit of 10,000 in the Mongol armies.

Tupac Amaru Also known as *Tupac Amaru II.* A descendant of the Inca emperor of the same name, he led a rebellion against Spanish rule in the 1780s.

Tutankhamen (too-TAHNK-ah-men) Boy pharaoh who ruled Egypt 1347–1339 B.C.E.

Twelve Tables The first written Roman law code; established *c.* 450 B.C.E.

ulama (oo-lah-MAH) Muslim religious scholars, usually specialists in Holy Law (see Shari'a); sometimes called *mullahs.*

Umayyad Dynasty (oo-MAHY-yad) The caliphs resident in Damascus from 661 to 750 C.E.

Umma (OO-mah) The entire Muslim community, meaning something like the Christian concept of the "Church."

unequal treaties Chinese name for the diplomatic and territorial arrangements foisted on the weak Qing Dynasty by European powers in the nineteenth century; also, the commercial treaties forced on just-opened Japan by the same powers and the United States.

Upanishads (oo-PAH-ni-shads) The ancient Hindu holy epics dealing with morals and philosophy.

urban migration A term for the widespread demographic event beginning in Europe in the early nineteenth century that saw millions of people moving into the towns and cities from the countryside.

Utopia *Nowhere*; Greek term used to denote an ideal place or society.

Utrecht, Treaty of Treaty signed in 1713 that ended the War of the Spanish Succession. A defeat for King Louis XIV of France, it gave Britain access to the valuable trade of the Spanish Caribbean Islands.

vassal In medieval Europe, a person, usually a noble, who owed feudal duties to a superior, called a *suzerain*.

Vedas (VAY-dahs) The four oral epics of the Aryans brought into ancient India.

Vedic Age/Vedic Epoch The period in Indian history when the Vedas were being recorded—roughly 1500 to 500 B.C.E.

Vishnu (VISH-noo) One of the high Hindu trinity of gods, the god who preserves the universe and karma.

vizier (vih-ZEER) An official of Muslim government, especially a high Turkish official equivalent to prime minister.

Wahhabism (wah-HAHB-ism) Movement begun by Muhammad Abd al-Wahhab in the mid-1700s to impose a fundamentalist Islamic law on Arabia. It became the foundation of Saudi Arabia as well as contemporary, radical—and sometimes violent—Islamic fundamentalism.

Wannsee Conference The 1942 meeting of Nazi leaders that determined the "final solution" for the Jews.

waqf (WAHK-f) An Islamic trust established by the devout to benefit a particular group of people or institution (a mosque, for example). Usually, the *ulama* administer these foundations much as lawyers oversee trusts.

Warsaw Pact An organization of the Soviet satellite states in Europe; founded under Russian aegis in 1954 to serve as a counterweight to NATO.

Wars of the Roses An English civil war between noble factions over the succession to the throne in the fifteenth century.

Waterloo The final defeat of Napoleon in 1815 after his return from Elban exile.

Wealth of Nations, The The short title of the path-breaking work on national economy by Adam Smith; published in 1776.

weapons of mass destruction (WMDs) Deadly nuclear, chemical, or biological weapons.

Weimar Republic (VEYE-mahr) The popular name for Germany's democratic government between 1919 and the Nazi takeover.

Westphalia, Treaty of The treaty that ended the Thirty Years' War in 1648; the first modern peace treaty, in that it established strategic and territorial gains as more important than religious or dynastic ones.

Whigs A nickname for British nineteenth-century liberals; opposite of Tories.

white man's burden A phrase coined by Rudyard Kipling to refer to what he considered the necessity of bringing European civilization to non-Europeans.

white settler colonies African colonies that experienced relatively large amounts of white European immigration during the colonial period—primarily Algeria, Kenya, (Southern) Rhodesia, Angola, Mozambique, and South Africa.

Wollstonecraft, Mary (1759–1797) Considered by many to be the founder of modern feminism. Mary Wollstonecraft advocated better education and more occupational opportunities for Enlightenment era women.

women's liberation Movement, begun in the 1960s, to improve the economic and social status of women.

Woodland civilizations A collection of closely-related Native American civilizations that thrived east of the Mississippi River, *c.* 1000 B.C.E. to 1000 C.E.

World Bank A monetary institution founded after World War II by Western nations to assist in the recovery effort and to aid the Third World's economic development.

xenophobia Prejudice against foreigners.

Yalta Conference Conference in 1945 in southern Prussia where Franklin D. Roosevelt, Josef Stalin, and Winston Churchill (the "Big Three") met to attempt to settle postwar questions, particularly those affecting the future of Europe.

Yom Kippur War (YAHM kih-POOR) A name for the 1973 conflict between Israel and its Arab neighbors.

Young Ottomans A group of Western-educated Turkish intellectuals and journalists who, in the 1870s, supported the transformation of the Ottoman sultanate into a constitutional monarchy.

Yuan Dynasty (YOO-an) Official term for the Mongol dynasty of the Great Khans in China, 1279–1368.

yurts (yerts) Tent-like Mongol dwellings usually made of felt.

zaibatsu Japanese corporate entities established during the Meiji Restoration to help control the economy.

Zama, Battle of Decisive battle of the Second Punic War; Roman victory in 202 was followed by absorption of most of the Carthaginian Empire in the Mediterranean.

Zanzibar Sultanate Sultanate (Arab government) established in 1832 on the East African island of Zanzibar by the former sultan of Oman, Sayyid Said bin Sultan al-Busaidi.

Zarathustra (ZAY-rah-THROOS-trah) The mythical founder and chief prophet of the ancient Persian religion known as Zoroastrianism, which influenced Jewish and later Christian belief.

zealots (ZEH-luhts) Jewish religious extremists at the time of Jesus who opposed Roman occupation and used guerilla methods and assassination against them to drive them out of Israel and Judea.

Zheng He (chung-huh) Chief eunuch of the Ming Yongle Emperor who led the Chinese Maritime Expeditions between 1405 and 1433. (*See* Maritime Expeditions.)

Zhou Dynasty (choh) The second historical Chinese dynasty; ruled from *c.* 1100 to *c.* 400 B.C.E.

ziggurat (ZIHG-goo-raht) The stepped and elevated temple structures that the ancient Mesopotamian civilization erected in honor of its gods.

Zionism (ZEYE-yuh-nism) A movement founded by Theodor Herzl in 1896 to establish a Jewish national homeland and to revive the study of Hebrew as a spoken language.

Zionists Those who believe in the ideals of Zionism.

Zulu War South African war fought in 1879 between Britain and the Zulu people. Its cause was Afrikaner expansion during the Great Trek and a British desire to defeat Africans who stood in the way of white settlement.

Answers to Test Your Knowledge

Chapter 22
1. c, 2. a, 3. a, 4. d, 5. b, 6. c, 7. d, 8. c, 9. a, 10. b

Chapter 23
1. c, 2. b, 3. c, 4. e, 5. a, 6. d, 7. a, 8. d, 9. a, 10, c

Chapter 24
1. d, 2. b, 3. d, 4. a, 5. b, 6. d, 7. b, 8. c, 9. a, 10. b

Chapter 25
1. e, 2. c, 3. a, 4. e, 5. d, 6. b, 7. a, 8. b, 9. d, 10. a

Chapter 26
1. b, 2. d, 3. e, 4. d, 5. d, 6. b, 7. c, 8. b, 9. c, 10. c

Chapter 27
1. d, 2. a, 3. c, 4. c, 5. b, 6. c, 7. c, 8. b, 9. d, 10. e

Chapter 28
1. b, 2. e, 3. c, 4. a, 5. e, 6. d, 7. a, 8. b, 9. b, 10. c

Chapter 29
1. b, 2. a, 3. b, 4. b, 5. d, 6. b, 7. c, 8. b, 9. a, 10. a

Chapter 30
1. a, 2. b, 3. b, 4. c, 5. e, 6.d, 7. d, 8. c, 9. e, 10. b

Chapter 31
1. c, 2. d, 3. b, 4. e, 5. a, 6. a, 7. b, 8. e, 9. b, 10. a

Chapter 32
1. e, 2. c, 3. a, 4. b, 5. b, 6. d, 7. c, 8. a, 9. c, 10. a

Chapter 33
1. c, 2. b, 3. d, 4. c, 5. e, 6. c, 7. e, 8. b, 9. d, 10. b

Chapter 34
1. b, 2. e, 3. d, 4. a, 5. c, 6. e, 7. a, 8. c, 9. d, 10. b

Chapter 35
1. b, 2. d, 3. a, 4. c, 5. e, 6. e, 7. d, 8. e, 9. b, 10. e

Chapter 36
1. d, 2. b, 3. b, 4. e, 5. c, 6. a, 7. b, 8. e, 9. d, 10. c

Chapter 37
1. a, 2. c, 3. c, 4. e, 5. c, 6. e, 7. b, 8. e, 9. b, 10. d

Chapter 38
1. a, 2. b, 3. c, 4. c, 5. b, 6. c, 7. e, 8. b, 9. b, 10. d

Chapter 39
1. c, 2. b, 3. e, 4. c, 5. c, 6. d, 7. a, 8. d, 9. e, 10. a

Chapter 40
1. a, 2. c, 3. d, 4. e, 5. c, 6. a, 7. d, 8. e, 9. e, 10. b

Chapter 41
1. a, 2. b, 3. b, 4. e, 5. c, 6. c, 7. a, 8. e, 9. a, 10. a

Chapter 42
1. b, 2. b, 3. c, 4. c, 5. c, 6. b, 7. e, 8. d, 9. b, 10. d

Chapter 43
1. a, 2. e, 3. a, 4. c, 5. a, 6. d, 7. b, 8. b, 9. c, 10. d

Chapter 44
1. c, 2. b, 3. d, 4. b, 5. e, 6. e, 7. d, 8. c, 9. a, 10. b

Chapter 45
1. c, 2. b, 3. b, 4. b, 5. c, 6. b, 7. c, 8. a, 9. d, 10. b

Chapter 46
1. a, 2. b, 3. e, 4. b, 5. b, 6. a, 7. c, 8. d, 9. c, 10. a

Chapter 47
1. d, 2. c, 3. e, 4. a, 5. c, 6. e, 7. c, 8. d, 9. a, 10. d

Chapter 48
1. e, 2. d, 3. c, 4. d, 5. b, 6. e, 7. b, 8. c, 9. a, 10. b

Chapter 49
1. b, 2. a, 3. e, 4. b, 5. a, 6. d, 7. b, 8. c, 9. d, 10. c

Chapter 50
1. c, 2. a, 3. b, 4. d, 5. c, 6. a, 7. e, 8. e, 9. b, 10. a

Chapter 51
1. b, 2. b, 3. d, 4. a, 5. a, 6. b, 7. b, 8. b, 9. c, 10. e

Chapter 52
1. d, 2. b, 3. a, 4. e, 5. b, 6. d, 7. e, 8. c, 9. d, 10. c

Chapter 53
1. e, 2. a, 3. c, 4. c, 5. a, 6. c, 7. b, 8. e, 9. d, 10. d

Index